THE THYSSEN-BORNEMISZA COLLECTION

Twentieth-century German painting

THE THYSSEN-BORNEMISZA COLLECTION

Twentieth-century German painting

Peter Vergo

GENERAL EDITOR IRENE MARTIN

Sotheby's Publications

for Caroline, Oliver and Emilia

First published 1992 for Sotheby's Publications by
Philip Wilson Publishers Ltd, 26 Litchfield Street, London WC2H 9NJ

Distributed in the USA and Canada by Rizzoli International Publications, Inc
300 Park Avenue South, New York, NY 10010

ISBN 0 85667 412 5
LC 91-060241

Distribuzione esclusiva in Italia: Electa, Milano
Elemond Editori Associati

Designed by Gillian Greenwood
Photography of the Thyssen Collection by Giuseppe Pennisi
Typeset in Photina by Southern Positives and Negatives (SPAN), Lingfield, Surrey
Printed and bound by Snoeck, Ducaju & Zoon, NV, Ghent, Belgium

Contents

Foreword 6

Introduction and acknowledgements 7

Notes on the catalogue 23

List of exhibitions 27

List of works 28

Catalogue 30

Bibliography 377

Photographic acknowledgements 382

Index of artists 385

Foreword

One of the ideas I had, after arriving at the Thyssen-Bornemisza Foundation in the summer of 1987, was an exhibition of Expressionist works from the Collection. It was obvious in going through the list of twentieth-century paintings that this was the area of greatest strength within the Collection; yet such an exhibition had never been proposed. We were fortunate to have Dr Peter Vergo of the University of Essex as curator of the exhibition and author of the catalogue. The exhibition, held in 1989, naturally led the way for the present catalogue of twentieth-century German paintings, the twelfth in the Thyssen-Bornemisza Collection series.

This volume appears at a time when there has been a renewed interest in the artists within the scope of Expressionism. The important exhibition *Degenerate Art* at the Los Angeles County Museum of Art in 1991 received international attention. Since then, Otto Dix, Karl Schmidt-Rottluff, Ludwig Meidner, Erich Heckel, Wassily Kandinsky and Gabriele Münter, just to name a few, have been the focus of major retrospective exhibitions in Europe.

Baron H.H. Thyssen-Bornemisza's interest in Expressionism goes back to 1961 when he attended the auction of the Stuttgarter Kunstkabinett. It was the 'bold colour range' of the Nolde watercolour, *Young Couple* [86] that caught the eye of the Baron and inspired him to make his first purchase in Modern Art. The seed of an interest in twentieth-century art was sown, and it grew to include not only German Expressionism, but most other movements of Modern Art in Europe and America.

Peter Vergo has written a brilliant catalogue for this most important section of the Thyssen-Bornemisza Collection of Modern Art. He has interviewed living sources whenever possible in his tireless search for missing data. Wrong dates on paintings have been corrected by stylistic analysis and archival research, as in the case of Kirchner's *Curving Bay* [48], a recent purchase. The name of the sitter in the portrait by Oskar Kokoschka [56] was correctly identified as Max Schmidt, and not Gino Schmidt, by locating relatives of the Schmidt family living in Vienna. The research for this volume has been thorough and detailed, often including visits to the locations where the paintings were executed; photographs of some of the actual views, streets and buildings as they are today are reproduced in the catalogue entries.

In the introductory essay, Dr Vergo gives a brief history of the main groups represented in the collection – Die Brücke, Der Blaue Reiter and Neue Sachlichkeit, and puts the works in perspective within the historical movements. Some artists in this catalogue who do not strictly belong to these main groups, but nonetheless fit into their general ambience, are placed in context as well.

This volume is of great importance for the Collection, scholars, art history students and the general public; it encompasses the latest scientific research on major works of Modern German painting, the results of which are published here for the first time.

Irene Martin
ADMINISTRATIVE DIRECTOR AND CURATOR

Introduction and acknowledgements

German art in the early 1900s was a broad torrent swelled by countless tributaries whose sources were often remote geographically or in time. It is, therefore, no accident that the earliest picture in this volume devoted to twentieth-century German painting in the Thyssen-Bornemisza Collection should be neither twentieth-century nor German (see [75]). Painted twelve years before the new century began, Edvard Munch's *Evening* is the work of an artist who was and remained stubbornly Norwegian in upbringing, in outlook and in his choice of subject-matter. He is, none the less, like van Gogh named as one of the great precursors of modern German painting in virtually every book and exhibition catalogue on Expressionism.[1] Nor is *Evening* the only 'cuckoo in the nest'. Leafing through the catalogue which follows, the reader will find discussed and reproduced a significant number of works by artists who, though they may have been active after (as well as in many cases before) 1900, were German neither by birth nor by adopted nationality.

Ensor, for instance, was Belgian, and lived for nearly his whole life in his native Ostend. Despite his remarkable longevity (he did not die until 1949), he had created virtually all his important paintings by 1895, after which he devoted himself increasingly to making copies or variants of his own compositions, an example of which is to be found in the Thyssen-Bornemisza Collection (see [9]).[2] His reputation, none the less, continued to spread rapidly throughout Germany and the German-speaking countries during the early 1900s, and his works were widely exhibited and reproduced. Though he himself travelled little, both Nolde and Heckel, two of the leading Expressionists, visited Ensor in Ostend,[3] undeterred by his suspicious demeanour and hermit-like existence. He also exerted a significant influence on a number of other German artists, for example Karl Hofer and Paul Klee.[4] Klee mentions Ensor with surprising frequency in his diaries from 1907 onwards, interested perhaps at this stage in his career as much in the Belgian artist's graphic production as in his paintings.[5] Hofer's repeated use of masks in his works of the same period echoes one of the dominant themes of Ensor's art of the 1880s and 1890s.

Kees van Dongen, to take another example, spent nearly all his life in France, though he was actually born in Holland. However, he maintained cordial relations with the Brücke group in Dresden, joining their association and participating in the exhibition of French avant-garde art held at the Kunstsalon Emil Richter in Dresden in 1908 concurrently with an exhibition of work by the Brücke artists themselves.[6] His early paintings have often been linked with Expressionism on account of their broad expressive brushstrokes and use of vivid, non-naturalistic colour. His watercolours in the Thyssen-Bornemisza Collection, on the other hand, date from his later Parisian period (see [7] and [8]) and have more in common with French art of the twenties and thirties than with Expressionism as such.

Perhaps the most striking case of 'elective affinities' is that of Munch, already referred to. Though Munch was Norwegian, some of his most influential works of the 1890s were created in Germany: many of the paintings belonging to his major cycle *The Frieze of Life* date from his years in Berlin between 1892 and 1895. During the early 1900s he was represented by important paintings, and groups of paintings, at exhibitions throughout Germany and Austria

Notes

1 In the major exhibition of Expressionism held in Florence in 1964, Munch was included (together with Ensor) in an introductory section entitled 'Precursors'. The catalogue noted that this prelude to the exhibition was intended to show the 'works of some of the major painters who are now considered – and whom the Expressionists themselves considered – the most important point of departure and stimulus for the development of the movement'; see *Espressionismo. Pittura, scultura, architettura*, exh. cat., Florence, Palazzo Strozzi, 1964, p.25

2 The chronology printed in the catalogue of the Ensor retrospective exhibition held in Paris in 1990 notes that the artist first copied one of his own earlier paintings, *Le Chou* of 1880, as early as 1893; thereafter failing inspiration accounted for the increasing numbers of replicas and variants painted during the late 1890s and early 1900s; see *James Ensor*, exh. cat., Paris, Musée du Petit Palais, 1990, pp.16–17, also Tricot (1985), pp.32–7

3 Nolde paid a visit to Ensor in April 1910: see the chronology printed in Urban (1987), p.18. Heckel encountered the Belgian artist while stationed as a member of a German army medical team in Flanders during the First World War: see Gabler (1983), pp.127f

4 Whether, strictly speaking, Klee is to be considered German or Swiss is open to debate. He was born in Switzerland (at Münchenbuchsee, near Berne, in 1879) and died there (at Muralto-Locarno, on Lake Maggiore, in 1940). However, he spent his entire working life in Germany, first in Munich before the First World War, then as a teacher at the Bauhaus, finally (until 1933) as professor at the Düsseldorf Academy. According to Felix Klee, his father would have been happy to remain in Germany even after 1933, but Klee's wife Lily pressed him to emigrate to Switzerland and apply for Swiss citizenship. Owing to bureaucratic delays, he was still technically a German citizen at the time of his death on 29

in cities as far afield as Berlin, Dresden and Vienna. It seems that in the main, he preferred to associate himself with established, even if avant-garde, exhibiting societies, and kept himself more or less aloof from the younger German artists, for example the painters of the Brücke. They, on the other hand, eagerly sought his participation in their exhibitions.[7] Though the Brücke artists themselves, perhaps out of pique at Munch's refusal to subscribe to their cause, later denied knowing his art at the crucial moment or being influenced by it,[8] their familiarity with his work both in the original (through exhibitions) and in reproduction can be easily demonstrated.[9]

A number of other artists who were not German by birth made their home in Germany, spending a major part of their working lives there and being usually regarded as part of the mainstream development of German art. Feininger, for example, was born in New York and retained American nationality, which caused him some difficulties, not least being treated as an enemy alien during the latter part of the First World War, but which enabled him to escape the increasingly repressive political situation during the 1930s when the Nazis' cultural purges began in earnest. By the time he left Germany in 1937, he had spent half a century in what he must have felt entitled to consider his second homeland; so deeply rooted was his art in German life and culture that he was frequently considered to be a German artist, even in America. Kandinsky and Jawlensky also spent by far the greater part of their careers in Germany; though they were Russian by birth, their contribution to German artistic life was so considerable both in its extent and in its influence that they too are often counted as German painters, however historically inaccurate such pigeon-holing might be.

Like Kandinsky, Johannes Itten was one of the 'first wave' of teachers appointed by Gropius to the newly established Bauhaus in Weimar after 1919. He also spent a crucial, though brief interlude in Stuttgart from 1913–16, from which dates one of the most important of his early paintings, now in the Thyssen-Bornemisza Collection, *Group of Houses in Spring* (see [30]). He was, however, Swiss, and made overall a more significant contribution to Swiss than to German art by virtue of his many years as director of the School of Applied Arts in Zurich. It is, in the end, more on account of his association with the other artists of the Bauhaus – Feininger, Kandinsky, Klee – than for any other reason that Itten's two paintings in the Thyssen Collection are included in the catalogue which follows.

Apart from these what one might term 'honorary Germans', virtually all the major German artists, and artistic groups, active during the period 1905–33 are represented in the present volume. Expressionism, Bauhaus and Neue Sachlichkeit are the three principal 'movements', art-historically speaking, but these broad categories embrace a number of sub-groups and artists working independently. There are also several artists who do not fall conveniently under any of the usual art-historical headings. Max Beckmann, for example, consistently rejected the label 'Expressionism', though his pronouncements on art occasionally sound a tone very similar to that of the Expressionists' own programmatic statements – for example, when he confessed to his 'crazy ambition' to 'build a tower in which mankind can shriek out all its rage and despair, all its poor hopes and joys and wild longing.'[10] Lovis Corinth, the most old-masterly of all the German painters of this century,[11] has at various times and in different contexts been linked with Academicism and Impressionism as well as Expressionism (see [5]), though he for his part disdained the Expressionists, considering himself to have nothing in common with the artistic ambitions and idealistic world view which characterized the work of the younger German painters. This, however, did not save his works from being confiscated

June 1940; see 'An Interview with Felix Klee', in Sabine Rewald, *Paul Klee*, New York (Metropolitan Museum of Art) 1988, pp.42f

5 See, e.g., Klee (1957), pp.230, 242, 249; also Jordan (1984), pp.19ff

6 See Reinhardt (1977): 146

7 For an account of Schmidt-Rottluff's attempts to involve Munch with the activities of himself and his comrades, see Werenskiold (1974): 140–8; also Reinhardt (1977): 106ff

8 Heckel, for example, maintained in a letter to Gustav Vriesen that Munch's work was 'unknown [to the artists of the Brücke] in the original or in reproduction during the first decisive years in Dresden 1904–8 or 1909'; cited after Reinhardt (1977): 107 and n.478

9 On the resemblances between Munch's works and those of the Brücke artists, especially Kirchner, see Gordon (1966), especially pp.339ff. Georg Reinhardt, however, has called in question the extent of Munch's stylistic influence, particularly in the case of Kirchner's paintings as opposed to graphic works; see Reinhardt: 110–14

10 Max Beckmann, 'Bekenntnis', in *Schöpferische Konfession*, Berlin (Erich Reiss), 1920, III of *Tribüne der Kunst und Zeit* (ed. Kasimir Edschmid), quoted after Diether Schmidt (ed.), *Manifeste, Manifeste. Künstlerschriften I*, Dresden (VEB Verlag der Kunst) n.d. [1965], p.142

11 For an excellent account, the first in English, of Corinth's life and work see Uhr (1990)

from the museums, along with theirs, when the National Socialists came to power in Germany in 1933.

Kokoschka and Schiele, by contrast, subscribed to a view of the purpose and function of art virtually identical to that held by other Expressionist artists, emphasizing the primacy of inner experience over the merely mechanical recording of external appearances. None the less, for much of the time both remained geographically remote from the principal centres of Expressionism, save for the short period Kokoschka spent in Berlin helping Herwarth Walden in editing the latter's periodical *Der Sturm* – in many ways the most important mouthpiece of Expressionism in literature and the visual arts.[12]

Within the ambit of Expressionism itself, what are generally regarded as the two principal artistic groupings, Die Brücke and Der Blaue Reiter, are both more than adequately represented in the Thyssen-Bornemisza Collection. Of the two it was, however, only the Brücke that was really a group in the strict sense of being a formally-constituted exhibiting society, founded in Dresden in 1905 in outspoken opposition to the art of the 'comfortably established older generation'.[13] Indeed, finding opportunities to exhibit the work of its members was one of the group's first aims, Erich Heckel shouldering much of the burden of endless correspondence with collectors and dealers and gallery owners. The record of exhibitions in which he and his comrades participated during the years between 1906 and 1913 makes clear how intensive their activities were, the Brücke artists showing either in mixed exhibitions or as a group on up to a dozen occasions in any one year.[14] They also used their graphic works as a means of publicizing their art, inviting collectors and art lovers to become 'passive members' of their association who, in return for a relatively modest subscription, were entitled to receive original prints by each of the artists, as well as a kind of newsletter or annual report detailing the group's activities.[15] To this body of passive members belonged some of the most important early supporters and protagonists of Expressionism in the visual arts, among them the jurist Gustav Schiefler, who championed Heckel and catalogued the graphic works of both Kirchner and Munch, the Hamburg art historian Rosa Schapire, who was a close friend of Schmidt-Rottluff, and the archaeologist Botho Graef, one of the first commentators to write sensitively about Kirchner's art.

It was also in the form of a print that the Brücke issued its first programmatic statement, the text of which Kirchner carved as a woodcut. It read:

> Putting our faith in a new generation of creators and art lovers, we call upon all youth to unite. We who possess the future shall create for ourselves a physical and spiritual freedom opposed to the values of the comfortably established older generation. Anyone who honestly and directly reproduces the force that impels him to create belongs to us.[16]

The tone of this appeal to youth – to those who 'possess the future' – and the language in which it is couched powerfully recall the writings of Nietzsche – not surprisingly, since there is ample evidence to show that the Brücke artists devoured and memorized and quoted at each other excerpts from the philosopher's works. The very name Brücke – 'bridge' – which Schmidt-Rottluff said signified a 'bridge to the future' echoes the frequently repeated phrase 'Brücke zum Übermenschen' – a bridge to the superman – in Nietzsche's *Thus Spake Zarathustra*.[17] That these young artists saw themselves in Nietzschean terms as superior beings, exalted above the

12 On the scope of Walden's activities as dealer, publisher, exhibition organizer and publicist of Expressionism see Georg Brühl, *Herwarth Walden und 'Der Sturm'*, Cologne (DuMont) 1983

13 On the founding and early history of the Brücke, see Reinhardt (1977), especially pp.18–36

14 Ibid., pp.50ff

15 See Hans Bolliger, 'Die Publikationen und Dokumente der Künstlergruppe "Brücke"', *Philobiblon*, 1 (1959): 46ff

16 Ibid., p.45

17 Reinhold Heller, while acknowledging the influence of Nietzsche on the artists of the Brücke, has also pointed to the similarity – which extends even to the metaphor of the 'bridge' – between the Brücke 'manifesto' and the stated aims of the slightly older and considerably larger, though scarcely less progressive, Deutscher Künstlerbund (Association of German Artists), founded in 1903; see Heller (1988), p.5 and notes 14, 15

'common herd' by virtue of their youth, their energy and their superabundance of creative (which Nietzsche linked with procreative) power is evident from their disdain for bourgeois morality, their 'shocking' lifestyle, living in crowded studios with erotic frescos and hangings promimently displayed on the walls, or disporting themselves naked in the open air in the company of their girl-friends and studio models. They also made their own élitist standpoint abundantly clear by contributing to a communal album which bore by way of a title a quotation from Horace's ode *Contentment* which begins 'odi profanum vulgus . . . ' – 'I hate the common herd'.[18]

The Brücke 'manifesto' has often been regarded as a manifesto of Expressionism itself, with some justification. While writers have tried in vain to define Expressionism in terms of any common characteristics of style, such coherence as the 'movement' (which in any case also embraced poetry and drama and music as well as the visual arts) may have possessed is rather to be found in a set of common aims and suppositions, a shared vision of the value and purpose of art. Central among these is the notion that it is the genuineness and force of the artist's urge to communicate, through no matter what medium, that confers upon the work of art its unique validity. Without wishing to rewrite the Brücke artists' manifesto for them, it is striking that their brief 'call to arms' claims as a kindred spirit *not* anyone who 'honestly and directly reproduces nature' nor even 'anyone who honestly and directly reveals the well-springs of human motivation', but instead unequivocally singles out the artistic urge itself: 'anyone who honestly and directly reproduces the *force that impels him to create* belongs to us.'

The extent to which, on the other hand, a coherent stylistic trend can be recognized in the work of the various members of the group remains open to debate. Much has been made of the fact that the artists of Die Brücke often worked together, sharing studios and setting up their easels side by side in the open air. Some writers even claim to have identified a specific 'Brücke-style', though the examples produced are almost invariably taken from the work of Kirchner and Heckel whose drawings, especially, from the period around 1910 are sometimes so similar in manner that they have even been confused.[19] But as for the other Brücke members, the differences between their works are often more striking than the similarities. Their activities were, moreover, characterized by constantly shifting allegiances; there were sub-groups within the group, alliances and friendships which included some members but excluded or marginalized others, so that rather than presenting itself as an organic whole, the association at times has more the aspect of some primitive life-form undergoing a constant and bewildering process of cellular division.

It has often been said that Schmidt-Rottluff was the outsider among the Brücke artists, probably because of his somewhat reserved and aloof manner. In truth, if there was an outsider it was really Pechstein, who was in Dresden infrequently after 1906 and moved to Berlin as early as 1908, whither the other Brücke artists eventually followed him, though not until 1911. He also played little part in the joint painting expeditions to distant and picturesque locations such as Dangast or Fehmarn, preferring to seek out for himself an even more remote destination, the village of Nidden at the extreme eastern end of the Baltic. He joined Kirchner and Heckel on their trips to the Moritzburg lakes near Dresden only once, in the summer of 1910 (see [89]). He visited Heckel and Schmidt-Rottluff at Dangast also on only one occasion,

18 See Reinhardt (1977): 26–7; also Beat Stutzer, 'Das Stammbuch "Odi Profanum" der Künstlergruppe "Brücke"', *Zeitschrift des deutschen Vereins für Kunstwissenschaft*, XXXVI, no.1–4 (1982): 87–105

19 Lucius Grisebach, for example, in his essay on Heckel's early work published in the catalogue of the 1983–4 Heckel retrospective exhibition, makes repeated allusion to the 'Brücke style of 1909–10'; see 'Erich Heckel und die "Brücke"', in Felix (1983), pp.9–23

20 Pechstein had broken the accord between the members of the Brücke that they would show their work only as a group by joining the Berlin Secession and participating in its exhibitions. Kirchner, in his *Chronicle of the Brücke*, noted in lapidary style merely that 'Pechstein betrayed the trust of the group, joined the Secession, and was expelled'; see Ernst Ludwig Kirchner, 'Chronik K.G.Brücke 1913', reprinted in Schmidt, op. cit., pp.46–7

21 Regarding the availability, either in the original or in reproduction, of examples of Post-Impressionist art to the painters of the Brücke, see the discussion on pp.180ff of the present volume. The influence of artists such as Gauguin and van Gogh may have been mediated not only directly, through exhibitions and publications, but also indirectly, for example through the work of Cuno Amiet who joined the Brücke group in autumn 1906: see Reinhardt (1977): 44f. I am grateful to Colin Rhodes for drawing my attention to Amiet's importance in this connection

22 In her article on the reception of van Gogh's art in Germany, Magdalena Moeller observes pertinently that in the works of the Brücke artists, unlike those of their Dutch precursor, colour and form 'are neither expressive of destiny nor charged with symbolic meaning; rather, the use of heavy impasto does not immediately conjure up an impression of substance, of coloured masses . . . it is more the expression of a liberated, unorthodox manner of painting freed from academic precepts . . .': see Moeller (1990), p.314

23 On German artists' attitudes to the primitive, whether real or imagined, see Lloyd (1991); also the article by Donald E. Gordon, 'German Expressionism', in William Rubin (ed.), *'Primitivism' in 20th Century Art. Affinity of the Tribal and the Modern*, exh. cat., New York, Museum of Modern Art, 1984, pp.369–403

24 The cult of nudism, health and the body beautiful was in any case widespread in Germany at this time, as is clear, for example, from the influential writings of the Dresden art historian Heinrich Pudor who, in his *Katechismus der Nacktkultur* of 1906, lists a number of establishments in the Dresden area which offered 'light, air and water bathing'. For an account of the relevance of such ideas to Expressionism, see Paul Reece, 'Edith Buckley, Ada Nolde and "Die Brücke". Bathing, Health and Art in Dresden, 1906–1911', in Brian Keith-Smith (ed.), *German Expressionism in the United Kingdom and Ireland*, Bristol (University of Bristol) 1986, pp.22–27

25 For a discussion of the range and variety of images reproduced in the *Blue Rider Almanac*, see Felix Thürlemann, 'Étonnantes résonances. Du discours des reproductions dans l'Almanach du Cavalier Bleu', in *Le Cavalier Bleu*, exh. cat., Berne, Kunstmuseum, 1987, pp.210–22

in 1910 – by contrast with Kirchner who, it appears, never set foot in Dangast. Kirchner and Heckel were personally close during these pre-war years; Kirchner and Schmidt-Rottluff, on the other hand, seemingly had little sympathy for one another, while most of the members of the group appear to have been somewhat jealous of Pechstein's early success and seized on a pretext to exclude him from their association in 1912.[20]

The other major factor they had in common was that, to a very large extent, they responded to the same influences, in particular that of French Neo- and Post-Impressionist painting, and most especially the art of van Gogh and Gauguin.[21] As regards style, it was van Gogh who made the greatest impact on the early work of both Kirchner and Heckel, as well as that of Schmidt-Rottluff and Nolde. It was, however, not so much his choice of subject-matter or his belief in the symbolic significance inherent in natural forms, but rather his expressive brushstroke and non-naturalistic use of colour which struck them most forcibly – a broad, gestural manner of painting in which pigment itself becomes the vehicle for the communication of profound emotional truths.[22]

The example of Gauguin, by comparison, manifests itself less in straightforward stylistic borrowings; while the younger German painters were deeply impressed by his art, what he stood for was even more important to them – his belief in the decadence of Western culture, in the need for a renewal of the creative impulse which could be achieved only by seeking out the very well-springs of creativity itself in the form of primitive cultures and societies, no matter how disastrous personally that search might in his own case have turned out to be. In later years, even an artist such as Schad – somewhat surprisingly – traced his first Dada experiments back to Gauguin's search for primitive sources of inspiration (see [92]), while two of the painters associated with the Brücke, Nolde and Pechstein, actually followed in the French artist's footsteps, embarking on the great voyage to the South Seas, in Nolde's case to New Guinea, in Pechstein's to Palau. Nor is it entirely fanciful to see, in the case of those Brücke members who stayed at home, their now celebrated excursions to 'remote' destinations such as Fehmarn or Moritzburg (even though Fehmarn was easily accessible by train, and Moritzburg only a short bicycle ride from Dresden) as a re-enactment of Gauguin's odyssey.[23] It was not geographical distance that mattered, nor even the encounter with actual primitive cultures (which both Nolde and Pechstein, true children of their time, persisted in seeing through unregenerately Western eyes), but rather the quest for a more 'natural' mode of existence, a one-ness with nature, symbolized by the fact that when the Brücke artists finally found themselves amid the tangled undergrowth or on some secluded beach, their first action was almost invariably to take their clothes off.[24]

The notion of the 'primitive' was equally crucial, albeit in a somewhat different context, to the artists of the Blue Rider circle in Munich. The famous *Blue Rider Almanac*, published in 1912 and edited by Kandinsky and Franz Marc, abounds in illustrations of various kinds of primitive art – 'primitive' here being understood in a very wide sense, embracing children's drawings, Romanesque sculpture and the work of Douanier Rousseau as well as Bavarian glass paintings, Easter Island carvings, Benin bronzes and Russian folk prints.[25] In marked contrast to the Brücke, however, the Blue Rider was properly speaking never a group nor indeed a movement. It was, first and foremost, a publication (the almanac) and two exhibitions, both held in

Munich, both of which derived their name from the almanac itself, despite the fact that they took place before the volume finally appeared in May 1912. There was no group manifesto, precisely because there was no group. There was no jury or hanging committee – just the 'editors of the *Blue Rider*' (Kandinsky and Marc), who selected like-minded artists to contribute to the almanac and to the two exhibitions, relying largely on their own judgment, behaving in what Kandinsky himself in a letter to Paul Westheim later described as a 'purely dictatorial manner'.[26] Nor was there any group style (and not just because there was no group). Rather, one of the most important messages contained in the almanac was that the 'question of form' (which was synonymous with 'style') was irrelevant, since the apparent diversity of styles which characterized the modern movement in art was at odds with the 'identity of inner striving' felt in all the best modern work.[27] Thus, the only question worth asking about 'external' form was whether it was that best suited to convey the inner message which it was the mission of the artist to communicate.

In the foreword to the catalogue of the 'First exhibition of the editors of the Blue Rider' (*Die Erste Austellung der Redaktion 'Der Blaue Reiter'*), Kandinsky wrote:

> In this small exhibition, we do not seek to propagate any *one* precise and special form; rather, we aim to show by means of the *variety* of forms represented how the *inner wishes* of the artist are embodied in manifold ways.[28]

Understanding this somewhat abstract theoretical standpoint is an important part of grasping the essential character of the Blue Rider itself.[29] Without such a standpoint, it is difficult to imagine what shared aesthetic could possibly unite the various personalities associated in one way or another with the almanac and with the exhibitions. Even if one considers only those artists who participated in the first Blue Rider exhibition in Munich in December 1911, any common characteristics of style would appear, at least at first sight, to be almost entirely lacking.

Perhaps closest to one another were Marc and Macke, both responding in obvious ways to the influence of French Orphism and Italian Futurism. Macke, in particular, was deeply affected by the example of Delaunay, even going so far as to pay a visit to the French painter in Paris in 1912, as Klee had done earlier in the same year (see [52]). The latter's work of this period seems, however, with its emphasis on linear form and element of fantasy, a world removed from the gentle, colourful lyricism of Macke, or the fragmented, crystalline forms of Marc's animal paintings. Münter, by comparison, reacted more to van Gogh and to the influence of French Synthetism, mediated via the ideas of Jawlensky. Kandinsky too, despite his dominant role in the creation of the Blue Rider, was really alone – and felt himself to be alone – in his dogged attempts not merely to invent, but also to justify a wholly non-representational form of art. Though most of the other Blue Rider artists – Marc, Macke and Münter among them – made isolated experiments with abstraction, none of them really resembles Kandinsky and none really imitated him – not even Münter, who was personally closest to him, but who was quite strong-minded enough to preserve her artistic independence confronted with personalities as overbearing as Kandinsky and Jawlensky.

Jawlensky's work occupies a somewhat anomalous position in relation to that of the 'Blue Riders' proper – though more for historical and personal than for stylistic reasons. He had left Kandinsky in the lurch in the autumn of 1911 when it came to a disagreement within the committee of the Neue Künstler-Vereinigung München (New Artists' Association of Munich) over the showing of the latter's *Composition V* at the society's third exhibition in December of

26 Westheim published Kandinsky's letter under the title 'Der Blaue Reiter (Rückblick)', in *Das Kunstblatt*, XIV, no.2 (February 1930): 57–60, translated in Lindsay (1982), pp.744–8

27 In his letter to Westheim recalling the origins of the Blue Rider (see n.26), Kandinsky defined the aim of the first *Blaue Reiter* exhibition as 'no advancement of any definite, exclusive "tendency", the juxtaposition of the most varied manifestations of the new painting, on an international basis and ... dictatorship'; cited after Lindsay (1982), p.747

28 Ibid., p.113

29 This distinction between outward form and inner content derives in essence from the philosophy of German Idealism; on the influence of Schopenhauerian philosophy, for example, on the ideas underlying the Blue Rider, see Peter Vergo, 'Kandinsky and the "Blue Rider Idea". The Unity of the Arts and the Beginning of Expressionism in Germany', in Anders Rosdahl (ed.), *Nya Perspektiv på Kandinsky/ New Perspectives on Kandinsky*, Malmö (Malmö Konsthall/ Sydsvenska Dagbladet) 1991, pp.49–58 that year. Thus, he was neither invited to participate in the first Blue Rider exhibition which, by way of a counter-blast, was held at the same time and on the same premises as the third exhibition of the NKVM, nor was his work reproduced in the almanac. He was, on the other hand, included along with the other Blue Riders in Herwarth Walden's *Erster Deutscher Herbstsalon* (First German *Salon d'Automne*) shown at the Sturm galleries in Berlin in autumn 1913. His rift with Kandinsky was, in any case, not permanent, and the two artists soon resumed friendly relations. During the 1920s and 1930s, both belonged to the group the Blue Four, conjured into existence by Jawlensky's admirer and protagonist Emmy (Galka) Scheyer, the other two members being Kandinsky's Bauhaus colleagues Feininger and Klee. Scheyer's active campaigning on behalf of 'her' artists contributed enormously to the spread of their reputation outside Germany, especially in the United States, during the period between the wars.

The Brücke and the Blaue Reiter have often been regarded as opposite poles of the Expressionist 'movement'.[30] In reality, there were numerous affinities, contacts, and resemblances between them. Despite Kandinsky's initial hesitation, works by Kirchner, Heckel and other members of the Brücke were in the end reproduced in the *Blue Rider Almanac*, albeit on a modest scale. Their inclusion came about partly as a result of prompting by Franz Marc, who had 'discovered' their latest work on a visit to Berlin at New Year 1912, when the almanac was still in the final stages of preparation.[31] They were also represented in large number in the second Blue Rider exhibition which opened in Munich in February 1912. Kandinsky thereby repayed the invitation extended to him more than five years earlier, when he had been represented by six prints at the Brücke artists' own first graphics exhibition in Dresden in the winter of 1906–7.[32]

There are also on occasion, though for the most part unremarked, uncanny resemblances between Kandinsky's work and that of Kirchner. The latter's painting *Curving Bay* (see [48]), which shows bathing figures abbreviated almost to the point of illegibility set against a cosmic landscape extraordinary in its vivid, non-naturalistic colours, evokes an apocalyptic mood that, for all the differences between the two artists, brings to mind that of Kandinsky's exactly contemporary abstract-eschatological compositions of the years immediately before the outbreak of the First World War in 1914. There was, on the other hand, no significant tendency towards abstraction in the work of any of the Brücke painters, their art remaining for the most part obstinately rooted in tangible reality. In a letter dating from after the war, Kirchner wrote to the art historian Will Grohmann (who was also Kandinsky's biographer), calling into question the very basis of abstract art, which he referred to as a

> completely new creation ... the abstract artist, without ever touching on the natural form, has to invent his forms; they can only arise from his mind, everything else to him is useless and not genuine ... But is this the desirable development? Could it not be that in this way art as such will cease to be art and will simply become a school discipline like geometry and algebra?[33]

The First World War marks, in many important respects, a major caesura within the development of German (and not only, of course, German) art during the period considered here. By 1914, the heyday of both the Brücke and the Blaue Reiter was over. The Brücke had, in fact, already dissolved under its own centrifugal force, the tensions and rivalries, the shifting alliances evident within the association from the very beginning having been brought to a head

30 One chapter of Horst Jähner's 1986 monograph on the Brücke is actually entitled 'Blauer Reiter als Gegenpol'; see Jähner (1986), pp.79f; compare also Günter Krüger, 'Le rôle des groupes "Die Brücke" et "Der Blaue Reiter" dans la percée de l'art moderne en Allemagne', in *Le Cavalier Bleu*, pp.252–60

31 See *Der Blaue Reiter. Herausgegeben von Wassily Kandinsky und Franz Marc. Dokumentarische Neuausgabe von Klaus Lankheit*, Munich (R.Piper & Co.) 1965, pp.264–5

32 Reinhardt (1977): 116–18

33 Kirchner to Grohmann, 8.7.1925, quoted after Grohmann (1961/2), p.24

with the publication of Kirchner's extremely one-sided account of their activities, under the title *Chronik K. G. Brücke* (Chronicle of the Brücke), in the spring of 1913. 1914 saw the printing of a second edition of the *Blue Rider Almanac*, almost identical to the first, save for an additional preface by each of the editors.[34] Kandinsky and Marc corresponded in a somewhat desultory fashion about plans for a new volume, to which it was suggested art historians such as Wilhelm Worringer might be invited to contribute,[35] but in the end, nothing came of it. Both Marc and Macke perished in the war, after which Kandinsky, quite understandably, evinced little enthusiasm at the prospect of trying to resurrect the 'Blue Rider idea' in some different form. Of the original Blue Riders, however, he and Klee were, as already noted, re-united during the post-war years both as colleagues at the Bauhaus and under the aegis of the group the Blue Four.

Of the principal artistic movements already mentioned, the Bauhaus – if, indeed, the Bauhaus may properly be called a movement – is least extensively represented in this catalogue: one watercolour by Schlemmer, two oils by Feininger, a painting and two watercolours by Kandinsky and three works by Klee out of a total of one hundred and six entries. In fact, there are in the Thyssen Collection other paintings and works on paper which date from the Bauhaus period and which might arguably have been included. These, however, apart from whether the artists in question were German or not, were felt to be more closely linked with examples of Constructivist art by Russian painters such as Lissitzky and Rodchenko, or by members of the De Stijl group in Holland, which will eventually be published in a separate catalogue. Moholy Nagy, Dexel, Kassak and other artists who were members of the Bauhaus or in one way or another associated with it but who have been excluded from the present volume will therefore be considered in due course within a stylistic context and against a historical background to which they more properly belong.

On the other hand, the collection also embraces a small number of Realist paintings from the 1920s which have nothing to do with Constructivism or with the abstract tendencies associated with the Bauhaus, but which represent none the less a crucial chapter in the development of art in Germany during the first half of this century. Throughout Europe, the period following the end of the First World War witnessed a revolt against subjectivism, against the communication of individual emotional states, artists instead favouring a more objective, even 'classical' manner of expression[36] – a 'return to order' which characterized music and poetry and drama as well as the visual arts. In painting it likewise became apparent that artists working in different countries were now rejecting the colouristic extravagance of the Fauve painters, the strident dynamism of the Futurists, the 'exorbitant, gushing ecstacies' of the Expressionists[37] in favour of a more studied, sober naturalism. The Neo-Classicism of Picasso and the exaggerated clarity and new spatial order developed by Carrà and the Italian painters associated with the movement known as 'pittura metafisica' were only the more obvious manifestations of this new tendency towards what Apollinaire, writing as early as 1916, referred to as the 'effort to rediscover the authentic tradition in art ... simplicity and freshness, and the disciplines to which these principles gave rise ... a blissful harmony, at once realistic and sublime.'[38]

This same tendency had its counterpart in the work of a number of German painters who, in

34 *Der Blaue Reiter ... Dokumentarische Neuausgabe ...*, pp.321–4

35 Ibid., p.277

36 On Neo-Classicism in twentieth-century European painting see the excellent catalogue by Elizabeth Cowling and Jennifer Mundy, *On Classic Ground. Picasso, Léger, de Chirico and the New Classicism 1910–1930*, exh. cat., London, Tate Gallery, 1990, which, however, pays no attention to the German Realist painters considered here

37 Rudolf Keyser, in *Die Neue Rundschau*, quoted after Peter Gay, *Weimar Culture. The Outsider as Insider*, Harmondsworth 1988, p.127

38 Guillaume Apollinaire, 'André Derain', in LeRoy C.Breunig (ed.), *Apollinaire on Art: Essays and Reviews 1902–1918*, London 1972, pp.444–5

39 The phrase was used by Paul Kornfeld, author of *Der beseelte und der psychologische Mensch*. Himself the author of several Expressionist dramas, for example *Die Verführung* (1917), by 1924 Kornfeld was advocating the rejection of Expressionism in favour of attention paid to 'other and smaller things'; see Gay, loc. cit., also H.A. and E.Frenzel, *Daten deutscher Dichtung*.

Chronologischer Abriss der deutschen Literaturgeschichte, II: *Vom Biedermeier bis zur Gegenwart*, Munich 1962, p.168
40 'Magic Realism' was the alternative title of Franz Roh's classic study *Nach-Expressionismus* (Post-Expressionism), published in 1925 in conjunction with the Mannheim exhibition *Neue Sachlichkeit – Deutsche Malerei seit dem Expressionismus*; see Franz Roh, *Nach-Expressionismus – Magischer Realismus. Probleme der neuesten europäischen Malerei*, Leipzig 1925. For an account of the various uses of the term, see also Seymour Menton, *Magic Realism Rediscovered, 1918–1981*, Brunswick, NJ (Associated University Presses, Inc.) 1983
41 The German word 'Sachlichkeit' might be thought in some ways closer to the English term 'sobriety', and indeed, the phrase 'the new sobriety' has in recent years gained ground as a translation of 'die neue Sachlichkeit'; see e.g. John Willett, *The New Sobriety. Art and Politics in the Weimar Period, 1917–33*, London 1978. The history of its use is also discussed by Fritz Schmalenbach, 'The Term Neue Sachlichkeit', *Art Bulletin*, XXII (1940), no.3: 161–5
42 Letter dated 18 May 1923, cited in 'Neue Sachlichkeit. Deutsche Malerei seit dem Expressionismus, Mannheim 1925', [kommentiert] von Caroline Hille, in Eberhard Roters (ed.), *Stationen der Moderne ... Kommentarband zu den Nachdrücken der zehn Ausstellungskataloge*, Cologne (Walther König) 1988, pp.134–5; see also Helen Adkins, 'Neue Sachlichkeit – Deutsche Malerei seit dem Expressionismus', in *Stationen der Moderne. Die bedeutenden Kunstausstellungen des 20. Jahrhunderts in Deutschland*, exh. cat., Berlin, Berlinische Galerie, 1988, pp.217–8. Hartlaub's letter is quoted in full in Schmalenbach
43 Five are listed in the catalogue; a further nine paintings, which had previously been on show in Hamburg, were added to the Mannheim exhibition a month after it opened, making Beckmann the artist most extensively represented, together with Kanoldt; see Hille, p.146
44 Max Beckmann, 'On My Painting', in Robert L.Herbert (ed.), *Modern Artists on Art*, Englewood Cliffs, NJ, 1964, p.132

the aftermath of the carnage brought about by the First World War and the subsequent uprisings in Germany, turned away from themes of 'war, revolution and the salvation of the world'[39] towards a preoccupation with mundane subjects and a more matter-of-fact style of painting. Their work was recognized at least by some critics as constituting a new direction or movement by the beginning of the 1920s. It was, however, not until 1925 that it impinged to any great extent on German public consciousness – a consequence of the major exhibition held that summer at the Kunsthalle in Mannheim which assured the movement a place in history by the simple expedient of giving it a name: 'Neue Sachlichkeit'.

The invention of the term has normally been credited to Gustav Hartlaub, director of the Mannheim Kunsthalle and organizer of the 1925 exhibition. In fact, he was merely voicing a demand for a 'new sobriety' which had already been advocated by critics and writers for some time – not just in the visual arts, but in literature and drama, indeed in cultural life generally. It was Hartlaub, however, who focused attention specifically on painting; and while other writers invented alternative names for the new movement, of which the most prevalent was 'Magic Realism' propagated by the art historian and critic Franz Roh,[40] it is the term Neue Sachlichkeit – difficult though it may be to translate elegantly into English – which has mostly prevailed.[41]

What Hartlaub himself understood by the term is clear from a letter of 1923 addressed to dealers, critics and fellow museum directors announcing his plans for the Mannheim exhibition, in which he alludes specifically to those painters 'who, in the last ten years, have been neither loosely Impressionist nor abstract-Expressionist ... those artists whom I would like to exhibit are the ones who have remained faithful to positive, tangible reality.'[42] It was, on the other hand, clear to observers even at the time that there were numerous links between Neue Sachlichkeit and the Expressionist movement in painting which it was supposed to have ousted. A number of artists actually represented in the exhibition, Dix and Grosz among them, started from unequivocally Expressionist beginnings; indeed, Hartlaub was sharply criticized for including several early Expressionist paintings by Grosz, among them his 1916–17 canvas *Metropolis* (see [17]).

Nor can the exhibition itself have presented a particularly unified picture, either stylistically or as regards the artists' political standpoint and choice of subject-matter. Even Hartlaub found himself obliged to distinguish within Neue Sachlichkeit between what he saw as two 'wings' of the movement: a 'right', or classicizing wing, represented in the main by Munich painters such as Alexander Kanoldt and Carlo Mense whose work concentrated on traditional and non-political subjects, especially landscape and still-life, and a 'left', or 'veristic' wing – 'verism' here being equated with a kind of social-critical realism, an art marked by overt political content, using irony and satire to attack the Weimar government and the militarist-capitalistic system. Grosz, Dix and Scholz were among the principal representatives of this latter tendency.

In reality, the picture was more complex than this seductively simple distinction between left and right might imply, since several artists who showed in Mannheim clearly belonged to neither camp – Beckmann, for example, represented in the exhibition by a total of fourteen paintings.[43] Though he himself later proclaimed his allegiance to a magic-realist aesthetic, declaring his aim to be 'to get hold of the magic of reality and to transfer this reality into painting ... it is, in fact, reality which forms the mystery of our existence',[44] his work was included in the 1925 exhibition probably for no other reason than because of Hartlaub's profound personal admiration, and can be no more easily subsumed under the heading of Neue Sachlichkeit than it can be accommodated within mainstream Expressionism. In the wake of the exhibition, moreover, writers and critics complicated matters still further by claiming to identify other, discrete sub-groups within the German Realist movement as a whole – the 'Naïve Realists' of Hanover (Mertens, Thoms), the Cologne 'Gruppe progressiver Künstler' (Hoerle, Seiwert). Even Schlemmer, somewhat implausibly, has been classed as a 'utopian Realist'.

In retrospect, Neue Sachlichkeit seems now a movement unified – if it all – only by certain very general characteristics of style. Of these, the most important were a certain precision in the recording of natural appearances, people and objects appearing in exaggeratedly sharp focus, inexpressive brushwork contrasting with the heavy impasto favoured by the Expressionists, a tendency to choose an unnaturally close standpoint, so that much of this kind of painting seems curiously myopic in character, and unified, undramatic lighting. The Neue Sachlichkeit artists also concentrated on a limited number of specific genres, especially portraiture and still-life, though portraiture in fact occupies a disproportionate place among their paintings in the Thyssen-Bornemisza Collection which contains, for example, only a small number of urban scenes and no interiors or still-lives – genres equally characteristic of the 'new sobriety'.

Works by the Neue Sachlichkeit artists are not only among the most recent German paintings in the collection; they are also some of the most recent acquisitions. Nearly all were purchased around 1979, at which point there was considerable interest generally in the 'new realism' of the twenties. This interest was fuelled in part by several major exhibitions, one of the most important of which was the Arts Council of Great Britain's historic survey *Neue Sachlichkeit and German Realism of the Twenties* shown at the Hayward Gallery in London in 1978–9, which included several works since acquired by the Thyssen-Bornemisza Collection. Before then, the modern German paintings in the collection had been, numerically speaking, dominated by examples of work by artists of the Brücke and Blaue Reiter groups, especially the Brücke. Among the present Baron Thyssen's earliest independent purchases had been paintings by Kirchner, who to this day remains one of his favourite artists, as evidenced by the recent acquisition of two works of major importance: the Fehmarn landscape *Curving Bay*, painted in all probability on the eve of the outbreak of the First World War,[45] and an alpine scene dating from the artist's last years in Switzerland, *Junkerboden under Snow*.[46]

It was, however, with the purchase in 1961 of a watercolour by Emil Nolde, only briefly a member of the Brücke group, that the acquisition of modern paintings began. Prior to this, the Thyssen-Bornemisza Collection had contained no modern works at all. Baron Heinrich Thyssen-Bornemisza, who during the 1920s and 1930s built up an extensive and remarkable collection of Old Master paintings, had no time for modern art as his son Hans Heinrich, the present Baron, ruefully recalled:

> During my youth my father had always brain-washed me that twentieth-century art was of little interest. For a long time I believed him and for fifteen years after his death I bought solely Old Master paintings. Gradually I began to think that every artistic effort that was being done in the first half of this century at a time when major achievements had been made in most areas could not be totally devoid of interest.[47]

The Nolde watercolour, *Young Couple*, was acquired for a record price at one of the last auctions held by the Stuttgarter Kunstkabinett[48] whose owner, the dealer and collector Roman Norbert Ketterer, was to play a decisive role in influencing the expansion of the Thyssen-Bornemisza

45 Acquired in 1987: see [48]
46 Acquired in 1983: see [51]
47 See Hans Heinrich Thyssen-Bornemisza, 'German Expressionism, a Personal Choice', *Apollo*, CXVIII, no.257 (July 1983), p.76, reprinted in Vergo (1989), pp.9f
48 See the article by Dieter Schnabel, 'Höchstpreis für Feininger und Nolde. Rückschau auf die 36. Auktion des Stuttgarter Kunstkabinetts Ketterer', *Bonner Rundschau*, 9 May 1961

Collection to include significant areas of modern art. Over and above his role as auctioneer, Ketterer had been appointed executor of Kirchner's estate, and as well as acquiring – and selling – paintings by the artist had succeeded in preserving a prodigious body of documentary and archive material – diaries, sketchbooks, photograph albums and the like – which has formed the basis of all subsequent research. During the 1960s, he and his assistant Wenzel Nachbaur helped the American art historian Donald Gordon to compile the first catalogue raisonné of Kirchner's paintings, to which frequent reference will be found in the present volume.[49] Ketterer was also personally acquainted with the surviving members of the Brücke group, Heckel and Schmidt-Rottluff in particular. A significant number of paintings by these and other Expressionist artists passed through his hands during the late fifties and early sixties. But, most important of all, he had himself accumulated an outstanding collection of Expressionist art which formed the basis of the major touring exhibition shown in Germany, Holland and Switzerland during 1960–61 under the title *Meisterwerke des deutschen Expressionismus*.[50]

Shortly afterwards, in 1962, he moved to Campione d'Italia on Lake Lugano, where he re-established his business under the name Galerie R.N.Ketterer. Not only did he continue dealing; he also, on occasion, sold works from his own personal collection. During this time, his relations with the present Baron Thyssen-Bornemisza (whose property, the Villa Favorita, was a short boat-ride away on the other side of the lake) were both close and cordial. The Baron frequently bought from the more or less annual sales of modern art, entitled simply *Moderne Kunst*, which Ketterer organized at Campione between 1963 and 1976; he also in many instances had first choice when Ketterer found himself obliged to sell works from his own collection. In this way some of the (qualitatively speaking) most important paintings by twentieth-century German artists, Kirchner in particular, entered the Thyssen-Bornemisza Collection. In an interview with the Baron, Ketterer himself recalled:

> My move from Stuttgart to Campione in 1962 brought me into financial difficulties, and so from time to time I would ring the Villa Favorita and announce my willingness to sell something from my private collection. With an extraordinary feeling for quality and incredible eye for colour you would then always choose the best from my collection – in every case, a painting that I was reluctant to sell.[51]

It was, however, as a source not merely of paintings, but also of advice and information, that Ketterer was important, 'a good friend who guided my first steps in the nearly unknown territory that was for me then twentieth-century art.'[52] His role in determining the direction the Baron's activities as collector were subsequently to take can scarcely be over-stressed.

The other factor which to some extent pre-destined the character of these early purchases was the fact that literally thousands of important paintings by Expressionist and other modern artists had been confiscated as 'degenerate' by the Nazis when they came to power in Germany in 1933.[53] To increase reserves of foreign currency, a number of these paintings were sold abroad during the years immediately before the Second World War, either through the intermediary of dealers such as Karl Buchholz and Ferdinand Möller in Berlin, or through the major auction held by the Galerie Fischer in Lucerne in June 1939. Other works were accepted on commission by Buchholz, Möller, Gurlitt and other dealers charged with 'realizing the value' of examples of 'degenerate' art, and were either sold covertly to German collectors still interested in movements such as Expressionism or Neue Sachlichkeit, or simply kept hidden until after the war, thus ensuring their survival at a time when significant numbers of important works of twentieth-century art were cynically destroyed.[54]

The present Baron was then too young to take advantage of the opportunites offered to

49 See Gordon (1968), especially pp.263f

50 For full reference see p.27

51 Ketterer (1988/1), pp.174f

52 See Thyssen-Bornemisza, loc. cit.

53 There is an extensive literature on the subject of 'degenerate' art. For an early account by an eye-witness of the Nazis' policies of *Kunstsäuberung* (artistic purification) see Roh (1962). The fiftieth anniversary, in 1987, of the notorious *Entartete Kunst* (Degenerate Art) exhibition shown in Munich and other German cities from 1937 onwards occasioned a spate of publications of which one of the most useful, dealing primarily with Munich, is the anthology edited by Peter-Klaus Schuster, see Schuster (1987). For a more recent survey, see Barron (1991) which includes essays by many of the principal experts on this subject, including Christoph Zuschlag, Mario-Andreas von Lüttichau and Andreas Hüneke

54 On the role of the dealers, see Andreas Hüneke, '"Dubiose Händler operieren im Dunst der Macht". Vom Handel mit "entarteter" Kunst', in *Alfred Flechtheim. Sammler, Kunsthändler, Verleger*, exh. cat., Düsseldorf, Kunstmuseum, 1987, pp.101–5.

acquire – indeed rescue – examples of 'degenerate' art, and his father, as already noted, was not interested in buying modern works. However, a number of these confiscated pictures began slowly to surface again after the war, turning up at auction with increasing frequency during the 1960s and 1970s, or being sold privately by their new owners. This time, Baron Hans Heinrich did not miss his chance to acquire pictures of a quality rarely seen in the salerooms today. Several of the most important paintings now in the collection once graced the walls of the major German museums and galleries: Grosz's *Metropolis*, from the Kunsthalle in Mannheim (see [17]), Pechstein's *Horse Fair*, from Berlin's Nationalgalerie (see [89]), Nolde's *Summer Clouds*, from the Kunsthalle in Kiel (see [79]).

For the buyer, increasingly recognized as one of the most active collectors of modern art on the international scene, the fact that these works had been scorned by the Nazis as degenerate and their authors victimized and oppressed gave an added fillip to his interest. Undoubtedly, rebellion against paternal taste was also a factor in his collecting. But most important of all was a growing passion for the Expressionists and an ever-wider understanding of the period which, coupled with an eye for quality, ensured the growth of what is now one of the most extraordinary collections of modern art still in private hands. Starting with the Expressionists, especially the painters of the Brücke, Baron Thyssen soon extended his knowledge and appreciation to embrace other artists and movements. His interest in the Blue Rider group in Munich, which included Kandinsky, led him to acquire works by other Russian artists as well, particularly of the abstract schools, so that the range of modern Russian works in the collection is now as interesting, if not quite as extensive, as that of the German paintings considered in this volume.

That the collection should offer so nearly complete a conspectus of this period of German art as a whole is all the more remarkable, given the fact that there was never really any such a thing as a 'purchasing policy' – or if there was, then it was a policy determined above all by personal taste. The acquisitions of many public collections are influenced by committee decisions, by the need for compromise, to satisfy the demands of a particular benefactor, or to fill a perceived gap. None of these factors, not even the last, really played any role here. By his own account, Baron Thyssen bought – and continues to buy – paintings out of 'love and passion, interest and enthusiasm',[55] not because some artist is under-represented or because the collection lacks an example of a particular historical style or tendency.

Partly because of the way the collection came about, it was in the end decided not to attempt to organize this catalogue chronologically or by 'school', though of course it would have been perfectly possible to envisage separate sections on the principal movements detailed above, each preceded by a historical introduction. There were, however, several arguments against such an arrangement which taken together appeared persuasive. Any number of artists – Rohlfs, Mammen, Hofer, Beckmann – fall under no convenient heading, so that such a system would leave little alternative other than to relegate them, quite inappropriately, to an appendix or supplement to the main catalogue. Itten is an artist often thought of in connection with the Bauhaus, but neither of his works in the collection is from the Bauhaus period, so it was again quite unclear where they should be placed. Worst of all, the works of some artists would, under such an arrangement, have to be split up, so that early paintings by Kandinsky, for example, would be found under the heading of the Blaue Reiter, while his later ones would appear many dozens of pages further on, in a section devoted to the Bauhaus[56] – and where would one put his one and only Paris period painting (see [39])?

55 In conversation with the author, Lugano, 28 July 1989

56 The same rule about not 'splitting up' works by a given artist also determined the inclusion in the present catalogue of two Dada pieces (by Grosz and Schad – see [18] and [92]) which it might otherwise have been thought more appropriate to include in a future catalogue devoted to the Dada and Surrealist paintings in the collection. In the end, however, dividing works by the same artist between two different volumes seemed the greater of two evils

In the end, a purely alphabetical arrangement seemed the only sensible and practical solution and has therefore been adopted here. Historical information, particularly concerning some of the lesser known artists, has been incorporated into the main body of the entries for each individual work. Further explanations of the principles on which the catalogue has been compiled will be found in the notes immediately following this introduction.

One of the privileges attendant upon undertaking a piece of research such as this is the opportunity of thanking in print the innumerable people who have helped in large ways and small. My thanks, first and foremost, to Baron and Baroness H. H. Thyssen-Bornemisza for their gracious hospitality, and for generously facilitating my researches in every way possible; further to Irene Martin, Curator and Administrative Director of the Thyssen-Bornemisza Collection, to Emil Bosshard, Head of Conservation, to Lucia Cassol, Elisabeth Nagy, Maria de Peverelli, Floriana Vismara, Maria Antonia Reinhardt and the entire staff of the Thyssen-Bornemisza Foundation. To all of these people who not merely answered my queries and provided me with materials, but who also supported, entertained, encouraged and – on occasion – consoled me, I owe an immense debt of gratitude and friendship.

On the other side of Lake Lugano at Campione d'Italia, almost within sight of the Villa Favorita, Dr Wolfgang Henze provided a wealth of information, photographs and other materials concerning Kirchner; I would also like to thank him – and through him his father-in-law, Mr Roman Norbert Ketterer – for supplying various details concerning the provenance of a number of works now in the Thyssen-Bornemisza Collection. North of the Alps, Mrs Anneliese Itten, Johannes Itten's widow, kindly welcomed me into her home in Zurich on more than one occasion, showed me her husband's works and patiently answered in person and subsequently by letter numerous questions about his two paintings in the collection. Angelica Jawlensky, the artist's grand-daughter, provided invaluable information from the files of the Alexej-von-Jawlensky Archiv, Locarno; I am most grateful to her for sharing with me the results of her researches prior to publication of the first volume of her catalogue raisonné of her grandfather's paintings. I am also deeply indebted to Dr Eberhard W. Kornfeld, who proved a mine of information not only concerning Kirchner but also a wide range of artists whose work had passed through his hands during the past three decades. It is difficult to know how to thank him adequately for the flood of information, advice, catalogues and photographs with which I was inundated, and for his kind hospitality and genial companionship during a memorable visit to Davos in which he enabled me to visit the three Kirchner houses and a number of other sites associated with the artist's last years in Switzerland.

In Germany, a large number of collectors, dealers, museum curators and scholars provided important information or assistance. I am especially grateful to Hans Geissler, administrator of the estate of Erich Heckel, for providing photographs, documents and otherwise unobtainable information from the Heckel archive at Hemmenhofen, and also for allowing me to reproduce the works by Heckel illustrated in this volume; to the late Bernd Hünlich, Radebeul, for unstinting advice, especially concerning the early work of the Brücke artists, for supplying photographs and other materials, and for taking at my request the photograph of the building depicted in Meidner's painting *The Corner House*; and to Dr Armin Zweite, at the time of my research director of the Städtische Galerie im Lenbachhaus and president of the Gabriele

Münter- und Johannes Eichner-Stiftung, Munich, for providing photographs and information concerning the work of both Kandinsky and Münter. Professor Dr Martin Urban, director of the Stiftung Seebüll Ada und Emil Nolde, graciously welcomed me to the artist's house at Seebüll which is now the home of the Nolde Foundation, and shared with me his unrivalled knowledge of Nolde's life and work. I also owe a special debt of gratitude to Professor Gerhard Wietek, Hamburg, for constant generous advice ever since the beginning of my research on this catalogue, for his kind hospitality at the time of my visit to North Germany in the spring of 1990, and for the very considerable quantity of rare, inaccessible or little-known material especially concerning Schmidt-Rottluff and the other members of Die Brücke which he has provided.

A large number of kind friends and colleagues assisted me during my brief visit to Denmark and Sweden in October 1989; my thanks to all of them, most especially Birgitta Schreiber of the Nordic Council of Ministers, Dr Bengt Lärkner of the University of Linköping for information concerning Kandinsky's 1915–16 stay in Sweden, and to Dr Marit Werenskiold of the University of Oslo for her advice in connection with the work of Edvard Munch.

In the United States, the list of those who have assisted me in various important ways is long indeed. I am particularly grateful to Vivian E. Barnett of the Solomon R. Guggenheim Museum, New York, for selflessly sharing with me at every stage of her work – and mine – the results of her extensive research on Kandinsky, and for providing information concerning other works formerly in the collection of the Guggenheim Museum; to Professor Kenneth Lindsay of the State University of New York at Binghamton, again for information and advice concerning Kandinsky based on a lifetime of study and research on the artist's work; to Peter M. Grosz, Princeton, New Jersey and to T. Lux Feininger, Cambridge, Massachusetts, for information concerning the work of George Grosz and Lyonel Feininger respectively; to Robert Gore Rifkind, Los Angeles, for information concerning works formerly in his collection, and for allowing me to reproduce the painting *The Waterfall* by Franz Marc; to Jane Kallir of the Galerie St Etienne, New York, for permitting me access to the material contained in her complete oeuvre-catalogue of the works of Egon Schiele prior to publication in the autumn of 1990, and for supplying photographs and information in connection with the artist's work; and to Professor Reinhold Heller of the University of Chicago for his advice on the one work by Otto Dix in the collection, and for sharing with me the results of his current research on the paintings of Gabriele Münter. To all of these, and the many others who have assisted me, my sincerest thanks.

Other friends and colleagues around the world have been generous with their time and knowledge, patiently answering my queries by letter, supplying documents and photographs or commenting on drafts of my text. Their names will for the most part be found in the notes accompanying the catalogue entries. I would, however, like to single out for particular mention Mr Günther Abels, Cologne; Dr Eva Badura-Triska, Vienna; Mrs Maja Beckmann, Murnau; Dr Vera J. Behal, Vienna; Mrs Jean Benjamin, New York; M. Heinz Berggruen, Paris; Dr Jane Block, Champaign-Urbana; Mr Ursus Dix, Jonquières; Professor Dr Alexander Dückers, Berlin; Dr Hanna Egger, Vienna; Mrs Marianne Feilchenfeldt, Zurich; Mr Richard L. Feigen, New York; Dr Wolfgang Fischer, London; Mr Stefan Frey, Berne; Dr Wolfram Gabler, Berlin; Dr Christian Geelhaar, Basle; Dr Barbara Göpel, Munich; Mrs Joan Morse Gordon, Pittsburgh; Mr Roy Graf, Reading; Mrs Roswitha Haftmann, Zurich; Dr Jelena Hahl-Koch, Pécrot; Mrs Melina Heering, Truchtlaching; Dr Ursula Heiderich, Syke-Okel; Dr Andreas Hüneke, Potsdam; Mr Florian Karsch, Berlin; Mr James Kirkman, London; Mrs Wilhelmine Corinth Klopfer, New York; Mrs

Olda Kokoschka, Villeneuve; Professor Dr Klaus Lankheit, Karlsruhe; Mme Francine-Claire Legrand, Brussels; Dr Diane Lesko, St Petersburg, Florida; Mr Bernd Lohse, Burghausen; Mrs Irene Lorenz, Vienna; Dr Annelise Loth, Darmstadt; Dr Ulrich Luckhardt, Hamburg; Dr Karin Frank von Maur, Stuttgart; Mr Achim Moeller, New York; Dr Sabine Rewald, New York; Mr G.A.Richter, Rottach-Egern; Professor Dr Eberhard Roters, Berlin; C.Raman Schlemmer, Oggebbio; Mrs Irene Schmidt, Vienna; Professor Dr Uwe M.Schneede, Hamburg; Professor Dr Heinz Spielmann, Schleswig; Mrs Margrit Sprengel, Hanover; Mr H.J.C.Stach, Zandvoort; Mrs Liselotte Bendix Stern, New York; Hofrat Mag. Dr Alice Strobl, Vienna; M.Xavier Tricot, Ostend; Professor Dr Paul Vogt, Essen; Professor David G.Wilkins, Pittsburgh; Mr Johann Winkler, Pöchlarn.

The directors and staff of many institutions have also been generous with their time and help in connection with my research; my particular thanks to the following: Agfa Foto-Historama in Wallraf-Richartz Museum/Museum Ludwig, Cologne, and especially Dr Bodo von Dewitz; Bayerische Staatsgemäldesammlungen, Munich, and especially Dr Ulrich Bischoff and Dr Christian Lenz; the Brücke-Museum, Berlin, and its director Professor Dr Magdalena M.Moeller; Bundesarchiv, Potsdam; the Busch-Reisinger Museum (Harvard University Art Museums) and Daimler-Benz Curator Peter Nisbet; Christie's, London; Frankfurter Kunstverein; Gabriele Münter- und Johannes Eichner-Stiftung, Munich, and especially Frau Ilse Holzinger; Galerie Beyeler, Basle; Galerie Brockstedt, Hamburg; Galerie Fischer, Lucerne, and especially Marco Crameri; Grace Borgenicht Gallery, New York; Karl Ernst Osthaus-Museum, Hagen; Kunstmuseum, Berne, Paul Klee Stiftung; Leonard Hutton Galleries, New York, and especially Mrs Ingrid Hutton; Louisiana Museum, Humlebaek, Denmark; Mills College Art Gallery, Oakland, California, and its assistant director Timothy Mosman; Minneapolis Institute of Arts, and especially archivist Brian J.Mulhern; Museum Folkwang, Essen, and especially Dr Hubertus Froning; Muzeum Narodowe, Wrocław; Norton Simon Museum, Pasadena; the Oakland Museum, Oakland, California, and especially Christine Droll; San Francisco Museum of Modern Art; Schweizerisches Institut für Kunstwissenschaft, Zurich, and especially Denise Vosseler; Sotheby's, New York; Staatliche Museen Preussischer Kulturbesitz, Berlin; Staatliche Museen zu Berlin, Nationalgalerie and Zentralarchiv, especially Dr Friedrich Künzel, Dr Annegret Janda and Dr Jörn Grabowski; Städtische Galerie im Lenbachhaus, Munich; Städtische Kunsthalle, Mannheim, and especially Dr Hans-Jürgen Buderer; the Ulmer Museum, Ulm, and its director Dr Brigitte Reinhardt; Wilhelm-Lehmbruck-Museum, Duisburg, and especially Dr Renate Heidt Heller; Zentralinstitut für Kunstgeschichte, Munich.

Nearer to home, several institutions in the United Kingdom went to quite extraordinary lengths to help me in my work and provide facilities of various kinds. I am especially grateful to the Tate Gallery, London, its director Nicholas Serota and the librarian and staff of the Tate Gallery Library; the Victoria and Albert Museum, London, and the librarian and staff of the National Art Library; and the Witt Library, Courtauld Institute of Art, University of London. Still closer to home, I am indebted to the Librarian and staff of Essex University Library for their unfailing courtesy and efficiency, especially the Inter-Library Loans Department under the able direction of Sandy Macmillen, who aided my work immeasurably; also to my friends and colleagues in the Department of Art History and Theory at Essex, particularly Professor Dawn Ades, who read and commented on some of my entries, to Professor Thomas Puttfarken and Professor Michael Podro, and to Barry Woodcock and Tim Laughton who advised me on photography and on various technical matters. In addition, I would like to thank several successive generations of postgraduate students on whom I took the liberty of trying out some of my ideas. I also relied heavily on the dedicated help and unstinting efforts of a small group of students and former students who acted as research assistants on this, as it turned out, mammoth project; I am particularly grateful to Christopher Short, who laid aside his own important work on Nietzsche and Expressionism in order to assist me in my researches; to Colin Rhodes, who as well as completing his Ph.D. and a book on Kirchner, somehow still found time to read and comment on my drafts and share with me his own ideas and enthusiasms; to Felicity Lunn, who likewise managed to combine her own demanding job as exhibitions officer at the Whitechapel Art Gallery with researching many of the provenances and exhibition histories of the works considered in this volume, and conducting the large amount of attendant correspondence; and to Jennifer Greitschus and Helen Skåtun, both of whom were especially helpful in connection with the three entries relating to the works of Edvard Munch. To all of them, and to the many other students and colleagues whom it has not been possible to name individually, I offer my sincerest thanks.

Finally, I am grateful to the staff of Philip Wilson Publishers, particularly Anne Jackson and Joan A. Speers, for all their efforts, also to Celia Jones, the copy-editor, and to Gillian Greenwood, the designer, who were meticulous in their attention to every detail, as well as offering much welcome advice.

My wife Caroline supported and encouraged me at every stage of this project, even when pressure of work threatened to engulf family life to an abnormal degree. She also discussed and criticized ideas, read drafts, fragments and proofs, and made suggestions and comments, always to my benefit. I am indebted to her more than I can say, and it is to her and to our two children that this book is dedicated in love and in gratitude.

Peter Vergo
UNIVERSITY OF ESSEX
March 1992

Notes on the catalogue

Arrangement

The catalogue which follows is arranged alphabetically by artist. Where the collection contains more than one work by a given artist, paintings are catalogued in chronological order followed by works on paper, except in the case of Klee, where a purely chronological sequence appeared more sensible. Each entry provides the following information: name of the artist with dates of birth and death; catalogue number and title of the work in English followed by original title (if any); date of execution; medium and support; dimensions; whether there is any signature or inscription on either recto or verso; a note on condition; and the accession number by which the work is known. Provenance, exhibition history and bibliographic references are summarized in concise form, followed by discussion of the work itself.

Title

For each work, I have tried to ascertain whether the title was that used by the artist. Many paintings are titled on the stretcher or back of the canvas, or the artist entered the work in a handlist or inventory. In such cases, this title is given in the original language immediately following the title in English. Titles found in early exhibition catalogues or dealers' lists which would have been compiled with the artist's knowledge or approval are likewise regarded as authentic. Where no such evidence exists, the title is given in English alone, and corresponds to that under which the work was sold, or by which it has most commonly been known.

Date of execution

Where the date of execution is known and is supported by documentary or other evidence, it is given as a single year. Where an earlier and a later date are given, separated by a hyphen (for example '1913–14'), work on the painting or drawing began in one year and finished in another. Where two dates are given, separated by a slash (for example '1914/25'), the available evidence indicates that the painting was left in a first or unfinished state, and that work then resumed or the picture was over-painted at a later date (as in the case of [49]). Where a date is given as '*c* ....', this is an assumption based on stylistic criteria or on secondary evidence (for example early exhibition history), unsupported by primary documentation. In cases where the date of execution is uncertain, the reasoning behind the date or dates suggested in this catalogue is discussed in the text.

Medium and support

Despite detailed technical examination, it has not always been possible to provide an exhaustive description of the various media employed. In general, the media described are those which were capable of being identified by purely visual inspection, under ultra-violet light or (in the case of *pentimenti* or underdrawing) by the use of infra-red reflectography. Invasive or destructive analytic techniques, however interesting these may be for the scientist, have been avoided. The most commonly used media proved to be, unsurprisingly, oil paint, tempera, gouache, watercolour, Indian or coloured inks and pencil. Supports included (most frequently) canvas, board, panel and paper. In the case of works on paper, it was not practicable to distinguish between the various brands of commercially available drawing paper, which are referred to simply as 'paper'. Where, however, the artist has employed, for example, a hand-made or high-quality art paper, or (at the other end of the scale) a poor-quality (for example wrapping) paper, this has been noted.

The designation 'board' proved to be especially problematic. As in the case of paper, during the period covered by this catalogue a very wide range of different qualities and different kinds of board was commercially available. At one end of the spectrum, artists often used a cheap, poor-quality material closely resembling (or identical with) ordinary every-day cardboard. At the other, they could if they wished buy commercially ready-prepared, even pre-primed artists' board. Also popular among artists was what is called in German *Hartfaserplatte* – in American usage 'masonite', usually translated into English as 'hardboard', though on closer examination hardboard turns out to be just as variable in quality and rigidity as other kinds of board. In the end, no attempt has been made to distinguish between these various kinds of rigid and semi-rigid support. (Any such attempt would in any case have been futile, since as often as not the original board layer has subsequently been stuck down on some other form of support, rendering it resistant to any kind of examination other than destructive chemical testing.) The one exception to this rule is in the case of what is sometimes referred to as 'canvasboard' (*Malkarton*), a kind of textured artists' board manufactured and ready-stamped so that its surface closely resembles that of a medium-to-loose weave canvas. This is a peculiarly deceptive form of support, since in reproduction, and even on cursory visual examination, it often passes for canvas. Even harder to distinguish between are canvasboard and cases where a canvas has actually been stuck down on board: thus, [32] (canvasboard) and [70] (canvas stuck down on board) appear to the naked eye virtually indistinguishable. Such instances have, therefore, been specifically noted.

Virtually all technical examinations were conducted together with Emil Bosshard, Head of Conservation of the Thyssen-Bornemisza Collection, for the most part in the conservation laboratory at Lugano. I am grateful to him for sharing with me his time, his expertise and his observations on many of the paintings. He was also responsible for the excellent photographs, taken in the course of examination by means of infra-red reflectography, which appear on pp.209, 288. Responsibility for any errors contained in the technical descriptions of the paintings, on the other hand, is entirely mine.

Dimensions/inscriptions

The dimensions given (in centimetres, height before width) are those of the canvas, board or sheet without frame or mount, unless otherwise indicated. The opportunity has been taken to correct many errors perpetrated in previous catalogues, particularly with regard to inscriptions. In one or two instances it was not possible to examine the back of a painting, because of the way it had been framed, or for conservation reasons. These instances are specifically noted. Some of the more widely-travelled paintings have, in the course of time, acquired an elaborate patina of dealers' or shippers' marks or labels affixed to the back of the frame or stretcher. The presence of these has in general been ignored, except where they shed light on early or otherwise unrecorded exhibitions, or on the identity of former owners.

Condition

Each entry includes a brief note on the condition of the work in question. Where this is considered to be good, without evidence of damage, over-painting or previous restoration, these notes have been kept to a minimum. Where the condition is fragile or poor, more detailed information is given. Instances in which a canvas has been re-lined or re-stretched are indicated. Paintings are varnished unless noted otherwise.

Provenance

Compiling a complete and accurate provenance for each work is a headache which afflicts every author of every catalogue raisonné. Apart from frequent difficulties in establishing the identity of previous owners, or persuading them to allow their names to be published, it is often a frustrating exercise to attempt to trace the progress of a work around the world from one saleroom or auction to another. In a number of cases, works acquired by dealers or commercial galleries such as Marlborough Fine Art in London, or the Galerie Nierendorf in Berlin, remained in their possession for a considerable time before being sold. In these instances the dealer or gallery is regarded as an owner, and named accordingly. Where, on the other hand, a work merely passed through the hands of a dealer or auction house in the course of its disposal, I have limited myself to naming the previous owner or collection from which it came, not the dealer or auction house. The manner in which each work was acquired by the present owner (as well as the date of acquisition, which may also be inferred from the accession number) is, however, indicated in every case. Thus, if a picture was purchased from a dealer or at auction, the dealer's name or that of the auction house immmediately precedes that of the Thyssen-Bornemisza Collection. In a few instances, especially in the case of private treaties, it proved impossible to discover the previous history of the work in question or, indeed, anything other than its date of acquisition.

The provenance of each work is given in chronological order. The phrase 'estate of the artist' means that the work was still in the artist's possession at the time of his or her death. 'Collection of the artist' indicates that the work remained in the artist's possession for some time – years rather than months – before being sold or otherwise disposed of.

Exhibitions/Literature

The lists of exhibitions, which are arranged in chronological order, are intended to be as comprehensive as possible. Frequently cited exhibitions are noted in short form (for example 'Bremen 1975'); for full references, see p.27. Otherwise the information given is as follows: city, museum or organizing institution, year, title of exhibition as recorded in the catalogue, catalogue number under which the work was exhibited. Where the same exhibition was shown at more than one venue, a slash separates the names of the participating cities and institutions (for example 'Schaffhausen, Museum zu Allerheiligen/Berlin, Schloss Charlottenburg, 1959, *Triumph der Farbe*'). If no catalogue number is given, it is because the works exhibited were unnumbered in the catalogue, or because there was no catalogue, or because the catalogue could not be located. In order to avoid perpetuating inaccuracies, or in dubious cases where a work is believed to have been included in a particular exhibition but no catalogue was published and no other record exists, the exhibition has been omitted from the present listings. The exhibition history of each work is complete to the end of 1990.

Literature references, on the other hand, are highly selective. In the case of some artists (for example Kirchner), the existing literature is vast; to list all of it against every entry would serve no purpose. Moreover, some works (for example [46]) have been reproduced on literally dozens of occasions, without commentary, more by way of decoration to articles and books on twentieth-century art than for the sake of any discussion of the picture's history or significance. It seemed pointless simply to confront the user of this catalogue with a list of such instances. Thus, those references included under Literature are precisely that, that is to say *references*: on looking up the relevant article, book or catalogue, the reader will find the work in question referred to, recorded or discussed. Where a reference is given in the form 'see . . .' or 'see also . . .', this indicates that the book or article includes important background information, rather than specific discussion of the particular painting, watercolour or drawing.

A small number works have, as far as can be ascertained, been neither exhibited nor written about. In the corresponding catalogue entries, the headings 'Exhibitions' and 'Literature' have therefore been omitted.

Bibliography

The bibliography, too, could scarcely be other than highly selective. A comprehensive bibliography of Expressionism alone would run to many volumes; a bibliography covering the whole of twentieth-century German art would be even more unwieldy. I have, therefore, included only those books and articles which are referred to in the catalogue entries, and which I have used in the course of my research. The individual entries contain on occasion more detailed references to some of the relevant periodical literature; not all of these references are included in the main bibliography. This for the most part consists of books and oeuvre-catalogues and is arranged alphabetically by author (or title of periodical or exhibition). Where there are several works by the same author, these are listed chronologically. In the catalogue entries, the majority of references are given in short form, for example 'Gordon (1968)', corresponding to the abbreviated reference which precedes each item included in the bibliography.

German institutions, etc.

As a consequence of the re-unification of Germany which happened while this book was being written, the names of a number of former East German institutions have changed. The proposed reorganization of many German museums and galleries, most especially the Berlin museums, makes it inevitable that further changes will occur. These, however, are far from complete at the time of writing, and for the sake of consistency with earlier publications the names and titles used in the present catalogue are for the most part those which obtained prior to 1990. By the same token, in discussing Kandinsky's 1915 journey from Russia to Sweden, I refer in passing to 'Petrograd', not 'St Petersburg' or 'Leningrad'; the same rule applies to other towns and cities whose names have changed in the course of time, e.g. Kristiania/Oslo, Breslau/Wrocław.

List of Exhibitions

In the catalogue entries which follow, frequently-cited exhibitions are referred to in abbreviated form; the full references are given below.

Australian tour 1979–80
Perth, Art Gallery of Western Australia/Adelaide, Art Gallery of South Australia/Brisbane, Queensland Art Gallery/Melbourne, National Gallery of Victoria/Sydney, Art Gallery of New South Wales/Wellington, NZ, National Art Gallery/Auckland, City Art Gallery/Christchurch, Robert McDougall Art Gallery, 1979–80, *America & Europe. A Century of Modern Masters from the Thyssen-Bornemisza Collection*

Bremen 1975
Bremen, Kunsthalle, 1975, *Moderne Kunst aus der Sammlung Thyssen-Bornemisza*

Brussels/Paris 1977–8
Brussels, Musée d'Ixelles/Paris, Musée d'Art Moderne de la Ville de Paris, 1977–8, *La Collection Thyssen-Bornemisza. Tableaux Modernes*

Budapest/Szombathely 1985–6
Budapest, Magyar Nemzéti Galéria/Szombathely, Képtár, 1985–6, *15.-20. századi remekmüvek a báró Thyssen-Bornemisza gyüjteményböl/Meisterwerke des 15.–20. Jahrhunderts aus der Sammlung Thyssen-Bornemisza*

Cologne 1986
Cologne, Galerie Gmurzynska, 1986, *Pioniere der abstrakten Kunst aus der Sammlung Thyssen-Bornemisza*

Essen 1958
Essen, Museum Folkwang, 1958, *Brücke 1905–1913, eine Künstlergemeinschaft des Expressionismus*[1]

***Expressionism, a German Intuition*, 1980–81**
New York, Solomon R. Guggenheim Museum/San Francisco, CA, Museum of Modern Art, 1980–81, *Expressionism. A German Intuition, 1905–1920*

***Expressionism and Modern German Painting*, 1989–90**
Washington, DC, National Gallery of Art/Forth Worth, TX, Kimbell Art Museum/San Francisco, CA, Fine Arts Museums, 1989–90, *Expressionism and Modern German Painting from the Thyssen-Bornemisza Collection*

Florence 1964
Florence, Palazzo Strozzi, 1964, *L'Espressionismo. Pittura, Scultura, Architettura*

Japanese tour 1976
Tokyo, Seibu Museum of Art/Kobe, Hyōgo Prefectural Museum/Fukuoka, Kitakyushu Municipal Museum, 1976, *The Origin of the 20th Century in the Collection Thyssen-Bornemisza*

Leningrad/Moscow 1988
Leningrad, Russian Museum/Moscow, Tretyakov Gallery, 1988, *Masterpieces of Twentieth-Century Painting from the Thyssen-Bornemisza Collection*

Lugano 1975
Lugano, Villa Malpensata, 1975, *Dalle collezioni d'arte private ticinesi. Maestri europei del XX secolo*

Lugano 1978
Lugano, Villa Malpensata, 1978, *Collezione Thyssen-Bornemisza. Arte Moderna*

Lugano 1989
Lugano, Villa Favorita, 1989, *Expressionism. Masterpieces from the Thyssen-Bornemisza Collection*

Luxemburg/Munich/Vienna, 1988–9
Luxemburg, Villa Vauban/Munich, Haus der Kunst/Vienna, Museum des 20. Jahrhunderts, 1988–9, *Wege zur Abstraktion. 80 Meisterwerke aus der Sammlung Thyssen-Bornemisza*

***Meisterwerke des deutschen Expressionismus*, 1960–61**
Bremen, Kunsthalle/Hanover, Kunstverein/The Hague, Gemeentemuseum/Cologne, Wallraf-Richartz Museum/Zurich, Kunsthaus, 1960–61, *Meisterwerke des deutschen Expressionismus*

***Modern Masters from the Thyssen-Bornemisza Collection*, 1984–6**
Tokyo, National Museum of Modern Art/Kumamoto, Prefectural Museum/London, Royal Academy of Arts/Nuremberg, Germanisches Nationalmuseum/Düsseldorf, Städtische Kunsthalle/Florence, Palazzo Pitti/Paris, Musée d'Art Moderne de la Ville de Paris/Madrid, Biblioteca Nacional, Salas Pablo Ruiz Picasso/Barcelona, Palacio de la Virreina, 1984–6, *Modern Masters from the Thyssen-Bornemisza Collection*

Munich 1949
Munich, Haus der Kunst, 1949, *Der Blaue Reiter. München und die Kunst des 20. Jahrhunderts; der Weg von 1908–1914*

Paris/Munich 1966
Paris, Musée National d'Art Moderne/Munich, Haus der Kunst, 1966, *Le fauvisme français et les débuts de l'expressionisme allemand/Der französische Fauvismus und der deutsche Frühexpressionismus*

Rome 1990–91
Rome, Palazzo Ruspoli, 1990–91, *Espressionismo. Capolavori della Collezione Thyssen-Bornemisza. Da van Gogh a Klee*

USA tour 1982–4
Washington, DC, National Gallery of Art/Hartford, CT, Wadsworth Atheneum/Toledo, OH, Museum of Art/Seattle, WA, Art Museum/San Francisco, CA, Museum of Modern Art/New York, Metropolitan Museum of Art/Phoenix, AZ, Art Museum, 1982–4, *20th-Century Masters. The Thyssen-Bornemisza Collection*

Note

1 A much reduced version of the exhibition, consisting of thirty paintings, was shown in Ulm at the Ulmer Museum during January – March 1959 under the title *Bilder der 'Brücke'*. There was no catalogue. I am grateful to Dr Brigitte Reinhardt, Director of the Ulmer Museum, for her assistance in confirming the precise contents of that exhibition

List of works

MAX BECKMANN
1 Self-portrait with Raised Hand
2 Quappi in Pink Jumper
3 Still-life with Yellow Roses
4 Circus Artists

LOVIS CORINTH
5 Fashion Show

OTTO DIX
6 Hugo Erfurth with Dog

KEES VAN DONGEN
7 Woman with Cigarette (Kiki de Montparnasse [?])
8 Nine Illustrations for Marcel Proust's *A la Recherche du temps perdu*

JAMES ENSOR
9 Theatre of Masks

LYONEL FEININGER
10 The White Man
11 Ships
12 Architecture II
13 Lady in Mauve
14 Magic River (Dream across the River)
15 La Belle
16 Street behind the Church. Treptow an der Rega

GEORGE GROSZ
17 Metropolis (View of the Metropolis)
18 Street Scene (Kurfürstendamm)
19 Nude
20 Twilight
21 Der Stammtisch

ERICH HECKEL
22 Brickworks
23 House in Dangast (The White House)
24 Female Head (Portrait of Siddi Heckel)
24 *verso* The Swing
25 In Front of Red Curtain
26 Bathers on the Beach

ALBERT HENRICH
27 Portrait of the Painter A.M.Tränkler

KARL HOFER
28 Church in Malcantone

KARL HUBBUCH
29 Twice Hilde II

JOHANNES ITTEN
30 Group of Houses in Spring
31 Kindly Light

ALEXEI VON JAWLENSKY
32 Child with Doll
33 Red Veil

WASSILY KANDINSKY
34 Murnau: Houses on the Obermarkt
35 Murnau: Top of the Johannisstrasse
36 The Ludwigskirche in Munich
37 Picture with Three Spots
38 In the Bright Oval
39 Around the Line
40 Untitled
41 Untitled
42 Delicate Tension

ERNST LUDWIG KIRCHNER
43 The Loam Pit
44 Doris with Ruff Collar
45 Woman in front of Birch Trees
45 *verso* Woman with Pointed Hat
46 Fränzi in front of Carved Chair
47 Kneeling Nude in front of Red Screen
47 *verso* Seated Nude with Bent Leg
48 Curving Bay
49 With Red Streetwalker
50 Alpine Kitchen
51 The Junkerboden under Snow

PAUL KLEE
52 View on to a Square
53 Revolving House
54 Still-life with Dice
55 Omega 5 (295) 'Dummy'

OSKAR KOKOSCHKA
56 Portrait of Max Schmidt
57 Pontresina
58 Flowers in a Vase
59 Tulips and Peonies
60 Bouquet of Flowers (Tulips and Lilac)
61 Tulips and Narcissi

AUGUST MACKE
62 Hussars (Hussars on a Sortie)
63 Circus
64 Promenade à Trois
65 Flowers
66 Woman on a Divan

JEANNE MAMMEN
67 Street Girl

FRANZ MARC
68 The Dream
69 Goblet with Fox and Deer

LUDWIG MEIDNER
70 The Corner House (Villa Kochmann, Dresden)

OTTO MUELLER
71 Two Female Nudes in a Landscape
72 Nude by a Woodland Pool

GABRIELE MÜNTER
73 Self-portrait
74 Murnau

EDVARD MUNCH
75 Evening
76 The Sick Child
77 Encounter in Space

EMIL NOLDE
78 Red Flowers
79 Summer Clouds
80 Flower Garden
81 Autumn Evening
82 Glowing Sunflowers
83 Head of a Woman

84 Summer Flowers (Red and White Poppies against Blue Sky)
85 Iris, Tiger-lilies, Poppies
86 Young Couple
87 Landscape with Farmhouses
88 Red Cloud

MAX PECHSTEIN
89 Horse Fair
90 Summer in Nidden

CHRISTIAN ROHLFS
91 Street in Soest

CHRISTIAN SCHAD
92 Composition en N
93 Maria and Annunziata 'from the Harbour'
94 Portrait of Dr Haustein

EGON SCHIELE
95 Houses on the River (The Old Town)
96 Self-portrait
97 Seated Girl (Poldi Lodzinski [?])
98 Nude Girl with Arms Outstretched
99 Boy in a Sailor Suit (Paul Erdmann)

OSKAR SCHLEMMER
100 Formation (Tri-partition)

RUDOLF SCHLICHTER
101 Portrait of an Oriental Journalist

KARL SCHMIDT-ROTTLUFF
102 The Little House
103 Autumn Landscape in Oldenburg
104 Sun over Pine Forest
105 The Village of Dangast
106 Reflecting Clouds

Max Beckmann 1884–1950

1 Self-portrait with Raised Hand

1908
Oil on canvas, 55 × 45 cm
Unsigned/undated
In good condition. The painting has received a coat of modern varnish, contrary to Beckmann's usual practice of leaving his paintings unvarnished
Accession no.1985.16

Provenance
Reinhard Piper, Munich [acquired before 1914; in his collection at his death in 1953]
Klaus Piper, Munich
Robert Gore Rifkind, Los Angeles, CA
Sotheby's, New York
Thyssen-Bornemisza Collection, 1985[1]

Exhibitions
Mannheim, Städtische Kunsthalle, 1928, *Max Beckmann: Das gesammelte Werk*, no.9
Munich, Haus der Kunst/Berlin, Schloss Charlottenburg, 1951, *Max Beckmann zum Gedächtnis, 1884–1950*, no.19 [as '1913']
Paris, Musée National d'Art Moderne, 1968–9, *Max Beckmann*, no.9[2]
Munich, Haus der Kunst, 1968–9, *Max Beckmann*, no.9
Bloomington, IN, Indiana University Art Museum, 1977, *German and Austrian Expressionism 1900–1920*, no.1
Bielefeld, Kunsthalle/Frankfurt am Main, Städelsches Kunstinstitut, 1982, *Max Beckmann: Die Frühen Bilder*, no.82
Los Angeles, CA, County Museum of Art, 1984–5, *Max Beckmann Retrospective*, no.9[3]
Lugano 1989, no.42
Expressionism and Modern German Painting, 1989–90, no.1
Leipzig, Museum der bildenden Künste/Frankfurt am Main, Städelsches Kunstinstitut, 1990, *Max Beckmann. Gemälde 1905–1950*, no.8
Rome 1990–91, no.1

Literature
Glaser (1924), p.76 [as '1913']
Reifenberg (1949), nos.68, 146
Reinhard Piper, *Mein Leben als Verleger*, Munich (R.Piper & Co.) 1964, p.336
Göpel (1976), no.99
Güse (1977), p.52
Erpel (1985), p.19
Max Beckmann. Gemälde 1905–1950, exh. cat., Leipzig, Museum der bildenden Künste, 1990, p.62
See also James D.Burke, 'Max Beckmann: An Introduction to the Self-Portraits', in Schulz-Hoffmann (1984), pp.53–68;[4] ibid., p.192

According to Beckmann's handlists,[5] this self-portrait was painted in the summer of 1908 in Hermsdorf, the northern suburb of Berlin where he had his studio. It appears that, having embarked on it, he then put it to one side for some considerable time – perhaps until as late as 1913 – while trying to decide whether to resume work on it or leave it unfinished. This is, perhaps, the cause of the conflicting dates to be found in some of the earlier literature. Glaser, in the first published catalogue of Beckmann's paintings, ascribed *Self-portrait with Raised Hand* to 1913, though without indicating on the basis of what evidence. Reifenberg, who compiled the 1949 catalogue of the artist's works from 1904 onwards, was evidently misled by Glaser's (unsubstantiated) dating; thus, the picture is, erroneously, entered twice in his listings, under 1908 (on the basis of Beckmann's handlists) and under 1913.[6]

Notes
1 Acquired at auction, 14 May 1985 (*Impressionist and Modern Paintings and Sculpture*, lot 53). I am grateful to Robert Gore Rifkind, Los Angeles, CA, his assistant, Margaret Amos, and registrar, Christine Vigiletti, for supplying additional information concerning the history and provenance of this painting
2 Exhibition also shown in Munich at the Haus der Kunst (with separate catalogue and in some cases different catalogue numbers: see following entry under 'Exhibitions') and in Brussels at the Palais des Beaux-Arts during 1968–9; the catalogue of the Brussels exhibition was identical with that used for the Paris showing
3 Centenary exhibition shown first in Munich, Haus der Kunst/Berlin, Nationalgalerie/Saint Louis, MO, City Art Museum, 1984–5; [1] was, however, shown only in Los Angeles
4 English language version of the catalogue of the Beckmann centenary exhibition: see n.3
5 See Göpel (1976), I, p.85
6 On the variant datings of the painting in the earlier Beckmann oeuvre-catalogues by Glaser and by Reifenberg and Hausenstein, as well as the arguments regarding the extent to which the work is to be regarded as unfinished, see Göpel (1976), I, note to p.86

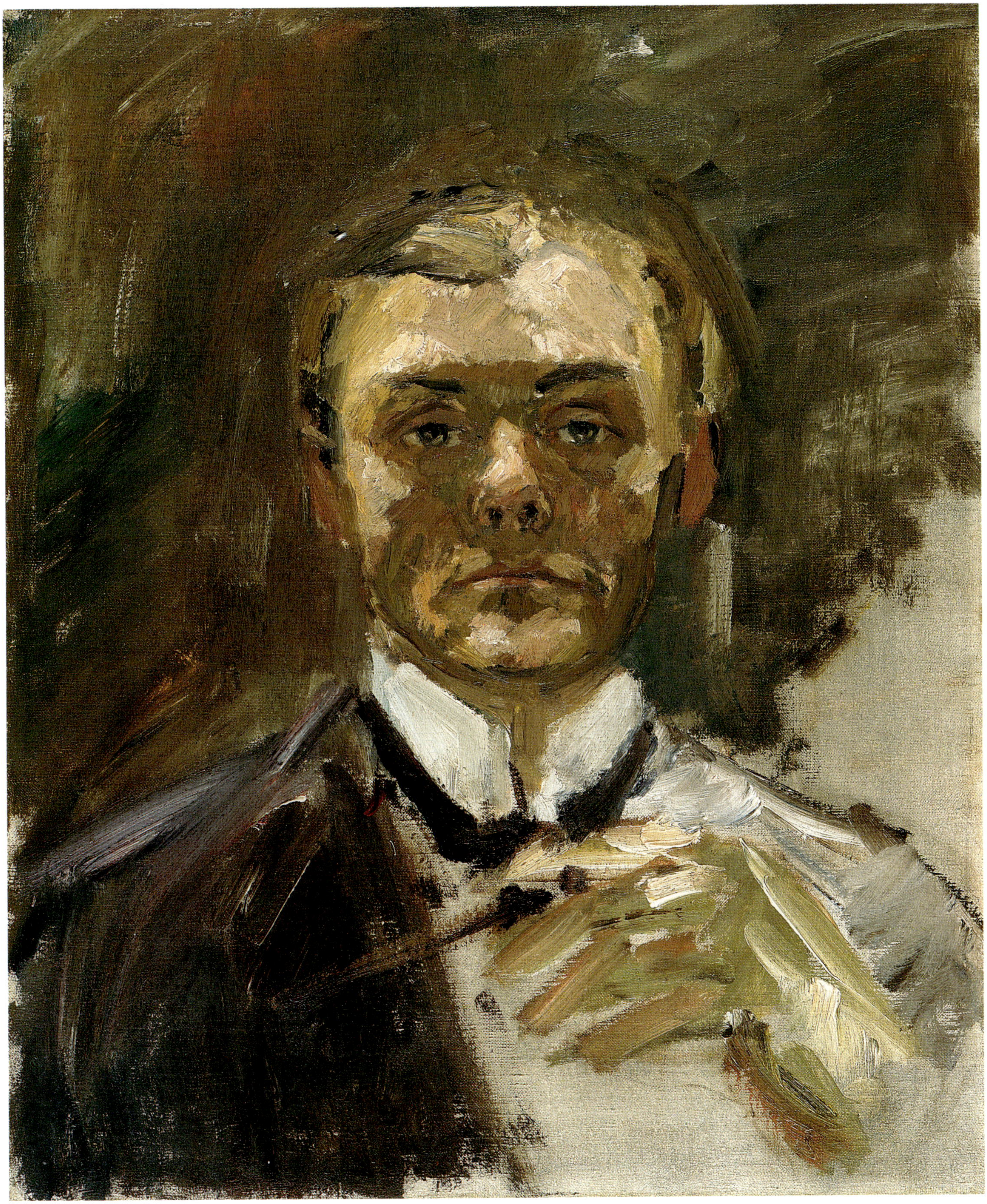

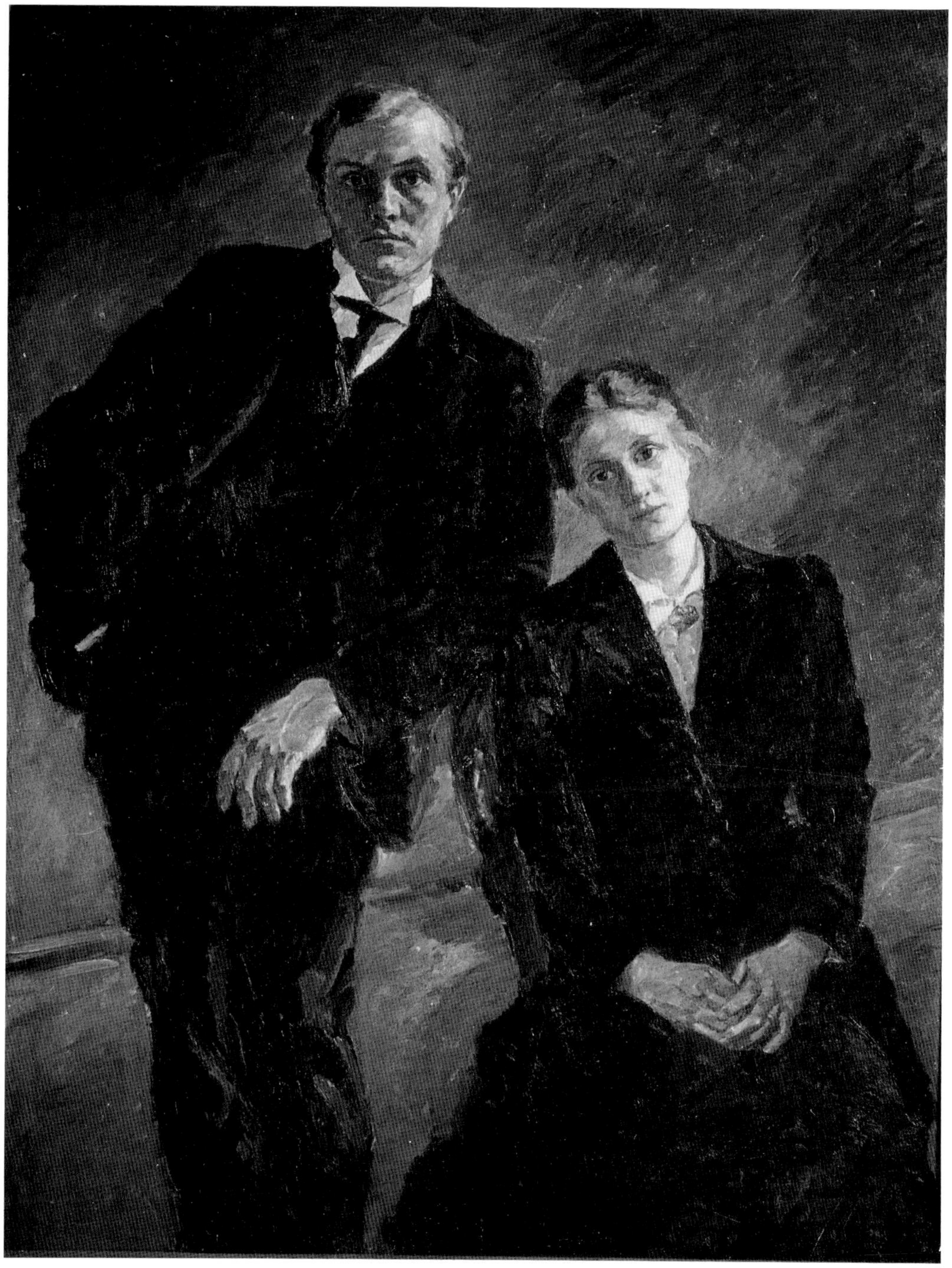

FIG 1 Max Beckmann, *Double Portrait of Mink and Myself*, oil on canvas, 142 × 109 cm (Halle, Staatliche Galerie Moritzburg, inv. no.1/131)

The title used here, *Self-portrait with Raised Hand*, is that given to the painting by its first owner, Reinhard Piper, one of Germany's foremost avant-garde publishers and a figure closely linked with Expressionism. A friend of Beckmann's, he collaborated with Reifenberg on the 1949 oeuvre-catalogue referred to above. He had also been intimately involved with the Blue Rider group in Munich before the First World War, having brought out both the *Blue Rider Almanac* of 1912 and Kandinsky's *Über das Geistige in der Kunst* (On the Spiritual in Art).[7] In his autobiography, Piper recalled: 'I acquired one of [Beckmann's] earliest paintings, the *Self-portrait with Raised Hand*, which is not entirely finished, shortly after the Samson.'[8] ('Samson' refers to Beckmann's *Samson and Delilah* of 1912,[9] which Piper had bought in the summer of that year on his first visit to the artist's Hermsdorf studio.) In his own inventory, Beckmann listed the present work merely as 'Selbstportrait (unvollendet) [Self-portrait (unfinished)]'.[10]

Notes

7 On Piper's career as publisher and collector, see Barbara Göpel, 'Reinhard Piper. Verleger und Sammler aus Passion', in the auction catalogue *Aquarelle, Zeichnungen und Graphik des 20. Jahrhunderts* (*Auktion 156*, 29–30 June 1981), Munich (Karl & Faber) 1981, pp.4–9

8 Piper, pp.315f

9 Göpel (1976), no.155

10 Ibid., 1, p.85

11 Piper, p.336
12 Leopold (1973), no.294; J.Kallir (1990), P.322
13 Güse (1977), loc. cit.
14 Ibid.; also Erpel (1985), p.300

The picture offers a striking, though slightly sombre view of the painter who, in later years, was to become one of his own most frequent subjects. (Piper observed that 'few contemporary artists have occupied themselves with their own appearance in so reflective and pictorial a manner as Beckmann has done in etchings, woodcuts and paintings from 1910 onwards.')[11] Among Beckmann's other early works, it most closely resembles the image of himself he presents in his celebrated double portrait with his first wife Minna, painted the following year (fig.1). The prominence given to the upraised hand, the vehicle by which the painter expresses himself, also links it with other portraits of Expressionist artists, for example Egon Schiele's depiction of the painter Albert Paris von Gütersloh of 1918 (Minneapolis Institute of Arts).[12] However, this early Beckmann painting is, by comparison, far more restrained in manner and in most important respects betrays few affinities with Expressionism or with other contemporary portraiture.

It has been suggested, not implausibly, that the frontality of the portrait head and the hand raised as if in benediction may be a deliberate reference to the Byzantine-inspired tradition of depicting Christ as ruler of the world (see fig.2).[13] On the other hand, whether the artist has here represented himself holding a paintbrush, as has repeatedly been stated,[14] or a cigarette, as in so many of the later self-portraits, remains open to question. Perhaps deliberately, or perhaps because the picture is unfinished, the object held between the second and third fingers of the left hand is too indistinctly painted for precise identification to be possible.

FIG 2 Christos Pantokrator, Greek, early 17th century, tempera on panel, 60.5 × 38.2 cm (Vienna, Österreichisches Museum für Angewandte Kunst, inv. no.Blg 242)

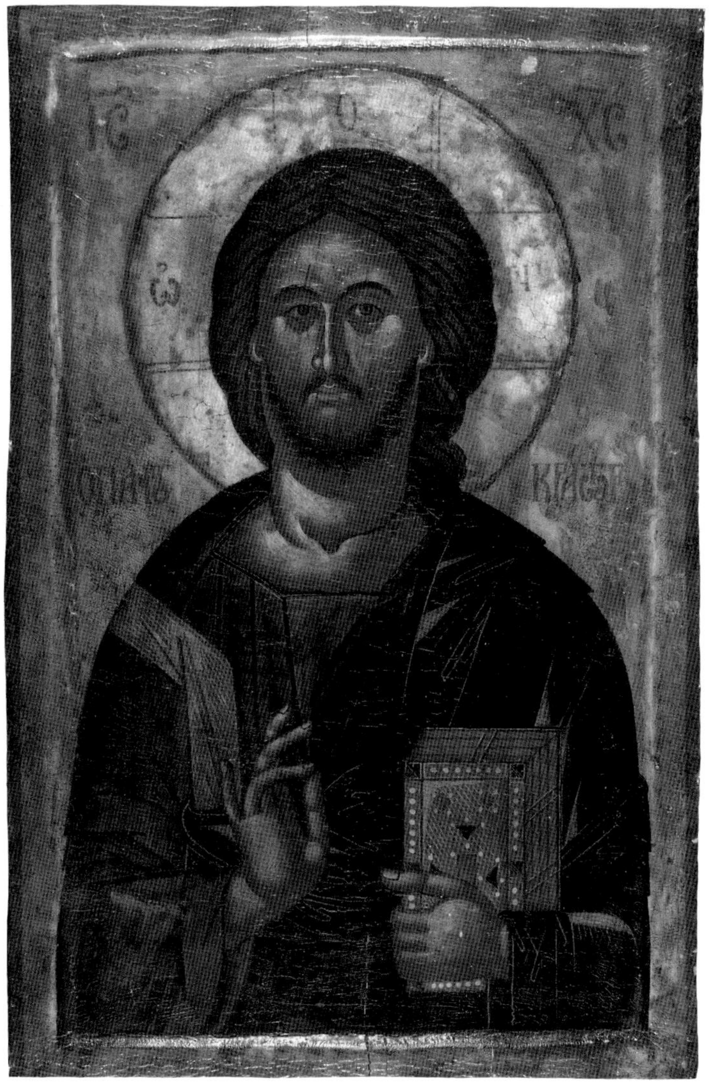

Max Beckmann 1884–1950

2 Quappi in Pink Jumper

Quappi in rosa Jumper[1]

1932–5
Oil on canvas, 105 × 73 cm
Signed/dated upper right: 'Beckmann 34'
The painting is unvarnished; despite its many travels, and the numerous occasions on which it has been exhibited, it is in pristine condition
Accession no.1969.19

Provenance
Collection of the artist
Stephan Lackner, Santa Barbara, CA
Galerie R.N.Ketterer, Campione d'Italia
Thyssen-Bornemisza Collection, 1969

Exhibitions
New York, Buchholz Gallery Curt Valentin, 1938, *Exhibition of Recent Paintings by Max Beckmann*, no.7[2]
Santa Barbara, CA, University Art Gallery, 1959, *Max Beckmann*, no.11
Downey, CA, Museum of Art, 1960, *Max Beckmann. Oils, Watercolors, Lithographs*, no.4
Karlsruhe, Badischer Kunstverein, 1963, *Max Beckmann. Das Portrait*, no.37
Pasadena CA, Art Museum, 1964, *A View of the Century*, no.13
Santa Barbara, CA, Museum of Art, 1965, *Works of Art from Santa Barbara and Vicinity*, no.1
Bremen, Kunsthalle, 1966–7, *Max Beckmann. Gemälde und Aquarelle der Sammlung Stephan Lackner*, no.2[3]
Paris, Musée National d'Art Moderne, 1968–9, *Max Beckmann*, no.50[4]
Munich, Haus der Kunst, 1968–9, *Max Beckmann*, no.48
Bremen 1975, no.3
Brussels/Paris 1977–8, no.4
Lugano 1978, no.4
Berlin, Staatliche Museen Preussischer Kulturbesitz, 1980, *Bilder von Menschen in der Kunst des Abendlandes*, no.57
USA tour 1982–4, no.12
Modern Masters from the Thyssen-Bornemisza Collection, 1984–6, no.5
Moscow/Leningrad 1988, no.3
Lugano 1989, no.43
Expressionism and Modern German Painting, 1989–90, no.2
Rome 1990–91, no.2

Literature
Reifenberg (1949), no.341 [as 'Portrait einer Amerikanerin']
R.N.Ketterer, *Moderne Kunst VI*, Campione d'Italia (Galerie R.N.Ketterer) 1969, p.16, no.7, ill. p.17
Kiel (1974), p.8, ill. p.9
Göpel (1976), no.404

Portraiture occupied an important place in Beckmann's work of the 1920s and 1930s. Apart from himself, one of his most frequent subjects was his second wife Mathilde von Kaulbach (1904–86), whom he married in 1925. Nicknamed Quappi, she was the youngest daughter of the eminent German painter Friedrich August von Kaulbach and was, like Beckmann's first wife the singer Minna Tube, a trained musician.

Notes
1 The title is taken from the artist's handlists; see Göpel (1976), I, p.271
2 Exhibition also shown in Kansas City, Los Angeles, San Francisco, Saint Louis, Portland and Seattle during 1938
3 Exhibition also shown in Berlin, Karlsruhe, Vienna, Linz and Lucerne during 1966–7
4 Exhibition also shown in Munich Haus der Kunst (with separate catalogue and in some cases different catalogue numbers: see following entry under Exhibitions)/Brussels, Palais des Beaux-Arts, 1968–9; the catalogue of the Brussels exhibition was identical with that used for the Paris showing

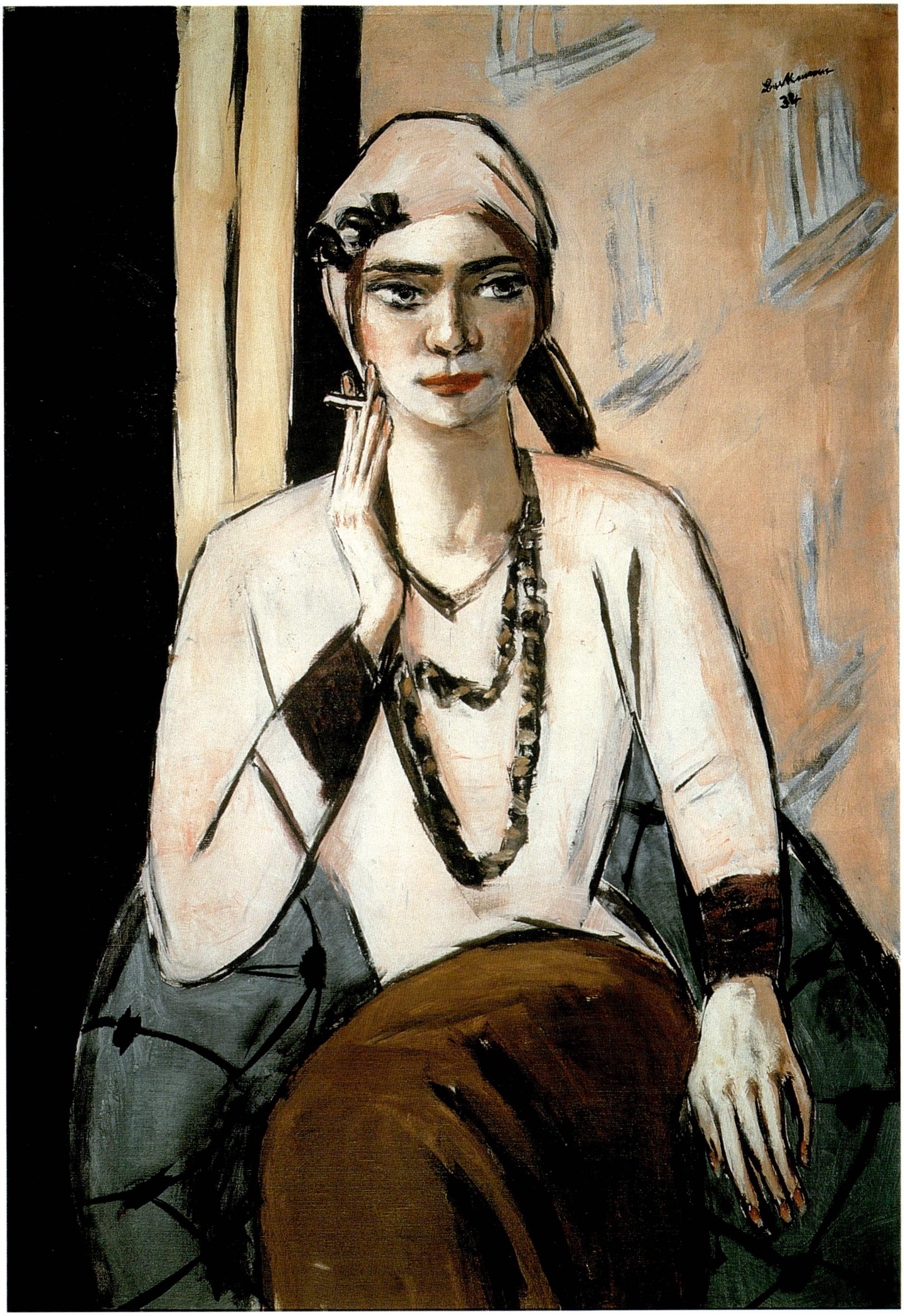

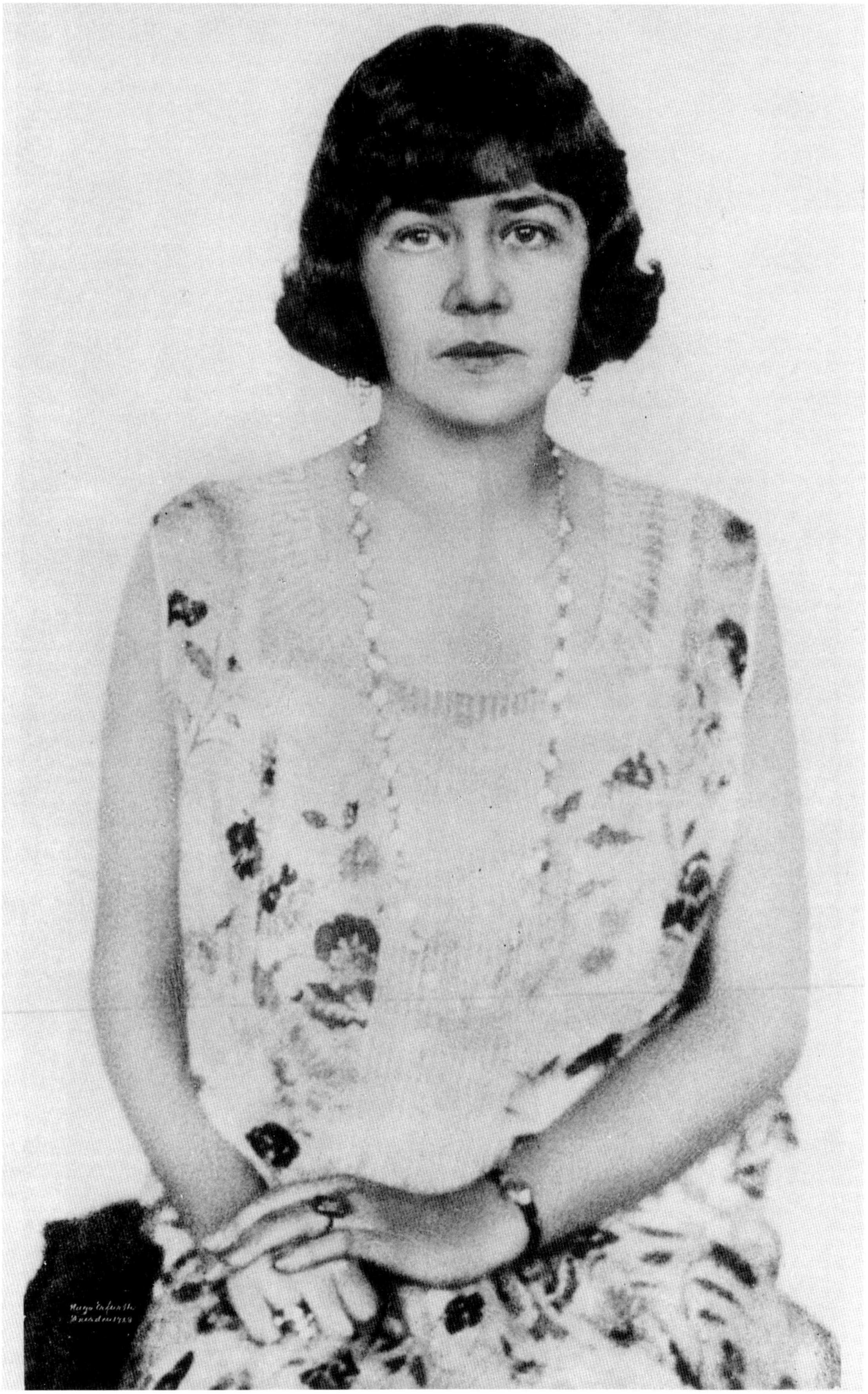

FIG 1 Portrait photograph of Mathilde (Quappi) Beckmann by Hugo Erfurth, inscribed 'Hugo Erfurth Dresden 1928' (archive Maja Beckmann, Murnau)

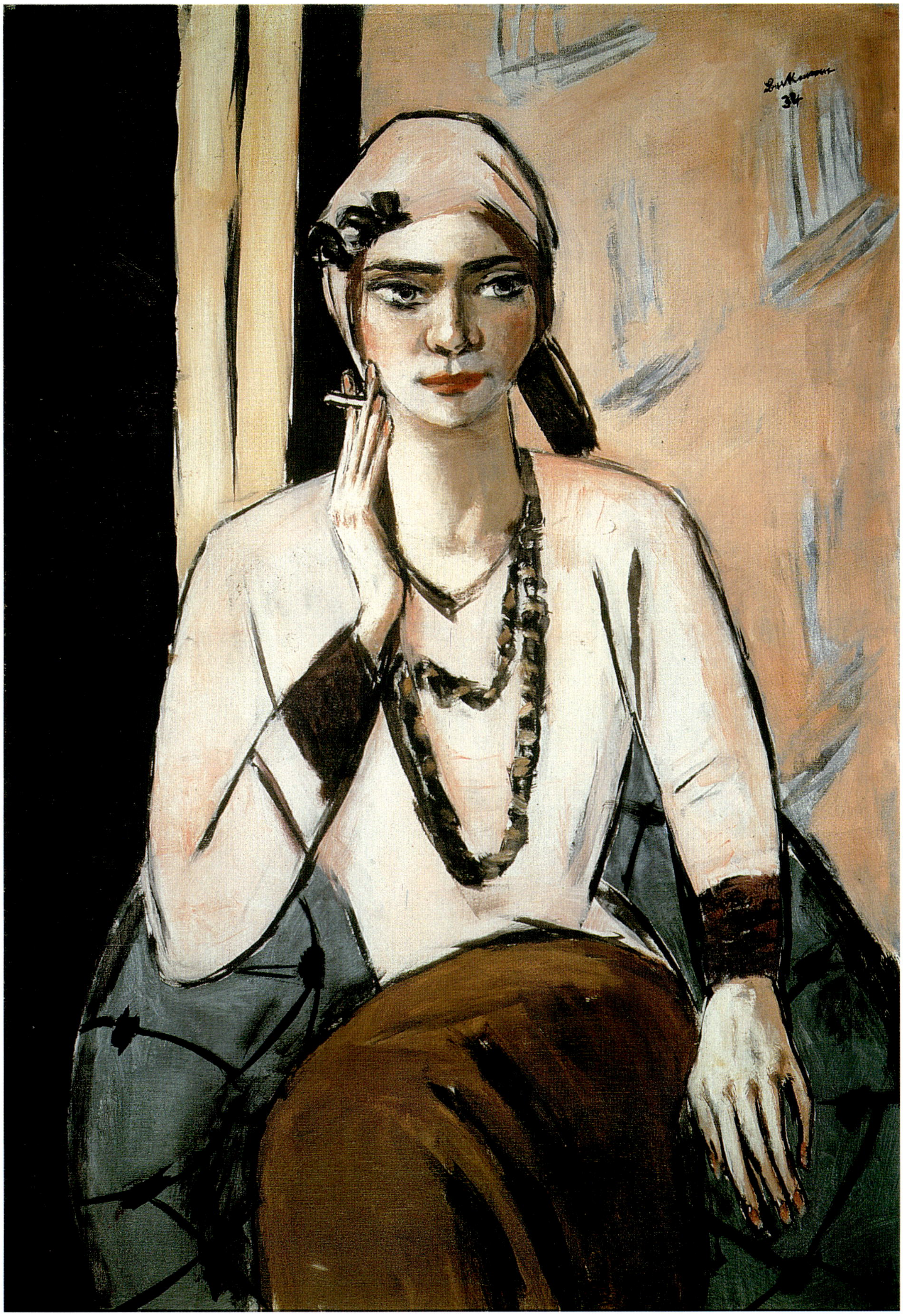

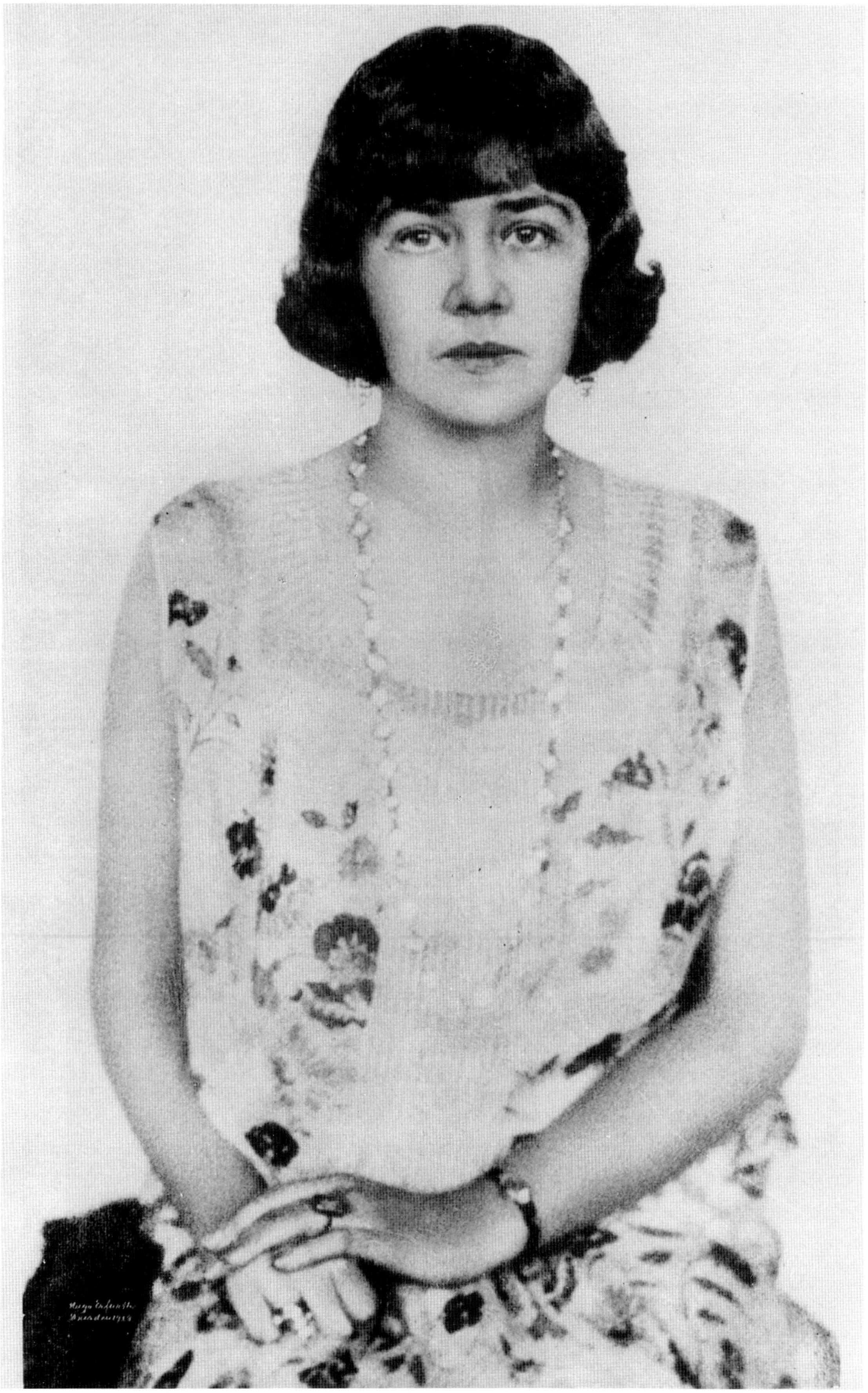

FIG 1 Portrait photograph of Mathilde (Quappi) Beckmann by Hugo Erfurth, inscribed 'Hugo Erfurth Dresden 1928' (archive Maja Beckmann, Murnau)

Quappi recalled that Beckmann, in painting her portrait, would sometimes be inspired by a particular item of clothing.[5] In this case it was a pink jumper with a grey thread running through it, bought in Frankfurt, together with a hat made of the same material. In its original state the painting was completed in Frankfurt in 1932; however, to judge by the signature and by the entry in the artist's own handlists,[6] Beckmann made certain changes to the picture in Berlin in 1934 and 1935, including those to the head and features of the sitter.

In the catalogue of the 1966 Bremen exhibition Stephan Lackner, the former owner of the painting and a close friend of Beckmann's, noted that Quappi had 'originally been painted with a broader smile, in addition to which [Beckmann] made a number of alterations to the head. The signature was painted over and it was re-dated 34.'[7] It is, however, evident even on purely visual inspection that the date has been altered; the original date '32' can still be faintly discerned, together with traces of over-painting around the face and mouth.

The portrait has on several occasions been reproduced under the mistaken title 'Amerikanerin' (American Woman).

Notes

5 Mathilde Q. Beckmann in *Max Beckmann. Das Portrait*, exh. cat., Karlsruhe, Badischer Kunstverein, 1963, n.p.

6 The entry in the artist's own inventory of paintings reads: '1932: Quappi (rosa, blau) – 1935: Beendet Quappi in rosa Jumper [1932: Quappi (pink, blue) – 1935 completed Quappi in pink jumper]': see Göpel, loc. cit.

7 Lackner also observes that 'the background was originally light blue; one admires the daring with which Beckmann now puts pink on top of pink, without the effect ever becoming sickly'; see *Max Beckmann. Gemälde und Aquarelle der Sammlung Stephan Lackner*, exh. cat., Bremen, Kunsthalle, 1966–7, p.30

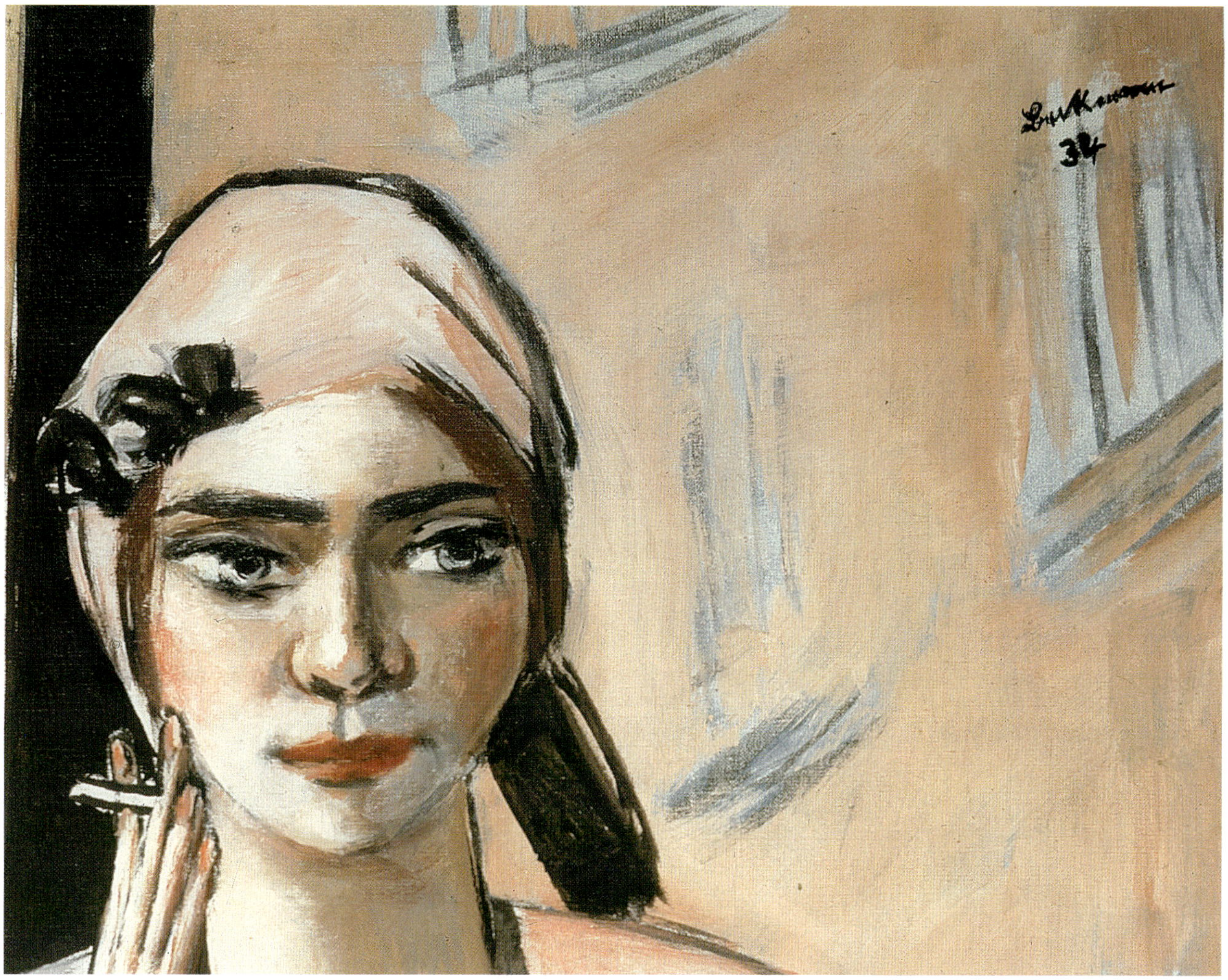

Detail [2]

Max Beckmann 1884–1950

3 Still-life with Yellow Roses
Stilleben mit gelben Rosen[1]

1937
Oil on canvas, 110.5 × 65.5 cm
Signed/dated upper left: 'Beckmann A 37'[2]
The painting is unvarnished. There is a horizontal crease at upper left. Otherwise condition is good
Accession no.1966.10

Provenance
Stephan Lackner, Santa Barbara, CA
Galerie R.N.Ketterer, Campione d'Italia
Thyssen-Bornemisza Collection, 1966

Exhibitions
Berne, Kunsthalle/Winterthur, Kunstmuseum, 1938, *Max Beckmann*, no.35[3]
Zurich, Galerie Aktuaryus/Basle, Galerie Bettie Thommen, 1938, *Max Beckmann. Gemälde und Graphik*[4]
New York, Buchholz Gallery Curt Valentin, 1940, *Max Beckmann Paintings 1936–1939*, no.7
Chicago, IL, Arts Club, 1942, *Max Beckmann Exhibition*, no.31
Santa Barbara, CA, University Art Gallery, 1959, *Max Beckmann*, no.19
Bremen 1975, no.2
Lugano 1975, no.35
Australian tour 1979–80, no.65
Munich, Haus der Kunst, *Max Beckmann Retrospektive*, 1984, no.83[5]
Rome 1990–91, no.3

Literature
R.N.Ketterer, *Moderne Kunst III*, Campione d'Italia (Galerie R.N.Ketterer) 1966, p.23, no.21, ill. p.22
Kiel (1974), p.10, ill. p.11
Göpel (1976), no.483
Schulz-Hoffmann (1984), p.270[6]
Not in Reifenberg (1949)[7]

On 19 July 1937, the notorious *Entartete Kunst* (Degenerate Art) exhibition opened in Munich. Having listened to Hitler's speech marking the inauguration of the Haus der Deutschen Kunst the day before, Beckmann left Germany for Amsterdam, where he eventually established himself in an apartment and studio at Rokin 85. Here he remained, trapped for much of the time by the war, until 1947. However, despite considerable privations and some dangers, especially during the last months of the German occupation, these were among his most productive years, accounting for one third of his total output of paintings. Among them were no fewer than five of the major triptychs, as well as a number of other allegorical compositions such as the horrifying *Birds' Hell* of 1938, in which his outrage at the cruelties perpetrated by

Notes
1 The title is taken from the artist's handlists: see Göpel (1976), I, p.310
2 The 'A' before the date indicates that the picture was painted in Amsterdam
3 At the 1938 Berne exhibition the painting was offered for sale for the sum of 2410 Swiss francs, according to Göpel (1976), I, note to p.310
4 Reduced version of the exhibition shown previously in Berne and Winterthur: see Göpel (1976), II, pp.99 (no.1646), 100 (nos.1656, 1657)
5 Centenary exhibition shown Munich, Haus der Kunst/Berlin, Nationalgalerie/Saint Louis, MO, City Art Museum/Los Angeles, CA, County Museum of Art, 1984–5
6 English language version of the catalogue of the Beckmann centenary exhibition: see n.5
7 In the catalogue *Moderne Kunst III* (Campione d'Italia, Galerie R.N.Ketterer, 1966, p.23) *Still-life with Yellow Roses* is mistakenly identified with Reifenberg (1949), no.392

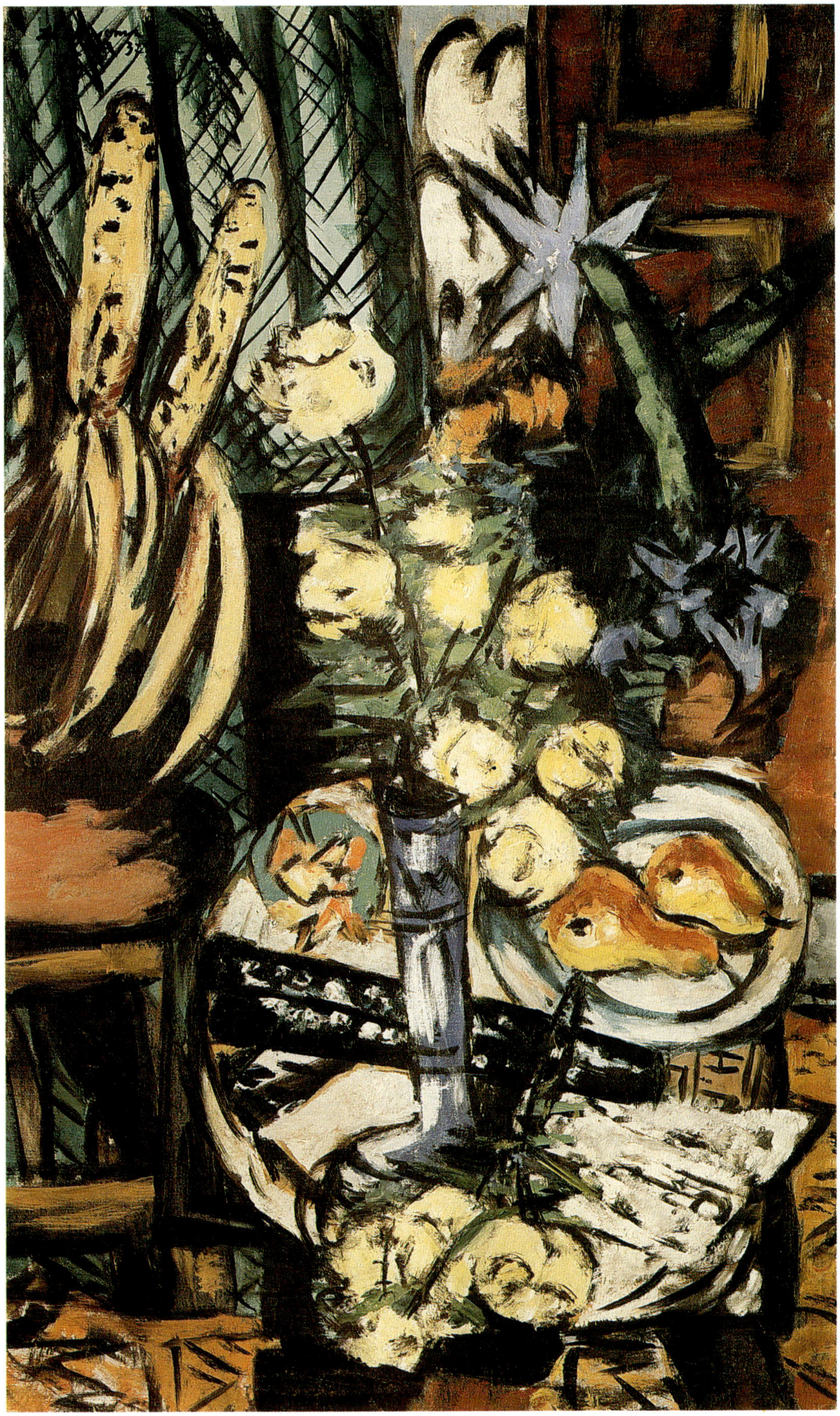

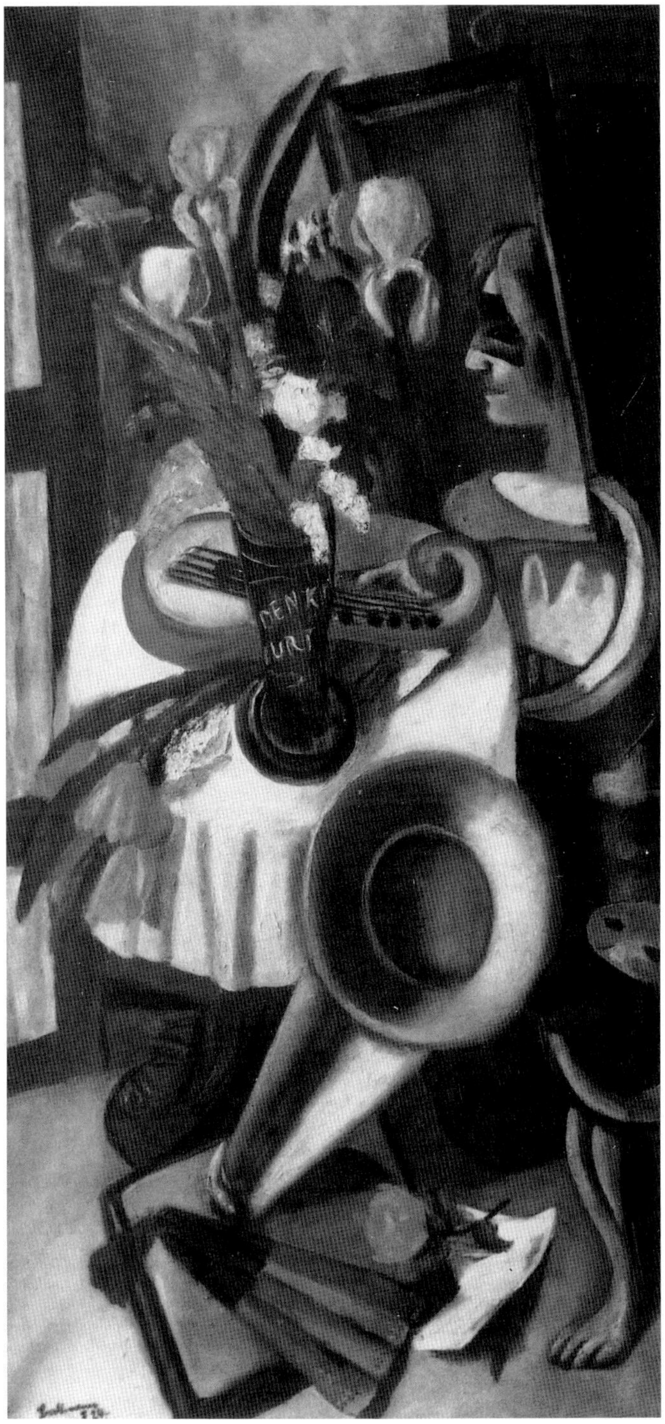

FIG 1 Max Beckmann, *Still-life with Gramophone and Irises*, 1924, oil on canvas, 114.5 × 55 cm (Private collection)

the Nazis finds symbolic expression.[8] By contrast, in other works of his first years in Amsterdam, especially the landscapes and still-lives including [3], no particular preoccupation with allegorical content or with the contemporary political situation is evident.

At this time, a prominent champion of Beckmann's art and opponent of the Nazis was the young Stephan Lackner. Then living in Paris, he did everything possible to promote the artist's reputation outside Germany, particularly in Switzerland and France. He was also involved in the exhibition *Twentieth Century German Art*, shown at the New Burlington Galleries in London in 1938, which brought together important paintings by artists whose work had been banned by the Nazis, among them Beckmann, Liebermann, Corinth, Feininger, Kandinsky, Klee, Schmidt-Rottluff, Kirchner, Nolde and Kokoschka. Beckmann and Lackner visited London in July in connection with the exhibition, the former delivering a lecture subsequently published in English under the title 'On My Painting'. Lackner and his family emigrated to the United States in April 1939, resuming correspondence with Beckmann from New York – contact severed by the outbreak of war in September that year.[9]

According to information provided by R.N.Ketterer, *Still-life with Yellow Roses* was acquired in Paris by Lackner in 1938, directly from Beckmann's Amsterdam studio.[10] Ketterer also cites Lackner's recollection that the chequered yellow forms which occur at upper left in the painting are dried corn-cobs sometimes found as decoration in Dutch interiors – a passing allusion, perhaps, to the environment in which the artist temporarily found himself. Some of the other still-life objects are, however, as Cornelia Stabenow observes, represented in so generalized a manner that their precise identification is somewhat problematic: a double flute, perhaps, and sheet music lying on the table.[11] Stabenow also suggests, plausibly, that Beckmann's 1924 painting *Still-life with Gramophone and Irises* (fig.1) may provide a compositional precedent for the present work.

Notes

8 Göpel (1976), no.506

9 On Beckmann's Amsterdam years and Lackner's early relations with the artist see Lackner (1967), pp.21ff; also idem., 'Beckmann's Exile in Amsterdam and Paris 1937–1947', in Schulz-Hoffmann (1984), pp.145–57

10 Ketterer, loc. cit. In September 1938, Beckmann entered into a contract with Lackner for two paintings a month in return for a guaranteed monthly payment: see the biography by Doris Schmidt printed in Schulz-Hoffmann (1984), p.462

11 Schulz-Hoffmann (1984), p.270

Max Beckmann 1884–1950

4 Circus Artists
Artisten

1948
Oil on canvas, 165 × 88.5 cm
Unsigned/undated
Contrary to Beckmann's usual practice of leaving his pictures unvarnished, the painting has been treated with a modern high-gloss varnish, so that the surface now appears excessively shiny. There is also extensive cupping and cracking in the pigment layer. The painting has been fitted to a new stretcher; the marks of the original stretcher are still visible
Accession no.1989.9

Provenance
Buchholz Gallery Curt Valentin, New York
Morton D. May, Saint Louis, MO
Marlborough Fine Art, London
Saul P. Steinberg, New York
Private collection
Christie's, London
Thyssen-Bornemisza Collection, 1989[1]

Exhibitions
Chicago, IL, Arts Club, 1951, *German Expressionists and Max Beckmann from the Collection of Mr and Mrs Morton D. May*, no.30
Saint Louis, MO, City Art Museum, 1956, *Max Beckmann Retrospective Exhibition*, without catalogue[2]
Madison, WI, Wisconsin Union Gallery, 1959, *Paintings from the Collection of Mr and Mrs Morton D. May*, no.1
Saint Louis, MO, Saint Louis University, 1960, *Paintings from the Collection of Mr and Mrs Morton D. May*, no.78
Cleveland, OH, Museum of Art, 1960, *Paths of Abstract Art*, no.17
Denver, CO, Art Museum, 1960–62, *German Expressionist Paintings from the Collection of Mr and Mrs Morton D. May*, no.83[3]
Jacksonville, FA, Art Museum/Nashville, TN, Fine Arts Gallery, 1966, *German Expressionist Paintings from the Collection of Mr and Mrs Morton D. May*, no.24
Portland, OR, Art Museum, 1967, *German Expressionist Paintings from the Collection of Mr and Mrs Morton D. May*, no.38
Bielefeld, Kunsthalle, 1968–9, *Deutsche Expressionisten aus der Sammlung Morton D. May*, no.24[4]
New York, Marlborough–Gerson Gallery/Saint Louis, MO, City Art Museum, 1970, *The Morton D. May Collection of 20th-Century German Masters*, no.47
London, Marlborough Fine Art, 1974, *Max Beckmann*, no.36

Literature
Reifenberg (1949), no.635
Fischer (1972), pp.199–202
Göpel (1976), no.762
Lackner (1977), p.154

Circus Artists was painted during the spring of 1948, while Beckmann was living in Saint Louis, Missouri. His diaries show that work on the picture began on 15 February and was finished by the end of March. An entry for 27 March 1948 reads: 'Allerletzte Hand an "Simon und Helene" . . .' (finishing touches to *Simon and Helen*).[5] The title *Simon und Helene* (or Helena), an allusion to the gnostic legend of Simon Magus,[6] is the one which occurs most frequently in Beckmann's diaries. Others include *Schlangenbändigerin und Clown* (Snake Charmer and Clown), *Zwei Köpfe* (Two Heads), and *Riesenzirkus* (which can mean either 'Giant Circus' or 'Circus of Giants'). In the artist's handlists, however, *Simon und Helena* is crossed out in favour of *Artisten*;[7] the latter title has therefore been adopted here.

Notes
1 Acquired at auction, 3 April 1989 (*Impressionist and Modern Paintings and Sculpture*, lot 39)
2 According to Göpel (1976), II, p.114
3 Exhibition also shown in Los Angeles, San Diego, San Francisco, Chicago, Youngstown, Akron, Pittsburgh, Washington, Baltimore and Kansas City
4 Exhibition also shown in Cologne, Essen, Bremen, Karlsruhe and Vienna during 1968–9
5 See Göpel (1976), I, p.458
6 On the influence of gnosticism and mysticism on Beckmann's work more generally, see Fischer (1972), pp.136ff, 200; also Göpel (1976), I, n. to p.290
7 Göpel (1976), I, p.458

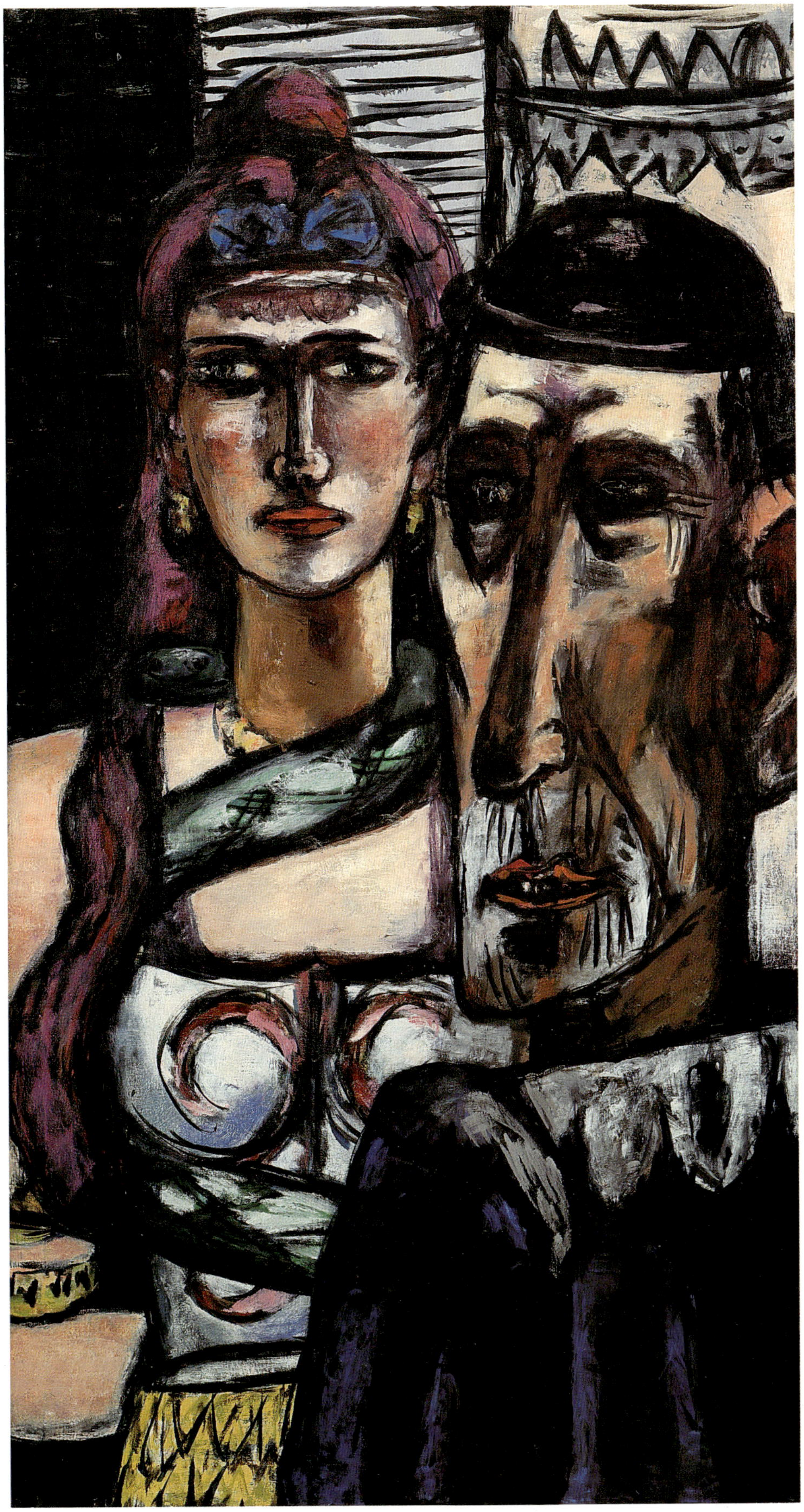

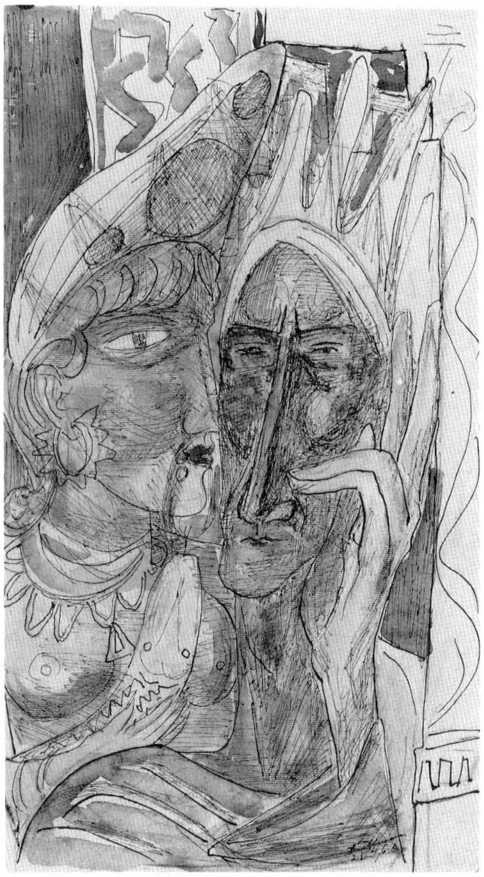

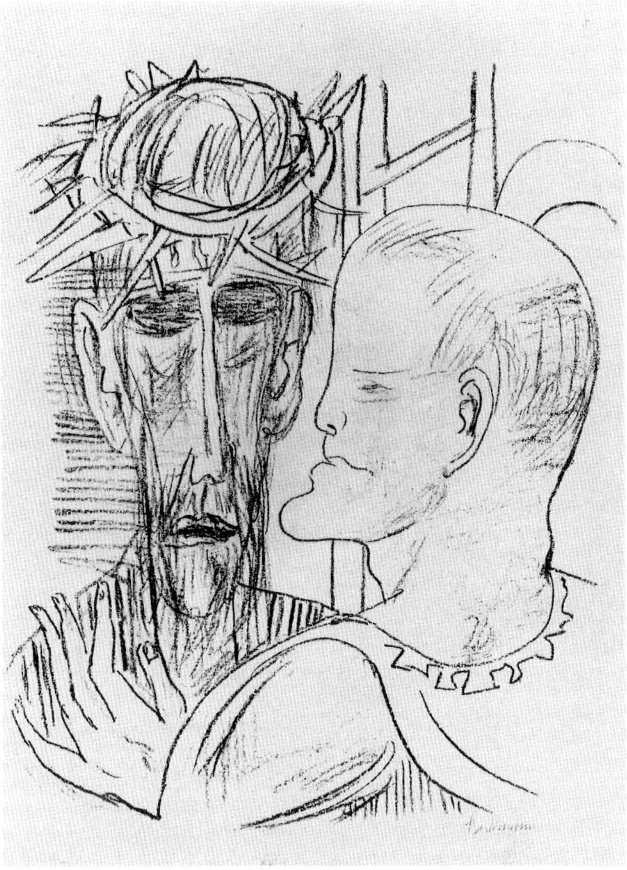

FIG 1 Max Beckmann, *Man, Woman and Snake*, 1946, ink and watercolour, 50.2 × 29.1 cm (formerly collection Samuel Magdoff, Bryn Mawr, PA)

FIG 2 Max Beckmann, *Christ and Pilate*, 1946, transfer lithograph, from the cycle *Day and Dream*, 35 × 27.5 cm (Saint Louis, MO, Art Museum, gift of the Buchholz Gallery, New York)

Several writers have linked the iconography of the painting with Gustave Flaubert's *Tentation de Saint Antoine*, a re-working of the legend according to which Simon and the young Helen (a reincarnation of Helen of Troy) appear to St Anthony. The same diary entry for 15 February 1948 in which Beckmann records starting work on the picture also mentions having embarked on a re-reading of Flaubert's prose drama – a book which had occupied him at various times over a period of many years, and which provided the starting point for his major triptych of 1936–7, *Versuchung* (Temptation).[8] He also considered making illustrations for a new edition of the Flaubert to be published by Curt Valentin in New York, as evidenced by a letter from Beckmann, then still living in Amsterdam, to Valentin dated 4 December 1946.[9] Fischer, however, in his detailed study of the artist's symbolism, questions the specific relevance of Flaubert for an interpretation of *Circus Artists*, pointing out that Beckmann's admiration was, at best, qualified.[10] On the fly-leaf of a copy of the book he had been sent by Rudolf von Simolin in 1935, Beckmann noted various criticisms including insufficient characterisation of St Anthony himself, describing it as an 'imperfect work of reference'. Elsewhere in the same copy are to be found further markings and critical marginalia.[11]

First ideas for the picture evidently go back as far as the artist's years in Amsterdam: a drawing in pen and ink dated '2.1.46 A' (fig.1) is clearly related to the iconography of *Circus Artists*, but contains no obvious allusion to the legend treated by Flaubert – something which is also true of the painting itself. There is, on the other hand, a close resemblance between the depiction of the old clown in this drawing and the head of Christ in Beckmann's 1946 lithograph *Christ and Pilate* from the portfolio *Day and Dream*, his last major cycle of prints (fig.2). Equally striking is the way in which, in each of these works, the two heads are brought into uncomfortably close proximity, while the crown of thorns (likewise a symbol of mockery) in *Christ and Pilate* finds its counterpart in the comical homburg hat perched on the head of the old clown in *Circus Artists*.

Notes
8 Ibid., no.439
9 New York, Museum of Modern Art archives; see Göpel (1976), I, n. to p.290
10 Fischer (1972), pp.138f
11 Göpel (1976), I, n. to p.290; also cited by Fischer (1972), loc. cit.

The parallel, suggested here, between the image of the Man of Sorrows and that of the clown is not wholly fanciful. Lackner, without referring specifically to the *Christ and Pilate* lithograph, remarks on the undertones of mockery and sadness with which *Circus Artists* is imbued:

> As a circus devotee of long standing, Beckmann knew that many funnymen are really very sad. The wide range of the clown's emotions imbues him with a deep human quality. His elongated face, his dark glance, his craggy cheek and thin shoulder evoke much pity and a little mirth. We may suspect that the fresh, strapping woman has caused him a good deal of suffering.[12]

It is also significant that the lithographic series *Day and Dream* to which *Christ and Pilate* belongs does not revolve around a single theme, but rather comprises a number of subjects which play a significant role in Beckmann's other works. He himself originally conceived it as what he called an 'all-in-one thing', including biblical, mythological and theatrical motifs as well as scenes from café and circus life,[13] thus linking the series even more closely with the iconography of *Circus Artists*. That the latter implies, none the less, a still wider range of references is demonstrated by the further allusion to Franz von Stuck's painting *Sin* (fig.3), one of the most famous, and most frequently reproduced of all turn-of-the-century images of the *femme fatale*, and one which Beckmann would certainly have known from his years in Germany.[14]

Circus Artists was originally sold by Curt Valentin's Buchholz Gallery in New York in 1950 to the department-store magnate and collector Morton D.May. May had become friendly with Beckmann as a consequence of the 1948 exhibition held at the Art Museum in Saint Louis, where the artist had taken up residence on emigrating from the Netherlands to the United States after the Second World War. Perry T.Rathbone, the director of the museum at that time and organizer of the exhibition, stressed the importance of May to Beckmann during the artist's years in America: 'May's purchases were a boost to Max's morale and a boon to his economic situation. In fact, May's devotion and collecting zeal rivalled, if it did not exceed, that of any Beckmann enthusiast, so that he became the principal patron of Beckmann's last years.'[15] Other works from the May collection are now in the Saint Louis Art Museum.

12 Lackner (1977), p.154

13 Schulz-Hoffmann (1984), p.438; Karen F.Beall, 'Max Beckmann Day and Dream', *Quarterly Journal of the Library of Congress*, (January 1970): 8

14 The painting exists in a number of variants, including an earlier version of 1893 now in the Bayerische Staatsgemäldesammlungen, Munich

15 In *Max Beckmann*, exh. cat., New York, Museum of Modern Art, 1964, p.128

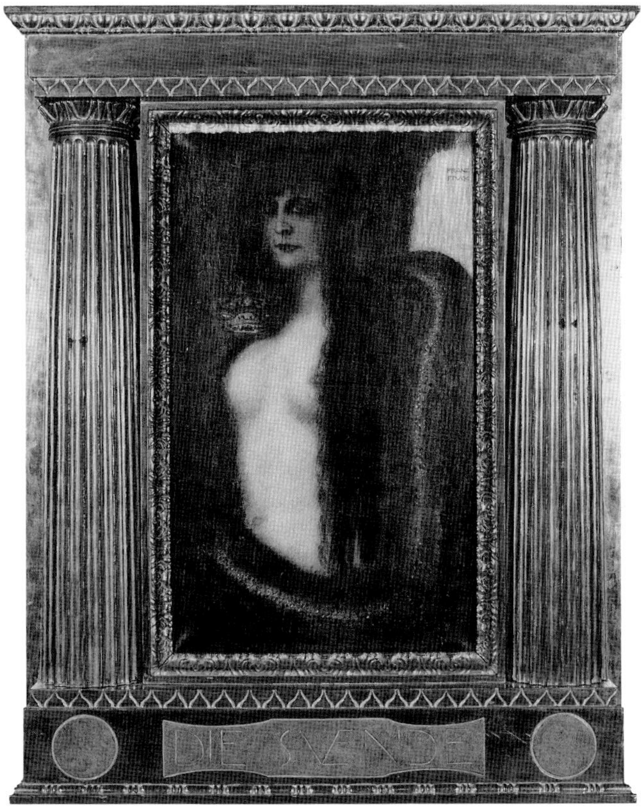

FIG 3 Franz von Stuck, *Sin*, *c*1912, oil on canvas, 88 × 53 cm, framed 124 × 99 cm (Munich, Museum in der Stuck-Villa)

Lovis Corinth 1858–1925

5 Fashion Show
Modeschau

1921
Oil on canvas, 201.5 × 100 cm
Inscribed lower left: 'Mode . . . [illegible] 1921 Lovis Corinth Januar/Februar'
The painting is unvarnished. There are considerable variations in the thickness of paint, ranging from a very heavy impasto in the centre to virtually bare areas of canvas at upper left and right. Some slight cupping and cracking, especially around the bodice of the figure. Otherwise condition is good
Accession no.1986.7

Provenance
Carl Steinbart, Berlin
Dora Stach-Steinbart, Amsterdam
Mr and Mrs Robert Stolper, London
Laura Barry, New York
James Kirkman Ltd, London[1]
Thyssen-Bornemisza Collection, 1986

Exhibitions
Berlin, Akademie der Künste, 1921[2]
Berlin, Nationalgalerie (Kronprinzenpalais), 1923, *Lovis Corinth*, no.107[3]

Literature
Berend-Corinth (1958), no.839, ill. p.756
See also Uhr (1990)

The last years of Corinth's life were overshadowed by illness and disability. In December 1911 he suffered a stroke affecting his left side which left him, for a time, partially paralysed.[4] After this, he experienced difficulty in working, due in part to a tremor in the right hand. In his autobiography, he recalled that 'illness, paralysis of the left side, violent trembling of the right hand exacerbated by exertion with the burin and caused by previous alcoholic excess' contributed to preventing any degree of technical finish in his works.[5]

In many respects, however, he made a remarkable recovery from this illness which, though it produced a profound psychological effect on him, in no way impaired his creative drive. On the contrary, more than half of his entire oeuvre dates from the years between 1912 and 1925, including nearly five hundred paintings and more than eight hundred prints, as well as

Notes

1 I am indebted to James H.Kirkman for helping me to establish a complete provenance for the painting; also to Mrs Raassen-Kruimel, Curator of the Singer Museum in Laren, and to Dr J.H.Kraan, of the Rijksbureau voor Kunsthistorische Dokumentatie, The Hague, for information concerning the Stach-Steinbart Collection

2 Reference taken from Berend-Corinth (1958), loc. cit. As far as it has been possible to ascertain, the painting has not been shown at exhibition since 1923

3 This exhibition comprised 170 works by the artist from private collections, according to the chronology printed in Corinth (1979), p.357

4 Ibid., p.152, fn.; on the contradiction between Corinth's apparent disability in attempting even simple physical movements and his sureness of touch when painting compare the account given by Fechter: 'Corinths Hände . . . zitterten ständig, waren unfähig zu den kleinsten Griffen – und waren sofort fest und sicher, wenn er Palette und Pinsel ergriff und zu malen begann' (Corinth's hands . . . shook continuously, were incapable of even the simplest movements – yet became at once firm and confident the moment he seized palette and brush and began to paint). See Paul Fechter, 'Lovis Corinth', *Menschen und Zeiten*, Berlin/Hamburg 1949, p.243, cited by Röthel in Berend-Corinth (1958), p.46

5 'Krankheiten, eine linksseitige Lähmung, ein ungeheueres Zittern der rechten Hand, durch Anstrengung mit der Nadel verstärkt und durch frühere Exzesse von Alkohol hervorgerufen, verhinderten schon eine handwerkliche Mache in meinen Arbeiten.' (Lovis Corinth, *Selbstbiographie*, Leipzig 1926, p.168)

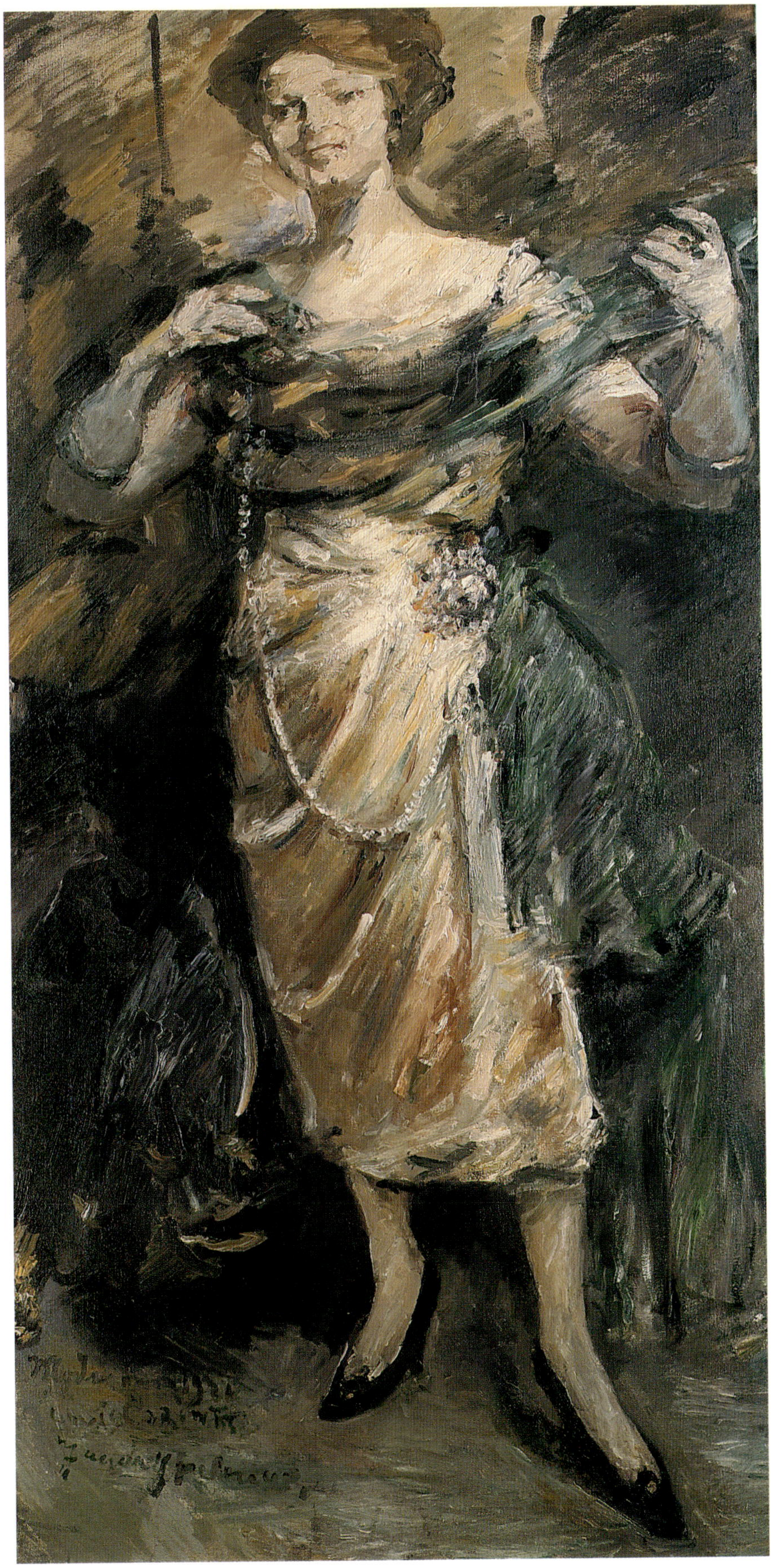

numerous drawings, watercolours and works on paper.[6] Moreover, little trace of any hindrance such as he refers to in his autobiography is evident in the magnificent sweeping impasto of his late oils whose pronounced gestural style inevitably invites comparison with the art of the Expressionists. These late paintings consist predominantly of landscapes, portraits, flower-pieces and scenes of society life, of which *Fashion Show* is an example; compare also Corinth's portrait of a woman in a fur coat (fig.1) of the same year, which in style and effect is closely related to the present painting.

According to his widow Charlotte Berend, *Fashion Show* was painted in the artist's apartment in Berlin at Klopstockstrasse 48 in 1921.[7] The inscription on the painting itself indicates that it was completed during January–February that year. Since Corinth was in Bavaria, at Urfeld on the Walchensee where he had acquired a property in 1918, until around 11 January 1921, it seems likely that work on the picture can only have been started towards the end of that month.[8]

Fashion Show was originally purchased from the artist by the Berlin collector Carl Steinbart, whose name can be found on a number of occasions in Corinth's correspondence. Steinbart was an important patron of the German Impressionists, including Liebermann, Corinth and Slevogt, but also collected works by more avant-garde painters such as Nolde, Kokoschka and Pechstein. After his death, the picture was inherited by his daughter Dora, who had in the meantime married Paul Stach (in 1914) and moved to the Netherlands (in 1920), where the couple obtained Dutch nationality in 1938.[9] On the death of Dora Stach-Steinbart in 1970, it was offered for sale by the firm of Wisselingh in the Netherlands, and was acquired by Mr and Mrs Robert Stolper, passing subsequently to their daughter Laura Barry in New York. Again offered for sale, this time by James Kirkman Ltd, London, it was purchased by the present owner in March 1986.[10]

Notes

6 For a sensitive account of Corinth's illness and recovery see Uhr (1990), pp.193ff

7 Berend-Corinth (1958), p.160

8 According to the chronology printed in Corinth (1979), p.355

9 I am grateful to Mr H.J.Stach, son of Paul Stach and Dora Stach-Steinbart and grandson of Carl Steinbart, for an account of his grandfather's activities as collector

10 I am indebted to the artist's daughter Mrs Wilhelmine Corinth Klopfer, New York, for commenting on the accompanying essay

FIG 1 Lovis Corinth, *Lady in a Fur Coat*, 1921, oil on canvas, 104.8 × 80.4 cm (Hanover, Niedersächsisches Landesmuseum, Landesgalerie, inv. no.KM 1949/143)

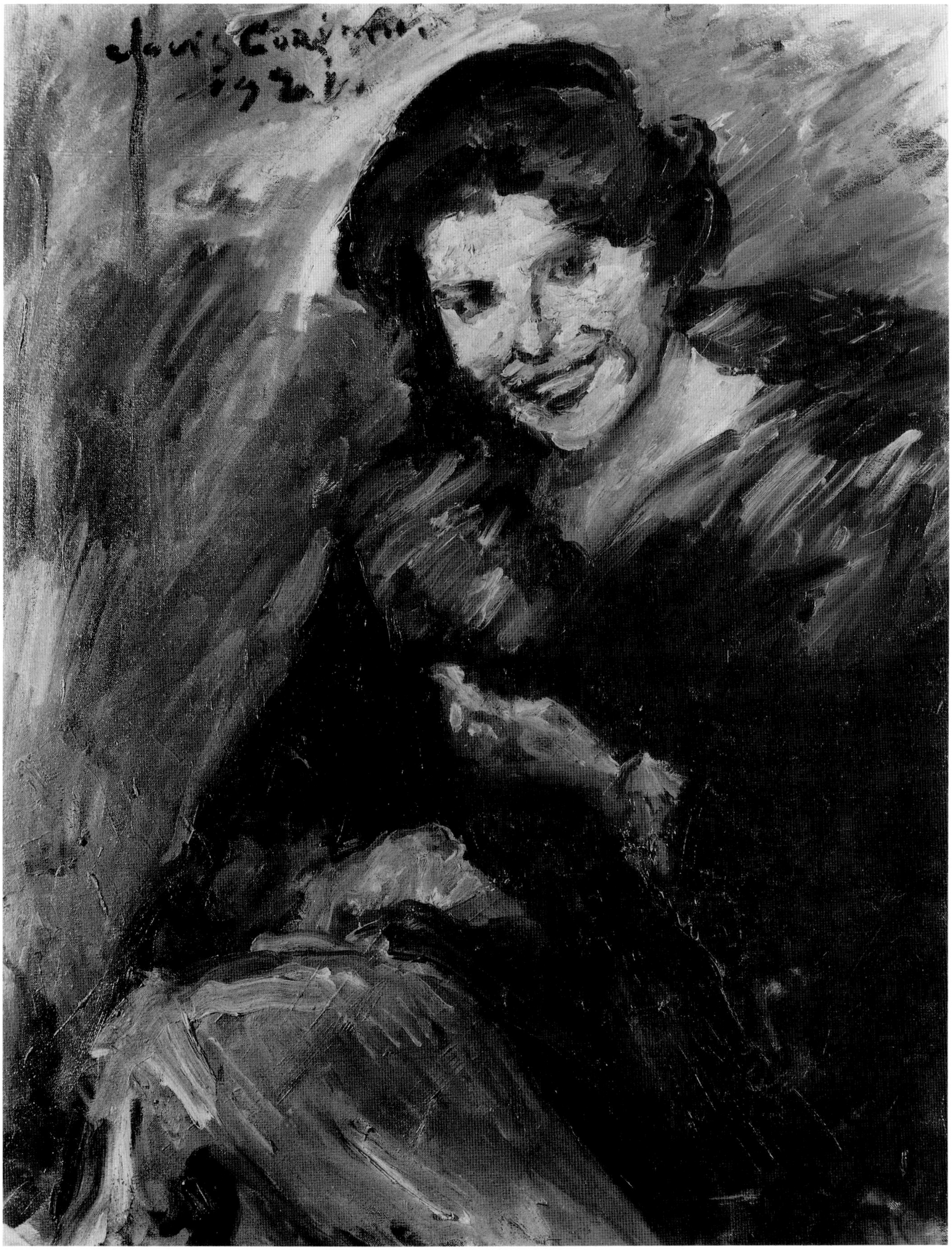

Otto Dix 1891–1969

6 Hugo Erfurth with Dog

1926
Tempera and oil on plywood panel, 80 × 100 cm
Initialled/dated upper left: 'D 1926'; also inscribed and signed on back of panel: 'Mischtechnik letzte Schicht Oelf[arbe] Leinöl. Darf vor Sept 27 *nicht* gefirnist werden. Dix.' (Mixed media top layer oil paint linseed oil. *Not* to be varnished before September [19]27. Dix.)
The painting was revarnished in 1975 using a Lucas matt varnish with addition of wax. The plywood panel is primed front and back, and shows a slight convex warp. There are scattered stains and scratches in the paint layer, which also shows some retouching. Otherwise condition is good
Accession no.1978.87

Provenance
Hugo Erfurth
Galerie Probst, Mannheim
Galerie Nierendorf, Berlin
Fischer Fine Art, London
Thyssen-Bornemisza Collection, 1978

Exhibitions
Freiburg im Breisgau, Kunstverein, 1950–51, *Otto Dix – Gemälde, Aquarelle und Zeichnungen* no.8[1]
Wuppertal, Städtisches Museum, 1957, *Otto Dix*, no.15a
Berlin, Galerie Nierendorf, 1966, *Otto Dix. Bilder – Aquarelle – Zeichnungen*, no.17
Hamburg, Kunstverein, 1966–7, *Otto Dix – Gemälde, Aquarelle, Zeichnungen, Graphik*, no.39
Berlin, Deutsche Gesellschaft für bildende Künste/Lausanne, Musée Cantonal des Beaux-Arts, 1968–9, *Berlin XX. Jahrhundert/Berlin XXe Siècle: de l'expressionisme à l'art contemporain*, no.121
Berlin, Galerie Nierendorf, 1970, *1920–1970: 50 Jahre Galerie Nierendorf. Jubiläumsausstellung*, no.5
Berlin, Galerie Nierendorf, 1971, *Die 20er Jahre II*, no.59
Bonn, Rheinisches Landesmuseum, 1976, *Die Zwanziger Jahre im Porträt*, no.22
Berlin, 1977, 15. *Europäische Kunstausstellung. Tendenzen der 20er Jahre*, no.4/44, ill. p.4/87
Paris, Centre Georges Pompidou, 1978, *Paris–Berlin, 1900–1933*, ill. p.191
London, Arts Council of Great Britain, 1978–9, *Neue Sachlichkeit and German Realism of the Twenties*, no.45
Modern Masters from the Thyssen-Bornemisza Collection, 1984–6, no.22
Leningrad/Moscow 1988, no.9
Madrid, Centro de Arte Reina Sofia, 1989, *Berlin, Punto de Encuentro*, no.5/8
Lugano 1989, no.49
Expressionism and Modern German Painting, 1989–90, no.3
Rome 1990–91, no.6

Literature
Löffler (1981), 1926/14
See also Bruce F.Miller, 'Otto Dix and his Oil-Tempera Technique', *Bulletin of the Cleveland Museum of Art*, LXXIV, no.8 (October 1987): 332–51; Anna Barbara Lorenzer, 'Studien zur Maltechnik von Otto Dix in der Schaffenszeit von 1910–1933', *Zeitschrift für Kunsttechnologie und Konservierung*, III, no.1 (1989): 113–48

Note
1 Exhibition also shown in Karlsruhe, Nuremberg, Cologne, Stuttgart and Heidelberg during 1950–51

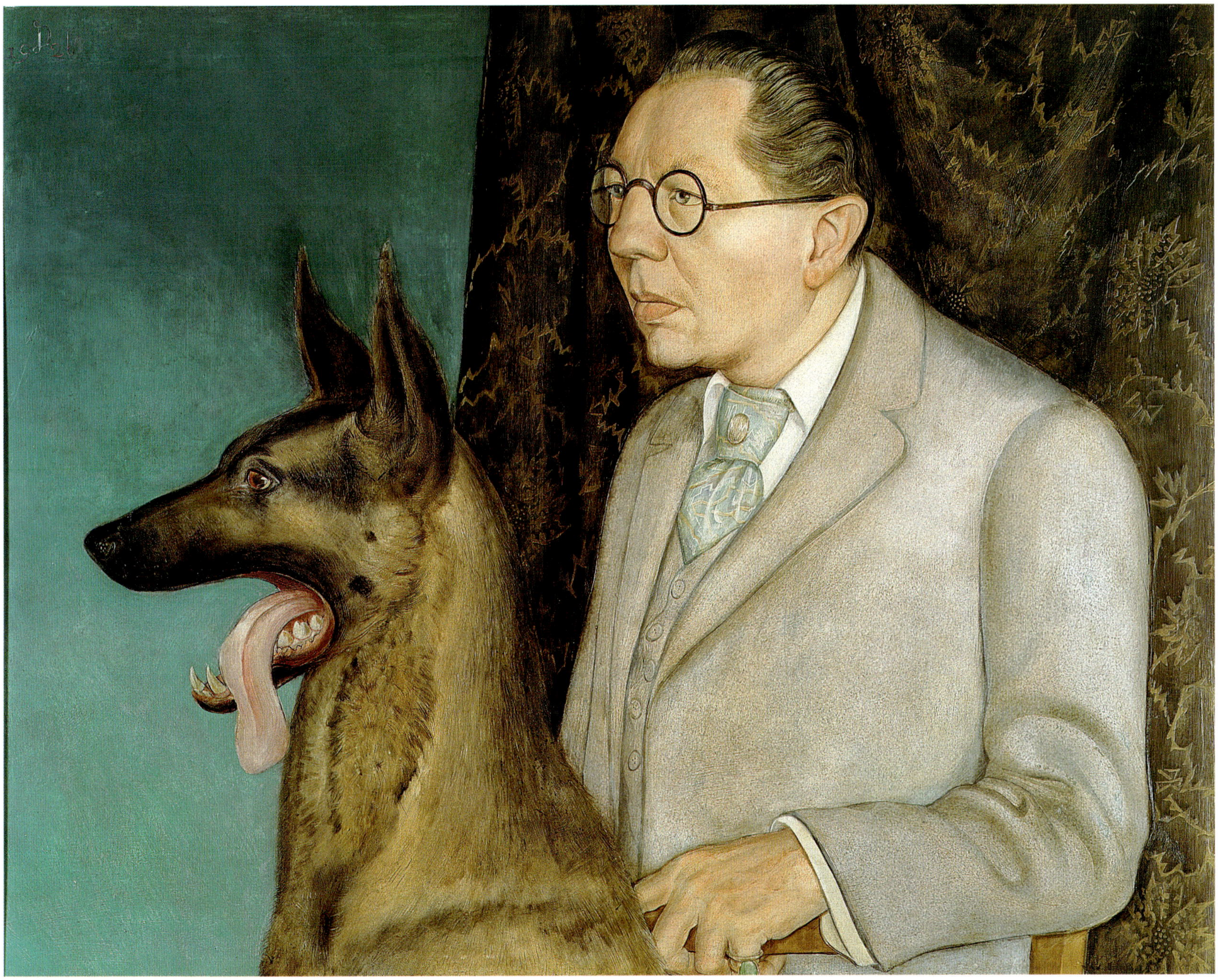

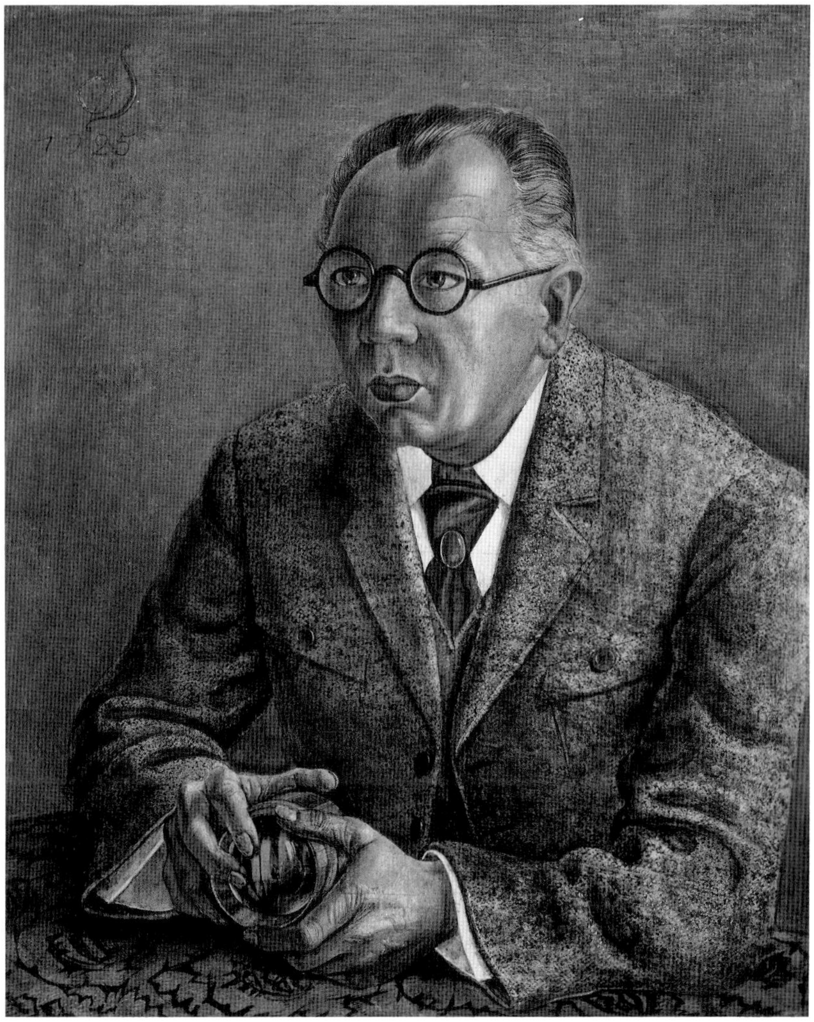

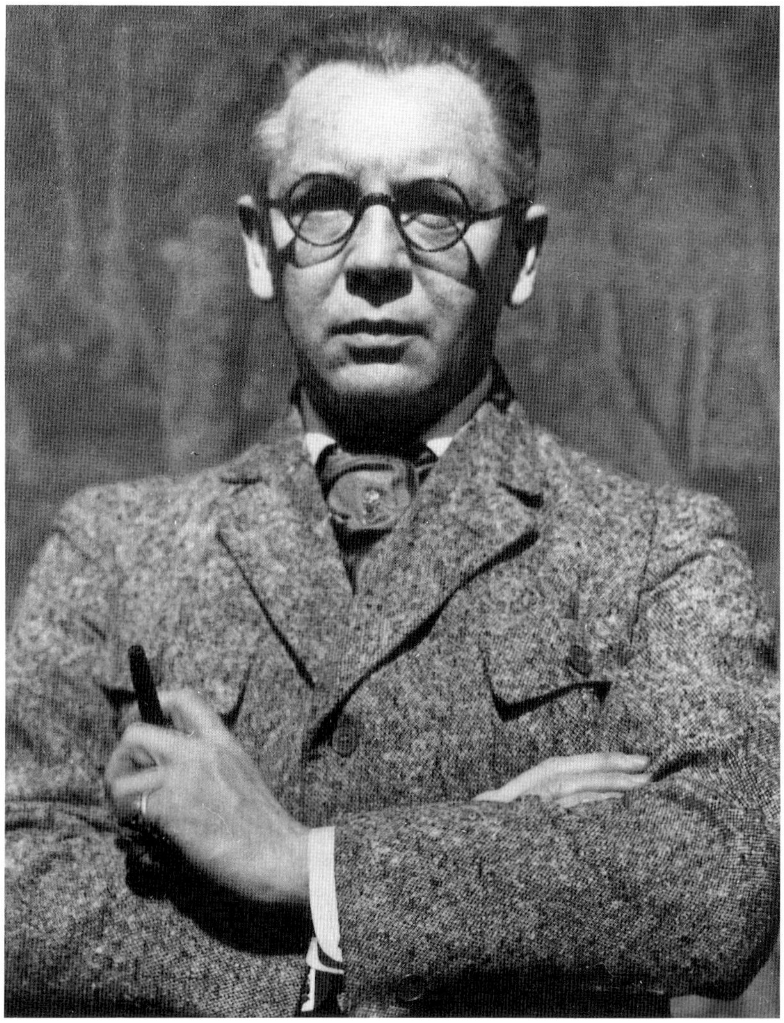

During the years after 1920 Dix created a plethora of works depicting scenes of horrifying ugliness and brutality, among them images of war victims and cripples, as well as of prostitutes and good-time girls, the flotsam and jetsam of city life. At the same time, he embarked on a succession of masterly portraits, in part images of the Bohemian and intellectual élite – figures such as the journalist Sylvia von Harden[2] or the art dealer Alfred Flechtheim[3] – in part likenesses of industrialists, lawyers and other pillars of a still unregenerately bourgeois society. These so enhanced his reputation that there were even suggestions that he should paint an official portrait of the then German Chancellor, Hans Luther. This idea was vetoed perhaps more on account of Dix's reputation as social critic and satirist, rather than any aesthetic criteria.[4] The commission went in the end to Max Slevogt.

The Thyssen Collection's *Hugo Erfurth with Dog* is less caricatured than the Flechtheim or Harden portraits, closer in style to some of Dix's society portraits of the mid-twenties. Erfurth himself is now remembered principally as a society photographer, one of the most successful of his day, who also captured the likenesses of eminent personalities from the world of literature and the arts, including Rabindranath Tagore, Walter Gropius, Käthe Kollwitz and Gret Palucca, as well as Dix himself.[5] In an interview with Bernd Lohse, Gottfried Erfurth recalled:

Notes

2 Löffler (1981), 1926/9

3 Ibid., 1926/10

4 Ibid., p.33; see also Kessler (1971), pp.288–9 (diary entry for 23 March 1926)

5 Reproduced in Bernd Lohse, *Hugo Erfurth 1874–1948. Der Fotograf der Goldenen Zwanziger Jahre*, Seebruck am Chiemsee (Heering Verlag) 1977, p.134. For a portrait photograph of Beckmann's wife Quappi by Hugo Erfurth, see [2] fig.1

FIG 1 Otto Dix, *Hugo Erfurth with Lens*, 1925, tempera on plywood panel, 75 × 60 cm (Munich, Bayerische Staatsgemäldesammlungen, Staatsgalerie moderner Kunst, gift of Sofie and Emanuel Fohn)

FIG 2 Hugo Erfurth photographed by his daughter, *c*1928 (Agfa Foto-Historama im Wallraf-Richartz-Museum/Museum Ludwig, Cologne)

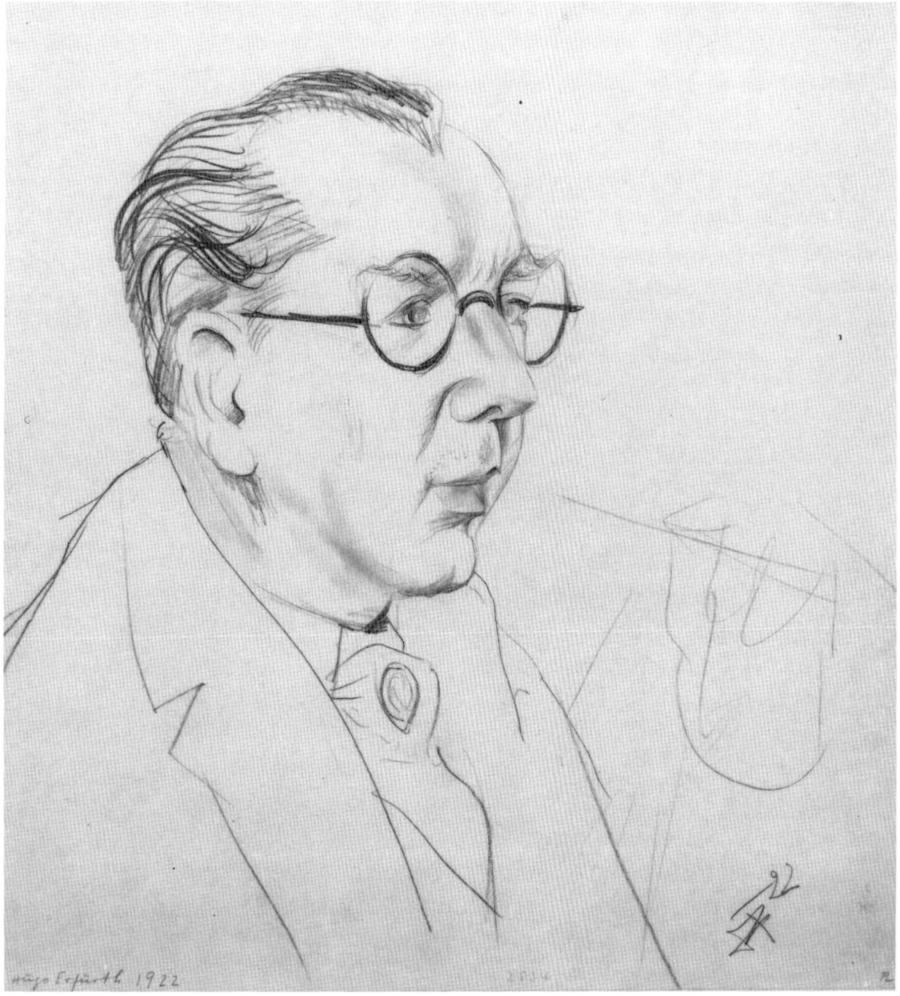

FIG 3 Otto Dix, *Hugo Erfurth*, 1922, pencil, 50 × 45.2 cm (Wuppertal, Von der Heydt-Museum, inv. no.KK 1954/71)

> Hugo Erfurth and Otto Dix were especially close . . . their friendship went back to a visit my father paid to the artist's studio. Dix had asked him to make some reproductions, for which he was not able to pay, but instead offered Hugo Erfurth the choice from among his paintings. Dix made several portraits of my father, and my father made even more of him and his family.[6]

Dix in fact painted two oil portraits of Hugo Erfurth, one in 1925 showing him holding a photographic lens (fig.1),[7] and the present version, which includes the family's Alsatian dog Ajax, painted in Erfurt in 1926. In this painting the dog is important not just for its size: whereas in the earlier portrait the photographer is identified by one of the implements of his trade, in *Hugo Erfurth with Dog* it is his position in society which is defined by the presence of the extremely large and doubtless pedigree animal – a symbol of possession and, at the same time, of status.[8] Two years later, Dix painted for Erfurth a picture of the dog.[9]

The two oil portraits and various portrait drawings of Erfurth all succeed in capturing a very precise physical likeness: not merely the physiognomy and character of the sitter, but even his affectations of dress and details of clothing.[10] A photograph taken by his daughter in about 1928 (fig.2) shows him wearing what appears to be the same jacket as in the Munich portrait, while an earlier drawing now in Wuppertal (fig.3) features a cameo tie-pin similar to that depicted both in the photograph and in the Thyssen Collection's painting. The tie-pin is, on the

6 Lohse, pp.26f
7 Löffler (1981), 1925/10
8 This point was made elegantly in a lecture by Professor Reinhold Heller entitled 'Constructions of Identity: Portraits of the Weimar Republic', which was given at the symposium *Primitivism, Modernity and Utopia. Painting in Germany 1905–1935* held at the Kimbell Art Museum, Fort Worth, TX, in January 1990 in conjunction with the exhibition *Expressionism and Modern German Painting from the Thyssen-Bornemisza Collection*. I am grateful to Professor Heller for providing me with a copy of his lecture, which is currently being revised for publication
9 Löffler (1981), 1928/13, present location unknown. The painting was offered for sale at auction in 1983 by Galerie Fischer, Lucerne (*Grosse Kunstauktionen in Luzern, 17. bis 20. Mai 1983*, lot 1472)
10 In his 'Thoughts on Portraiture', Dix referred to the folds of garments, posture of the person portrayed, hands and even ears as 'more revealing of the personality of the sitter than the expression of eyes and mouth'; see Otto Dix, 'Gedanken zum Portraitmalen', quoted in Lorenzer (1989), p.118

other hand, absent from the full-scale transfer drawing (fig.4), which must have immediately preceded the execution of the present work. This elaborate and highly finished cartoon otherwise prefigures the final composition in almost every detail save that, curiously, it contains no hint of the curtain which dominates the right-hand background, and which was perhaps painted as an after-thought. In the completed version of *Hugo Erfurth with Dog*, this curtain with its elaborate decorative pattern introduces a jarringly fussy note into an otherwise sparse and economical picture.

After about 1925, Dix largely abandoned canvas, which he had used extensively during the early 1920s, in favour of rigid supports such as hardboard or, as in the case of [6], plywood panel. In his paintings of this period, he strove to reproduce the effects achieved by the great masters of the Early Renaissance whose works he had admired since his student days in Dresden – 'that refined luminosity and transparency' which, by his own account, he found impossible to achieve using only commercially available oil paints.[11] It is, however, unlikely that he studied the methods of the Old Masters at first hand. Rather, his unconventional mixed-media technique, especially the juxtaposition of oil-based paints with tempera and aqueous colours, probably reflects his particular interest during the period from 1926 onwards in Doerner's famous treatise on the use of pigments, published five years earlier.[12] Not only the formula Dix used for his egg–oil emulsion but also his working methods appear virtually identical with those prescribed in Doerner's book, which clearly was written with a wide audience in mind and significantly influenced a number of artists at this date.[13]

Following Doerner's precepts, having transferred the main outlines of the composition on to the prepared panel Dix would then paint in tempera those forms and details, especially the principal contours with their areas of high tone, that demanded the greatest clarity and precision of execution. He would then overlay these with transparent and translucent glazes and passages of opaque oil-based pigment. The jewel-like effect and remarkable luminosity which are the immediately striking characteristics of *Hugo Erfurth with Dog* are the direct product of this unusual combination of techniques. It has also been suggested that the priming of panel or board on both sides such as is found in [6] may likewise reflect the influence of Doerner's theories.[14]

Notes

11 Ibid., p.127. Compare, however, Dix's 1926 portrait of the industrialist Dr Julius Hesse (private collection, Düsseldorf): see Löffler (1981), 1926/7. Hesse was the owner and manager of the Düsseldorf firm of H.Schminke & Co., which manufactured artists' materials; no doubt out of deference to his sitter, Dix used Schminke colours in painting this portrait

12 Max Doerner, *Malmaterial und seine Verwendung im Bilde*, 1st edn., Munich 1921.

13 There are numerous descriptions of Dix's 'method', including those by the artist himself. The most useful are Dix's own 'Lesson', written for an American correspondence college (Otto Dix, 'Painting a Figure Composition in Tempera and Oils', *Lesson 20*, Washington School of Art, 1958); the chapter by Ursus Dix on his father's techniques, in Rainer Beck (ed.), *Otto Dix, 1891–1969*, Munich 1985; and the articles by Miller and Lorenzer

14 Lorenzer, p.131. I am grateful to Emil Bosshard for drawing this article to my attention, and for discussing with me in detail aspects of Dix's technique in relation to Doerner's ideas

FIG 4 Otto Dix, *Hugo Erfurth with Ajax*, pencil and black chalk with white heightening, 84.3 × 100.2 cm (Berlin, Staatliche Museen Preussischer Kulturbesitz, Kupferstichkabinett)

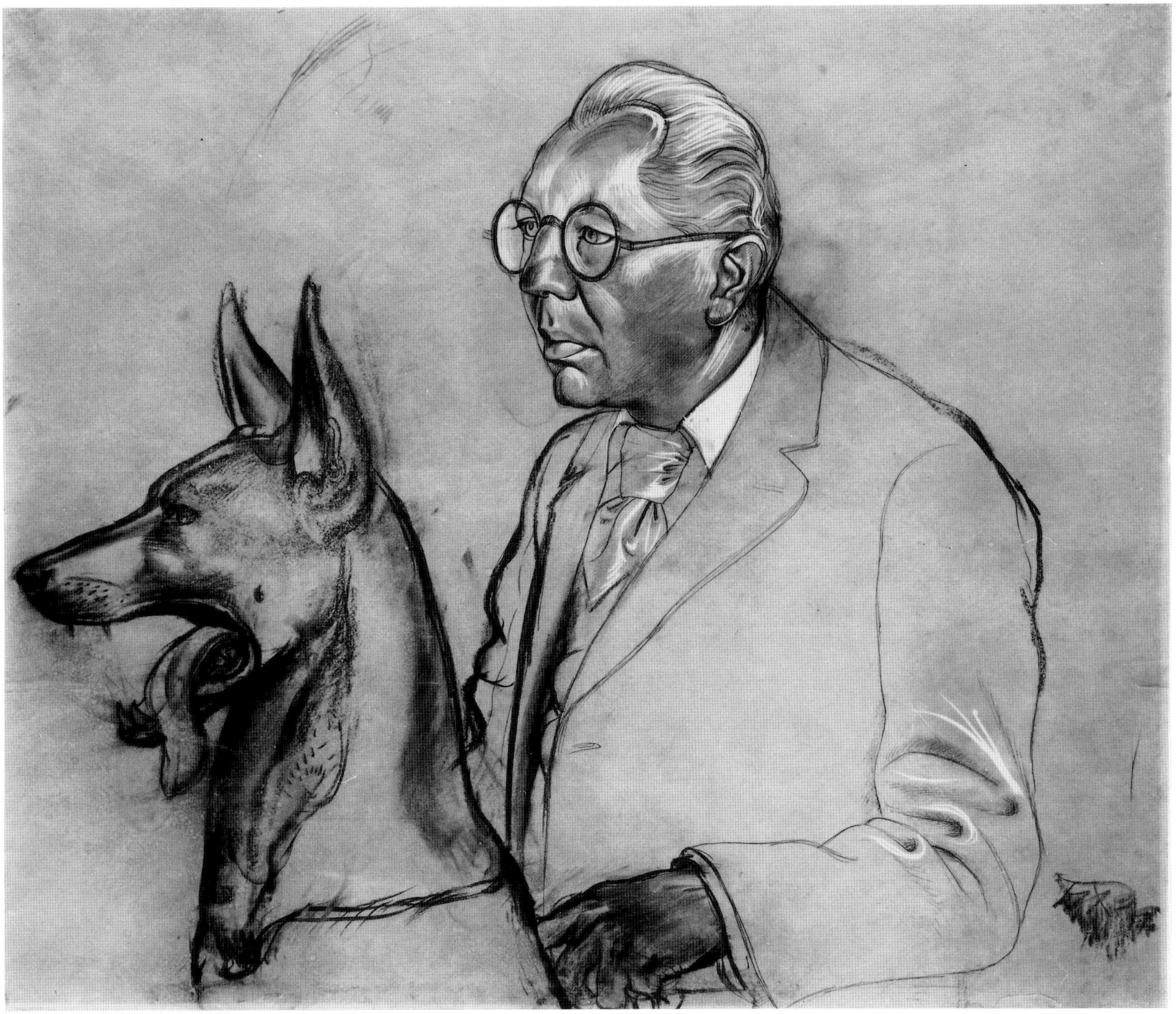

Kees van Dongen 1877–1968

7 Woman with Cigarette (Kiki de Montparnasse [?])

*c*1922–4
Watercolour on paper, 49.5 × 35.4 cm
Signed lower right: 'Van Dongen'
Some fading; otherwise condition is good
Accession no.1980.65

Provenance
Private collection
Andrew Crispo Gallery, New York
Thyssen-Bornemisza Collection, 1980

Exhibitions
Rome 1990–91, no.7

Literature
See Kiki [Alice Prin], *Kiki Souvenirs*, Paris (Henri Broca) 1929; Neil Baldwin, *Man Ray*, London (Hamish Hamilton) 1988; Billy Klüver and Julie Martin, *Kiki's Paris. Artists and Lovers 1900–1930*, New York (Abrams) 1989

Van Dongen has been considered at various times both a Fauvist and an Expressionist. He responded to many of the same influences as the German Expressionists, most particularly that of his compatriot van Gogh. He maintained links with the Brücke artists in Dresden, having met Pechstein in Paris in 1908, and been offered membership of the group the following year.[1] In the early years of this century van Dongen was, however, more closely allied with Matisse and the Parisian Fauve painters, with whom he exhibited at the famous 'Fauve salon' of 1905. He also participated in the exhibition of French avant-garde painting shown concurrently with the Brücke artists' own work at the Kunstsalon Emil Richter in Dresden in September 1908.[2] He made as significant a contribution to French as he did to Dutch art, living mainly in Paris after the First World War where he became known principally as a society painter, working in a style that might best be described as 'post-Fauvist'. He took French citizenship in 1929.

The sitter in this evocative watercolour is unidentified, but is thought to have been Kiki de Montparnasse. 'Kiki'[3] was the most celebrated of all the artistically gifted, sexually liberated women who haunted the studios and cafés of Montparnasse, that quarter of Paris on the left bank of the River Seine which, during the 1920s and 1930s, considered itself the centre of the artistic universe. Remembered with affection by those who met her, she published her memoirs in 1929 and acted in eight films, including Léger's experimental *Ballet Mécanique* of 1924 in which her features, fragmented and endlessly repeated, constitute a recurrent motif. She also apparently had several exhibitions of her paintings, of which the most significant was in March 1927 at the Galerie Au Sacre du Printemps on the rue du Cherche-Midi in Paris.[4]

Though the identification of the sitter in the present portrait is not supported by any documentation, there is an evident resemblance between the image presented here and Kiki's features captured in numerous photographic studies by Man Ray, who became her lover towards the end of 1921.[5] Her relationship with Man Ray lasted six years and was, in Kiki's own mind at least, the nearest thing to marriage; she even called herself 'Kiki Man Ray'. She was also the model in what has become perhaps the most famous of all his photographic images, *Ingres' Violin*. This, coupled with the fact that he and Kiki moved in the same circles as van Dongen during the early 1920s, frequenting the same parties and attending the same balls, makes the date suggested here, *c*1922–4, seem likely.[6]

The work is extremely delicate in execution, with passages of heavier impasto being reserved principally for the black feather boa worn by the sitter. Fleeting touches of blue indicate eye-shadow, while even fainter passages of pale grey wash are used to suggest smoke from the cigarette, or perhaps the smoky atmosphere of the café interior.

Notes
1 As evidenced by a postcard from Schmidt-Rottluff to Cuno Amiet dated 8 January 1909, now in the Brücke-Museum, Berlin; see Reinhardt (1977), p.146 and n.734
2 Ibid., p.146. The exhibition was reviewed in *Dresdner Journal*, no.213 (12 September 1908), p.6
3 Real name Alice Ernestine Prin, born at Châtillon-sur-Seine in Burgundy, 2 October 1901; see Klüver and Martin, op. cit., p.60
4 Ibid., pp.134, 160–1
5 Baldwin, op. cit., pp.104, 105ff, 111
6 The dating of van Dongen's work is fraught with difficulties, as was made clear by the retrospective exhibition held in Rotterdam during 1989–90: see *Kees van Dongen*, exh. cat., Rotterdam, Boymans–van Beuningen Museum, 1989, pp.9–10, 45, 152ff

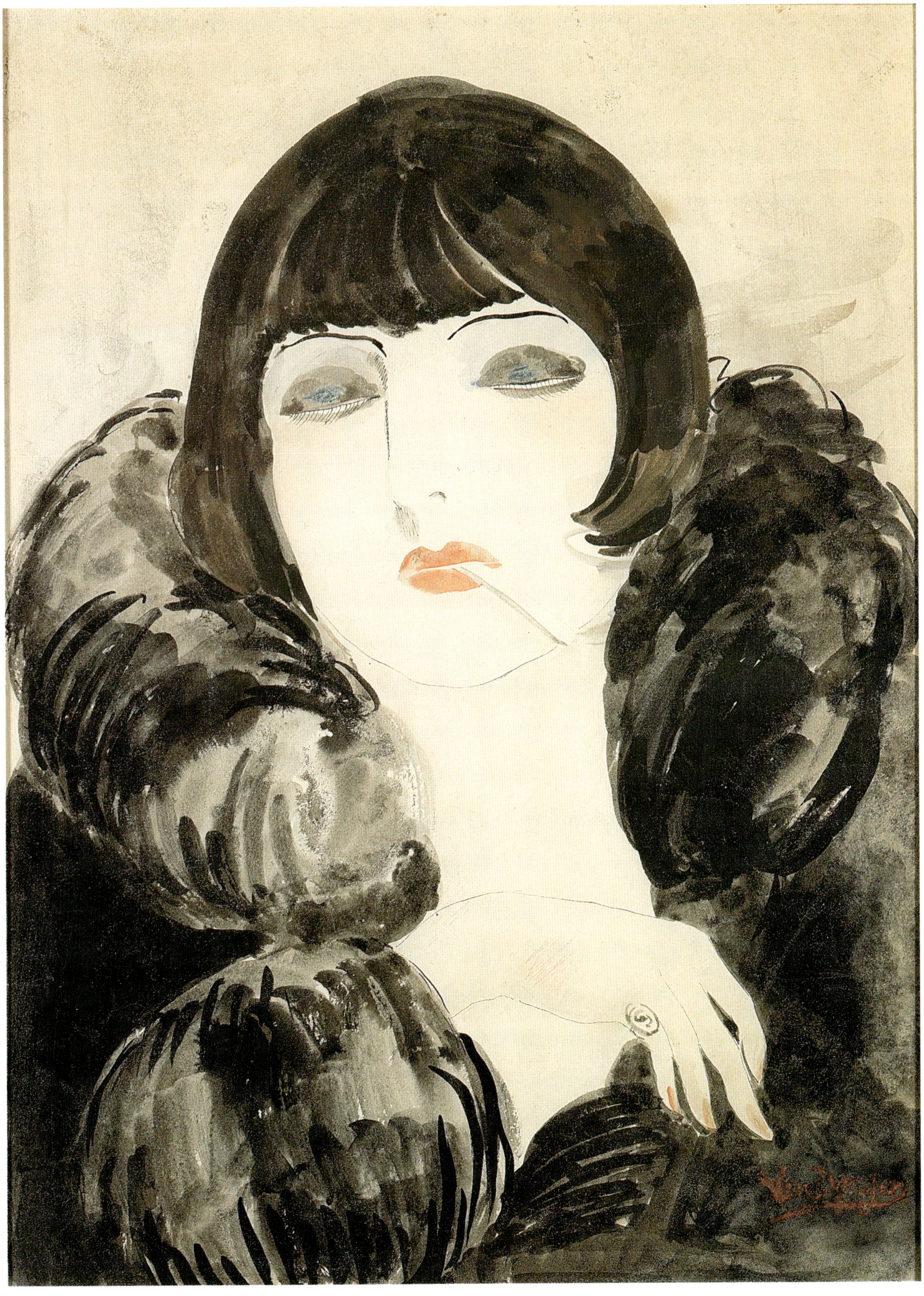
Van Dongen

Kees van Dongen 1877–1968

8 Nine illustrations for Marcel Proust's A la Recherche du temps perdu

1946–7
Each stamped with signature: 'van Dongen'
The watercolour medium is thickly applied, often consisting of multiple layers, especially of cobalt and Prussian blue; occasional cracks in the pigment layers are to be found in the passages of heaviest impasto. Otherwise condition of all nine sheets is good

Provenance
Estate of Marcel Proust
Sotheby's, London
Thyssen-Bornemisza Collection, 1976[1]

Literature
Marcel Proust, *A la Recherche du temps perdu*, 3 vols., Paris (Gallimard) 1947

Notes
1 Of the nine illustrations now owned by the Thyssen-Bornemisza Collection, all except [8e] and [8h] were acquired at the sale held by Sotheby's, London, on 30 June 1976 (*Impressionist and Modern Drawings and Watercolours*, lots 235, 236, 241, 250, 268, 281, 295). The two remaining illustrations, which had been lots 260 and 289 at the Sotheby's sale, were bought in October the same year from the Galerie Muzac, Paris

The Pavilion at Armenonville (a)
Le Pavillon d'Armenonville
Proust, I, facing p.192

Watercolour, pencil and Indian ink, 24.6 × 21.3 cm
Inscribed in right border: 'Proust No.8, page 73. Odette et Swann – restaurant d'Armenonville.'
Accession no.1976.43

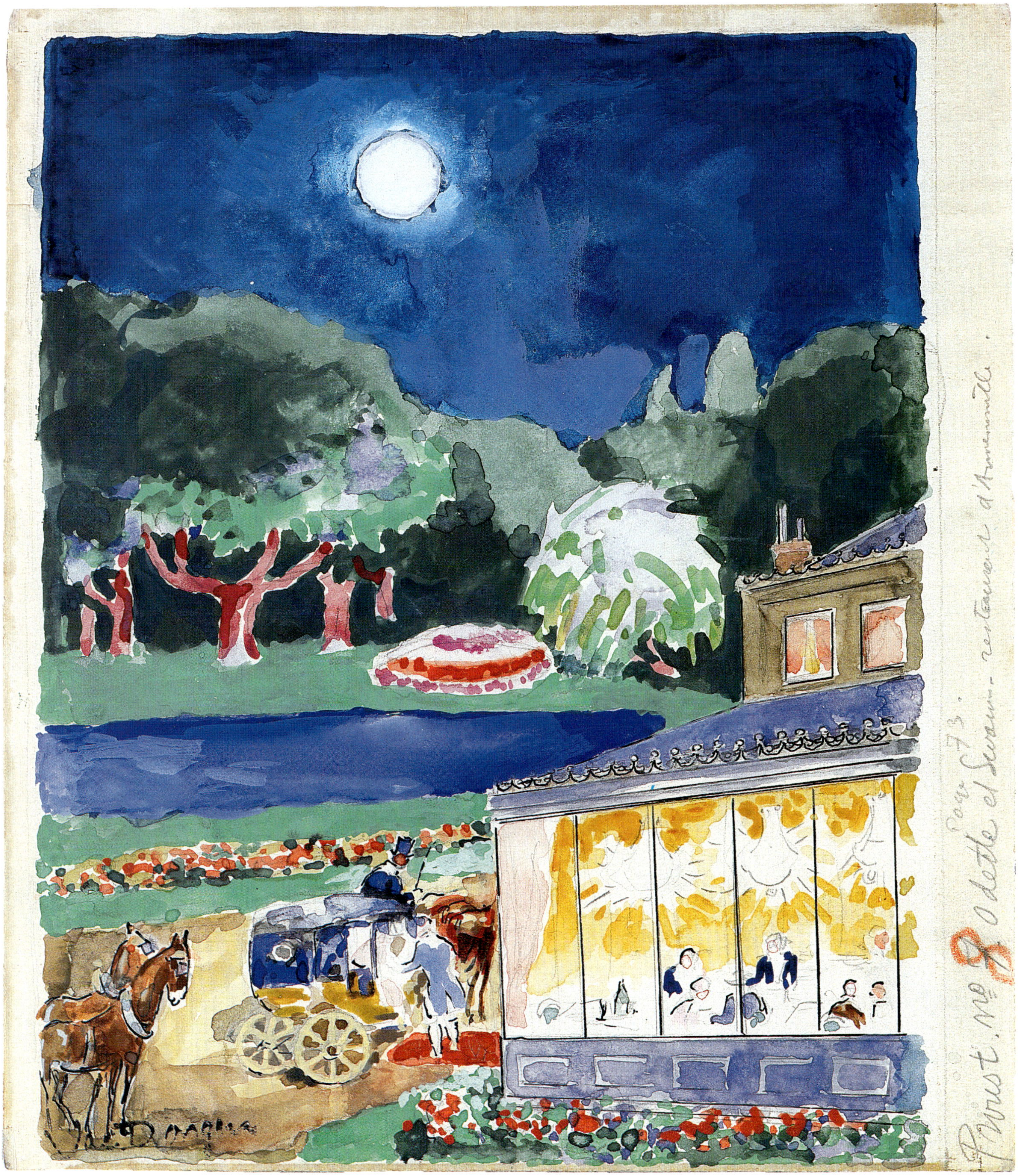
Proust. No 8 Odette et Swann - restaurant d'Armenonville.
Page 73.

a

Swann and the Marquis de Forestelle (b)
Swann et le marquis de Forestelle
Proust, I, facing p.208

Watercolour and pencil with white heightening, 24.5 × 21.2 cm
Inscribed in right border: 'Proust No.9. Swann et le marquis de Forestelle.'
Accession no.1976.44

Soirée at the house of Mme de Saint-Euverte (c)
Soirée chez Mme de Saint-Euverte
Proust, I, facing p.232

Watercolour and pencil with white heightening, 24.4 × 21.2 cm
Inscribed in right border: 'Proust No.10. La soirée chez Mme. de Saint-Euvert [sic].'
Accession no.1976.103

The Bathers (d)
Les Baigneuses
Proust, I, facing p.632

Watercolour and pencil, 24.4 × 21.2 cm
Inscribed in right border: 'Proust No.26 les baigneuses.'
Accession no.1976.40

The Kiss (e)
Le Baiser
Proust, II, facing p.248

Watercolour and pencil with white heightening, 24.5 × 21.2 cm
Inscribed in right border: 'Proust No.36. Baiser Albertine.'
Accession no.1976.71

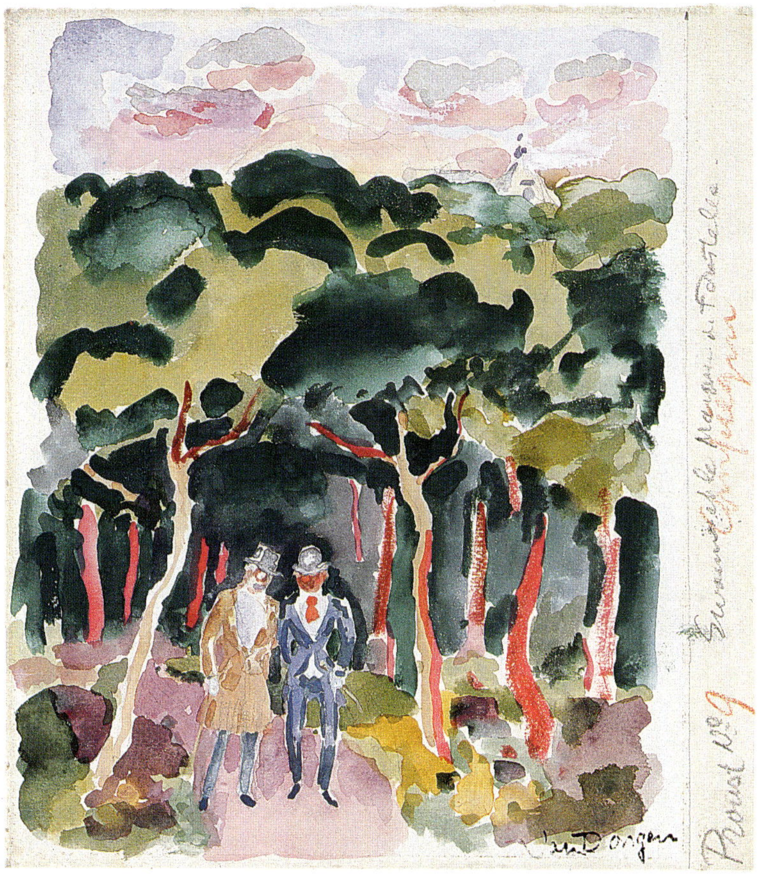
Proust N° 9
VanDongen

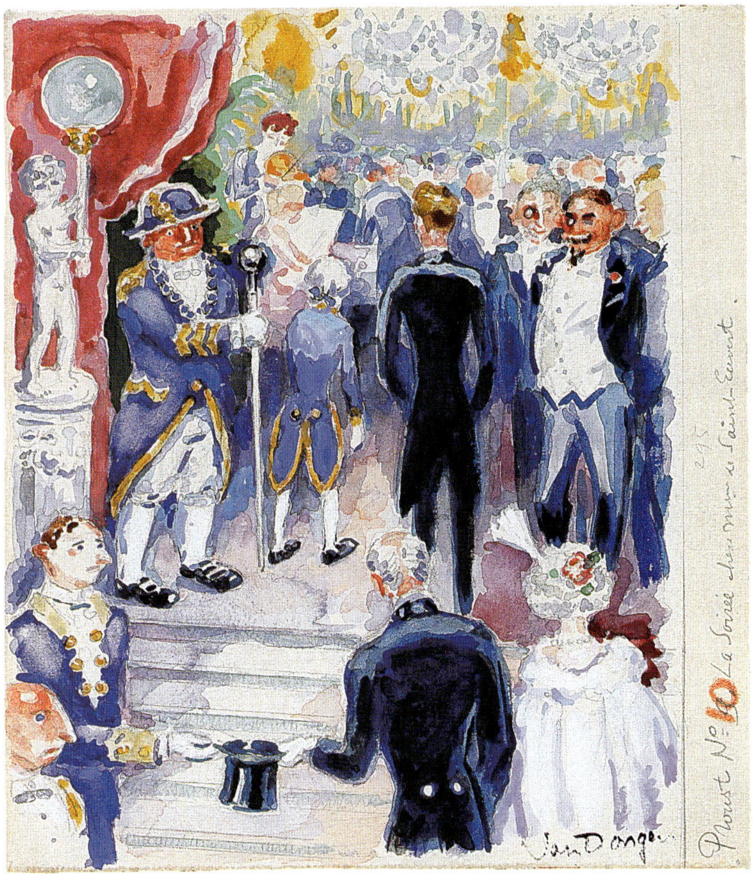
Proust N° 10
VanDongen

b/c

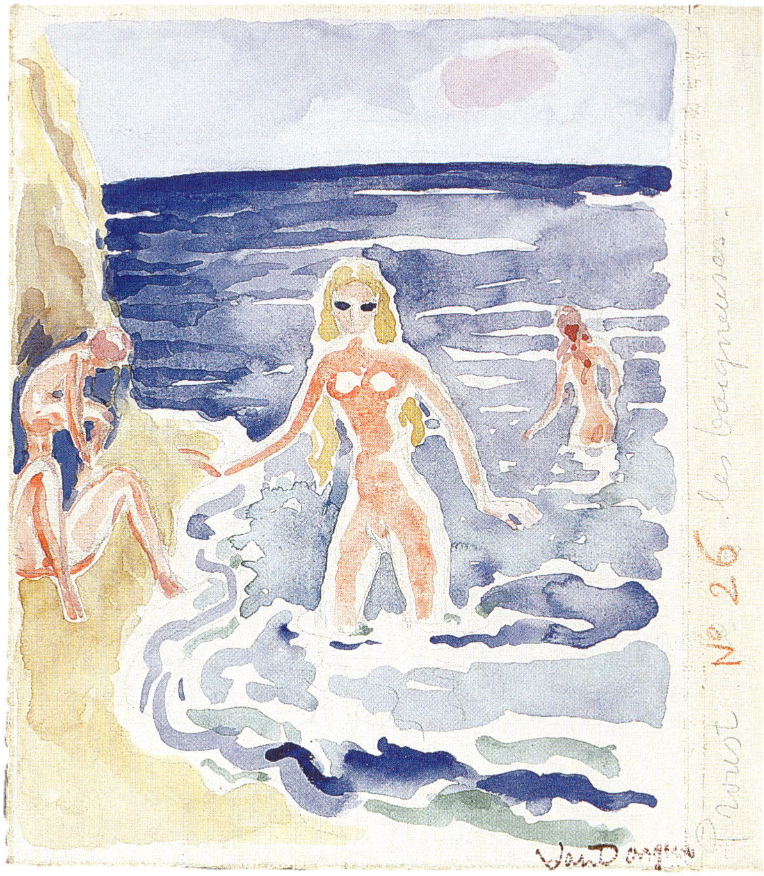
Proust N° 26 les baigneuses
VanDongen

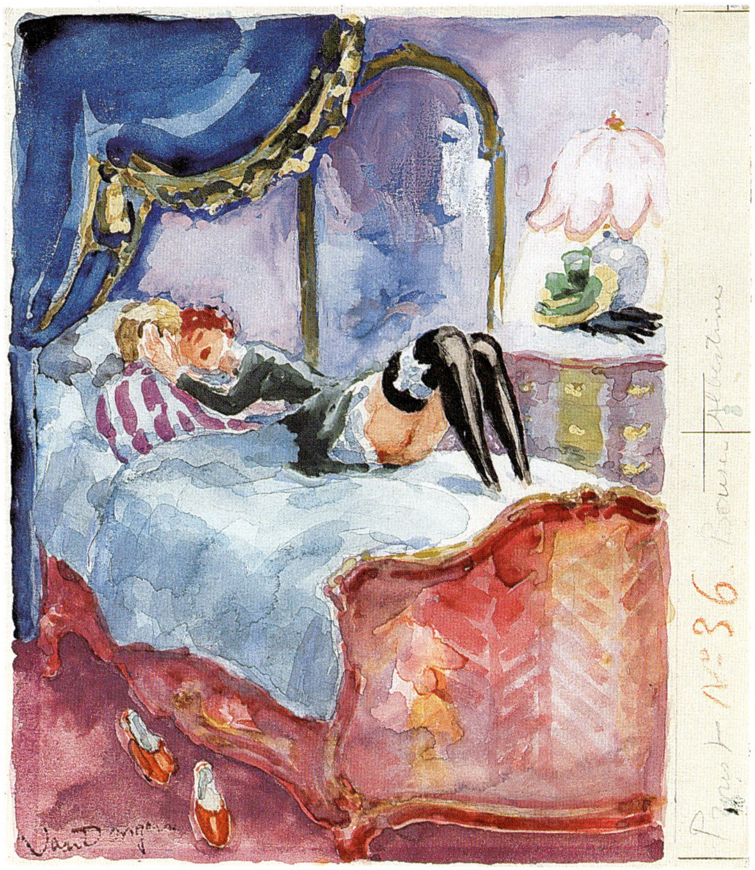
Proust N° 36
VanDongen

d/e

Albertine at the house of the narrator (f)
Albertine chez le narrateur
Proust, II, facing p.496

Watercolour and pencil with white heightening, 24.2 × 21.2 cm
Inscribed in right border: 'Proust No.46. Albertine chez Proust.'
Accession no.1976.39

Decline of Charlus (g)
Déchéance de Charlus
Proust, III, facing p.144

Watercolour and pencil with white heightening, 24.4 × 21.5 cm
Inscribed in right border: 'Proust No.59. Charlus vieux – tapettes professionelles.'
Accession no.1976.41

Albertine and Andrée (h)
Albertine et Andrée
Proust, III, facing p.248

Watercolour and pencil with white heightening, 24.5 × 21.2 cm
Inscribed in left border: 'Proust No.63. Albertine et Andrée dans leur chambre.'
Accession no.1976.70

Evocations (i)
Évocations
Proust, III, facing p.568

Watercolour and pencil, 25.2 × 20.4 cm
Inscribed in right border: 'Proust No.75 ... [illegible] évoque le passé.'
Accession no.1976.42

In 1946–7, the French pubishing house of Gallimard commissioned van Dongen to produce seventy-seven illustrations for a new three-volume version of Proust's *A la Recherche du temps perdu*, published in 1947 in an edition of 8,750 copies. The original watercolours initially remained in the collection of the Proust family; all but seven of them were offered for sale at Sotheby's in London in June 1976, each stamped with a signature and accompanied by a certificate of authenticity by Mme Kees van Dongen. The nine illustrations acquired by the Thyssen-Bornemisza Collection are listed above in the order in which they appear in the book.

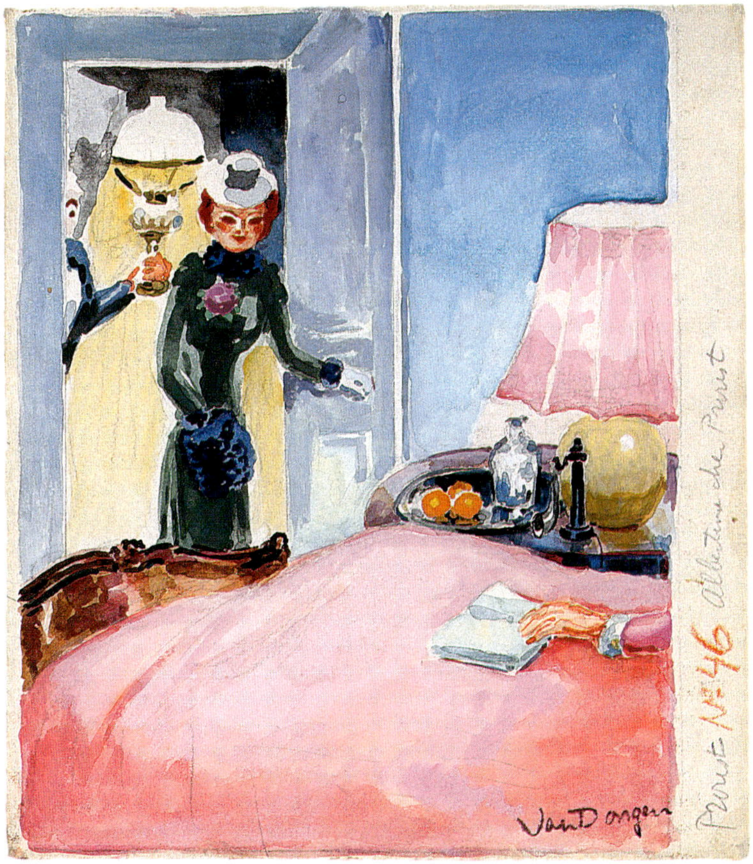
Proust Nº46
VanDongen

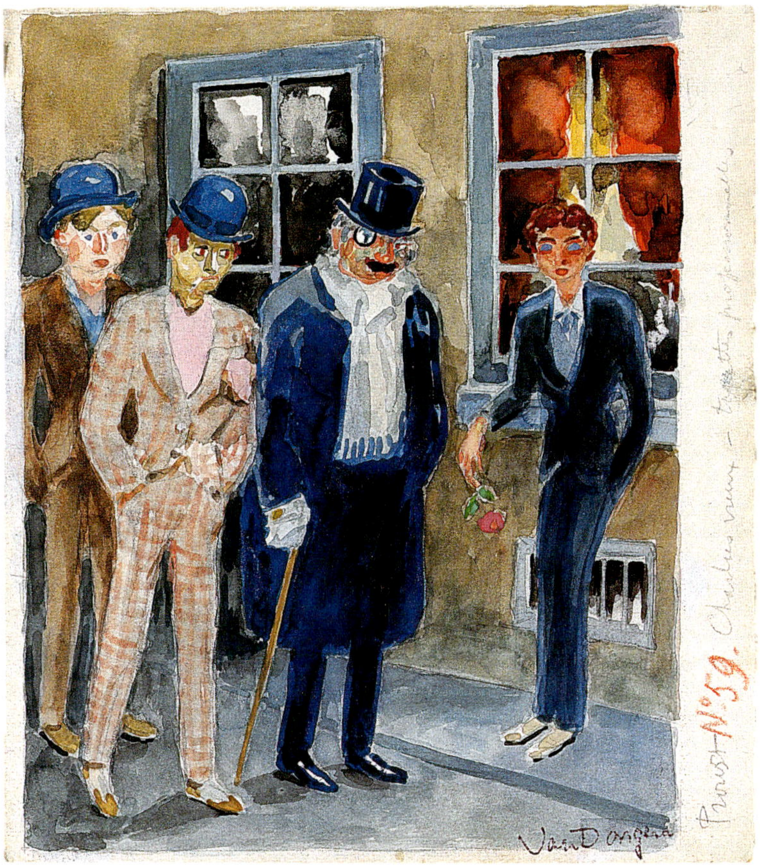
Proust Nº59.
VanDongen

f/g

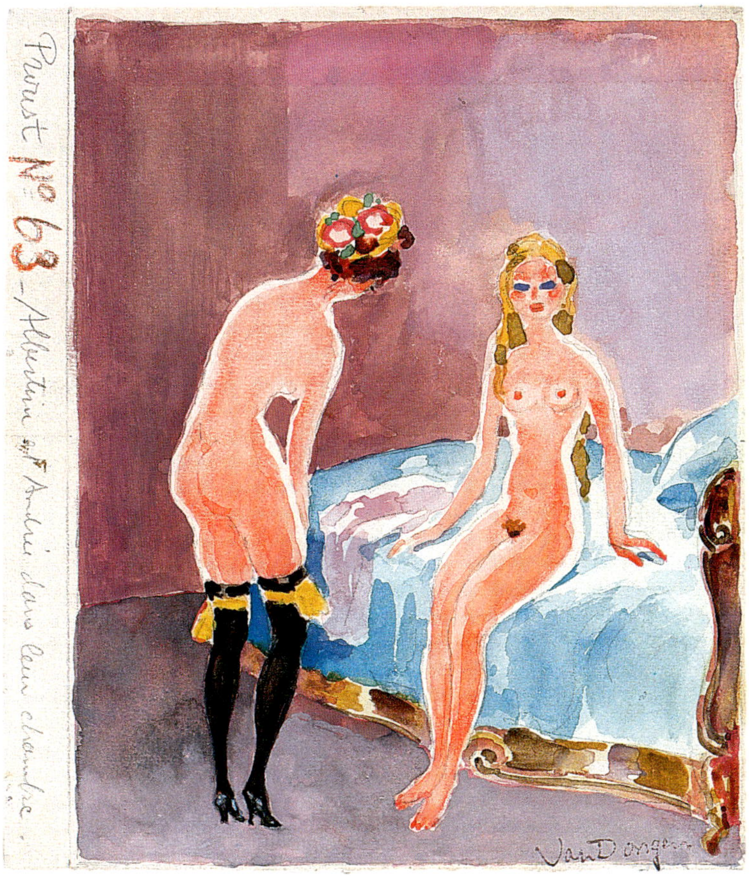
Proust Nº63
VanDongen

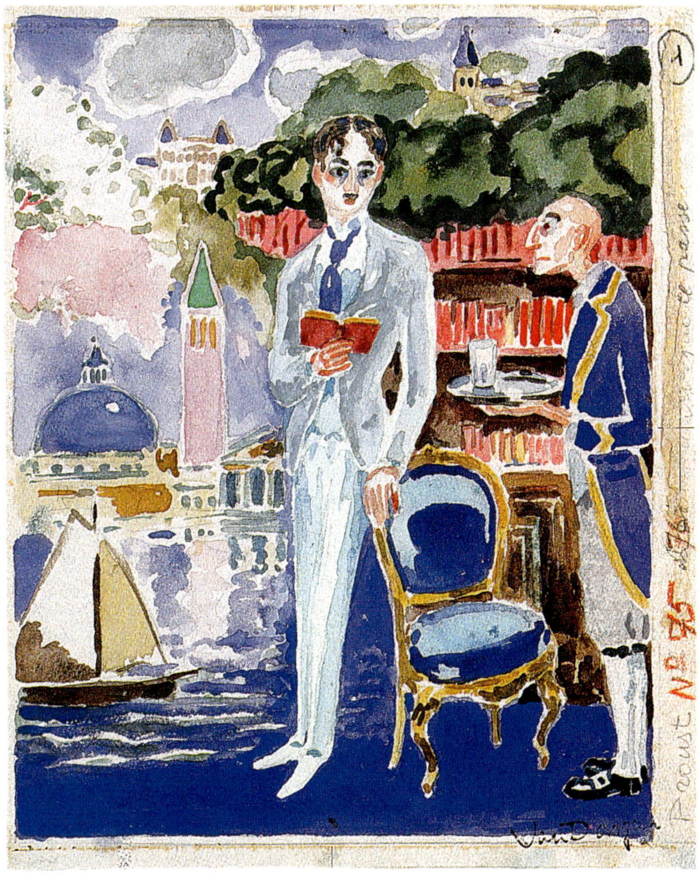
Proust

h/i

James Ensor 1860–1949

9 Theatre of Masks

1908
Oil on canvas, 72 × 86 cm; framed 93.5 × 113.5 cm
Signed/dated lower right: 'Ensor 1908'
In good condition. Original frame
Accession no.1977.61

Provenance
R.Sostberg, Berlin
W.Kleinberg, Antwerp
Fritz Trüssel, Berne
Mme Julien Rossat-Trüssel, Féchy
François Daulte, Lausanne
Thyssen-Bornemisza Collection, 1977[1]

Exhibitions
Hanover, Kestner-Gesellschaft, 1919, *James Ensor – Künstler des Café du Dome. XXVIII. Sonder-Ausstellung*, no.4 [as 'Carnaval' ?][2]
Hanover, Galerie von Garvens, 1920, *Erste Ausstellung: James Ensor, Paula Modersohn-Becker, Alt-Tibetanisches Kunstgewerbe*, p.6 [as 'Maskenszene' ?]
Dresden, *Internationale Kunstausstellung*, 1926, no.28
Hanover, Kestner-Gesellschaft/Dresden, Galerie Neue Kunst Fides, 1927, *James Ensor*, no.37 [as 'Maskentheater in Brügge, 1896']
Berlin, Galerie Paul Cassirer, 1927, *James Ensor*[3]
Mannheim, Städtische Kunsthalle, 1928, *James Ensor*, no.32 [as 'Maskentheater in Brügge, ca. 1896']
Leipzig, Kunstverein, 1928, *James Ensor*, no.27 [as 'Maskentheater in Brügge, ca. 1896']
Brussels, Palais des Beaux-Arts, 1929, *James Ensor*, no. 256 [as 'Le Grand Théatre des Masques']
Amsterdam, Kunsthandel Huinck and Scherjon, 1930, *James Ensor*, no.13
Brussels, Galerie Georges Giroux, 1931, *L'art vivant en Belgique*, no.4
Basle, Kunsthalle/Münster, Westfälisches Landesmuseum, 1963, *James Ensor*, no.80
Chicago, IL, Art Institute/New York, Solomon R.Guggenheim Museum, 1976–7, *Ensor*, p.37
Brussels/Paris 1977–8, no.19
Lugano 1978, no.23
Modern Masters from the Thyssen-Bornemisza Collection, 1984–6, no.23
Hamburg, Kunstverein, 1986–7, *James Ensor*, no.31, ill. p.86b
Lugano 1989, no.4
's-Hertogenbosch, Noordbrabants Museum, 1990, *Een feest van kleur. Post-impressionisten uit particulier bezit*, no.23
Rome 1990–91, no.8

Literature
Luc and Paul Haesaerts, *Flandre, L'Impressionisme*, Paris 1931, p.357
Legrand (1971), p.116, cat. no.199
Tricot (1985), p.35, cat. no.24(b)[4]

Apart from its slightly larger dimensions, *Theatre of Masks* is a virtually exact replica of Ensor's composition of the same title painted in 1889, now in Antwerp (fig.1).[5] The Thyssen picture differs from this earlier work principally in the artist's handling of paint, which in the 1889 version is far more plastic and virtuoso. The later copy appears somewhat flat and ghostly by comparison. Given, however, the close resemblance between the two paintings, it is hardly surprising that they have on occasion been confused.[6]

Notes
1 Acquired directly from the previous owner
2 In the case of this and the following exhibition, it is not absolutely certain that it was the Thyssen Collection's painting that was shown: see also n.6
3 There was no catalogue for this exhibition which was, however, the same as that shown earlier the same year at the Kestner-Gesellschaft in Hanover (information supplied by Xavier Tricot, Ostend: letter to the author, 17 July 1990)
4 This study by Tricot of aspects of Ensor's art includes a section 'Repliques et Versions des Tableaux' (pp.32–7) listing all the copies and variants of the artist's paintings: comprising 45 entries and in some instances as many as three versions of the same composition, it makes clear how frequent was Ensor's practice of copying from or repeating his own earlier works
5 James Ensor, *Maskertoneel*, 1889, oil on canvas, 59 × 72 cm: see *Catalogus schilderijen 19de en 20ste eeuw*, Antwerp (Ministerie van Nederlandse Cultuur/ Koninklijk Museum voor Schone Kunsten Antwerpen) n.d. [1977], p.152, cat. no.1855; also Haesaerts (1957), cat. no.171
6 I am grateful to Xavier Tricot, Ostend, for helping to resolve numerous problems, including that of identification; information given here concerning the early exhibition history of the Thyssen painting is drawn largely from the catalogue of the 1986–7 Hamburg exhibition, for which he was responsible. I am also indebted to Dr Diane Lesko, Curator of Collections at the Museum of Fine Arts, St Petersburg, FA, for her advice on the painting

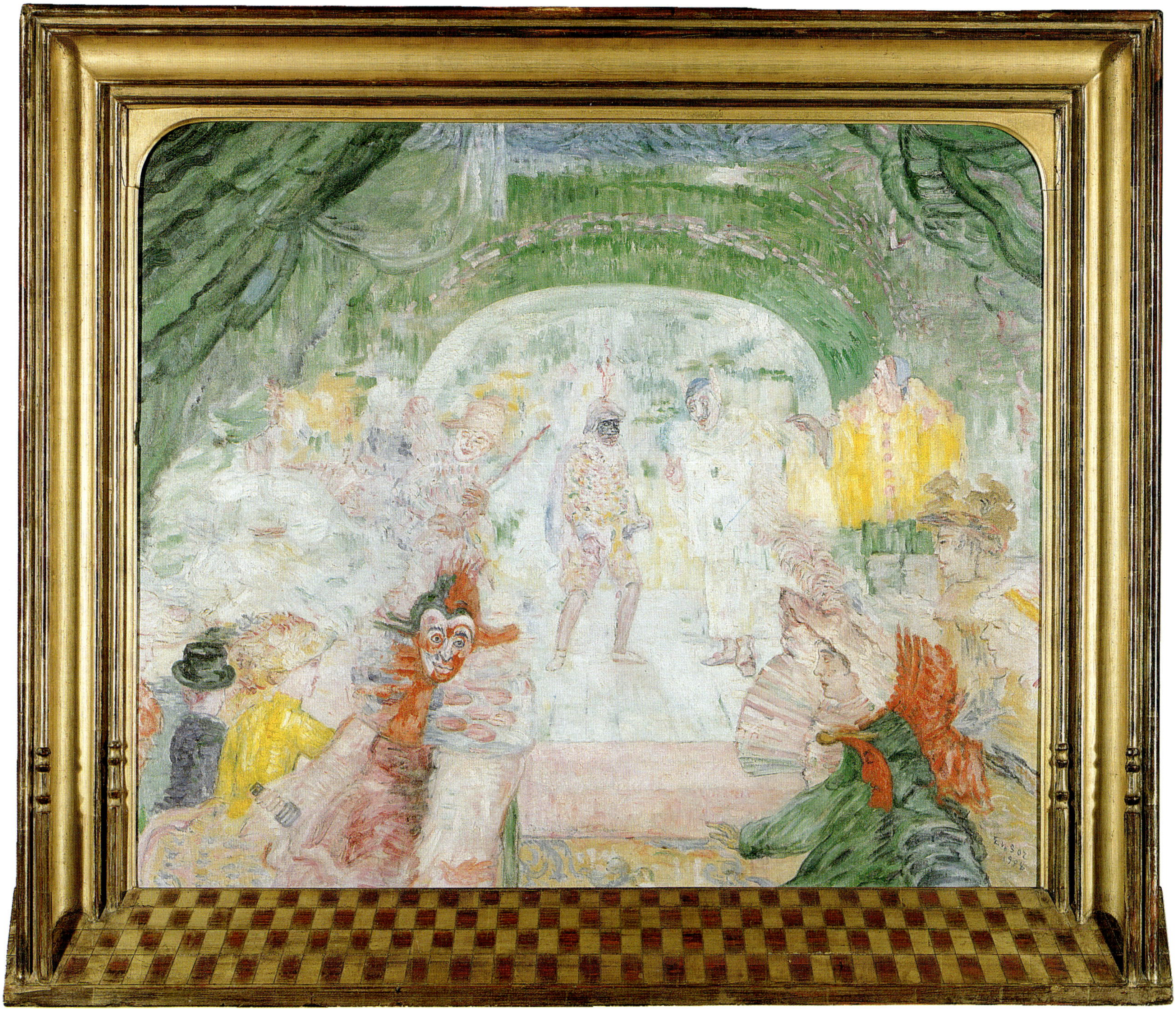

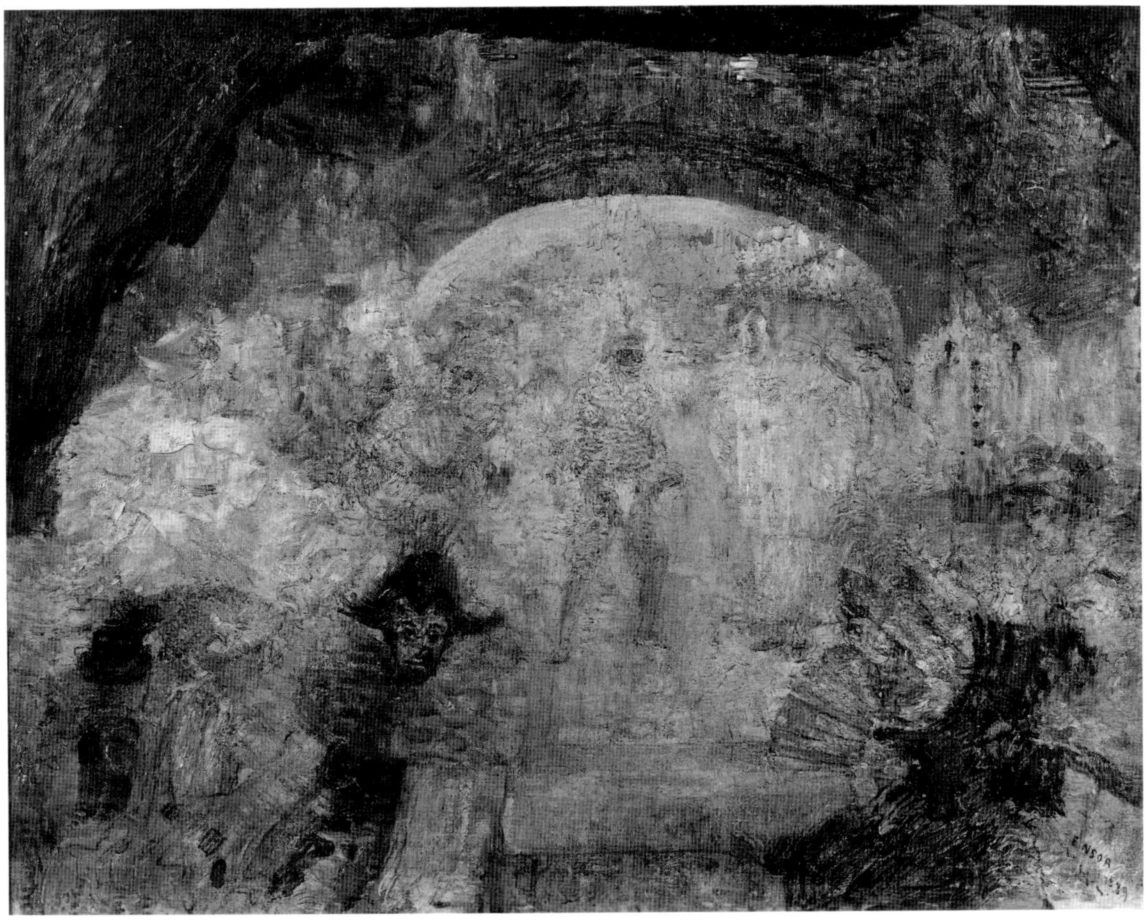

FIG 1 James Ensor, *Theatre of Masks*, 1889, oil on canvas, 59 × 72 cm (Antwerp, Koninklijk Museum voor Schone Kunsten, inv. no.1855)

The original version of the composition dates from a period during which Ensor's relations with other Belgian avant-garde groups were, to say the least, ambivalent. Though clearly anxious to play a significant role in exhibiting societies such as Les Vingt and La Libre Esthétique, his own sense of being an outsider, verging at times on paranoia, made him an awkward member of any such association. His feelings of isolation, of being persecuted, find pictorial expression in the subject matter of many of his works at this time, especially in his repeated use of skeletons and masks, frequently mocked or mocking, always ironic or satirical, as in his great canvas of the preceding year, the *Entry of Christ into Brussels* (fig.2).

Like so many of Ensor's paintings, *Theatre of Masks* is a work laden with a particular, and peculiar, personal symbolism. Quite apart from any expression of feelings of paranoia, it would have had at least two further levels of personal significance: his recollections of carnival time in Ostend, where his mother and aunt kept a souvenir shop selling masks, sea-shells and other such items, and his admiration for Watteau, in particular his theatre scenes, of which Ensor made a number of copies.[7] It also seems as if, in this instance, he wished to paint a theatre scene of his own in which Pierrot is protagonist. The inspiration of the Italian *commedia dell'arte*, as well as that of Watteau, is unmistakable.

It has not been possible to establish precisely why the later version was made, but Ensor's practice of painting variants of his own compositions was extensive. In a letter to the author dated 6 September 1989, the Ensor scholar Xavier Tricot observes that among the reasons for the numerous versions and copies, which mostly date from after the turn of the century, was the fact that increasingly frequent invitations to participate in foreign exhibitions meant that the artist became concerned about the fate of his works: fearing that they might be lost or destroyed, he 'immortalized' his subjects by copying. The growing number of his admirers and buyers also meant that prospective purchasers wanted copies of works already sold, which

Notes

7 See the chapter 'Variations d'Ensor sur les themes de Rubens et Watteau' in Tricot (1985), pp.16–20

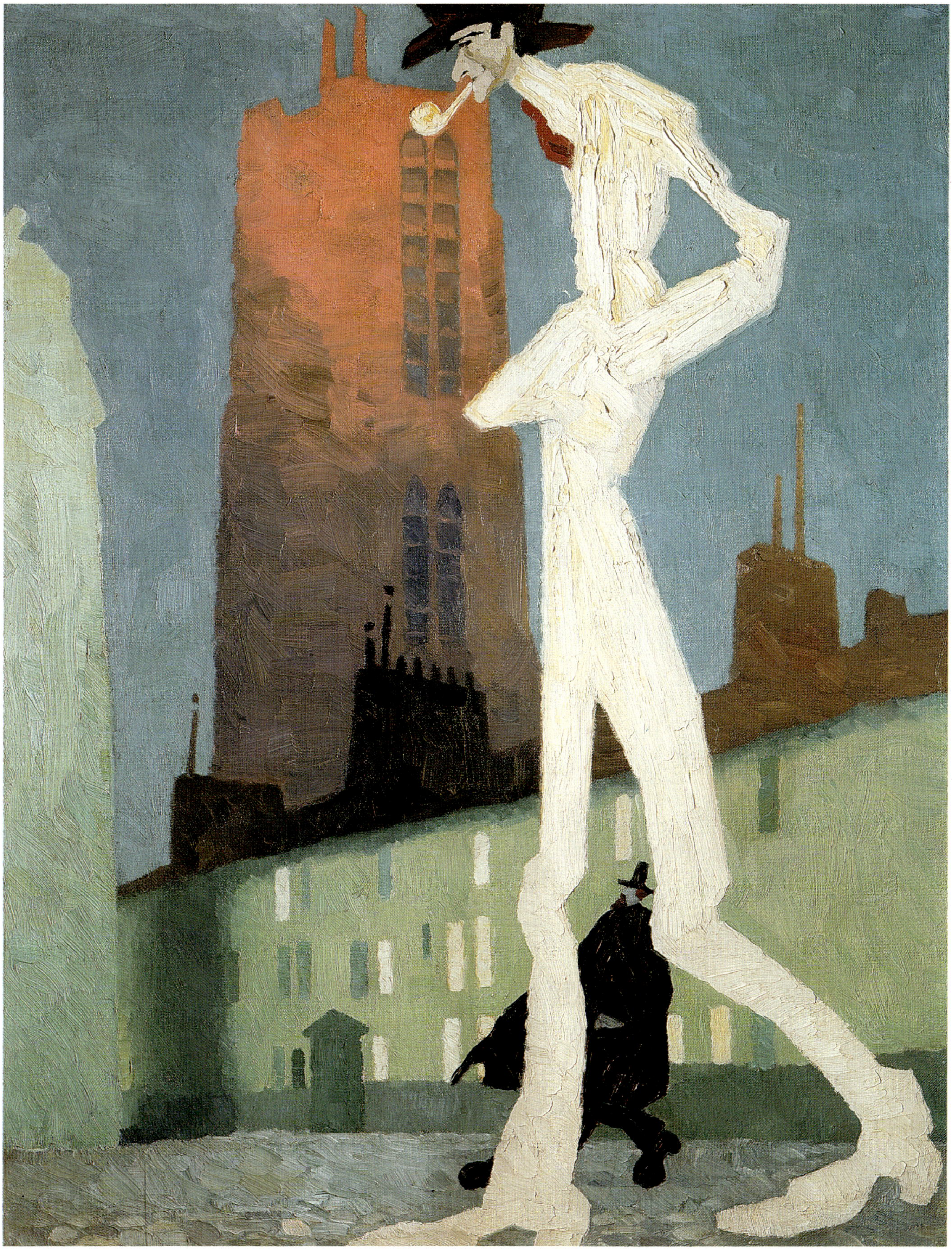

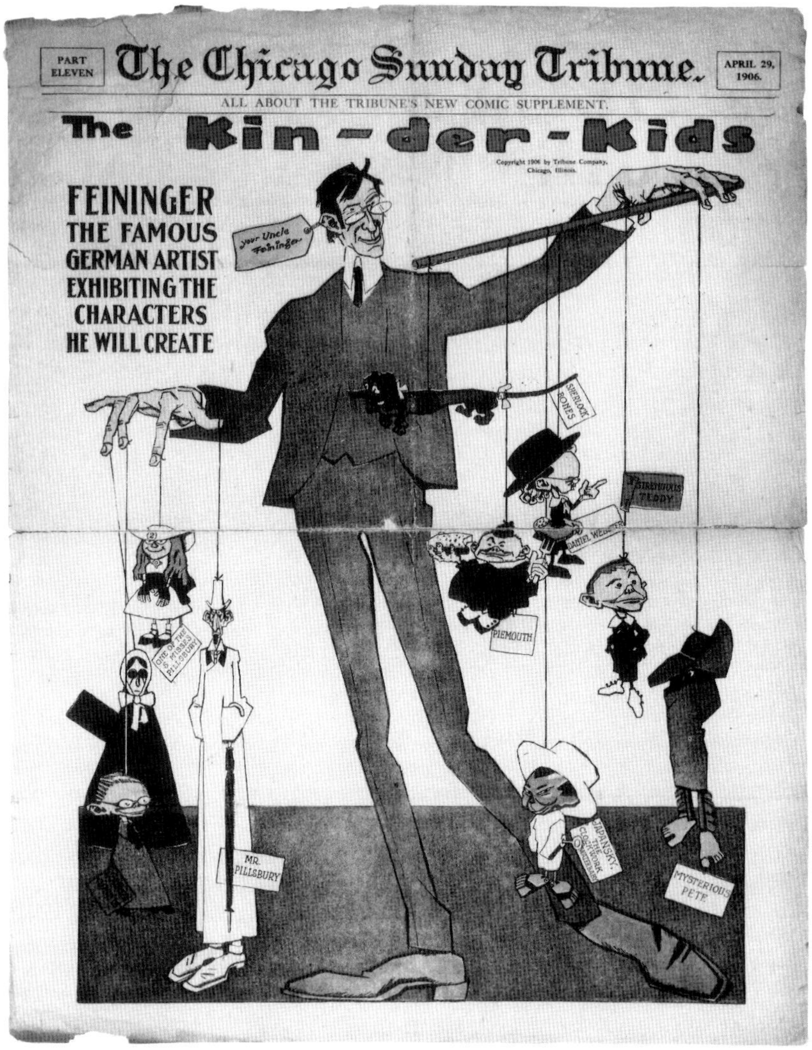

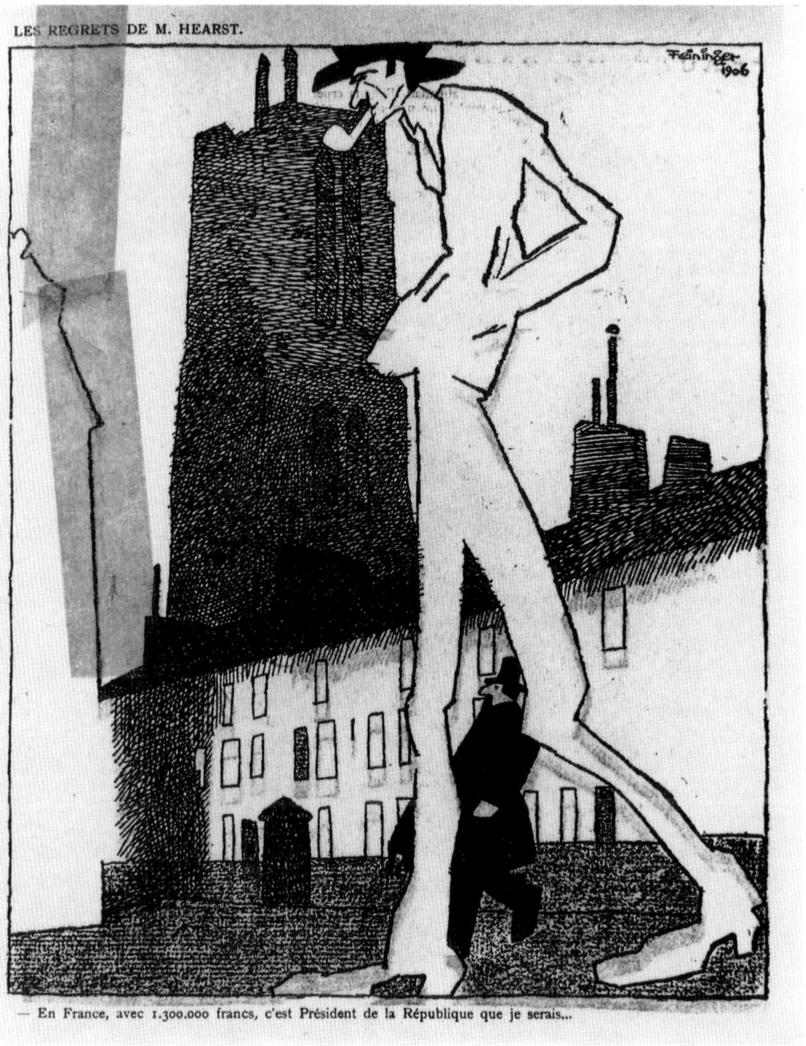

Having previously worked as a caricaturist for a succession of mainly humorous or satirical German magazines and periodicals, it was perhaps natural that Feininger should gravitate towards literary and journalistic circles on his arrival in Paris in July 1906. Among the Parisian magazines for which he provided illustrations was the journal *Le Témoin*, founded the same year by Dagny Björnson-Langen and edited by the designer Paul Iribe (see also [13]).[4] One of these illustrations was a drawing, compositionally identical to the present painting, published as a cartoon in one of the first issues of *Le Témoin* in autumn 1906 under the title 'Les regrets de M. Hearst' (fig.2).

The subject-matter of both caricature and painting has lent itself to a number of quite different interpretations. The title 'Les regrets de M. Hearst . . .', together with the accompanying caption 'In France with 1,300,000 francs I could be president of the Republic', was undoubtedly the work of the editor, rather than the artist. To Feininger's Parisian contemporaries, the tall man in the white suit with hat and pipe may well have suggested an American newspaper baron. That the image was not, on the other hand, intended as a portrait of William Randolph Hearst is beyond question; nor, indeed, is there anything to identify the figure as specifically American. Alois Schardt, one of the first German critics to write about the painting and a staunch champion of Feininger, believed the 'white man' to be a travelling Englishman:

Notes

4 Björnson-Langen was the wife of Albert Langen, publisher of the German satirical magazine *Simplicissimus*. *Le Témoin* continued to publish cartoons by Feininger until 1910: see Luckhardt (1987), pp.39f; also Luckhardt (1989), p.175

5 Schardt, loc. cit.; I have followed the translation printed in Luckhardt (1989)

6 See *Lyonel Feininger – Marsden Hartley*, exh. cat., New York, Museum of Modern Art, 1944, p.18

7 Luckhardt (1989), p.50

8 Hans Hess, in his account of the painting, alludes merely to the 'white man' as 'shadowing his counterpart, a small dark man . . .'; see Hess (1961), p.40

FIG 1 'The Kin-der-Kids', *Chicago Sunday Tribune*, 29 April 1906, title-page to part II

FIG 2 'Les regrets de M.Hearst', cartoon from *Le Témoin*, I (1906), no.6

FIG 3 Feininger photographed on the beach at Graal (Rügen), 1905 (Harvard University, Lyonel Feininger Archive)

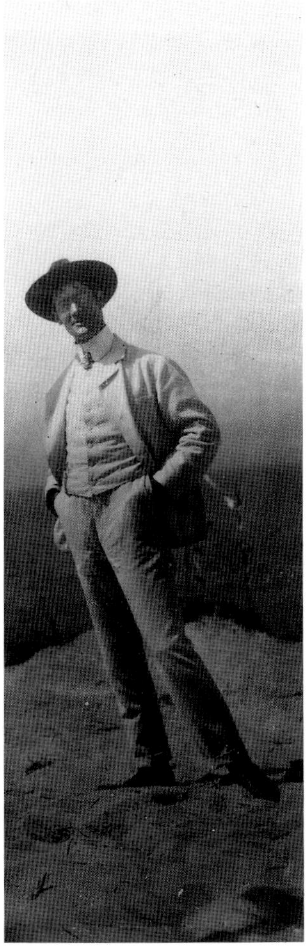

> A white man strides through the world slowly, deliberately, slightly bent, his pipe in his mouth, looking before him as he walks. He will never look up, he will never stop. There will be no excitement of mind or body, no expenditure of force, no end to his staying power; he will walk forever, hands in coat pockets. Between his legs, a black man runs through a flurry of wind, driven on in busy haste. He is running as fast as he can, but he will never catch up. The white man must be walking faster than we thought. Beneath him we see a three-storey building shimmering in a green light. He must be larger than we thought. Behind him a tower, a bit smaller than he is, stands in the reddish evening light. The man is huge, bigger than the picture frame, he has to bend slightly as he walks, for he reaches out beyond the frame, beyond its limited space into infinity. The suspended relation between ... the real tower, the real person and the white man, between real space and lack of space, between time and timelessness – this suspension seems restrained, grotesque, but so superhumanly grotesque that we cannot laugh.[5]

Aside from any debate as to the painting's intended meaning, Schardt's analysis of its compositional aspect is revealing. One of the most striking things about *The White Man* is the discrepancy in scale between the treatment of the principal figure and the surrounding architecture. This was clearly a deliberate device, employed to a quite specific end. In a letter of 1906, Feininger wrote:

> The slightest difference in relative proportions creates enormous differences with regard to the monumentality and intensity of the composition. Monumentality is not attained by making things larger – how childish! – but by constrasting large and small in the same composition. On the size of a postage stamp one can represent something gigantic, while yards of canvas may be used in a smallish way and squandered ...[6]

By contrast, Hans Hess, Feininger's biographer, identifed *The White Man* as representing the artist himself, whom he described as 'a tall, angular, boyishly jerky man': 'There he stands, as high as the Tour St Jacques, hands in his pocket, an American in Paris, a painter looking at his world.' This suggestion is not wholly implausible. There is an undeniable resemblance between the figure of the 'white man', with spindly legs and enormous feet, and the artist's own depiction of himself in the *Chicago Sunday Tribune* (29 April 1906), introducing the paper's 'new comic supplement' (fig.1), accompanied by the caption: 'The Kin-der-Kids: Feininger the famous German artist [sic] exhibiting the characters he will create.' There is also something about the pose of an old family snapshot (fig.3) taken in 1905 showing Feininger on the beach at Graal, dressed in a summer suit with high collar and hat, which calls irresistably to mind the figure in the 1907 painting. Ulrich Luckhardt, on the other hand, the most recent author to write extensively about Feininger, believes that the image of the 'white man', though closely related to the artist's caricatures, is itself without specific reference.[7]

Other than that by Schardt, none of the interpretations of the picture published hitherto has devoted much attention to the significance of the figure of the 'black man';[8] indeed, such is the 'difference in relative proportions' between the two figures, about which Feininger writes, that it is easy, at least at first glance, to overlook him altogether. If, however, the suggestion that the 'white man' may have been intended as a self-portrait is at least plausible, then the 'black man' must surely be some kind of alter ego, representing perhaps the saturnine side of the artist's personality or even, in a more general sense, the darker powers that threaten the human psyche: scurrying along in the background behind the 'white man', distracting him, tripping him up, diverting the purposefully striding figure from attaining its true objective.

Lyonel Feininger 1871–1956

11 Ships

1917
Oil on canvas, 71 × 85.5 cm
Signed/dated upper left: 'Feininger 17'
History of flaking and scattered losses. There is some cupping and lifting of the paint surface, and small areas of discolouration corresponding to earlier repairs. The original edges of the canvas have been trimmed off, and the canvas lined with wax–resin adhesive
Accession no.1967.2

Provenance
Gustav Jung, Hagen
Galerie Aenne Abels, Cologne
Thyssen-Bornemisza Collection, 1967

Exhibitions
Turin, Galleria Civica d'Arte Moderna, 1971, *Il Cavaliere Azzurro*, ill. p.153
Bremen 1975, no.20
Cologne 1986, p.26, ill. p.27
Luxemburg/Munich/Vienna 1988, no.24

Literature
Hess (1961), no.180
Kiel (1974), p.34, ill. p.35

1917 was for Feininger a year marked by both difficulties and success. In April, the United States entered the war; thereafter, as an alien resident in Germany he was regarded with suspicion, and his movements restricted. He experienced problems in obtaining adequate materials as the war progressed, in particular, paints of reasonable quality. He was, moreover, increasingly concerned about his financial position and relative lack of public acclaim. These worries were to some extent alleviated by his first one-man show, held in Berlin at Herwarth Walden's Sturm Gallery in September that year. Though, as Feininger predicted, it did not lead to prodigious numbers of sales, the exhibition was none the less favourably regarded, and his work widely discussed by public and press; thereafter, his reputation in Germany continued to grow, particularly during thc immcdiatcly post-war years.

In *Ships*, one of seventeen paintings executed during the course of 1917,[1] Feininger gave expression to his childhood wish to become a marine painter. Marine subjects had preoccupied him on and off for the best part of a decade, his interest re-kindled by repeated visits made both before and during the war to Germany's Baltic coast. Interestingly, *Ships* is among his first pictures in which ships and the sea are the sole subject of the composition; as Luckhardt remarks, in Feininger's earlier work such scenes are usually peopled by figures standing on jetty, beach or shore.[2] Only with paintings such as *Side Wheeler* of 1913 (Private collection)[3] or *Leviathan*, done in the same year as the present picture,[4] did he dispense with the human figure, which in any case began to assume diminished importance in his work of the post-war years.

With its crystalline forms and intersecting planes, *Ships* also reflects the artist's continuing interest in Parisian Cubist painting, particularly the Orphism of Delaunay, which Feininger had the opportunity to see in Paris in 1911 and again at Walden's *Erster Deutscher Herbstsalon* in Berlin in the autumn of 1913. Though sceptical about Delaunay, referring to the French artist in a letter to Alfred Kubin as a 'totally mechanized mind',[5] Feininger continued working through the consequences of Orphism for his own art for a considerable time, into the late 1920s and even beyond (see also [16]).

Notes
1 According to Luckhardt (1989), p.176
2 Ibid., p.84
3 See Luckhardt (1989), no.18, ill. p.85
4 Hess (1961), no.176
5 Letter dated 5 October 1913, quoted after Luckhardt (1989), p.30

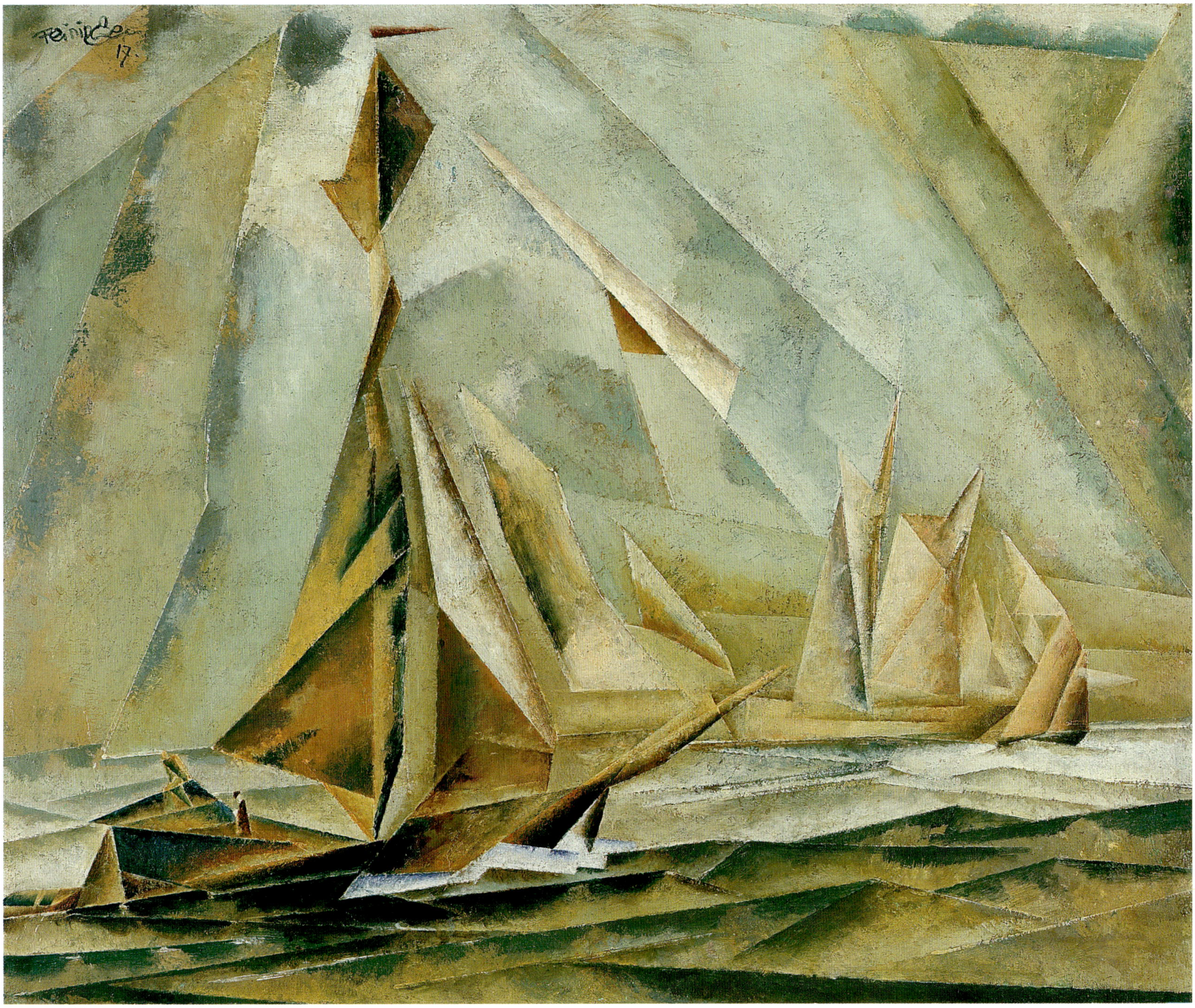
Feininger 17.

Lyonel Feininger 1871–1956

12 Architecture II

1921
Oil on canvas, 101 × 80.5 cm
Signed/dated lower right: 'Feininger 1921'; inscribed on back of stretcher: 'Lyonel Feininger "Architecture II"'
The paint layer is brittle, and shows some cracking. There is slight cupping around some of the cracks, and the canvas is cockled in places. The surface is slightly glossy and appears to have been treated with a natural resin varnish which has discoloured with age. Otherwise condition is good
Accession no.1977.12

Provenance
Estate of the artist
Pat and Lux Feininger, Cambridge, MA
Mr and Mrs Harry W. Anderson, Atherton, CA
Marlborough Fine Art, London
Thyssen-Bornemisza Collection, 1977

Exhibitions
Oakland, CA, Mills College Art Gallery, 1937, *2nd Feininger Exhibition* [as 'Architecture I']
New York, Curt Valentin Gallery, 1952, *Lyonel Feininger*, no.5 [as 'Architecture I']
New York, Willard Gallery, 1958, *Lyonel Feininger*, no.2
San Francisco, CA, Museum of Art, *Lyonel Feininger Memorial Exhibition*, 1959–61, no.21[1]
New York, Willard Gallery, 1961, *Lyonel Feininger. Architecture Paris–New York*, no.21
New York, Marlborough–Gerson Gallery, 1969, *Lyonel Feininger*, no.27
Munich, Haus der Kunst/Zurich, Kunsthaus, 1973, *Lyonel Feininger 1871–1956*, no.103
Brussels/Paris 1977–8, no.28
Lugano 1978, no.32
USA tour 1982–4, no.29
Modern Masters from the Thyssen-Bornemisza Collection, 1984–6, no.26
Cologne 1986, p.28, ill. p.29
Lugano 1989, no.37
Rome 1990–91, no.10

Literature
Hess (1961), no. 221 and p.94f
R.N.Ketterer, *Moderne Kunst IV*, Campione d'Italia (Galerie R.N.Ketterer) 1967, p.28, no.16, ill. p.29
Luckhardt (1989), p.116

When the Bauhaus was established in Weimar in 1919 under the direction of Walter Gropius, Feininger was one of the first teachers to be appointed. The majority of his paintings of the Bauhaus years are concerned with the depiction of architectural form. Few give such prominence to the human figure as do *Architecture II* and *Lady in Mauve* [13], though it is only in the latter that the human form dominates; in *Architecture II*, the significance of the three figures represented is overshadowed by the man-made environment surrounding them.

The two pictures have usually been regarded as closely related, both because of their subject matter and because of their almost identical dimensions. Luckhardt has even suggested that *Lady in Mauve*, painted a year later, may have been conceived as a pendant to *Architecture II*.[2]

Notes
1 This large touring exhibition was also shown in Minneapolis, Cleveland, Buffalo, Boston, and (in reduced form) in England at York City Art Gallery and at the Arts Council Gallery in London during the course of 1959–60
2 Luckhardt (1989), loc. cit.

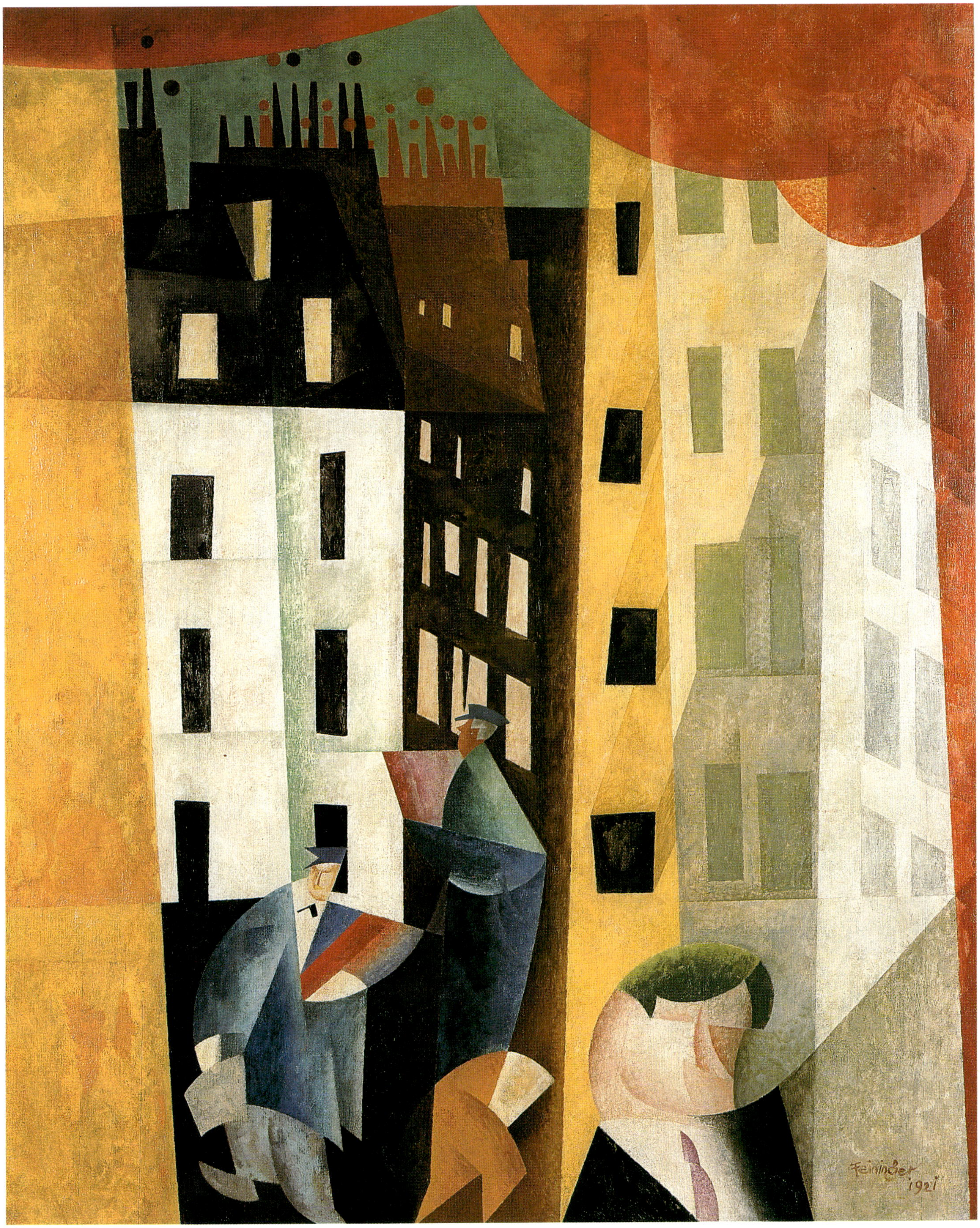
Feininger
1921

Hans Hess described both paintings as recollections of Paris. This may be true in two senses. Not only does the architecture depicted evoke the façades and rooftops of the French capital, but also both *Lady in Mauve* and *Architecture II* make use of geometric planes of colour which overlap one another in a way which seems reminiscent of Parisian Cubist painting.[3] However, the latter work is, as Luckhardt observes, unusual in Feininger's oeuvre, in that these geometric colour planes are intensely painted and relatively opaque, depending for their effect principally on the use of saturated colour: a far cry from the crystalline forms more often associated with the artist's work of this period.

FIG 1 Still from *The Cabinet of Dr Caligari* (Robert Wiene, 1919)

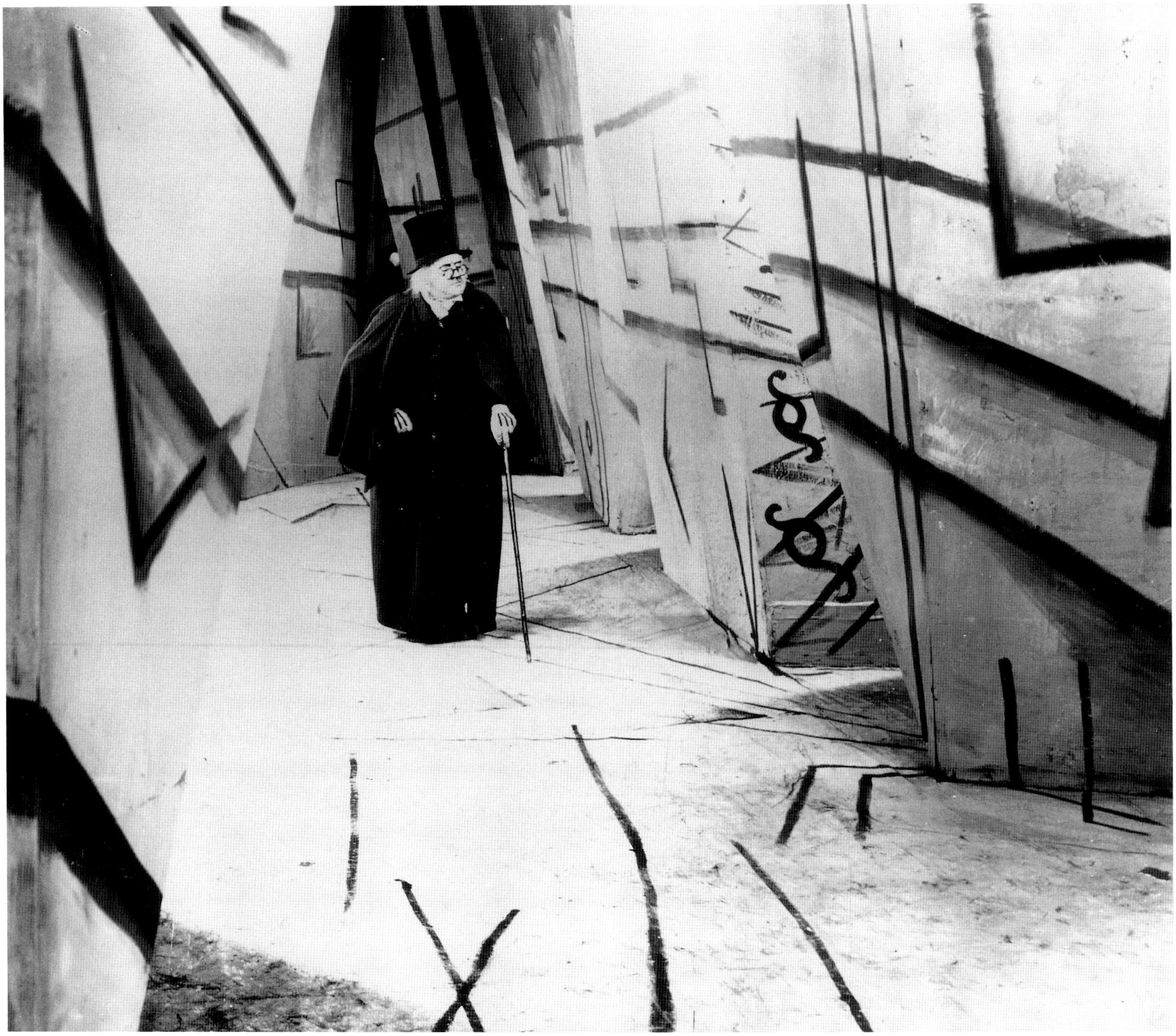

It has also been suggested that the architecture, in particular the crooked buildings which bear down upon the human figures or, as in *Lady in Mauve*, lean back to allow them to pass, seems curiously akin to the backdrops utilized in some of the earliest masterpieces of Expressionist cinema – what Lotte Eisner called the 'haunted screen' – such as the epoch-making *The Cabinet of Dr Caligari* of 1919 (see fig.1). Feininger himself, on the other hand, in a letter of 1944 to the film historian Siegfried Kracauer, denied that there was any truth in this suggestion – indeed, denied all knowledge of *Caligari* or of the artists of Walden's circle – Hermann Warm, Walter Röhrig and Walter Reimann – who painted the scenery for the film.[4]

It has proved impossible to trace any record of exhibitions in which [12] was shown prior to 1937. In that year, however, Feininger visited Mills College in Oakland, California, spending the summer teaching there, as he had done the previous year. His visits were the outcome of an invitation by the art historian Alfred Neumeyer (probably prompted, as Luckhardt suggests, by Emmy Scheyer)[5] extended to Feininger in 1935 while the artist was still in Germany. To coincide with these two visits, Mills College Art Gallery mounted important retrospective exhibitions of Feininger's work; according to handlists preserved by the gallery, the present painting was included in the second of these exhibitions, albeit under the title *Architecture I*.[6]

Despite the misleading title, the dimensions and date indicated on the gallery's handlist and the presence of an old label of Mills College Art Gallery on the back of the picture make it virtually certain that it was the Thyssen Collection's painting that was exhibited on that occasion. Whether the variant title was simply a mistake, or whether the artist subsequently changed his mind as regards the numbering of his *Architecture* series is impossible to ascertain. It seems, however, that the painting was exhibited again as *Architecture I* when shown at the Curt Valentin Gallery in New York in 1952.[7]

The painting has also long been known as *The Man from Potin*. It is not clear exactly how this name first came about, but it probably began as a joke between his parents, according to the artist's son, T. Lux Feininger.[8] 'Potin' alludes to the well-known Parisian supermarket chain Félix Potin, which in the years before the First World War was a high-class grocery store offering a home delivery service. The figure in the foreground perhaps reminded the Feiningers of the 'man from Potin' who brought purchases to the door of the apartment they occupied on the boulevard Raspail during the years around 1907. This allusion is interesting not merely in itself, but also because, quite apart from the unmistakably Parisian façades of the buildings represented, it confirms that the artist did indeed have the experiences of his Parisian sojourn in mind when painting this picture.

See also [13].

Notes

3 Hess (1961), p.94

4 Siegfried Kracauer, *From Caligari to Hitler. A Psychological History of the German Film*, Princeton, NJ, 1947, repr. 1966, p.69 and n.11

5 See Luckhardt (1989), p.179

6 I am grateful to Timothy Mosman, assistant director of Mills College Art Gallery, for making available information from the gallery's files regarding the 1936 and 1937 exhibitions of Feininger's work

7 New York, Curt Valentin Gallery, 1952, *Lyonel Feininger*, no.5 ('*Architecture I*, 1921, 39½" × 31"'). The dimensions are identical with those of the present picture

8 Letter to the author, 9 June 1991. I am grateful to Mr Feininger for his comments and advice concerning other works by his father now in the Thyssen-Bornemisza Collection

Lyonel Feininger 1871–1956

13 Lady in Mauve

1922
Oil on canvas, 100.5 × 80.5 cm
Signed/dated lower left: 'Feininger 22'
The canvas has been lined with wax–resin adhesive; perhaps as a result, the paint surface now appears to the eye somewhat lustreless. The artist evidently primed his own canvas; a visually disturbing effect is produced by the broad brushstrokes of the priming, clearly visible beneath the pigment layer. The paint surface is abraded, with scattered in-painting; earlier restoration was evidently of inferior quality, and the picture has been poorly cleaned, though it is not clear at what date[1]
Accession no.1964.12

Provenance
Estate of the artist
Julia Feininger, New York
Pat and Lux Feininger, Cambridge, MA
Galerie R.N.Ketterer, Campione d'Italia
Thyssen-Bornemisza Collection, 1964

Exhibitions
New York, Museum of Modern Art, 1944, *Lyonel Feininger – Marsden Hartley*, p.46
New York, Curt Valentin Gallery, 1952, *Lyonel Feininger*, no.7
San Francisco, CA, Museum of Art, *Lyonel Feininger Memorial Exhibition*, 1959–60, no.24[2]
Hamburg, Kunstverein/Essen, Museum Folkwang/Baden-Baden, Staatliche Kunsthalle, 1961, *Lyonel Feininger 1871–1956. Gedächtnis-Ausstellung*, no.25
Dallas, TX, Museum of Contemporary Arts, 1963, *Lyonel Feininger Retrospective*
New York, Marlborough–Gerson Gallery, 1969, *Lyonel Feininger*, no.28
Munich, Haus der Kunst/Zurich, Kunsthaus, 1973, *Lyonel Feininger 1871–1956*, no.104
Bremen 1975, no.21
Japanese tour 1976
Brussels/Paris 1977–8, no.29
Lugano 1978, no.33
USA tour 1982–4, no.30
Modern Masters from the Thyssen-Bornemisza Collection, 1984–6, no.27
Lugano 1989, no.36
Expressionism and Modern German Painting, 1989–90, no.5
Rome 1990–91, no.11

Literature
Hess (1961), no.227 and pp.94f
Kiel (1974), p.36, ill. p.37
Luckhardt (1987), pp.43, 84f
Luckhardt (1989), p.120

One of the early drawings Feininger did for Paul Iribe during his 1906–7 stay in Paris[3] was a pen-and-ink study entitled *La Belle*, also in the Thyssen-Bornemisza Collection (see [15]). It was published in the magazine *Le Témoin* in 1907 under the title 'L'Impatiente', together with the caption: 'He said he'd be here at eight, it's now ten . . . I'll wait a bit longer, but at midnight, I'm going' (fig.2). As in the case of the drawing which preceded Feininger's painting *The White Man* [10], likewise published in *Le Témoin*, it seems certain that both title and caption appended to the caricature were the work of the editor, having little or nothing to do with the artist's own intentions.

Notes
1 A letter from Feininger to the New York restorer William Suhr, 9 October 1944 (copy in the archive of the Thyssen-Bornemisza Collection, Lugano-Castagnola), refers to *Lady in Mauve* having been 'repaired'; it is not clear to what extent the painting was restored at this time
2 This large touring exhibition was also shown in Minneapolis, Cleveland, Buffalo, Boston, and (in reduced form) in England at York City Art Gallery and at the Arts Council Gallery in London during the course of 1959–60. *Lady in Mauve* was no.12 in the English version of the exhibition
3 See p.70

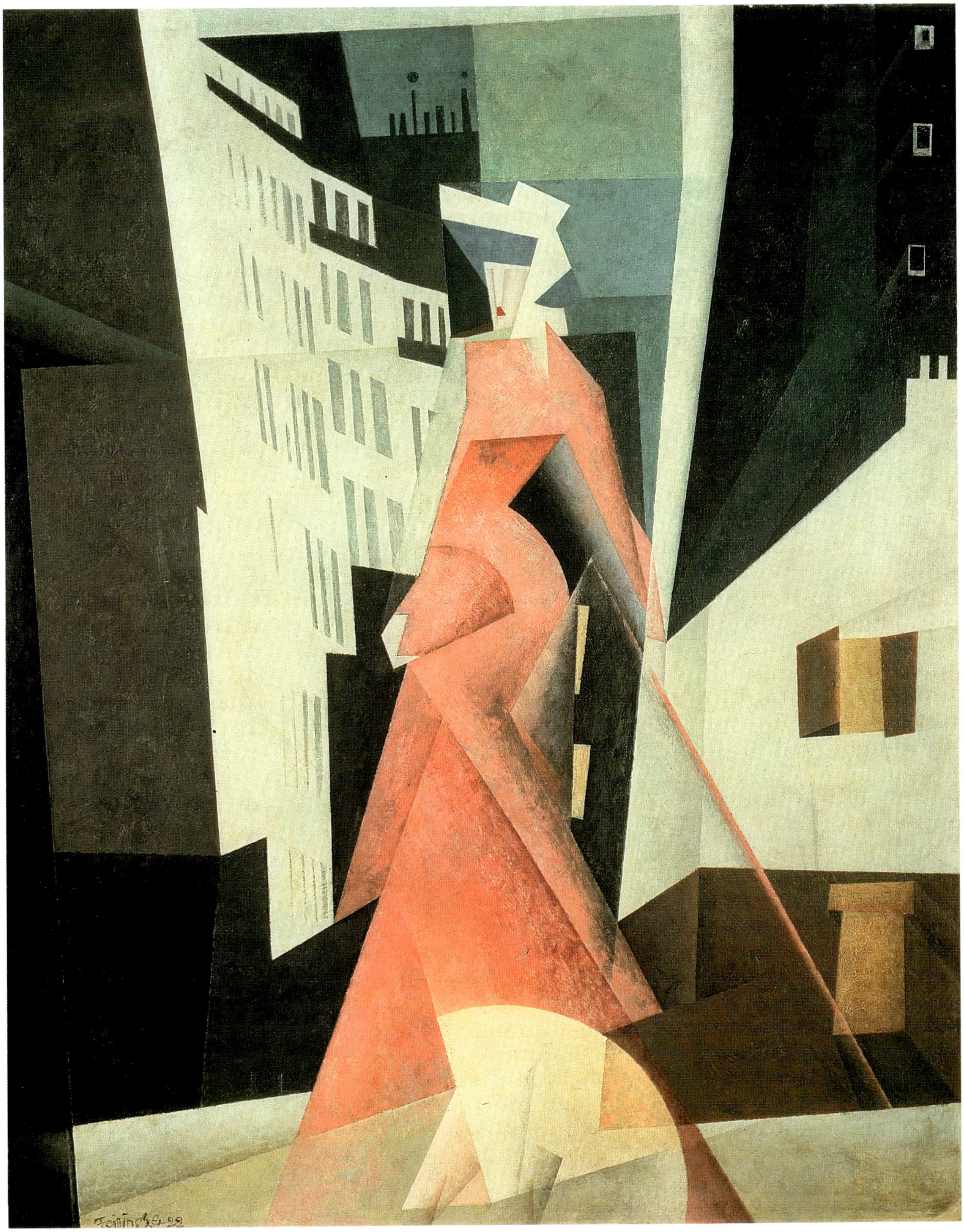

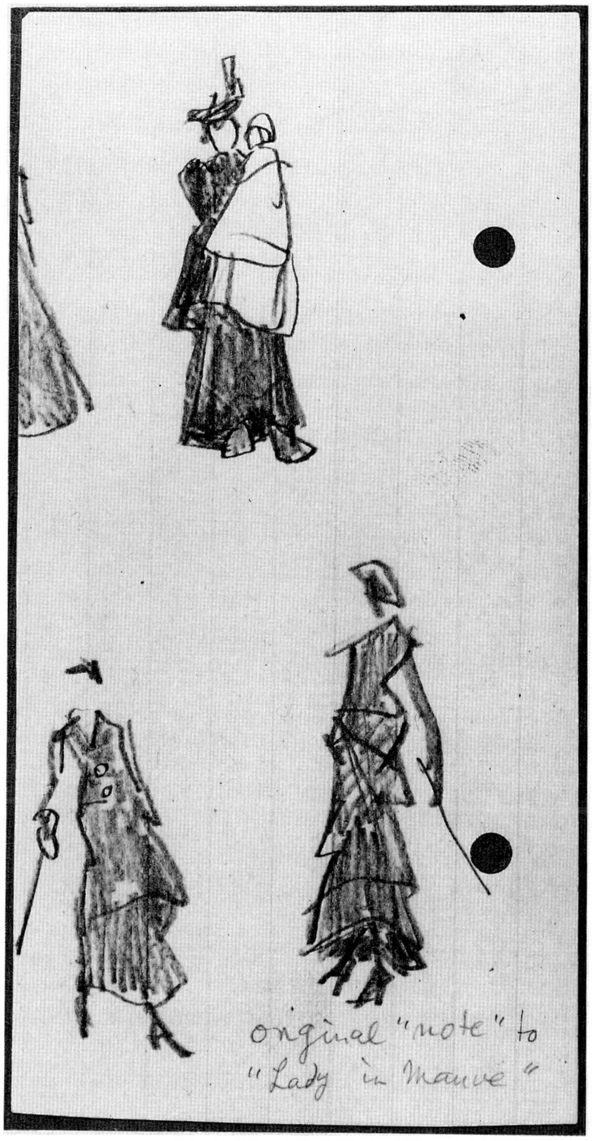

FIG 1 Lyonel Feininger, sheet of figure studies including original 'note' to *Lady in Mauve*, graphite, 14.7 × 7.3 cm (Harvard University, Busch-Reisinger Museum, gift of Julia Feininger, inv. no.BR 1963.3923 *recto*)

FIG 2 'L'Impatiente', cartoon from *Le Témoin*, II, no.20 (1907)

Interestingly, Feininger returned to this ink drawing as the starting point for *Lady in Mauve*, painted more than fifteen years later when he was already at the Bauhaus, which presents an identical compositional structure. There also exists a preliminary study of the figure of the woman (fig.1)[4] – one of Feininger's numerous 'nature notes', as he called them, fleeting sketches in which he sought to capture some detail glimpsed and hastily set down on paper: in this case the momentary pause of a figure in motion. This study bears an inscription by the artist: 'original "note" to "Lady in Mauve"'.

Under examination by means of infra-red reflectography it emerges that the painting underwent considerable changes in the course of its evolution. By comparison with the abstract, geometrical appearance of the picture as it presents itself to the naked eye, the artist's first intention was evidently to treat the figure, in particular, in more conventional terms. Especially striking are the changes made to the head and face of the 'woman in mauve', who was originally depicted with naturalistically painted eyes and hair.

In this work, as in *Architecture II*, painted the preceding year, it is easy to discern influences both of French Cubist painting, and of Italian Futurism. Hans Hess, Feininger's biographer, regarded *Lady in Mauve* as a 'fleeting compliment to Cubism'; he also claimed to detect 'a slightly ironic remnant of Futurist speed in the movements of the lady's feet (shades of Balla's dog) . . .'[5]

See also [12].

Notes

4 I am grateful to Mr T. Lux Feininger, Cambridge, MA, and to Peter Nisbet, Daimler-Benz Curator, Busch-Reisinger Museum, Harvard, for helping me to locate this early drawing; see also Hess (1961), p.94

5 Hess (1961), loc. cit.

L'IMPATIENTE

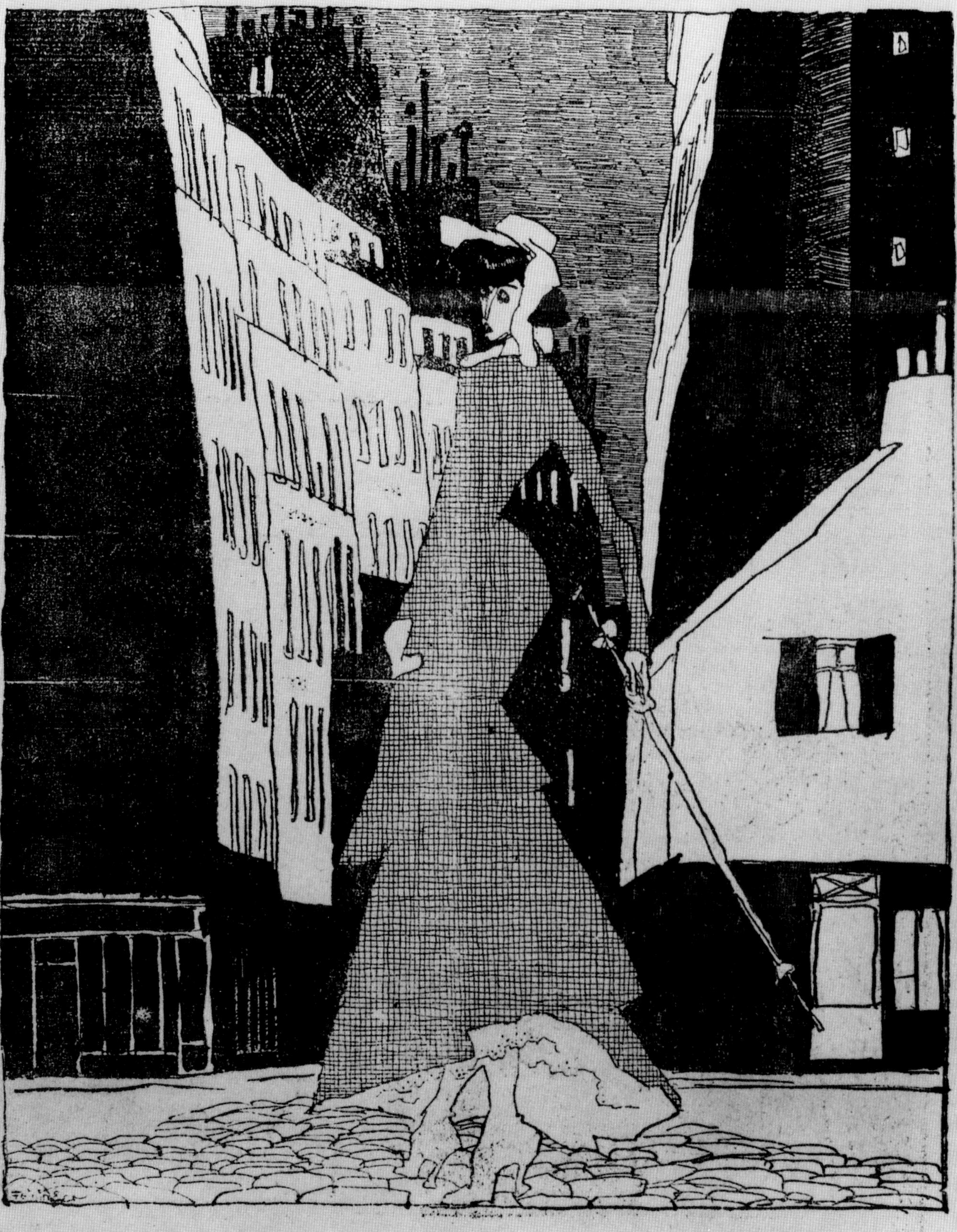

— Il m'a dit : « Je serai là à 8 heures »,... il en est dix, je vais encore attendre un peu, mais à minuit... je pars...

Lyonel Feininger 1871–1956

14 Magic River (Dream across the River)

1937
Oil on canvas, 36 × 70 cm
Signed upper left: 'Feininger'; inscribed on stretcher: 'Feininger 1937 "Magic River"'[1]
In good condition
Accession no.1963.6

Provenance
Nancy Wilson Ross (Mrs Stanley Young), Old Westbury, Long Island, NY
Galerie R.N.Ketterer, Campione d'Italia
Thyssen-Bornemisza Collection, 1963

Exhibitions
Oakland, CA, Mills College Art Gallery, 1937, *2nd Feininger Exhibition*
Turin, Galleria Civica d'Arte Moderna, 1971, *Il Cavaliere Azzurro*, ill. p.154
Bremen 1975, no.23
Lugano 1978, no.34
Budapest/Szombathely 1985–6, no.33
Cologne 1986, p.30, ill. p.31
Luxemburg/Munich/Vienna 1988, no.25

Literature
Hess (1961), no.381
R.N.Ketterer, *Moderne Kunst*, Campione d'Italia (Galerie R.N.Ketterer) 1963, n.p.
Kiel (1974), p.40, ill. p.41

Soon after the National Socialists came to power in 1933, Feininger began to realize that Germany held no future for him. In accepting an invitation from Mills College, California, to teach there in the summer of 1936 (see [12]), he was no doubt testing the water, already contemplating a return to his native America which he had not seen for more than forty years.

1937, the year in which *Magic River* was painted, was the last Feininger spent in Germany; he produced only seven paintings, all done during the early part of that year. He did not, however, wait to see his works pilloried in the *Entartete Kunst* (Degenerate Art) exhibition in Munich in July. He and Julia set sail for New York on 11 June, pinning their hopes on a new career in a land in which 'imagination in art and abstraction are not an utter crime, as they are here . . .' (letter to his son Lux, 31 May 1937).[2]

As in his exactly contemporary picture, *Mid-Ocean* of early 1937 (Emden, Kunsthalle),[3] the artist's hopes for the future and thoughts of the impending voyage permeate *Magic River*. It is, in essence, an imaginary scene, though his memories of Deep, the estuary of the River Rega and the Pomeranian coast, that flat landscape of dunes and empty horizon which he had visited so often, probably provided the starting point. The dark colours, however, like the 'black wave' in *Mid-Ocean*, convey a sombre mood: despite his opposition to the Nazis and despair at the apparent triumph of evil, the decision to leave Germany cannot have been an easy one, and his future in the United States, where he was in effect an unknown artist, must have seemed at best uncertain.

Notes
1 The alternative title *Dream across the River* is that recorded in the oeuvre-catalogue of Feininger's work compiled by Hans Hess, with the collaboration of the artist's widow Julia. The titles contained therein are generally regarded as authentic
2 Quoted after Luckhardt (1989), p.44
3 See Luckhardt (1989), no.50, ill. p.149

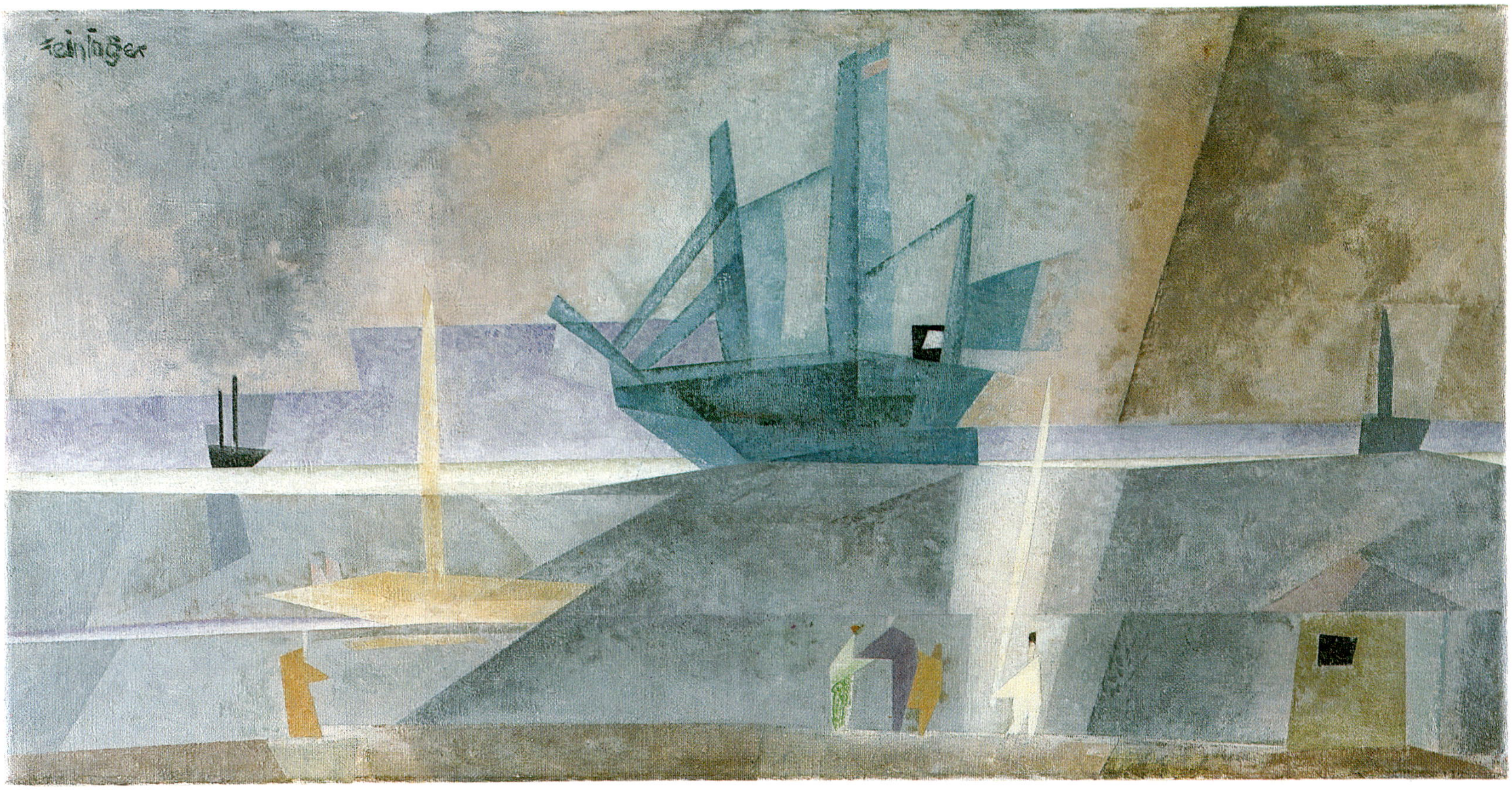
Feininger

Lyonel Feininger 1871–1956

15 La Belle

1906
Black ink on paper, 26.5 × 21 cm
Signed/dated lower left: 'Feininger 1906'; inscribed lower centre: 'La Belle'
In good condition
Accession no.1976.62

Provenance
Estate of the artist
Julia Feininger, New York
Marlborough Fine Art, London
Thyssen-Bornemisza Collection, 1976

Exhibitions
Berlin, Nationalgalerie (Kronprinzenpalais), 1931, *Lyonel Feininger*, no.9
New York, Willard Gallery, 1964, *Feininger. Oils and watercolors 1906–1955*
Pasadena, CA, Art Museum/Milwaukee, WI, Art Center/Baltimore, MD, Museum of Art, 1966, *Lyonel Feininger 1871–1956. A Memorial Exhibition*, no.70
Brussels/Paris 1977–8, no.27
Lugano 1978, no.30

Literature
Kiel (1974), p.36
Luckhardt (1987), pp.43, 84 and note 354

See entry for [13].

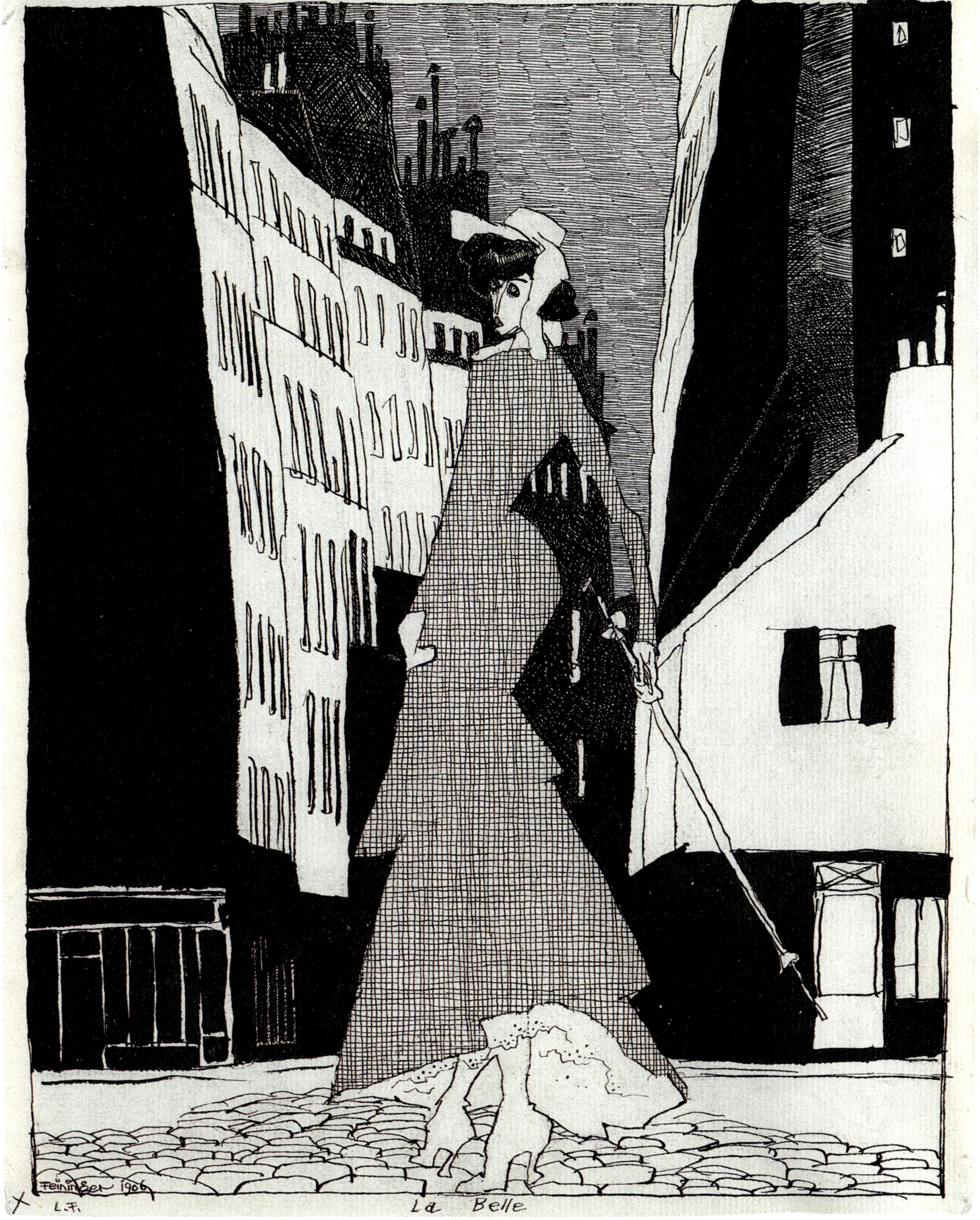
Feininger 1906
L.F.
La Belle

Lyonel Feininger 1871–1956

16 Street behind the Church. Treptow an der Rega
Strasse hinter der Kirche. Treptow an der Rega

1931
Watercolour and ink on hand-made paper, 29.4 × 23.5 cm
Signed lower left: 'Feininger'; dated lower right: '1931'; inscribed lower centre: 'Strasse hinter der Kirche. Treptow a.R.' With a handwritten dedication: 'Dr Jeanette Sackheim in Verehrung'
Paper shows cockling on left side, and has somewhat yellowed with age
Accession no.1976.36

Provenance
Dr Jeanette Sackheim, New York
Serge Sabarsky Gallery, New York
Galerie R.N.Ketterer, Campione d'Italia
Thyssen-Bornemisza Collection, 1976

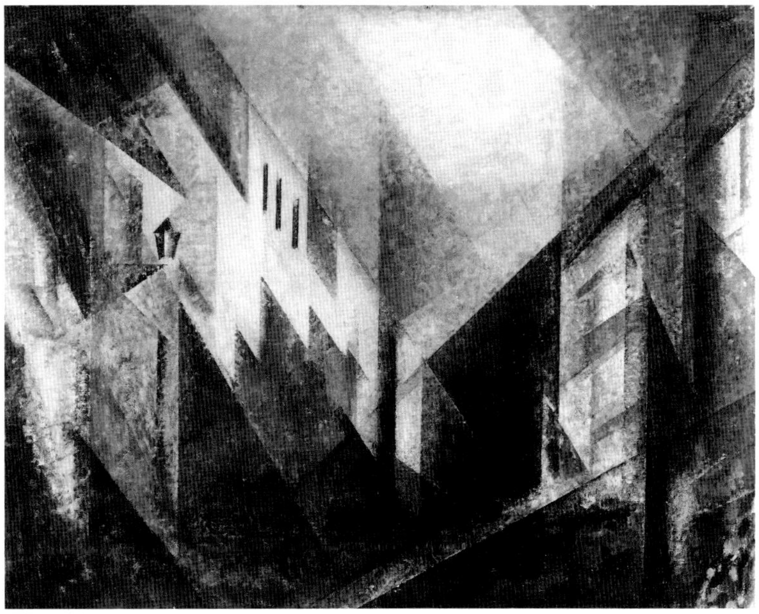

FIG 1 Lyonel Feininger, *Street in Treptow II (Afternoonlight)*, 1932, oil on canvas, 80 × 100 cm (Cologne, Galerie Gmurzynska)

Feininger first visited Deep, on the Pomeranian Baltic coast, in 1924, while still employed as one of the masters at the Weimar Bauhaus.[1] He was to return there every summer until 1935. From Deep, according to his biographer Hans Hess, he would embark on lengthy walking tours, visiting neighbouring localities including the old town of Treptow on the River Rega,[2] where this watercolour was painted.

As regards both style and the subject depicted, *Street behind the Church* closely resembles the oil painting *Street in Treptow II (Afternoonlight)*, formerly in the Thyssen-Bornemisza Collection (fig.1), done the following year.[3] In both watercolour and oil painting, Feininger's continuing interest in adapting the formal language of French Cubist painting, especially the crystalline forms characteristic of the Orphist works of Delaunay, is equally evident.

The dedicatee of this drawing, Jeannette Sackheim, was a doctor forced to flee Nazi Germany in 1939. Emigrating to the United States, she became a friend of the Feiningers (and for a time their physician) in New York.[4] She may have been given the drawing as a token of friendship, or possibly gratitude, on the part of the artist.

Notes
1 Two years later, at his own instigation, Feininger was released from his teaching obligations at the Bauhaus. He remained a master, however, at Gropius's request: see Luckhardt (1989), pp.177–8
2 Hess (1961), p.100
3 See *Lyonel Feininger*, exh. cat., Cologne, Galerie Gmurzynska, 1989, p.46; Kiel (1974), p.38, ill. p.39
4 According to the artist's son, T.Lux Feininger (letter to the author, 15 April 1991)

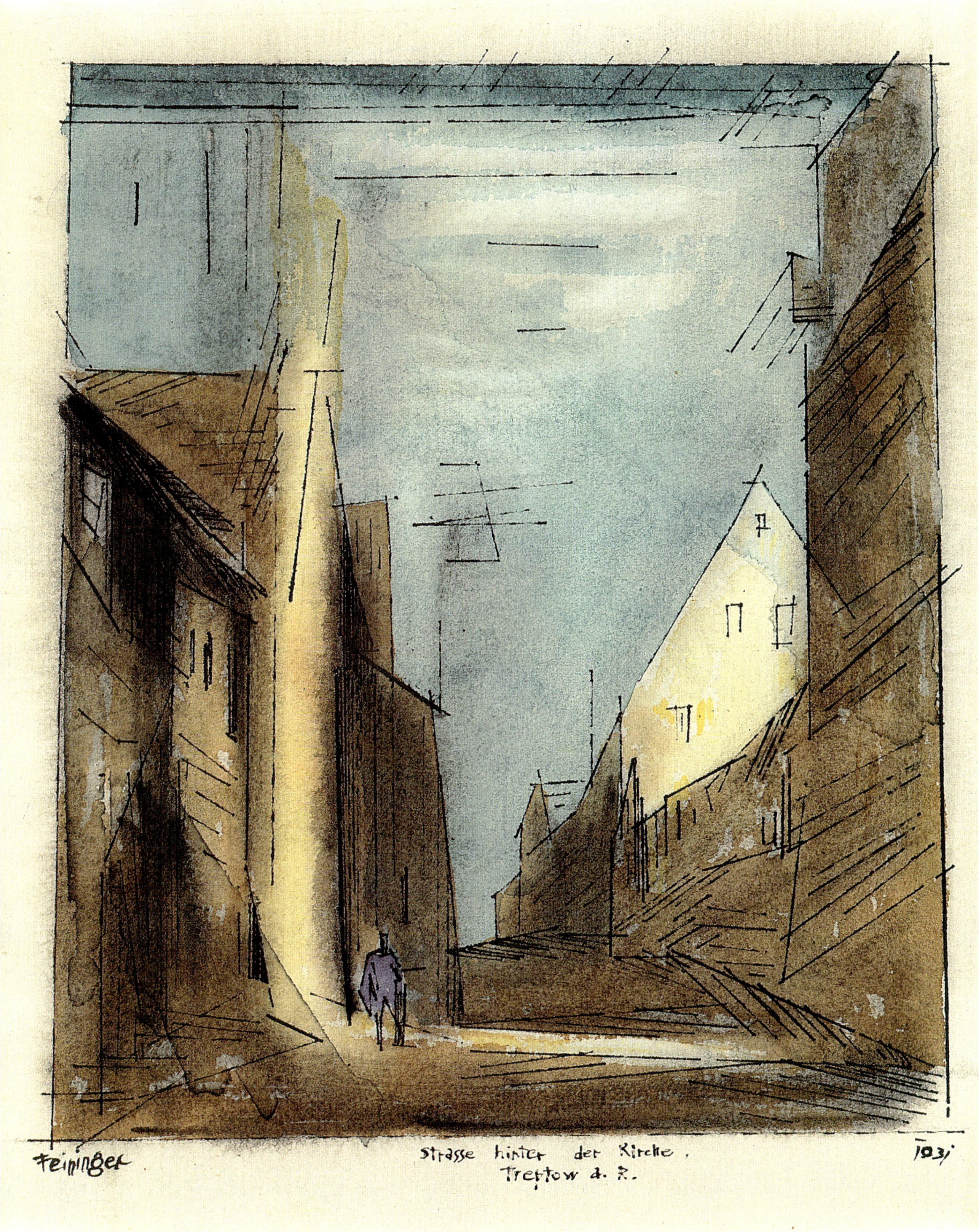
Feininger
Strasse hinter der Kirche,
Treptow a. R.
1931

George Grosz 1893–1959

17 Metropolis (View of the Metropolis)

Die Grosstadt (Blick in die Grosstadt)

1916–17
Oil on canvas, 100 × 102 cm
Signed/dated on verso: 'Grosz Dezember 1916 bis August 1917'
In good condition
Accession no.1978.23

Provenance
Kunsthalle, Mannheim
Buchholz Gallery Curt Valentin, New York
Herman Shulman, New York
George Grosz, Huntington, Long Island, NY
Richard L.Feigen, Chicago, IL/New York
Thyssen-Bornemisza Collection, 1978

Exhibitions
Mannheim, Städtische Kunsthalle, 1925, *Neue Sachlichkeit. Deutsche Malerei seit dem Expressionismus*, no.40 [as 'Blick in die Grosstadt 1917 (Südende)'][1]
Mannheim, Städtische Kunsthalle, 1933, *Kulturbolschewistische Bilder*[2]
Munich, Archaeologisches Institut, 1937, *Entartete Kunst*[3]
Boston, MA, Institute of Modern Art, 1939, *Contemporary German Art*, no.14
New York, Museum of Modern Art, 1941–2, *George Grosz*[4]
New York, Museum of Modern Art, 1953–6, *Early Works of Modern Artists*[5]
Chicago, IL, Richard L.Feigen Gallery, 1961, *George Grosz*, no.4
Pasadena, CA, Art Museum, 1961, *German Expressionism*, no.17
Berlin, Akademie der Künste/Dortmund, Museum am Ostwall, 1962–3, *George Grosz 1893–1959*, no.4
York, City Art Gallery/London, Arts Council Gallery/Bristol, City Art Gallery, 1963, *George Grosz 1893–1959*, no.2
Cleveland, OH, Museum of Art, 1966, *Fifty Years of Modern Art, 1916–1966*, no.7
Paris, Centre Georges Pompidou, 1978, *Paris–Berlin*, ill. p.141
Expressionism, a German Intuition, 1980–81, no.308
USA tour 1982–4, no.28
Modern Masters from the Thyssen-Bornemisza Collection, 1984–6, no.41
Venice, Palazzo Grassi, 1986, *Futurismo e Futurismi*, ill. p.290
Berlin, Berlin-Museum, 1987, *Stadtbilder. Berlin in der Malerei vom 17. Jahrhundert bis zur Gegenwart*, no.145
Los Angeles, CA, County Museum of Art, 1988–9, *German Expressionism 1915–1925. The Second Generation*, no.85[6]
Expressionism and Modern German Painting, 1989–90, no.6
Los Angeles, CA, County Museum of Art/Chicago, IL, Art Institute, 1991, *'Degenerate Art'. The Fate of the Avant-Garde in Nazi Germany*, p.245, ill. p.244

Literature
Däubler (1916): 167–70
Däubler (1919), pp.38–9
Gemälde und Plastiken moderner Meister aus deutschen Museen, Lucerne (Galerie Fischer) 1939, no.42
Roh (1962), p.212
Hess (1974), pp.70f
Grosz (1979), pp.53–4
Irit Rogoff, 'Representations of Politics: Critics, Pessimists, Radicals', in C.M.Joachimides, N.Rosenthal and W.Schmied (eds.), *German Art in the 20th Century*, exh. cat., London, Royal Academy of Arts, 1985, p.133
Peter-Klaus Schuster (ed.), *Delaunay und Deutschland*, exh. cat., Munich, Haus der Kunst, 1985–6, pp.270–2 and no.214[7]
Gordon (1987), p.108
Mario-Andreas von Lüttichau, 'Rekonstruktion der Ausstellung "Entartete Kunst", München, 19. Juli–30. November 1937', in Schuster (1987), p.164.
Entartete Kunst – Beschlagnahmeaktionen in der Städtischen Kunsthalle Mannheim 1937 (Kunst + Dokumentation 10), exh. cat., Mannheim, Städtische Kunsthalle, 1987, p.52

Notes
1 Exhibition also shown in Dresden, Chemnitz, Erfurt and (in revised form) Dessau, Halle and Jena: see Helen Adkins, 'Neue Sachlichkeit – Deutsche Malerei seit dem Expressionismus', in *Stationen der Moderne. Die bedeutenden Kunstausstellungen des 20. Jahrhunderts in Deutschland*, exh. cat., Berlin, Berlinische Galerie, 1988, p.217
2 Exhibition shown in reduced form at the Kunstverein in Munich and at the Orangerie in Erlangen during June–August 1933; see Christoph Zuschlag, 'An "Educational Exhibition". The Precursors of *Entartete Kunst* and Its Individual Venues', in Barron (1991), pp.83ff, 98
3 Exhibition shown in revised form in Berlin, Leipzig, Düsseldorf and other German cities, and also in Vienna and Salzburg during 1938–41. *Metropolis* had, however, been sold by June 1939 at the Galerie Fischer auction in Lucerne: see Barron (1991), pp.135ff, 155
4 Circulating exhibition
5 Circulating exhibition
6 Exhibition also shown at the Modern Art Museum of Fort Worth, TX, and (under the title *Expressionismus. Die Zweite Generation 1915–1925*) at the Kunstmuseum, Düsseldorf, and the Staatliche Galerie Moritzburg, Halle, during 1988–9
7 Though the painting is included under this number in the catalogue of the exhibition *Delaunay und Deutschland* held at the Haus der Kunst, Munich, during 1985–6, it was not in fact shown, since it was then on tour as part of the exhibition *Modern Masters from the Thyssen-Bornemisza Collection*: for full reference see p.27

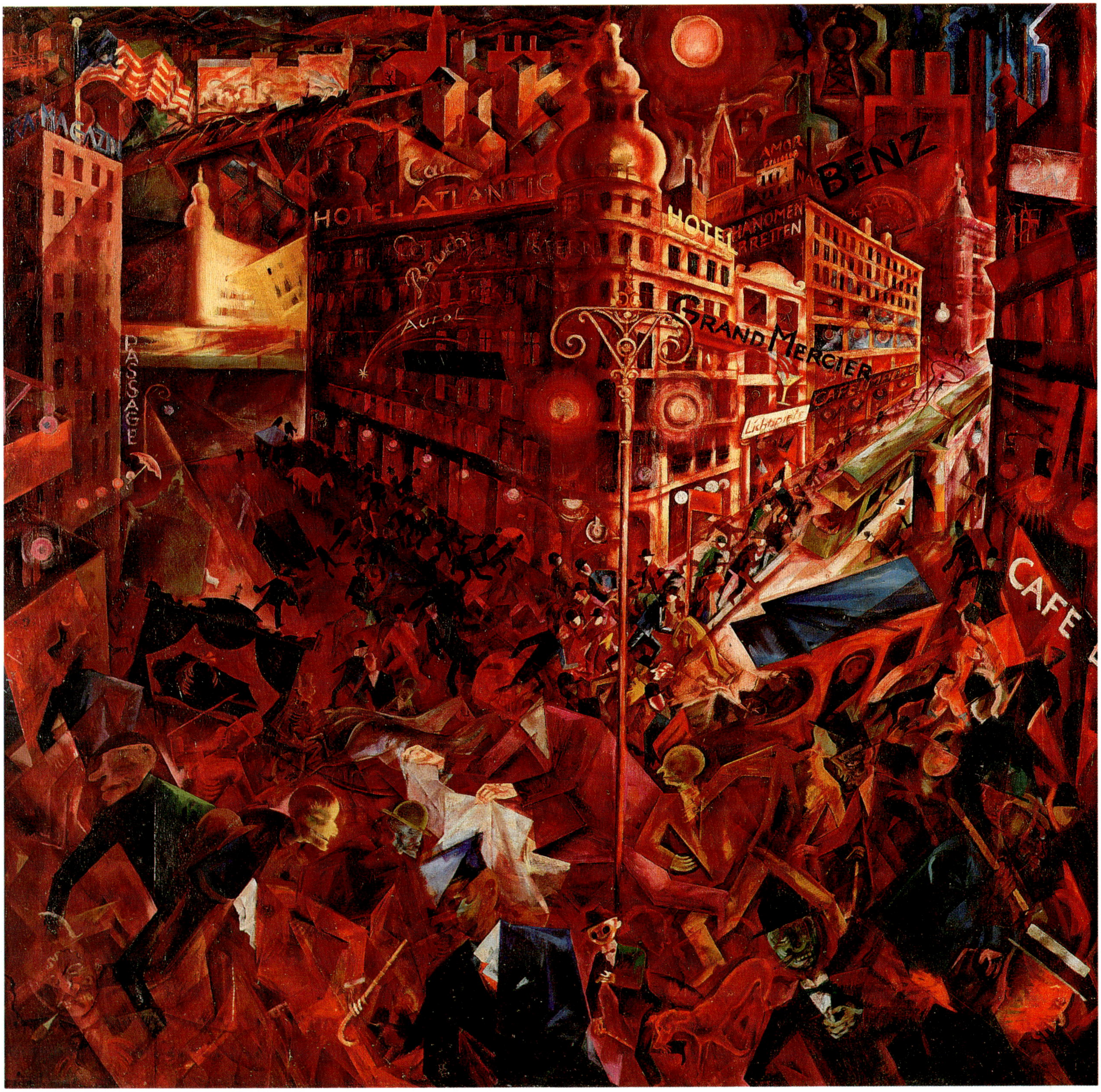
MAGAZIN
HOTEL ATLANTIC
HOTEL
BENZ
AMOR
HANOMEN
GRAND MERCIER
CAFE
PASSAGE
CAFE

Dominik Bartmann *et al.* (eds.), *Stadtbilder. Berlin in der Malerei vom 17. Jahrhundert bis zur Gegenwart*, exh. cat., Berlin, Berlin-Museum, 1987, pp.270–2
Barron (1988), p.16
Stephanie Barron, 'The Galerie Fischer Auction', in Barron (1991), pp.135ff, 155

Metropolis is a picture of considerable importance not only for aesthetic but also for historical reasons. Purchased in 1924 by the Kunsthalle in Mannheim, it was one of the first works by Grosz to enter a German public collection. The following year it formed part of the famous exhibition *Neue Sachlichkeit – German Painting since Expressionism* organized by the director of the Kunsthalle, G.F.Hartlaub, and shown in Mannheim and other German cities during the course of 1925–6.[8] The inclusion of paintings by Dix, Grosz, Scholz and other social-critical artists was intended to represent what Hartlaub called the 'left (veristic) wing' of the new 'movement' he himself had been instrumental in defining.[9] However, their contributions – and those of Grosz especially – contrasted uncomfortably with those of the 'classical realists' of the Munich school, the other dominant group within the exhibition, led by artists such as Alexander Kanoldt, Georg Schrimpf and Carlo Mense. Kanoldt, in particular, objected violently to Grosz's early works, writing to Hartlaub that he was astounded by the presence of these 'wildest expressionistic daubings by Grosz from the years 1916–1919', which had nothing in common with the theme of the exhibition.[10] It would undoubtedy have been paintings such as *Metropolis* and *Dedicated to Oskar Panizza* (fig.1) which provoked his strongest resentment.

However deprecating, Kanoldt's remark about 'expressionistic daubings' at least reveals that he was alive to Grosz's stylistic antecedents. *Metropolis*, in particular, shows clearly the influences of both Expressionism and, to an even greater extent, Futurism. The repetition of forms, the chaotic throng of human figures and, especially, the 'lines of force' which divide the composition, immediately recall the works of the Italian Futurist painters which Grosz must have encountered by 1913 at the latest through the exhibitions of Walden's Der Sturm gallery in Berlin.[11] The content of his painting could, on the other hand, scarcely be more different. While the Futurists glorified the city, Grosz conjures up a setting which, like Meidner's townscapes, speaks unequivocally of apocalypse and impending dissolution, linking his work with aspects of pre-war Expressionism.

Significantly, in the catalogue of the 1939 Lucerne auction at which the painting was offered for sale, it is described as a 'wild-fantastic big-cityscape with people falling over one another, quaking buildings and strident advertisements in tones of red and blue. Especially characteristic of the artist's expressionistic phase'.[12] *Metropolis* also anticipates certain works of his Dada period in that it is, in a sense, a collage, not of physical, but of mental elements: forms seen are juxtaposed with forms remembered or invented. It may be considered more than just coincidence that Grosz, influenced by the beginnings of Dada, was starting to experiment with actual collage at just about the same time, for example in the prospectus for the *Kleine Grosz-Mappe* of 1917.[13]

The picture was painted in Berlin over an eight-month period beginning in December 1916, during part of which Grosz was recalled for further military service. (He had initially been discharged from the army in May 1915; called up again on 4 January 1917, he was eventually discharged as permanently unfit on 20 May that year after periods spent in hospital and under medical observation.)[14] Though it contains no specific allusion to the war, like his two other major canvases of this period, *Dedicated to Oskar Panizza* and *Germany: a Winter's Tale*, *Metropolis* sums up his revulsion at the horrors he had witnessed. These assume allegorical form in this depiction of the infernal and chaotic city, of a society seemingly hell-bent on its own destruction.

The greater part of the work on the picture was probably done during the summer of 1917, as evidenced by a letter to Otto Schmalhausen dated 30 June that year:

Notes

8 See n.1

9 G.F.Hartlaub, 'Zum Geleit', in *Ausstellung 'Neue Sachlichkeit'. Deutsche Malerei seit dem Expressionismus*, exh. cat., Mannheim, Städtische Kunsthalle, 1925, n.p.

10 Letters dated 24 November and 1 December 1912 (Städtische Kunsthalle, Mannheim), cited in 'Neue Sachlichkeit. Deutsche Malerei seit dem Expressionismus, Mannheim 1925', [kommentiert] von Caroline Hille, in Eberhard Roters (ed.), *Stationen der Moderne ... Kommentarband zu den Nachdrücken der zehn Ausstellungskataloge*, Cologne (Walther König) 1988, pp.140–41, 149 and n.12

11 In his first article on Grosz, published in 1916, the critic Theodor Däubler alluded to him as 'augenblicklich das futuristische Temperament Berlins': see Däubler (1916), p.167. He also specifically linked Grosz's city visions with the influence of Delaunay's Simultanism: 'Auch George Grosz mit seiner von der Schnellbahn gesehenen Grosstadtperspektive, führt uns raschest zum gleichen Ursprung [i.e. Delaunay] zurück.' (Daubler (1919), p.39: see also *Delaunay und Deutschland*, pp.270, 454)

12 'Wildphantastisches Grosstadtbild mit übereinanderstürzenden Menschen, wankenden Häusern und schreienden Reklamen in roten und blauen Farbtönen. Besonders charakteristisch für die expressionistische Periode des Künstlers'; see the auction catalogue *Gemälde und Plastiken moderner Meister aus deutschen Museen*, Lucerne (Galerie Fischer) 1939, no.42

13 Schneede (1979), fig.71; see also *Delaunay und Deutschland*, p.455

14 See chronology published in Hess (1974), p.260; also Lewis (1971), pp.51–2

FIG 1 George Grosz, *Dedicated to Oskar Panizza*, 1917–18, oil on canvas, 140 × 110 cm (Stuttgart, Staatsgalerie, inv. no.2338)

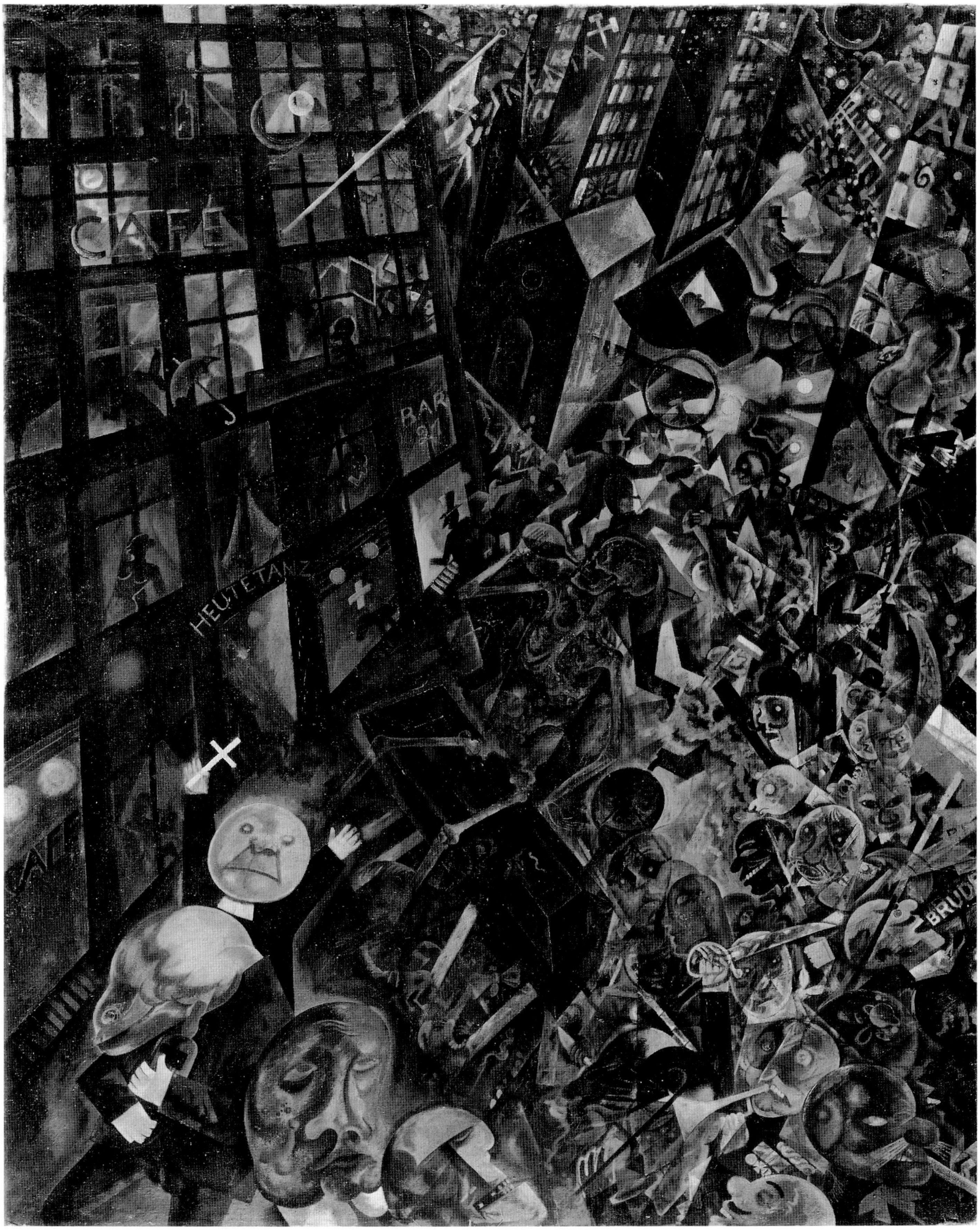
CAFÉ
BAR
HEUTE TANZ
BRUD

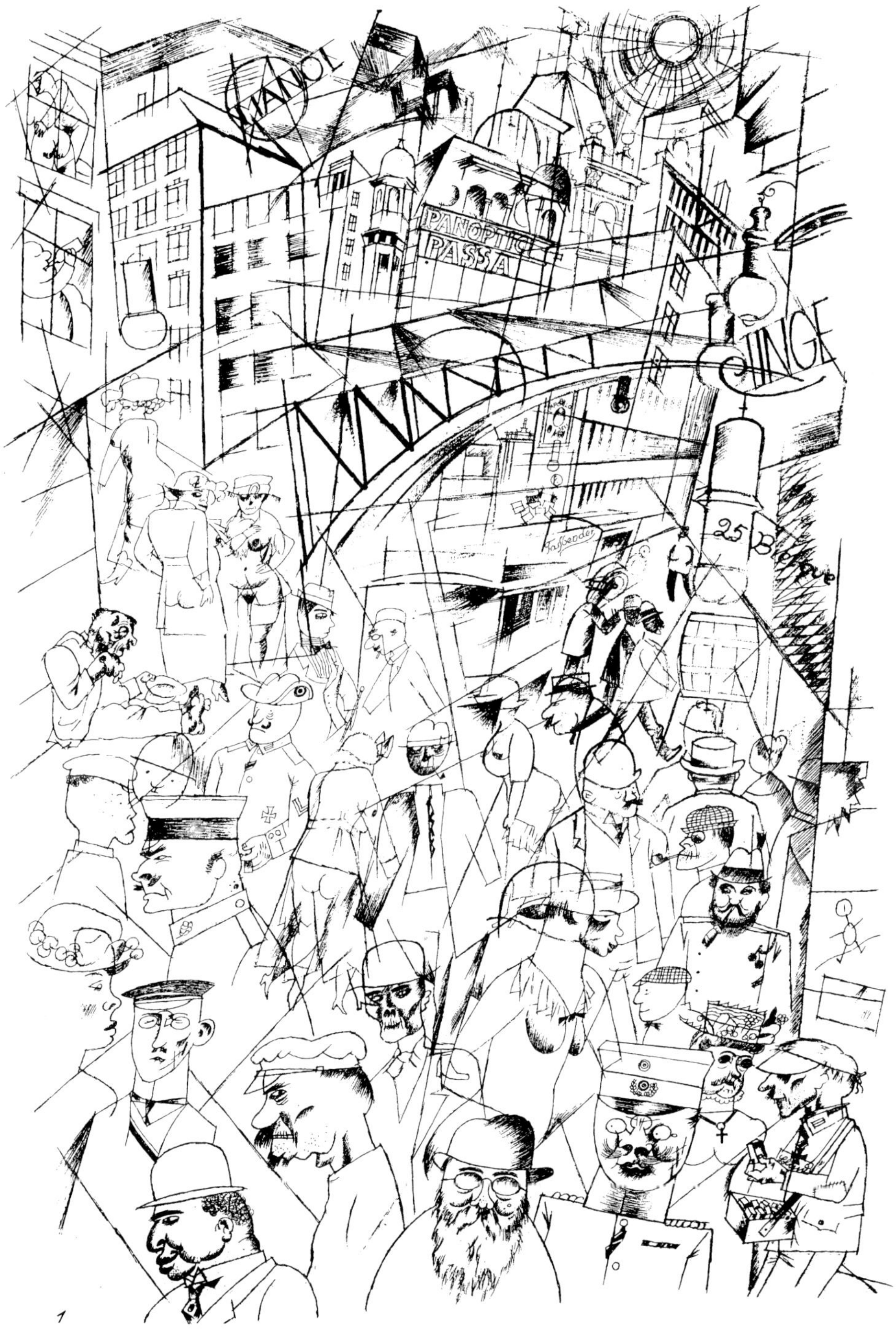

FIG 2 George Grosz, *Berlin, Friedrichstrasse*, 1918, lithograph reproduced in *Ecce Homo*, Berlin (Malik) 1923, fig. 1

> I am painting a lot: a big city-scape and a smaller picture (reds, lots of reds!); evenings and nights I perch in front of my easel with my quiver of reed pens and black-magic ink. I am up to my neck in visions . . . a starry sky circling above a red head, a tram bursting into the picture, telephones ringing, a woman in labour crying out, while knuckle-duster and flick-knife sleep peaceably in the pimp's trouser pocket . . . the port-red, wine-sodden nights where the moon is side by side with infection and cursing cab drivers, and where strangulations take place in dusty coal cellars – oh emotion of the big cities![15]

That the painting was conceived as an image of Berlin is made clear not only by Grosz's own statements, but also by the caption printed in the 1925 Mannheim catalogue, which includes the designation 'Südende' – the name of the predominantly proletarian district where he had his studio until 1918. The location and, especially, the architecture also recall the area around Berlin's Friedrichstrasse railway station and the Central Hotel which he depicted in a compositionally related lithograph of 1918 (see figs.2 and 3). There was, however, no 'Hotel Atlantic', and the American flag unfurled at the upper left implies that the image in the back of his mind is that of the great American cities, Chicago and New York, which at this juncture he had never seen, but for whose noisy bustle and frenetic way of life he evinced an uncritical enthusiasm. In his works of this period, Grosz would frequently combine mental images of America with impressions of Berlin, as in the lithograph *Memory of New York*,[16] where American-style skyscrapers sprout the leaded onion-dome cupolas characteristic of the Prussian capital – an architectural feature which recurs in *Metropolis*, and for which, according to Däubler, the artist had a particular predilection.[17]

For various reasons, not least of them being his political affiliations, Grosz's work was particularly offensive to the Nazis. *Metropolis*, in particular, was one of the first paintings to fall victim to the new régime's policy of *Kunstsäuberung* or 'artistic purification', being included in the exhibition of 'images of cultural bolshevism' (*Kulturbolschewistische Bilder*) organized by the National Socialists and shown in Mannheim immediately after they came to power in Germany in 1933.[18] Confiscated from the Kunsthalle as 'degenerate' on 8 July 1937, it was included in the exhibition *Entartete Kunst* which opened in Munich on the 19th of the same month.[19] According to a law enacted the following year, the 1937 'confiscations' became 'expropriations' by the state; thus, strictly speaking, the legal owner of the picture at the time of its disposal in 1939 was the German Reich itself.[20] Offered for sale at auction on 30 June that year by the Galerie Fischer in Lucerne, together with numerous other modern works which had been removed from German museums, *Metropolis* was bought by the New York dealer Curt Valentin for 700 Swiss francs.[21] It was subsequently purchased by the collector Herman Shulman, from whom Grosz himself, already in America, was later able to re-acquire it. In 1958 Grosz sold the painting to the collector and dealer Richard Feigen, from whom it was acquired by the present owner.[22]

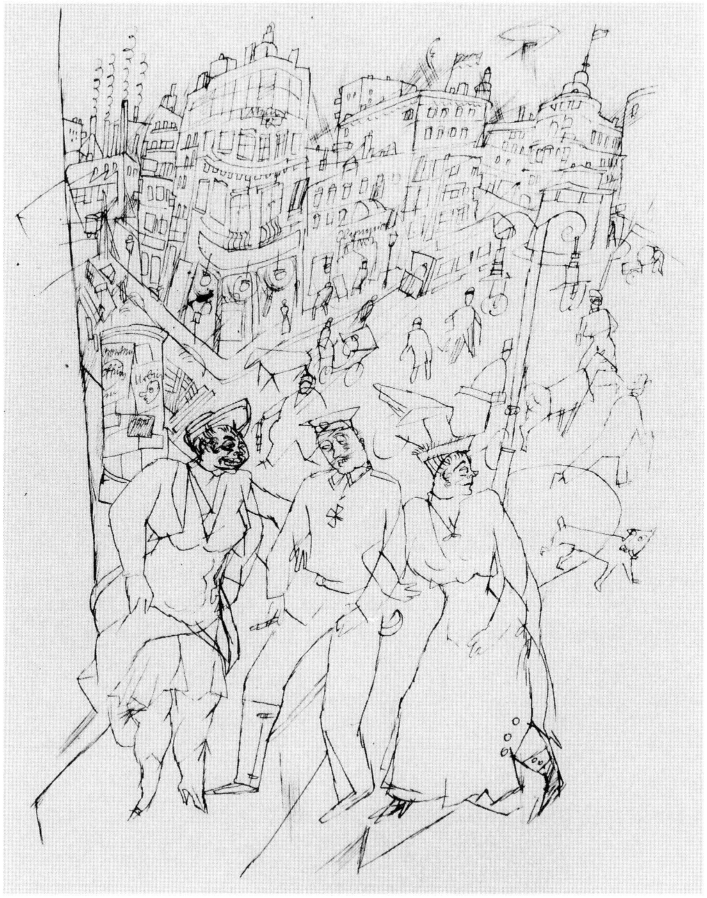

FIG 3 George Grosz, *Olympia Cinema Berlin*, 1917, pen, 29 × 22.6 cm (Princeton, NJ, collection of Mr and Mrs Peter M. Grosz)

Notes

15 Grosz (1979), pp.53–4. I have for the most part followed the translation of this letter published in Schneede (1979), p.48

16 *Erste George Grosz-Mappe*, 1917; Schneede (1979) fig.72

17 See *Stadtbilder*, exh. cat., Berlin, 1987, p.272

18 Zuschlag, loc. cit.; see also the catalogue *Entartete Kunst – Beschlagnahmeaktionen in der Städtischen Kunsthalle Mannheim 1937*, Mannheim, Städtische Kunsthalle, 1987, p.52

19 Inv. no.16194: see Mario-Andreas von Lüttichau, 'Rekonstruktion der Ausstellung "Entartete Kunst"', in Schuster (1987), loc. cit.; also idem., '*Entartete Kunst*, Munich 1937. A Reconstruction', in Barron (1991), pp.45–81

20 The edict of 31 May 1938 expropriating the works confiscated from German museums is reprinted in Roters (1984), pp.166–7

21 In Germany after 1933, Valentin had been assistant to Karl Buchholz, who from 1938 onwards was one of the small number of dealers comissioned with 'realizing the value' of the works of art confiscated as 'degenerate' from the German museums. When he moved to New York in 1937, Valentin established his own gallery, initially on West 46th Street, under the Buchholz name; see the obituary in the *New York Times*, Saturday, 21 August, 1954. The gallery changed its name to Curt Valentin Gallery in 1951

22 I am grateful to Richard L. Feigen, New York, and to his assistant Samuel Lorin Trower, for their help in enabling me to confirm the exact provenance of the painting

George Grosz 1893–1959

18 Street Scene (Kurfürstendamm)[1]

1925
Oil on canvas, 81.3 × 61.3
Signed/dated on back of canvas (upper right): 'George Grosz 1925 Feb'; inscribed (upper left): '24 Chicago "Streetscene 1925" 1925'[2]
The painting is unvarnished, and shows ingrained surface grime. There are some abrasions, especially to the lower edges. Otherwise condition is good
Accession no.1981.69

Provenance
Collection of the artist
Erich Cohn, New York
Richard L.Feigen, New York
Siegfried Adler, Montagnola
Galerie R.N.Ketterer, Campione d'Italia
Hans Grote
Galerie Thomas, Munich
Thyssen-Bornemisza Collection, 1981

Exhibitions
New York, Whitney Museum, 1954, *George Grosz*, no.2[3]
Berlin, Akademie der Künste/Dortmund, Museum am Ostwall, 1962–3, *George Grosz*, no.12
York, City Art Gallery/London, Arts Council Gallery/Bristol, City Art Gallery, 1963, *George Grosz 1893–1959*, no.7
Modern Masters from the Thyssen-Bornemisza Collection, 1984–6, no.42
Berlin, Berlin-Museum, 1987, *Stadtbilder. Berlin in der Malerei vom 17. Jahrhundert bis zur Gegenwart*, no.173
Madrid, Centro de Arte Reina Sofia, 1989, *Berlin, Punto de Encuentro*, no.5/14
Lugano 1989, no.44
Expressionism and Modern German Painting, 1989–90, no.7
Rome 1990–91, no.13

Literature
Grosz (1946), ill. following p.64[4]
R.N.Ketterer, *Moderne Kunst VI*, Campione d'Italia (Galerie R.N.Ketterer) 1969, p.38, no.20, ill. p.39
R.N.Ketterer, *Moderne Kunst VII*, Campione d'Italia (Galerie R.N.Ketterer) 1971, p.68, no.34, ill. p.69
Hess (1974), pp.134–6, ill. p.139
Sammlung Rheingarten, exh. cat., Munich, Galerie Raimund Thomas, 1981, p.39, ill. p.38
Kurt Winkler, 'Abbilder Berlins – Spiegelbilder der Metropole', in Dominik Bartmann *et al.* (eds.), *Stadtbilder. Berlin in der Malerei vom 17. Jahrhundert bis zur Gegenwart*, exh. cat., Berlin, Berlin-Museum, 1987, pp.330–1

In June 1925 Grosz participated in Hartlaub's epoch-making exhibition *Neue Sachlichkeit – Deutsche Malerei seit dem Expressionismus* at the Kunsthalle in Mannheim (see [17]). He remained, however, suspicious of much of the 'new realism', on account of what he saw as its bourgeois tendency and lack of social commitment, and in his essay 'Art is in Danger', published the same year, questioned the value of traditional easel painting, a genre he had effectively abandoned some three years earlier. None the less, in the course of 1925 he himself resumed painting in oils. Alluding once again to his ambition to be the 'German Hogarth',[5] he evidently had in mind to embark on a new succession of social-critical paintings in the manner

Notes
1 Although the title 'Kurfürstendamm' does not appear on the work itself (see n.2), it formed part of the catalogue caption when the painting was exhibited at the Whitney Museum in 1954. Since the exhibition was held in New York at a time when the artist himself was living and teaching there, it may reasonably be considered authentic
2 The painting has been framed within a 'false frame', leaving the edges of the original stretcher exposed; this frame, together with the painting itself, has now been sealed from behind in such a way that it proved impracticable to examine the back of the canvas for inscriptions. Evidently, however, such an examination was undertaken at the time of the 1987 Berlin exhibition (see Exhibitions); a label affixed to the backing board at that time records the original inscriptions as noted here
3 Exhibition also shown at the William Rockhill Nelson Gallery of Art, Kansas City, KS, the Pasadena Art Institute, CA, and the San Francisco Museum of Art, CA during 1954
4 In this 1946 publication, the painting was reproduced with the misleading caption: 'Street Scene (1923)'
5 As recorded by Count Harry Kessler, who in March 1926 took part in a meeting of the newly established Society for Politics, Science and Art which was also attended by Grosz; see Kessler (1971), p.287; also Flavell (1988), pp.58–9. Grosz had first confided in Kessler regarding his ambition to be the 'German Hogarth' as early as 1919: see Kessler, op. cit., p.64 (diary entry for 5 February 1919)

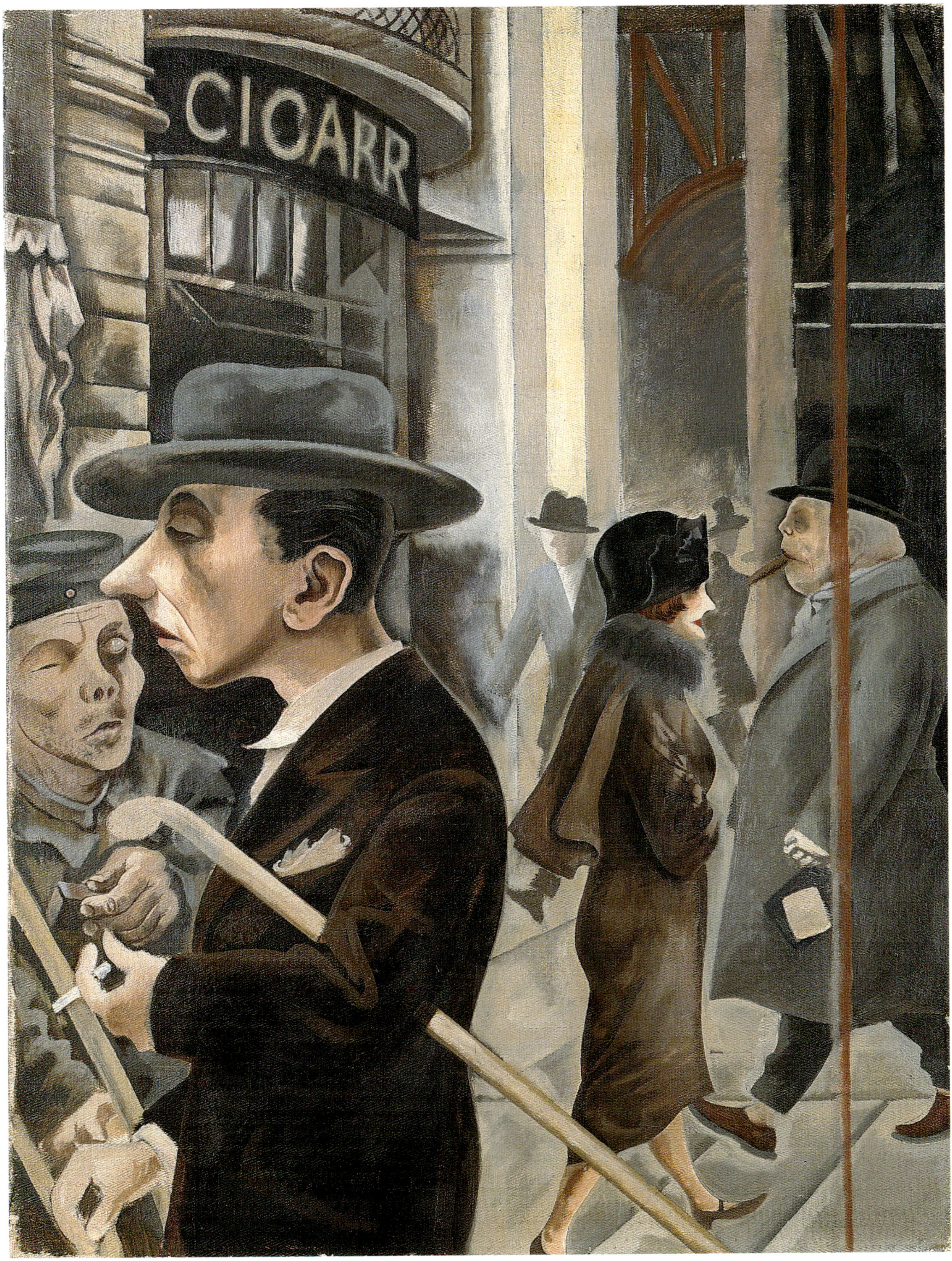
CIOARR

of his earlier *Dedicated to Oskar Panizza* or *Germany: a Winter's Tale*. The product of this ambition was his two great canvases of 1926, *Eclipse of the Sun* and *Pillars of Society*.

Much of Grosz's work of this period betrays an increasing tension between his role as satirist and politically committed artist on the one hand and his growing professional success on the other. Already in some of his works of 1925, the mordant tone of his earlier caricatures is noticeably lacking. A comparison between the drawings included in his anthology *Ecce Homo* of 1923 (see [20]) and the series *Der Spiesser-Spiegel* (Mirror of the Bourgeoisie), published in 1925, is instructive. The latter, as Hess points out, seems merely to catalogue in a relatively innocuous manner the affectations of the middle classes, by contrast with the castigation of their vices characteristic of the earlier drawings. Economic factors may well have played a part; the fact that Grosz had recently been 'taken on' by Alfred Flechtheim, Berlin's most successful and worldly dealer who sold widely to museums and to a prosperous bourgeois clientele, is scarcely a coincidence.[6] By 1927, Grosz himself was prepared to admit in a letter to his brother-in-law, Otto Schmalhausen, that he was largely abandoning 'offensive' subject matter, even if only in order to buy himself the freedom to go on painting works such as *Eclipse of the Sun* or *Pillars of Society*.[7]

Against this background, *Street Scene* can be seen to occupy a transitional place between Grosz's earlier politically engaged work and his paintings of the later twenties. The subject is not new: he had treated the theme of cripples and war veterans, for example, during the early twenties in numerous paintings and drawings which are a searing indictment of a bourgeois militaristic society (fig.1). The note of anger and scorn which characterizes these earlier works is, however, absent here: *Street Scene* has more in common with Grosz's contemporary watercolours than with his earlier oil paintings, being closely related in both feeling and subject to a work such as *Insider and Outsider* (1926),[8] in which the contrast between the 'haves' and the 'have-nots' (epitomized in *Street Scene* by the crippled match-vendor and the fat man smoking a cigar) is likewise viewed with a new detachment. As Lewis observes, in his later urban scenes Grosz's 'polemical' treatment of capitalists, prostitutes and the military gives way to a still caricatured but more sensitive depiction of actual people whose actions are not pilloried from an ideological standpoint but simply recorded.[9] This greater sense of remoteness, of being merely reportage, marks the beginnings of a transition towards the more 'acceptable' manner of painting to which he himself referred.

The inscription on the back of the painting '24 Chicago' might prove puzzling, were it not for the fact that Grosz's American fantasies, and his obsession with role-playing, are well-documented. His mode of dress, his dandyism and affectations of speech, even the fact that he changed his name from 'Georg' to 'George' all have their origin in his fascination with everything American, gained in part from early Westerns and from books by Karl May and James Fenimore Cooper.[10] He signed drawings and letters with American pen-names; one visitor to his studio in around 1916 even recalled how Grosz had pointed out the various features of a big picture of New York harbour with the kind of familiarity one would expect only from someone who had been there.[11] (Grosz visited New York for the first time in 1932, in response to an invitation from the Art Students' League.) As Schneede has observed, the artist's American dreams were nourished not only by images of the rugged freedom of the Wild West, but also of skyscrapers and the urban environment.[12] Thus, the sleazy urban scene depicted in [18] may well have 'reminded' him of the street life of Chicago as represented in American novels or films.

Street Scene was originally owned by Erich Cohn, one of the first people in New York to buy Grosz's work after the artist moved to the United States in 1933. During the 1970s it was acquired by the German collector Hans Grote, who had amassed a number of masterpieces of twentieth-century German painting, including paintings by Corinth, Beckmann, Kirchner and Mueller. These were offered for sale by the Galerie Raimund Thomas in Munich in autumn 1981 under the pseudonym 'The Rheingarten Collection',[13] whence *Street Scene* was purchased by the present owner.

Notes

6 Compare Hess: 'With Flechtheim he was in the world of expensive art. Flechtheim's gallery had become the first in Berlin to show the works of the modern French masters, and was the most fashionable and expensive establishment in Berlin ..' (Hess (1974), p.122). On Flechtheim and his relations with the artists he represented, see *Alfred Flechtheim. Sammler, Kunsthändler, Verleger*, exh. cat., Düsseldorf, Kunstmuseum, 1987

7 Letter dated 27 May 1927; see Grosz (1979), p.101

8 Hess (1974), loc. cit. and fig.132

9 Lewis (1971), pp.176–81

10 Ibid., pp.25f

11 Walter Mehring, *Berlin Dada: eine Chronik mit Photos und Dokumenten*, Zurich 1959, p.31, cited after Lewis (1971), pp.25f

12 Schneede (1979), p.50

13 See *Die Zeit*, no.42 (9 October 1981)

FIG 1 George Grosz, *Welfare Officer for War Wounded (Grey Day)*, 1921, oil on canvas, 115 × 80 cm (Berlin, Staatliche Museen Preussischer Kulturbesitz, Nationalgalerie, inv. no.B97)

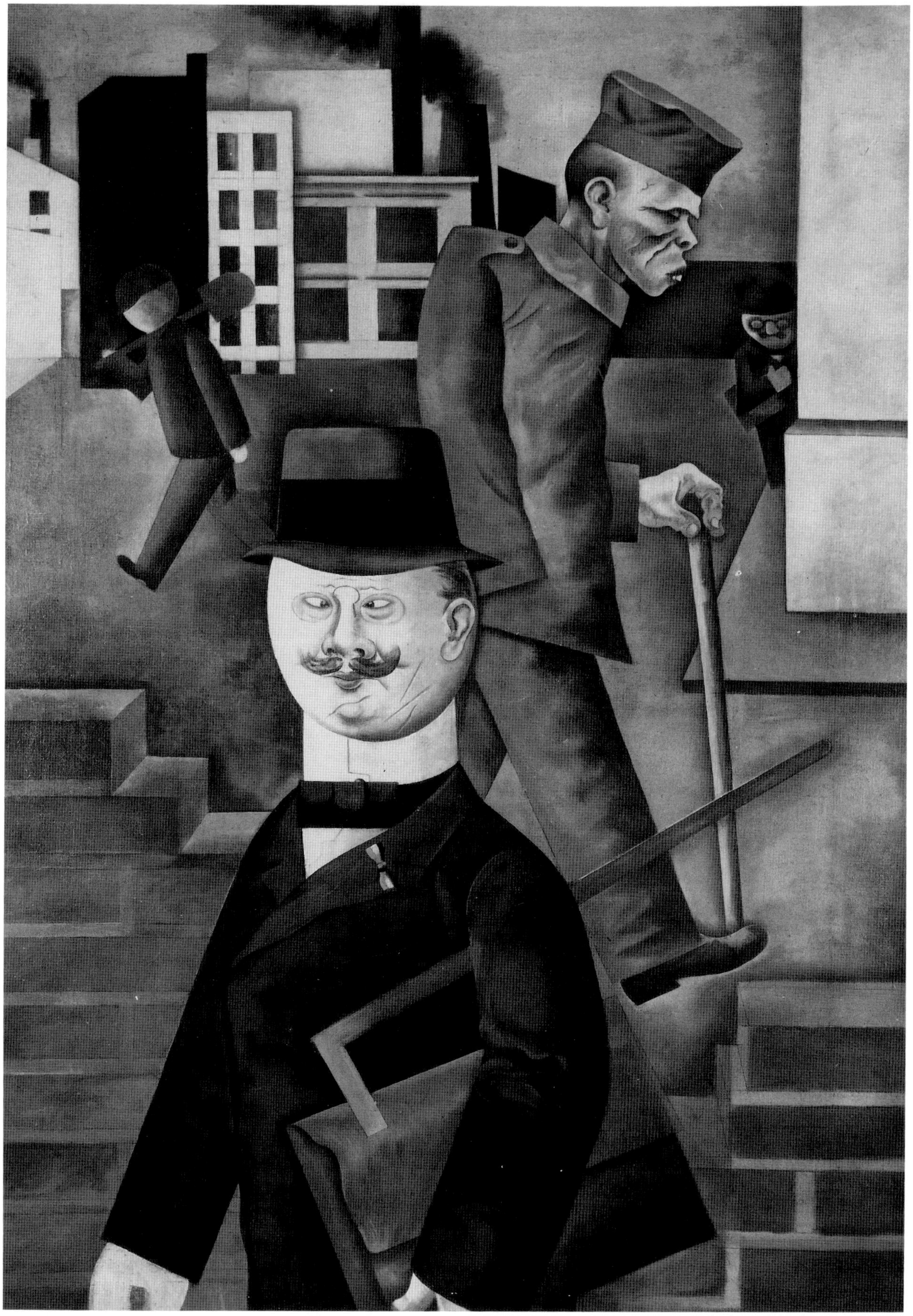

George Grosz 1893–1959

19 Nude

1920
Mixed media on paper, 40 × 29.2 cm
Unsigned/undated
The paper shows slight bulging; otherwise condition is good
Accession no.1978.6

Provenance
Fischer Fine Art, London
Thyssen-Bornemisza Collection, 1978

Exhibitions
Berlin, Kunsthandlung Dr Otto Burchard, 1920, *Erste Internationale Dada-Messe*, no.56 [as 'Tatlinistischer Plan']
Berlin, 1977, 15. *Europäische Kunstausstellung. Tendenzen der Zwanziger Jahre*, no.3/590 [as '*c.*1919']
Frankfurt am Main, Städelsches Kunstinstitut, 1977–8, *Dada in Europa, Werke und Dokumente*, no.3/590 [as '*c.*1919']
London, Arts Council of Great Britain, 1978, *Dada and Surrealism Reviewed*, no.4.26 [as '*c.*1919']
Paris, Centre Georges Pompidou, 1978, *Paris–Berlin*, ill. p.169 [as '1919']
Venice, Palazzo Grassi, 1979, *La Pittura Metafisica*, no.114 [as '*c.*1919']
Minneapolis, MN, Institute of Arts/Chicago, IL, Museum of Contemporary Art, 1980–81, *German Realism of the Twenties. The Artist as Social Critic*, no.56 [as 'about 1919']
Berlin, Berlinische Galerie, 1987, *Ich und die Stadt*, no.53 [as '1919']
Berlin, Berlinische Galerie, 1988–9, *Stationen der Moderne*, no.4/11
Madrid, Centro de Arte Reina Sofia, 1989, *Berlin, Punto de Encuentro*, no.3/9

Literature
George Grosz, *Mit Pinsel und Schere. 7 Materialisationen*, Berlin (Malik) 1922
Schneede (1975), ill. p.65
Eberhard Roters and Bernhard Schulz (eds.), *Ich und die Stadt. Mensch und Grosstadt in der deutschen Kunst des 20. Jahrhunderts*, exh. cat., Berlin, Berlinische Galerie, 1987, p.160

Nude was first shown at the provocative First International Dada-Fair in Berlin in 1920. Like other works of Grosz's Dada period, it consists at first sight of a seemingly random, though evocative, juxtaposition of for the most part unrelated images. In style and technique, as well as in the central role of the erotically conceived nude figure, it is closely related to another watercolour and collage composition entitled *'Daum' marries ...* (fig.1), with which Grosz

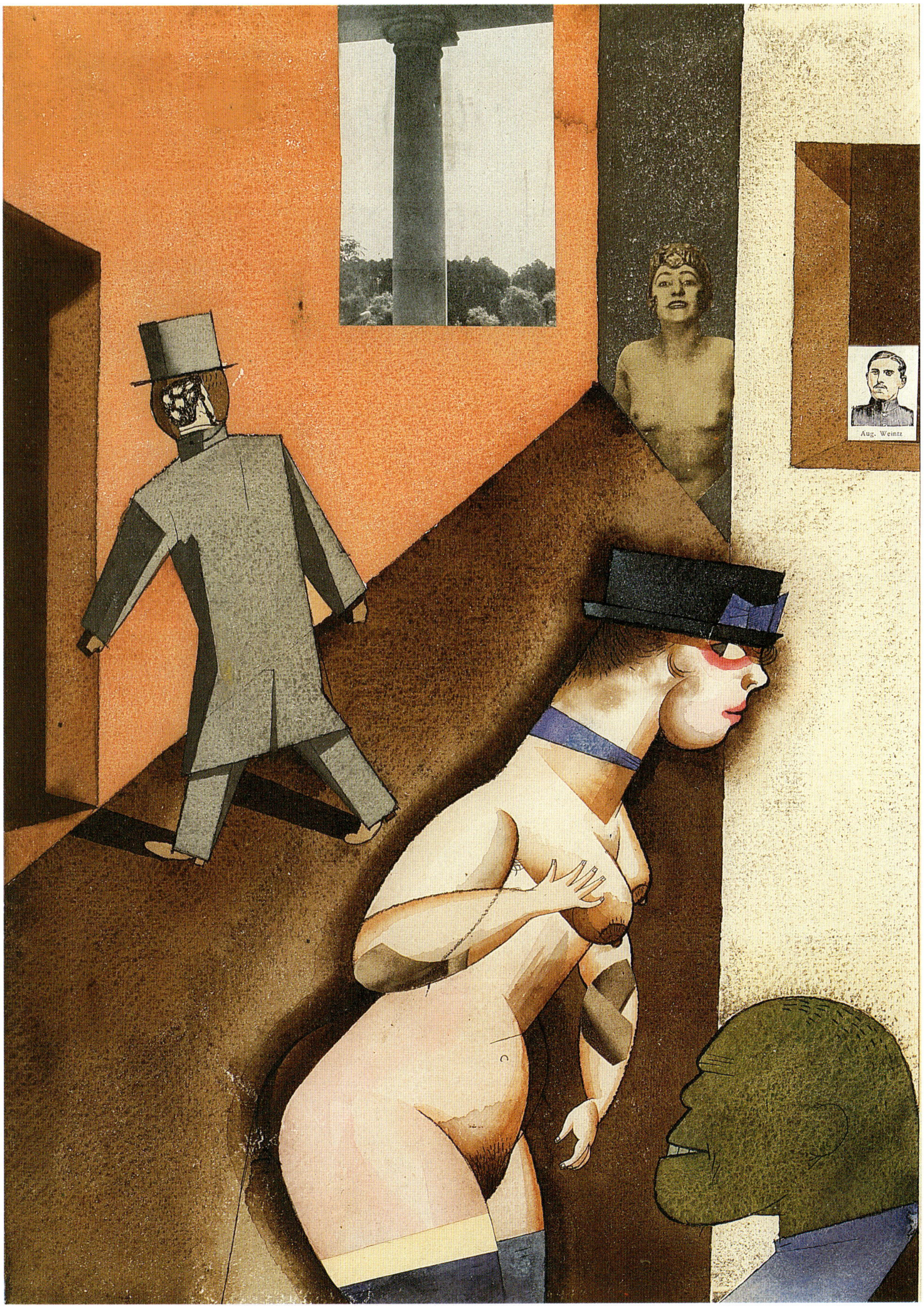
Aug. Weintz

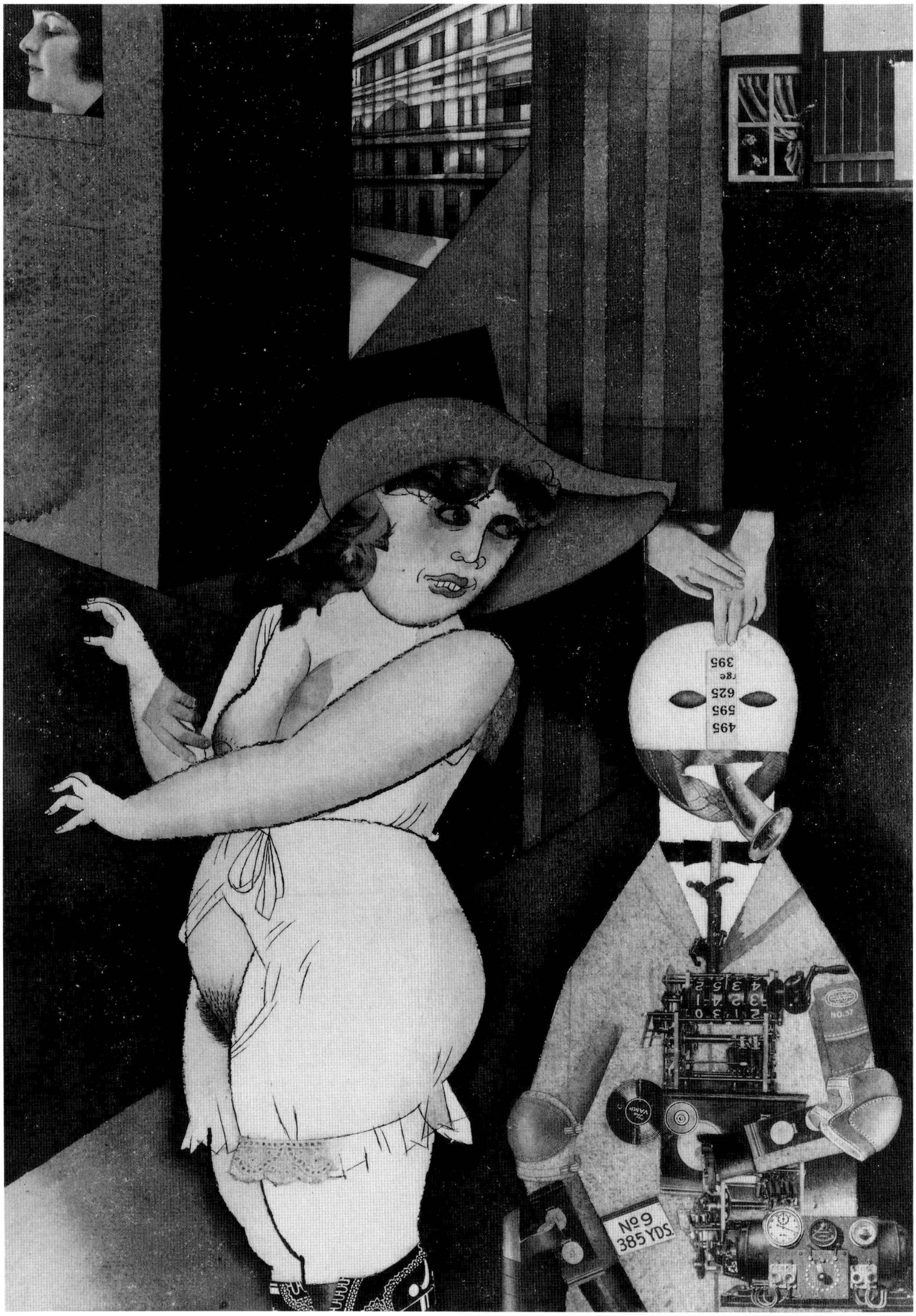
No 9
385 YDS.

marked the occasion of his marriage to Eva Peter in May 1920. Though *Nude* is undated, the manifest similarity between the two works, and the fact that both were exhibited at the International Dada-Fair which opened at the end of June makes a date of execution some time in the spring or early summer of 1920 virtually certain.

In the catalogue of the exhibition (in reality, a large-format broadsheet), the present work is listed under the title *Tatlinistischer Plan* (Tatlinesque Plan). In fact, the Dada artists probably knew very little about Tatlin's work at this time. Not until the so-called *Erste Russische Kunstausstellung* (First Russian Art Exhibition) at the Galerie van Diemen in Berlin in 1922 was there the opportunity of finding out at first-hand anything much about the developments that had taken place in Russian avant-garde art during the years of war and revolution.[1] None the less, the Berlin Dadaists were captivated by the image associated in their minds with Tatlin – an image which had more to do with his being a revolutionary and a Communist and an engineer than with his acutal works. A number of Dadaist manifestations were conceived as 'acts of homage' to Tatlin, among them the International Dada-Fair itself: a frequently reproduced photograph taken at the exhibition shows Grosz and Heartfield ostentatiously holding a placard which read 'Art is Dead. Long Live the Machine Art of Tatlin'.[2]

The similarities between *Nude* and other contemporary works by Grosz are in several respects suggestive of its intended meaning. There is, for example, an evident resemblance between the somewhat sinister bald-headed profile which appears at bottom right and Grosz's Dada portrait of *The Engineer John Heartfield*, likewise of 1920 (New York, Museum of Modern Art). Though interpreting the iconography of Dada works can be a somewhat risky occupation, it is also perhaps not wholly fanciful to recognize in the nude female figure a depiction of 'Daum' (Grosz's nickname for Eva, an anagram of her pet-name 'Maud'), and in the smartly-attired male figure disappearing into the doorway an image of Grosz himself, whose dandyesque affectations were well known. If this identification is correct, then given its full title both *'Daum' marries ...* (properly entitled *'Daum' marries her psychic automaton 'George' in May 1920, John Heartfield is very glad of it*) and *Nude* might, not implausibly, be regarded as a form of commentary, however oblique, on the relationship between Heartfield, Grosz and Eva.

Nude is executed principally in watercolour, with some outlines drawn in pen and Indian ink, together with what appear to be faint traces of crayon, drawn lightly across the rough surface of the heavily textured watercolour paper. There are also fragments of photographs and other *papiers collés*, cut and pasted on to the surface. However, it is not, strictly speaking, a photomontage, as it has on occasion been called,[3] since the superimposed elements are merely interpolations within an essentially watercolour composition, not all of them photographic in origin. More accurate would be to describe it as a watercolour and collage of photographic and other images, cut and pasted on to the surface of the paper. There are eight such collage elements, evidently taken from different sources: (1) the space within the outline of the head of the figure on the left wearing a hat is occupied by an image of a smaller head of a bearded man seen from behind, apparently cut from a newspaper; (2) a photograph, perhaps from an illustrated magazine, taken from within a Doric portico looking out on to a park; (3) a photograph, again perhaps from an illustrated magazine, of what appears to be a cabaret girl; (4) a line etching, hand coloured, of the features of a man, with the printed insciption 'Aug. Weintz'; (5, 6) two small fragments of what might be machine forms which have been pasted into the spaces occupied by the elbow and arm of the principal figure, and (7, 8) two pieces of cut and pasted paper representing her eye and garter.

Like *'Daum' marries ...*, *Nude* was reproduced in the album *Mit Pinsel und Schere. 7 Materialisationen* (With Brush and Scissors. 7 Materializations), published in Berlin in July 1922 – one of a number of collections of Grosz's work which appeared under the imprint of Wieland Herzfelde's Malik publishing house between 1917 and 1923.[4] The original, framed, can be seen in the background of a photograph of the artist himself taken in his Berlin studio in 1920, known under the title *George Grosz at home* (fig.2).

Notes

1 See Andrei B. Nakov, 'This Last Exhibition which was the "First"', and Peter Nisbet, 'Some Facts on the Organizational History of the van Diemen Exhibition', in *The 1st Russian Show. A Commemoration of the Van Diemen Exhibition Berlin 1922*, exh. cat., London, Annely Juda Fine Art, 1983, pp.6–47, 67–72

2 Originally published in Richard Huelsenbeck, *Dada-Almanach*, Berlin 1920

3 See, e.g. Roters and Schulz, loc. cit.

4 On the history of the firm, in which both Herzfelde's brother John Heartfield and Grosz himself played a leading role, see *Der Malik-Verlag 1916–1947*, exh. cat., Berlin, Deutsche Akademie der Künste, 1967

FIG 1 George Grosz, *'Daum' marries her psychic automaton 'George' in May 1920, John Heartfield is very glad of it*, 1920, mixed media, 42 × 30.2 cm (Berlin, Galerie Nierendorf)

FIG 2 *George Grosz at home*, photograph 1920

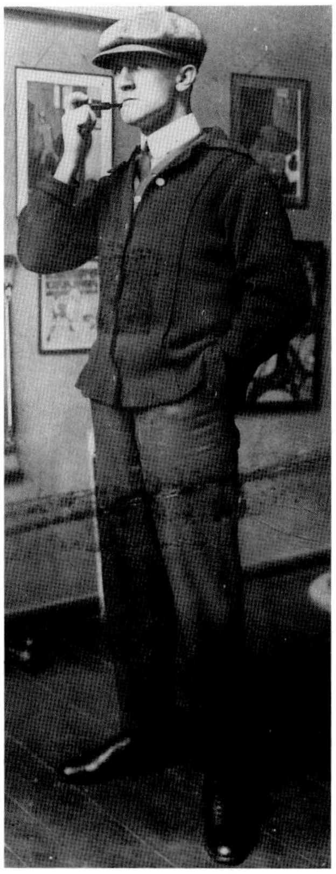

George Grosz 1893–1959

20 Twilight

1922
Watercolour and Indian ink on brownish paper, 52.3 × 40.5 cm
Signed lower right: 'Grosz'
The paper has become discoloured and shows several pin-holes. Otherwise condition is good
Accession no.1973.65(a)

Verso Study for 'Twilight'

1922
Ink on brownish paper
Accession no.1973.65(b)

Provenance
Count Harry Kessler, Berlin/Weimar
Marlborough Fine Art, London
Galerie R.N.Ketterer, Campione d'Italia
Thyssen-Bornemisza Collection, 1973

Exhibitions
Vienna, Kunsthandlung Würthle, 1923, *George Grosz*, no.1
London, Marlborough Fine Art, 1972, *Masters of the 19th and 20th Centuries*, no.28
Bremen 1975, no.25
Lugano 1978, no.40

Literature
Hess (1974), ill. p.79
R.N.Ketterer, *Moderne Kunst VIII*, Campione d'Italia (Galerie R.N.Ketterer) 1973, p.56, no.29, ill. p.57

This watercolour was originally owned by Harry, Graf Kessler (1868–1937), the so-called 'Red Count'. Kessler, a diplomat and collector known for his left-wing sympathies, promoted (and to some extent protected) radical artists such as John Heartfield and his brother Wieland Herzfelde during the violent and troubled period in Berlin following the end of the First World War.[1] He also encouraged plans for the satirical-political review *Jedermann sein eigner Fussball* (Everyman his own Football), published by Herzfelde's Malik Verlag in Berlin in 1919 with illustrations by Grosz.

The title and date given here are based on the close resemblance between the present work and another street scene by Grosz which was included among sixteen watercolours reproduced

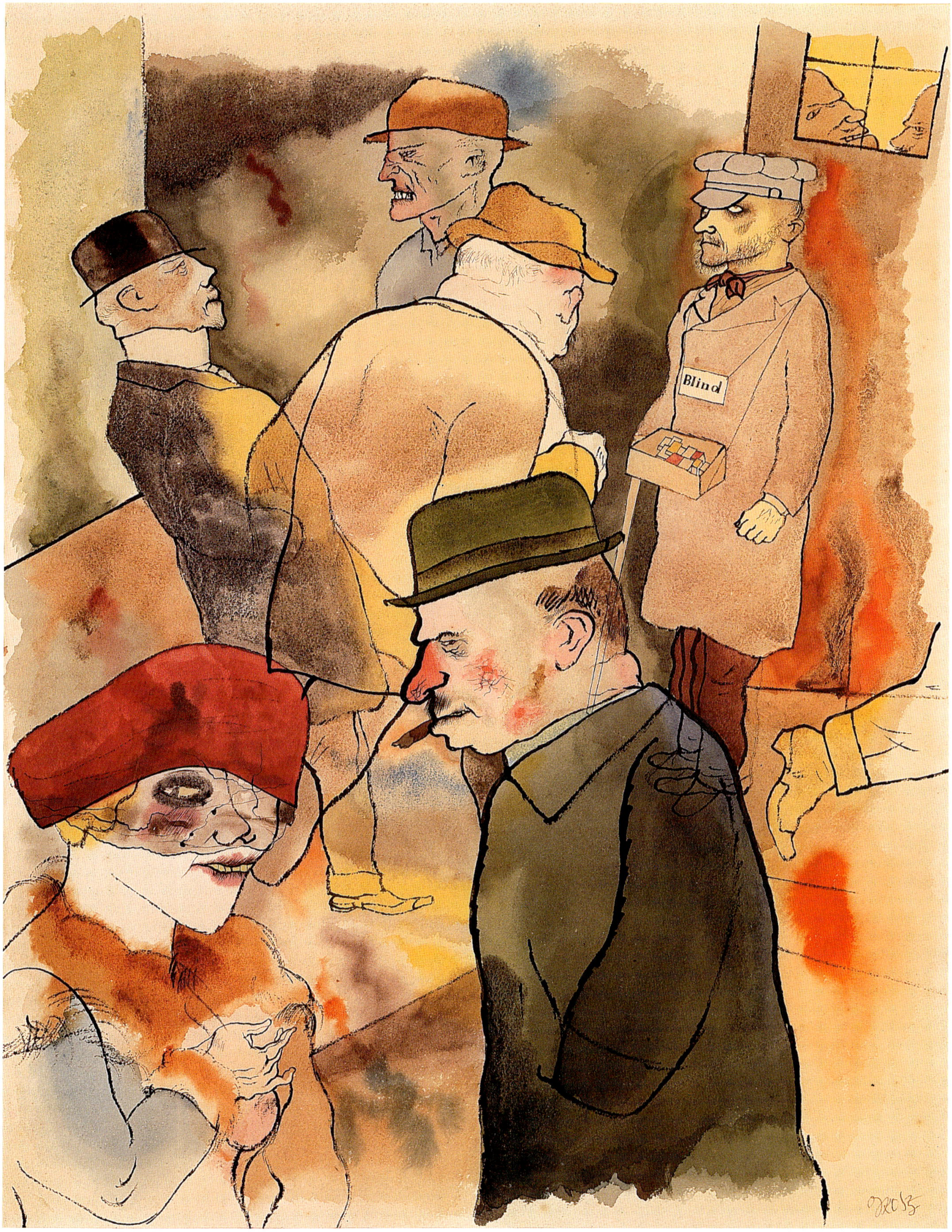
Blind

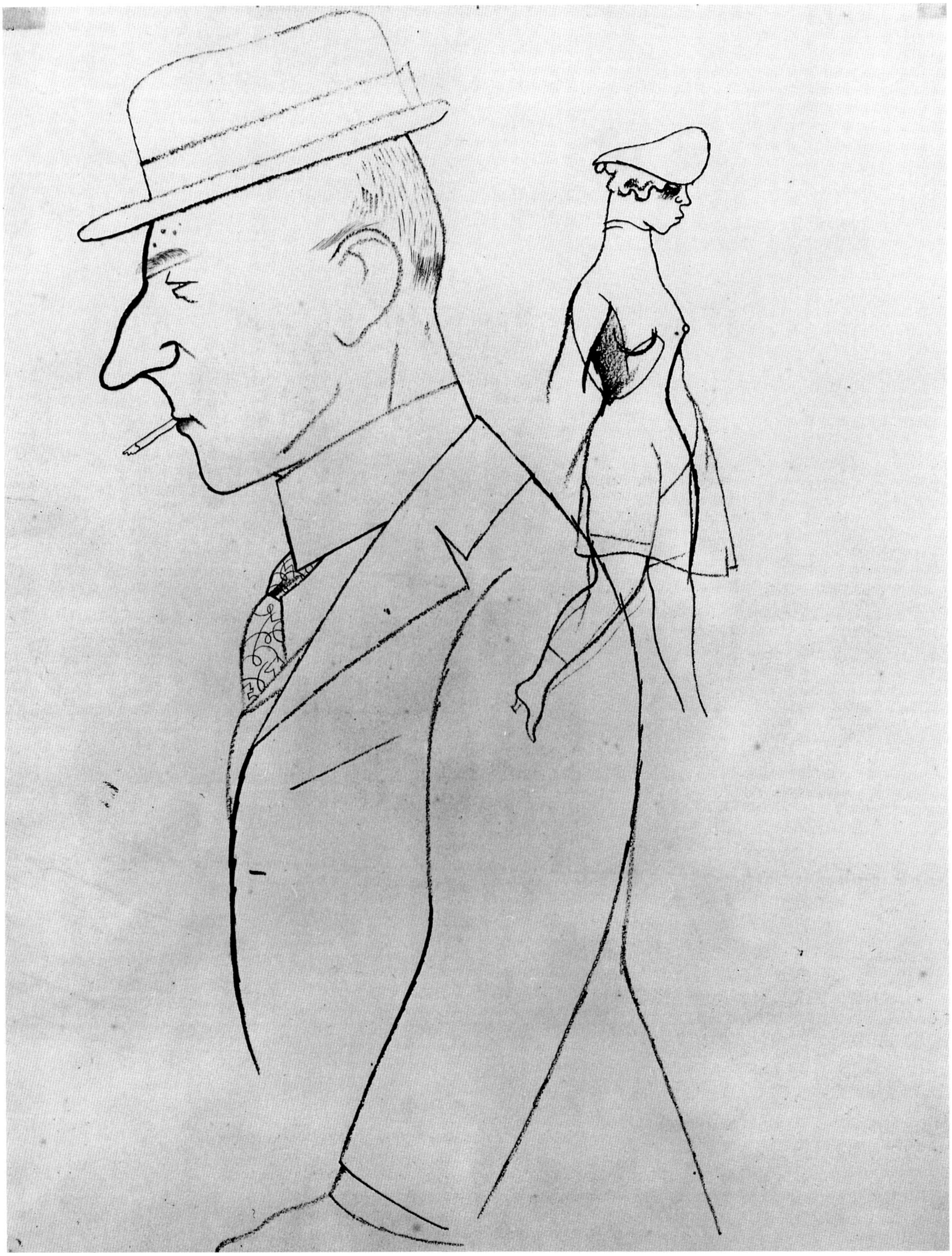

[20] *verso*
George Grosz,
Study for 'Twilight'

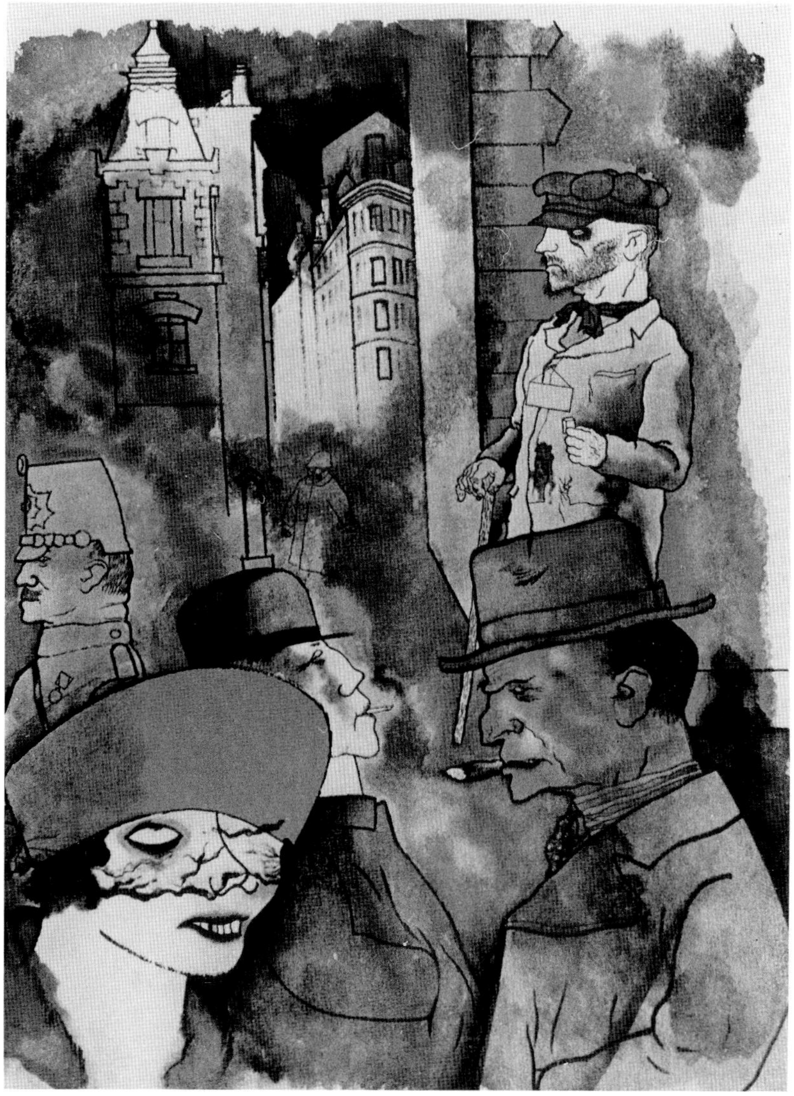

FIG 1 George Grosz, *Twilight*, 1922, watercolour reproduced in *Ecce Homo*, Berlin (Malik) 1923, pl.XVI

in *Ecce Homo*, the 1923 collection of the artist's work also published by Malik Verlag (see fig.1).[2] Dated 1922 and entitled *Dämmerung* (Twilight), this published variant is compositionally almost identical with the Thyssen painting and contains most of the same figures. The principal difference is in the architectural background, which seems more evocative of New York than of Berlin.[3] The figures, on the other hand, are unmistakably German. As in many of his works of the early 1920s, Grosz here conjures up an unflattering but immediately recognizable picture of Prussian society at that time: not only stereotypes of the urban bourgeoisie, self-satisfaction and greed etched on their faces, but also the tarts and pimps and beggars who existed on the fringes of that society, and whose image recurs in many of the other drawings and watercolours included in *Ecce Homo*.

Grosz himself referred to *Ecce Homo* as 'a document of that period of inflation, with its vices and its immorality', and called its impact 'as brutal as the time which suggested it to me ... All of the work I have produced which has led to charges against me has emerged in the same way; it can only be understood in the light of the people and the period I have known.'[4] In 1924, he was tried and convicted on grounds of obscenity, largely on the basis of the predominantly erotic subject-matter of the drawings published in *Ecce Homo* – one of a number of prosecutions brought against him during this period, including in 1928 an action for blasphemy.

On the back of the sheet is an ink drawing for the male figure on the recto, together with a smaller sketch of a woman.

Notes

1 On Kessler and his activities as political go-between and patron of the arts, see the historical introduction by Otto Friedrich, in Kessler (1971), pp.ix-xv; also Beatrice von Bismarck, 'Harry Graf Kessler und die französische Kunst der Jahrhundertwende', *Zeitschrift des Deutschen Vereins für Kunstwissenschaft*, XLII, no.3 (1988): 47–62

2 Hans Hess wrongly identified the present watercolour with that published in *Ecce Homo*: see Hess (1974), p.118 and fig.62

3 On Grosz's American fantasies, see [18]

4 George Grosz, autobiographical fragment, quoted after Flavell (1988), p.314

George Grosz 1893–1959

21 Der Stammtisch

*c*1928–30 (?)
Watercolour and black ink with white heightening on paper, 59 × 46 cm
Signed lower right: 'Grosz'; inscribed lower left, in pencil: 'PN', lower right: 'No.21'
Paper is cockled and slightly discoloured
Accession no.1979.86

Provenance
Collection of the artist
Herman Shulman, New York
Associated American Artists, New York
Private collection, New York
Andrew Crispo Gallery, New York
Thyssen-Bornemisza Collection, 1979

Der Stammtisch belongs to a group of works in pen or pencil, sometimes with the addition of watercolour, executed during the artist's last years in Germany. In these, the culimination of more than a decade spent acutely observing and recording the social and political life of the Weimar republic with all its blemishes, vices and moments of grim humour, Grosz treated subjects drawn mostly from the street and café life of Berlin in the period of depression and economic crisis which saw Hitler's inexorable rise to power.

The title employed here is derived from the inscription on the centrepiece of the table around which the group of 'regulars' is seated. It is virtually untranslatable, there being no real equivalent in the English-speaking world. A *Stammtisch* is a table in a particular restaurant or café regularly reserved for a like-minded group of customers who meet to exchange anecdotes, discuss business affairs, or simply put the world to rights. In 1979 the watercolour was offered for sale to the Thyssen Collection under the title *Political Conversation*, though it is far from clear whence this title derives; it has also been known as *German Café*. It has not been possible to establish which, if any, of these titles was used by the artist himself.

Though it is neither titled nor dated, *Der Stammtisch* is close in style to other works by Grosz datable to the late twenties, for example the watercolour *Inflation* of 1929 (Princeton, NJ, estate of George Grosz).[1] It is on the basis of stylistic similarity with such works that the date *c*1928–30 is suggested here.[2]

Notes
1 Schneede (1979), fig.189
2 I am grateful to Mr Peter M.Grosz, Princeton, NJ, for his advice and assistance, in particular his opinion on the dating of the present work which he likewise ascribes to 'around 1929–31 or perhaps slightly earlier' (letter to the author, 7 July 1991)

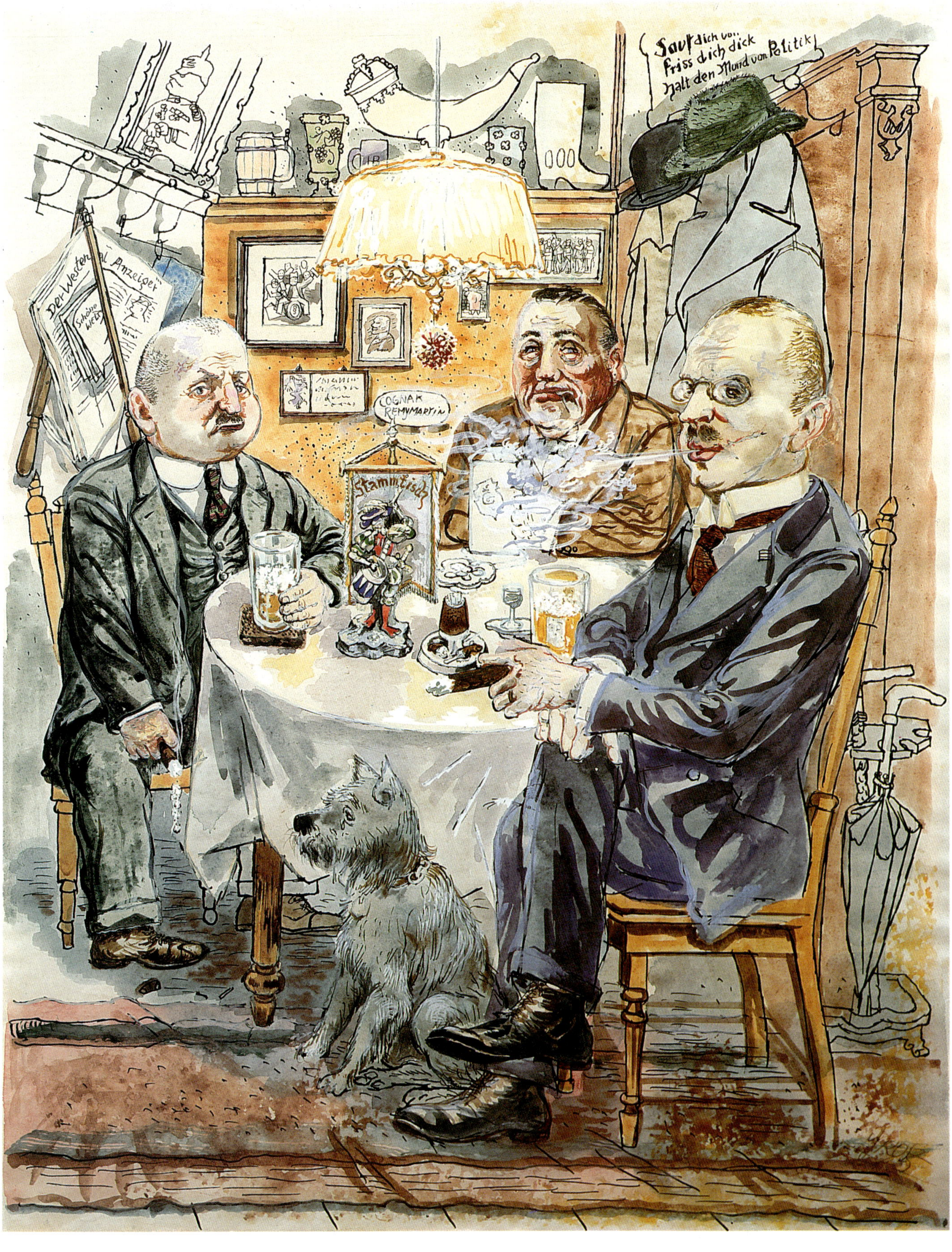
Sauf dich vo
friss dich dick
halt den Mund von Politik
Der Westen
Anzeiger
Schöne Welt
COGNAK
REMYMARTIN
Stammtisch

Erich Heckel 1883–1970

22 Brickworks
Ziegelei

1907
Oil on canvas, 68 × 86 cm
Initialled/dated lower right: 'EH 07'; inscribed on stretcher: 'Erich Heckel Ziegelei 1907'
The canvas shows occasional warping along the edges. The painting is unvarnished. The paint layer consists of a thick, dry impasto, with scattered cracking and minor losses
Accession no.1965.12

Provenance
Collection of the artist
Collection Roman Norbert Ketterer
Thyssen-Bornemisza Collection, 1965[1]

Exhibitions
Münster, Westfälisches Landesmuseum, 1953, *Erich Heckel. Zur Vollendung des siebenten Lebensjahrzehntes*, no.2
Oldenburg, Kunstverein, 1957, *Maler der Brücke in Dangast von 1907 bis 1912*, p.87, no.5
Amsterdam, Stedelijk Museum, 1957, *Europa 1907*, no.30
Stuttgart, Württembergischer Kunstverein, 1957, *Erich Heckel. Werke der Brückezeit 1907–1917*, no.3
Essen 1958, no.11
Ulm, Ulmer Museum, 1959, *Bilder der 'Brücke'*[2]
Meisterwerke des deutschen Expressionismus, 1960–61, no.96
Essen, Museum Folkwang/Hamburg, Kunstverein, 1963–4, *Erich Heckel. Zur Vollendung des achten Lebensjahrzehntes*, no.2
Munich, Haus der Kunst, 1970, *Europäischer Expressionismus*, no.5
Paris, Musée National d'Art Moderne, 1970, *L'Expressionisme Européen*, no.73
Turin, Galleria Civica d'Arte Moderna, 1971, *Il Cavaliere Azzurro*, ill. p.124
Bremen 1975, no.28
Lugano 1975, no.31
Lugano 1978, no.41
Expressionism, a German Intuition, 1980–81, no.89
Essen, Museum Folkwang/Munich, Haus der Kunst, 1983–4, *Erich Heckel 1883–1970. Gemälde, Aquarelle, Zeichnungen und Graphik*, no.5
Modern Masters from the Thyssen-Bornemisza Collection, 1984–6, no.44
Lugano 1989, no.13
Rome 1990–91, no.14

Literature
Vogt (1965), 1907/4
Vogt (1972), p.100, ill, p.99
Dube (1972), p.54, ill. p.55
Kiel (1974), p.46, ill. p.45
Paul Vogt, *Expressionism. German Painting 1905–1920*, New York 1980, p.64
Henze (1983), pp.25f
See also Gerhard Wietek, 'Dangast am Jadebusen', in Wietek (1976), pp.170–77; Felix (1983), pp.210f

The artists of the Brücke tended to flee the city during the summer months. Singly, or in twos and threes, they sought out for themselves remote locations where they might paint undisturbed and at the same time immerse themselves in what seemed to them a more 'natural' or 'primitive' way of life. Landscape motifs, rural architecture and studies of bathing figures are the principal ingredients of the works they brought back from these summer painting expeditions.

Notes
1 Acquired directly from the previous owner; on the Stuttgarter Kunstkabinett, the Ketterer collection and the Galerie R.N.Ketterer, see pp.16–17
2 See n.1 to p.27

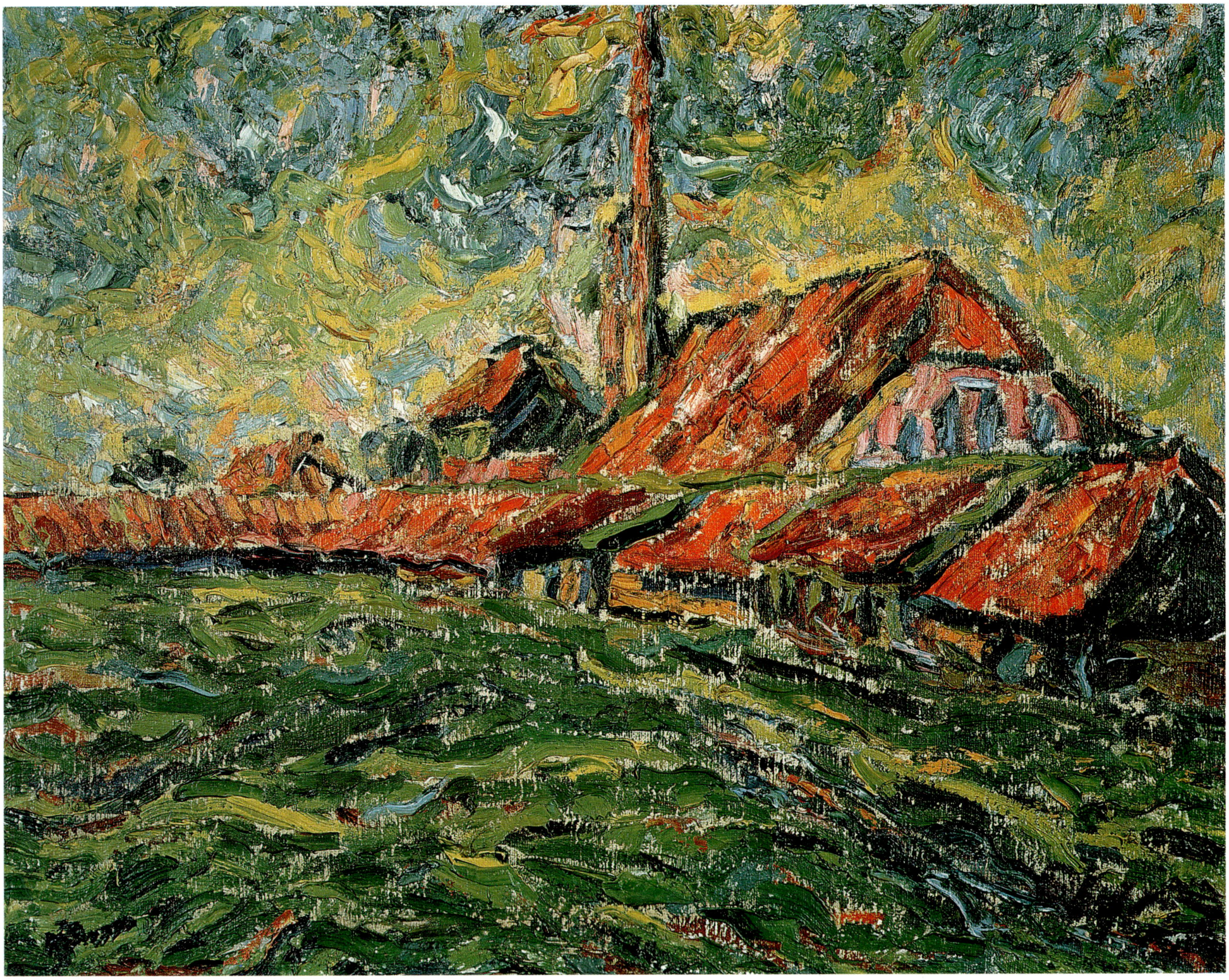

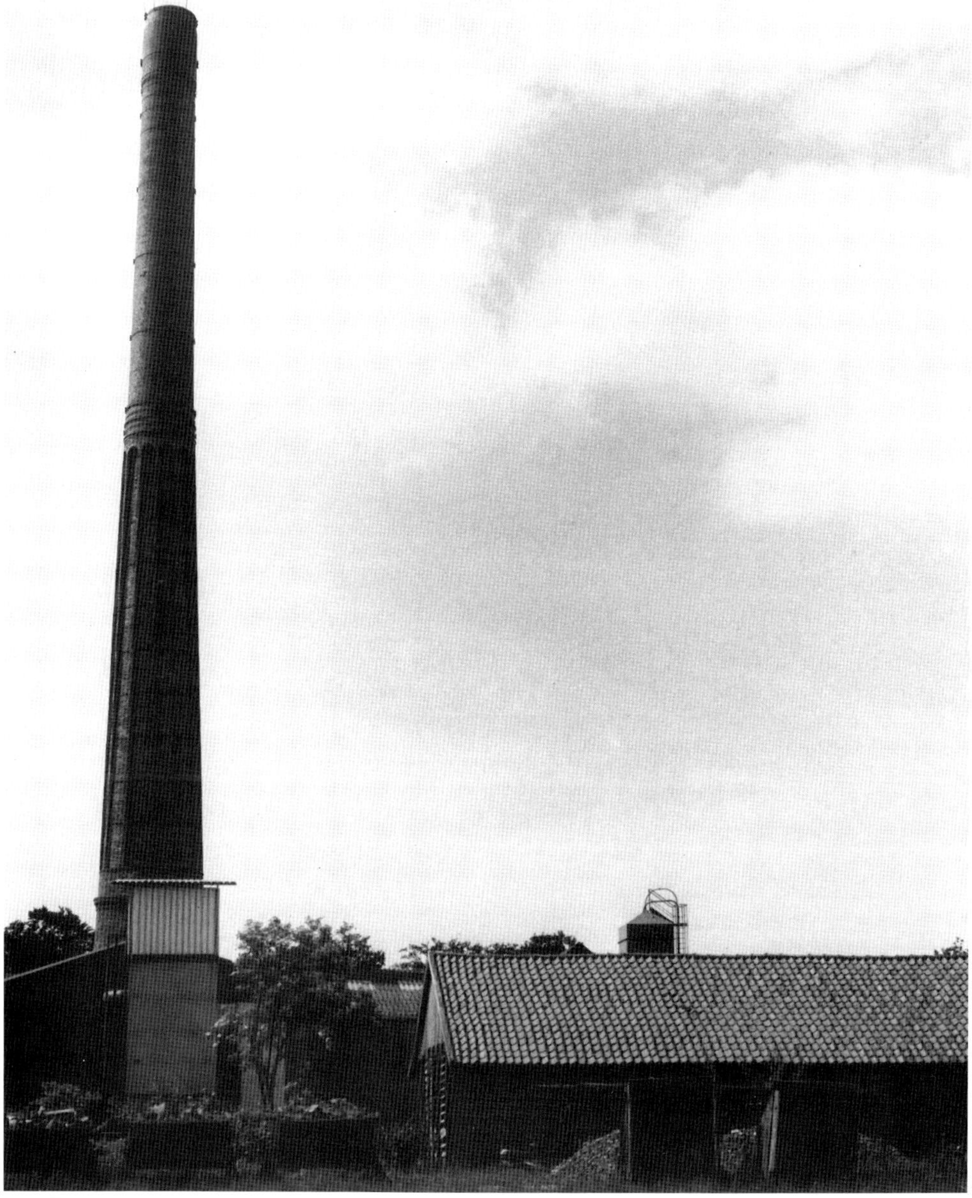

FIG 1 Brickworks in the vicinity of Obenstrohe near Varel, 1990

By his own account, it was Heckel who, in search of a rural retreat where he and Schmidt-Rottluff might spend the summer of 1907 painting, put his finger on a large-scale map of the region to the north of Oldenburg, on Germany's North Sea coast. In an interview given many years afterwards, he recalled:

> Schmidt-Rottluff and I wondered where to go in search of new subjects. I turned up a big atlas and we looked for a bit of coastline, because we wanted to go to the sea-side, somewhere really remote. In the atlas was a detailed map of the Jadebusen in Oldenburg. It appeared there were sand dunes and dykes, an artificial dam and in the other direction moorland. We said to ourselves this was the place for us, we had to go there because it was completely unknown. Schmidt-Rottluff travelled up there first. He wrote to me saying that the region was quite fantastic, everything simply demanding to be painted ...[3]

Their choice fell on the little village of Dangast, near Varel, which lays claim to being Germany's oldest seaside resort,[4] at that date consisting of little more than a few houses penned in between the marshes and the sea. They both seem to have fallen in love with the place: Schmidt-Rottluff, in particular, returned there every year until 1912, Heckel joining him for part of each summer or autumn until, in 1911, he abandoned Dangast in favour of Prerow on the Baltic.[5]

Notes

3 Erich Heckel in conversation with Roman Norbert Ketterer (1958): see Ketterer (1988/11), p.53

4 The origins of the resort go back to the late eighteenth century: see Wietek (1976), p.170; also Wietek (1957), p.10; Reinhardt (1977): 134

5 See chronology printed in Felix (1983), p.211

6 See n.3 above
7 Gordon (1966): 338f; Feilchenfeldt (1988), pp.20–21
8 Erich Heckel, *Brickworks*, 1908 (Oldenburg, Landesmuseum): see Vogt (1965), 1908/13

In those days, a dominant feature of the landscape around Dangast was the large number of brickworks with their tall chimneys and long, low drying sheds. (A few of these old factory buildings from the early years of this century survive today: see fig.1.) Their red-tiled roofs as depicted in *Brickworks* afforded a colourful motif to which both Heckel and Schmidt-Rottluff returned in numerous paintings and watercolour studies dating especially from their first visits to the area. Half a century later, Heckel still remembered vividly how the buildings 'introduced a note of red into the landscape; the long sheds emphasized the horizontal, while the tall chimneys, as it were, brought the sky into the picture.'[6]

At this point in their development, the dominant influence on the work of both Heckel and Schmidt-Rottluff was the art of van Gogh, whose paintings they could have seen, not only in reproduction, but also in the original in the exhibition organized by the Berlin dealer Paul Cassirer, shown in November 1905 at the Galerie Arnold in Dresden.[7] This influence is revealed most clearly in their use of strident, non-naturalistic colours and heavy impasto, of which the first version of *Brickworks* offers a particularly striking example.

It is instructive to compare Heckel's 1907 version of this subject with his depiction of the same building seen from a different angle, painted the following year.[8] By contrast with the relative flatness of the later version, in *Brickworks* form is created primarily by means of colour, the pigment piled up in heavy masses almost as tangible as the tiled roof of the building itself. So rapid, however, was the pace of his development at this time that in his treatment of the same subject painted only a year later, he is evidently bent on creating form more by means of outline than colour or brushwork, marking the beginnings of a transition to the greater clarity of his mature style.

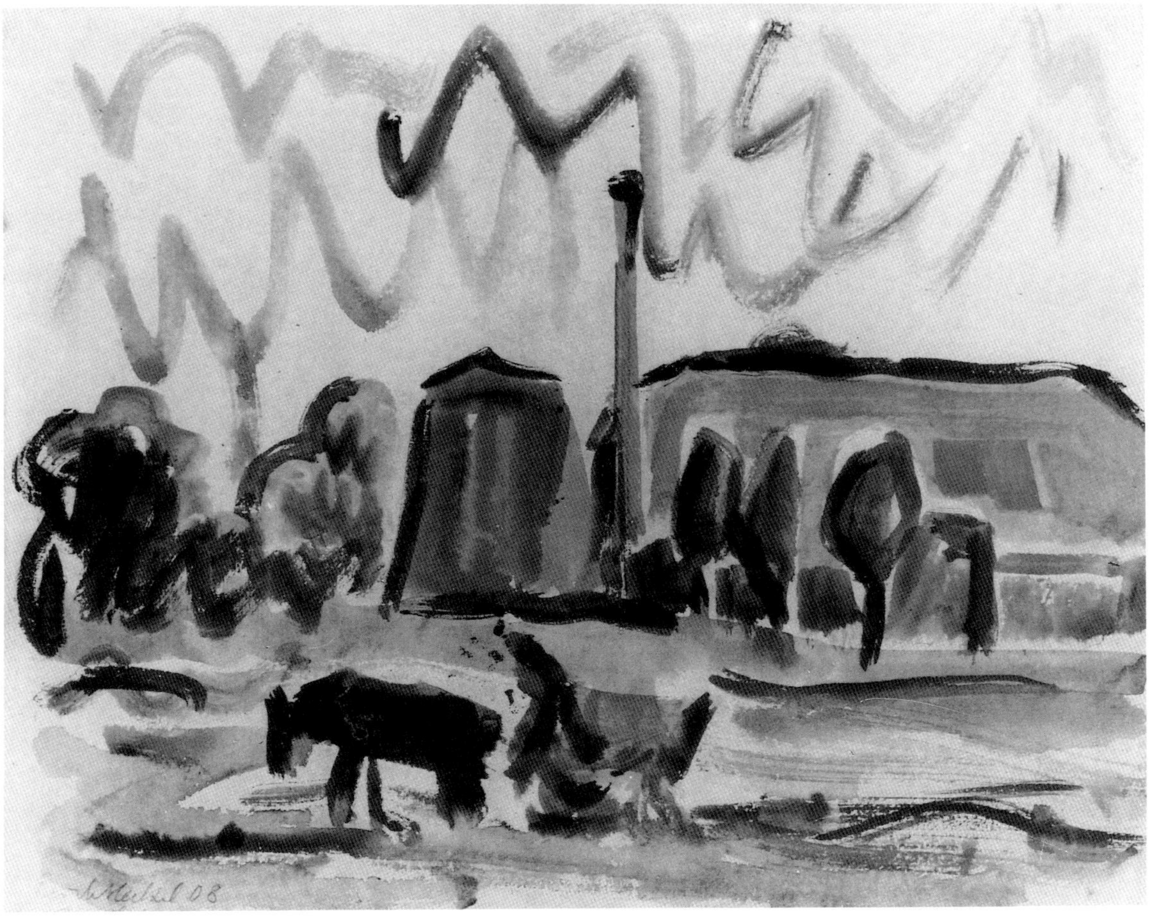

FIG 2 Erich Heckel, *Brickworks in Dangast*, 1908, watercolour, 35.8 × 44.3 cm (Essen, Museum Folkwang, inv. no.A 6/80)

Erich Heckel 1883–1970

23 House in Dangast (The White House)[1]
Haus in Dangast

1908
Oil on canvas, 71 × 81 cm
Signed/dated lower right: 'Heckel 08'; inscribed (twice) on back on stretcher: 'Heckel 1908. Haus in Dangast'; '1908 Haus in Dangast'
The paint layer shows some minor flaking. Otherwise condition is good. The painting is unvarnished
Accession no.1961.13

Provenance
Collection of the artist
Collection Roman Norbert Ketterer
Thyssen-Bornemisza Collection, 1961[2]

Exhibitions
Berlin, Kunst-Salon Fritz Gurlitt, 1914, no.17[3]
Oldenburg, Kunstverein, 1957, *Maler der Brücke in Dangast von 1907 bis 1912*, p.88, no.30 [as 'Weisses Haus (Altes Posthaus Dangast)'][4]
Duisburg, Städtisches Kunstmuseum, 1957, *Erich Heckel*, no.8
Stuttgart, Württembergischer Kunstverein, 1957, *Erich Heckel. Werke der Brückezeit 1907–1917*, no.6
Essen 1958, no.18
Ulm, Ulmer Museum, 1959, *Bilder der 'Brücke'*[5]
Schaffhausen, Museum zu Allerheiligen/Berlin, Schloss Charlottenburg, 1959, *Triumph der Farbe. Die europäischen Fauves*, no.91 [as 'Weisses Haus in Dangast']
Meisterwerke des deutschen Expressionismus, 1960–61, no.97
Essen, Museum Folkwang/Hamburg, Kunstverein, 1963–4, *Erich Heckel. Zur Vollendung des achten Lebensjahrzehntes*, no.7
Florence 1964, no.118
London, Tate Gallery, 1964, *Painters of the Brücke*, no.5
Paris/Munich 1966, no.148
Ottawa, National Gallery/Winnipeg, Art Gallery, 1971, *Erich Heckel*, no.5
Schaffhausen, Museum zu Allerheiligen, 1972, *Die Künstler der 'Brücke'*, no.19
Bremen 1975, no.27
Lugano 1975, no.32
Brussels/Paris 1977–8, no.35
Expressionism, a German Intuition, 1980–81, no.90
USA tour, 1982–4, no.6
Modern Masters from the Thyssen-Bornemisza Collection, 1984–6, no.43
Lugano 1989, no.14
Expressionism and Modern German Painting, 1989–90, no.8
Essen, Museum Folkwang, 1990, *Vincent van Gogh und die Moderne 1890–1914*, no.147
Amsterdam, Rijksmuseum Vincent van Gogh, 1990–91, *Vincent van Gogh en de moderne Kunst 1890–1914*, no.115

Literature
Vogt (1965), 1908/8
Kiel (1974), p.48, ill. p.47
See also Wietek (1957), p.88

Notes
1 See n.4
2 Acquired directly from the previous owner; on the Stuttgarter Kunstkabinett, the Ketterer collection and the Galerie R.N.Ketterer see pp.16–17
3 Mixed exhibition of paintings by Adolf Erbslöh, Erich Heckel, Otto Hettner and others, shown from 20 March–10 April 1914. According to a list of exhibitions compiled by the artist's widow, Siddi Heckel, [23] was included in this 1914 exhibition (information kindly provided by Hans Geissler, Hemmenhofen). If this was the case, it can only have been the painting listed in the catalogue as no.17, under the title 'Landschaft mit Haus'
4 The titles of paintings recorded in the catalogue of the 1957 Oldenburg exhibition are, in almost every case, those furnished by the Brücke artists themselves, most of whom were then still alive. I am grateful to Professor Gerhard Wietek, the organizer of the exhibition and author of the catalogue, for confirming the authenticity of these titles, and for information concerning the localities depicted
5 See n.1 to p.27

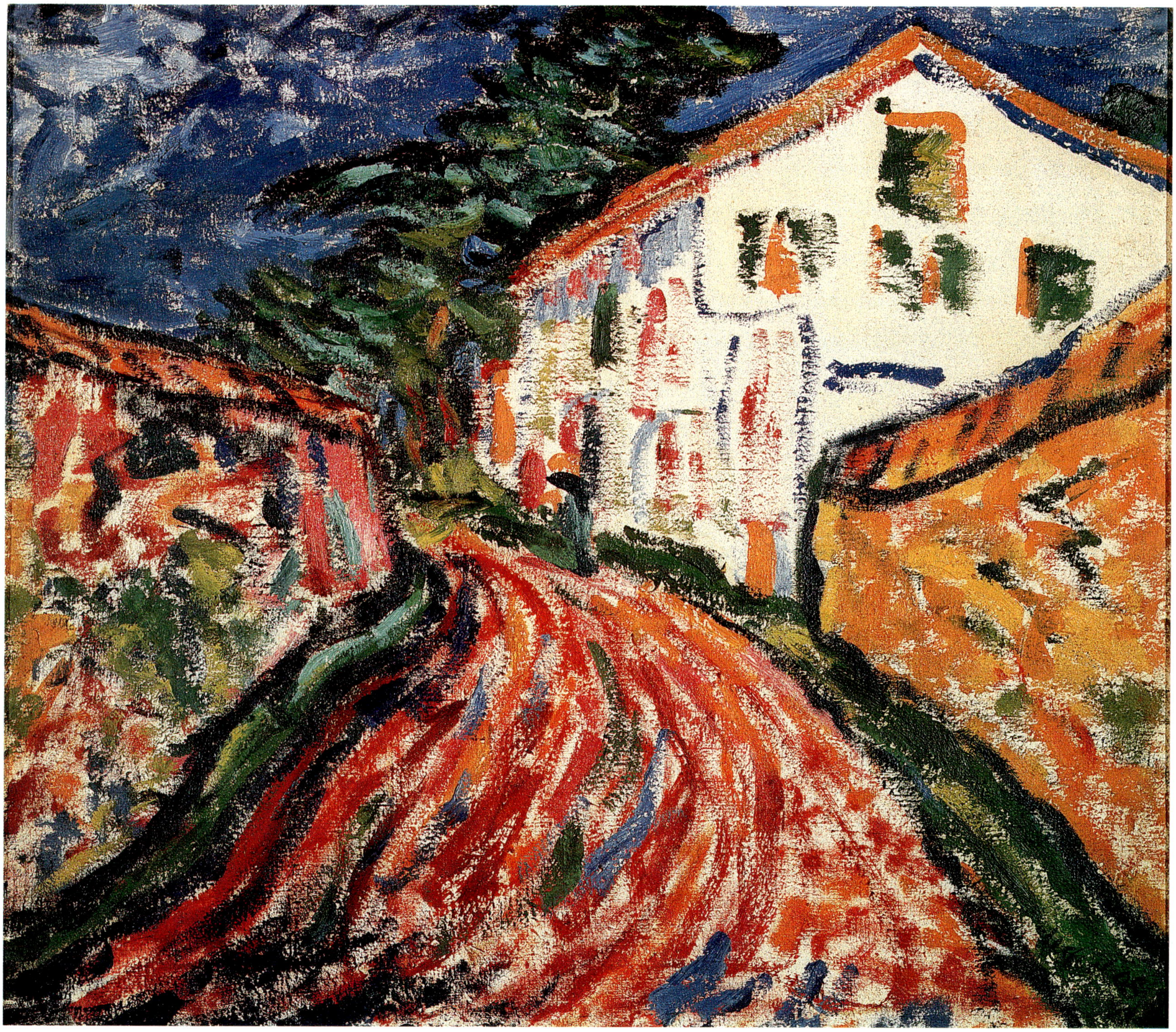

The Old Post House in Dangast – the 'White House' depicted in Heckel's painting – still stands, a short distance from the shoreline and mud-flats of the so-called Wattenmeer, the curving bay which describes a semi-circle between the town of Varel and the port of Wilhelmshaven and whose proper name is the Jadebusen. The immediate surroundings, however, are now so changed that it is difficult to visualize the locality as it must have appeared in the early years of this century. In particular, the main asphalt road now runs not alongside the building, but past the further gable end of the house. The house itself is also overshadowed by trees to such extent that one can scarcely imagine it in the dazzling sunlit colours of Heckel's painting. The accompanying photograph (fig. 1) conveys an idea of its present appearance. Schmidt-Rottluff and, in later years, the painter Franz Radziwill also depicted the same building on several occasions.[6]

FIG 1 The Old Post House, Dangast, 1990

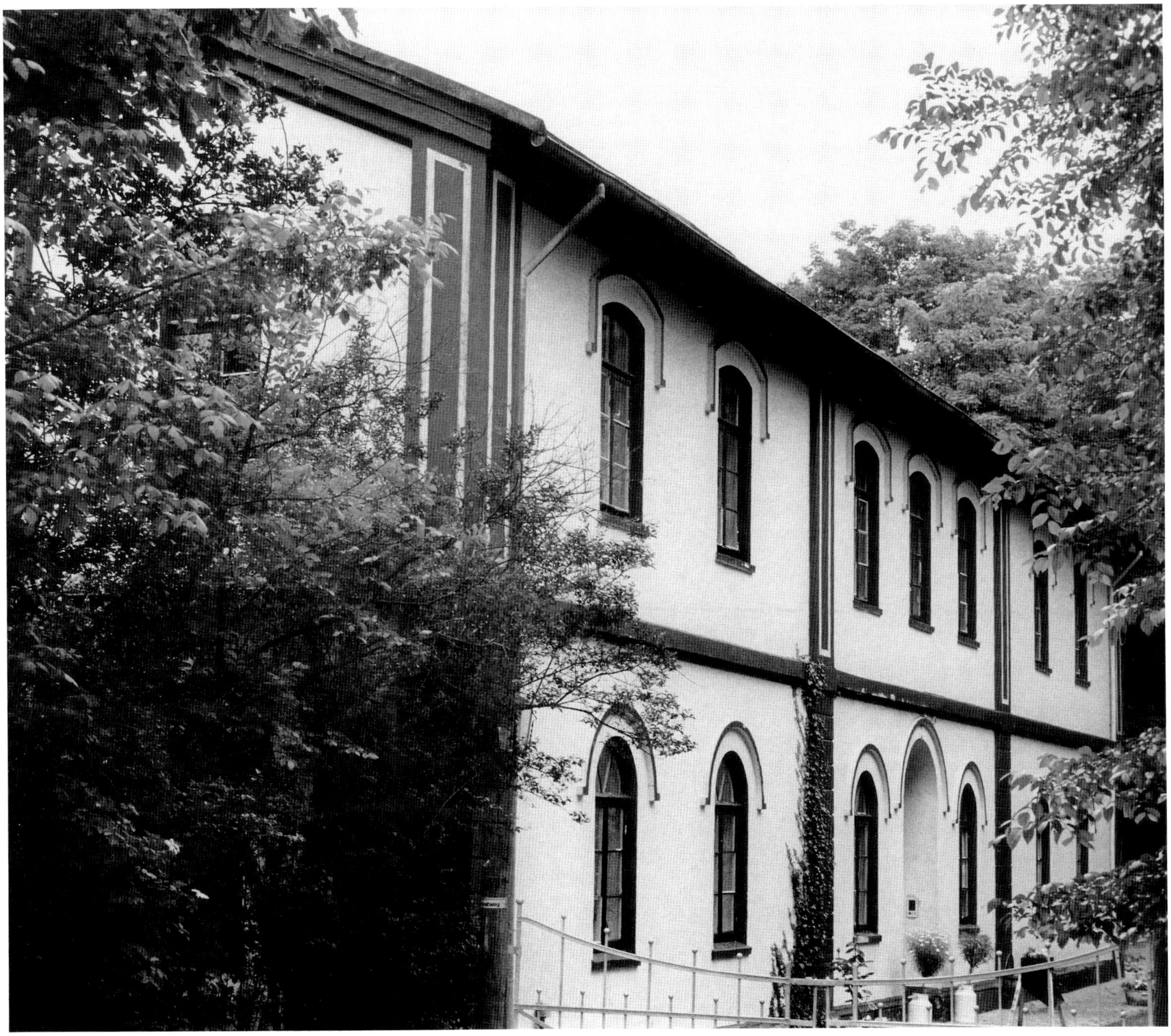

Notes
6 Radziwill in fact stayed at the Old Post House when he first visited Dangast in 1921: see Franz Radziwill, *Raum und Haus*, Munich 1987, pp.21f. I am indebted to Professor Gerhard Wietek, Hamburg for drawing this reference to my attention
7 Henze (1983), pp.26–7
8 Heckel himself, in an interview with Roman Norbert Ketterer held in 1958, not only dismissed the idea of any profound affinity between the art of the Brücke and that of the Fauves, but also denied any knowledge of the work of the younger French artists prior to the Cologne Sonderbund exhibition of 1912: see Ketterer (1988/II), p.54
9 Pechstein (1963), pp.33f
10 No.213 (12 September 1908): see Reinhardt (1977), p.146 and n.734
11 See Gisela Fiedler-Bender's account of Matisse's relations with Germany, in *Matisse und seine deutschen Schüler*, exh. cat., Kaiserslautern, Pfalzgalerie/Regensburg, Ostdeutsche Galerie, 1988, esp. pp.16–20
12 See n.8

The picture dates from Heckel's second visit to Dangast in the summer of 1908. It signals a dramatic move away from the heavy impasto characteristic of his works done the preceding year towards a flatter, clearer manner of painting. Compared with *Brickworks* [22], the pigment is in many places now sparingly applied, the composition dominated in part by flat, luminous planes of colour. Henze notes that Heckel at this time started diluting his paints with varnish or even paraffin, experimenting with ground pigments and attempting to devise a kind of thin distemper that might suit his increasingly rapid and impulsive brushwork.[7]

In style, *House in Dangast* marks perhaps the closest point of contact between any of the Brücke artists and the Fauves. It would not be difficult to convince oneself that, instead of the cold sunlight of Germany's North Sea coast, these were the brilliant colours of the Mediterranean captured by a painter such as Vlaminck or Derain.[8] To what extent Heckel might have been aware of their work at so early a date remains open to question, though it is possible that such influences could have been mediated through the example of Pechstein, who had discovered the art of the Fauves at first hand in Paris during the winter of 1907–8.[9] According to a notice printed in the *Dresdner Journal*, paintings by Fauvist artists, including Derain, van Dongen, Friesz, Marquet and Vlaminck, were exhibited in Dresden at the Kunstsalon Richter in September 1908 at the same time as a showing of the Brücke members' own work.[10] Matisse, too, was known in Germany by 1909 at the latest, in part through the intermediary of his numerous German pupils, in part as a consequence of his exhibition in January of that year at Cassirer's in Berlin.[11] On the other hand, *House in Dangast* had been painted as early as the preceding summer, and it is perfectly possible that Heckel had arrived independently at similar conclusions, and that his later statement that he was unaware of contemporary French art at this time should be taken quite literally.[12]

Erich Heckel 1883–1970

24 Female Head (Portrait of Siddi Heckel)
Weiblicher Kopf

1913
Oil on canvas, 70 × 60 cm
Initialled/dated lower right: 'EH 13'. Inscribed on the original stretcher (since discarded): 'Weiblicher Kopf'[1]
The painting had been put on a new stretcher prior to its acquisition by the present owner, and a number of repairs undertaken to secure areas of flaking and paint loss to the portrait on the recto. At some point prior to this, a coat of varnish had been applied to the painting on the verso: this may have led to a darkening or discolouration of the portrait which, according to Roman Norbert Ketterer, comparing it with his recollections of the 1950s was originally brighter and more intense in its colours[2]
Accession no.1986.20 (a)

Verso The Swing

Provenance
Collection of the artist
Galerie Ferdinand Möller, Berlin
Museum für Kunst und Landesgeschichte, Hanover
Galerie Ferdinand Möller, Berlin, subsequently Cologne
Susanne Wenzl-Möller, Lucerne
Robert Gore Rifkind Collection, Los Angeles, CA
Thyssen-Bornemisza Collection, 1986[3]

Exhibitions
Frankfurt am Main, Kunstsalon Ludwig Schames, 1919, no.15
Hanover, Kestner-Gesellschaft, 1919, *XXII. Sonderausstellung. Erich Heckel. Gemälde, Graphik*, no.19
Cologne, Galerie Ferdinand Möller, 1951–2, *Die alten Meister der modernen Kunst in Deutschland*, no.10
Venice, 1952, *XXVI Biennale. (Germania)*, no.5
Lucerne, Kunstmuseum, 1953, *Deutsche Kunst. Meisterwerke des 20. Jahrhunderts*, no.19
Stuttgart, Württembergischer Kunstverein, 1957, *Erich Heckel. Werke der Brückezeit 1907–1917*, no.47
Essen 1958, no.48 [as 'Frauenbildnis']
Berlin, Deutsche Gesellschaft für bildende Künste/Lausanne, Musée Cantonal des Beaux-Arts, 1968–9, *Berlin XX. Jahrhundert/Berlin XXe Siècle: de l'expressionisme à l'art contemporain*, no.34
Lugano 1989, no.15
Expressionism and Modern German Painting, 1989–90, no.9
Rome 1990–91, no.15

Literature
Museum der Gegenwart, II, no.2 (1931–2): 88, ill. p.85
Vogt (1965), 1913/4
Roters (1984), pp.287, 289
See also Felix (1983), pp.211f; Gabler (1983), p.75

Notes
1 I am grateful to Robert Gore Rifkind, Los Angeles, and to Christine Vigiletti, Registrar of the Robert Gore Rifkind Collection, for supplying numerous details regarding the previous history of the work, and especially inscriptions and old labels on the original stretcher, which was removed during restoration of the painting
2 Letter dated 30 September 1987 to Baron H.H. Thyssen-Bornemisza; Lugano-Castagnola, Thyssen-Bornemisza Collection, archive
3 Acquired directly from the previous owner

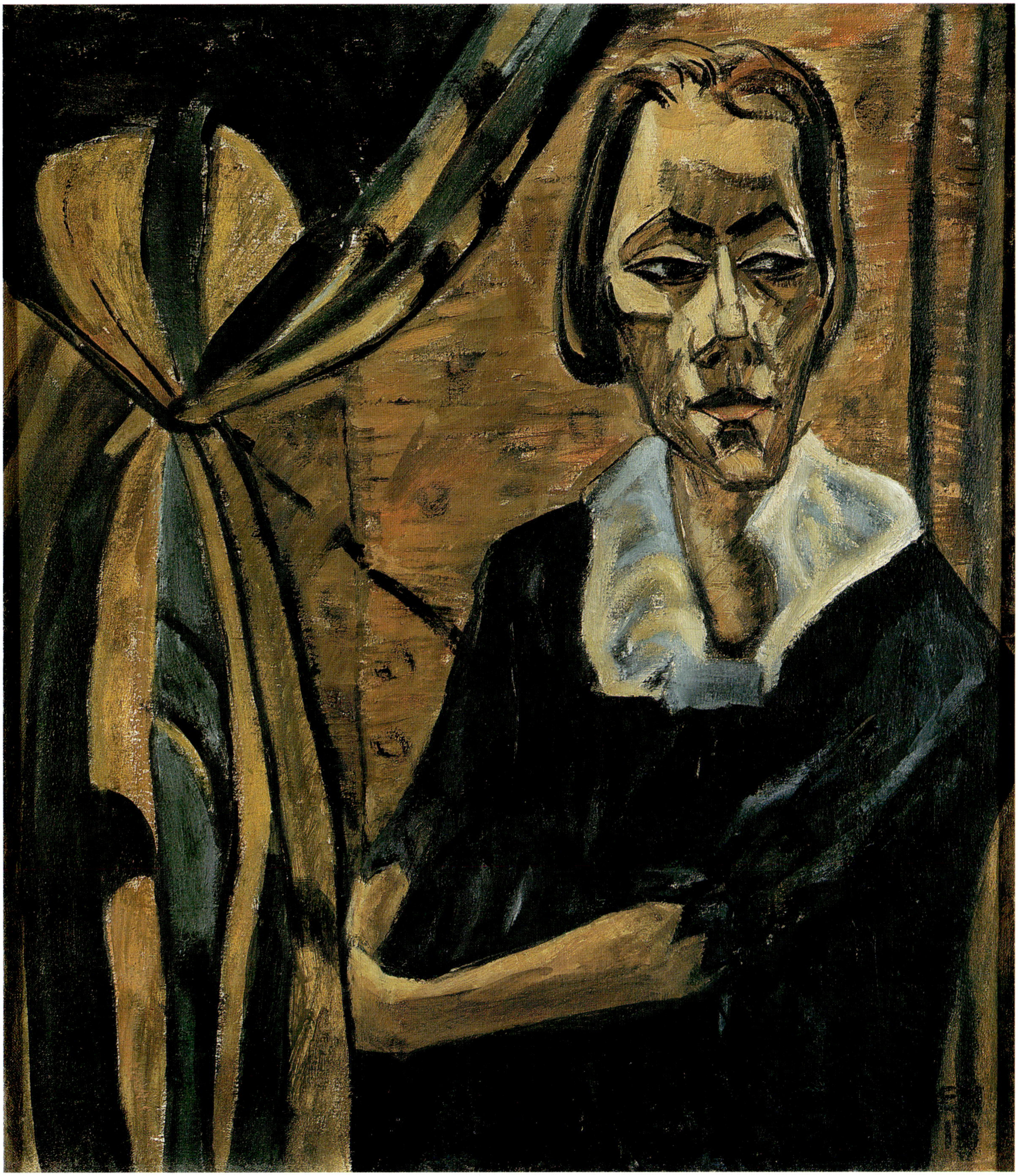

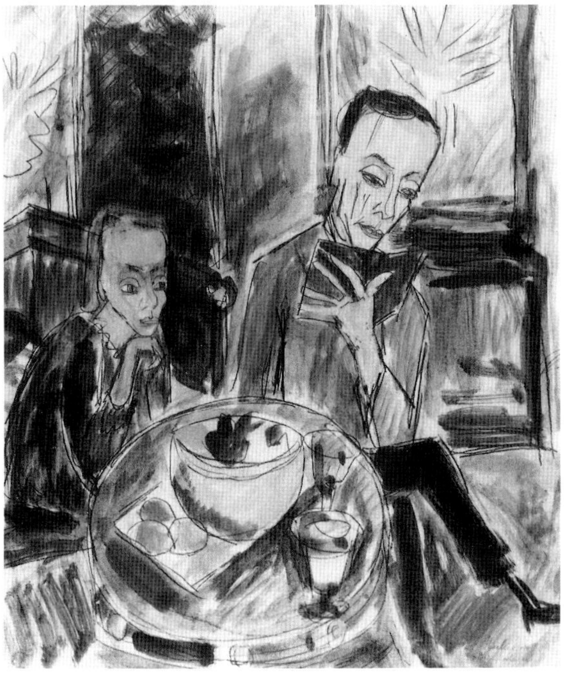

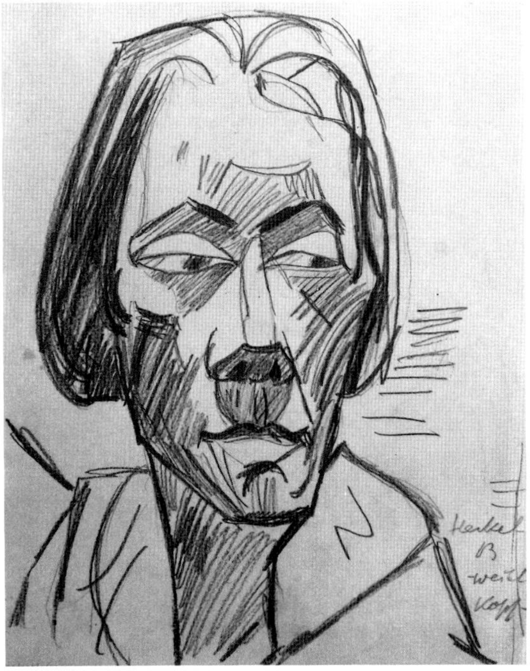

FIG 1 Erich Heckel, *Reading Aloud*, 1913–14, watercolour and pencil, 45.4 × 37.3 cm (Berlin, Brücke-Museum, gift of Siddi Heckel in memory of the artist)

FIG 2 Erich Heckel, *Female Head*, 1913, pencil, 27.5 × 22.4 cm (Hemmenhofen, estate of Erich Heckel)

FIG 3 Erich Heckel, *Reading Aloud*, 1914, oil on canvas, 95 × 80 cm (Private collection)

The sitter in *Female Head* is Heckel's wife, the dancer Sidi (later Siddi) Riha (real name Milda Frieda Georgi). The couple first became acquainted in 1910, and were eventually married on 19 June 1915. Siddi may have been the cause of a somewhat greater distance which Heckel seemed inclined to put between himself and the other members of the Brücke. In a rueful addendum to a postcard to Otto Mueller dated 19 December 1910, Kirchner noted disconsolately: 'A little dancer has lured him away from us wretches'.[4] Siddi apparently played an active role in the discussions of art and literature, and readings of literary works, which were a central feature of Heckel's life in Berlin. Her features are easily recognizable in a number of his other paintings and graphic works dating from this period,[5] as well as a watercolour of 1913–14 entitled *Reading Aloud* which shows Siddi together with Walter Kaesbach, later director of the Angermuseum in Erfurt and commander of Heckel's army medical unit in Flanders, presumably taking part in just such a literary séance (see fig.1).[6] This watercolour is related to an oil painting of 1914, likewise entitled *Reading Aloud* (fig.3) which, though compositionally similar, includes in addition a depiction of Heckel himself.[7] There is also preserved among the artist's drawings a pencil study for the present painting (fig.2).

The picture has had a chequered history. It was purchased from the Galerie Ferdinand Möller in Berlin in 1930 by the then Museum für Kunst und Landesgeschichte, Hanover.[8] It is listed under PNM 592 in the museum's handwritten inventory of paintings, which also shows that it was confiscated, together with other works by modern masters, in 1937.[9] It was, however, evidently considered saleable, in accordance with the Nazi régime's policy of disposing of at least some works of 'degenerate' art in exchange for hard currency, since it subsequently appeared on a list of paintings acquired by its original vendor, Ferdinand Möller, presumably from the so-called Depository for Degenerate Art at Schloss Niederschönhausen, just outside Berlin.[10] (Möller was one of four dealers primarily responsible for 'converting' – which in many instances was identical with rescuing – works of 'degenerate art' confiscated from the German museums; the others were Bernhard A.Boehmer, Hildebrand Gurlitt and Karl Buchholz.)[11] This list, which also includes paintings by Nolde and Schmidt-Rottluff, is dated 17 April 1940; although Möller's records show that the picture was then valued at $30,[12] a further document

Notes

4 Gabler (1983), ill. p.76

5 For example the oil painting *Müde Tänzerin*: see Vogt (1965), 1911/2

6 Compare also Heckel's 1914 woodcut of the same subject: see Dube (1964), no.272

7 Vogt (1965), 1914/4; see also the auction catalogue *Auktion 206, I. Teil (150 ausgewählte Kunstwerke des 19. und 20. Jahrhunderts)*, Berne (Galerie Kornfeld) 1991, lot 45

8 See *Museum der Gegenwart*, loc. cit. ('Nachrichten. Erwerbungen von Werken neuerer Kunst ...'), pp.85ff

9 I am grateful to Dr Hans Werner Grohn, Director of the Niedersächsisches Landesmuseum Hannover, for helping to confirm the details given here regarding the acquisition and confiscation of the picture; see also Roh (1962), p.194

10 Roters (1984), p.287, Doc.110

11 See Andreas Hüneke, '"Dubiose Händler operieren im Dunst der Macht". Vom Handel mit "entarteter" Kunst', in *Alfred Flechtheim. Sammler, Kunsthändler, Verleger*, exh. cat., Düsseldorf, Kunstmuseum, 1987, pp.101–5

12 See n.12 to p.325

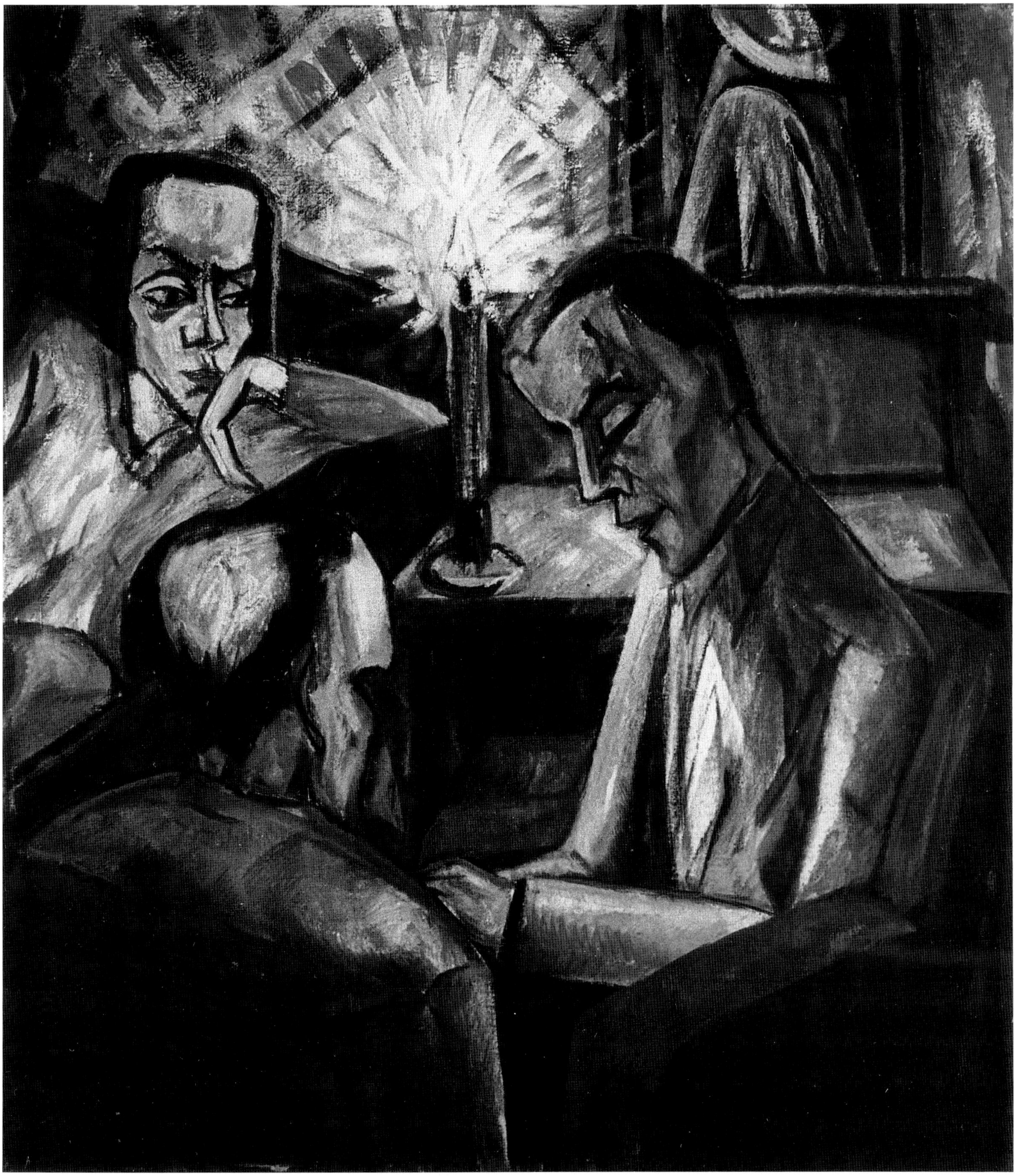

dated 5 March 1941 makes clear that it was not actually sold but exchanged, together with twenty-seven further works mainly by artists of the Brücke, against a landscape painting with castle and knight by F.E. Oehme.[13]

Contrary to the repeated directives of Goebbels's propaganda ministry regarding the necessity of selling works of 'degenerate' art abroad, Möller, it appears, simply kept the painting until after the war, when it was shown by the newly re-established Galerie Ferdinand Möller in Cologne as part of their 1951 exhibition *The Old Masters of Modern Art in Germany*. It remained in the possession of the gallery until at least 1957, after which it passed into the private collection of Möller's daughter, Susanne Wenzl-Möller, in Lucerne. In 1977 it was offered for sale at auction by the firm of Kornfeld & Klipstein in Berne[14] and subsequently acquired by the American collector Robert Gore Rifkind; hence, in 1986, directly to the present owner.

On the verso of the canvas is an earlier painting by Heckel, *The Swing*, depicting a couple with two children.

Notes
13 Roters (1984), p.287, Doc.112, also p.289
14 Kornfeld & Klipstein, Berne, 8–9 June 1977 (*Auktion 162*, lot 352)

24 *verso* The Swing

1910
Oil on canvas, 70 × 60 cm
Unsigned/undated
Varnished using a high-gloss varnish
Accession no.1986.20(b)

Literature
Vogt (1965), 1910/15

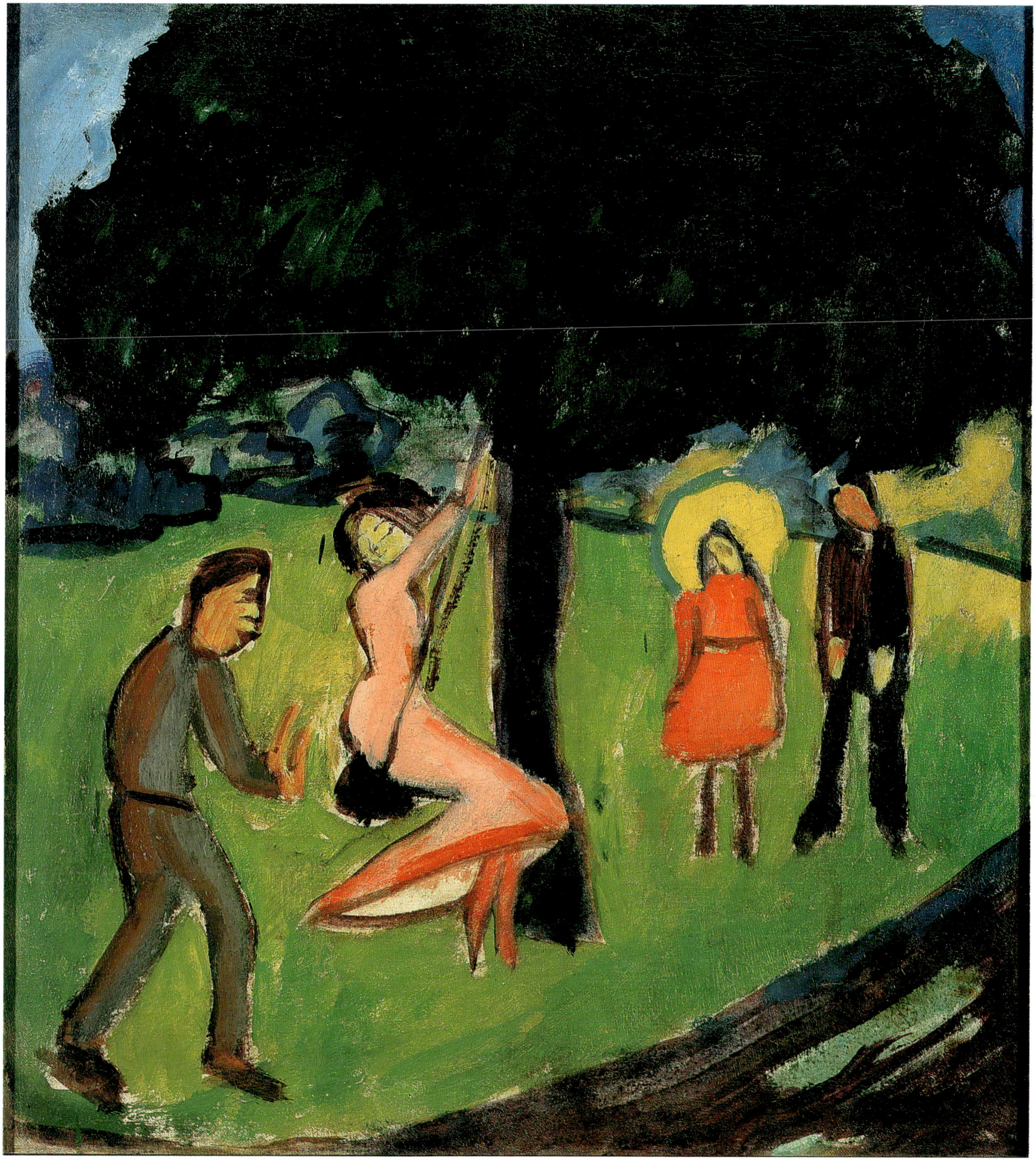

Erich Heckel 1883–1970

25 In Front of Red Curtain
Vor rotem Vorhang

1912
Pencil and watercolour on paper, 44 × 36 cm
Signed/dated lower right: 'Heckel 12'; inscribed: 'Vor rotem Vorhang'
The paper is slightly yellow, and shows some bulging. Otherwise condition is good
Accession no.1974.17

Provenance
Estate of the artist
Galerie R.N.Ketterer, Campione d'Italia
Thyssen-Bornemisza Collection, 1974

Exhibitions
Stuttgart, Württembergischer Kunstverein, 1957, *Erich Heckel. Werke der Brückezeit 1907–1917*, no.67
Bremen 1975, no.26

Literature
R.N.Ketterer, *Moderne Kunst VII*, Campione d'Italia (Galerie R.N.Ketterer) 1971, p.84, no.43, ill. p.85
Kiel (1974), p.50, ill. p.51

The interior depicted evokes vividly the atmosphere of the Brücke artists' studios of the Dresden and early Berlin periods – in this instance Heckel's Berlin studio located at no.60 Mommsenstrasse, which he took over from Otto Mueller in autumn 1911, and which he proceeded to decorate with figurative textiles and wall-hangings.[1] The studio was also apparently furnished with hand-carved pieces such as the primitivizing stool on which, in *In Front of Red Curtain*, the female nude is seated.

Note
1 Among the drawings preserved in Heckel's estate are a number of designs from late 1911 onwards for textiles and other decorations for the Mommsenstrasse studio: see, e.g., Gabler (1983), p.87

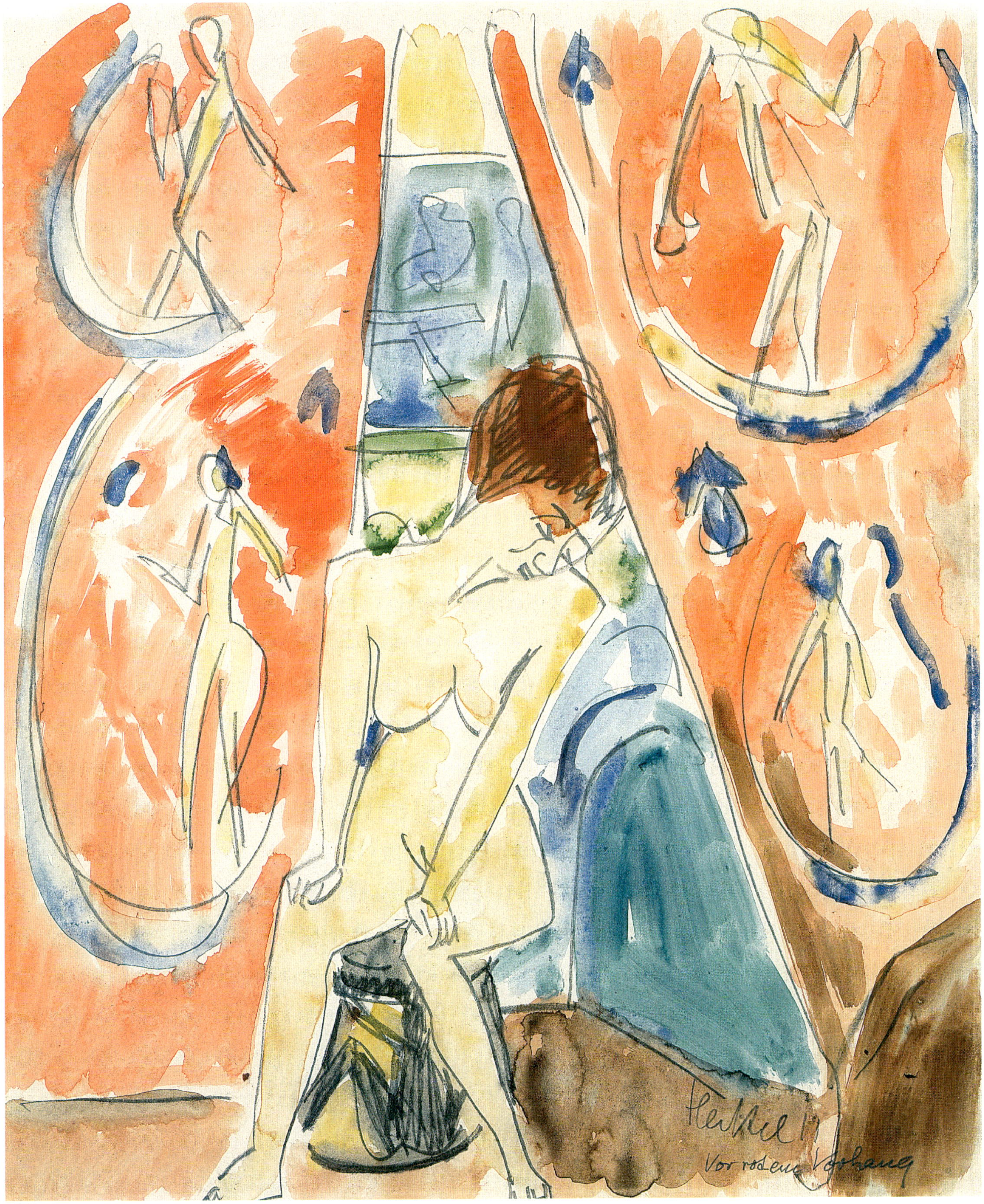

Though the watercolour does not show sufficient detail for precise identification to be possible, this particular stool appears to consist of a naked crouching figure supporting a carved seat, a device characteristic of items of furniture made at this period for their own use by both Kirchner and Heckel (compare *Fränzi in front of Carved Chair* [46]). The angular form of the sitter also betrays the influence exerted by primitive art on Heckel's own stylistic development at this time, in particular examples of African sculpture he had seen in the ethnographic collections in Dresden and Berlin.

For reasons that are unclear, this watercolour has hitherto been ascribed to 1913.[2] It is, however, signed and dated by the artist 'Heckel 12'; it is also closely related in subject and composition to his painting of the same year *Two Girls beneath Red Curtain* (fig.1).[3] Two further watercolours, dated 1911 and 1912, in the estate of the artist show a similar scene: a studio interior with parted curtains forming an inverted 'v', revealing glimpses of primitivizing decor and including in each case a naked female figure.[4] Evidently, this group of related works, to which [25] also belongs, must have been executed within a few weeks, or at the most months of each other, in the course of winter 1911–12.

Notes

2 See, e.g., Kiel (1974), p.50

3 Vogt (1965), 1912/4 (present whereabouts unknown)

4 See *Erich Heckel*, exh. cat., Reutlingen, Hans Thoma-Gesellschaft, 1988, no.11, fig.10 (*Girl between Curtains*, 1911) and no.18, fig.17 (*Nude in a Room*, 1912). I am indebted to Herr Hans Geissler, administrator of the estate of Erich Heckel, for drawing these watercolours to my attention

FIG 1 Erich Heckel, *Two Girls beneath Red Curtain*, 1912, oil on canvas, 120 × 60 cm (present location unknown)

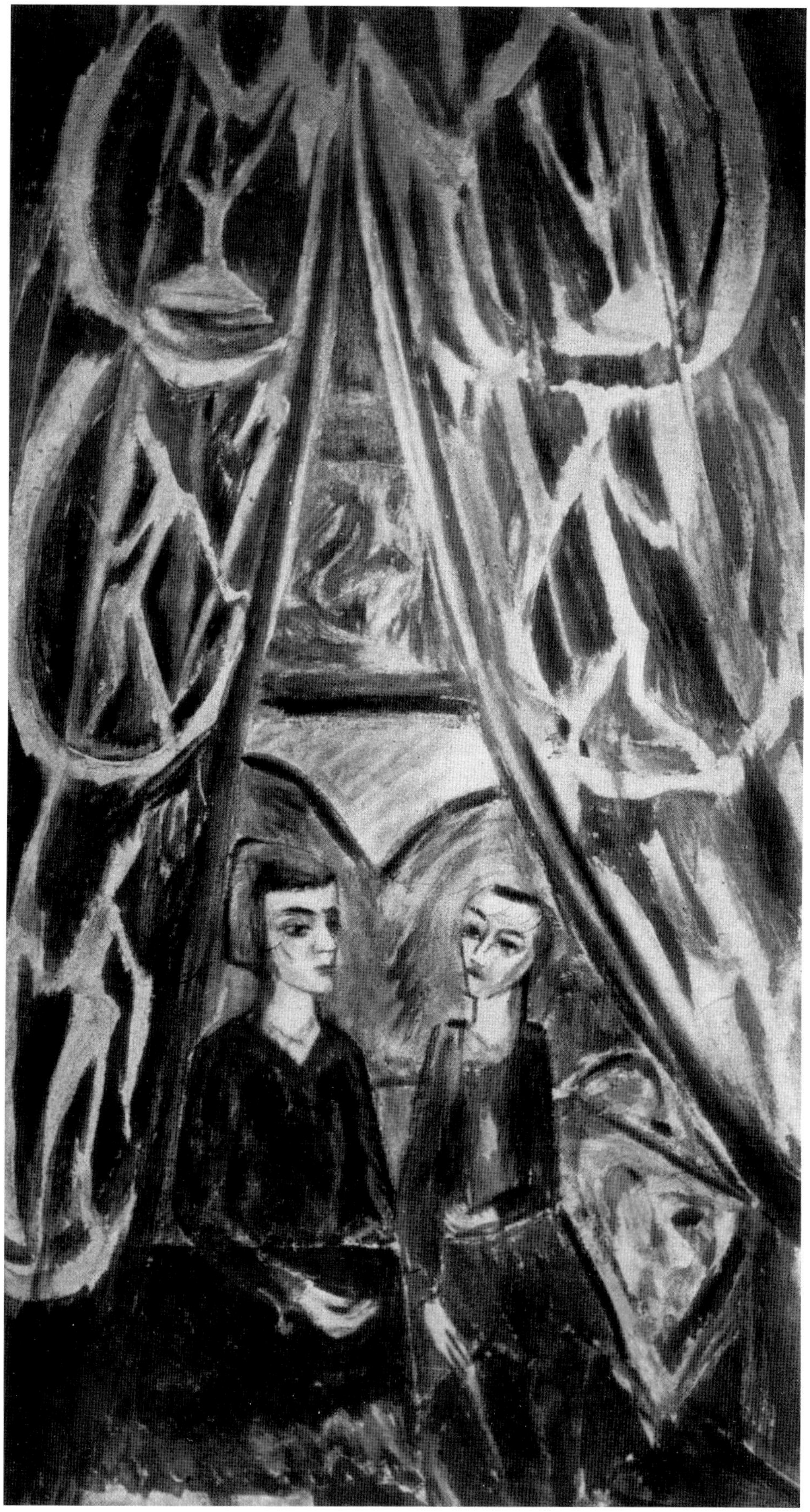

Erich Heckel 1883–1970

26 Bathers on the Beach

1913
Pencil and watercolour on paper, 38 × 49 cm
Signed/dated lower right: 'Erich Heckel 13'
Paper slightly distorted at corners; otherwise condition is good
Accession no.1970.36

Provenance
Galerie Motte, Geneva
Thyssen-Bornemisza Collection, 1970[1]

Literature
Kiel (1974), p.50, ill. p.49

On the basis of subject matter and date, this beach scene can be ascribed to Heckel's first visit to Osterholz, on the German Baltic coast in the region of Flensburg, in the summer of 1913. Osterholz in later years was to play an important part in his life, as working retreat and a haven from public attention during the period of Nazi oppression.

According to the recollections of his widow, Siddi, Heckel had set out on an exploration of the Schleswig-Holstein peninsula with the express intention of finding a stretch of countryside in which he would 'be able to work for many years to come.'[2] After spending a few days at Mellingstedt near Hamburg as guests of Gustav Schiefler, one of the principal early patrons and supporters of the Brücke, in mid-June 1913 she and Heckel first travelled up the German North Sea coast as far as Niebüll, where years later Nolde was to build his last house, then crossed the peninsula to reach the Baltic port of Flensburg, a short distance from the island of Alsen. In the course of a boat trip which took the couple up Flensburg Sound and around Alsen, Heckel recognized, even from the water, the undulating landscape around Osterholz as the environment he was seeking. Following the advice of the ship's captain, he rented an old barn from a shipwright by the name of Peter Hansen; in 1918, he was able to purchase the property, together with the adjoining house.[3]

Notes
1 Acquired at auction, Geneva, 9 December 1970, lot 163
2 Siddi Heckel's account of her and Heckel's first visits to Mellingstedt and Osterholz are published in Wietek (1974), pp.144ff
3 Ibid., pp.145–6

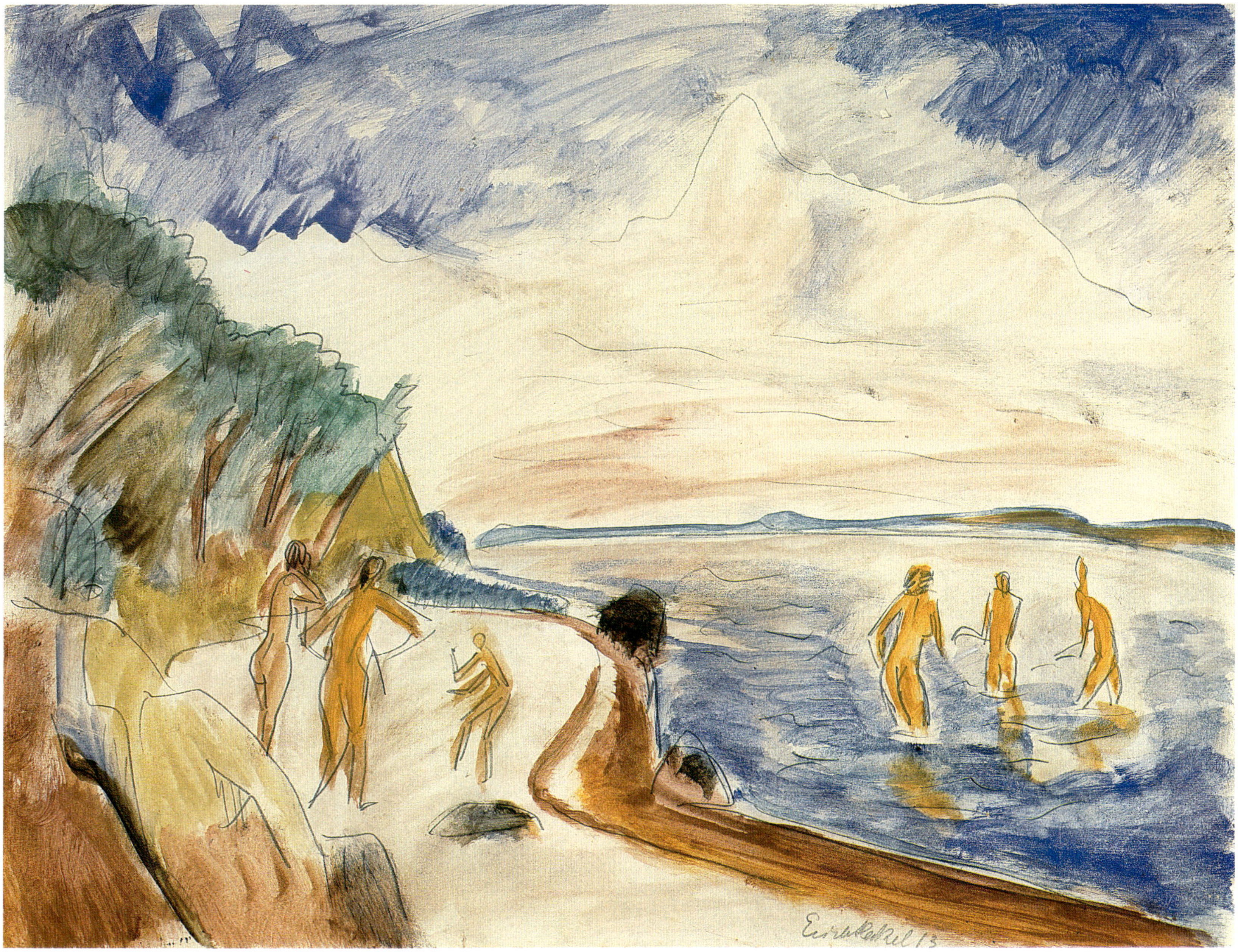

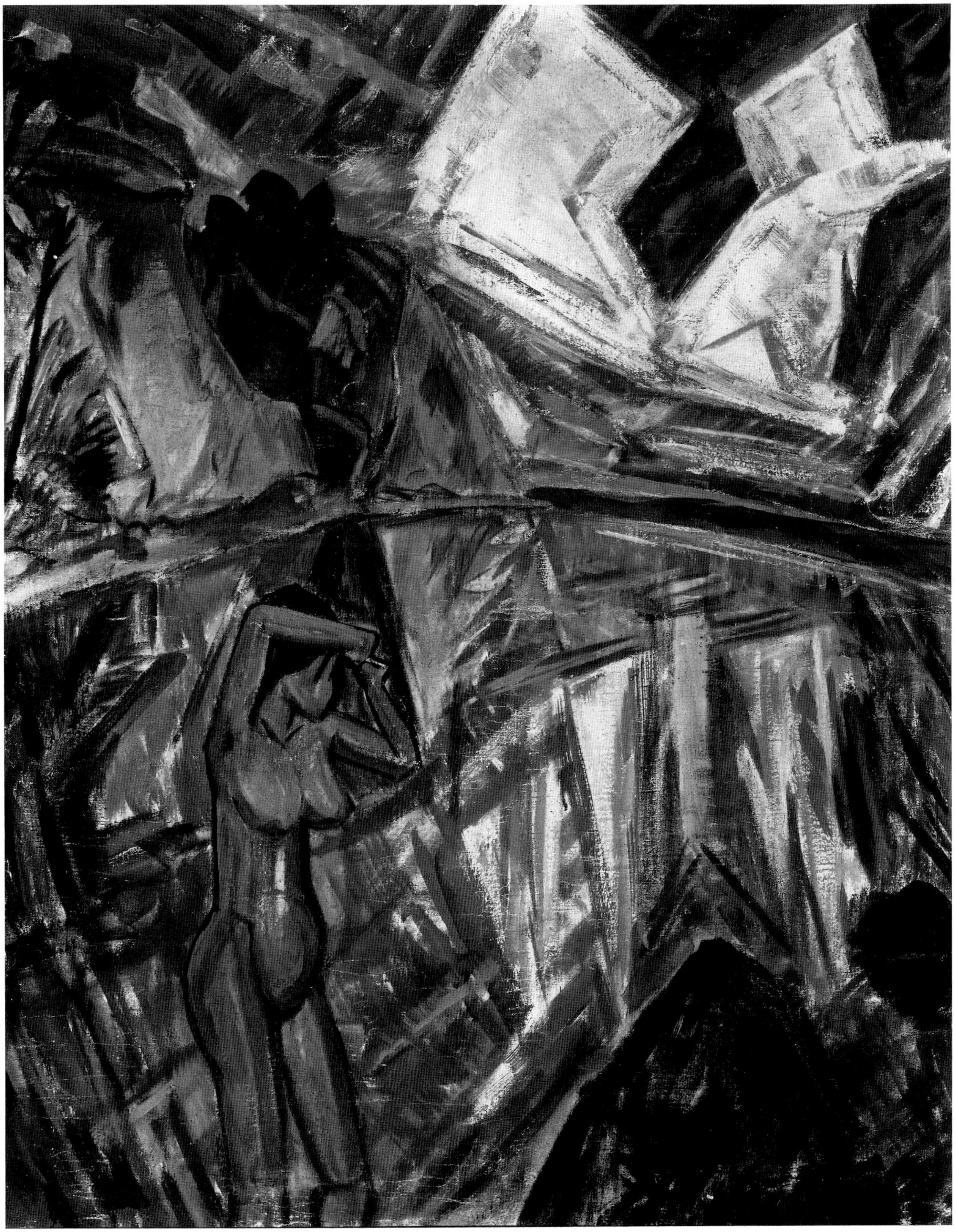

FIG 1 Erich Heckel, *Glass Day*, 1913, oil on canvas, 117 × 92 cm (Munich, Bayerische Staatsgemäldesammlungen, Staatsgalerie moderner Kunst, gift of Markus and Martha Kruss, inv. no.14534)

Gerhard Wietek, in the catalogue of the Heckel exhibition shown at the Altona Museum in Hamburg in 1971, has pointed to the particular significance of this still relatively little-known region in the context of the artist's development, emphasizing the central theme of naked figures in a landscape in the Osterholz drawings and watercolours which, rather than the better-known paintings, capture the essence of the 'undulating rhythm of the fields and meadows and shaded coves, whose colours change with the seasons ... the steeply shelving coastline with its ravines overgrown with trees and bushes, and its beaches irregularly dotted with huge boulders.'[4]

In 1913, however, Heckel was to some extent still feeling his way in his treatment of these novel surroundings, despite the fact that they provided the setting for one of the greatest of all his pre-war paintings, the celebrated *Glass Day*, also of 1913 (fig.1). He himself described the fruits of his labours of this first summer at Osterholz in rather modest terms, writing several times between July and September to Walter Kaesbach about his studies, 'among them a number of drawings which may perhaps survive ...',[5] and about his attempts to evoke the particular charm of the landscape, 'the huge rocks on the foreshore and the cliffs falling steeply away to the beach ...'[6] And on another occasion, also to Kaesbach: 'The sun has meanwhile grown even yellower, and the foliage browner. Naked forms, brilliant yellow, leap about in thc blue-black water, while the rocks, blue and dark-toned, and the limestone cliffs cast long shadows on the shore.'[7]

Notes

4 *Erich Heckel 1883–1970*, exh. cat., Hamburg, Altonaer Museum, 1971, quoted after Felix (1983), p.232; see also ibid., p.212

5 To Kaesbach, 23 August 1913: Gabler (1983), p.120

6 Ibid. (letter of 9 July 1913)

7 Undated (September 1913): Gabler (1983), loc. cit.

Albert Henrich 1899–1971

27 Portrait of the painter A.M.Tränkler

1926
Oil on canvas, 81 × 62 cm
Signed/dated lower right: 'A.Henrich 26'
There is a history of flaking and some losses, which have been retouched, also scattered abrasions throughout. The varnish, which is glossy, shows some drips at the left-hand edge of the painting
Accession no.1980.27

Provenance
Collection of the artist
Michael Henrich
Galleria del Levante, Milan/Munich
Fischer Fine Art, London
Thyssen-Bornemisza Collection, 1980

Exhibitions
Wuppertal, Kunst- und Museumsverein/Von der Heydt-Museum, 1967, *Magischer Realismus in Deutschland 1920–1933*, no.39
Milan, Rotonda di via Besana, 1971–2, *Il Realismo in Germania*, ill. p.66
Saint Étienne, Musée d'Art et d'Industrie/Chambéry, Musée d'Art et d'Histoire, 1974, *Réalismes en Allemagne, 1919–1933*, no.61
Vienna, Museum des 20. Jahrhunderts, 1977, *Neue Sachlichkeit und Realismus*, no.79
Modern Masters from the Thyssen-Bornemisza Collection, 1984–6, no.45
Lugano 1989, no.50
Rome 1990–91, no.16

Literature
See Schmied (1969), figs.122, 205; *Düsseldorf, Stadt der Künstler*, exh. cat., Düsseldorf-Stockum, Vortragszentrum der Neuen Messe, 1971, n.p.

A pupil of Keller, Männchen, Spatz and Ederer at the Düsseldorf Academy, Albert Henrich remains one of the least known representatives of the realist tendency in German art of the 1920s and 1930s. His work consists predominantly of landscapes, portraits, and above all still-life, in which the influence of Dutch seventeenth century painting is clearly evident.[1] Though his style in many ways resembles that of the realist artists associated with the Neue Sachlichkeit movement, he does not appear to have shared their political convictions and, unlike the majority of them, continued to enjoy professional success during the Nazi era in Germany. He was a prominent member of the Society for the Promotion of Visual Art in Düsseldorf (Gesellschaft zur Förderung der Düsseldorfer bildenden Kunst e.V.), and showed repeatedly at their exhibitions held at the Düsseldorf Kunsthalle during the 1930s. He was also represented by three paintings at the *Grosse Kunstausstellung* in Düsseldorf in 1937, which consisted largely of the kind of anaemically realistic depictions of heroic subjects favoured by the Nazi régime. He founded the Düsseldorfer Künstlergruppe in 1949, and was its first president. He died in Düsseldorf in 1971.

It has so far proved impossible to discover anything whatever about the sitter other than his name, Alfons Maria Tränkler, and the fact that he was a painter. This portrait, in its sober, understated naturalism, in some ways recalls Schlichter's *Oriental Journalist* [101]; Henrich's handling of paint is, however, far more restrained than Schlichter's, and the colouring of the portrait more subdued, allowing only the hands and face of the sitter to stand out as the dominant elements of the composition.

Note
1 For illustrations of other works by Henrich, see Schmied, loc. cit.

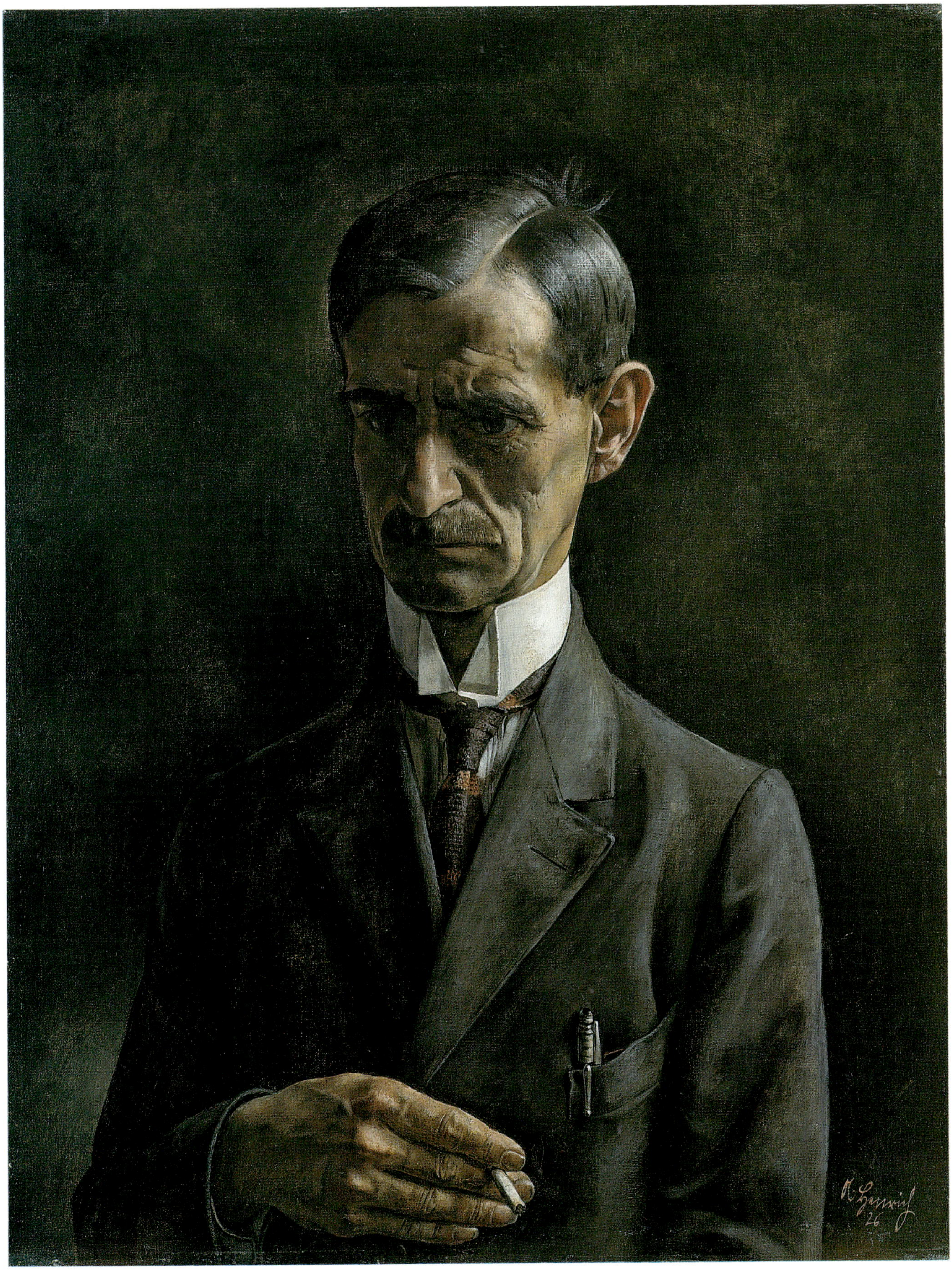

Karl Hofer 1878–1955

28 Church in Malcantone

1938
Oil on canvas, 57.5 × 78 cm
Initialled/dated lower left: 'H 38'
In good condition. The painting is unvarnished
Accession no.1962.3

Provenance
Stuttgarter Kunstkabinett, Stuttgart
Thyssen-Bornemisza Collection, 1962[1]

Literature
Kiel (1974), p.52, ill. p.53
See also Ida Katherine Rigby, *Karl Hofer*, New York 1976

Often classed as an Expressionist (a label which, like Beckmann, he explicitly rejected),[2] Hofer's relationship with Expressionism was, though enduring, oblique and problematic. As Rigby observes, his oeuvre was essentially conservative in form, communication and sources. He acknowledged no affinities between his own works and those of his contemporaries, and though his art on occasion betrays reminiscences of Cubism, Surrealism and even abstraction, his dalliance with these avant-garde movements was at best superficial.[3] By far the most lasting influence was that of the so-called *Deutsch-Römer*, the German classicists of the nineteenth century. In Hofer's art, the dark, even tortured visions evoked in a small number of works painted in the aftermath of the Great War – visions that surfaced again in his painting with the advent of Fascism – coexist with classicising nudes and rigorously composed landscapes which clearly emulate the model of German nineteenth-century predecessors such as Hans von Marées.

An outspoken opponent of the Nazis, Hofer was stripped of his teaching position almost as soon as the National Socialists came to power in Germany in 1933, and branded as a 'degenerate' artist. During the 1930s, he spent much of his time in Ticino, the Italian-speaking part of Switzerland, where he had bought a house at La Torrazza di Caslano, not far from Lugano. From this period prior to the outbreak of the Second World War dates an important group of paintings of the surrounding landscape, including *Church in Malcantone*, the subject in this case being taken from the area of Malcantone, the region which extends westward from Lake Lugano towards Lake Maggiore and the border with Italy. It has not, however, been possible so far to locate the church depicted in the present painting, and indeed, some parts of the region are now so built up as to render precise identification of the particular topography somewhat problematic.

Notes
1 Acquired at the 37th auction of the Stuttgarter Kunstkabinett, Pt.1, 3–4 May 1962, lot 165
2 Rigby (1976), p.109
3 Ibid., p.xiv

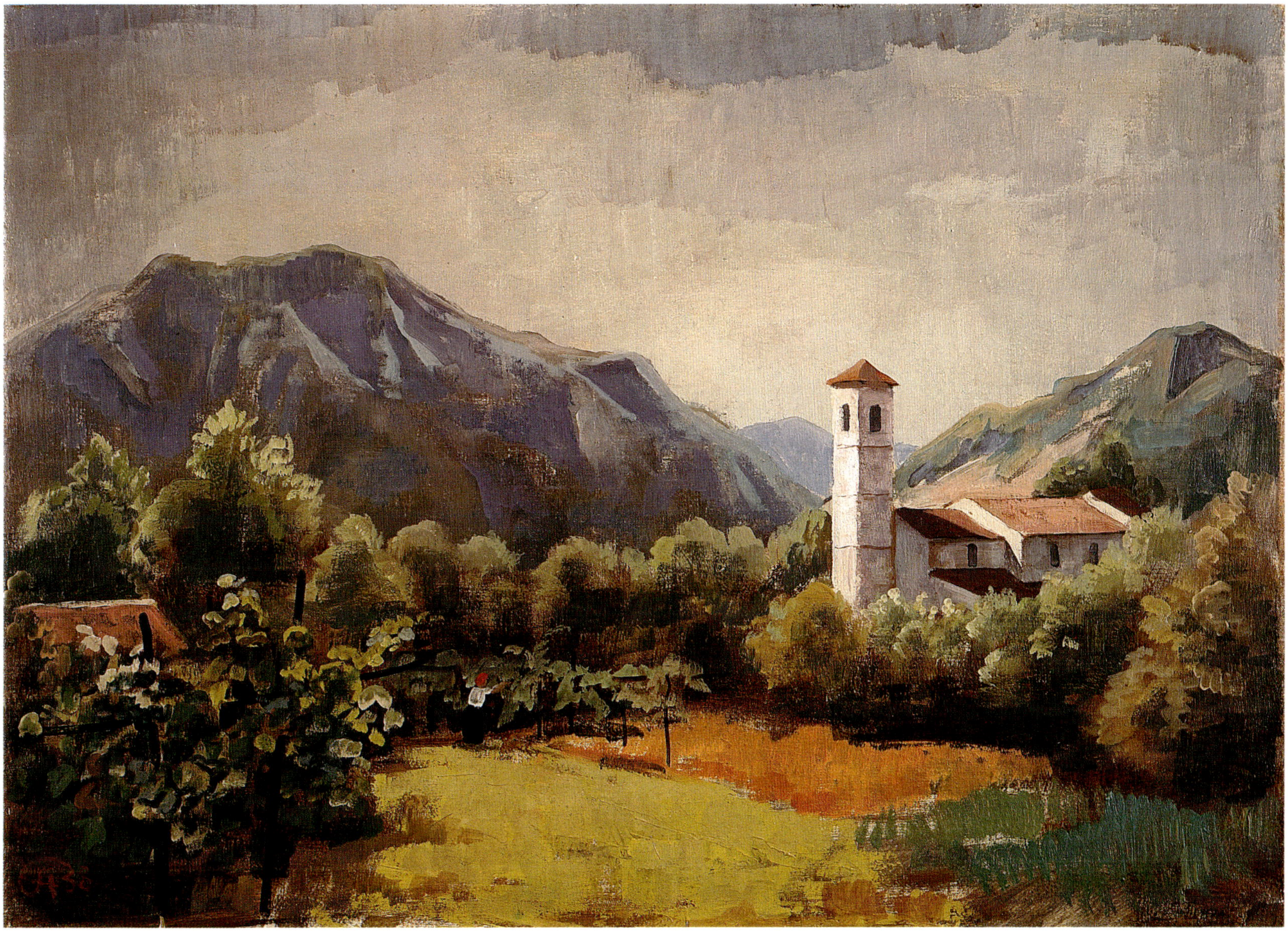

Karl Hubbuch 1891–1979

29 Twice Hilde II

*c*1929[1]
Oil on canvas mounted on board, 150 × 77 cm
Signed lower left: 'Hubbuch'
The original canvas has been cut at the right-hand side and mounted on board. The paint layer is brittle, with scattered losses. Extensive drying cracks throughout background and numerous surface scratches. Otherwise condition is good. The painting is unvarnished
Accession no.1978.88

Provenance
Collection of the artist
Galleria del Levante, Milan/Munich
Private collection
Fischer Fine Art, London
Thyssen-Bornemisza Collection, 1978

Exhibitions
Stuttgart, Württembergischer Kunstverein, 1971, *Realismus zwischen Revolution und Machtergreifung 1919–1933*, no.64 [as '1923']
Milan, Rotonda di via Besana, 1971–2, *Il Realismo in Germania*, ill. p.76 [as '1923']
Oldenburg, Kunstverein, 1972, *Maler der Wirklichkeit. Deutschland 1920–1932*, no.14 [as '1923']
Saint Étienne, Musée d'Art et d'Industrie/Chambéry, Musée d'Art et d'Histoire, 1974, *Réalismes en Allemagne, 1919–1933*, no.66 [as '1923']
Berlin, Staatliche Museen, Nationalgalerie, 1974, *Realismus und Sachlichkeit. Aspekte deutscher Kunst 1919–1933*, no.154 [as '1923']
Vienna, Museum des 20. Jahrhunderts, 1977, *Neue Sachlichkeit und Realismus*, no.91
London, Arts Council of Great Britain, 1979–80, *Neue Sachlichkeit and German Realism of the Twenties*, no.149 [as '1923']
Minneapolis, MN, Institute of Arts/Chicago, IL, Museum of Contemporary Art, 1980–81, *German Realism of the Twenties. The Artist as Social Critic*, no.3 [as '1923']
Karlsruhe, Badischer Kunstverein/Berlin, Staatliche Kunsthalle/Hamburg, Kunstverein, 1981–2, *Karl Hubbuch 1891–1979*, no.239 [as '*c*.1929']
USA tour 1982–4, no.48 [as '1923']
Modern Masters from the Thyssen-Bornemisza Collection, 1984–6, no.48 [as '1923']
Lugano 1989, no.47
Rome 1990–91, no.17

Literature
Wolfgang Hartmann, 'Karl Hubbuch. Leben und Werk', in Hubbuch (1981), pp.8ff, 25

Hubbuch, who studied with the graphic artist and designer Emil Orlik in Berlin, first made a name for himself during the early 1920s as a draughtsman and lithographer.[2] Only after he joined the staff of the Karlsruhe Academy (then known as the Badische Landeskunstschule) in 1924 as teaching assistant, where from 1928 he was professor, did he begin to devote himself to painting, as well as drawing and print-making. In 1926, he got to know Hilde Isai, a student at the school; they were married in 1927. Hilde later studied at the Bauhaus under the mathematician and photographer Walter Peterhans;[3] it was she who furnished their home with items of Bauhaus furniture, among them the famous tubular steel chairs designed by Marcel Breuer. These figure in a number of Hubbuch's drawings and paintings including *Twice Hilde II*, in fact a double portrait of his wife.

Notes
1 For discussion of proposed dating, see accompanying essay
2 For a detailed account of Hubbuch's training and early career, see Hartmann, op. cit., especially pp.8–20
3 Ibid., p.24

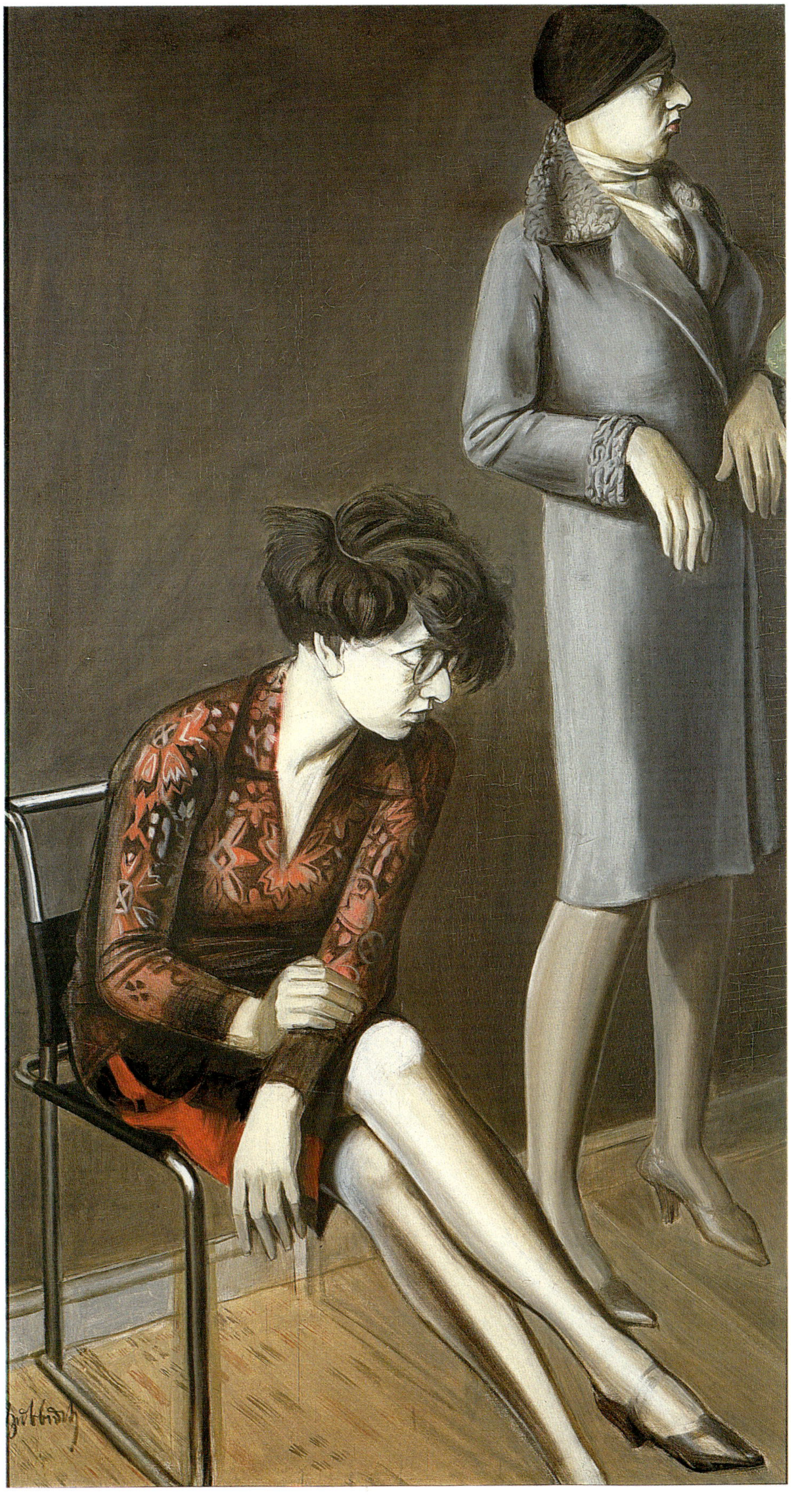

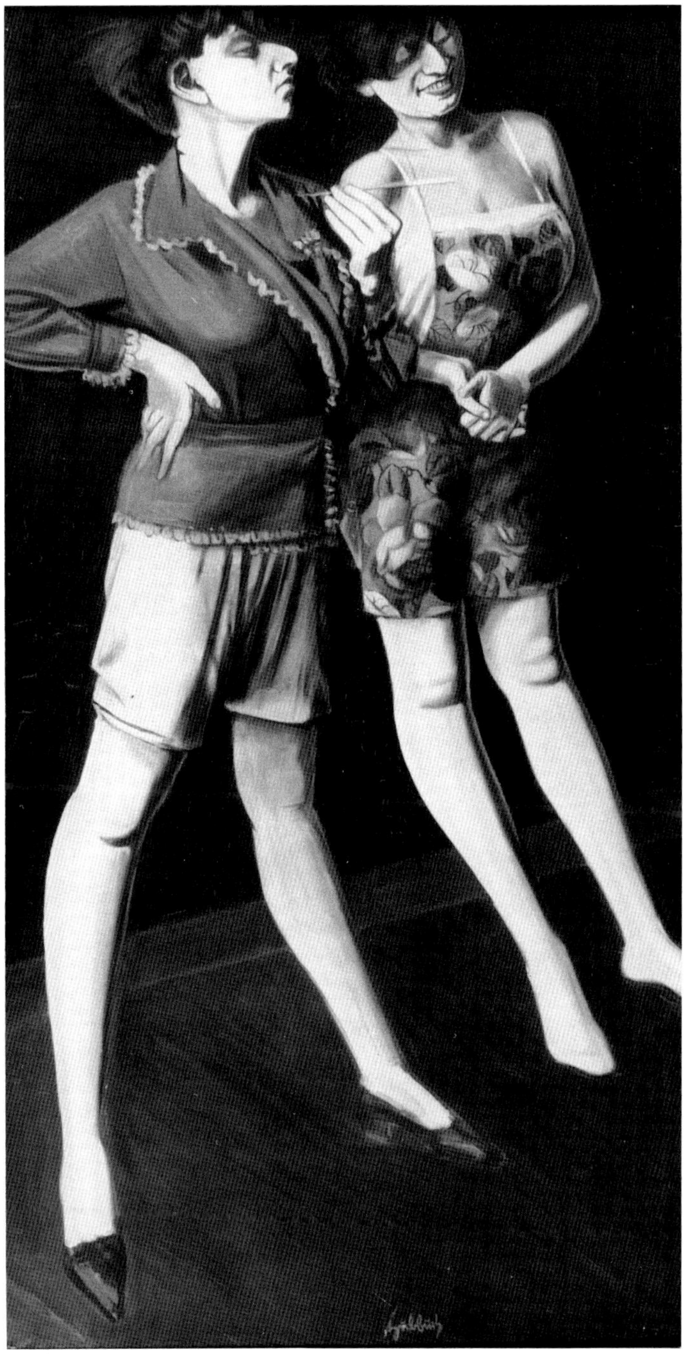

FIG 1 Karl Hubbuch, *Twice Hilde I*, *c*1929, oil on board, 150 × 77 cm (Munich, Bayerische Staatsgemäldesammlungen)

As preparatory studies reveal, the painting was originally conceived as a quadruple portrait which was later divided vertically into two halves, one half being eventually acquired by the Thyssen-Bornemisza Collection. The other half, which shows a more coquettish aspect of Hilde (fig.1), now belongs to the Bayerische Staatsgemäldesammlungen, Munich.[4] The Munich painting is known under the title *Twice Hilde I*; a related drawing (fig.2), now in Karlsruhe, showing the whole of the original composition makes clear, however, that the four images represented a progression from left to right, and that the composition was intended to be read in that way, the Thyssen painting being the left-hand half, the Munich painting the right-hand half of the originally more-or-less square picture.[5] Whether, seen in this light, the quadruple portrait may have been intended to represent stages in the evolution of Hilde's personality (from sullen spinster to joyous spouse?) remains open to speculation.

Notes

4 The Lugano and Munich paintings were shown reunited both in the 1979–80 Arts Council exhibition *Neue Sachlichkeit and German Realism of the Twenties* (nos.149 and 148) and in the Hubbuch retrospective exhibition shown in Karlsruhe, Berlin and Hamburg in 1981–2 (nos.239 and 238)

5 Two further drawings relating to the two halves of the composition were illustrated in *Les Réalismes*, exh. cat., Paris, Centre Georges Pompidou, 1980–81, p.521

Given that there are no known paintings by Hubbuch in oil or tempera which can be securely dated earlier than 1925,[6] and that he did not make Hilde's acquaintance until the following year, it is difficult to understand why *Twice Hilde II*, when exhibited and reproduced on numerous occasions during the 1970s and 1980s, should have repeatedly been ascribed to the impossibly early date of 1923. The foreword to the catalogue of the Hubbuch retrospective exhibition of 1981–2, the first serious attempt to examine his work in its entirety, warns of the uncritical stance adopted by earlier literature on the artist, the lack of any stylistic analysis or convincing account of his development, the neglect of considerations such as the iconography employed or the known circumstances of his life.[7] Not until that exhibition was the date '*c*.1929' first advanced for both halves of the painting, as well as for the Karlsruhe drawing – presumably for all the reasons outlined above. Though unsupported by any other documentation, the same date, *c*1929, for *Twice Hilde II* is likewise suggested here, on the grounds of technique, subject and style.[8]

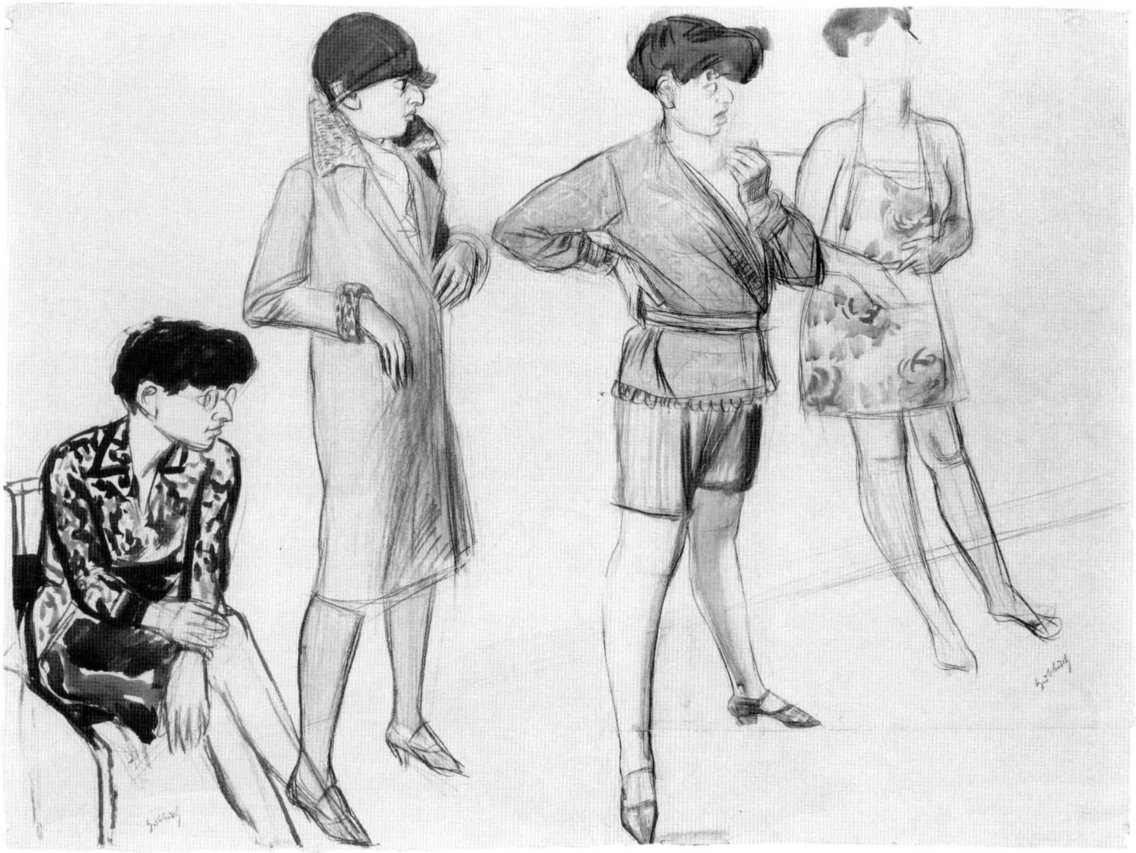

FIG 2 Karl Hubbuch, *Four Times Hilde*, pencil, black chalk and watercolour, 37.5 × 100 cm (Karlsruhe, Staatliche Kunsthalle)

According to information supplied by the Bayerische Staatsgemäldesammlungen, Munich, *Twice Hilde I* was sold by the artist to the Galerie Brockstedt in Hamburg at some point prior to 1972.[9] At that time, Hubbuch informed the purchaser that it was he himself who had cut up the quadruple portrait, ostensibly because it was damaged. By his own account, he also cropped the Munich painting at the left-hand edge and the Thyssen picture at the right-hand edge in order to remove traces of an obtrusive watermark, which presumably ran vertically down what must have been more or less the centre of the original composition. Though some traces of staining remain, there has been no way of substantially verifying this account, and it remains possible that other considerations may have influenced the artist's decision to divide the picture into two.

6 Hubbuch's *Die Schulstube* of 1925 has been identified as the artist's first known painting in oil: see Hartmann, 'K.H., Leben und Werk', in Hubbuch (1981), p.23, also fig.176

7 Hartmann, op. cit., p.8

8 It has also been suggested that the original painting *Four Times Hilde* may have been one of two works still in progress in the spring of 1929 which were entered by Hubbuch for the exhibition *Badisches Kunstschaffen der Gegenwart* held at the Kunsthalle in Mannheim during May–June that year. Both paintings were, however, rejected by the jury, though they accepted other works; see Hartmann, op. cit., p.25

9 It was subsequently acquired by the Galleria del Levante, Milan/Munich, by whom it was sold to the Bayerische Staatsgemäldesammlungen. I am grateful to the Galerie Brockstedt, Hamburg, and to Dr Ulrich Bischoff, Munich, for providing me with information concerning the history of the painting

Johannes Itten 1888–1967

30 Group of Houses in Spring
Häusergruppe im Frühling

1916
Oil on canvas, 90 × 75 cm
Signed on back of canvas: 'Itten'
The paint-ground complex is extremely brittle. There is a history of scattered flaking, some of which has been retouched. There is also evident surface grime. The painting is unvarnished
An old label formerly affixed to the stretcher bears an inscription in the artist's hand: '5. Häusergruppe im Frühling 1916. Itten'[1]
Accession no.1962.2

Provenance
Collection of the artist
Stuttgarter Kunstkabinett, Stuttgart
Thyssen-Bornemisza Collection, 1962[2]

Exhibitions
Zurich, Kunstgewerbemuseum, 1923[3]
Berlin, Der Sturm, 1923, *123. Sturm-Ausstellung (2. Gesamtausstellung Johannes Itten)*
Weimar, Landesmuseum, 1923, *Bauhausmeister*
Lübeck, Overbeck-Gesellschaft, 1931–2[4]
Amsterdam, Stedelijk Museum, 1957, *Johannes Itten*, no.5
Baden-Baden, Staatliche Kunsthalle, 1958–9, *Max Ackermann, Johannes Itten, Boris Kleint, Friedrich Vordemberge-Gildewart*, no.82 [as '1915']
Stuttgart, Württembergischer Kunstverein, 1961, *Hoelzel und sein Kreis*, no.197
Zurich, Kunsthaus, 1964, *Johannes Itten*, no.6
Düsseldorf, Kunstverein, 1965–6, *Johannes Itten*, no.14
Berne, Kunsthalle, 1971, *Johannes Itten*, no.25
Bremen 1975, no.29
Münster, Westfälisches Landesmuseum, 1980, *Johannes Itten. Gemälde, Gouachen, Aquarelle, Tuschen, Zeichnungen*, no.15
Modern Masters from the Thyssen-Bornemisza Collection, 1984–6, no.49
Luxemburg/Munich/Vienna 1988, no.34
Lugano 1989, no.41
Expressionism and Modern German Painting, 1989–90, no.10
Rome 1990–91, no.18

Literature
Kiel (1974), p.58, ill. p.57
Rotzler (1978), no.73
See also Karin von Maur, 'Es wuchs ein Kristall. Johannes Itten in Stuttgart 1913–1916', in *Johannes Itten. Künstler und Lehrer*, exh. cat., Berne, Kunstmuseum, 1984, pp.55–65; Dieter Bogner and Eva Badura-Triska, *Johannes Itten. Meine Symbole, meine Mythologien werden die Formen und Farben sein*, Vienna (Löcker) 1988

Group of Houses in Spring was painted in Stuttgart early in 1916.[5] It appears at first sight surprising by comparison with Itten's other paintings of the same period: its colourful lyricism and Cubist-influenced deformation of nature contrast strikingly with more abstract compositions such as *The Meeting*, also of early 1916 (fig.2). Given that the canvas itself is undated, it might have been tempting to place it somewhat earlier, were it not for a closely related study, signed and dated 'Itten 1916' (fig.1), which was illustrated as early as 1919 in an article published by the Viennese art historian Hans Tietze.[6] This drawing is identical with that reproduced as no.74 in Willy Rotzler's oeuvre-catalogue of the artist's work, entitled '*Häuser im Frühling* (1916)'.[7]

Notes

1 The label is now preserved in the archive of the Thyssen-Bornemisza Collection, Lugano-Castagnola. It was evidently fixed to the picture at the time of the exhibition of Itten's work held at the Stedelijk Museum, Amsterdam, in 1957; *Group of Houses in Spring* was no.5 in the catalogue of that exhibition (as 'huizengroep in de lente, 90 × 75,5'). I am grateful to Mrs Anneliese Itten, Zurich, for drawing this catalogue to my attention

2 Acquired at the 37th auction of the Stuttgarter Kunstkabinett, Pt.I, 3–4 May 1962, lot 171

3 Exhibition of works by Itten, together with objects produced by the workshops of the Staatliches Bauhaus Weimar: see Rotzler, p.430

4 Travelling exhibition of the work of Itten and the Itten-Schule in Berlin, also shown at Hamburg, Danzig, Krefeld, Königsberg, Berlin and Zurich during 1931–2

5 For information on the artist's Stuttgart period, see Bogner and Badura-Triska, op. cit., pp.8–13. I am grateful to Dr Eva Badura-Triska, Vienna, for her opinion on questions of style and dating in Itten's paintings of these years

6 Hans Tietze, 'Die Zeichnungen von Johannes Itten', *Die Bildenden Künste* (Wiener Monatshefte, im Kunstverlag Anton Schroll & Co.), II, no.4 (1919): 89–96; Itten's drawing related to *Group of Houses in Spring* is reproduced on p.92, entitled simply 'Landschaft'

7 The drawing was evidently unknown to Rotzler in the original. Sold at auction in 1982 by the Galerie Kornfeld, Berne, it was acquired on that occasion by the Piccadilly Gallery, London (letter from Anneliese Itten to the author, 14 August 1989); it was also included as no.58 in *Johannes Itten. Künstler und Lehrer*

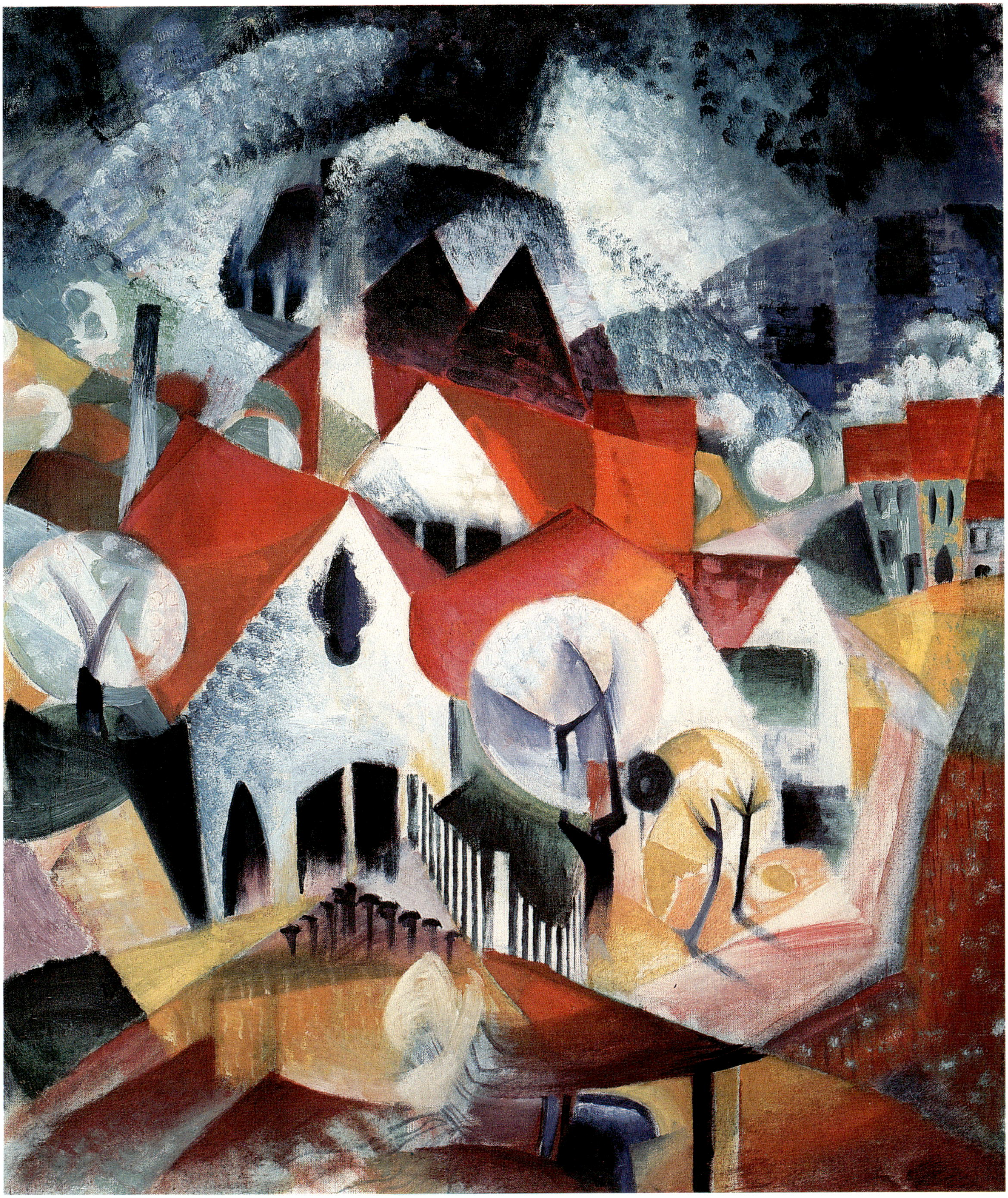

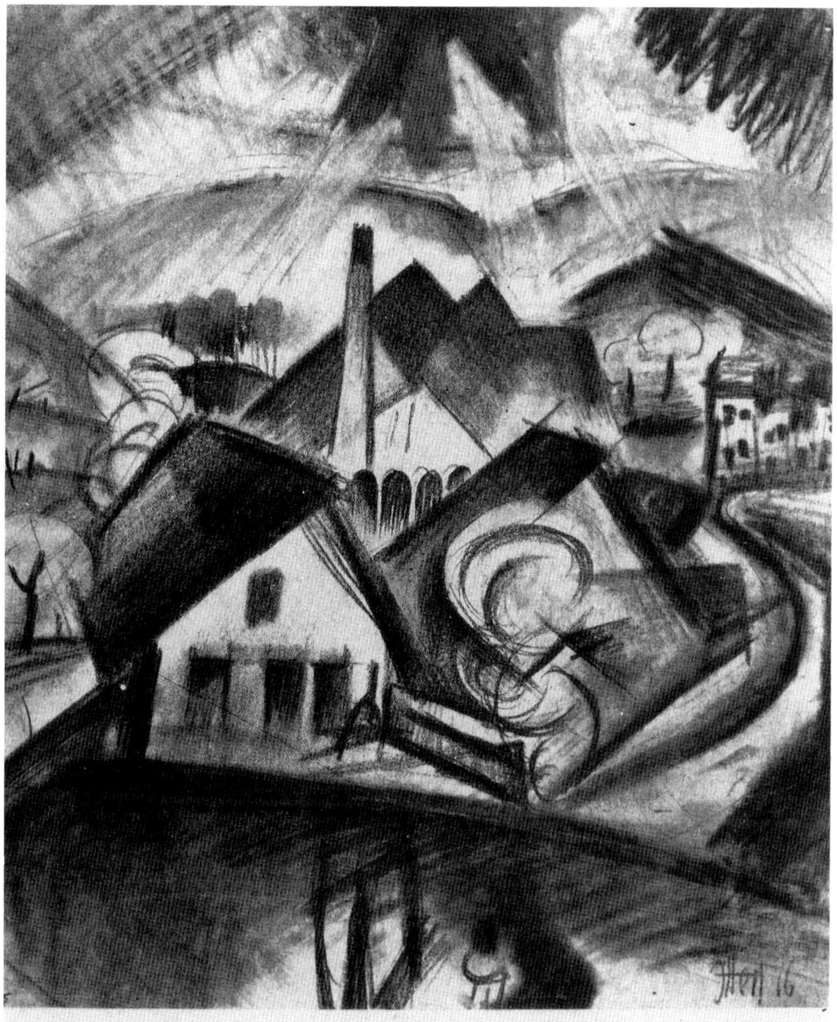

Johannes Itten, Landschaft

FIG 1 Johannes Itten, *'Landscape'*, 1916, pencil, 30 × 26 cm, taken from the reproduction published in *Die Bildenden Künste*, II, no.4 (1919), p.92

The present work has frequently been both illustrated and exhibited under the title *Stuttgart am Killesberg*. This title is not authentic, and there is no reason to suppose that it is correct. In conversation with the author,[8] Anneliese Itten, the artist's widow, ventured that the location depicted is more likely to have been the Gänsheide, another of the wooded hills above Stuttgart, where Itten on his arrival in October 1913 rented a tiny garden house in the grounds of a villa owned by the family of a typesetter called Girbich.[9] From these cramped and chilly quarters, which served as lodging-cum-studio, he enjoyed a view into the garden of the adjacent Villa Reizenstein which, it has been suggested, may form the architectural subject of the present picture.

This supposition, however, also seems dubious, for two reasons. If, as noted above, the related drawing supports the dating of 1916 for the finished painting, then it cannot have been executed in the Gänsheide studio, which Itten gave up in autumn 1915 for the sake of other, more central accomodation on Stuttgart's Friedenstrasse. Secondly, the drawing, though closely related to the painting in composition and in many of its details, is far more representational, allowing one to recognize not a hill, but a deep, winding river valley traversed by bridges. The structures in the foreground, moreover, resemble not so much a villa or any kind of domestic architecture as a group of industrial buildings, with a factory chimney clearly visible in the drawing. This chimney, though subjected to a more radical process of abstraction, remains the dominant element in the finished painting.

Notes

8 In conversation with the author, Zurich, 3 April 1989

9 See Itten's autobiographical essay 'Aus meinem Leben', written in 1948, published in Rotzler (1978), pp.15ff. His encounter with the Girbich family and his first studio are described in a lengthy passage beginning on p.24

In a letter to the author dated 22 December 1989, Dr Karin Frank von Maur, of the Staatsgalerie Stuttgart, also expressed the opinion that the view depicted in the 1916 drawing must be from one of the hills surrounding Stuttgart looking down into the so-called 'Talkessel', the saucer-shaped valley in which the city is situated, and that the buildings are probably industrial or commercial.[10] She suggests that perhaps a brewery such as the former Brauerei Wulle on the Neckarstrasse, which according to her recollection had large arched windows along the façade like those shown in the drawing, might have provided a starting point. There is, however, no river flowing through the centre of Stuttgart; if the industrial complex was situated on the River Neckar, then a factory located in the outskirts such as the Daimler-Werke in Untertürkheim springs to mind. Itten's topography should not, in any case, be taken too literally: the surrounding hills are in reality not nearly as precipitous as he makes them appear – a poetic exaggeration, perhaps, of the unfamiliar landscape with which he found himself confronted.

Seen in the context of his early development, *Group of Houses in Spring* marks an important stage in the artist's evolution of an abstract language of painting: by contrast with the related drawing, in the painted version precise details of architecture and topography are largely submerged in the overall abstract rhythm of colour and form. For Itten, however, abstraction never constituted an end in itself (any more than it did for Klee). Rather, one of the most important functions of art was to reveal the principles of order and coherence inherent in nature, principles of which the 'laws' of music were merely another manifestation. Significantly, in his works which immediately succeeded *Group of Houses in Spring*, he frequently sought to apply the abstract organizational principles of musical composition to painting.[11]

Itten himself, in a letter to Baron H.H. Thyssen-Bornemisza dated 4 February 1964, referred to *Group of Houses in Spring* as 'among the most significant of my early works'.[12] Certainly, he chose to include it in a number of important exhibitions held during the 1920s and 1930s, as well as after the war.[13] In 1964, at Itten's particular request, it was lent by the Thyssen-Bornemisza Collection to the major retrospective of his work shown at the Kunsthaus in Zurich.

10 I am indebted to Dr Karin Frank von Maur for her opinion on the painting and for providing other valuable information

11 Itten had studied music under Hans Klee, father of the painter Paul Klee; in a speech acknowledging the award of an honorary doctorate from the Technische Hochschule in Darmstadt in 1965, he himself confessed to having been in some doubt whether to pursue a career as a painter or as a musician: see Rotzler (1978), p.280

12 Lugano-Castagnola, Thyssen-Bornemisza Collection, archive

13 See Exhibitions; information regarding early exhibitions in which [30] was included is based on that printed in the catalogue of the 1962 auction of the Stuttgarter Kunstkabinett, and on the list of exhibitions published in Rotzler, op. cit., pp.430ff

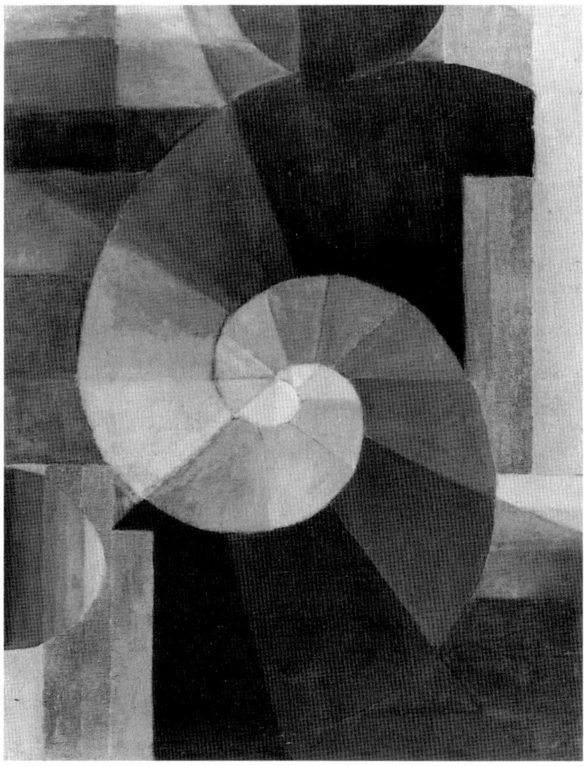

FIG 2 Johannes Itten, *Meeting*, 1916, oil on canvas, 105 × 80 cm (Zurich, Kunsthaus, inv. no.1964/5)

Johannes Itten 1888–1967

31 Kindly Light
Gütiges Licht[1]

1963
Oil on canvas, 100 × 72 cm
Signed/dated on back of canvas: 'Itten 1963'
In good condition. The painting is unvarnished
Accession no.1964.10

Provenance
Collection of the artist
Thyssen-Bornemisza Collection, 1964[2]

Exhibitions
Zurich, Kunsthaus, 1964, *Johannes Itten*, no.134
Aarau, Aargauer Kunsthaus, 1964, *Willi Baumeister, Hans Brühlmann, Johannes Itten, Ida Kerkovius, Otto Meyer-Amden, A.H.Pellegrini, Oskar Schlemmer, Hermann Stenner*, no.149
Venice, 1966, *XXXIII Biennale (Svizzera)*, no.15
Berne, Kunsthalle, 1971, *Johannes Itten*, no.174
Münster, Westfälisches Landesmuseum, 1980, *Johannes Itten. Gemälde, Gouachen, Aquarelle, Tuschen, Zeichnungen*, no.52
Berne, Kunstmuseum/Krefeld, Kaiser-Wilhelm-Museum/Stuttgart, Galerie der Stadt Stuttgart, 1984–5, *Johannes Itten. Künstler und Lehrer*, no.244
Budapest/Szombathely 1985–6, no.41

Literature
Rotzler (1978), no.1165

In 1953, after a lifetime of pedagogy, Itten retired from his position as director of the Museum and School of Applied Arts in Zurich.[3] Thereafter, he gradually divested himself of his last teaching responsibilities, and during a long and fruitful retirement devoted himself increasingly to his own creative work, reaping a prolific harvest of oil paintings, watercolours and drawings, and gouaches.

His works of this late period may be divided into three main categories: those inspired by the direct impression of external nature, the (predominantly brush and ink) drawings which explore the expressive potential of line and form, and – especially during the last twelve years of his life – an important series of geometric-constructive paintings, including *Kindly Light*.

Two years after his retirement, Itten moved into a new studio overlooking the valley of the River Limmat, on which Zurich stands – a studio unusual in that, being south-facing, it was exposed to strong sunlight. This prompted him to embark on a series of pictorial experiments in which he sought to capture the various effects of direct and indirect light, including effects such as that of light filtered through blinds or curtains.[4] These experiments became the starting point for a group of paintings on the theme of light, many of them with very similar titles – *Against the Light, Early Summer Light* – to which *Kindly Light* also belongs.

Notes
1 The title is that which appeared in the catalogue of the 1964 Zurich exhibition, which was prepared in collaboration with the artist
2 Acquired directly from the artist
3 Though formally retired, Itten in fact stayed on as acting director of the School of Applied Arts until the end of March 1954: see Rotzler (1978), p.430
4 According to Anneliese Itten, in conversation with the author, Zurich, 3 April 1989

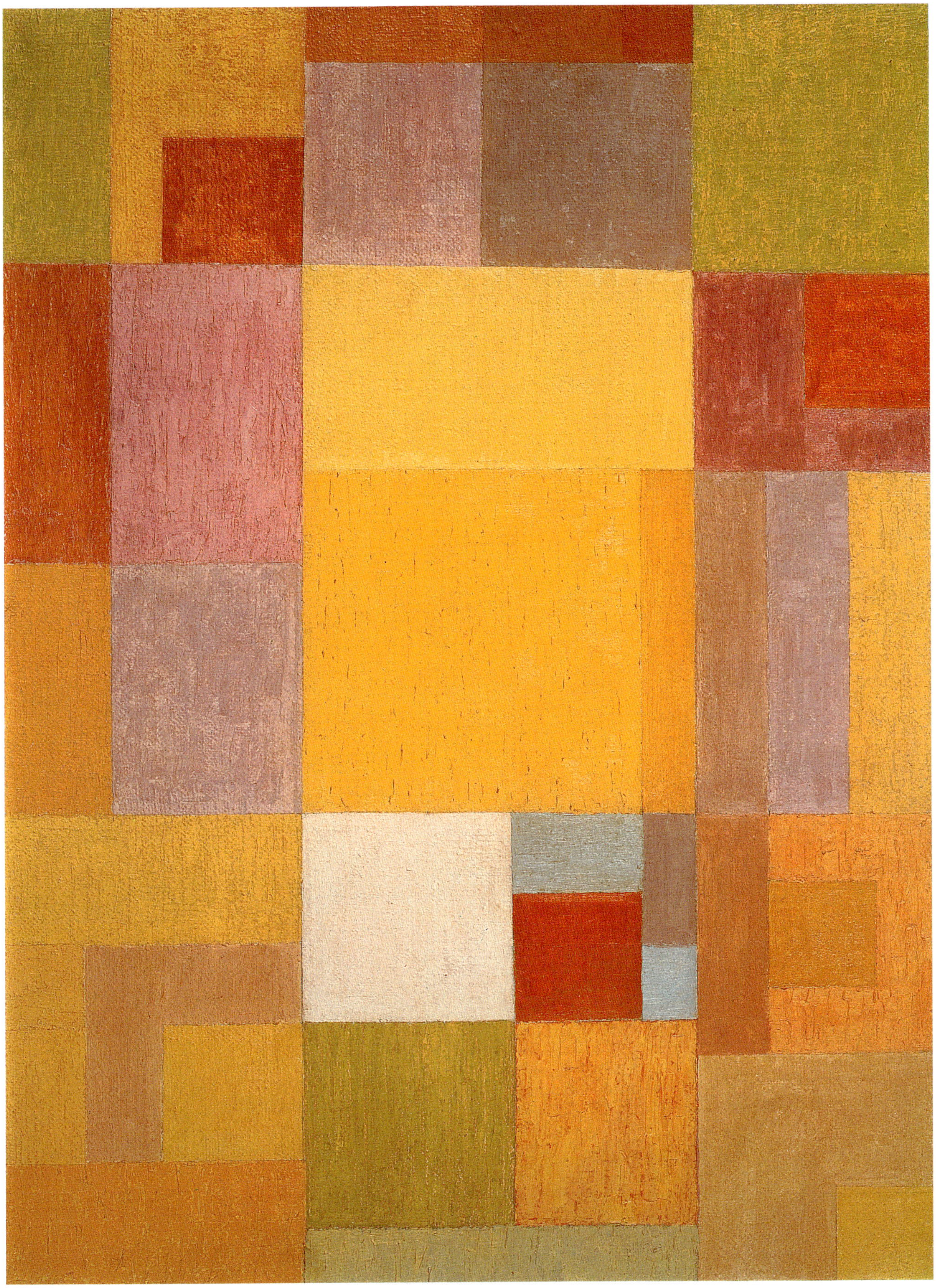

Alexei von Jawlensky 1864–1941

32 Child with Doll

1910
Oil on board, 61 × 50.5 cm[1]
Signed/dated upper left: 'A. Jawlensky 10'
The heavy textured board on which the picture is painted is slightly convex-warped. Otherwise condition is good
Accession no. 1983.14

Provenance
Bernhard Hirsch[2]
Estate of Gerta Hirsch, Berlin
Leonard Hutton Galleries, New York
Thyssen-Bornemisza Collection, 1983

Exhibitions
Modern Masters from the Thyssen-Bornemisza Collection, 1984–6, no. 50
Leningrad/Moscow 1988, no. 38
Lugano 1989, no. 30
Rome 1990–91, no. 19

Literature
See Zweite (1983);[3] *Jawlensky Father and Son*, exh. cat., New York, Leonard Hutton Galleries, 1987; Jelena Hahl-Koch, 'Jawlenskys Studien- und Geniezeit', in Chiappini (1989), pp. 32–96
Not in Weiler[4]

Jawlensky was one of a number of Russian artists who sought residence in Munich during the 1890s and early 1900s. On his arrival in the Bavarian capital in 1896 together with his compatriots Igor Grabar and Dmitri Kardovsky, he enrolled in the private art school run by the painter Anton Ažbè. Unlike Kandinsky, whom he met at the Ažbè school shortly afterwards, Jawlensky could by this time already boast of a thorough academic training as a painter, having been a student of the celebrated Russian realist Il'ya Repin at the St Petersburg Academy. Like Kandinsky, during the years after 1900 Jawlensky travelled widely, in particular to France, acquainting himself with recent developments in Post-Impressionist and avant-garde art. The influence of Neo-Impressionist theory and practice is evident in his work

Notes

1 The support is a kind of textured cardboard, known in German as *Malkarton*, which simulates the surface appearance of canvas. It is sometimes referred to as 'canvasboard'; see p. 24

2 Affixed to the back of the original board is a label inscribed in pen: 'Eigentum Bernhard Hirsch . . .' (property of Bernhard Hirsch . . .); the rest of the inscription, though faintly visible, is now indecipherable

3 Catalogue of the exhibition held at the Städtische Galerie im Lenbachhaus, Munich, in 1983

4 See n. 8

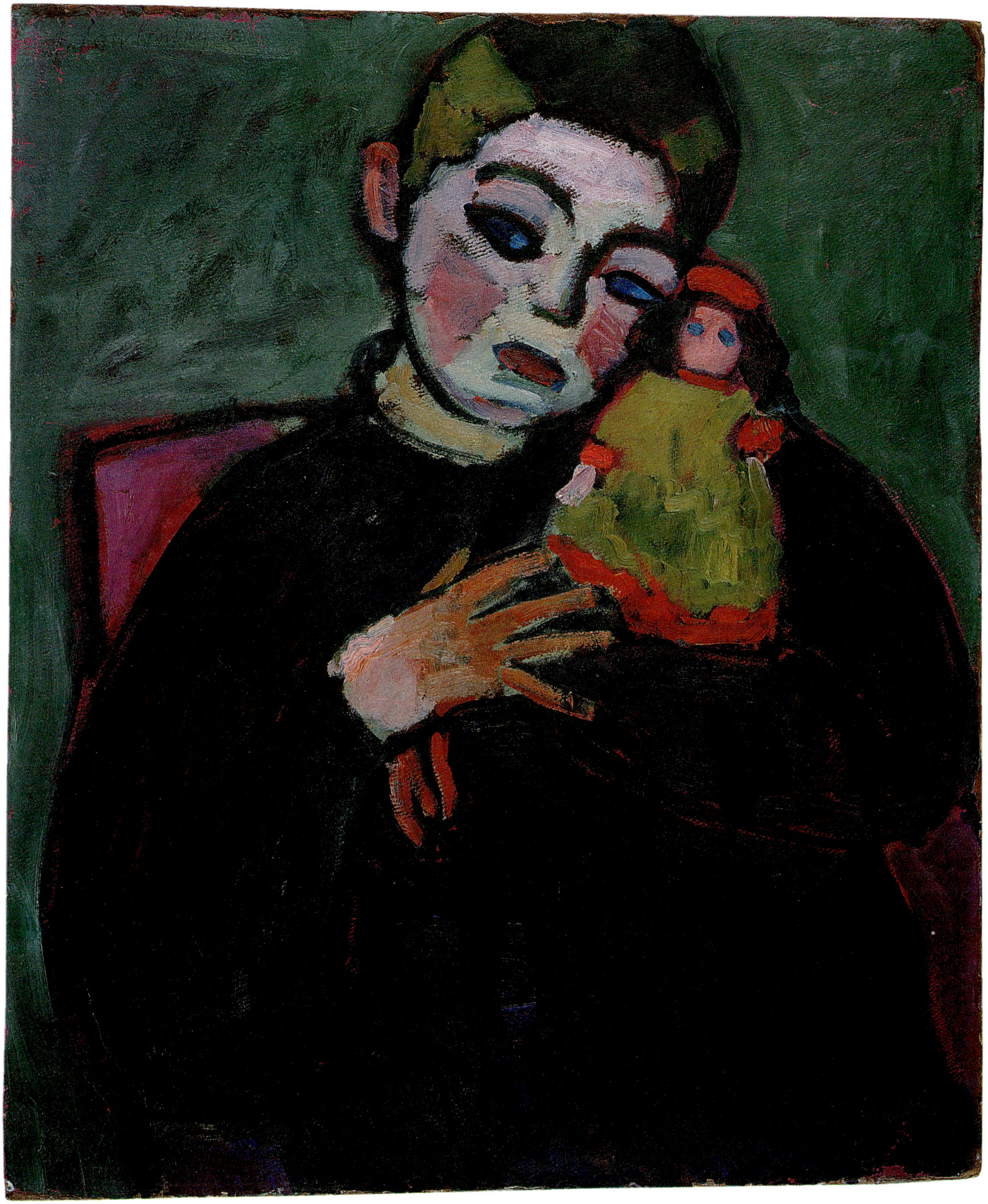

until at least 1905, the year in which he met Matisse. Thereafter, his use of vivid, often non-naturalistic colour in part reflects the impression made on him by Fauve painting which, together with the example of Gauguin and van Gogh, constitutes one of the major influences on his development at this time.

The subject of this portrait is the artist's 8-year-old son Andreas Jawlensky (1902–84). Andreas was born on 18 January 1902 at Ansbaki in the province of Vitebsk, the only child of Jawlensky and Helene Nesnakomoff.[5] Helene is described affectionately in the recollections of several of those who knew the family,[6] as a quiet and devoted person who accompanied the Jawlensky household on their frequent travels and looked after the growing boy. She and Jawlensky were married in 1922.

Andreas inherited his father's talent. His contact with art, not only his father's paintings but also those of other avant-garde artists, went back to his earliest years. As a young boy, he was part of the familial circle in and around Murnau which included Jawlensky, Marianne von Werefkin, Kandinsky and Gabriele Münter. A photograph taken by Kandinsky in Murnau, probably in 1908 or 1909, shows Andreas accompanied by Münter (fig.1).

Jawlensky himself greatly esteemed his son's gifts as an artist. In his reminiscences, he recalled how, from the age of four, Andreas had worked alongside him in his Munich studio, and how, during the years of exile in Switzerland, Hodler had remarked on the boy's abilities as a draughtsman, exchanging two of his own drawings for one by Andreas.[7] In 1987, an exhibition organized by the Leonard Hutton Galleries in New York under the title *Jawlensky Father and Son* provided a valuable insight into the extent of his accomplishment as a painter.

The portrait was for many years in a private collection in Berlin and evidently remained unknown to Clemens Weiler, compiler of the first oeuvre-catalogue of Jawlensky's paintings.[8] When sold to the present owner it was accompanied by a photo-certificate signed by Andreas Jawlensky and dated Munich, 24 February 1983, confirming the authenticity of the painting. The inscription on the back of the photograph reads:

> Picture on reverse *Child with Doll* 1910 was painted by the hand of my father Alexej v. Jawlensky in his studio Giselastr. 23, Munich. Size 61 × 50.5 cm. Signed and dated upper left. The picture depicts me as a boy of eight years of age.[9]

Notes

5 See chronology printed in Chiappini (1989), pp.255ff

6 For example, by Elisabeth Macke, wife of the painter August Macke, in her recollections of her husband: see Erdmann-Macke (1962), pp.190ff

7 Weiler (1970), p.117

8 Clemens Weiler, *Alexej Jawlensky*, Cologne 1959. The painting is included in the catalogue by Maria Jawlensky, Lucia Pieroni-Jawlensky and Angelica Jawlensky, *Alexej Jawlensky, Catalogue Raisonné of the Oil-Paintings, I, 1890–1914*, London (Sotheby's) 1992

9 'Umseitiges Bild "Kind mit Puppe" 1910 ist von meinem Vater Alexej v. Jawlensky eigenhändig im Atelier Giselastr. 23, München eigenhändig gemalt worden. Grösse 61 × 50,5 cm. Oben links signiert und datiert. Das Bild stellt mich dar als achtjährigen Knaben.' (Lugano-Castagnola, Thyssen-Bornemisza Collection, archive)

FIG 1 Andreas Jawlensky as a boy, together with Gabriele Münter, photographed by Kandinsky in Murnau, *c*1908–9. Jawlensky himself appears at extreme left (Gabriele Münter- und Johannes Eichner-Stiftung, Munich)

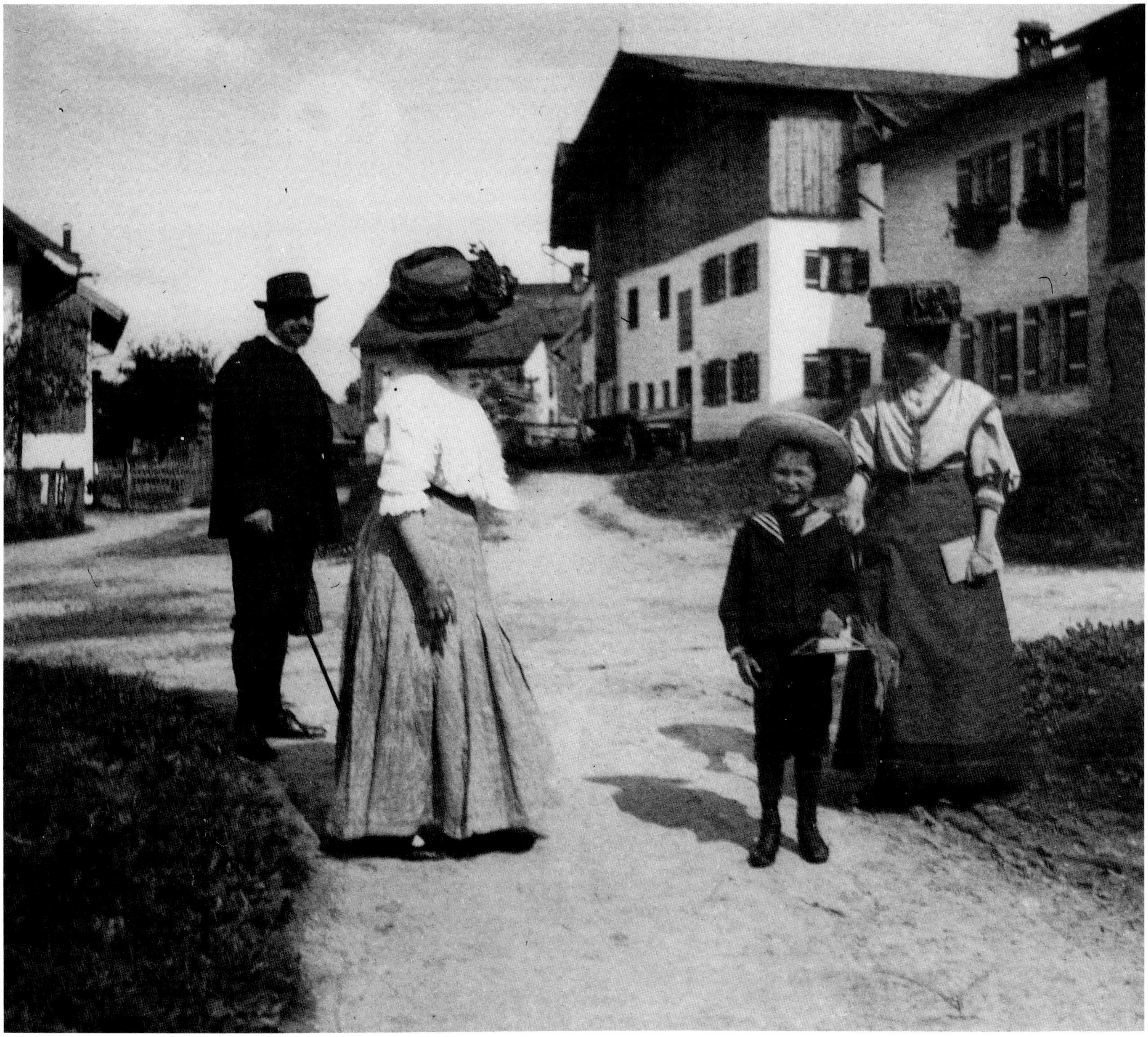

Alexei von Jawlensky 1864–1941

33 Red Veil
Roter Schleier

1912
Oil on board, 64.5 × 54 cm
Signed lower left: 'A.Jawlensky'; inscribed on back of board: 'VK Roter Schleier 1912/A.Jawlensky N.76'[1]
Faint traces of another portrait head can be discerned on the verso. These have been partially obliterated by a layer of dark over-painting, on top of which have been added signature and inscription as noted above. Apart from a large convex bulge in the centre of the board, and minor surface scratches and abrasions to the recto, condition is good
Accession no.1975.20

Provenance
Estate of the artist
Private collection, New York
Forberg Collection, Düsseldorf
Galerie Wilhelm Grosshenig, Düsseldorf
Thyssen-Bornemisza Collection, 1975

Exhibitions
Düsseldorf, Galerie Alex Vömel, 1956, *Oelbilder von Alexej von Jawlensky*, no.7
London, Marlborough Fine Art, 1959, *Art in Revolt. Germany 1905–25*, no.47
Frankfurt am Main, Kunstverein/Hamburg, Kunstverein, 1967, *Alexej Jawlensky*, no.28
Brussels/Paris 1977–8, no.38
Lugano 1978, no.45
Australian tour 1979–80, no.28
USA tour 1982–4, no.8
Modern Masters from the Thyssen-Bornemisza Collection, 1984–6, no.51
Leningrad/Moscow 1988, no.39
Lugano 1989, no.31
Expressionism and Modern German Painting, 1989–90, no.11
Rome 1990–91, no.20

Literature
Weiler (1959), no.135
Ewald Rathke, *Alexej Jawlensky*, Hanau (Hans Peters) 1968, p.50, no.28
See also Weiler (1970); Rudy Chiappini, 'Mit kühnen Farben die Finsternis herausfordern', Jelena Hahl-Koch, 'Jawlenskys Studien- und Geniezeit', Angelica Jawlensky, 'Der Weg zur Abstraktion', in Chiappini (1989), pp.11–28, 32–96, 100–46

During the years around 1912, Jawlensky devoted himself increasingly to the treatment of a single theme, that of the female face. Landscape and still-life begin to occupy an increasingly unimportant place within his art, while conventional portraiture is likewise abandoned in favour of what are in essence representations of a type. Numerous works of this period bear merely the title *Head* or *Female Head*. Even where the sitter can be identified, as for example in portraits of his future wife Helene, his concern is primarily with the general characteristics of the human countenance, rather than particularities. Like so many Expressionist artists, he was not interested in capturing a precise physical likeness, observing that in a hundred years no one would remember what the sitter looked like, and then the 'portrait' would be extremely faithful.

Note
1 The inscription is part of a system which Jawlensky adopted during the years after the First World War, albeit not altogether consistently, of categorizing his paintings according to period and subject – portraits, landscapes, etc. In the present instance, 'VK' stands for 'Vorkriegsköpfe' (pre-war heads); the designation 'N.76' alludes to a numerical handlist of the artist's paintings, according to information supplied by Angelica Jawlensky, Locarno

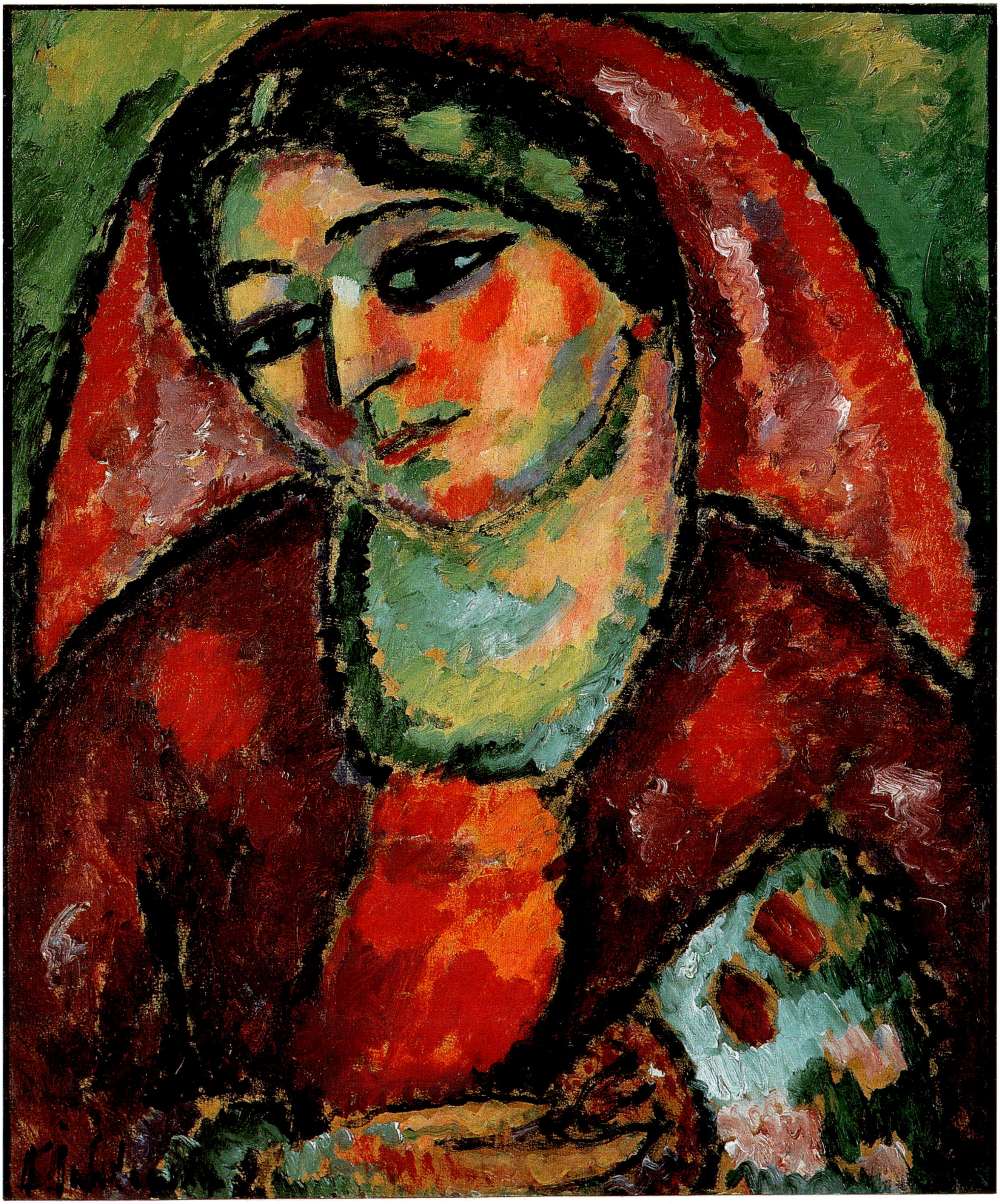

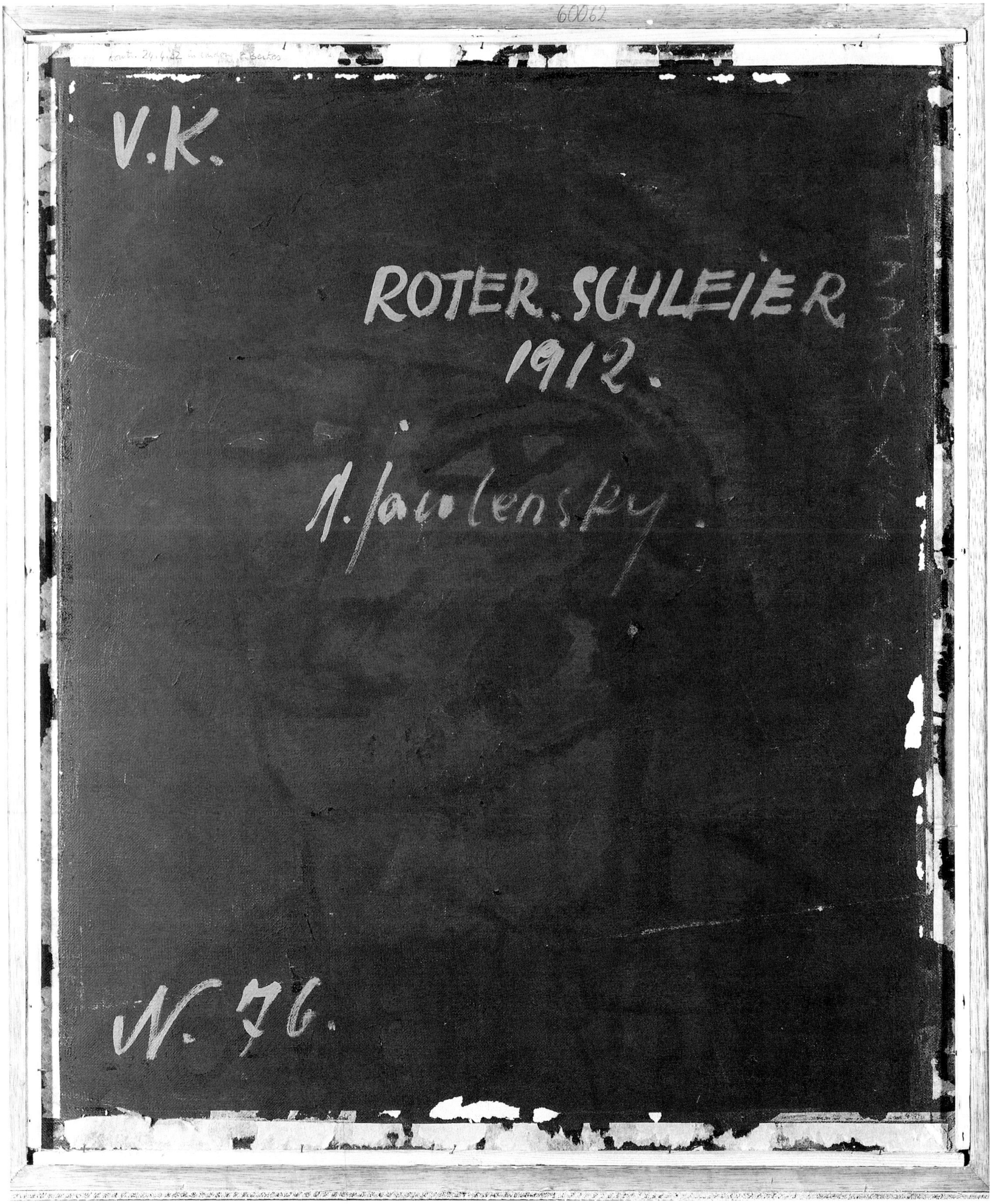
V.K.
ROTER. SCHLEIER
1912.
A. Jawlensky.
N. 76.

Notes
2 Hahl-Koch, op. cit., pp.84ff
3 See the chronology printed in Chiappini (1989), p.255; also Weiler (1970), pp.102f
4 Weiler (1970), p.105
5 Quoted after Hahl-Koch, op. cit., p.32
6 Weiler (1970), p.112
7 Hahl-Koch, p.80

Rather, his paintings draw attention to the abstract, expressive character of the face, the representation of which is raised to a level of the utmost stylization.

It has recently been suggested that these works are, in several important ways, deeply influenced by Russian icons,[2] as in *Red Veil*, where the veil thrown over the head of the figure and the jewel-like colours both evoke medieval representations of the Madonna. This suggestion seems highly plausible. A devout Orthodox, Jawlensky counted among his formative experiences that of traditional icon painting, both (as a child) in Russian churches, and subsequently in the museums in St Petersburg, to which city he had succeeded in arranging a transfer in 1889 as an officer in the Alexander Nevsky regiment, in order to pursue the study of art.[3] In his reminiscences, dictated shortly before his death, he still recalled the impression made on him by seeing 'whole rooms of icons ... even complete iconostases' in the Imperial Russian Museum in St Petersburg;[4] while in a letter of 1939 concerning the origins of his art, he observed: 'My Russian soul was always akin to old Russian art, to Russian icons, Byzantine art, the mosaics of Ravenna, Venice, Rome and Romanesque art. All these art forms caused in my soul a beatific vibration, for I sensed therein a profound spiritual language.'[5]

This influence appears most prevalent in the powerful stylized heads of 1912–13, in which the eyes, preternaturally large, are accentuated by dark outlines, while the head itself is set against a neutral, indeterminate ground, corresponding to the white or gold ground of medieval icons. The notion that Jawlensky's purpose in these works was the increasing spiritualization of the human visage is borne out by several of his own statements. In retrospect, he referred to his paintings of this period as having been born as if out of an 'inner ecstasy';[6] while concerning his work of the years after 1914 he wrote in a letter to the Symbolist painter Jan Verkade: 'I had grasped that great art could only be created out of religious feeling. And this was something I could achieve only through the human face. I understood that every artist must express through his art, through form and colour, the divine within him. In this way, the work of art is a visible God, and art itself is the yearning for God.'[7] During the 1920s and 1930s, the same concern was to lead him to create a lengthy series of portrait heads simplified to the verge of illegibility, consisting of little more than abstract geometric planes of colour.

[33] *Verso*

Wassily Kandinsky 1866–1944

34 Murnau: Houses on the Obermarkt

1908
Oil on board, 64.5 × 50.2 cm
Signed on back of board: 'Kandinsky'
Some minor flaking. Otherwise condition is good
Accession no.1977.68

Provenance
Estate of the artist
Nina Kandinsky, Paris
Leonard Hutton Galleries, New York
Thyssen-Bornemisza Collection, 1977

Exhibitions
Sydney, David Jones Ltd, 1976, *Aspects of 20th Century Art*, no.17 [as 'The Market at Murnau']
New York, Leonard Hutton Galleries, 1977, *Der Blaue Reiter und sein Kreis*, no.25
Brussels/Paris 1977–8, no.39
Lugano 1978, no.47
Modern Masters from the Thyssen-Bornemisza Collection, 1984–6, no.54
Leningrad/Moscow 1988, no.11
Lugano 1989, no.23
Rome 1990–91, no.22

Literature
P.Kaplan and S.Manso (eds.), *Major European Art Movements, 1900–1945. A Critical Anthology*, New York (Dutton) 1977, p.81
Roethel (1982), no.202
See also Eichner (1957), pp.87ff

For Kandinsky, the years between 1904 and 1908 were years of travel. Much of this time was spent in the company of the young German artist Gabriele Münter, whom he had met in Munich in 1902. During 1904–5 they visited Holland, Italy and North Africa. The couple was in Paris from 1906–7, and spent six months in Berlin in the winter of 1907–8, finally returning to Munich in the summer of 1908. From then on, they divided their time between the Bavarian

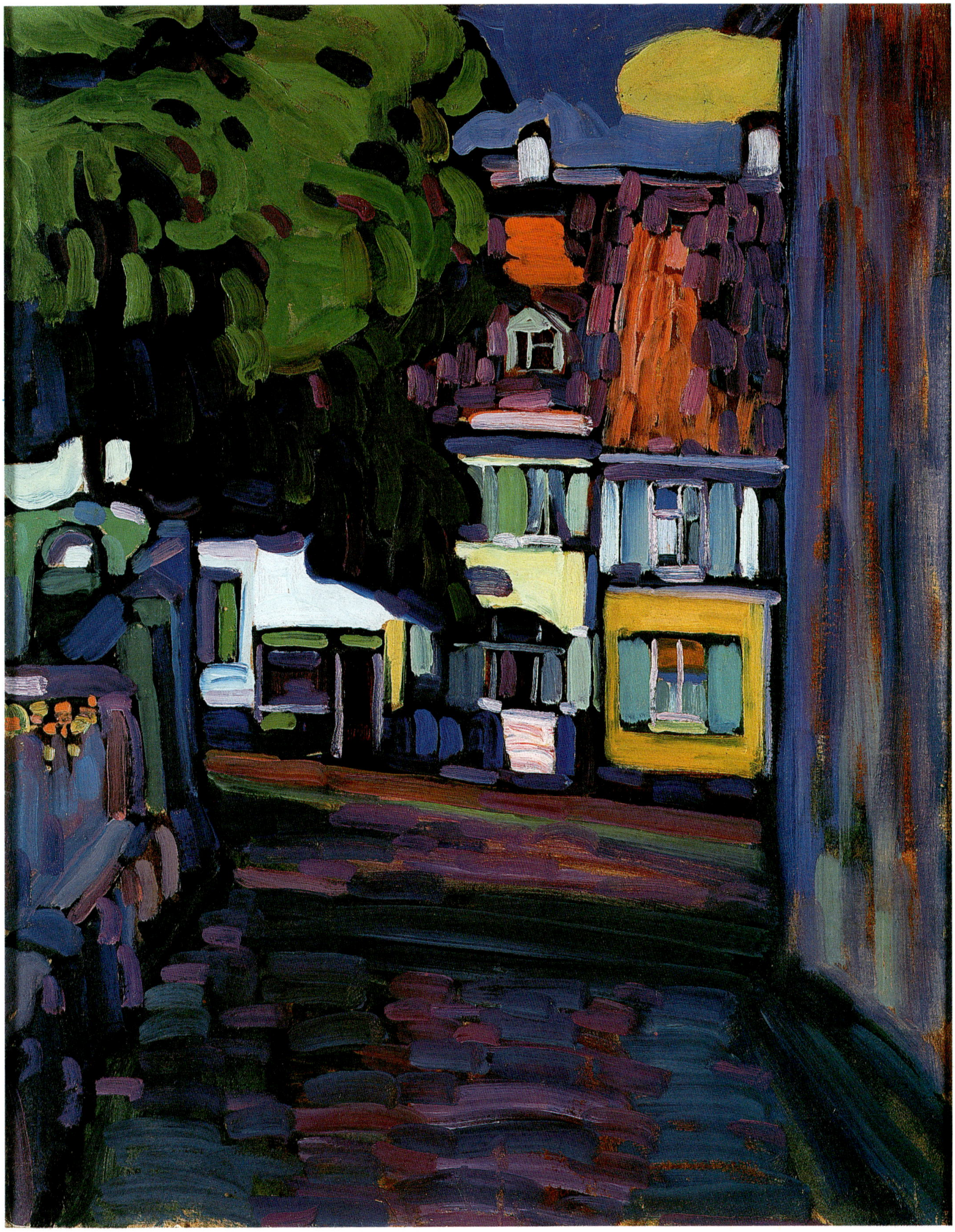

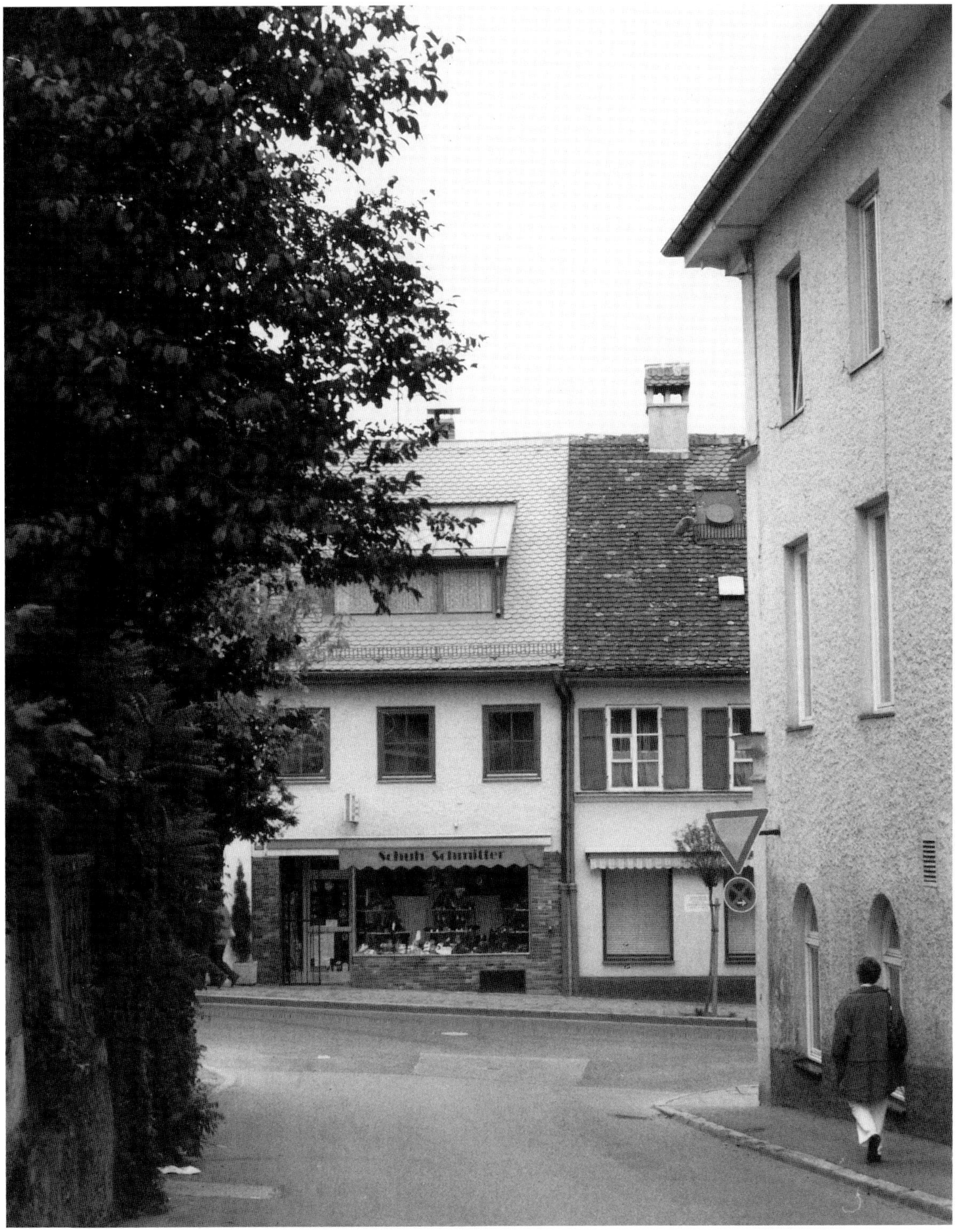

FIG 1 Murnau, looking towards the Obermarkt, 1988

capital and the village of Murnau, some fifty miles to the south of Munich, which they first visited together in the course of a brief excursion in mid-June 1908.[1]

Falling in love with the place, Münter bought a house there the following year. From 1909 until the outbreak of war in 1914 she and Kandinsky, often joined by other artists including Kandinsky's compatriots Alexei Jawlensky and Marianne von Werefkin, spent part of every year in Murnau, especially the summers.[2] The village and its surroundings (Murnau is picturesquely situated in the foothills of the Bavarian Alps) provided a repertoire of subjects to

Notes

1 Eichner, loc. cit.

2 See chronological table in ibid., pp.208f

3 See Roethel (1982), p.202
4 Ibid., pp.16ff

which Kandinsky returned constantly during these crucial years which also saw his increasingly radical development towards an abstract style of painting.

Though *Houses on the Obermarkt* is undated, the artist's stylistic evolution during these years is so rapid, and so decisive, that there can be little doubt that this is a work of 1908, done at a time when the influence of Fauve paintings he had seen in Paris is still apparent. Further evidence for the dating of the work is provided by the fact that the picture, which had lain unnoticed for many years in the artist's last apartment in Neuilly-sur-Seine, and which was rediscovered by Kandinsky's widow, was found wrapped in a copy of a Munich newspaper, the *Münchner Neueste Nachrichten*, dated 1908.[3] The title, however, is not original, nor is the work entered in the artist's handlists in which he recorded all his major paintings:[4] *Houses on the Obermarkt* is merely the title used in the catalogue raisonné compiled by Roethel and Benjamin, and by which the picture has subsequently been known.

The painting depicts the main street of Murnau, seen from a shady side street which runs alongside the Griesbräu Inn. The locality has changed so little, even today, that it is possible to identify exactly the point at which the artist must have set up his easel (see fig.1). The scale of the painting and the freedom in the handling of paint make it likely that the picture was painted *en plein air*, perhaps in a single session.

Wassily Kandinsky 1866–1944

35 Murnau: Top of the Johannisstrasse
Murnau: Ausgang der Johannisstrasse

1908
Oil on board, 70 × 48.5 cm
Signed/dated on back of board: 'Kandinsky 1908'; inscribed: 'Murnau Ausgang der J ... [illegible]'
The painting is unvarnished. There is some damage to the paint layer along the lower edge of the board. Otherwise condition is good
Accession no.1987.20

Provenance
Gabriele Münter, Murnau
Marlborough Fine Art, London
Sotheby's, New York
Thyssen-Bornemisza Collection, 1987[1]

Exhibitions
London, Marlborough Fine Art, 1961, *Kandinsky: The Road to Abstraction*, no.26 [as 'The End of the Johannesgasse, Murnau 1908']

Literature
Roethel (1982), no.208
See also Eichner (1957), pp.87f, 162ff, 181–2

The work is not recorded in the artist's handlists,[2] and the inscription on the reverse may be by Münter rather than Kandinsky. The picture is, however, generally accepted as authentic, including by the present author, on the basis of both style and provenance.

Murnau: Top of the Johannisstrasse was evidently among the considerable number of works which Kandinsky left with Gabriele Münter when he was forced as an enemy alien to return to Russia at the outbreak of war in 1914, and which remained in her possession for more than forty years. Some of the most important of these were given to the Städtische Galerie im Lenbachhaus in Munich in 1957 on the occasion of her eightieth birthday, and now form the core of the gallery's outstanding collection of works by artists of the Blue Rider circle. Münter, however, kept a number of smaller paintings, including [35], some of which were sold during her lifetime, others being disposed of after her death by the executors of her estate.[3]

The painting depicts the intersection between the Johannisstrasse and the Obermarkt, looking from the former to the latter (see fig.1). The building to the right on the far side of the street is the Griesbräu Inn, where Kandinsky and Münter stayed during their second visit to Murnau in August–September 1908.[4] To modern eyes accustomed to the dun colours of the majority of Bavarian rural buildings as they appear today, the bright pistachio green of the façade seems startling. It is none the less possible that the artist in this instance merely recorded faithfully what he saw in front of him: in earlier times many eighteenth- and nineteenth-century buildings in Bavaria and Austria had painted façades in a variety of vivid colours: bright blue, strawberry pink and pistachio green among them.[5]

Notes
1 Acquired at auction, 11 November 1987 (*Impressionist and Modern Paintings and Sculpture, Part I*, lot 54)
2 See n.4 to p.155
3 I am indebted to Dr Armin Zweite, president of the board of trustees of the Gabriele Münter- und Johannes Eichner-Stiftung, Munich, for information regarding the provenance and subsequent history of a number of paintings formerly in Münter's possession, including the present work
4 See chronological table published in Eichner, op. cit., p.208; also Rosel Gollek, 'Murnau im Alpenvorland', in Wietek (1976), pp.178ff
5 On Baroque painted façades in Austria, see Ivo Hammer *et al.*, 'Dürnstein – Untersuching, Analyse, Restaurierung', *Stift Dürnstein: eine Restaurierung*, 1 of *Denkmalpflege in Niederösterreich*, Vienna (Amt der NÖ Landesregierung) n.d., pp.44f

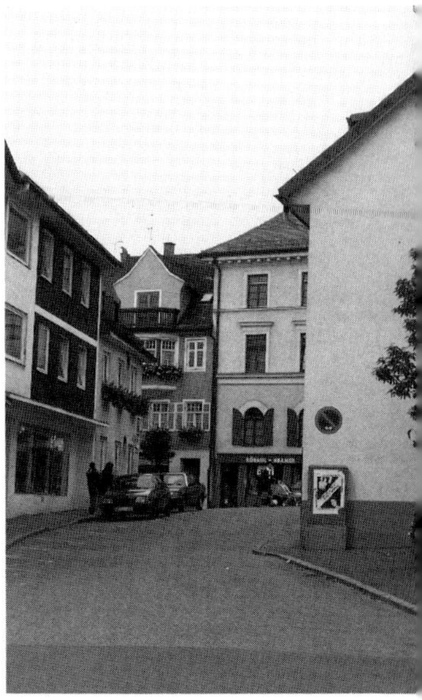

FIG 1 Murnau, looking from the Johannisstrasse towards the Griesbräu Inn, 1988

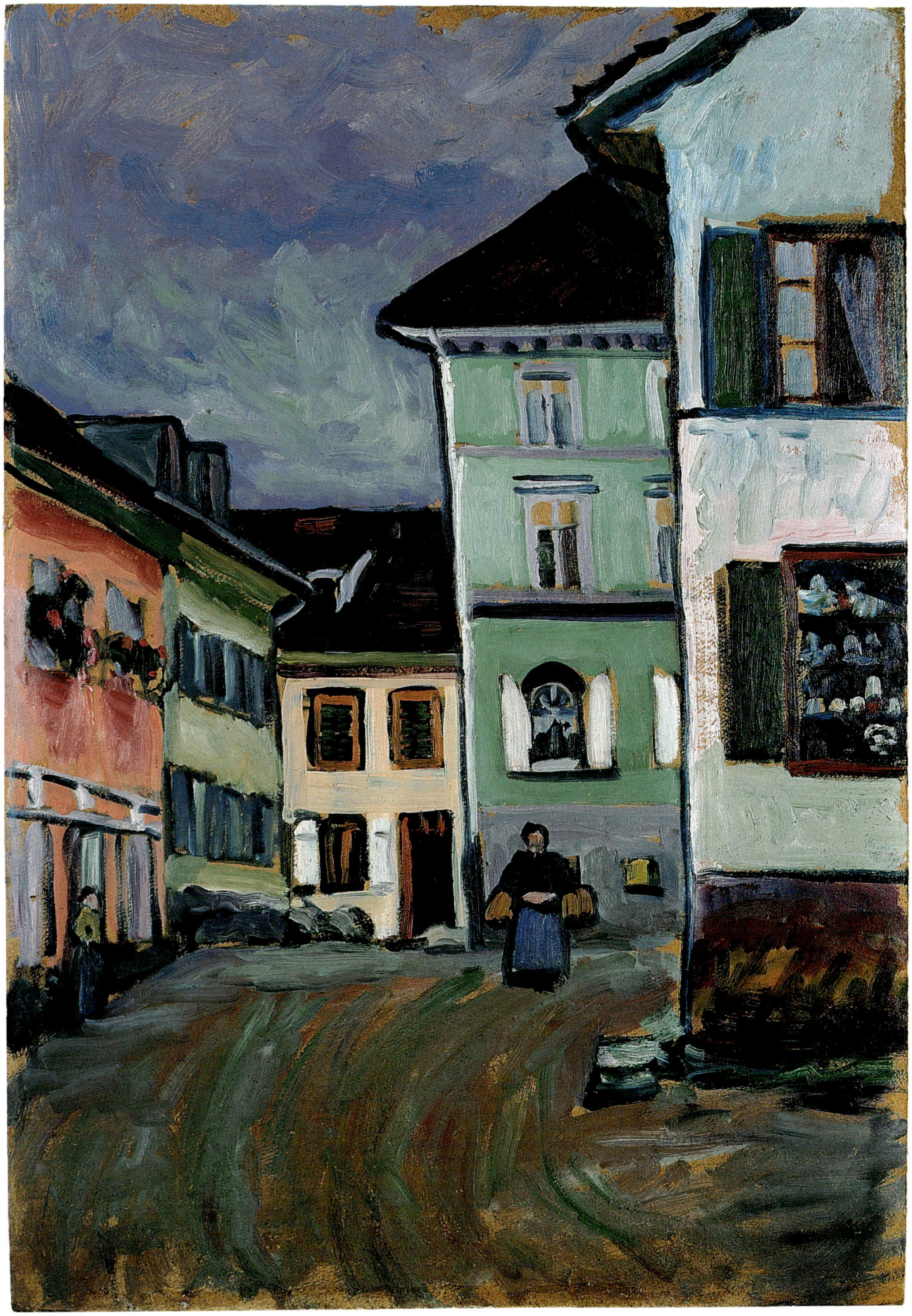

Wassily Kandinsky 1866–1944

36 The Ludwigskirche in Munich
Ludwigskirche in München

1908
Oil on board, 67.3 × 96 cm
Signed/dated lower left: 'Kandinsky 1908'; inscribed on back of board: 'Ludwigskirche in München'
The cardboard support is uneven, with some convex deformations. Otherwise condition is good
Accession no.1977.101

Provenance
Arthur Jerome Eddy, Chicago, IL
Katharine Kuh, Chicago, IL
John Pratt, Southern Rhodesia
Inez Stark Boulton, Washington, DC
David L. Kreeger, Washington, DC
Richard L. Feigen & Co., New York
Thyssen-Bornemisza Collection, 1977

Exhibitions
New York, Museum of Non-Objective Painting, 1945, *Wassily Kandinsky Memorial Exhibition*, no.2
Washington, DC, Corcoran Gallery/Baltimore, MD, Baltimore Museum, 1965, *The Kreeger Collection*, no.8
Australian tour, 1979–80, no.24
Modern Masters from the Thyssen-Bornemisza Collection, 1984–6, no.53
Cologne 1986, p.114, ill. p.115
Luxemburg/Munich/Vienna 1988, no.36
Lugano 1989, no.24
Expressionism and Modern German Painting, 1989–90, no.12
's-Hertogenbosch, Noordbrabants Museum, 1990, *Een feest van kleur: Post-impressionisten uit particulier bezit*, no.32
Rome 1990–91, no.21

Literature
C.J.Bulliet, 'Around the Galleries', *Chicago Daily News*, 24 September 1938
Grohmann (1961/1), p.345
Henri Dorra, *The Kreeger Collection*, Washington, DC (H.K.Press) 1970, pp.86–7
Roethel (1982), no.254

This work, like many of Kandinsky's early landscape studies and paintings in small format, is not entered in the artist's handlists.[1] It has, however, always been accepted as authentic, including by Grohmann in the supplement to his oeuvre-catalogue of Kandinsky's paintings.

As early as 1914, the picture had been acquired by the American collector and writer on art Arthur Jerome Eddy, author of *Delight, the Soul of Art* and *Recollections and Impressions of James A. McNeill Whistler*.[2] No doubt impressed by work he had seen both at the Armory Show in New York in 1913 and during his travels in Europe, Eddy amassed an important collection of paintings by Kandinsky, some of which, according to the terms of his will, eventually passed to the Art Institute in Chicago.[3] In 1914 he published *Cubists and Post Impressionism*, featuring a chapter on the 'New Art in Munich' which included an extended appreciation of Kandinsky and long extracts from letters he had received from him. This, together with the English translation of Kandinsky's treatise *Über das Geistige in der Kunst*, enormously enhanced the artist's reputation in both Britain and America during and after the First World War.

Notes
1 See n.4 to p.155
2 The present painting, referred to as 'Ludwigskirche Prozession', is entered in a handwritten list (not Kandinsky's hand) dated 11.XII.13 and headed 'An Eddy [to Eddy]'; this list is now preserved in the archive of the Gabriele Münter- und Johannes Eichner-Stiftung, Munich. I am grateful to Vivian E. Barnett, New York, for drawing this document to my attention
3 Not, however, *Ludwigskirche in München*, which subsequent to Eddy's death in 1921 was acquired by the Chicago collector and dealer Katharine Kuh. The painting was still in her possession in 1950, as revealed by a letter from Miss Kuh to Professor Kenneth Lindsay, Binghamton, NY, dated 27 March that year. I am grateful to Professor Lindsay for information regarding the Eddy bequest, and the subsequent history of the present painting

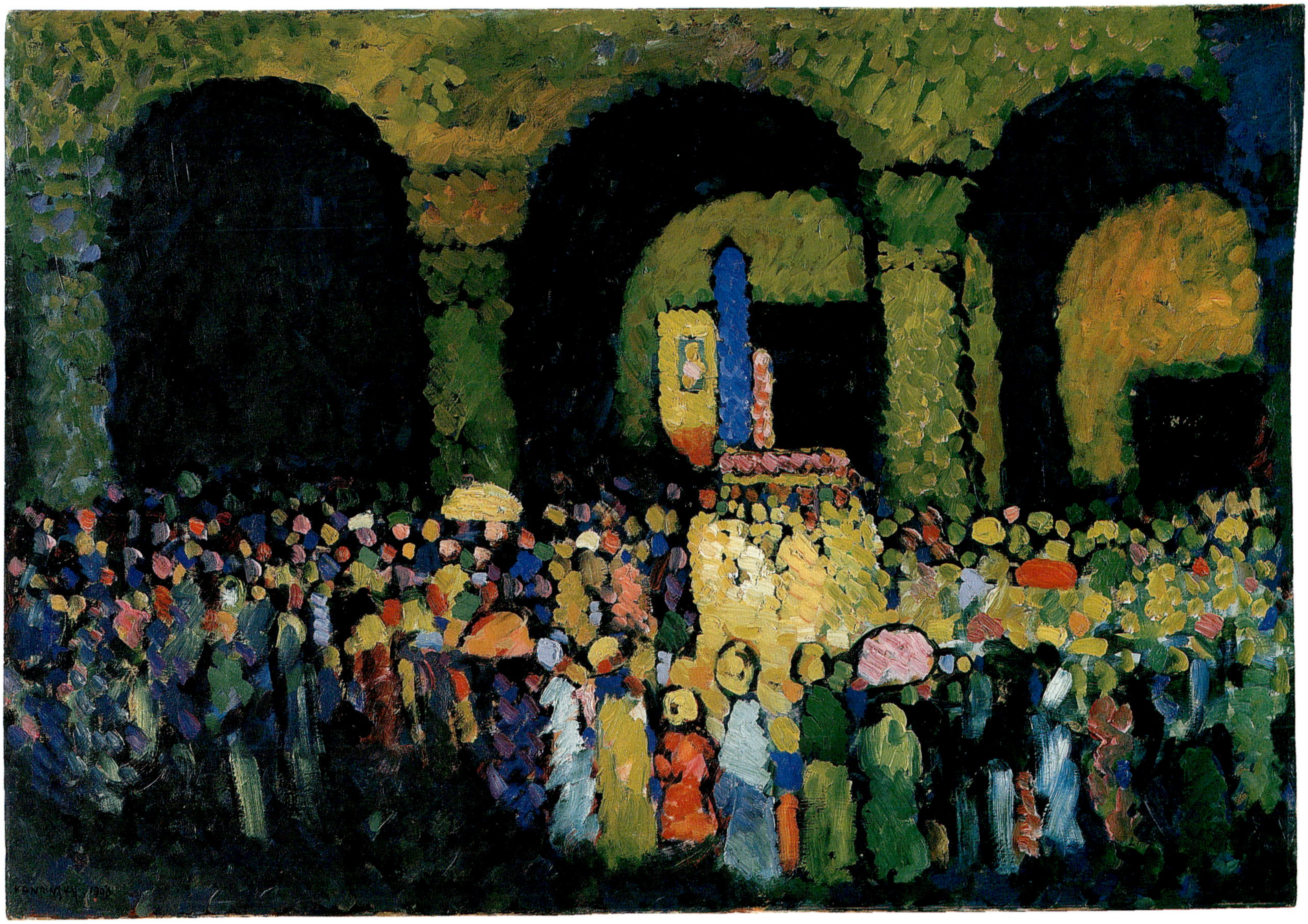

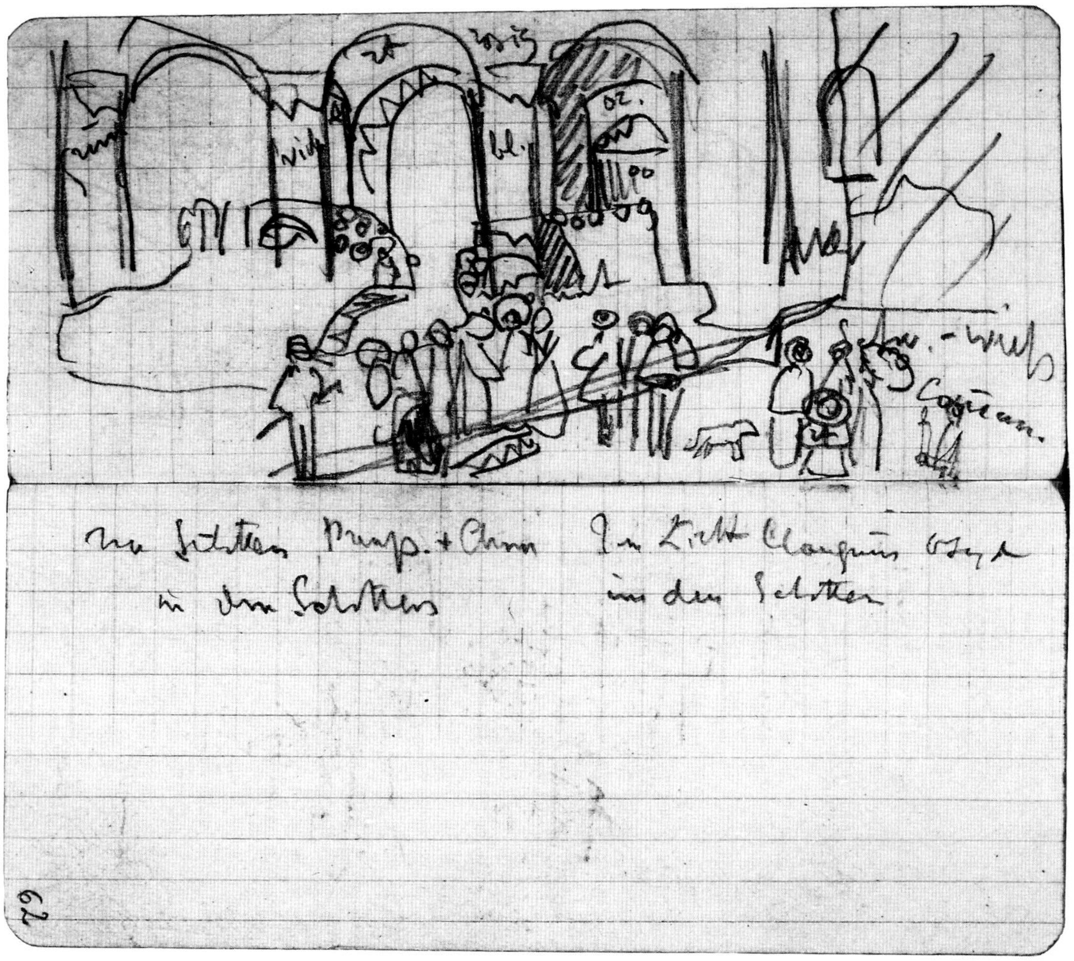

FIG 1 Kandinsky, pencil study for *Ludwigskirche in München*, 1908, from sketchbook GMS 328 (Munich, Städtische Galerie im Lenbachhaus)

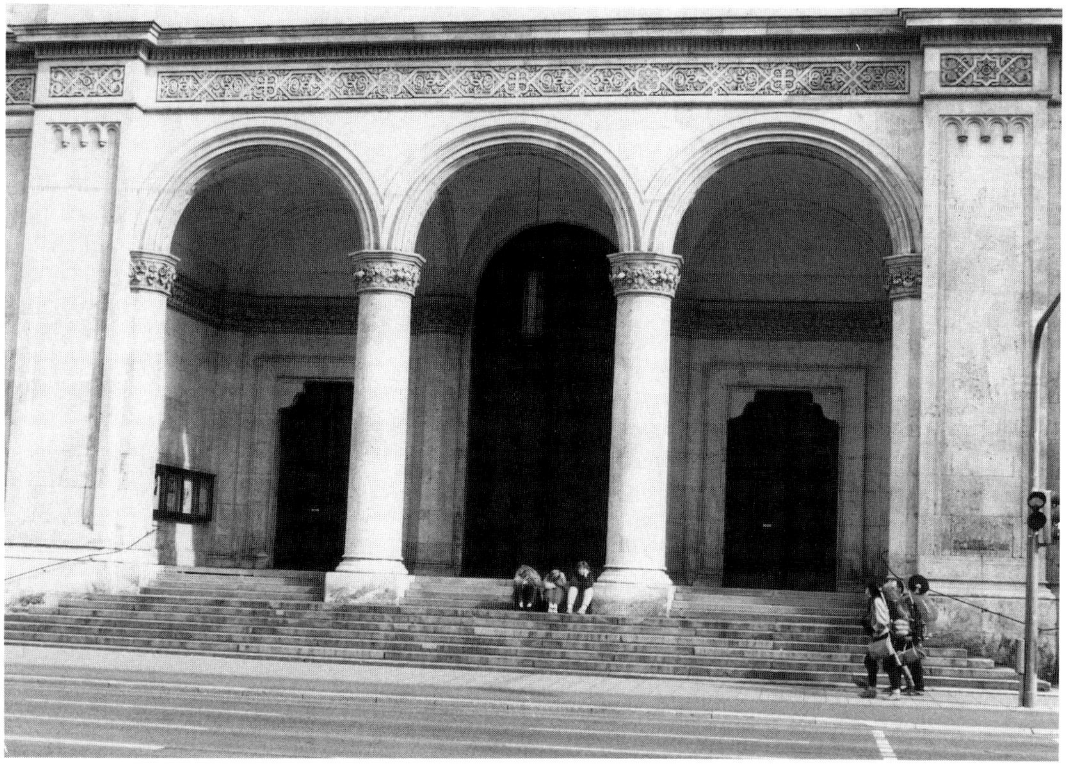

FIG 2 Munich, the Ludwigskirche, 1988, detail of façade

FIG 3 Kandinsky, *Riding Couple*, 1906–7, 55 × 50.5 cm (Munich, Städtische Galerie im Lenbachhaus, GMS 26)

Ludwigskirche in Munich depicts the lower part of the street façade of the church of St Ludwig (built 1829–40) with its unmistakable triple-arched portico, one of the most important works of the early nineteenth-century architect Friedrich von Gärtner (1792–1847). The church is located not far from Schwabing's Ainmillerstrasse, in the 'artists' quarter' of Munich, where Kandinsky rented an apartment and studio in September 1908. The picture was, in all probability, painted during the autumn of that year; a preparatory pencil drawing, closely related to the final composition, occurs on page 61 of a small-format notebook in use during 1908–9 (fig.1). The drawing differs from the final painting only in the way the foreground figures are more clearly separated into groups, and in taking a somewhat more distant standpoint from the church, allowing us to see rather more of the right-hand part of the façade. The drawing also bears numerous colour indications: 'red' and 'rose pink' above the portico, 'green' 'violet' and 'blue' beneath the arches, as well as several references to the treatment of the shadows. Evidently, the marked contrast of tonal values found in the painting was a matter of some importance to Kandinsky, and one he wished to establish clearly in his own mind before taking his brush in his hand.

In the picture as actually executed, the porch is thronged with a brightly-coloured multitude, presumably worshippers. The banners beneath the central archway and the group of priests in their yellow vestments suggest they are witnessing a procession to mark one of the great feasts of the church. The application of paint and jewel-like colours recall Kandinsky's immediately preceding 'fairy-tale' paintings of the period 1906–7, often depicting Russian scenes with knights on horseback and onion-domed churches, done under the influence of French Neo-Impressionism (see fig.3). The brilliant sunshine, however, casts the porch into deep shadow, giving the painting an abstract-decorative quality which is new in his work at this time, while the handling of pigment and high tonal values betray the impact of Matisse and the Fauve painters whom he had the opportunity of studying in Paris during 1906–7.

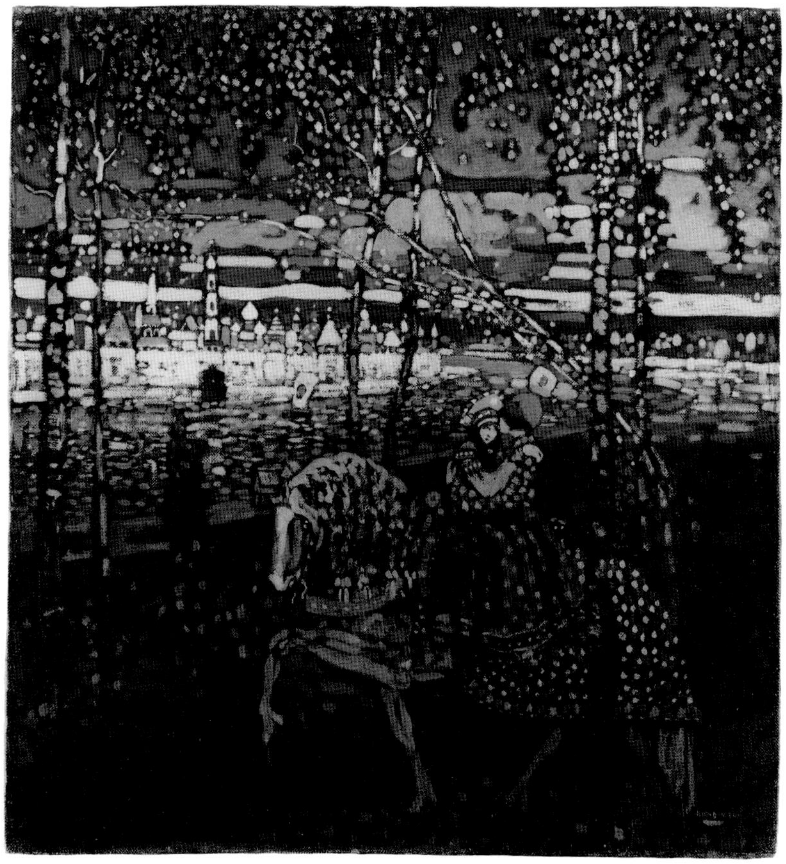

Wassily Kandinsky 1866–1944

37 Picture with Three Spots
Bild mit drei Flecken

1914
Oil on canvas, 121 × 111 cm
Signed/dated lower left: 'Kandinsky 1914'[1]
Condition is good, apart from some slight paint losses to the extreme edges of the canvas, especially at the corners, also a small indentation at top right. The painting is unvarnished, and has been fitted to a new stretcher
Accession no.1975.36

Provenance
Herwarth Walden [?]
Max Leon Flemming, Hamburg[2]
Rudolf Bauer, Berlin
Solomon R.Guggenheim, New York
Museum of Non-Objective Painting, subsequently Solomon R.Guggenheim Museum, New York
Galerie Beyeler, Basle
Galleria Internazionale, Milan
Thyssen-Bornemisza Collection, 1975

Exhibitions
Berlin, Der Sturm, 1916, *44. Ausstellung. Kandinsky, Gemälde und Aquarelle*, no.25
Dresden, Galerie Arnold, 1919, *Sonderausstellung Der Sturm: Expressionisten, Futuristen, Kubisten*, no.124
Charleston, SC, Gibbes Memorial Art Gallery, 1936, *Solomon R.Guggenheim Collection of Non-Objective Paintings*, no.70
Philadelphia, PA, Art Alliance, 1937, *Solomon R.Guggenheim Collection of Non-Objective Paintings*, no.78
Charleston, SC, Gibbes Memorial Art Gallery, 1938, *Solomon R.Guggenheim Collection of Non-Objective Paintings*, no.108
New York, Solomon R.Guggenheim Foundation, 1939, *Art of Tomorrow*, no. 242 [as '1913']
New York, Museum of Non-Objective Painting, 1945, *Wassily Kandinsky Memorial Exhibition*, no.26 [as '1913'][3]
Munich 1949, no.72 [as '1913']
Pasadena, CA, Art Museum, 1963–4, *Vasily Kandinsky 1866–1944. A Retrospective Exhibition*, no.25[4]
Marseilles, Musée Cantini, 1965, *Expressionisme Allemand, 1900–1920*, no.93
Buffalo, NY, Albright-Knox Art Gallery/Dayton, OH, Art Institute/Cleveland, OH, Museum of Art, 1970–71, *Color and Field 1890–1970*, ill. p.38
Brussels/Paris 1977–8, no.40
USA tour 1982–4, no.14
Modern Masters from the Thyssen-Bornemisza Collection, 1984–6, no.52
Tokyo, National Museum of Modern Art/Kyoto, National Museum of Modern Art, 1987, *Kandinsky*, no.26
Leningrad/Moscow 1988, no.10
Lugano 1989, no.25
Expressionism and Modern German Painting, 1989–90, no.13
Rome 1990–91, no.23

Literature
Grohmann (1961/1), p.333
Frank Whitford, *Kandinsky*, London (Hamlyn) 1967, p.23
Roethel (1982), no.490

The work is recorded under no.196 in the artist's own handlists of paintings;[5] it has on occasion been known by the title *Picture with Three Spots, No.196*. It was purchased from the artist Rudolf Bauer (1889–1953) by Solomon R.Guggenheim, acting on the advice of Baroness Hilla Rebay, the first director of the Museum of Non-Objective Painting in New York. In 1937, it was given by Guggenheim to the foundation which bore his name, as part of the important group of

Notes
1 According to information supplied by the Solomon R.Guggenheim Museum, New York, the painting was inscribed on back of stretcher 'Kandinsky Bild mit [drei Flecken] no.196'; the original stretcher has since been discarded. I am grateful to Vivian E.Barnett, Curator, and Holly Fullam, Program Co-ordinator, for providing me with details concerning this and other works formerly in the Guggenheim Museum collection
2 The painting is illustrated (upside down) in an article by Paul Erich Küppers, 'Die Sammlung Max Leon Flemming in Hamburg', *Der Cicerone*, XIV, no.1 (January 1922), entitled *Komposition 2* (information supplied by Vivian E.Barnett, New York). Flemming almost certainly acquired it directly from Walden, who had included [37] in two exhibitions organized by Der Sturm between 1914 and 1921, while Kandinsky was in Russia
3 Exhibition shown in revised form Chicago, IL, Arts Club/ Pittsburgh PA, Carnegie Institute, during 1945–6; *Picture with Three Spots* was no.5 in Chicago, no.11 in Pittsburgh
4 There were two exhibitions under this title, both organized by the Solomon R.Guggenheim Museum, New York, both of which began in January 1963. The one, international exhibition, which included 89 oil paintings, was shown in New York, Paris, The Hague, and Basle, and did not include *Picture with Three Spots*. The other exhibition, including 65 oil paintings, started in Pasadena and was shown at various cities throughout the United States and Canada during 1963–4, including San Francisco, Portland, Baltimore, Saint Louis and Montreal, but not New York; *Picture with Three Spots* was no.25 in this exhibition
5 See Roethel (1982), p.491

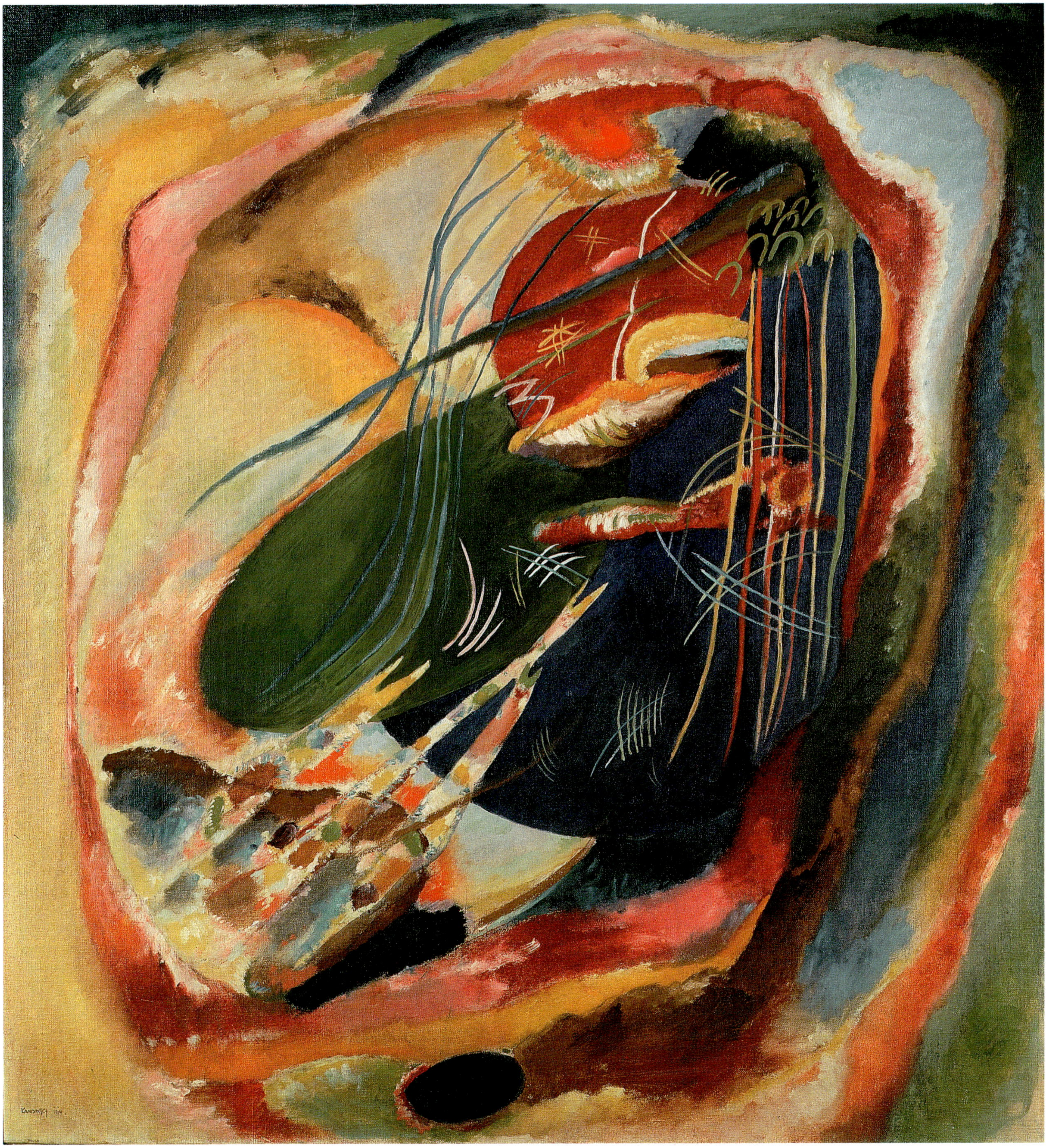

paintings by early abstract masters which formed the core of what was subsequently to become the Solomon R.Guggenheim Museum.[6] Between 1954 and 1960 the picture was on extended loan to the Museum of Fine Arts in Richmond, Virginia. It was 'de-accessioned' by the Guggenheim Museum and sold at auction by Parke-Bernet Galleries, Inc., New York, on 20 October 1971.[7] Subsequently acquired by the Galerie Beyeler in Basle, in 1975 it was sold by the Galleria Internazionale, Milan, to the present owner.

Picture with Three Spots belongs among a group of works executed during the first half of 1914 in which Kandinsky carried his experiments in abandoning recognizable imagery to the very brink of pure abstraction. To many of these works, including the present painting, he gave purely 'abstract' titles – *Black Lines, Picture with Red Spot* – offering little clue as to their content or meaning. By 1914, when this work was painted, the possibility of an entirely abstract art had tantalized him for some time. As early as 1909, he had written at length about the symbolic language of colours and forms, but warned of the danger that abstract painting might descend to the level of mere decoration, 'like a tie or a carpet'.[8] And in his autobiographical 'Reminiscences' of 1913 he poses the question: what is to replace the missing object? – a question which he was at this date still unable to answer.

This uncertainty is clearly reflected in his works of 1913 and 1914, in fact one of the most prolific periods of his life. At first sight, his paintings of these years appear devoid of any identifiable subject-matter. Only on closer acquaintance are most found to contain some distant allusion to natural, usually landscape forms, though such allusions are often impossible to recognize except by examining preparatory drawings, studies and other related works.

In the case of *Picture with Three Spots*, an ink drawing, now in Munich (fig.1), offers a valuable insight into the underlying imagery on which Kandinsky draws. Here, it is possible to recognize at lower left a group of figures seated in two coracle-like boats, and to the right of the boats a succession of wavy lines indicating water, though these forms are abstracted to the level almost of hieroglyphs. The motif of storm-tossed boats, which occurs widely in his work at this time, is usually associated with apocalyptic or eschatological themes; its presence here raises the question whether the painting is meant to evoke some cataclysmic or even apocalyptic event.[9]

Other forms identifiable in the drawing are, however, less specific in their associations. At extreme right, attenuated vertical lines suggest a group of standing figures, their heads inclined to the right, while at the very top a semi-circular form, marked 'Kr[asnoe]' ('red' in Russian) is surely meant to denote the sun. This allusion was perhaps considered too specific, or too easily recognizable, since it does not appear in this form in the finished painting. The drawing also bears further annotations in Russian indicating colours: 'white' and 'grey' at lower right, 'green' for the large ellipse which dominates the centre of the composition. This schema is largely adhered to in the painting as actually executed.

Of Kandinsky's other works of 1914, *Picture with Three Spots* is closest in style to the cycle of four paintings known as the *Campbell Panels* (Museum of Modern Art, New York),[10] which have been tentatively identified as depicting the four seasons.[11] The present picture, on the other hand, offers no such recognizable programme. Rather, it produces its effect on the viewer mainly by means of its clashing and even discordant combinations of colours and forms, calling to mind a frequently quoted passage from 'Reminiscences', in which he describes the genesis of the work of art as being like the creation of the cosmos; he also likens painting to a 'thundering collision of different worlds'.[12] Many of his other works of this period are based, how ever distantly, on the depiction of apocalyptic subjects. Like the storm-tossed boats, the violent clash of colours and forms also calls to mind the possibility that *Picture with Three Spots* conceals within itself some hidden eschatalogical meaning.

Notes

6 For a brief history of the Solomon R.Guggenheim Foundation, the Museum of Non-Objective Painting, and the Solomon R.Guggenheim Museum see the introductory essay by Peter Lawson-Johnston, in Rudenstine (1976), p.1ff

7 *Important 20th Century Paintings, Watercolours and Drawings from the Solomon R.Guggenheim Foundation, New York*, lot 11

8 Lindsay (1982), p.197. The quotation is taken from Kandinsky's treatise *On the Spiritual in Art*, the manuscript of which is dated August 1909

9 For a more detailed discussion of the persistance of recognizable imagery, often of an apocalyptic character, in Kandinsky's works of 1913–14 having no obvious representational starting point, see the chapter 'Paintings with Titles Emphasizing Form and Colour, 1912–1914', in Rose-Carol Washton Long, *Kandinsky. The Development of an Abstract Style*, Oxford (Clarendon Press) 1980, pp.123–36.

10 Roethel (1982), nos.492–5; see also Kenneth C.Lindsay, 'Kandinsky in 1914 New York: Solving a Riddle', *Art News*, LV (May 1956): 32–3, 58–60

11 This identification, by Lindsay (see n.10), of the four Campbell Panels with the four seasons has, more recently, been questioned both by Rudenstine (1976), pp.284f, and by Roethel (1982), p.493

12 Lindsay (1982), p.373

FIG 1 Wassily Kandinsky, *Sketch for 'Picture with Three Spots'*, 1914, ink, 26.7 × 31.3 cm (Munich, Städtische Galerie im Lenbachhaus, GMS 494)

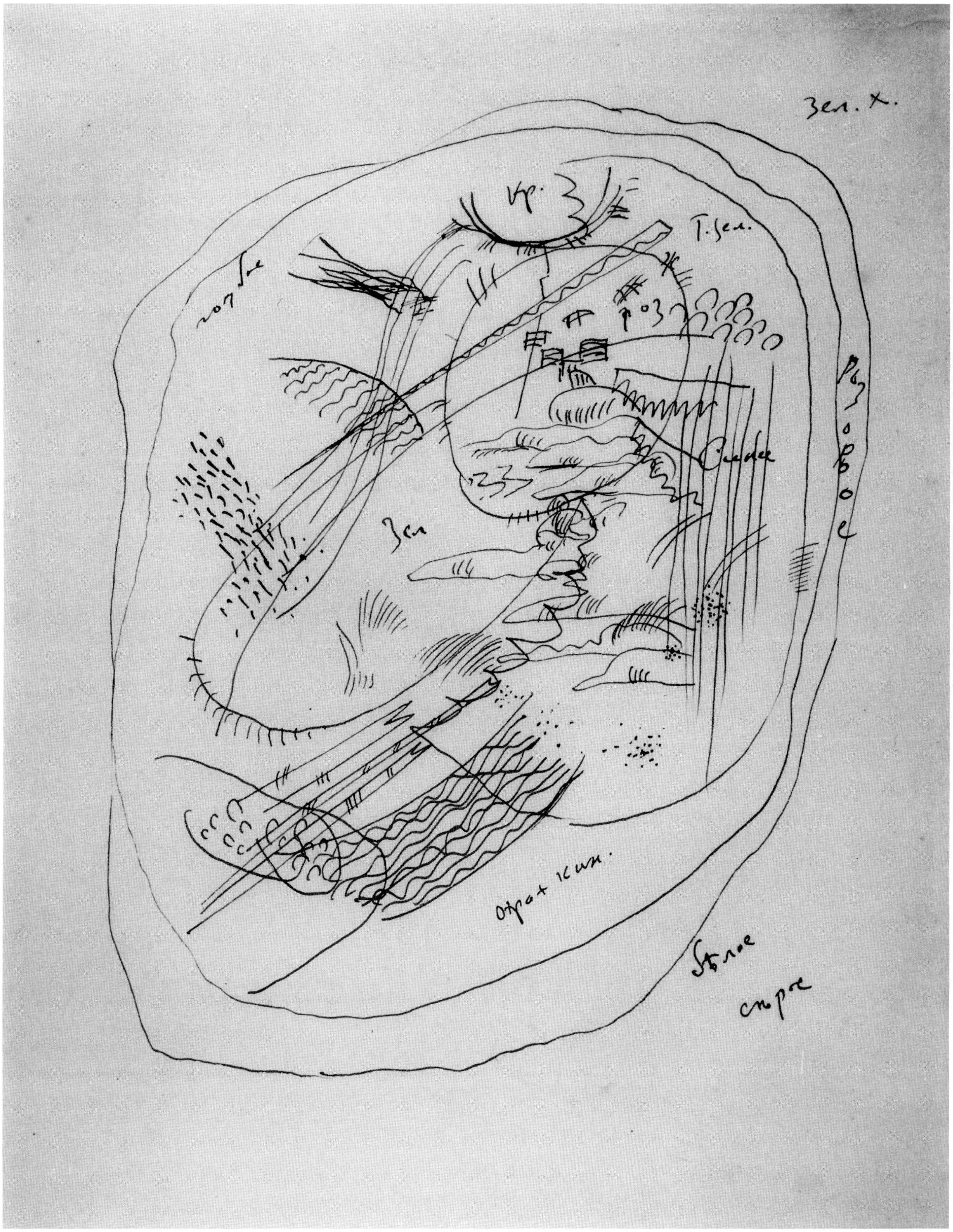
Зел. х.
Кр.
Т. зел.
Зел

Wassily Kandinsky 1866–1944

38 In the Bright Oval
Im hellen Oval

1925
Oil on board, 73 × 59 cm
Initialled/dated lower left: 'K 25'
The thick cardboard support shows a slight convex warp; otherwise condition is good
Accession no.1975.31

Provenance
Charlotte Mack, San Francisco, CA
Alexander Rabow Gallery, San Francisco, CA
Galleria Internazionale, Milan
Thyssen-Bornemisza Collection, 1975

Exhibitions
Berlin, Galerie Neumann-Nierendorf, 1925, *Die Maler der Gegenwart* [?]
Brunswick, Gesellschaft der Freunde junger Kunst, 1926, *Jubiläums-Ausstellung W. Kandinsky*, no.17
Dresden, Galerie Arnold/Berlin, Galerie Neumann–Nierendorf, 1926, *Kandinsky*, no.41[1]
Munich, Neue Kunst Hans Goltz, 1927, *Kandinsky*, no.20[2]
Oakland, CA, Art Gallery, 1929, *Kandinsky*, no.27 [as 'In a Light Oval']
Los Angeles, CA, Braxton Gallery, 1930, *The Blue Four: Kandinsky*, no.4[3]
Oakland, CA, Art Gallery, 1931, *The Blue Four* [Kandinsky] no.8 [as 'Inside Light Oval']
Japanese tour 1976
Brussels/Paris 1977–8, no.41
Australian tour 1979–80, no.51
Budapest/Szombathely 1985–6, no.32
Tokyo, Museum of Modern Art/Kyoto, Museum of Modern Art, 1987, *Kandinsky*, no.59
Luxemburg/Munich/Vienna 1988, no.37
Lugano 1989, no.26
Expressionism and Modern German Painting, 1989–90, no.14
Rome 1990–91, no.24

Literature
Grohmann (1961/1), p.335
Roethel (1984), no.756

Arriving back in Russia at the very end of 1914, having been forced as an enemey alien to leave Germany on the outbreak of the Great War, Kandinsky must have been taken aback by the rapid strides in the development of avant-garde art during the relatively short time he had been away.[4] For several years, he had wrestled with the theoretical question of the possibility of an entirely abstract manner of painting. Now, it seemed, younger artists such as Malevich and Tatlin saw no difficulty in envisaging a far more radical form of art than he himself had hitherto been able to contemplate.

Notes
1 Jubilee exhibition in celebration of the artist's sixtieth birthday; on the various Kandinsky 'jubilee' exhibitions which took place throughout Germany during 1926–7, see Roethel (1982), p.29. The Dresden–Berlin exhibition of autumn 1926 was shown subsequently in Dessau at the Anhaltischer Kunstverein and in Munich at Hans Goltz's gallery Neue Kunst
2 See n.1
3 Exhibition recorded by Roethel (1984), p.708
4 For an account of Kandinsky's movements during this period see Barnett (1989), pp.10ff. He had last been in Russia for about six weeks during July–August 1913: see chronological table printed in Eichner (1957), p.209

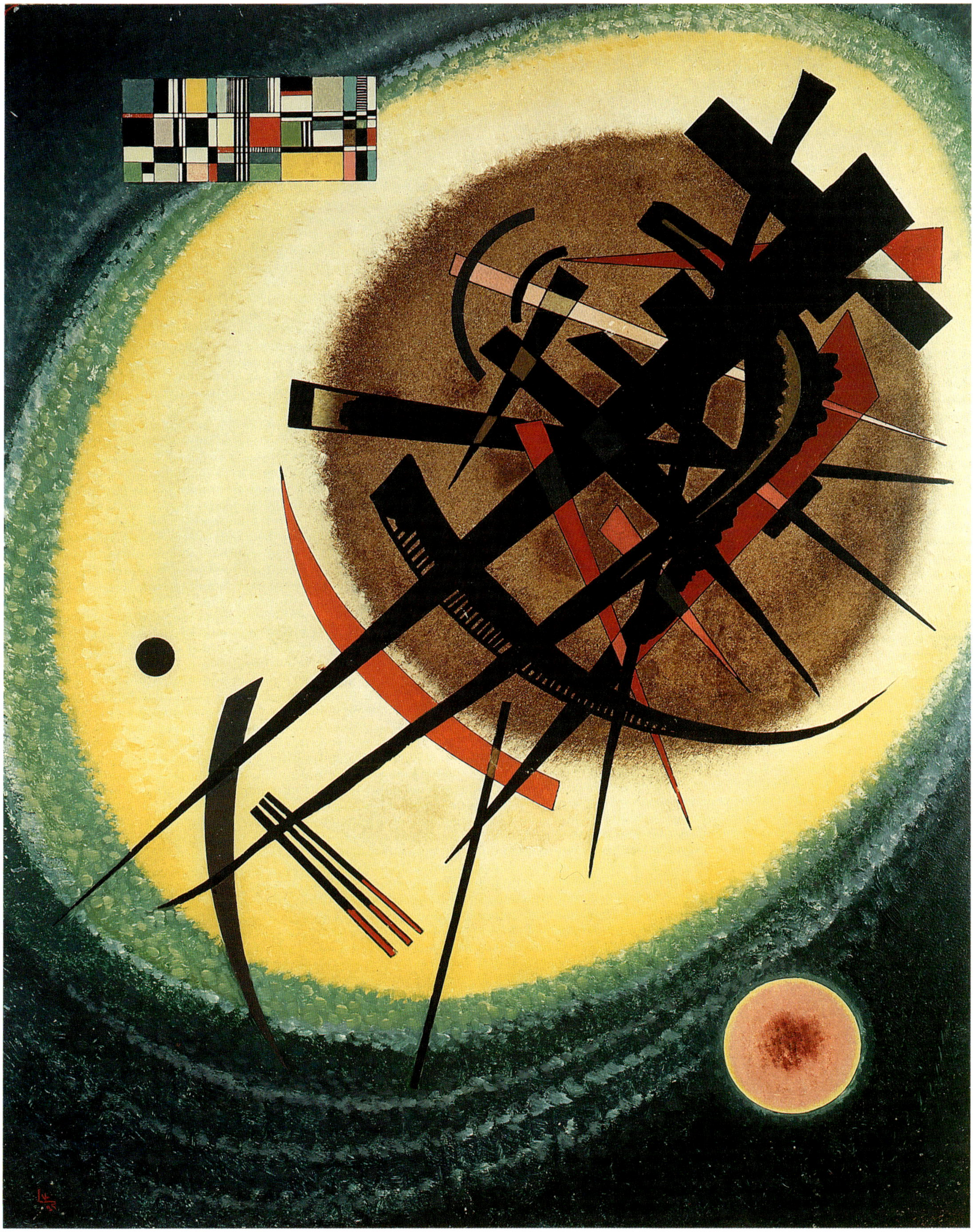

Just how quickly Kandinsky succeeded in picking up the threads of artistic life in Russia it is impossible to say. There is, on the one hand, no doubt that he was soon in close touch with a number of avant-garde artists: Rodchenko and Stepanova, for example, even lived in Kandinsky's house in Moscow for a time during 1915.[5] It is also possible that he saw the remarkable exhibition *0–10* in Petrograd in December 1915 while on his way to Sweden. The most practicable route from Moscow to Stockholm in wartime was via Petrograd, where it would have been necessary to change trains. Though a visit to the exhibition is not documented, it seems highly likely that he would have seized this opportunity of acquainting himself with the work of other radical artists. If indeed he did so, he must surely have been astonished to find Malevich exhibiting a very considerable body of entirely abstract, geometric work to which he gave the name 'Suprematism': paintings based on no apparent system or reminiscence of natural form, but seemingly consisting only of floating squares, rectangles, circles and other geometric elements.[6]

It was, on the other hand, only gradually that Kandinsky himself began to assimilate the new formal vocabulary of the Russian abstractionists. Much of his work of these years is, in essence atavistic, recalling either his lyrical abstractions of immediately before the war, or else the straight-forwardly realistic 'fairytale' paintings with riders and castles and figures in folk costume done in Munich in some cases more than a decade earlier (see [40]). Only gradually, for the most part after 1919, do geometric shapes begin to play a significant role in his work, often co-existing – at times uneasily – with more playful or capricious motifs which still often evoke natural or landscape forms. Not until the very last paintings of his Russian period, executed just prior to his departure for Germany at the end of 1921, is it possible to detect a new confidence and deftness of touch in his handling of purely geometric abstract form.

At almost every stage in Kandinsky's career, formal innovation went hand in hand with theoretical speculation, even if, in the end, he firmly believed that the irrational or inspirational element in art took precedence over rational investigation. Significantly, it was also only in 1919 that he published his first essay on the elementary resources of purely abstract painting, point and line, which appeared under the general heading 'Little Articles on Big Questions'.[7] This essay, printed in *Iskusstvo*, the journal of the Fine Arts Section of the People's Commissariat of Enlightenment in which Kandinsky and other avant-garde artists for a time played a leading role, in many important respects foreshadows his theoretical writings of the 1920s, in which he sought to formulate his ideas and researches as a teacher at the Bauhaus from 1922 onwards – ideas which found fullest expression in his 1926 treatise *Point and Line to Plane*.[8]

Point and Line to Plane, the manuscript of which was completed in November 1925, the year *In the Bright Oval* was painted, devotes considerable space to an examination of the purely abstract language of painting, particularly the compositional significance of various colours and forms, regarded as independent, autonomous elements within the picture. In his own paintings of the same period, Kandinsky employed primarily, though not exclusively geometric forms: rectangles, circles, ovals. The use of the oval, in particular, may be traced back to an earlier sequence of important canvases, begun while he was still in Russia, in which similar forms play a dominant role: works such as *Two Ovals* (1919), *Red Oval* (1920) and *White Oval* (1921).[9]

It would, however, be mistaken to see these pictures as merely exemplifying his theories concerning the significance of abstract geometric form. Like many of his works from the years before the war, paintings such as *In the Bright Oval* also convey the impression of being spiritual or cosmic depictions. Particularly striking in this work is the lunar form of the circle which features at the bottom right of the composition, while the more diffuse, circular brownish form which occupies more or less the centre of the picture perhaps evokes the 'darkened sun' which also occurs in Kandinsky's earlier, more theosophically influenced paintings, and to which he refers in his pre-war treatise, *On the Spiritual in Art*.[10] More unusual is the purely rectilinear, multi-coloured 'box' at upper left, which seems almost like some kind of rebus or even key to the

Notes

5 See chronology printed in *Kandinsky: Russian and Bauhaus Years, 1915–1933*, exh. cat., New York, Solomon R. Guggenheim Museum, 1983, p.350; on Kandinsky's relationship with other members of the Russian avant-garde see Clark V. Poling, in ibid., pp.13ff and especially pp.30–6

6 Kandinsky also participated, together with Malevich, in the Moscow exhibition *The Year 1915* in which, however, it appears that only a-logistic paintings by Malevich were shown: see Rakitin (1979), p.80

7 Lindsay (1982), pp.423–7

8 Ibid., pp.527–699

9 Roethel (1984), nos.659, 668 and 680

10 Lindsay (1982), p.142; on Kandinsky's involvement with theosophy and mysticism see Sixten Ringbom, *The Sounding Cosmos. A Study in the Spiritualism of Kandinsky and the Genesis of Abstract Painting*, Åbo (Åbo Akademi) 1970

colours deployed in the composition. Though various kinds of chequer-boards and grids are to be found frequently in Kandinsky's paintings of these Bauhaus years, similar 'boxes of colours' occur in only a small number of works, of which the most important are *Black Accompaniment* and *Capricious Line*, both of 1924.[11]

In the Bright Oval is entered as no.313 in the artist's handlist of paintings, according to which it was completed in May 1925.[12] It was shown as early as October the same year in an exhibition at the Galerie Nierendorf in Berlin, as well as at the various jubilee exhibitions of 1926–7 to mark the artist's sixtieth birthday. It seems, however, to have travelled to the United States shortly thereafter, being shown at the Oakland Art Gallery in 1929 as part of a one-man exhibition which, according to the catalogue, had been 'assembled in Europe last year by Mme Galka E. Scheyer.'[13] In an exhibition of the work of the Blue Four, again at the Oakland Art Gallery, in 1931, the painting is recorded as belonging to the collection of Charlotte Mack.[14]

11 See Roethel (1984), nos.713 and 722
12 See ibid., p.708
13 The reference is to Emmy Scheyer, a close friend of Jawlensky, who was largely responsible for promoting the reputation of the Blue Four – Kandinsky, Klee, Feininger and Jawlensky – in the United States
14 I am grateful to Christine Droll, of the Oakland Museum, for making copies of these and other early catalogues of the Oakland Art Gallery available to me

Wassily Kandinsky 1866–1944

39 Around the Line
Autour de la Ligne

1943
Oil on board, 42 × 57.8 cm
Initialled/dated lower left: 'K 43'; also initialled and dated on back of board: 'K no.710 1943'[1]
The work is painted in oil on what was probably a piece of commercially pre-prepared, sized cardboard; there is a history of numerous abrasions and water stains which have been restored. The oil paint is very dry, so that it has the appearance almost of tempera. The painting is unvarnished
Accession no.1972.8

Provenance
Estate of the artist
Nina Kandinsky, Paris
Thyssen-Bornemisza Collection, 1972[2]

Exhibitions
Paris, Galerie René Drouin, 1949, *Kandinsky, Époque Parisienne, 1933–44*, no.20
Berne, Kunsthalle, 1955, *Gesamtausstellung Wassily Kandinsky*, no.108
Bremen 1975, no.31
Lugano 1975, no.54
Japanese tour 1976
Brussels/Paris 1977–8, no.42
Lugano 1978, no.49
New York, Solomon R.Guggenheim Museum, 1985, *Kandinsky in Paris*, no.151[3]
Milan, Palazzo Reale, 1985, *Kandinsky a Parigi*, no.121
Cologne 1986, p.120, ill. p.121
Leningrad/Moscow 1988, no.12

Literature
Grohmann (1961/1), p.342
Kiel (1974), p.60, ill. p.61
Roethel (1984), no.1147

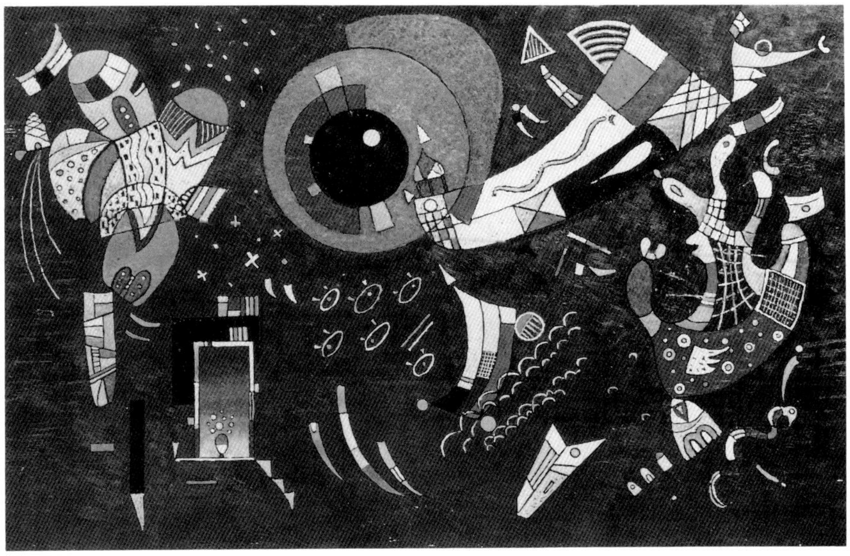

FIG 1 Wassily Kandinsky, *Sketch for 'Autour du Cercle'*, 1940, oil on mahogany panel, 40 × 60 cm (formerly Basle, Galerie Beyeler)

In 1933, the Bauhaus, then in Berlin, was forced to close by Germany's new National Socialist government. Kandinsky emigrated to Paris, where he spent the remainder of his life; he died there in December 1944. His paintings of this last Parisian period are more playful in spirit than his often severely geometric works of the Bauhaus years, and are frequently inhabited by seemingly anthropomorphic forms which exhibit an unmistakable affinity with the works of Joan Miró.

Notes
1 The work is entered under number 710 in the artist's handlist of paintings, according to which it was done in February 1943; see Roethel (1984), p.1041; Grohmann (1961/1), p.342
2 Acquired directly from the previous owner (letters from Mme Nina Kandinsky to A.S.Berkes and to Baron H.H.Thyssen-Bornemisza, 9 May and 13 June 1972; Lugano-Castagnola, Thyssen-Bornemisza Collection, archive)
3 Shown in revised form Houston, TX, Museum of Fine Arts/Vienna, Museum des 20. Jahrhunderts, 1985

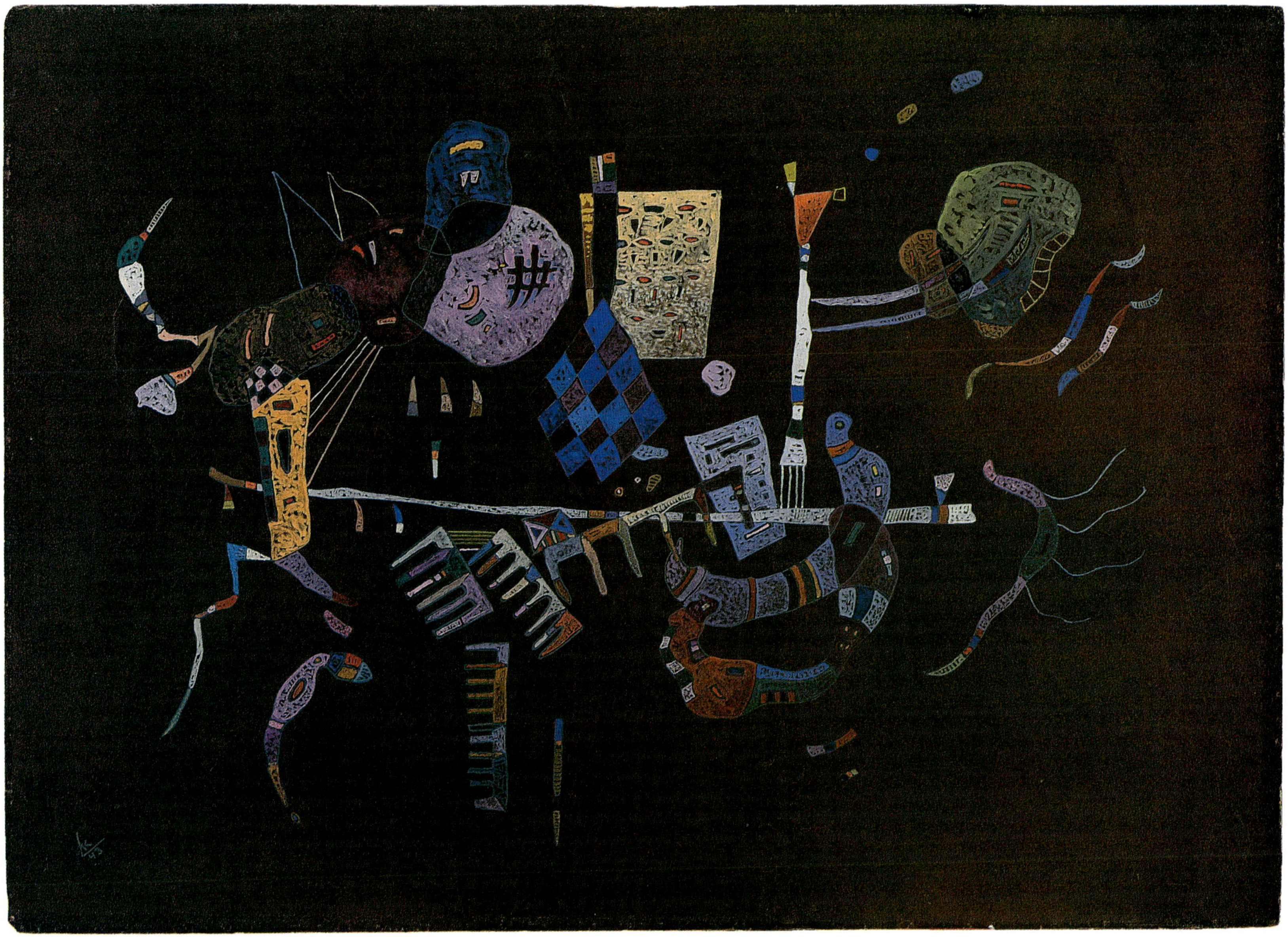

4 Handlist no.677; Roethel (1984), no.1115
5 Handlist no.675; Roethel (1984), no.1113
6 Ibid., p.1006

Kandinsky was still, on the other hand, intrigued by what he termed the 'fundamental elements' of painting, which he set out to explore in theoretical terms in his writings of the Bauhaus period, in particular his 1926 treatise *Point and Line to Plane*. Many of his late paintings, including *Around the Line*, exploit the expressive potential of abstract, geometric forms, especially circle and line.

Closely related in theme to *Around the Line*, though much larger, is the painting *Autour du Cercle* (New York, Solomon R. Guggenheim Museum), completed between May and August 1940.[4] For this earlier painting, Kandinsky made a compositionally almost identical oil study on mahogany panel (fig.1), whose dimensions are very nearly the same as those of *Around the Line*.[5] Both *Around the Line* and the sketch for *Autour du Cercle* were shown in the exhibition *Kandinsky, Époque Parisienne* at the Galerie René Drouin, Paris, in 1949.[6] Given the subject of the Thyssen Collection's painting, its dimensions, the medium employed, and the context in which it was first exhibited, it seems likely that [39] may also have been an oil study for an intended, but unexecuted, larger painting of the same title.

Wassily Kandinsky 1866–1944

40 Untitled

1915
Pencil, Indian ink and watercolour on paper, 45 × 61 cm
Initialled/dated lower left: 'K [in triangle] 15'
In good condition
Accession no.1982.47

Provenance
Johnny Roosval, Stockholm[1]
Private collection, Sweden
James Kirkman Ltd, London
Thyssen-Bornemisza Collection, 1982[2]

Exhibitions
Stockholm, Carl Gummesons Konsthandel, 1916, *Kandinsky: Oljemålninger och Grafik*, no.13
Malmö, Konsthall/Stockholm, Moderna Museet, 1989–90, *Kandinsky och Sverige*, no.22

Literature
J.R.[Johnny Roosval], 'Kandinsky', *Saisonen*, 1 (1916): 4–5
Eichner (1957), p.175 and fig.73
Barnett (1989), p.29, ill. p.157
Barnett (1990), p.101
Barnett (1992), no.430

This watercolour dates from December 1915. In all probability, it was executed in Moscow prior to Kandinsky's departure for Stockholm, where he arrived on 23 December, in time to spend Christmas with Gabriele Münter. It was included, together with a number of other watercolours which the artist entitled 'Bagatelles', in the important one-man exhibition of his work organized by the dealer Carl Gummeson and shown in Stockholm in February 1916.[3]

Kandinsky's work of 1915–16 is puzzlingly ambivalent in style and intention. On the one hand, there are numerous glass-paintings and watercolours, including the Bagatelles, which are unashamedly figurative and literal in their depiction of mostly allegorical or fairy-tale subjects. On the other, there are drawings and watercolours which continue in the same vein as his most 'advanced' works of immediately before the outbreak of war such as the *Campbell Panels* or the Thyssen Collection's *Painting with Three Spots* [37], in which the artist employs a highly abstract formal language. These two categories of work may perhaps correspond to two quite different publics: while the figurative paintings were doubtless more immediately

Notes
1 See n.8
2 The heirs of the former owner had previously offered the work for sale at auction at Sotheby's, London (*Impressionist and Modern Drawings and Watercolours*, 1 July 1981, lot 338), where it was acquired by James Kirkman Ltd and Waddington Galleries, London. I am grateful to James Kirkman, London, and to Vivian E.Barnett, New York, for supplying information which enabled me to confirm the exact provenance of this watercolour
3 Barnett (1989), p.34

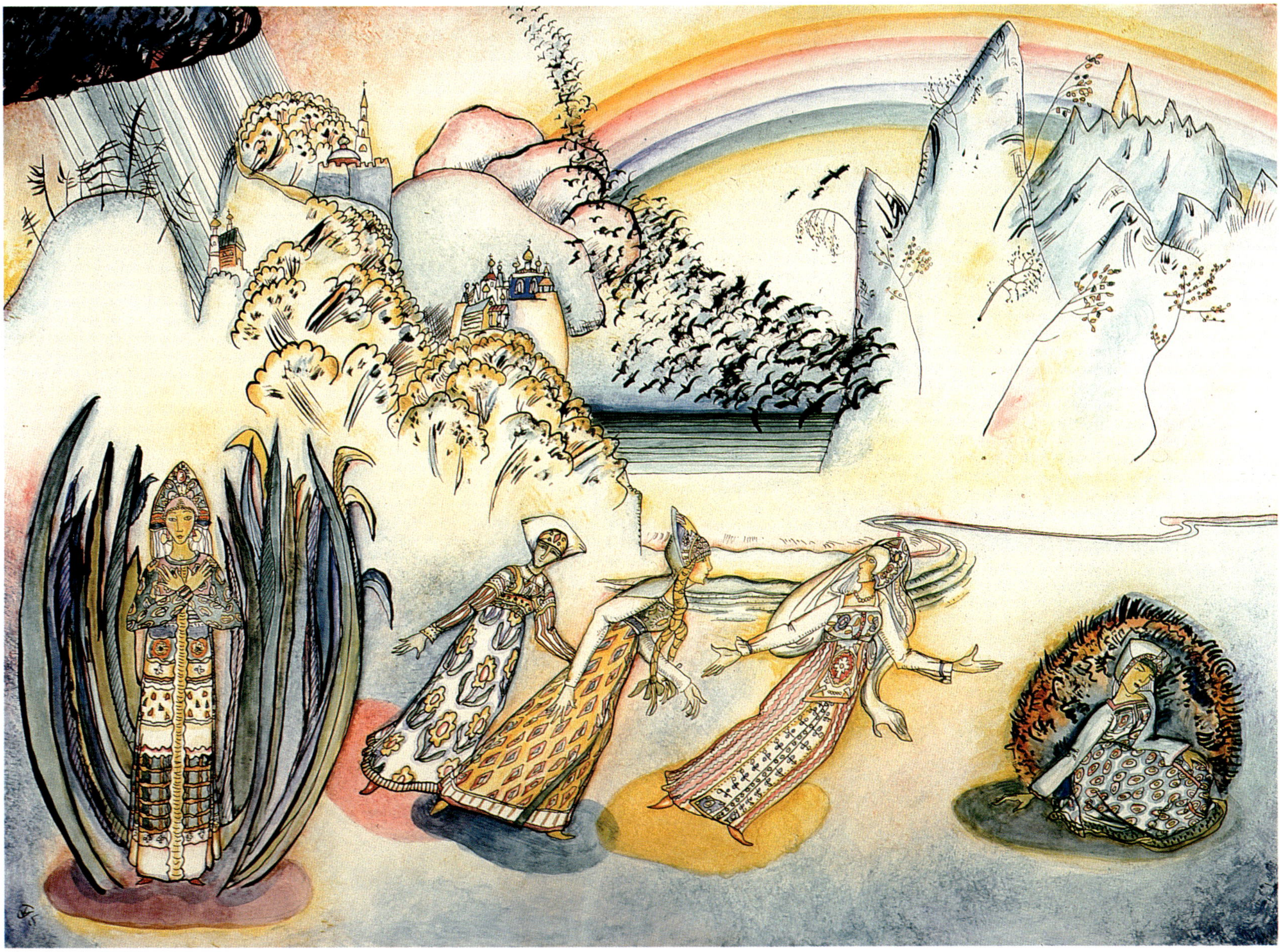

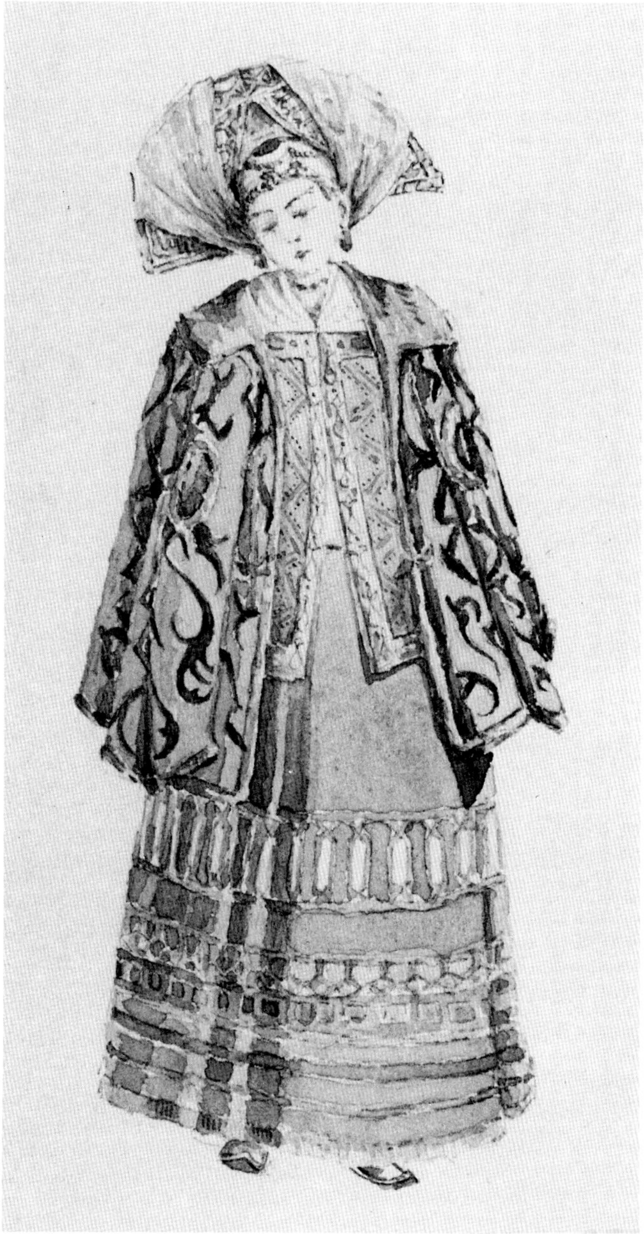

FIG 1 Wassily Kandinsky, *Costume drawing*, c1901–2, pencil and watercolour, 19.3 × 10.8 cm (Munich, Städtische Galerie im Lenbachhaus, GMS 465)

FIG 2 Wassily Kandinsky, *Untitled*, December 1915, watercolour, 46.8 × 63.8 cm (Private collection)

attractive and potentially saleable, there was also, at least in Sweden, a number of avant-garde collectors deeply interested in Kandinsky's experiments in pushing non-figuration to the limits in his search for an entirely new kind of painting.[4]

The subject of the present watercolour remains uncertain. The work has an undeniably Russian 'feel', and is in some ways akin to the jewel-like fairy-tale illustrations produced by Kandinsky's compatriot Ivan Bilibin. Some of the costumes also recall studies of Oriental and Russian peasant attire executed more than a decade previously (see fig.1), while the non-naturalistic sequence of colours in the rainbow may well reflect a renewed interest in mysticism, in Russian folk tales, or in the shamanistic legends which have been identified as a possible source of inspiration.[5] But the dream-like mood of the work, especially the sleeping female figure, also evokes the mysterious world conjured up by the Belgian dramatist Maurice

Notes

4 On Kandinsky's Swedish patrons see ibid., especially pp.40ff, 56ff

5 On the influence of shamanism on Kandinsky's work see in particular Peg Weiss, 'Kandinsky and "Old Russia". An Ethnographic Exploration', in Gabriel P. Weisberg and Laurinda S. Dixon (eds.), *The Documented Image. Visions in Art History*, Syracuse, NY, University Press 1987, pp.187–222

6 In *On the Spiritual*, Kandinsky referred to *Les Sept Princesses* as representing 'not figures of ancient times, as the stylized heroes of Shakespeare appear to us … [but] souls searching in the mist, threatened with suffocation, over whom hovers a dark invisible power…'; see Lindsay (1982), p.146

7 The first page of this list, inscribed 'Bagatelles (Petites aquarelles)' and dated '*Stockholm*, Januar 1916' is reproduced in Barnett (1989), p.30, fig.4. It is now part of the Kandinsky archive in the collection of the Musée National d'Art Moderne, Centre Georges Pompidou, Paris

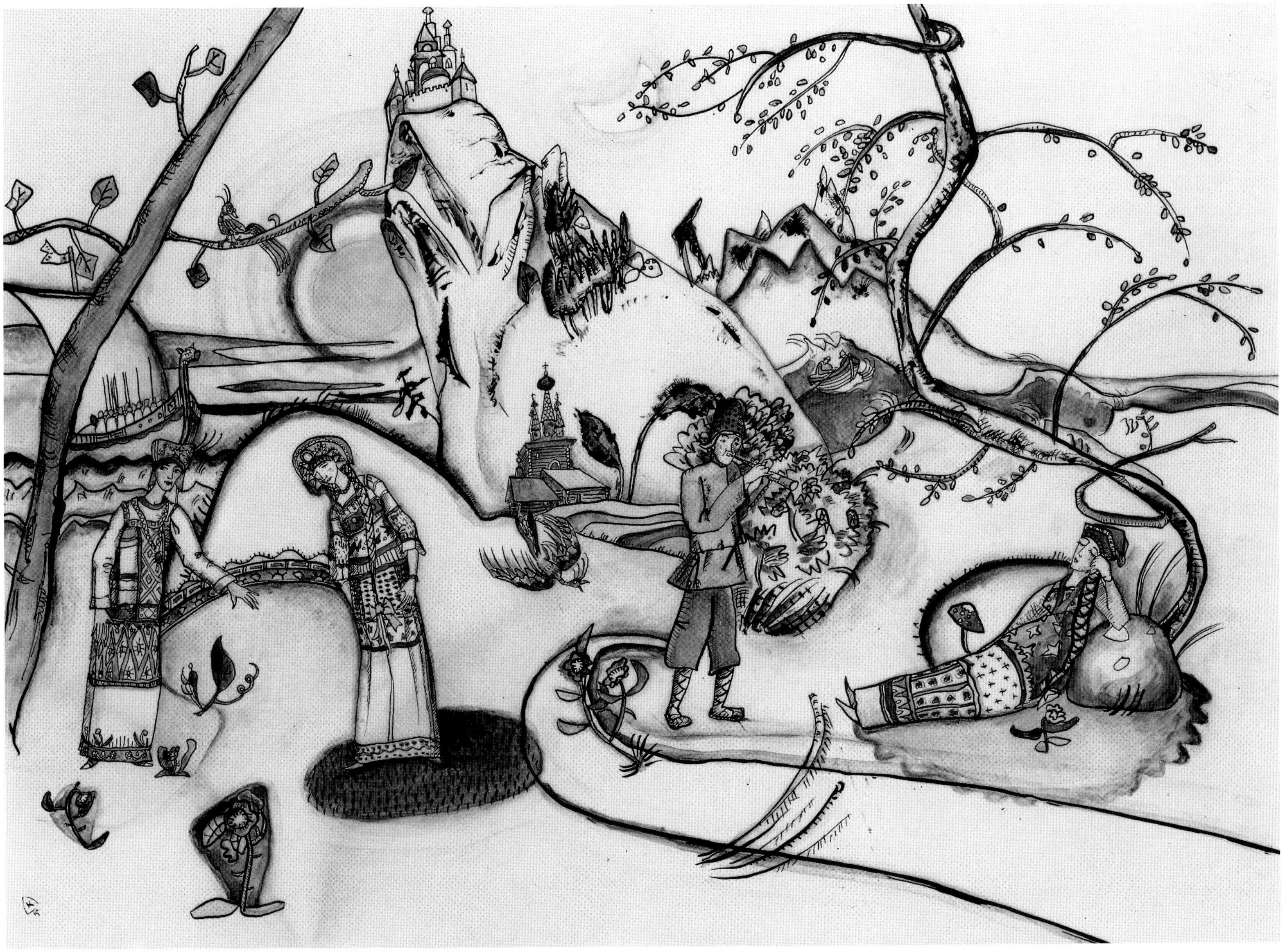

8 Kandinsky's handwritten entry refers merely to the work having been sold to 'Dr Roosval'; however, the illustration reproduced in the article in *Saisonen* referred to above names Roosval's wife Ellen (née von Hallwyl) as the owner of the watercolour. She may also have been the actual purchaser. I am indebted to Dr Bengt Lärkner of the University of Linköping, Sweden, for drawing this to my attention, and for information about members of the Roosval family

Maeterlinck, in particular his play *Les Sept Princesses* (The Seven Princesses), to which Kandinsky makes specific allusion in his treatise *On the Spiritual in Art*.[6] Maeterlinck's dramas were in any case extremely well-known in Russia at this time.

The work is entered as the second item in the handlist of Bagatelles begun by the artist in Stockholm in the winter of 1916, which Gabriele Münter completed.[7] The entry notes that it was sold, presumably by Gummeson, to the art-historian and collector Johnny Roosval for 500 crowns.[8] It may plausibly be regarded as a pendant to the first item on the list, another untitled watercolour of similar dimensions and closely comparable in subject-matter and style, also datable to December 1915 (see fig.2). Though the Thyssen Collection's watercolour has often been called 'Maerchen' (Fairy Tale), this was not Kandinsky's title, and the work is untitled in both versions of the artist's handlist of his own works.

Wassily Kandinsky 1866–1944

41 Untitled[1]

1922
Watercolour and Indian ink on heavy watercolour paper, 26 × 35 cm
Initialled/dated lower left: 'K 22'
Some discolouration and staining, in particular adjacent to the edges of the sheet. Otherwise condition is good
Accession no.1974.50

Provenance
Robert von Hirsch, Basle
Galerie Beyeler, Basle
Galerie R.N.Ketterer, Campione d'Italia
Thyssen-Bornemisza Collection, 1974

Exhibitions
Cologne 1986, p.116, ill. p.117
Tokyo, National Museum of Modern Art/Kyoto, National Museum of Modern Art, 1987, *Kandinsky*, no.51

Literature
Kiel (1974), p.60, ill.
The work will be included in the second volume of Vivian E.Barnett's catalogue raisonné of Kandinsky's watercolours.[2]

This watercolour, like a number of works dating from Kandinsky's first years at the Bauhaus, combines purely abstract, geometric elements (circles, triangles, straight lines) with more 'spontaneous' forms which appear to have been freely composed, and which in some instances recall the motivic vocabulary of his pre-war paintings. At upper right, a boat with a triangular sail (which in Kandinsky's earlier work is associated thematically with the Biblical flood) is here juxtaposed with what may be a rowing boat, highly schematized, and consisting of little more than a circle surmounted by the hunched figure of a lone oarsman. At lower left, a succession of extended, in some cases curving lines form a criss-cross pattern, like clashing swords. This area of the composition is unexpectedly similar to the lower-left quarter of Kandinsky's oil painting *In the Bright Oval* [38], painted some three years later, while the dominant arch form, so striking in [41], is also found tipped on its side and partially obscured in the later painting.

Notes
1 The work is not entered in the artist's handlist of watercolours, according to a letter from Vivian E.Barnett to the author, 30 October 1989
2 The first volume, Barnett (1992), covers the years 1900–21. A second volume, devoted to the works of 1922–44, is scheduled for publication in 1993

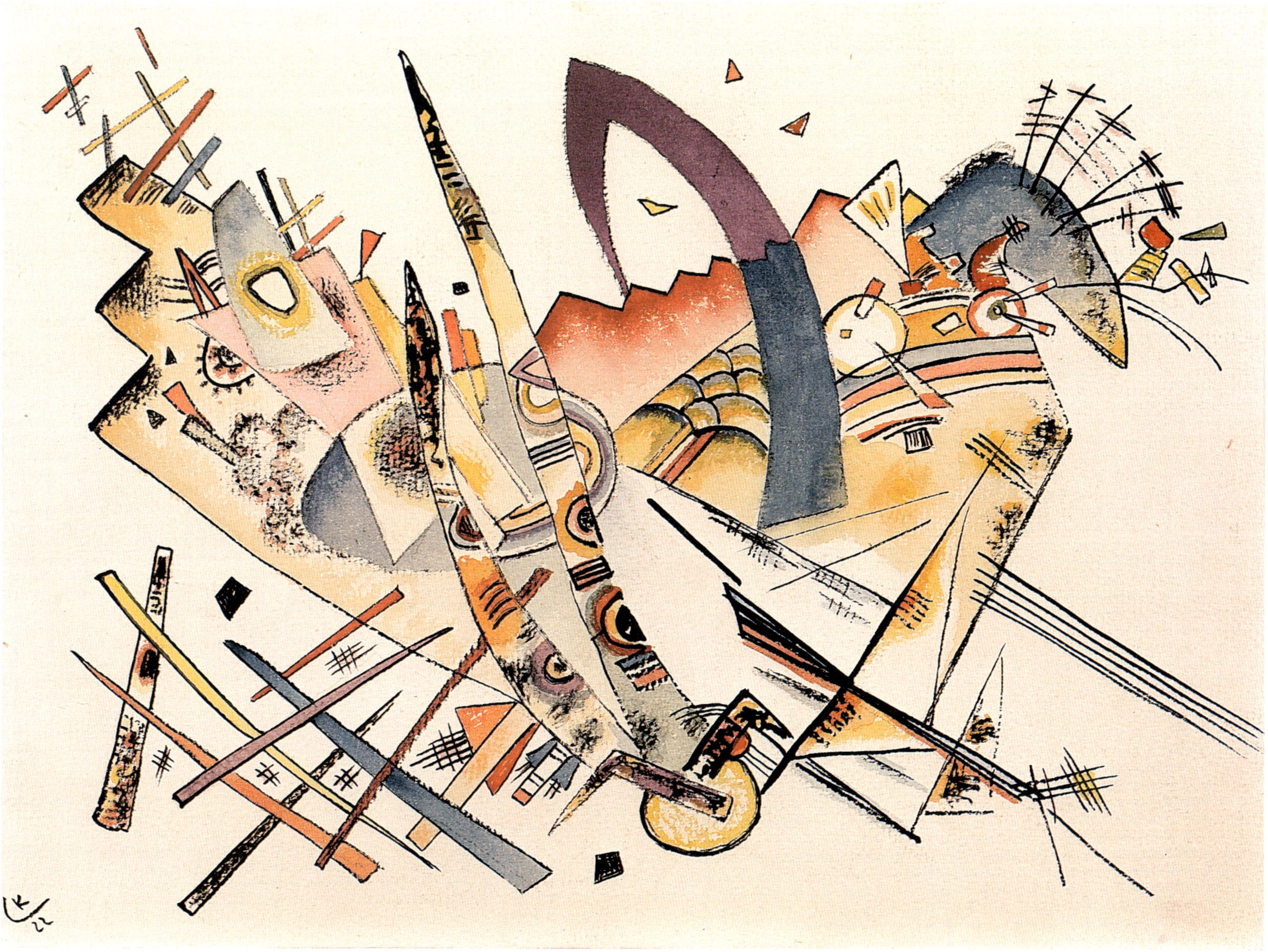

Wassily Kandinsky 1866–1944

42 Delicate Tension
Zarte Spannung[1]

1923
Watercolour and Indian ink on heavy watercolour paper, 35.5 × 25 cm
Initialled/dated lower left: 'K 23'
There are minor stains close to the right-hand edge of the sheet. Otherwise condition is good
Accession no.1977.77

Provenance
Galerie Ferdinand Möller, Berlin
Rudolf Bauer, Berlin
Hilla Rebay, New York
Solomon R. Guggenheim, New York; given to the Guggenheim Foundation, 1938[2]
Private collection
Andrew Crispo Gallery, New York
Thyssen-Bornemisza Collection, 1977

Exhibitions
Charleston, SC, Gibbes Memorial Art Gallery, 1936, *Solomon R. Guggenheim Collection of Non-Objective Paintings*, no.75
Philadelphia, PA, Art Alliance, 1937, *Solomon R. Guggenheim Collection of Non-Objective Paintings*, no.85
Charleston, SC, Gibbes Memorial Art Gallery, 1938, *Solomon R. Guggenheim Collection of Non-Objective Paintings*, no.115
New York, Solomon R. Guggenheim Foundation, 1939, *Art of Tomorrow*, no.261
New York, Museum of Non-Objective Painting, 1945, *Wassily Kandinsky Memorial Exhibition*, no.56
Lugano 1978, no.48
Cologne 1986, p.118, ill. p.119
Tokyo, National Museum of Modern Art/Kyoto, National Museum of Modern Art, 1987, *Kandinsky*, no.57

Literature
The work will be included in the second volume of Vivian E. Barnett's catalogue raisonné of Kandinsky's watercolours[3]

A number of Kandinsky's watercolours and other works on paper (including prints) dating from his early years at the Weimar Bauhaus are untitled, while the titles of others are purely descriptive of the colours and forms employed: *Grey*,[4] *Black Lines*,[5] *On Violet*.[6] However, to a group of works of 1922–3, among them *Delicate Tension*, the artist gave titles that are purposely more allusive, albeit enigmatic: *Free Relationship*,[7] *Joyful Ascent*,[8] *Bright Sound*.[9] In its dimensions and format, *Delicate Tension* is closely related to *Bright Sound*, also of 1923, now in the Solomon R. Guggenheim Museum, New York. In its use of exclusively geometric form, on the other hand, it is more akin to the watercolour *Free Relationship*, painted in the same month. As already noted in connection with *In the Bright Oval* [38], even as late as 1925 Kandinsky would still from time to time combine purely geometric shapes with seemingly more 'spontaneous' forms which on occasion recall natural or landscape motifs, or the iconography of his earlier, pre-war paintings.

The work is entered under no.85 in the artist's handlist of watercolours, according to which it was painted in July 1923.[10]

Notes
1 The title derives from the artist's handlist of watercolours: see note 10 below
2 *Delicate Tension* was 'de-accessioned' by the Guggenheim Museum and sold at auction by Parke-Bernet Galleries, Inc., New York, 20 October 1971 (*Important 20th Century Paintings, Watercolours & Drawings from the Solomon R. Guggenheim Foundation, New York*, lot 15); see also n.1 to p.162
3 See n.2 to p.176
4 Barnett (1980), no.15
5 Roethel (1970), no.184
6 Barnett (1980), no.14
7 Ibid., no.12
8 Roethel (1970), no.177
9 Barnett (1980), no.11
10 Letter from Vivian E. Barnett to the author, 30 October 1989

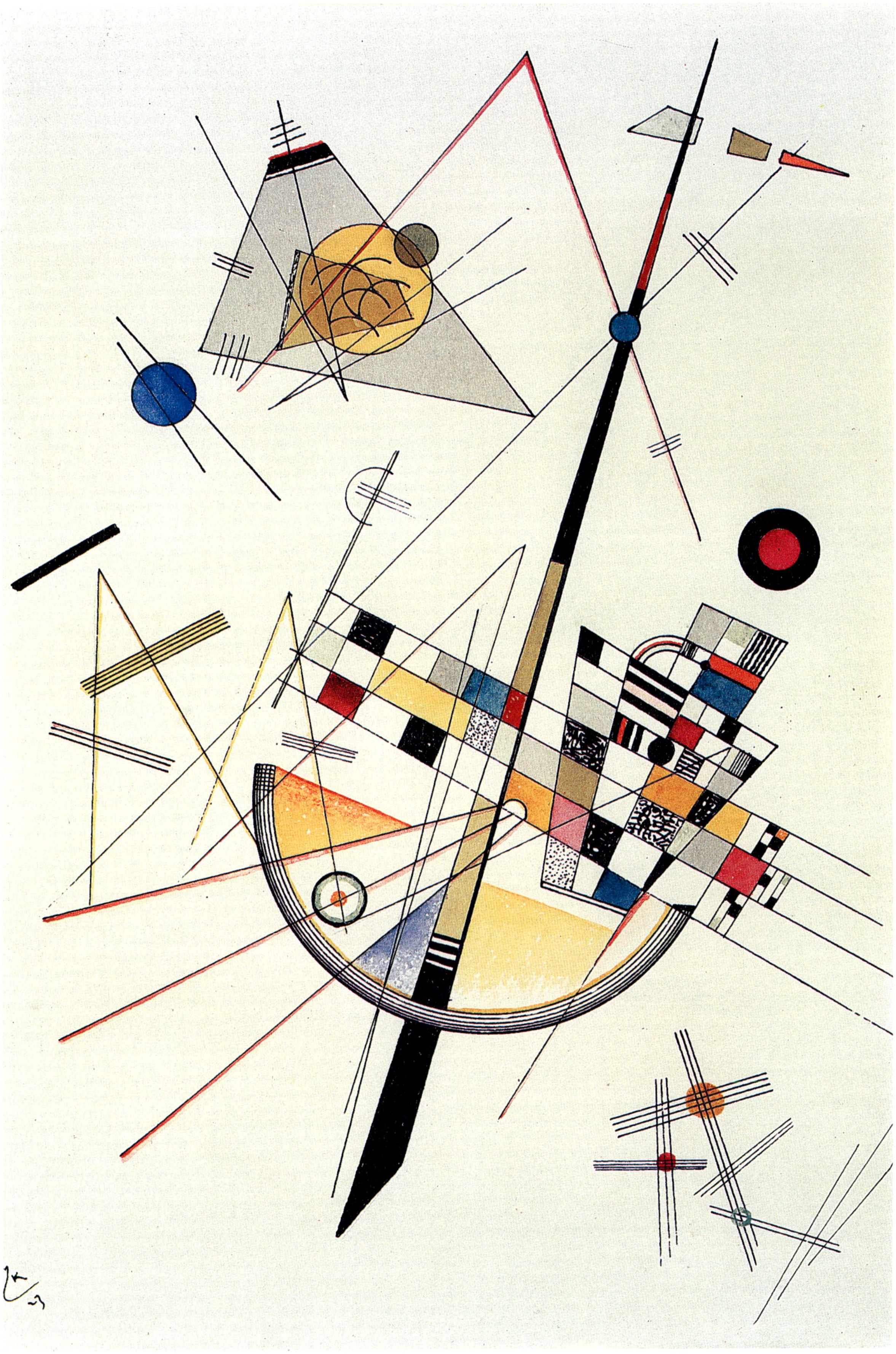

Ernst Ludwig Kirchner 1880–1938

43 The Loam Pit[1]

*c*1906
Oil on board, 51 × 71 cm
Signed lower left: 'E.L.Kirchner'; estate stamp on back of board, inscribed: 'Dre/Aa 5'[2]
The painting is unvarnished, and the paint surface has become rather grimy. The support is slightly convex-warped. Otherwise condition is good
Accession no.1964.13

Provenance
Estate of the artist
Collection Roman Norbert Ketterer
Galerie R.N.Ketterer, Campione d'Italia
Thyssen-Bornemisza Collection, 1964[3]

Exhibitions
Meisterwerke des deutschen Expressionismus, 1960–61, no.2
Florence 1964, no.169
Basle, Kunsthalle, 1967, *E.L.Kirchner und Rot-Blau*, no.6
Berlin, Brücke-Museum, 1973, *Künstler der Brücke. Gemälde der Dresdener Jahre 1905–1910*, no.14
Bremen 1975, no.34
Villingen-Schwenningen, Beethovenhaus, 1979, 50. *Städtische Kunstausstellung: Ernst Ludwig Kirchner. Gemälde, Aquarelle, Zeichnungen, Graphik*, no.1
London, Royal Academy of Arts, 1979–80, *Post-Impressionism. Cross-Currents in European Painting*, no.253
Washington, DC, National Gallery of Art, 1980, *Post-Impressionism. Cross-Currents in European Painting*, no.187
Rome 1990–91, no.25

Literature
R.N.Ketterer, *Moderne Kunst*, Campione d'Italia (Galerie R.N.Ketterer) 1963, n.p.
Gordon (1968), no.15 and pp.48–50
Kiel (1974), p.66, ill. p.65
See also Gordon (1966): 338ff

One of the most important formative influences on Kirchner's early work was the art of van Gogh, whose paintings were exhibited in Germany on a number of occasions during the early years of the century, notably at the Galerie Arnold in Dresden in 1905.[4] Kirchner, like the other artists of the Brücke group, could scarcely have been immune to the effect of such events taking place on his own doorstep. He was also, almost certainly, familiar with the Dutch artist's work in illustration. His personal library, sent for auction in 1951, was found to contain two copies of Julius Meier-Graefe's influential and richly illustrated three-volume *Entwicklungsgeschichte der modernen Kunst*, containing reproductions of paintings by van Gogh and other 'modern' artists.[5] The German periodical *Kunst und Künstler*, the first issue of which appeared in 1903, also contained numerous illustrations of works by Neo- and Post-Impressionist artists, including Cézanne, van Gogh, Pissarro and Signac. That the young Dresden artists regularly devoured the latest illustrated German and foreign periodicals is confirmed by the recollections of another of the founder-members of the Brücke, Fritz Bleyl.[6] The impact of van Gogh's painting on the development of Kirchner's style is seen clearly in *The Loam Pit* with its strident colour contrasts, loose brushwork and heavy impasto.

Notes
1 The work has been known by the German title *Die Lehmgrube*, and is thus entitled in Gordon's oeuvre-catalogue of Kirchner's paintings: see Gordon (1968), p.267
2 After the death of Kirchner's companion Erna Schilling in 1945, scholars at the Kunstmuseum, Basle, under the direction of Georg Schmidt compiled an inventory of works from the artist's estate and devised a chronological ordering of the paintings based in the first instance on their place of execution. They also affixed a seal to the verso of the paintings, a rubber stamp in the form of a horizontal cartouche bearing the words 'Nachlass E.L.Kirchner' (referred to in this catalogue as 'estate stamp') to which was added a handwritten inscription consisting of both letters and numbers, beginning in each case with 'Dre' (Dresden), 'Be' (Berlin) or 'Da' (Davos). Despite occasional inaccuracies, subsequent research has shown the general reliability of this system, which was followed in the main by Gordon in compiling his 1968 oeuvre-catalogue, still the basic reference work on Kirchner's paintings. On the ordering of the estate, see further Gordon (1968), pp.263f; also Ketterer (1982), pp.9f
3 On the Stuttgarter Kunstkabinett, the Ketterer collection, and the Galerie R.N.Ketterer, see pp.16–17
4 Gordon (1966): 338–9, 341; on the reception of van Gogh's art in Germany during this period, see Feilchenfeldt (1988), also Moeller (1990), especially pp.312–7
5 One of these sets was apparently a first edition of 1904: see Hans Bolliger, 'Die Publikationen und Dokumente der Künstlergruppe "Brücke"', *Philobiblon*, I (1959): 43; also Gabler (1980), p.358 for a complete list of the contents of the 1951 auction
6 Wentzel (1968): 94

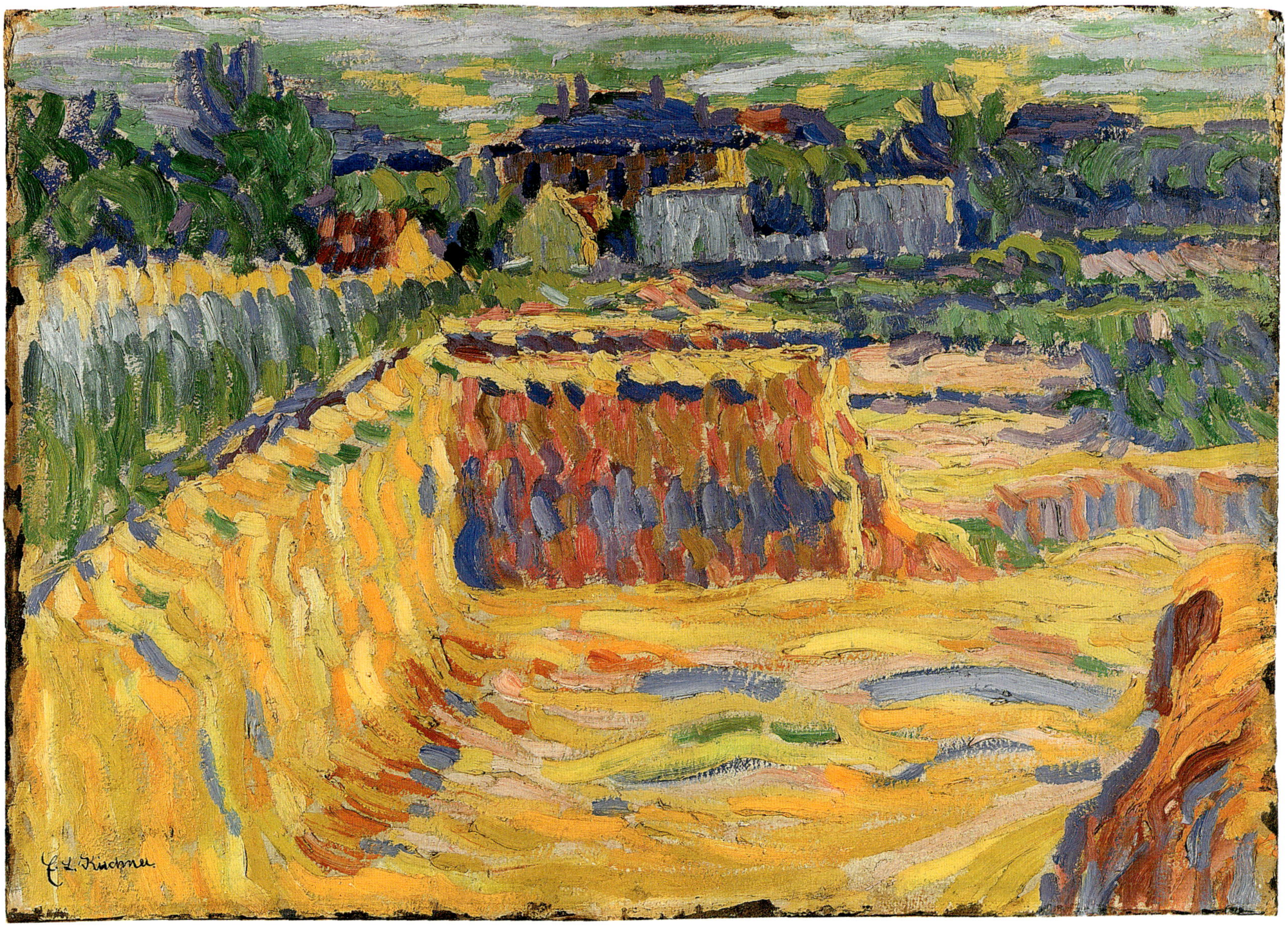

The dating of Kirchner's earliest Dresden paintings is fraught with difficulties. In general it may be stated that few, if any, of his works in oil can convincingly be dated earlier than the end of 1905. By 1908, the influence of French Neo- and Post-Impressionism had begun considerably to diminish, to be replaced by a flatter, more abbreviated style which owes more, perhaps, to the impact of Munch's art.[7] In the absence, however, of any significant number of documented works, suggested dates of 1906 and 1907 must be regarded as at best tentative, and are based principally on stylistic criteria.

Donald Gordon, both in his oeuvre-catalogue of Kirchner's paintings and in his 1966 article 'Kirchner in Dresden', has discussed at length the question of the various influences to which the artist responded, in attempting to construct a convincing chronology of the early works. As noted, however, many of these remain undocumented, including [43], which Gordon identifies as belonging to a group of *plein-air* paintings done in all probability during spring-summer 1906, of which the best known is the 'reliably dated' *Lake in Dresden Park*.[8]

7 Kirchner probably became acquainted with the Norwegian artist's work through the Munch exhibition shown in Dresden in February 1906. He was, however, as Gordon notes, at that date 'not yet able to enlarge upon the more expressive aspects of post-Impressionist art'. His interest in Munch was rekindled by the exhibition he saw at the Berlin Secession in autumn 1908, which included several recent paintings: see Gordon (1966): 340, 345–6, also Werenskiold (1974): 143f

8 Gordon (1968), no.13; also pp.48–50

Ernst Ludwig Kirchner 1880–1938

44 Doris with Ruff Collar
Doris mit Halskrause[1]

*c*1906
Oil on board, 70.5 × 51 cm
Unsigned/undated
The original painting, on cardboard, has been stuck to a piece of hardboard, which has in turn been affixed to another piece of cardboard backing. On the verso of the backing board is a painted device, in the form of a cartouche, with the inscription: 'Nachlass E.L.Kirchner Dre/Ba 3'.[2] The painting on the recto shows some evidence of restoration at extreme lower-left corner, also at upper right. Otherwise condition is good
Accession no.1961.7

Provenance
Estate of the artist
Collection Roman Norbert Ketterer
Thyssen-Bornemisza Collection, 1961[3]

Exhibitions
Essen 1958, no.54 [as 'Mädchen mit Halskrause']
Ulm, Ulmer Museum, 1959, *Bilder der 'Brücke'* [as 'Mädchen mit Halskrause'][4]
Meisterwerke des deutschen Expressionismus, 1960–61, no.10
Lausanne, Palais de Beaulieu, 1964, *Chefs-d'oeuvre des collections suisses de Manet à Picasso*, no.186 [as 'Femme à l'écharpe rouge']
Paris/Munich 1966, no.197
Basel, Kunsthalle, 1967, *E.L.Kirchner und Rot-Blau*, no.7 [as 'Mädchen mit Halskrause']
Hamburg, Kunstverein/Frankfurt, Kunstverein, 1969–70, *E.L.Kirchner. Gemälde, Aquarelle, Zeichnungen und Druckgraphik*, no.1
Bremen 1975, no.33
Wrocław, Muzeum Narodowe, 1978–9, *Die Künstlergruppe 'Brücke', 1905–1913/Grupa 'Die Brücke'*, no.8a [as '1906/08']
Poznan, Muzeum Narodowe, 1979, *Die Brücke 1905–1913*, no.9 [as '1906/08']
London, Royal Academy of Arts, 1979–80, *Post-Impressionism. Cross-Currents in European Painting*, no.255
Lugano 1989, no.5
Expressionism and Modern German Painting, 1989–90, no.15

Literature
Grohmann (1961/2), pp.34, 38, ill. p.11 [as 'Girl with Ruff']
Gordon (1968), no.16 [as '1906/1908–9']
Kiel (1974), p.70, ill. p.69
Grisebach (1968), p.43
Hünlich (1988): 137–47

'Doris' was Doris Grosse, nicknamed 'Dodo', Kirchner's second girl-friend of his years in Dresden. It seems he was already acquainted with her prior to his departure for Munich in the autumn of 1903, according to the recollections of his artist friend, Fritz Bleyl.[5] She appears in numerous single and group portraits, and is undoubtedly one of the nude figures posing in some of the studio compositions and in the studies of bathers painted during Kirchner's visits to the Moritzburg lakes in 1909 and 1910.

Notes
1 The work is recorded on p.28 of the first of the artist's four photograph albums preserved in the Kirchner estate, on which Gordon's titles are largely based: see Gordon (1968), pp.263f, 268
2 This appears like a crude imitation of the Kirchner estate stamp (see n.2 to p.180) such as occurs on the verso of other paintings. It is possible that during some previous restoration, in the course of which the original cardboard support was made secure by being attached to the present backing, an inscription on the verso of the original was transcribed on to the new backing board
3 Acquired directly from the previous owner: on the Stuttgarter Kunstkabinett, the Ketterer collection, and the Galerie R.N.Ketterer, see pp.16–17
4 See note 1 to p.27
5 Wentzel (1968): 94–5

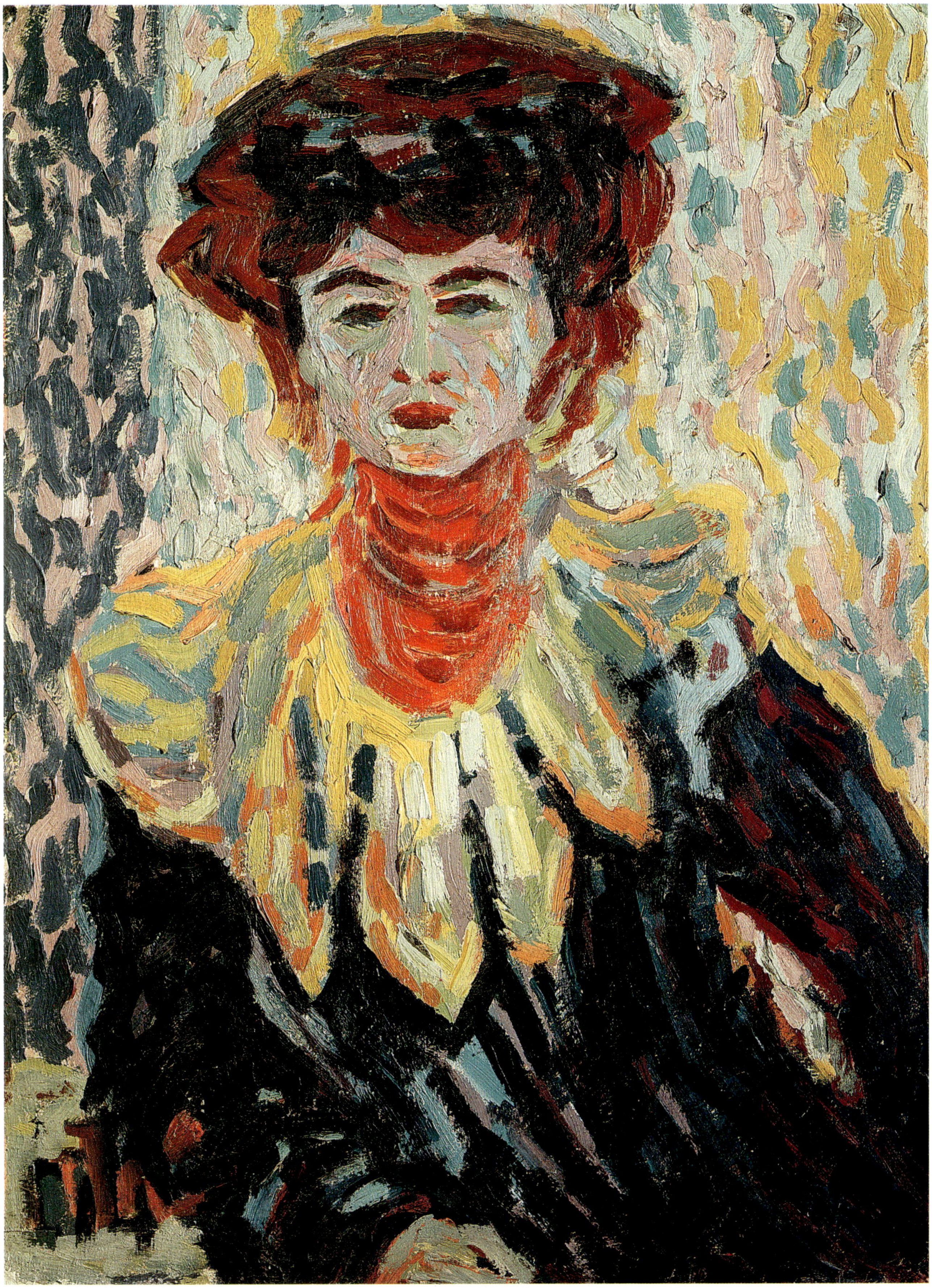

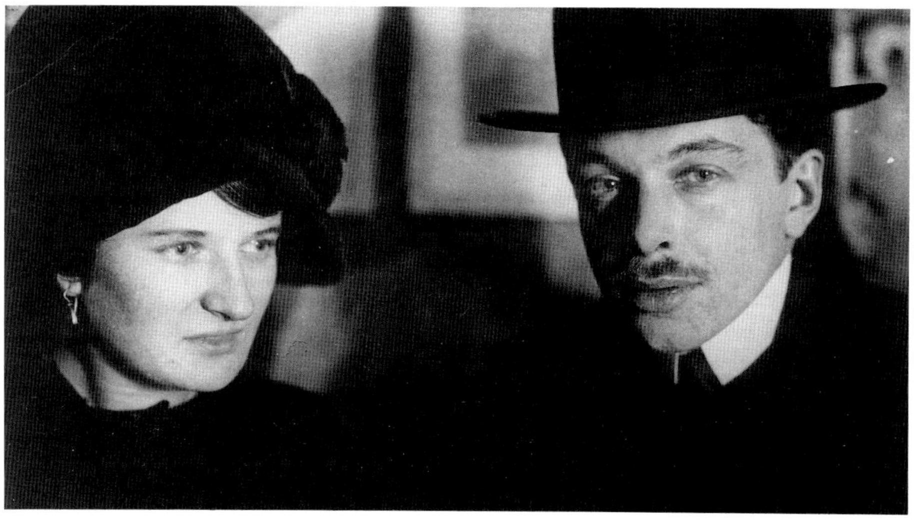

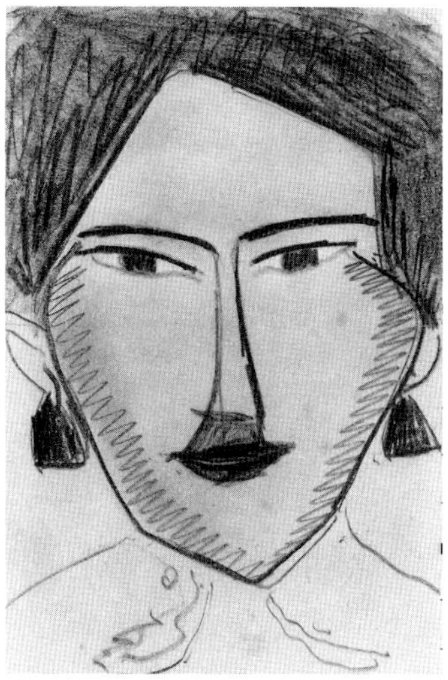

FIG 1 Ernst Ludwig Kirchner and Doris Grosse photographed in Dresden, c1909 (Foto-Archiv Hans Bolliger–Roman Norbert Ketterer)

FIG 2 Doris Grosse, *Self-portrait* (Hamburg, Altonaer Museum, Norddeutsches Landesmuseum, inv. no.1964/272)

Bernd Hünlich, whose researches first established the identity of Doris Grosse, has cast doubt on whether the 'Doris' portrayed in *Doris with Ruff Collar* is identical with the 'Dodo' who features in the later paintings.[6] However, the 'narrow feline eyes' familiar from an old photograph of 'Dodo' with Kirchner (fig.1), and which Hünlich acknowledges as characteristic of those portraits which demonstrably are of Doris Grosse, seem – at least to the eye of this author – no less recognizable in the present work. Indeed, the features portrayed in *Doris with Ruff Collar* appear to be unmistakably Dodo's: a comparison with Kirchner's painting *Dodo and her Brother* of 1908 (fig.3), as well as with Doris's own *Self-portrait* (fig.2), drawn on a postcard from Ernst Ludwig Kirchner to Erich Heckel dated 2 November 1910,[7] is persuasive.

Kirchner was by all accounts deeply attached to Dodo. Years later, in Switzerland, he began a lengthy diary entry with a curiously moving passage in praise of her beauty and 'refined sensuality'.[8] His relationship with her apparently came to an end only with (possibly because of) his move from Dresden to Berlin in the autumn of 1911.

In later years, Kirchner dated *Doris with Ruff Collar* to 1903,[9] which on stylistic grounds is wholly implausible. Will Grohmann, in his 1961 monograph on Kirchner, raises the question of the dating of *Doris* in relation to Kirchner's other paintings, noting: 'Either the "Lake in Dresden Park" and the "Girl with Ruff" are earlier, or the studio pictures with the nudes painted in large surface planes and cruder contours are later.'[10] In the opinion of the present author, the Thyssen Collection's portrait can scarcely be dated earlier than 1906, the most obvious influence being that of French Neo-Impressionist painting, examples of which Kirchner may have seen in the original in Dresden in the autumn of that year (see also [45]). The exact dating of his work of this early period is, however, notoriously problematic.

A photograph in the Kirchner estate, almost certainly taken by the artist himself during his first years in Davos, appears to show a slightly different state of the picture, with minor differences in the hair, around the collar, and in the lower left corner (fig.4). It was perhaps because of these differences, which are stylistically consistent with Kirchner's other work of his Dresden period, that Gordon in his oeuvre-catalogue of the paintings suggested a date of 1906/1908–9 for the execution of [44].[11] Had over-painting occurred during the 1920s, as was more usually the case, this would almost certainly have consisted of covering the earlier rapid, nervous brushwork with broader, more opaque areas of paint, as in *With Red Streetwalker* [49].[12] These differences may, on the other hand, be due to a distortion of tonal values in the old photograph. Visual examination of the picture itself shows little trace of over-painting. On the contrary, the top layer of vermilion paint around the collar, though mostly lying on top of the other paint layers, is in one or two places intermingled with lower layers of yellow and green, so that either this whole passage is the product of very extensive re-working, or else the painting is as orginally executed.

Notes

6 Hünlich (1988), p.146

7 The card is addressed to Heckel's new studio, Dresden-A, An der Falkenbrücke 2a Parterre; see Dube-Heynig (1984), no.83, pp.211 (ill.), 276. A postcard from Kirchner addressed to Otto and Maschka Mueller (Staatliche Museen zu Berlin, Kupferstichkabinett und Sammlung der Zeichnungen) with another self-portrait by Dodo is reproduced in ibid., no.83(a)

8 Grisebach (1968), p.43

9 See Gordon (1968), p.268. At least some of the dates Kirchner gave to his own paintings were intended deliberately to mislead. Reidemeister alludes specifically to the artist's 'inclinination always to pre-date his pictures, in order to ensure the priority of his own artistic development'; see Reidemeister (1970), p.18

10 Grohmann, op. cit., p.34. Without having very much by way of documentary evidence at his disposal, Grohmann grapples courageously with the tangled chronology of Kirchner's early work, trying to construct a more plausible sequence based on little

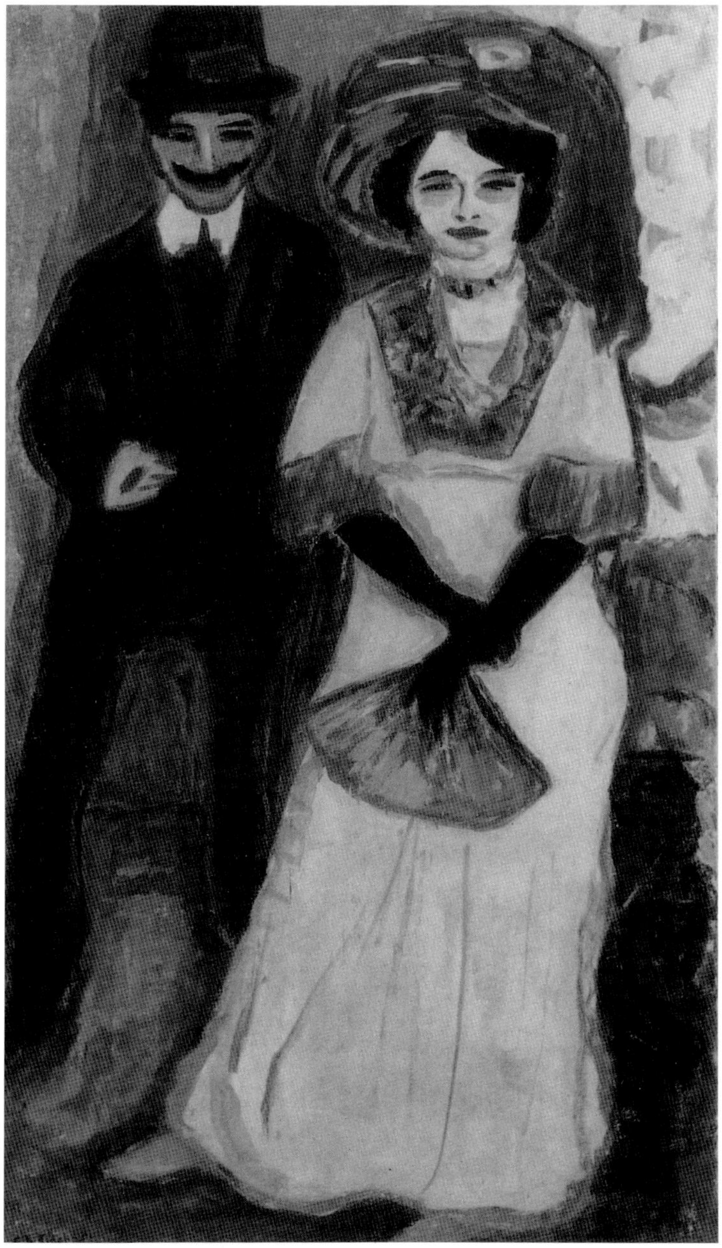

FIG 3 Ernst Ludwig Kirchner, *Dodo and her Brother*, 1908, oil on canvas, 171 × 95 cm (Northampton, MA, Smith College Museum of Art)

FIG 4 Archive photograph of [44], probably taken by Kirchner, *c*1923 (Foto-Archiv Hans Bolliger–Roman Norbert Kettterer)

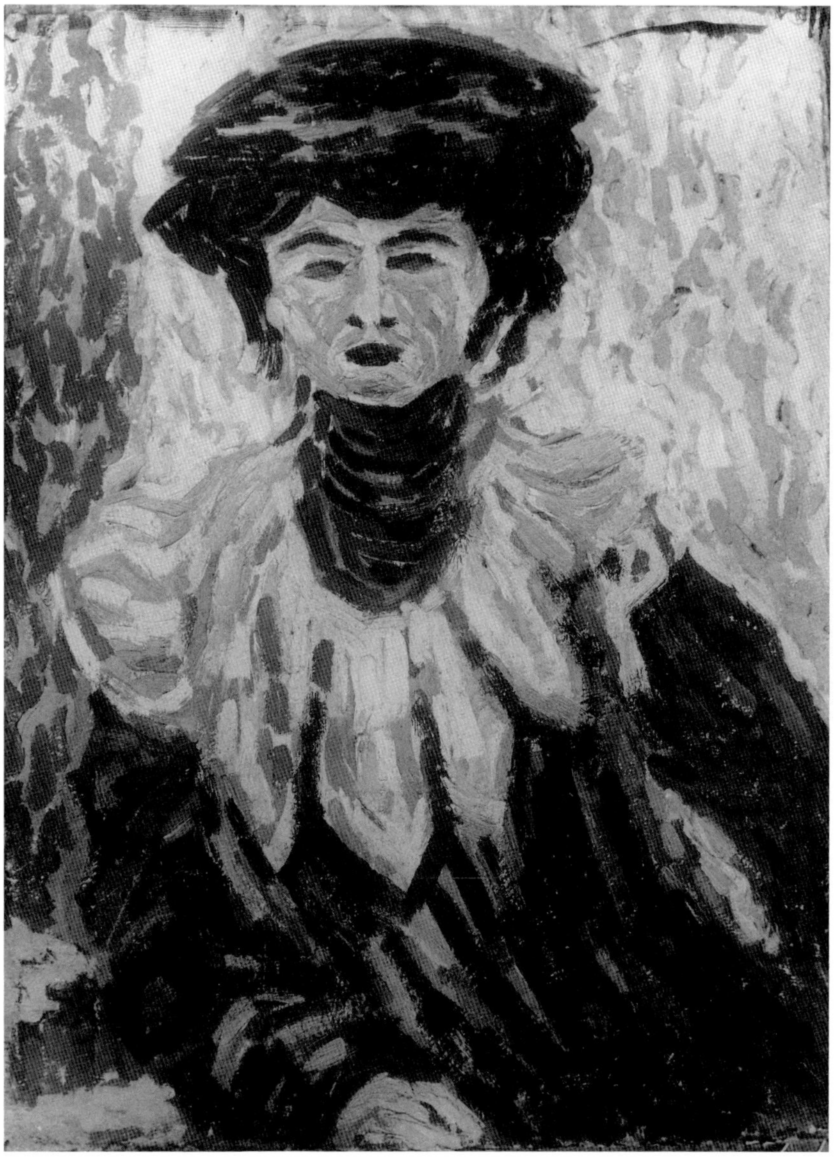

other than purely stylistic judgments. He does not, however, arrive in the end at any very definite conclusions: see Grohmann, loc. cit., also pp.44ff

11 See Gordon (1968), p.268; the corresponding entry indicates that Gordon considered the photograph in the Kirchner estate as recording a first or earlier state of the picture

12 Kirchner's custom of photographing and then re-painting his earlier works during his Swiss years is described in Ketterer (1982), pp.7–8; see also Gordon (1966): 336, ns.12, 13

Ernst Ludwig Kirchner 1880–1938

45 Woman in front of Birch Trees[1]

*c*1907
Oil on canvas, 68.5 × 78 cm
Unsigned/undated
The painting is unvarnished. Very heavy impasto with dirt in the hollows, also cracking and flaking of paint surface. Some evidence of previous restoration and additions, particularly at vertical edges of canvas. New stretcher
Accession no.1963.7(a)

Verso Woman with Pointed Hat

Provenance
Estate of the artist
Collection Roman Norbert Ketterer
Galerie R.N.Ketterer, Campione d'Italia
Thyssen-Bornemisza Collection, 1963

Exhibitions
Meisterwerke des deutschen Expressionismus, 1960–61, no.3
Florence 1964, no.170
Berlin, Brücke-Museum, 1973, *Künstler der Brücke. Gemälde der Dresdener Jahre 1905–1910*, no.22
Bremen 1975, no.32
Lugano 1975, no.27
London, Royal Academy of Arts, 1979–80, *Post-Impressionism. Cross-Currents in European Painting*, no.254 [as 'Woman in a Birch Wood, 1906']
Washington, DC, National Gallery of Art, 1980, *Post-Impressionism. Cross-Currents in European Painting*, no.188 [as 'Woman in a Birch Wood, 1906']

Literature
R.N.Ketterer, *Moderne Kunst*, Campione d'Italia (Galerie R.N.Ketterer) 1963, n.p.
Gordon (1966): 342 and n.45
Gordon (1968), no.22
Frank Whitford, *Expressionism*, London (Hamlyn) 1970, p.39, ill. p.50
Kiel (1974), p.68, ill. p.67

It has generally been acknowledged that with *Woman in front of Birch Trees* Kirchner's involvement with French Neo- and Post-Impressionist painting reached its peak.[2] Exactly when he first became aware of Neo-Impressionism is unclear. He himself recalled seeing an exhibition which included works by Neo-Impressionist artists in Munich in 1903.[3] Several writers have identified this exhibition with one staged by Kandinsky's Munich society, the Phalanx.[4] If it was one of the Phalanx shows Kirchner had in mind, this can only have been the organization's tenth exhibition, which took place in May 1904 and included work by Signac, van Rysselberghe and Vallotton.[5] However, this date conflicts with the frequently repeated assertion that his visit to Munich took place from November 1903 to March 1904, after which he returned to Dresden to resume his studies,[6] and it remains possible that he did not begin to interest himself seriously in the methods of the Neo-Impressionists until somewhat later.

Notes

1 The work has been known by the German title *Frau vor Birken*, and is thus entitled in Gordon's oeuvre-catalogue of Kirchner's paintings: see Gordon (1968), p.268

2 See e.g. *Post-Impressionism. Cross-Currents in European Painting*, exh. cat., London, Royal Academy of Arts, 1979, p.160

3 This recollection, some two decades after the event, may be part of Kirchner's continued attempts to make his own early development appear more precocious than it really was; see 'Die Arbeit E.L.Kirchners', an autobiographical essay written in 1925 or 1926, first published in Kornfeld (1979), pp.331ff. Kirchner also mentioned what was presumably the same Neo-Impressionist exhibition in a letter to the dealer Curt Valentin, 17 April 1937, published in *E.L.Kirchner*, exh. cat., New York, Curt Valentin Gallery, 1952; see also 'A Letter from Ernest [sic] Ludwig Kirchner', *Minneapolis Institute of Arts Bulletin*, XLII, no.8 (21 February 1953): 37–8

4 There was, however, no 'exhibition organized by *Phalanx* and on show from November 1903 until January 1904' containing Neo-Impressionist paintings, as stated by Bolliger; see Ketterer (1982), pp.233–4

5 See Roethel (1970), pp.434–5, for a detailed listing of all the Phalanx exhibitions

6 Several sources state, however, that Kirchner spent two semesters studying in Munich, for which the period November–March would have been far too short; see Gordon (1968), pp.15–16. Gordon also notes that 'the first or winter semester in the German university calendar then as now runs from November to March', and that Heckel himself recalled, albeit in an interview given as late as 1954, that following their meeting in Dresden, Kirchner returned to Munich for the summer semester (ibid., p.455, fns.13, 14). This is directly contradicted by Bleyl's statement, likewise made long after the event, that Kirchner spent only one semester in Munich: see Wentzel (1968): 95

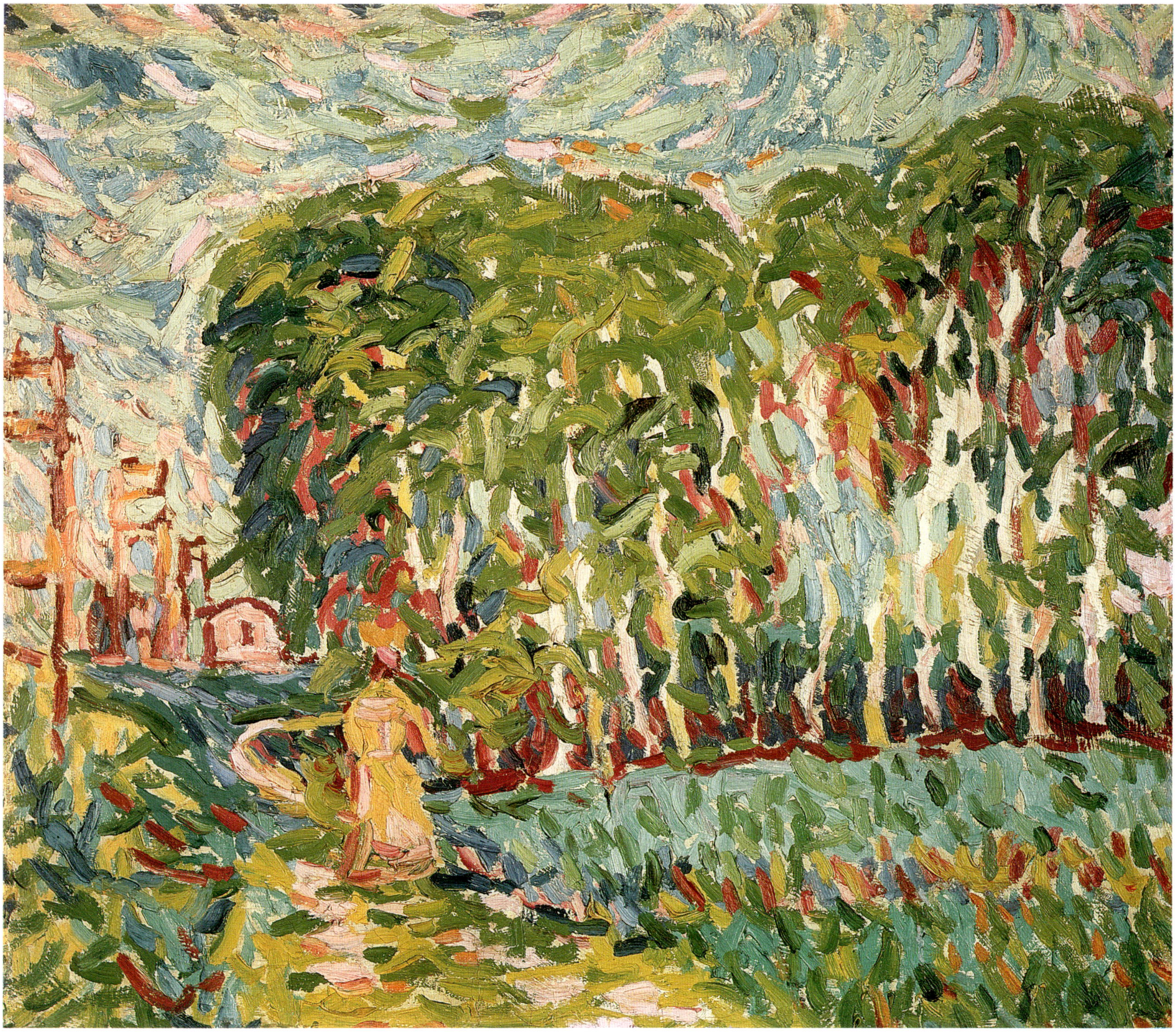

Gordon mentions an exhibition held at the Galerie Arnold in Dresden in November 1906 which included works by Signac, Luce, Cross, van Rysselberghe and Seurat.[7] Though Kirchner does not refer to it, this exhibition may well have been his first real opportunity of seeing Neo-Impressionist paintings in the original. But equally, the influence of Neo-Impressionism could have been mediated through the example of Nolde, who joined the Brücke group in the same year. In *Woman in front of Birch Trees*, the heavy impasto and expressive brushstrokes are in reality far closer to Nolde's manner of painting than to the Neo-Impressionist dot, which Kirchner said 'failed to satisfy him', and which by his own account he soon abandoned 'in order to study thoroughly the technique of the old masters.'[8]

Like many of his German contemporaries, Kirchner was less interested in the scientific theories underlying Neo-Impressionism than in the expressive potential of pure, unmixed colour applied directly to the canvas. As in Kandinsky's works of the same period, the Divisionist dot or point characteristic of the art of Seurat or Signac is transformed in his early Dresden paintings into broad, flowing brushstrokes, often widely separated, in places revealing bare areas of canvas in between.

In Gordon's 1968 oeuvre-catalogue of Kirchner's paintings, *Woman in front of Birch Trees* is the first painting listed under 1907, which would imply a date of execution early in that year. In his earlier article 'Kirchner in Dresden', he tentatively identifies [45] with the painting *Aus Dresden* shown at an exhibition of the Sächsischer Kunstverein in Dresden in June 1907.[9]

Notes

7 Gordon also cites a review of the exhibition by Paul Fechter in the *Dresdener Neueste Nachrichten*, no.305 (10 November 1906), in which a number of the paintings shown are identified by name; see Gordon (1966): 341 and n.40

8 'Die Arbeit E.L.Kirchners', p.334

9 Gordon (1966), loc. cit.

10 The work has been known by the German title *Frau mit spitzem Hut*: see Gordon (1968), p.268

11 Gordon (1968), p.268, refers to a 'K' scratched lower right on the canvas; a visual inspection, however, now reveals no trace of any date or signature

45 *verso* Woman with Pointed Hat[10]

*c*1936–7
Oil on canvas, 78 × 68.5 cm
Unsigned/undated[11]
The canvas bears the Kirchner estate stamp, inscribed: 'Da/Ba 31'
In good condition. The painting is unvarnished
Accession no.1963.7(b)

Literature
Gordon (1968), no.22v
Kiel (1974), p.68

According to Kirchner's biographer, Donald Gordon, the painting dates from the last years of the artist's life: Kirchner commited suicide close to the village of Frauenkirch, near Davos in Switzerland, in May 1938. The sitter is almost certainly Erna Schilling, his common-law wife (fig.1), whom during the last months of his life he had expressed an intention to marry. Erna, his companion from the years in Berlin, had faithfully accompanied him to his last domicile in Switzerland after his discharge from military service and departure from Germany towards the end of the First World War. She and Kirchner were to spend the rest of their lives mostly in the region around Davos. The portrait is unfinished.

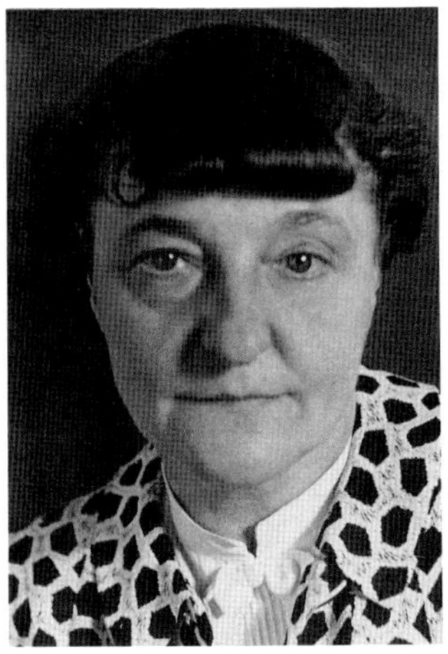

FIG 1 Erna Schilling, *c*1934 (archive Dr Eberhard W.Kornfeld, Berne)

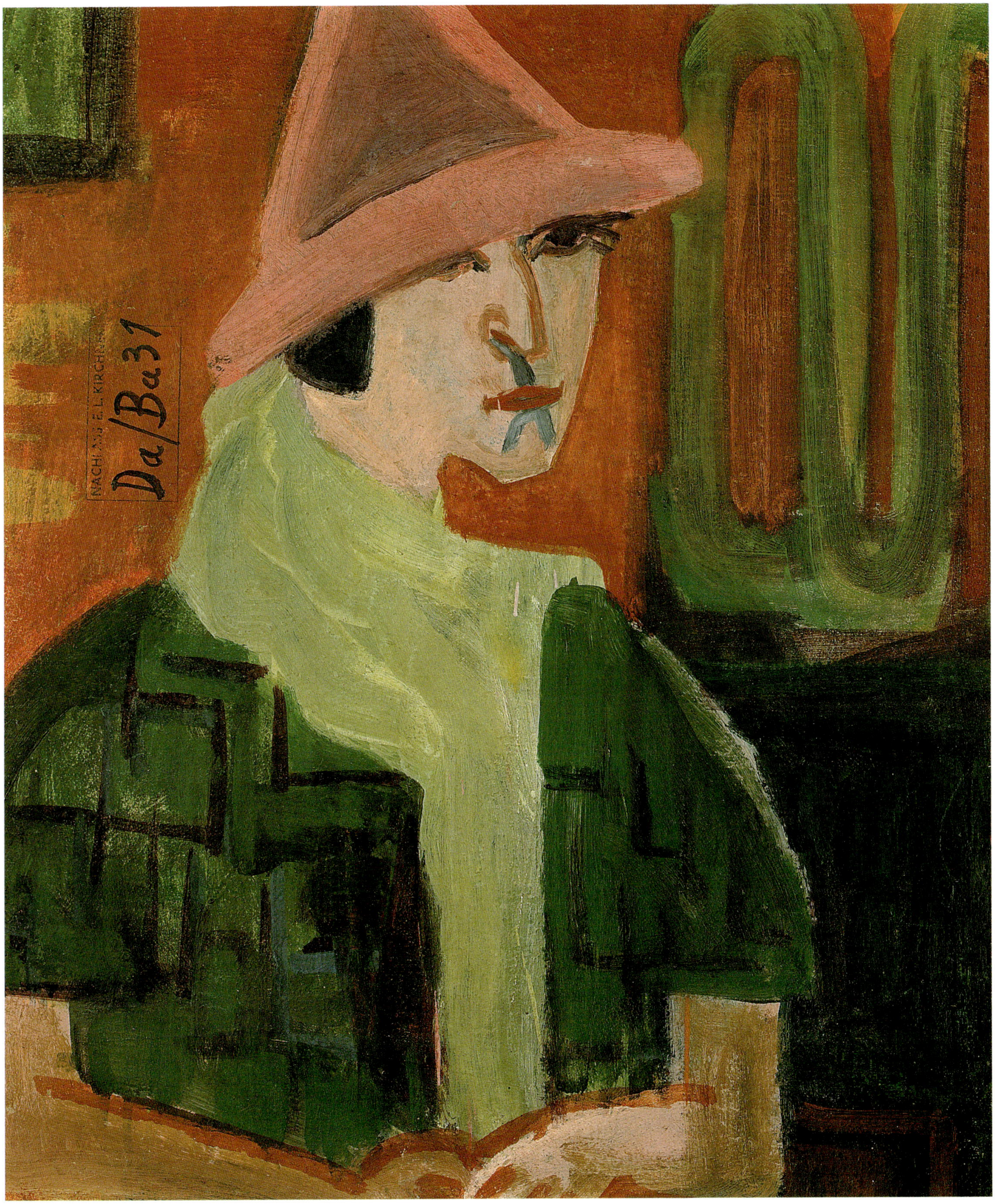
Da/Ba 31

Ernst Ludwig Kirchner 1880–1938

46 Fränzi in front of Carved Chair

Fränzi vor geschnitztem Stuhl[1]

1910[2]
Oil on canvas, 71 × 49.5 cm
Estate stamp on back of canvas, inscribed: 'Dre/Ba 14a'
Most sources describe the picture as being signed at lower right; neither visual inspection nor examination by means of infra-red reflectography now reveals any trace of a signature, save for what might be an 'E', lightly scratched in the paint surface.[3]
The painting is in fragile condition. There is a history of scattered losses in both paint and ground layers, also extensive cracking, most especially around the forehead of the sitter
Accession no.1961.8

Provenance
Estate of the artist
Collection Roman Norbert Ketterer
Thyssen-Bornemisza Collection, 1961[4]

Exhibitions
Munich, Galerie Günther Franke, 1958, *Bildnisse aus dem 20. Jahrhundert*, no.15a [as 'Fränzikopf 1907']
Essen 1958, no.60 [as 'Fränzikopf 1907/08']
Ulm, Ulmer Museum, 1959, *Bilder der 'Brücke'* [as 'Fränzikopf 1907/08'][5]
Meisterwerke des deutschen Expressionismus, 1960–61, no.13 [as 'Fränzikopf (vor geschnitztem Stuhl) 1908–9']
Lausanne, Palais de Beaulieu, 1964, *Chefs-d'oeuvre des collections suisses de Manet à Picasso*, no.187 [as 'Portrait de Fränzi, 1908–1909']
London, Tate Gallery, 1964, *Painters of the Brücke*, no.63 [as 'Fränzi in front of a carved bench, 1910']
Paris/Munich 1966, no.204 [as '1908/09']
Basle, Kunsthalle, 1967, *E.L.Kirchner und Rot-Blau*, no.14 [as '1908/09']
Seattle, WA, Art Museum/Pasadena, CA, Art Museum/Boston, MA, Museum of Fine Arts, 1968–9, *Ernst Ludwig Kirchner, a retrospective exhibition*, no.19
Turin, Galleria Civica d'Arte Moderna, 1971, *Il Cavaliere Azzurro*, ill. p.122
Berlin, Brücke-Museum, 1973, *Künstler der Brücke. Gemälde der Dresdener Jahre 1905–1910*, no.45
Bremen 1975, no.35
Lugano 1975, no.28
Brussels/Paris 1977–8, no.43
Lugano 1978, no.50
Wrocław, Muzeum Narodowe, 1978–9, *Die Künstlergruppe 'Brücke', 1905–1913/Grupa 'Die Brücke'*, no.11 [as '1908/09']
Poznan, Muzeum Narodowe, 1979, *Die Brücke 1905–1913*, no.12 [as '1908/09']
Villingen-Schwenningen, Beethovenhaus, 1979, *50. Städtische Kunstausstellung: Ernst Ludwig Kirchner. Gemälde, Aquarelle, Zeichnungen, Graphik*, no.2
Berlin, Nationalgalerie, 1979–1980, *Ernst Ludwig Kirchner 1880–1938*, no.82[6]
Expressionism, a German Intuition, 1980–81, no.130
Hamburg, Kunsthalle, 1981–2, *Der zerbrochene Kopf. Picasso zum 100. Geburtstag*, ill. p.115
USA tour 1982–4, no.7
Modern Masters from the Thyssen-Bornemisza Collection, 1984–6, no.56
Lugano 1989, no.6
Expressionism and Modern German Painting, 1989–90, no.16
Rome 1990–91, no.26

Literature
Grohmann (1961/2), pp.34, 38, 44f
Gordon (1966): 355 and n.119
Gordon (1968), no.122 and pp.64–6 [as '1910']
Vogt (1972), p.98 and fig.50
Kiel (1974), p.72, ill. p.71
Henze (1980), pp.24f
Erika Billeter, 'Ich sehe Dich in tausend Bildern', *Du*, 6 (1983): 47–52
Herbert (1983), pl.IX
Gordon (1987), p.30
Lloyd (1987), pp.142–3

Notes
1 The work is recorded on p.163 of the first of the artist's four photograph albums preserved in the Kirchner estate, on which Gordon's titles are largely based: see Gordon (1968), pp.263f, 283
2 For discussion of the documentary and other evidence for the dating of the picture, see below
3 A draft catalogue entry relating to the picture, compiled shortly after the work was acquired by the present owner, refers to 'vestiges of a signature' at the lower right (Lugano-Castagnola, Thyssen-Bornemisza Collection, archive), as does the entry in the catalogue of the 1960–61 exhibition *Meisterwerke des deutschen Expressionismus*, cat. no.13; traces of a signature can also be detected on an old archive photograph of the painting (letter from Dr Wolfgang Henze to the author, 4 October 1989). In conversation with the author (Campione d'Italia, 6 April 1989), Dr Henze observed that Kirchner would on occasion sign his paintings in fugitive media such as pencil or pen, and that the passage of time, or excessive restoration might in this case have obliterated a previously existing signature
4 Acquired directly from the previous owner; on the Stuttgarter Kunstkabinett, the Ketterer collection, and the Galerie R.N.Ketterer, see pp.16–17
5 See n.1 to p.27
6 Exhibition to mark the centenary of the artist's birth, also shown in Munich, Cologne and Zurich during 1979–80

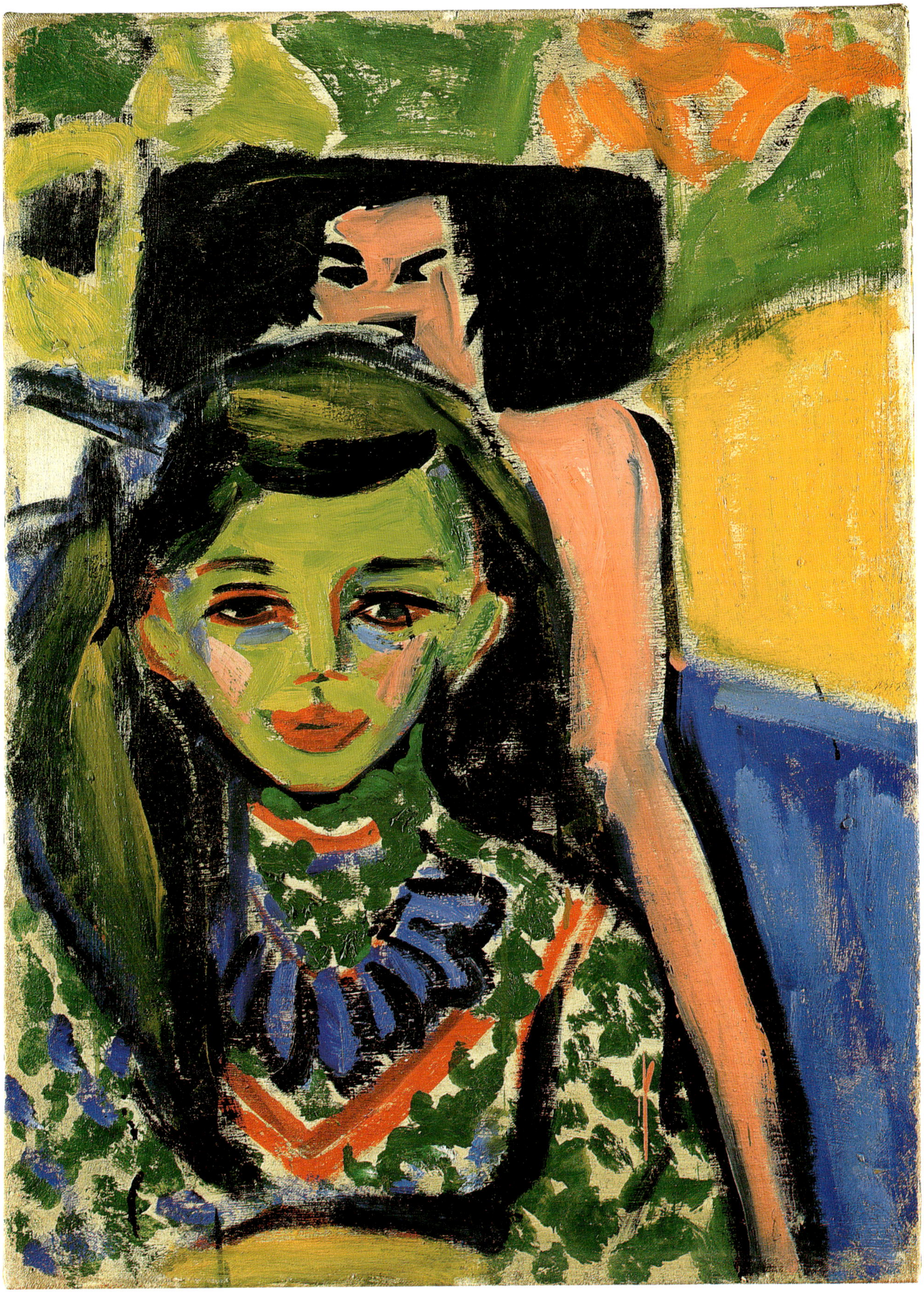

Fränzi in front of Carved Chair must be among the most frequently reproduced images of twentieth-century German painting; it has also generally been regarded as one of the outstanding masterpieces of early Expressionist art. There is hence a certain irony in the fact that both its subject and its date of execution are to some extent problematic. 'Fränzi' herself was evidently one of the many juvenile models who frequented the Brücke artists' studios in Dresden. That she existed is attested by the fact that her name features in the titles of various works from around 1910 not only by Kirchner but also by other painters of the Brücke. An old archive photograph (fig.1), thought to have been taken in Kirchner's studio, shows a leggy, pubescent girl of perhaps twelve or thirteen, purportedly 'Fränzi', with a knowing expression and in a highly provocative pose, together with a boy of about the same age, sometimes identified – though apparently on the basis of no evidence whatever – as her brother.[7] A lost painting by Heckel, dated 1910 in Paul Vogt's oeuvre-catalogue of the artist's work, depicts what appear to be the same two children in a very similar pose.[8] Whether the title given to Heckel's painting, 'Fränzi and her Playmate', derives from that by which the photograph has been known or vice versa is impossible to determine.

It has often been claimed that 'Fränzi' had an older sister named Marcella (or Marzella), and that the two girls were orphans from the Friedrichstrasse quarter of Dresden whom the Brücke artists 'adopted'. This is almost certainly false. A postcard from Heckel to Dr Rosa Schapire in Hamburg, postmarked 18 February 1910, bears a drawing in ink and coloured crayon depicting two girls shooting arrows, with the inscription: 'Hier zwei Schwestern, die ich neulich entdeckte ... [Here are two sisters whom I recently discovered ...]'[9] Frustratingly, the names of the two sisters are not mentioned; however, the same motif of two girls playing with bows and arrows is also featured on a postcard from Kirchner to Heckel postmarked '12.5.10' bearing a message, in Kirchner's hand: 'Meine beiden kleinen Mädel sehr nett ... [My two little girls are very nice ...]', plus two additions, presumably written by the 'two little girls' in question: 'Ich will einen Krebs haben. Marzella. [Bring me back a crab. Marzella.]' 'Gruss und Kuss. Senta. [Love and kisses. Senta.]' The drawing in pen and ink and crayon on the verso depicting, one presumes, the same two girls casts doubt on whether Heckel's card to Rosa Schapire necessarily represents 'Fränzi' and Marzella, as has previously been assumed.

Pechstein, recalling the Brücke years in Dresden, gives a somewhat different account. According to his Reminiscences, the porter who looked after the studios at the Academy of Fine Arts procured for them two teenage girls, daughters of a deceased variety artist, who accompanied the painters on their summer 1910 expedition to the Moritzburg lakes (see [89]) in order to act as models. If his story is to be believed, the girls' mother consented to the trip and even visited her daughters on several occasions during their stay.[10] Again, the girls' names are not revealed.

The tale about 'Fränzi' and Marzella being sisters may also rest upon a confusion. An undated letter from Kirchner to Heckel mentions that Marzella 'brachte ihre Freundin mit. 12 Jahre alt, hat eine Schwester von 15. Das wird was für uns, hoffe ich ... [Marzella brought a friend with her: 12 years old, with a 15-year old sister. I hope that might be something for us ...]'.[11] The description of Kirchner's feelings for Marzella in this letter is overtly sexual in tone, leading one to suspect that his interest in some of the other juvenile models, including perhaps 'Fränzi', may have gone beyond the purely artistic.

Though we learn from the Kirchner–Heckel correspondence the names of many of the other studio girls,[12] the name 'Fränzi' never crops up in any of the letters or postcards.[13] Her existence is, on the other hand, further substantiated by a small piece of evidence dating from a brief and curious postlude to the Brücke years. According to the artist's biographer, Will Grohmann, Kirchner went looking for 'Fränzi' when he revisited Dresden early in 1926, and actually found her: 'When Kirchner visited Dresden ... for a month, one of his first walks was to the Friedrichstrasse to search for Fränzi, the model after whom the now famous pictures were named. He found her, and the reunion was a great joy to both.'[14] Kirchner in fact stayed with

Notes

7 I am grateful to Dr Wolfgang Henze, Campione d'Italia, for supplying a copy of the original photograph in the Kirchner estate

8 Vogt (1965), 1910/10; compare the woodcut *Children on a Bench* of 1910 (Dube (1967), no.191), reproduced in Heller (1988), no.6, with further discussion of the possible identification of the figures. See also Gabler (1983), p.67

9 Tel Aviv, Tel Aviv Museum; see Ketterer (1982), p.8

10 Pechstein (1963), pp.45f; also Gordon (1987), p.30, presumably based on the same account

11 Dube-Heynig (1984), p.238, letter 31, undated (Dresden, between 30 March and 2 April 1910). The rather precise statement, in *Ernst Ludwig Kirchner. Zeichnungen, Pastelle, Aquarelle* exh. cat., Aschaffenburg, Museum der Stadt Aschaffenburg, 1980, p.106, that 'Fränzi' and Marzella were 'two sisters aged twelve and fifteen' may depend upon a misreading of this same letter

12 See for example Dube-Heynig (1984), p.90, postcard no.34 (Kirchner to Heckel, spring 1910) which, in addition to Kirchner's signature, bears greetings from 'Dori Pauli Gerdi Hedi Julietti Melani'. Hünlich has suggested that the first two signatures are most likely those of Doris Grosse ('Dodo') and her elder sister Paula: see Hünlich (1988), p.141; also Moeller (1991), no.16

13 In the excellent and detailed commentary to her edition of the Kirchner-Heckel correspondence, Dube-Heynig observes: 'aus den vielen Namen der mitunterzeichnenden Mädchen der folgenden Karten ... wird die Schwierigkeit deutlich, auf den Arbeiten bestimmte Modelle erkennen und mit Namen belegen zu wollen. So taucht eigenartigerweise in den hier vorliegenden Postkarten und Briefen der Name "Fränzi" nicht auf. Auch Erinnerungen, mündlich oder schriftlich von den Brücke-Künstlern später mitgeteilt, können völlig unbeabsichtigt trügen. So schnitt Heckel 1910 für den Katalog der Ausstellung der Künstlergruppe "Brücke" in der Galerie Arnold Kirchners Gemälde *Marzella* in Holz und nannte es in seinem Werkverzeichnis 1964 "Fränzi"...'; see Dube-Heynig (1984), pp.285f

14 Grohmann (1961/2), p.38

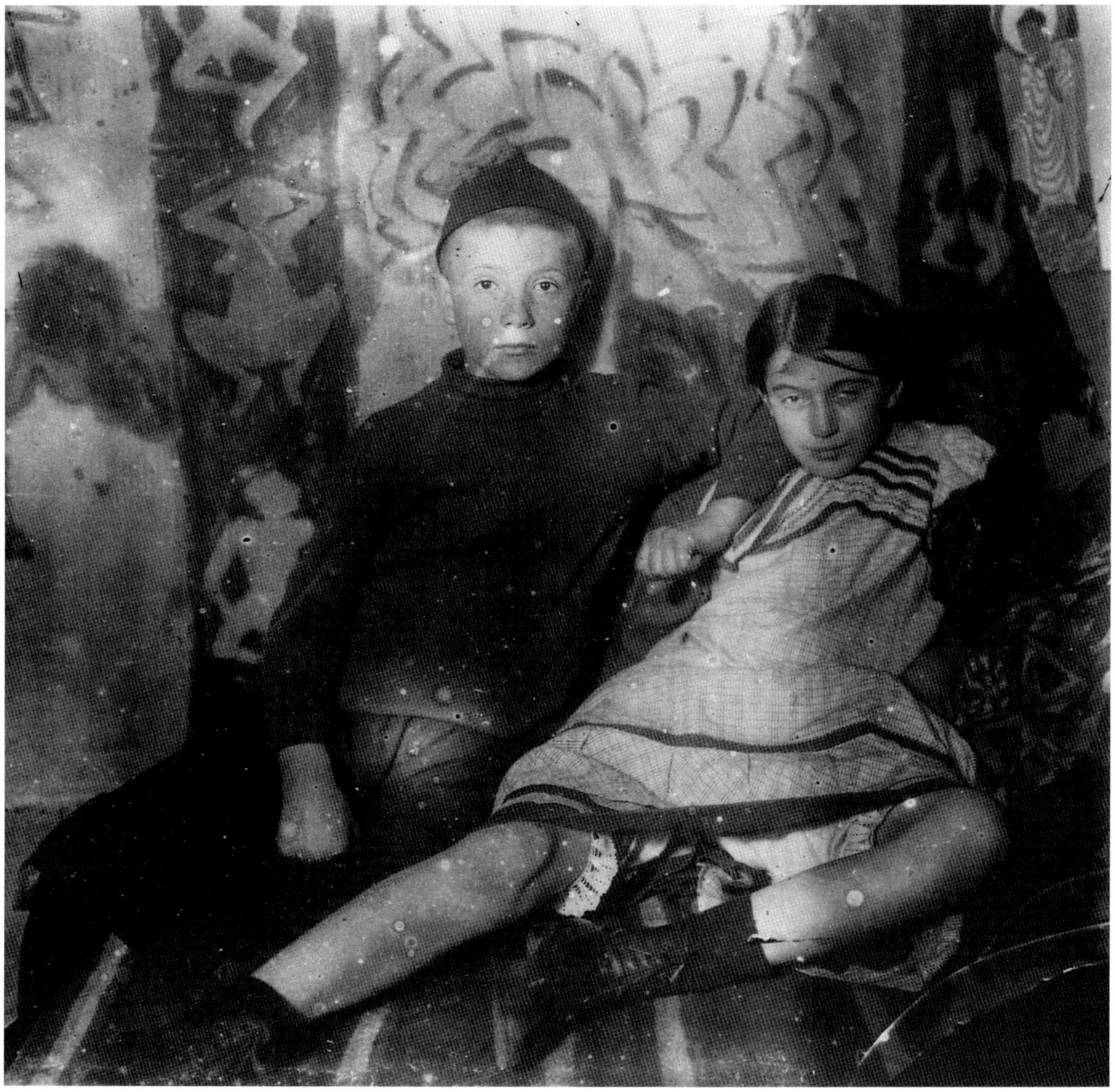

FIG 1 'Fränzi' together with an unidentified youth, photograph taken supposedly in Kirchner's Dresden studio, c1910 (Foto-Archiv Hans Bolliger–Roman Norbert Ketterer)

Grohmann in Dresden; the latter's memory appears to be at fault only in ascribing the visit to the spring of 1925.[15] Kirchner in fact visited Dresden twice in 1926 (which is perhaps how the confusion arose): at the beginning of the year, as part of an extended journey which also took in Zurich, Basle, Frankfurt, Chemnitz and Berlin,[16] and again in June for the opening of the Internationale Kunstausstellung.[17] Ominously, there is no mention of his having attempted to find 'Dodo' again (see [44]), despite the fact that she and her younger sister Armgart, both unmarried, apparently continued to live in Dresden until at least 1937.[18]

Identifying the odd-looking piece of furniture on – or, more accurately, against – which 'Fränzi' is seated poses almost as many difficulties as identifying 'Fränzi' herself. It is, in all probability, a high-backed bench or chair, one of a number of crudely-carved wooden pieces which Kirchner, spurred on by his interest in primitive art, created both during his years in Dresden and Berlin and later in Davos (though during his Swiss period his earlier passion for African and Oceanic cultures had significantly diminished).[19] In the absence of a complete catalogue of his sculptures, it is difficult to draw any firm conclusions from surviving photographs and drawings; it seems likely, however, that many of the objects Kirchner made for his own use have been destroyed, including the chair or bench depicted in [46]. That it existed, on the other hand, is beyond question. Though no photograph of it survives, what is

15 Ibid., p.72
16 See biography by Hans Bolliger printed in Ketterer (1982), p.243
17 In an interview he gave to Roman Norbert Ketterer in 1964, Grohmann corrected his recollection of Kirchner's Dresden visit, linking it specifically with the *Grosse Kunstausstellung* of 1926: see Ketterer (1988/II), p.79
18 Hünlich (1988): 143. Kirchner also alludes briefly and nostalgically to Fränzi in a diary entry written at Davos, dated 7 July 1919: see Grisebach (1968), p.45
19 For a personal recollection regarding Kirchner's later distrust of the Orient, see Llewelyn Powys, 'Ernst Ludwig Kirchner', *Swiss Essays*, London (John Lane) 1947, p.20

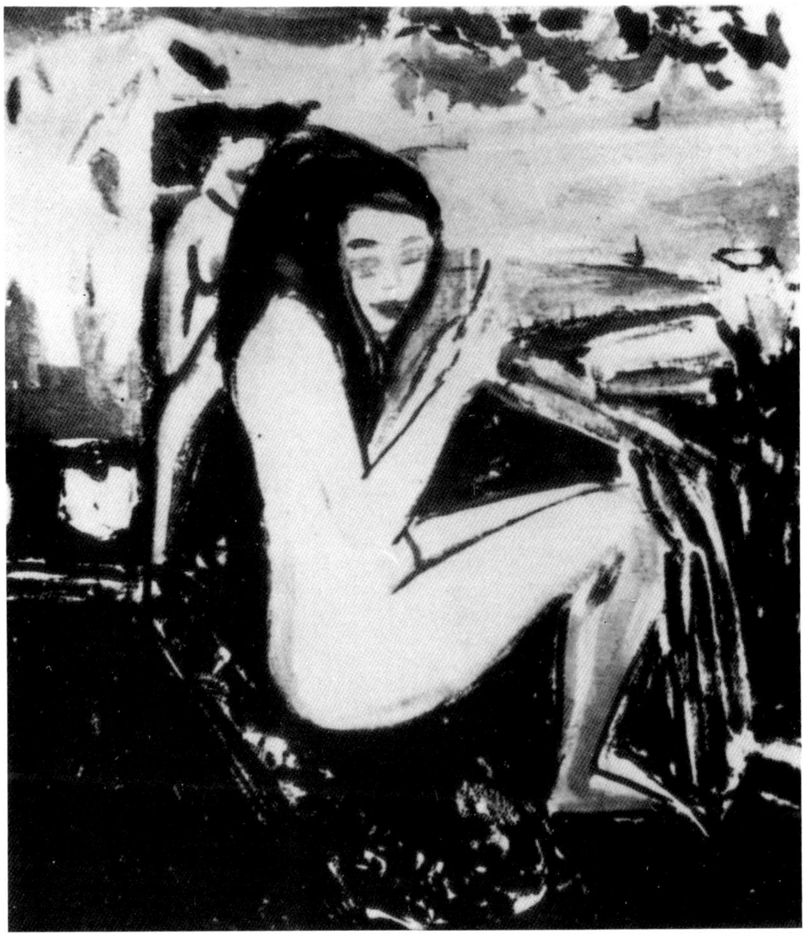

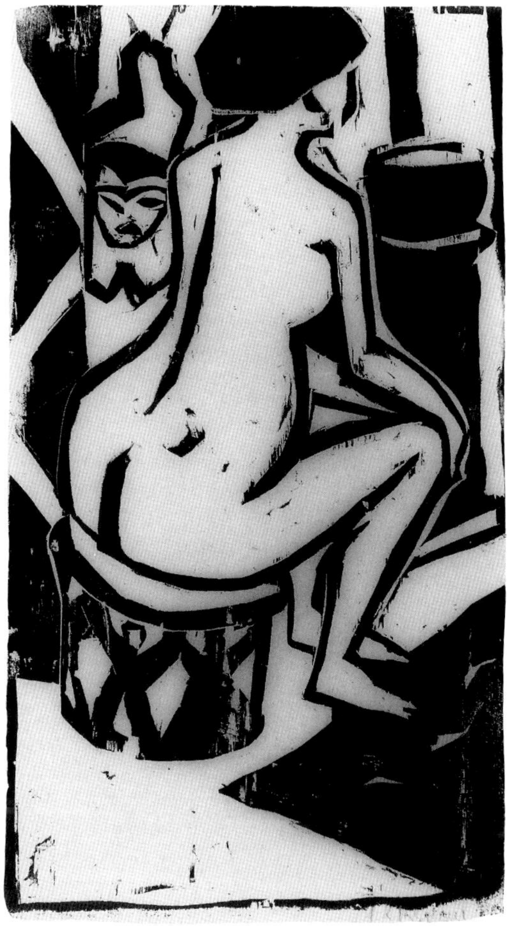

FIG 2 Ernst Ludwig Kirchner, *Naked Fränzi in Profile*, 1910 (location unknown)

FIG 3 Ernst Ludwig Kirchner, *Seated Female Nude*, 1910, woodcut (Frankfurt am Main, Städelsches Kunstinstitut)

evidently the same piece turns up in a number of works almost certainly executed during the latter part of 1910, including the now lost painting *Naked Fränzi in Profile* (fig.2).[20] In this picture, the pose of the model suggests that, rather than facing forwards on a chair with a narrow, high back (as might at first sight appear in *Fränzi in front of Carved Chair*), 'Fränzi' may have been seated on or against a more unusual kind of long bench with carved sides[21] such as features in Kirchner's woodcut *Seated Female Nude* of 1910 (fig.3).[22] Heckel also depicted a seemingly identical bench on a postcard dated 16 December 1910 addressed to Gustav Schiefler's wife Luise, which shows Kirchner seated astride – rather than on this same piece of furniture.[23]

The precise date at which Kirchner first discovered primitive artefacts and began to adapt them to his own purposes is not certain. Heckel, in an interview given in April 1954, recalled that the chair in the Thyssen Collection's portrait of Fränzi was carved by Kirchner in the winter of 1908–9: 'apparently the first piece of Brücke furniture to derive from Cameroon sources . . . it was carved out of linden planks and painted pink and black.'[24] Cameroon was a German protectorate before 1918; its artefacts consituted a likely source of inspiration for artists familiar with German ethnographic collections which displayed such objects in quantity from about 1906 onwards.[25] Strikingly, however, no genuine primitive objects are depicted in works by any of the Brücke artists securely datable before 1910 (or, at the earliest, late 1909), and it was only in the autumn 1910 Brücke exhibition at the Galerie Arnold in Dresden that primitivizing sculptures by Kirchner and Heckel made their first appearance – sculptures which, as Gordon observes, are diminutive in scale. None the less, by the time of his departure for Berlin in autumn 1911 Kirchner had evidently made quite a number of such pieces, which not only feature in his paintings but are also in many cases visible in photographs of his studios.

Notes

20 *Nackte Fränzi im Profil*, Gordon (1968), no.150 (location unknown). The existence of the painting is documented in the first of the artist's four photograph albums preserved in the Kirchner estate; see ibid., p.287

21 The catalogue of the 1964 Tate Gallery exhibition *Painters of the Brücke* is, it seems, unique in entitling the painting *Fränzi in front of a carved bench*

22 *Sitzender Weiblicher Akt*: see Dube (1967), no.155

23 Ketterer (1982), p.86; see also Gabler (1983), p.65

24 Gordon (1966), p.354 and n.119. Despite his interest in African sculpture, it appears that Kirchner owned only one

Apart from tribal art, the other most important – indeed obvious – influence apparent in *Fränzi in front of Carved Chair* is that of Gauguin, whose allegorical use of primitive motifs in his Tahitian pictures finds an exact parallel in Kirchner's art. The painting which suggests the closest comparison with [46] is Gauguin's *Ancestors of Teha'amana* of 1893 (fig.4), which likewise includes a carved figure of demonic aspect – in this instance part of a decorative frieze or relief – visible behind the seated female figure. Kirchner was well acquainted with the French artist's work by 1910, in part through reproductions published in periodicals and anthologies such as Meier-Graefe's *Entwicklungsgeschichte der modernen Kunst*.[26] There was also an exhibition which opened in Dresden at the Galerie Arnold in September that year comprising twenty-six paintings by Gauguin, for which Kirchner made a woodcut poster based on the former's 1893 portrait of his mother.[27] That he saw the exhibition is beyond doubt, since it took place at the same time and in the same gallery as the Brücke artists' own autumn show.[28]

genuine Cameroon piece: the so-called 'leopard stool' now in Bündner Kunstmuseum in Chur, which is represented on a postcard from the artist to Luise Schiefler dated 24 December 1910. Chemical tests on the wood of the stool, which were conducted at the suggestion of Bernd Hünlich, show it to be an original African piece: see Lloyd (1987), pp.142, 416 and n.45

25 For a detailed account of the Brücke artists' experiments with primitivizing sculpture and their undoubted knowledge of original primitive sources from around 1910 onwards, see Lloyd (1987) especially pp.132ff

26 See n.5 to p.180

27 Gordon (1966): 355 and n.122. It has not been possible to establish whether the *Teha'amana* painting was in the 1910 exhibition

28 See Gordon (1966), figs.47, 48. In addition, there are in the Kirchner archive photographs made by the artist after Gauguin's paintings: see ibid., n.126

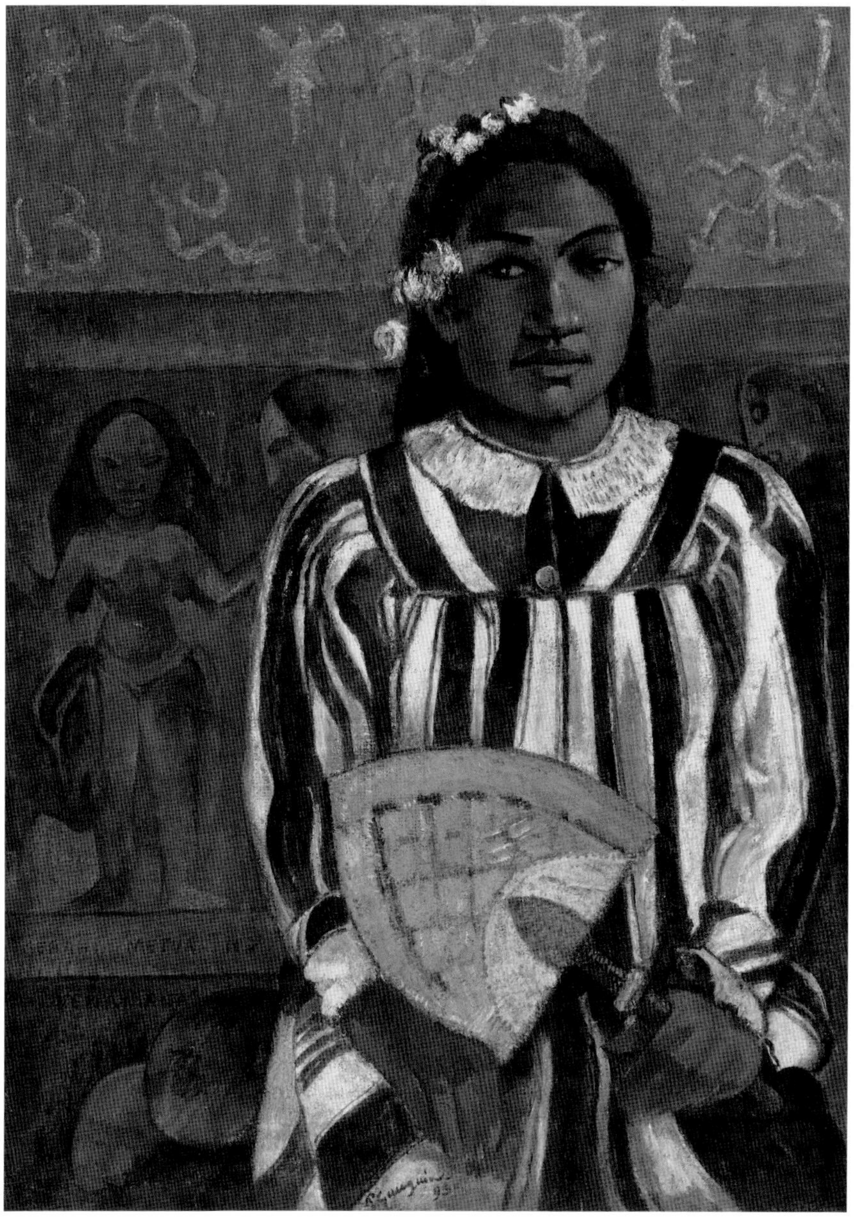

FIG 4 Paul Gauguin, *Ancestors of Teha'amana*, 1893, oil on canvas, 76.3 × 54.3 cm (Chicago, IL, Art Institute, gift of Mr and Mrs Charles Deering McCormick, inv. no.1980.613)

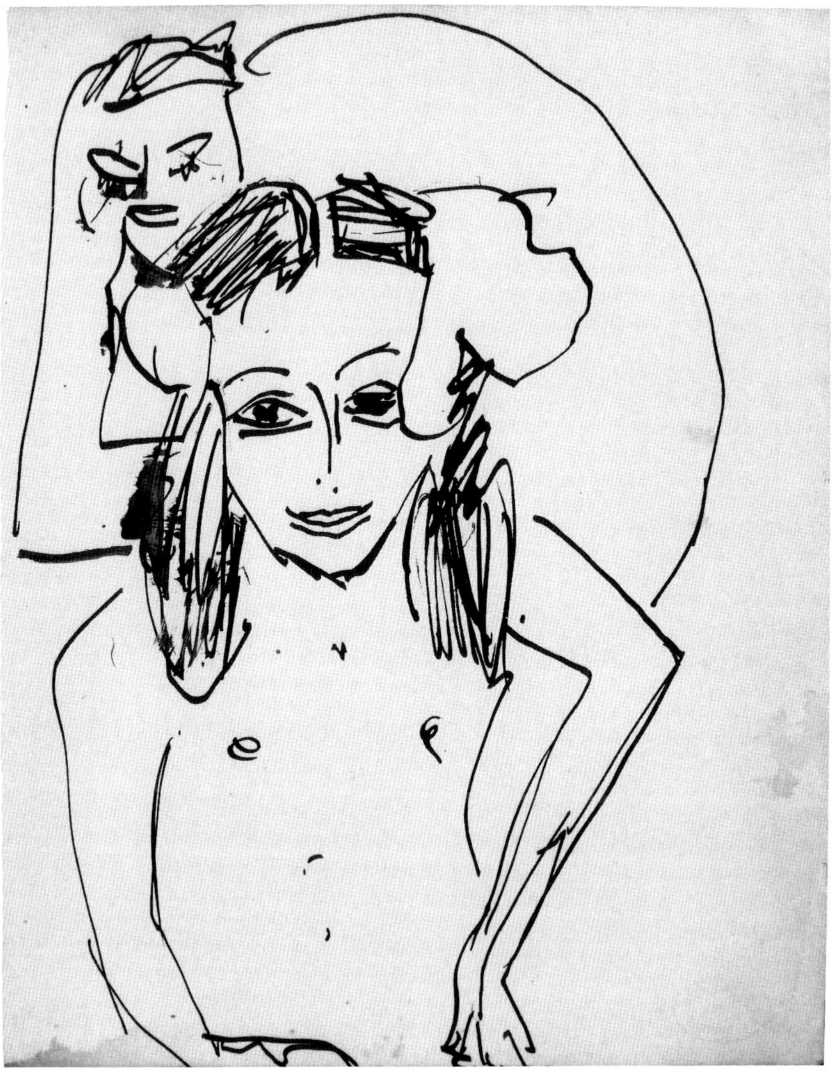

FIG 5 Ernst Ludwig Kirchner, *Fränzi in front of Sculpture*, 1910, ink, 20.8 × 13.9 cm (formerly Galerie Utermann, Dortmund)

In his article 'Kirchner in Dresden', Donald Gordon sees Kirchner's experience of this Gauguin exhibition as an important milestone in his development, observing that prior to this, primitive artefacts had merely constituted 'objects of aesthetic contemplation, curiosities whose "otherness" was provocative in suggesting decor for studio appointments and stylizations for a drawing shorthand', whereas 'after the Gauguin exhibition, non-Western sources became for Kirchner the essential raw material for the ultimate attainment of personal style'.[29] This observation appears to be borne out by a consideration of the probable genesis of *Fränzi in front of Carved Chair* which, to judge from studies and other related works, seems to have extended over a considerable period of time – perhaps even the greater part of 1910.

Two works, in particular, enable us to trace the development of the artist's ideas in some detail: an ink drawing entitled *Fränzi in front of Sculpture* (fig.5), which appears to represent not a chair, but a grinning mask placed immediately behind the sitter, and the study in coloured chalk and pastel now in Frankfurt, which is also known by the title *Fränzi in front of Carved Chair* (fig.6). In the drawing, which should probably be ascribed to some time early in 1910, the primitive mask is indeed employed merely as a decorative prop or accoutrement as Gordon suggests, while the head of the sitter and its 'reflection' created by the mask-like carving behind are more widely separated than in the finished painting. In the pastel, the anthropomorphic aspect of the carved chair is accentuated by the way the artist has depicted it with 'naturalistic' hair and breasts and flesh tones produced by a combination of the delicate pastel and the light

Notes

29 Ibid., pp.356f. Lloyd also points to Gauguin's *Teha'amana* (as well as Edvard Munch's 1894 painting *Puberty*) as a possible source for [46], but takes issue with Gordon over the extent to which the 1910 Gauguin exhibition acted as a 'catalyst' on the development of Kirchner's primitivist style: see Lloyd (1987), pp.75, 142–3

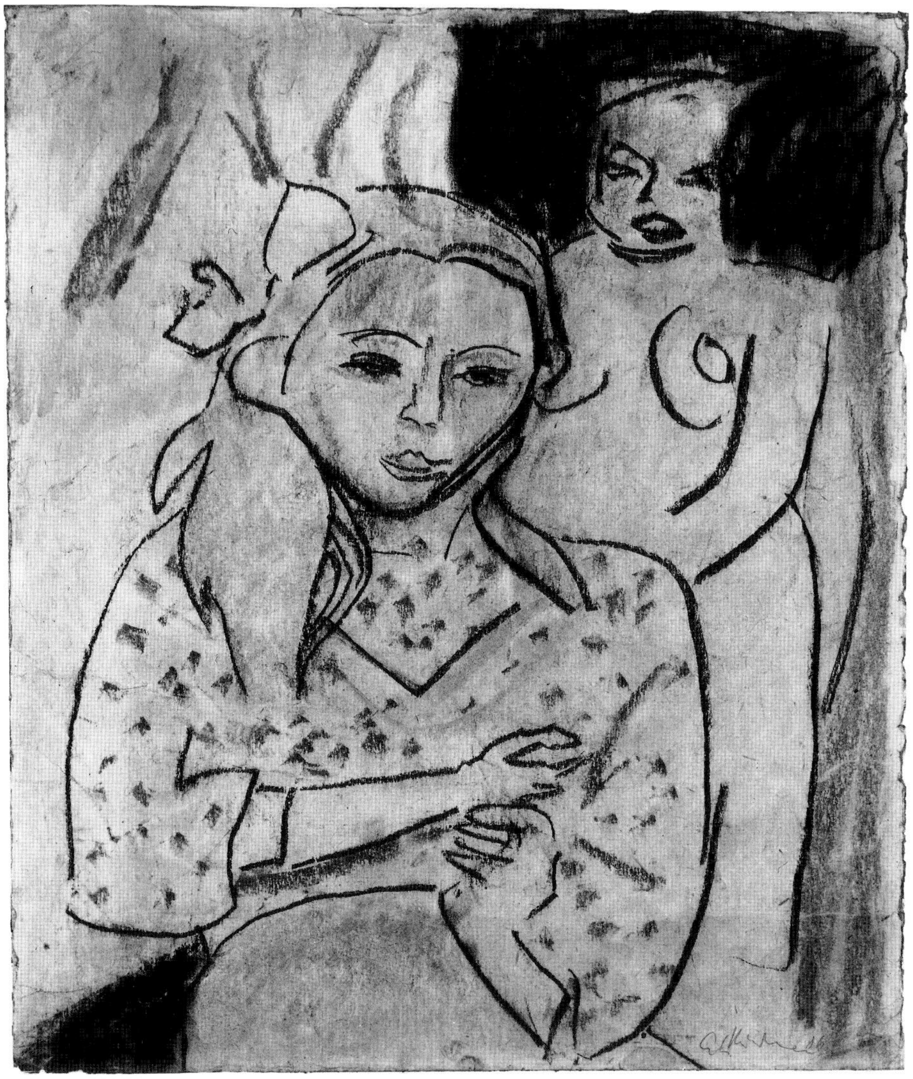

FIG 6 Ernst Ludwig Kirchner, *Fränzi in front of Carved Chair*, 1910, coloured chalk, pastel and charcoal, 59.8 × 49.5 (Frankfurt am Main, Städelsches Kunstinstitut)

brown colour of the paper. The carved chair is, none the less, still quite clearly separated from the figure of Fränzi, and seems to fulfil the role of a commentary on the principal theme of the composition. This is, in part, also true of the painting itself, which still exhibits one of the most striking features of the pastel: the ironic reversal created by the quasi-naturalistic flesh tones in which the chair is painted, contrasting with the unnatural green of the real human visage in the foreground – a deliberate visual pun. In the painting, however, the commentary is more mordant: the fixed grimace of the carving, which creates the illusion that there is another, leering countenance immediately behind that of 'Fränzi', also serves to emphasize the precociously sensual expression of the sitter.

It is, on the other hand, only in the painting that figure and carving become fully integrated, while for the first time the crude handling of the carved primitivizing artefact here extends to the angular, awkward treatment of the human figure with its garish, non-naturalistic colours. It was almost certainly Kirchner's experience of Gauguin's paintings in the original which provided the impetus for this closer interplay between figure and primitivizing background; thus, the finished painting should in all probability be dated to the latter part of the year, after the autumn Gauguin exhibition at Arnold's.

On the basis both of style and of the documentary and other evidence summarized above, dates such as 1907 or 1907–8 suggested for [46] in the catalogues of several of the earlier exhibitions in which the painting was shown can no longer be considered tenable.[30]

30 Questioned as to the date at which Kirchner first became acquainted with 'Fränzi', Heckel, in an interview with Roman Norbert Ketterer given in 1958, suggested (not implausibly) 1909: see Ketterer (1988/II), p.47

Ernst Ludwig Kirchner 1880–1938

47 Kneeling Nude in front of Red Screen[1]

*c*1911–12
Oil on canvas, 75 × 56 cm
Signed lower left: 'Kirchner'
There is a history of flaking and earlier restoration; the paint surface is now abraded, and exhibits an irregular texture. The structure of the paint layer is brittle. The paint losses have been retouched, especially around the edges of the painting
Accession no.1973.66(a)

Verso Seated Nude with Bent Leg

Provenance
Estate of the artist
Galerie R.N.Ketterer, Campione d'Italia
Thyssen-Bornemisza Collection, 1973

Exhibitions
Turin, Galleria d'Arte Contemporanea, 1964, *Ernst Ludwig Kirchner*, no.4
Florence 1964, no.178 [as '1909']
Bremen 1975, no.36
Rome 1990–91, no.27

Literature
Gordon (1968), no.240
R.N.Ketterer, *Moderne Kunst VI*, Campione d'Italia (Galerie R.N.Ketterer) 1969, p.86, no.48, ill. p.87
Kiel (1974), p.77, ill. p.75

Throughout his years in both Dresden and Berlin, Kirchner occupied himself with the age-old theme of the female nude. Bathers compositions, nudes in a landscape, studio models depicted singly or in twos and threes constitute a major part of his work. Only after his move to Switzerland does this preoccupation with figure compositions, which dominate his early work, yield to an ever more profound absorption in landscape painting.

The exact dating of *Kneeling Nude* is problematic. The date 1912 suggested by Gordon is not supported by documentary evidence, and on the basis of style alone, the work would appear to

Note
1 The work has been known by the German title *Kniender Mädchenakt vor rotem Wandschirm*, and is thus entitled in Gordon's oeuvre-catalogue of Kirchner's paintings: see Gordon (1968), p.300

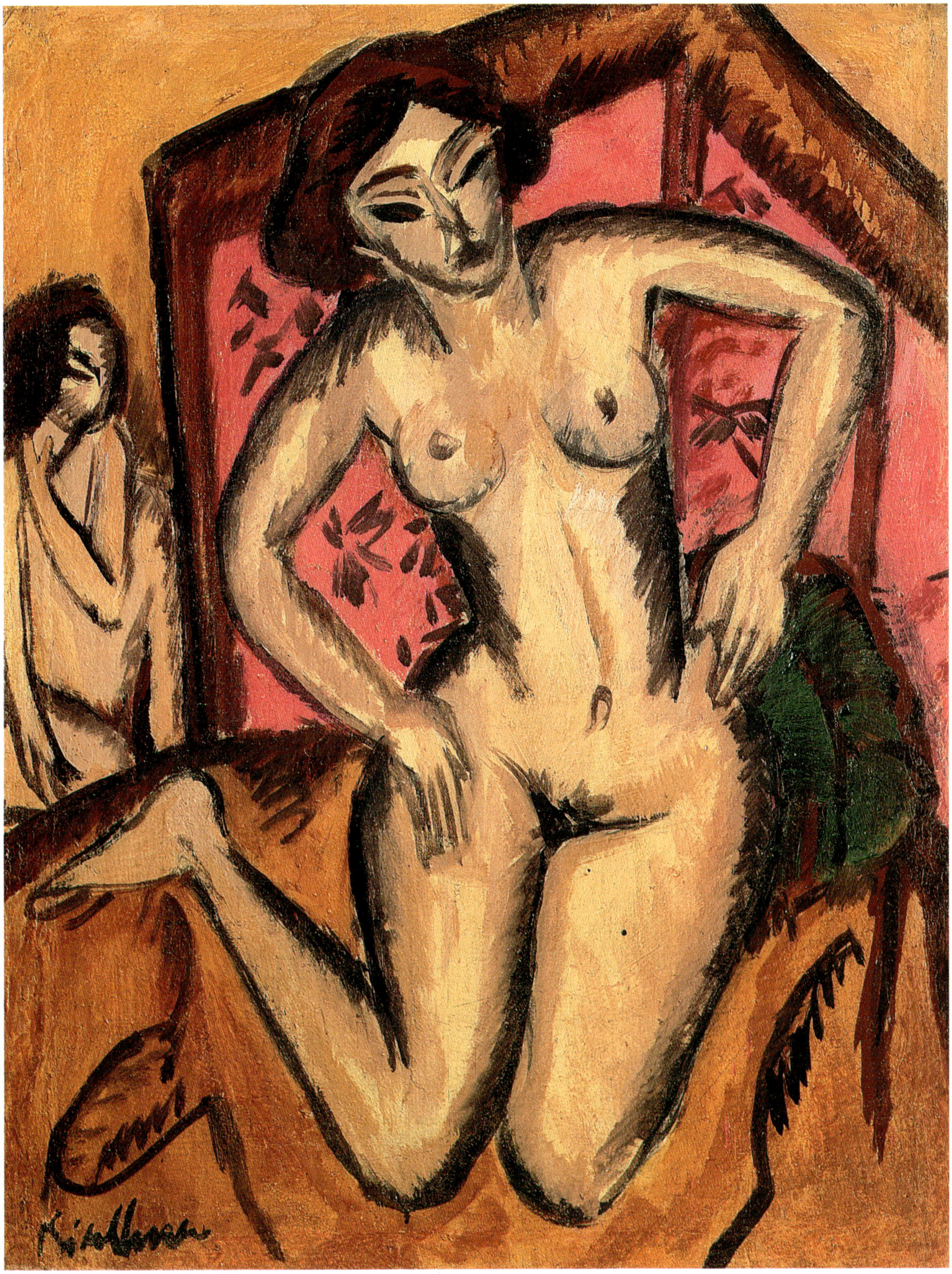

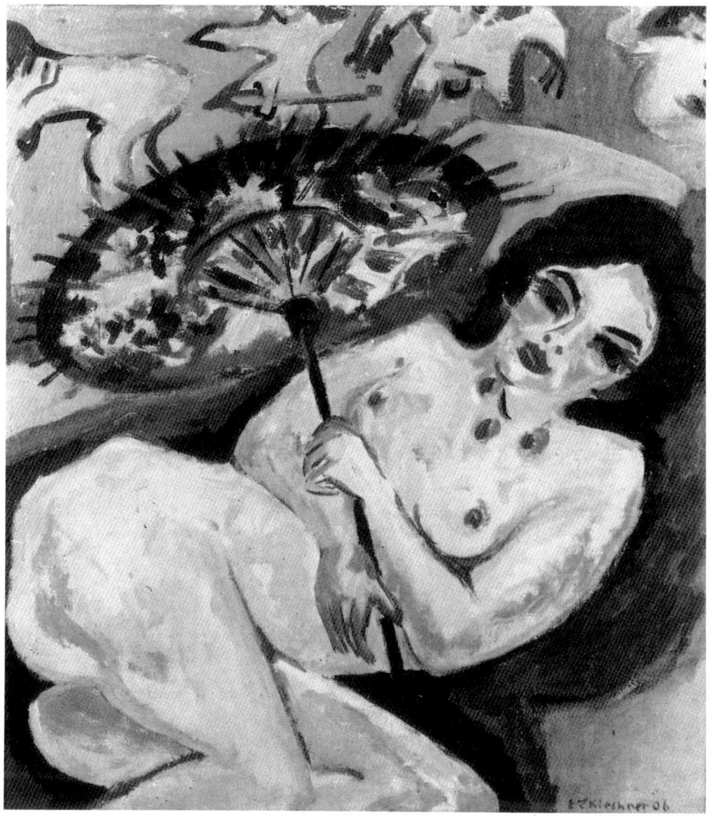

FIG 1 Ernst Ludwig Kirchner, *Girl under Japanese Umbrella*, 1909, oil on canvas, 92 × 80 cm (Düsseldorf, Kunstsammlung Nordrhein-Westfalen)

span the Dresden and Berlin periods. Though the date 1909 given in the catalogue of the 1964 Florence exhibition is probably too early, in many ways the treatment of figure and depth, the severe anatomical distortion and flattening of foreground space recall works such as *Girl under Japanese Umbrella*, which almost certainly was painted in that year (fig.1).[2] On the other hand, the angular appearance of the figure and nervous brushwork suggest a kinship with other paintings of Kirchner's first months in Berlin, so that a date of *c*1911–12 appears to the present author not improbable.

The verso of the painting bears another nude composition, tentatively dated by Gordon to 1921–3; this, on the basis of style, seems plausible.

Notes

2 Gordon (1968), no.57, signed and dated '06'. An old photograph of the work preserved in the Kirchner estate is dated '04'; see Gordon (1968), p.274

3 The work has been known by the German title *Sitzender Mädchenakt mit angezogenem Knie*, and is thus entitled in Gordon's oeuvre-catalogue of Kirchner's paintings: see Gordon (1968), p.300

47 *verso* Seated Nude with Bent Leg[3]

*c*1921–3
Oil on canvas, 75 × 56 cm
Unsigned/undated
The canvas bears the Kirchner estate stamp, inscribed 'Da/Bg 2'
The painting is unvarnished and in good condition
Accession no.1973.66(b)

Literature

Gordon (1968), no.240v
Kiel (1974), p.77, ill. p.76

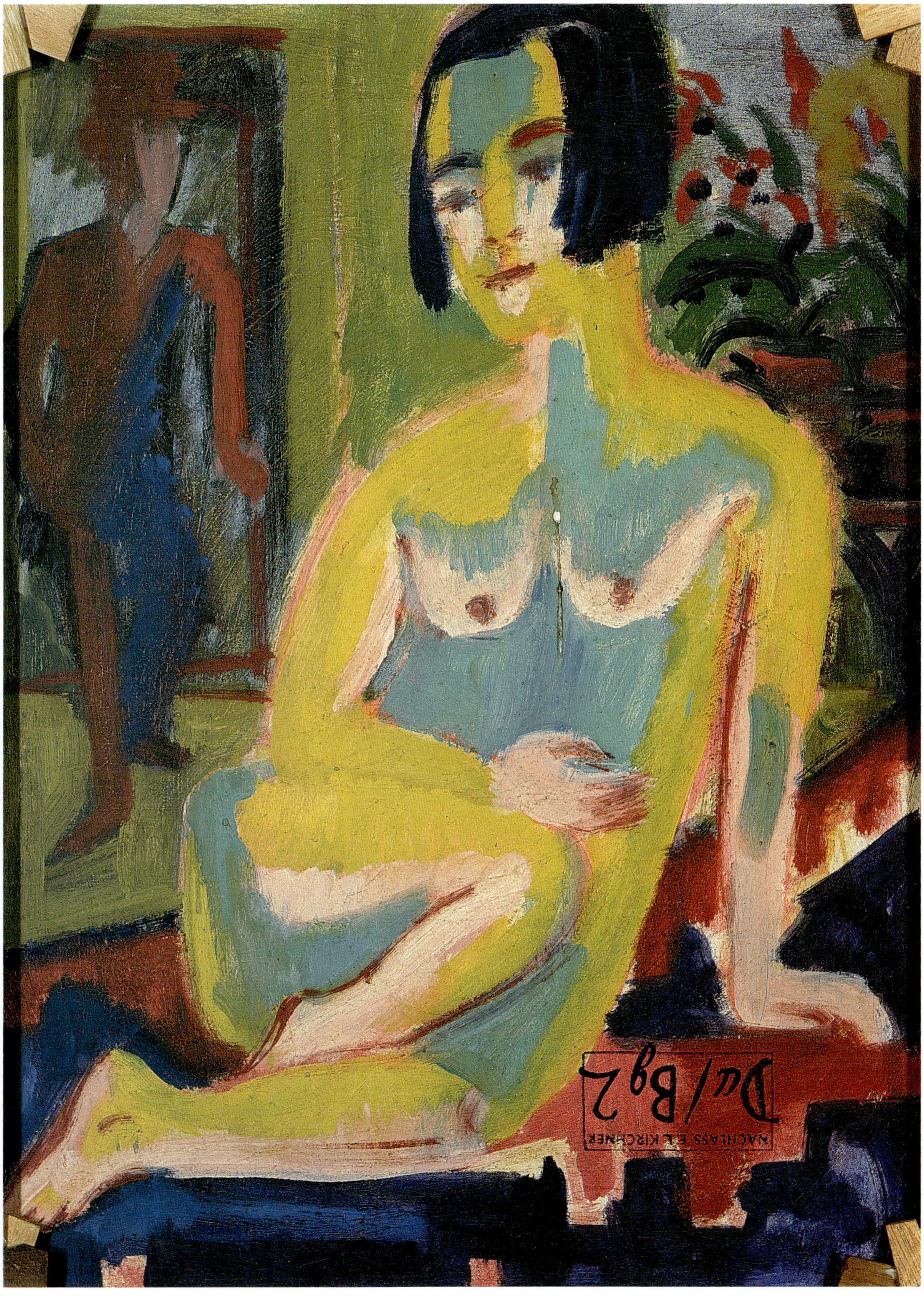
NACHLASS E.L.KIRCHNER
Du/Bg 2

Ernst Ludwig Kirchner 1880–1938

48 Curving Bay[1]

1914 (?)
Oil on canvas, 146 × 123 cm
Unsigned/undated
The painting has not previously been restored, is unvarnished, and is in fragile condition. The paint film is brittle and shows a number of vertical cracks
Accession no.1987.8

Provenance
Schlegel Collection, Uttwil
M. Kesser, Zurich
Galerie Aenne Abels, Cologne
Lehmann Collection, Cologne
Private collection, Ambach
Galerie R.N.Ketterer, Campione d'Italia
Thyssen-Bornemisza Collection, 1987

Exhibitions
Lugano 1989, no.7[2]
Expressionism and Modern German Painting, 1989–90, no.17
Rome 1990–91, no.28

Literature
Gordon (1968), no.479 [as '1917']

According to notes taken by the late Donald Gordon, a photograph of this work is contained in the third of the artist's photo-albums preserved in the Kirchner estate, p.69, inscribed 'Goldregenbaum 1917, 150 × 120, Frau Schlegel, Uttwil'.[3] It was presumably on the basis of this inscription that Gordon dated the picture to 1917 in his oeuvre-catalogue of Kirchner's paintings. Such a date appears, however, highly implausible. It was wartime; there were no more nude bathing parties to secluded lakes or beaches, and indeed, there are no other bathers compositions from that period. Nor does *Curving Bay* resemble in style any of the artist's other known paintings of 1917. Kirchner himself was ill, and in and out of sanatoria for much of the time. The summer of that year was, moreover, spent on top of a mountain in Switzerland (see [50]): an unlikely setting in which to paint a picture of nudes on a beach.

Interestingly, in his own, unpublished notes Gordon hazarded a date of 1913–14 for the present work. This suggestion seems far more probable. The subject depicted is undoubtedly the Bay of Fehmarn, the island in the Baltic which Kirchner visited for three consecutive summers – 1912, 1913 and 1914.[4] In style, *Curving Bay* is closely related to several paintings ascribed by

Notes
1 See n.5
2 It has proved impossible to trace any record of previous exhibitions. According to Gordon (1968), p.336, [48] was shown at the Modern Art Center in Zurich in 1949 under no.426; this appears to have been an auction held by the Galerie Max G.Bollag at which the painting was sold. I am grateful to Mr Bollag and to Denise Vosseler, of the Schweizerisches Institut für Kunstwissenschaft, Zurich, for their efforts to assist me in establishing the early history of the painting
3 Donald Gordon's personal archive and papers are now preserved at the University of Pittsburgh. According to his wishes, in due course they will be made accessible to other scholars for further research. Meanwhile, I am greatly indebted to Professor Gordon's widow, Joan Morse Gordon, and to Professor David G.Wilkins, Director of the University Art Gallery and Chair of the Henry Clay Frick Fine Arts Department at the University of Pittsburgh, for making material from the Gordon archive available to me
4 Kirchner had first visited Fehmarn in the summer of 1908: see Hans Bolliger, 'Biography', in Ketterer (1982), p.235

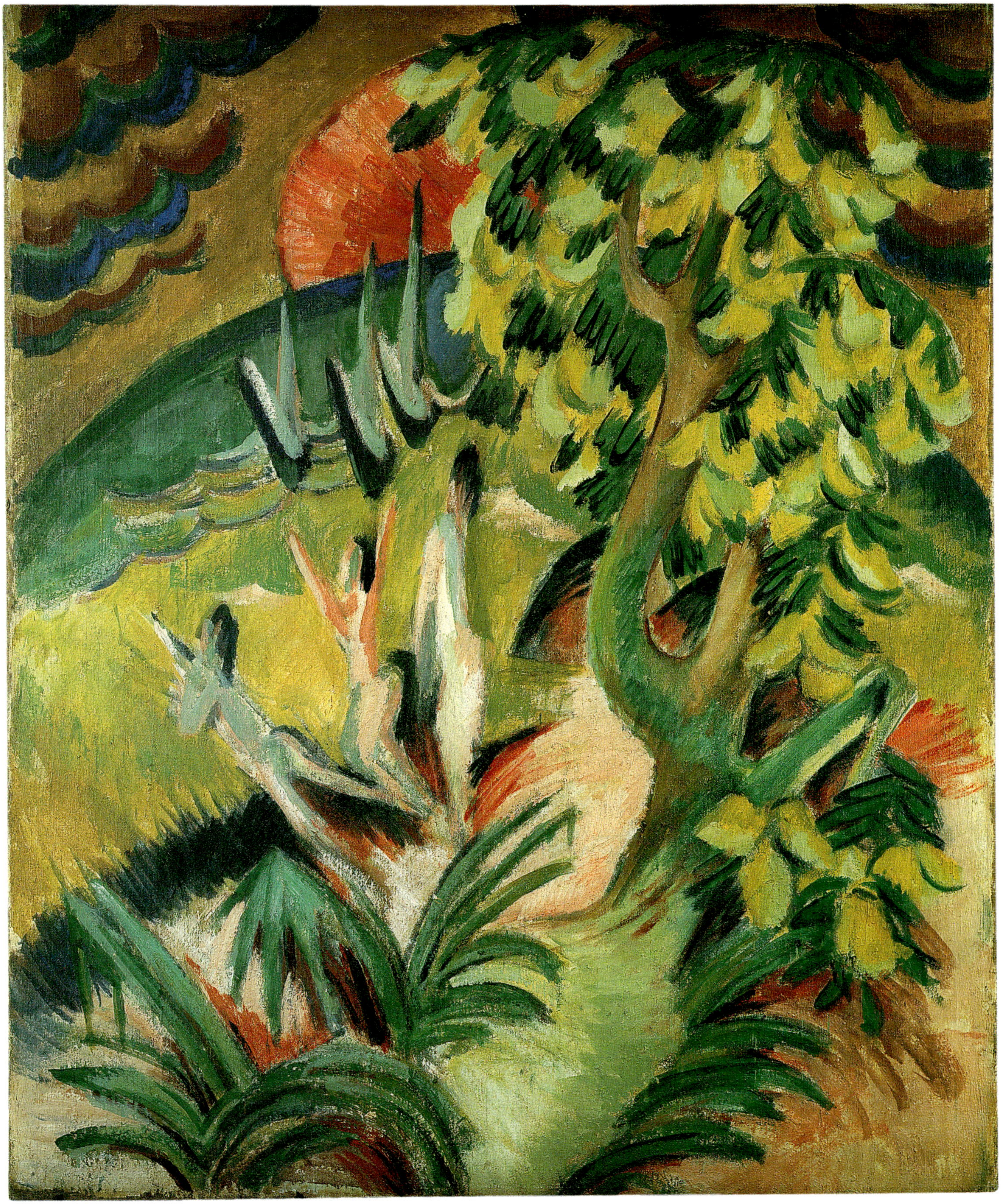

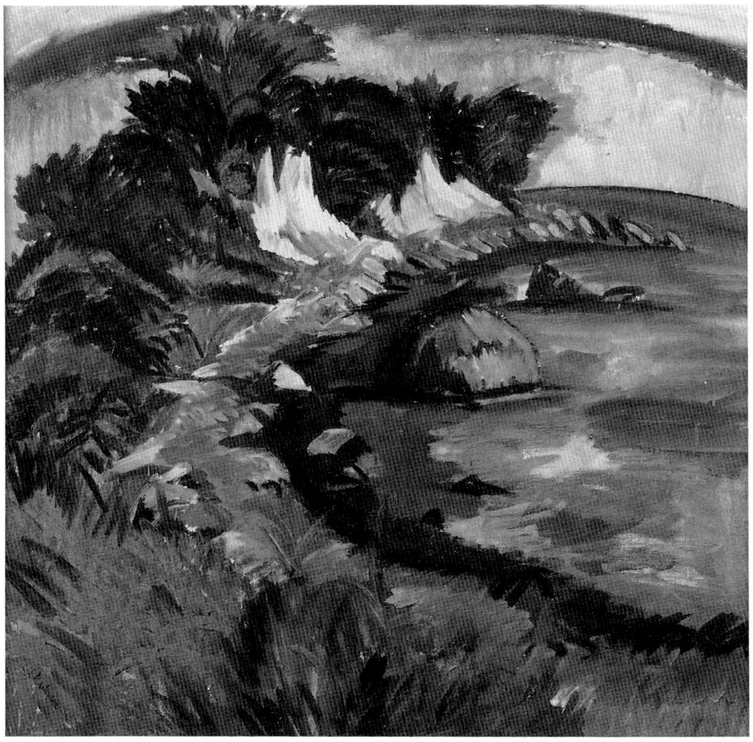

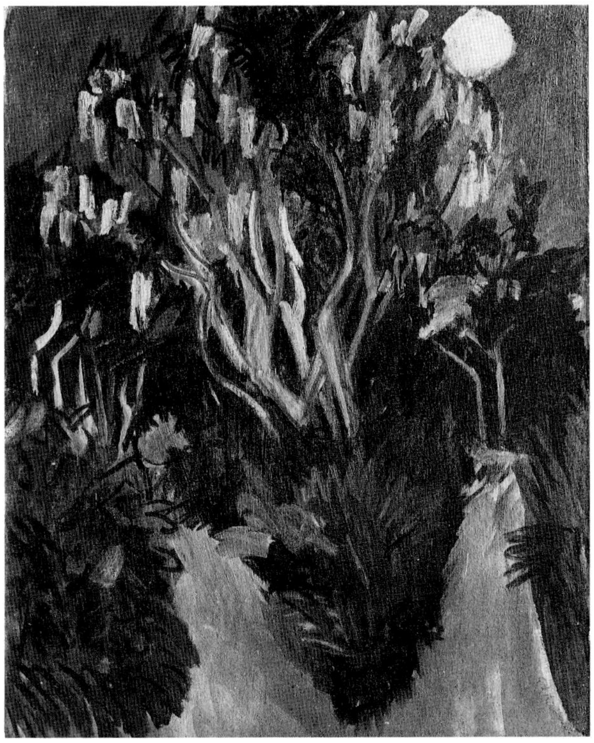

Gordon to the summer of 1913, particularly *Coast at Fehmarn* (fig.1). There is also a manifest similarity with a further picture of 1913, now in the collection of Colby College Art Museum, Waterville, Maine, entitled *Laburnum Tree* (fig.2), the alternative title by which [48] has been known.[5]

In a letter to the author dated 7 May 1989, Dr Wolfgang Henze pointed out the resemblance between the figures represented in *Curving Bay* and those which occur in Kirchner's woodcut *Three Bathers in the Waves*, also of 1913.[6] On the other hand, he also ventured the opinion that the 'ecstatic pictorial language, composition and use of colour' in *Curving Bay* are closer to works done after Kirchner's return from Fehmarn in the summer of 1914, and even raised the possibility that the painting could have been executed from memory, perhaps as late as 1915.[7]

In the opinion of the present author, *Curving Bay* is, in style, closest of all to the woodcut *Beach and Cliffs with Curving Bay* (fig.3) which, in the oeuvre-catalogue of Kirchner's graphic works compiled in 1967, is again ascribed to 1913.[8] However, in 1985 the Galerie Kornfeld in Berne offered for sale an original example of this print (inscribed 'Eigendruck'), which had been dated by the artist in pencil: '14'.[9] This, together with the mood of the painting, the sense that it is not a depiction of a real landscape, but rather a cosmological scene with semi-circular horizon, heraldic sun and non-naturalistic colours, would likewise argue for a date of 1914 for *Curving Bay*, and it is on this basis that the painting has – albeit tentatively – been dated here.[10] Whether it was actually executed *sur le motif* or, as Henze suggests, after the artist's return to Berlin is impossible to say.

Kirchner himself, by his own account, regarded his painting visits to Fehmarn as of particular importance for the development of his art. After the summer he spent there in 1912, he wrote to Schiefler: 'I painted pictures of absolute maturity, so far as I myself can judge. Ochre, blue and green are the colours of Fehmarn, a wonderful coast formation often of South Sea opulence, absurd flowers with fat stems ...'[11] And in December 1914, his friend Botho Graef wrote to Karl Ernst Osthaus, director of the then Folkwang-Museum in Hagen, about Kirchner's latest work, singling out for particular praise '... landscapes which will probably delight even the old academicians, figure paintings most intense in their effects ... I asked him for permission to write to you to say how wonderful I find his work ...'[12]

Notes

5 In his notes, Gordon several times refers to [48] by the title *Runde Bucht* (Curving Bay); it is not, however, clear whence this title derives. I have used *Curving Bay*, rather than *Laburnum Tree*, for the Thyssen Collection's painting principally in order to distinguish it from the Colby College Museum's picture

6 Dube (1967), no.222. Similar figures also occur in the woodcut *Three Bathing Women*, likewise of 1913; see ibid., no.225

7 I am grateful to Dr Wolfgang Henze, Campione d'Italia, for his opinion on this painting

8 Dube (1967), no.220

9 *Auktion 189, Ernst Ludwig Kirchner. Werke – Dokumente – Bücher*, Berne 1985, no.70

10 If this supposition is correct, the date 1917 given by Gordon may well derive from a mis-reading of the handwritten inscription in the Kirchner photograph album referred to above: it would be relatively easy to mistake a '4' for a 'continental' crossed '7'

11 Letter dated 31 December 1912, quoted after Gordon (1968), p.24; see also Lloyd (1987), pp.208, 430 and n.66

12 H. Hesse-Frielinghaus, 'E.L. Kirchner und das Folkwang-Museum Hagen', *Westfalen*, LII (1974), nos.1–2: 17–18; cited after Bolliger, loc. cit., p.237

FIG 1 Ernst Ludwig Kirchner, *Coast at Fehmarn*, 1913, oil on canvas, 85.5 × 85.5 cm (Darmstadt, Hessisches Landesmuseum)

FIG 2 Ernst Ludwig Kirchner, *Laburnum Tree*, 1913, oil on canvas, 99 × 75 cm (Waterville, ME, Colby College Art Museum)

FIG 3 Ernst Ludwig Kirchner, *Beach and Cliffs with Curving Bay*, 1913 (1914?), woodcut (Cleveland, OH, Cleveland Museum of Art, CMA 73.235, gift of Moselle Taylor Meals)

FIG 4 Coast at Fehmarn between Katharinenhof and Staberhuk

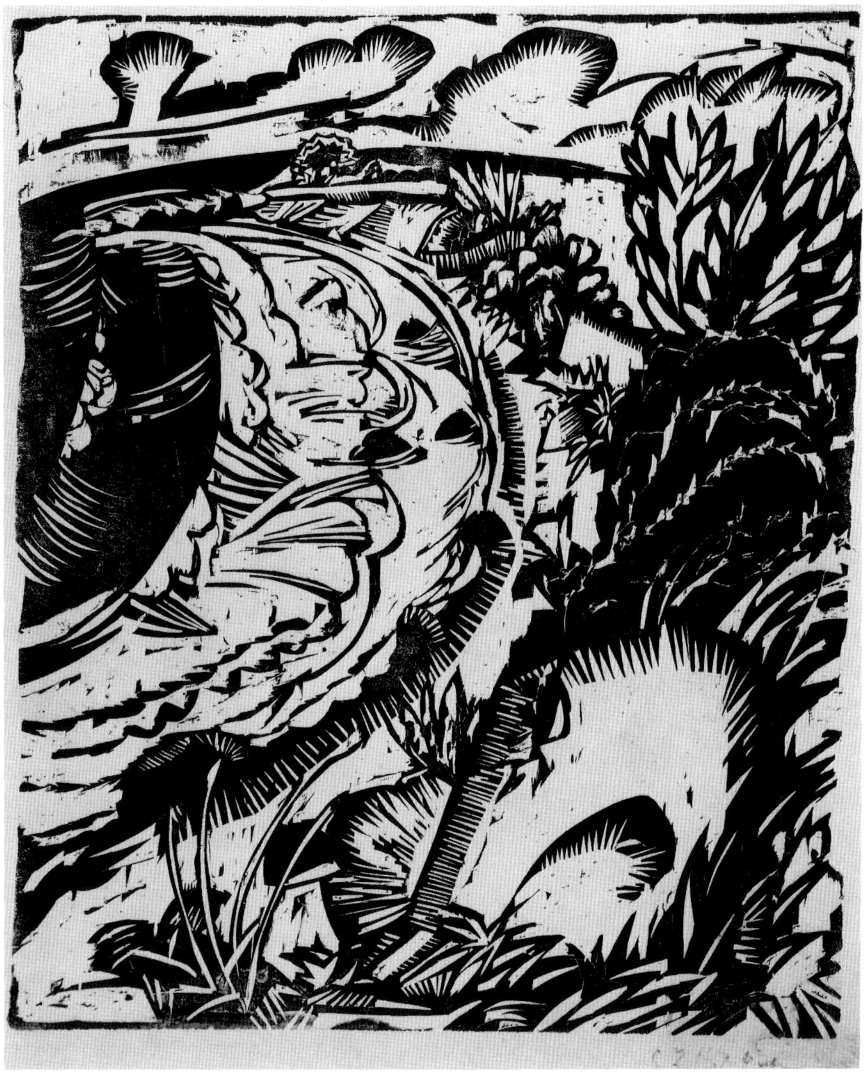

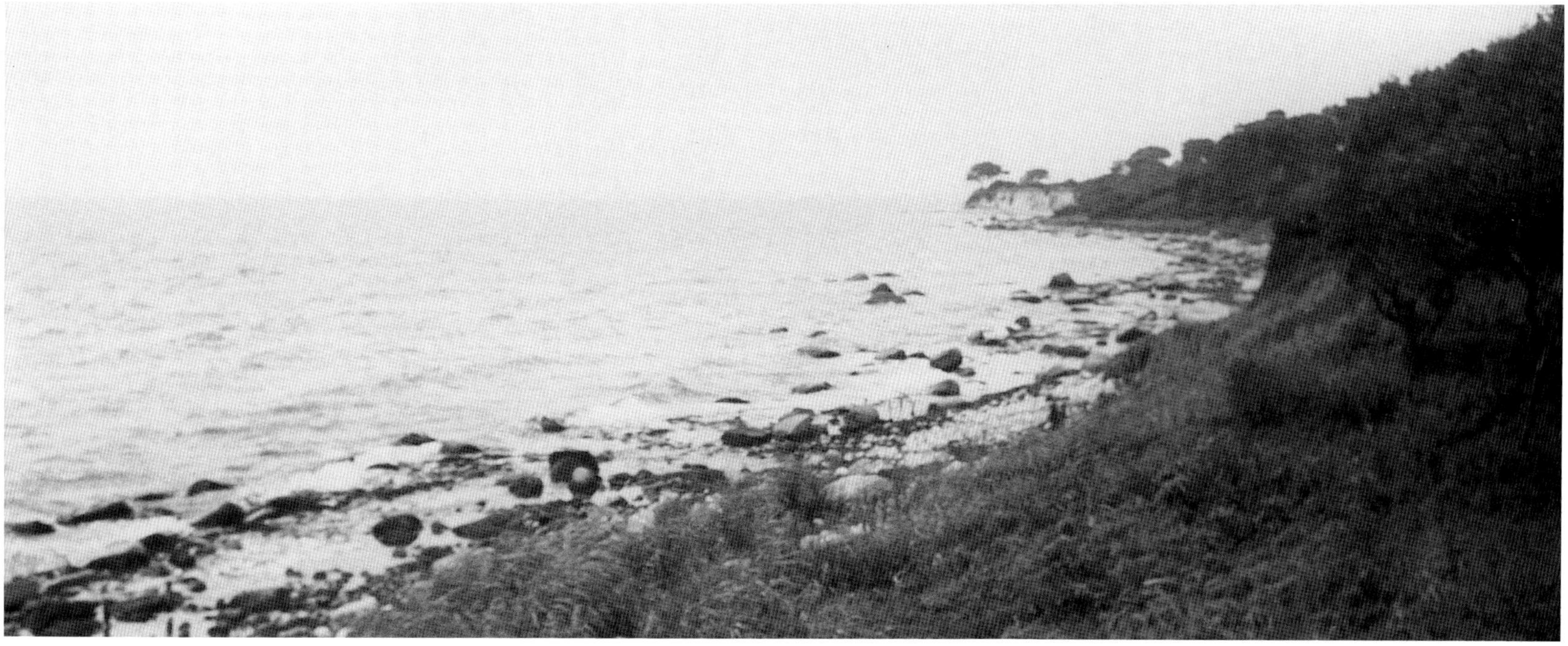

Ernst Ludwig Kirchner 1880–1938

49 With Red Streetwalker
Strasse mit roter Kokotte

1914/1925
Oil on canvas, 125 × 90.5 cm
Inscribed on back of canvas: 'E.L.Kirchner. Strasse mit roter Kokotte. Berlin 14', with estate stamp, inscribed: 'Be/Bb 2'
There is a history of cracking and lifting of the paint layers, especially around the head of the principal figure. The surface shows some cupping, especially around the cracks. The painting is unvarnished. Frame probably original
Accession no.1973.63

Provenance
Estate of the artist
Dr Ferdinand Ziersch, Wuppertal[1]
Ilse Ziersch, Feldafing
Thyssen-Bornemisza Collection, 1973[2]

Exhibitions
Munich, Neue-Secession, 1929, *XV. Sommer-Ausstellung*, no.142
Berne, Kunsthalle, 1933, *Ernst Ludwig Kirchner*, no.20
St Gallen, Kunstmuseum, 1950, *Ernst Ludwig Kirchner*, no.16
Düsseldorf, Kunsthalle, 1960, *Ernst Ludwig Kirchner. Zum Gedächtnis an die 80. Wiederkehr des Geburtstages*, no.42 [as '1913']
Kassel, Alte Galerie/Museum Fridericianum/Orangerie, 1964, *documenta III, internationale ausstellung*, no.9 [as '1913']
Bielefeld, Kunsthalle, 1969, *Ernst Ludwig Kirchner aus Privatbesitz*, no.10
Bremen 1975, no.37
Berlin, Nationalgalerie, 1979–80, *Ernst Ludwig Kirchner 1880–1938*, no.184[3]
Expressionism, a German Intuition, 1980–81, no.137
Modern Masters from the Thyssen-Bornemisza Collection, 1984–6, no.57
Berlin, Berlinische Galerie, 1987, *Ich und die Stadt*, no.112
Lugano 1989, no.8
Expressionism and Modern German Painting, 1989–90, no.19

Literature
Gordon (1968), no.366
Grisebach (1968), p.96
Kiel (1974), p.74, ill. p.73
Eberhard Roters and Bernhard Schulz (eds.), *Ich und die Stadt. Mensch und Grossstadt in der deutschen Kunst des 20. Jahrhunderts*, exh. cat., Berlin, Berlinische Galerie, 1987, p.68
See also Ketterer (1982), p.124; Rosalyn Deutsche, 'Alienation in Berlin: Kirchner's Street Scenes', *Art in America* (January 1983): 65–72

Although Kirchner had repeatedly depicted city scenes – streets and tramways and bridges – during his years in Dresden, with his move to Berlin in the autumn of 1911 the city as subject took on a heightened significance, as if the capital's frenetic pace of life provoked a new excitement in him. But it was the darker side of city life that he recorded in his Berlin paintings, seeming to align himself with those – cabaret artists, circus folk and prostitutes in particular – whose existence was on the fringes of society, inhabiting a shifting, uncertain, twilight world – a world to which, from a Nietzschean perspective, artists also belonged.[4]

Notes
1 The painting is referred to in an exchange of letters between Kirchner and the Berlin dealer Ferdinand Möller dating from the spring of 1929. Möller asked Kirchner to send him two pre-war paintings, *With Red Streetwalker* and *Russian Dancer*, to show potential buyers. Whether the Thyssen painting was in fact sold at that time is not clear from the correspondence, copies of which are in the archive of the Thyssen-Bornemisza Collection, Lugano-Castagnola. The provenance given by Gordon appears to show that the work was acquired by Ferdinand Ziersch in 1954 directly from the Kirchner estate: see Gordon (1968), p.319
2 Acquired directly from the previous owner
3 Exhibition to mark the centenary of the artist's birth, also shown in Munich, Cologne and Zurich, 1979–80
4 On the Nietzschean content of Expressionist art generally, and that of Die Brücke in particular, see Donald E.Gordon, 'Content by Contradiction', *Art in America* (December 1982): 76–89, also Gordon (1987), especially ch.1

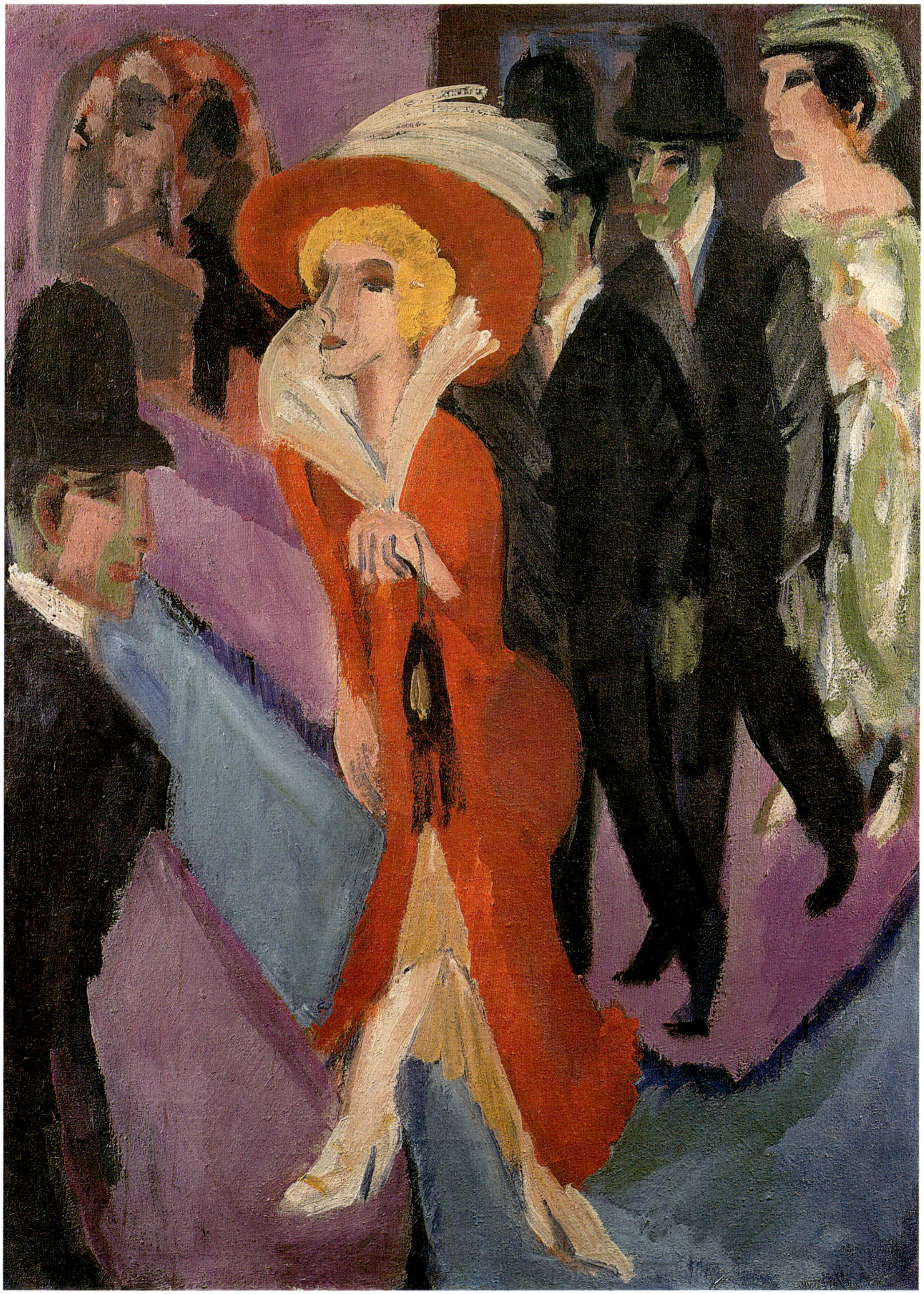

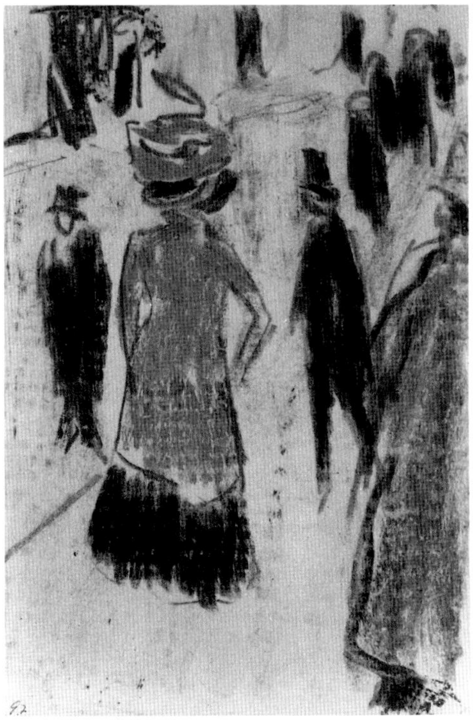

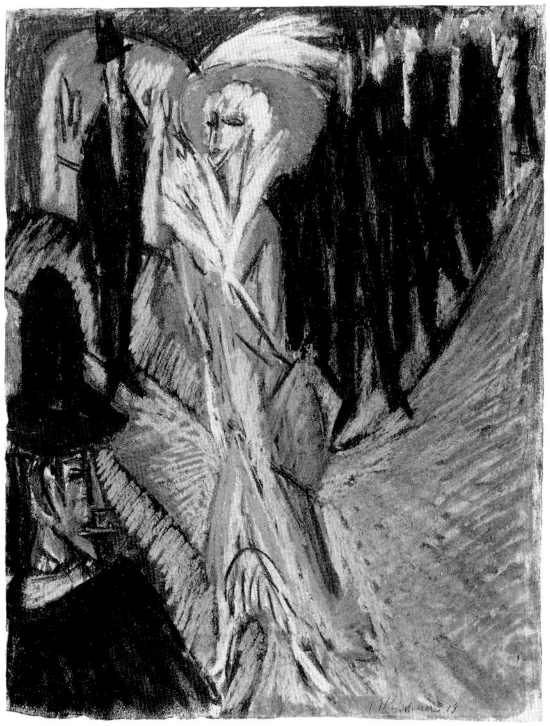

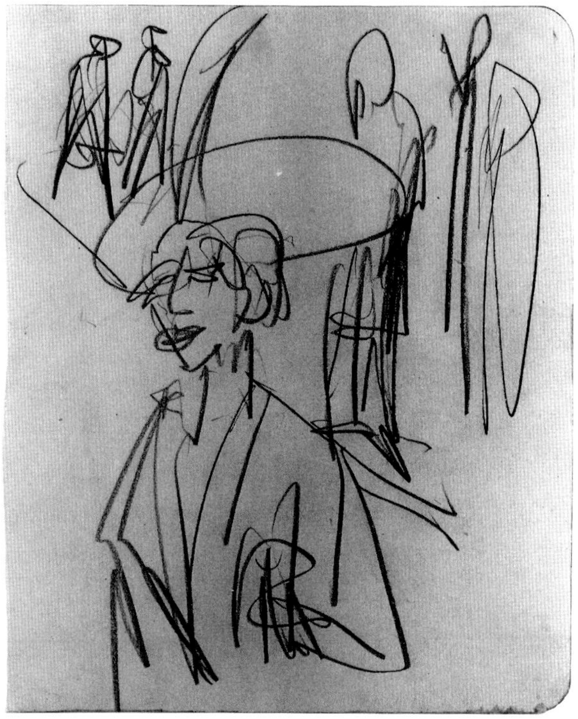

According to the painter Werner Gothein, who had accompanied Kirchner on his 1913 visit to Fehmarn, most of the Berlin streetwalker pictures were painted between February and April 1914.[5] *With Red Streetwalker* almost certainly belongs among this group of paintings executed during the early part of that year. However, a related drawing on a postcard sent by Kirchner to Heckel postmarked 4 April 1910 (fig.1) shows a very similar composition, with a streetwalker in red flanked by a diagonal line of men going off to the right, lending substance to the notion that Kirchner's paintings of the Berlin years are on occasion reworkings of much earlier ideas. The principal differences between the postcard and the painting are that, in the former, the central figure is turned away from us, while the observer in the extreme foreground appears here at bottom right, rather than bottom left as in [49].

Also closely related to *With Red Streetwalker* is a highly-finished pastel, now in Stuttgart (fig.2), which like the painting is dated 1914. Here, the differences are more telling. Though the pastel exhibits what is in essence the same composition, it is immediately distinguished from the painting by its much greater immediacy and stronger emotional charge. In particular, the overall structure in the form of a large 'x', found in many of Kirchner's major works of this period, directs our attention specifically to the genital area of the female figure in red – an undisguised sexual suggestion which is reinforced by the fact that the gaze of the male onlooker at lower left is clearly fixed on the same spot. It is as if all eyes, all lines converge upon that which is the focus of the client's, if not the artist's, interest. In the painting, this erotic theme is made less explicit by subtle changes to the composition, underlining a somewhat eerie sense of alienation, as if the artist is in this instance merely a dispassionate onlooker, calmly observing a scene which is of no concern to him.[6]

Whether these, from a psychological viewpoint, highly significant changes reflect the evolution of Kirchner's ideas between the execution of the pastel and the completion of the original version of the painting, some time early in 1914, appears questionable. On taking up permanent residence in Switzerland, he began reworking – and in some cases substantially repainting – the pictures that had been stored in his Berlin studio during the First World War. This, almost certainly, is what happened to [49]. Examination by means of infra-red reflectography reveals extensive reworking, especially around the bodice and left arm of the

Notes

5 Letter dated 14 November 1960 to Roman Norbert Ketterer, cited in *Ernst Ludwig Kirchner 1880–1938*, exh. cat., Berlin, Nationalgalerie, 1979–80, p.192; see also Roters and Schulz loc. cit.

6 Ketterer, commenting on the Stuttgart pastel which he describes as 'clearly the greatest of all [Kirchner's] street scenes of prostitutes', raises the question whether the male figure in the extreme left foreground, who in the painting seems more like an uninvolved witness to the scene than a potential client, is a portrait of the artist himself or, if not a self-portrait as such, 'a kind of alter ego'; see Ketterer (1982), p.124

7 Grisebach (1968), p.98; see also n.12 to p.185

FIG 1 Ernst Ludwig Kirchner, postcard addressed to Erich Heckel dated 4 April 1910 (Hamburg, Altonaer Museum, Norddeutsches Landesmuseum, inv. no.1964/220)

FIG 2 Ernst Ludwig Kirchner, *Street with Red Cocotte*, 1914, pastel and coloured chalk, 41 × 30.3 cm (Stuttgart, Staatsgalerie, Graphische Sammlung, inv. no.C57/745)

FIG 3 Ernst Ludwig Kirchner, drawing related to *Street with Red Cocotte*, pencil, 20.5 × 16.5 cm (Berlin, Dr Wolfram Gabler)

FIG 4 Detail of *Street with Red Streetwalker* under infra-red reflectography

main figure and the upper part of face and hat (see fig.4), as well as changes to the brothel scene glimpsed at top left. The hypothesis that the picture was over-painted at this time is supported by a diary entry Kirchner wrote at Davos dated 30 September 1925, in which he notes that he had 'finished' *Red Streetwalker*.[7] This over-painting appears at first sight to have consisted mainly in covering the nervous, rapid brushwork typical of his works of 1913–14 with larger, flat, generally opaque areas of paint. A comparison with the febrile quality and the nervous vibrancy of execution of the Stuttgart pastel conveys an idea of what the painting must originally have looked like.

However, the changes made at this time were not confined merely to details of brushwork and anatomy. The underlying composition as revealed by infra-red reflectography likewise appears far closer to that of the pastel: as in the pastel, the figure of the streetwalker herself as first painted seems to have been taller and thinner, occupying a space which extends vertically much further in the direction of the bottom edge of the canvas. Thus, the purpose of reworking the picture more than a decade later may well have been not merely to bring it up to date, in the sense of being painted in what Kirchner then conceived of as a more 'modern' style, but also to lower the emotional temperature of the original composition, more in keeping with the increased detachment characteristic of the majority of his figure paintings executed during the years in Switzerland.

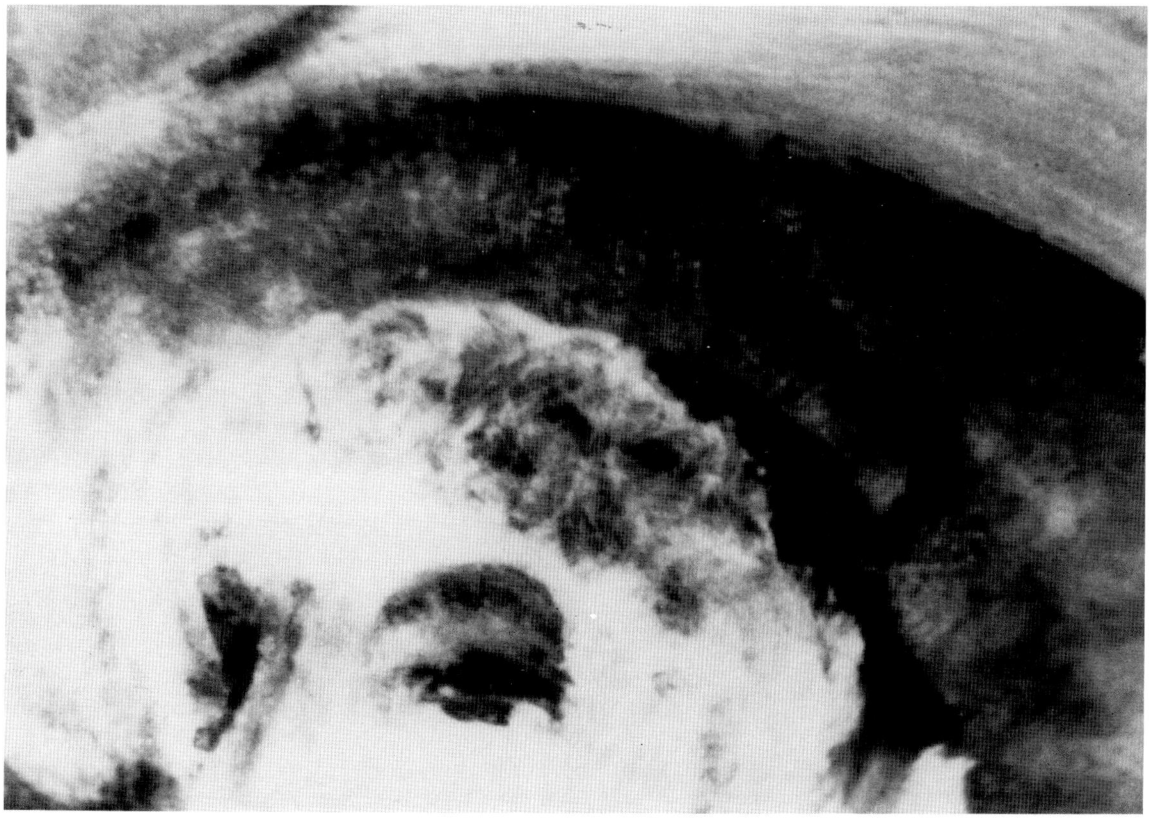

Ernst Ludwig Kirchner 1880–1938

50 Alpine Kitchen
Alpküche

1918[1]
Oil on canvas, 121.5 × 121.5 cm
Signed lower right: 'E.L.Kirchner'; inscribed on back of canvas: 'Alpküche', also estate stamp, inscribed: 'Da/Ad 2'
There is some cracking towards the upper edges of the canvas, with slight cupping of the paint layer in the area of the cracks. The corners of the canvas are beginning to tear. Otherwise condition is good
Accession no.1983.30

Provenance
Estate of the artist
Galerie R.N.Ketterer, Campione d'Italia
Thyssen-Bornemisza Collection, 1983

Exhibitions
Frankfurt am Main, Kunstsalon Ludwig Schames, 1922, *Schweizer Arbeit von E.L.Kirchner*, no.7
Berlin, Galerie Paul Cassirer, 1926, *Ernst Ludwig Kirchner*, no.6
Winterthur, Kunstmuseum, 1975, *Expressionismus in der Schweiz, 1905–1930*, no.185
Berlin, Nationalgalerie, 1979–80, *Ernst Ludwig Kirchner 1880–1938*, no.281[2]
Modern Masters from the Thyssen-Bornemisza Collection, 1984–6, no.55
Lugano 1989, no.9
Expressionism and Modern German Painting, 1989–90, no.18
Rome 1990–91, no.29

Literature
Gordon (1968), no.518 and p.114
R.N.Ketterer, *Moderne Kunst VII*, Campione d'Italia (Galerie R.N.Ketterer) 1971, p.123, no.60, ill. p.122
R.N.Ketterer, *Moderne Kunst VIII*, Campione d'Italia (Galerie R.N.Ketterer) 1973, p.119, no.60, ill. p.118
Kornfeld (1979), pp.84, 89, 117ff
See also L.de Marsalle [pseud.], 'Über die Schweizer Arbeiten von E.L.Kirchner', in Carl Einstein and Paul Westheim (eds.), *Europa Almanach*, Potsdam (Gustav Kiepenheuer) 1925, pp.66–71; Eberhard W.Kornfeld, '"Das Wohnzimmer" – Ein Gemälde Ernst Ludwig Kirchners in der Hamburger Kunsthalle', *Idea ... Jahrbuch der Hamburger Kunsthalle*, VIII (1989): 197f

Having suffered a severe mental and physical collapse, Kirchner was discharged from the German army as unfit for military service in December 1915. He at first sought a cure at Dr Oscar Kohnstamm's sanatorium at Königstein in the Taunus, but in January 1917 travelled to Switzerland in order to consult the lung specialist Dr Lucius Spengler in Davos.[3]

Kirchner's biographer, Donald Gordon, maintains that for much of that year the artist was too ill to paint, and dismisses many of his works of 1917–18 as uncompleted or unsatisfactory.[4] This statement is to some extent belied by the spontaneity and freshness of some of the earliest Swiss paintings, as if the mountain landscape around Davos, which provided a new and unfamiliar range of subject matter, inspired Kirchner to a new outburst of creative energy.

Kirchner was back in Switzerland in the early summer of 1917 and, though still largely suffering from the after-effects of his illness, insisted on renting a remote alpine cabin, poorly

Notes
1 On the basis of style and the known chronology of Kirchner's first years in Davos
2 Exhibition to mark the centenary of the artist's birth, also shown in Munich, Cologne and Zurich during 1979–80
3 See the biography by Hans Bolliger in Ketterer (1982), pp.237f
4 Gordon (1968), p.107

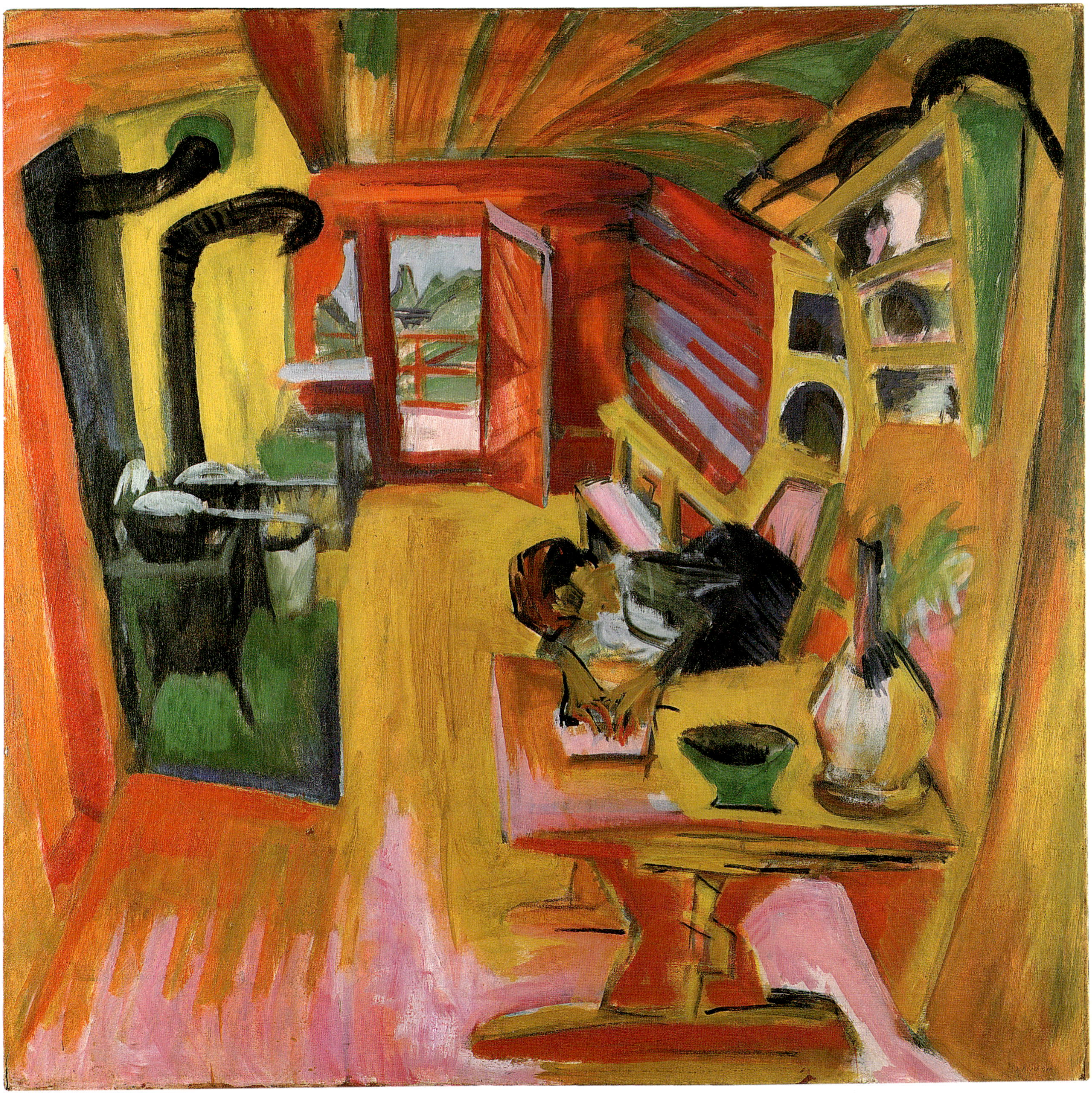

equipped and difficult to reach, on the Stafelalp above the village of Frauenkirch, a little way to the south of Davos (see fig.1). The cabin was owned by a local family called Rüesch; Kirchner subsequently sculpted a triple-portrait in wood of the three Rüesch sisters, as well as the related triple-portrait in oil *The Three Old Women* of 1925.[5]

From the Stafelalp house he wrote to the architect Henry van de Velde during that first alpine summer, describing his new environment with some relish: 'The rooms up here are most unusual, the gaps in the walls filled in with moss, and a wonderful pot-bellied stove, embellished with brass ...'[6] He returned there for two months the following summer, accompanied by Erna, who had succeeded in obtaining permission to visit him in Switzerland even before the cessation of hostilities in autumn 1918. In late September of that year, however, he moved down the mountain, closer to the village, and rented an all-weather house, christened In den Lärchen (House Amid the Larches), which was to remain his home until 1923.

Gordon ventures the opinion that the interior shown in the present work is that of the house In den Lärchen.[7] This is incorrect: the painting clearly depicts the still sparsely-furnished and somewhat inhospitable-looking kitchen of the Stafelalp hut, looking south towards the Tinzenhorn, the most dramatic of the distant mountain peaks and the leitmotif of Kirchner's Swiss period (see [51]; compare also the ground plan of the house, fig.2). The painting, however, makes the narrow confines of the room appear much larger than they are in reality.[8]

It has also been suggested that the painting shows Kirchner himself, bent over the kitchen table, preparing a lithographic stone.[9] This seems unlikely, for a number of reasons. It was only in January 1919 (i.e. after the picture was painted) that he had his hand-printing press brought from Berlin to Davos. Until then, he had been unable to produce any lithographs at all in Switzerland, and only a relatively limited quantity of prints in other media.[10] The action represented, moreover, clearly involves considerable downward pressure, the movement of the wrists and arms being quite unlike those involved in hand-carving or any other graphic process, but more akin to planing, sanding or scrubbing. This hypothesis is borne out by the fact that the picture shows the table-top as comprising two quite distinct areas of colour, or possibly texture, the one to which pressure is being applied being darker, rougher and redder. Nor does the figure portrayed bear any resemblance to the artist's other depictions of himself. Indeed, though indicated only summarily by means of a few lines and daubs of colour, it would appear to be undeniably female: in all probability Erna. That it does not, in any event, represent Kirchner seems on the basis of visual evidence alone virtually certain.[11]

Notes

5 Ibid., no.805

6 Kornfeld (1979), p.89

7 Gordon (1968), p.114

8 The house still exists, largely unaltered since Kirchner's time

9 By Roman Norbert Ketterer, the adminstrator of Kirchner's estate, according to *Modern Masters from the Thyssen-Bornemisza Collection*, exh. cat., London, Royal Academy of Arts, 1984, p.172

10 See biography by Hans Bolliger published in Ketterer (1982), p.240; also Eberhard W.Kornfeld, *Ernst Ludwig Kirchner: Davoser Werke 1917–1923*, exh. cat., Davos, Ernst Ludwig Kirchner-Museum, Davos-Platz, 1989, p.116. Dube (1967) ascribes to 1918 a group of six lithographs (nos.334–9) apparently depicting motifs from the vicinity of the Stafelalp; it is not clear, however, on what evidence this dating is based. Though Kirchner returned once again to the Stafelalp house in the summer of 1919, it would certainly have been impossible to have his printing press – an iron monster weighing more than 200lb – carted up there: see Kornfeld (1979), p.132

11 I am grateful to Colin Rhodes, who reinforced my suspicions that the figure portrayed cannot be Kirchner and who shared with me his own views on the probable actions depicted in the painting, as well as the scope offered for a new interpretation

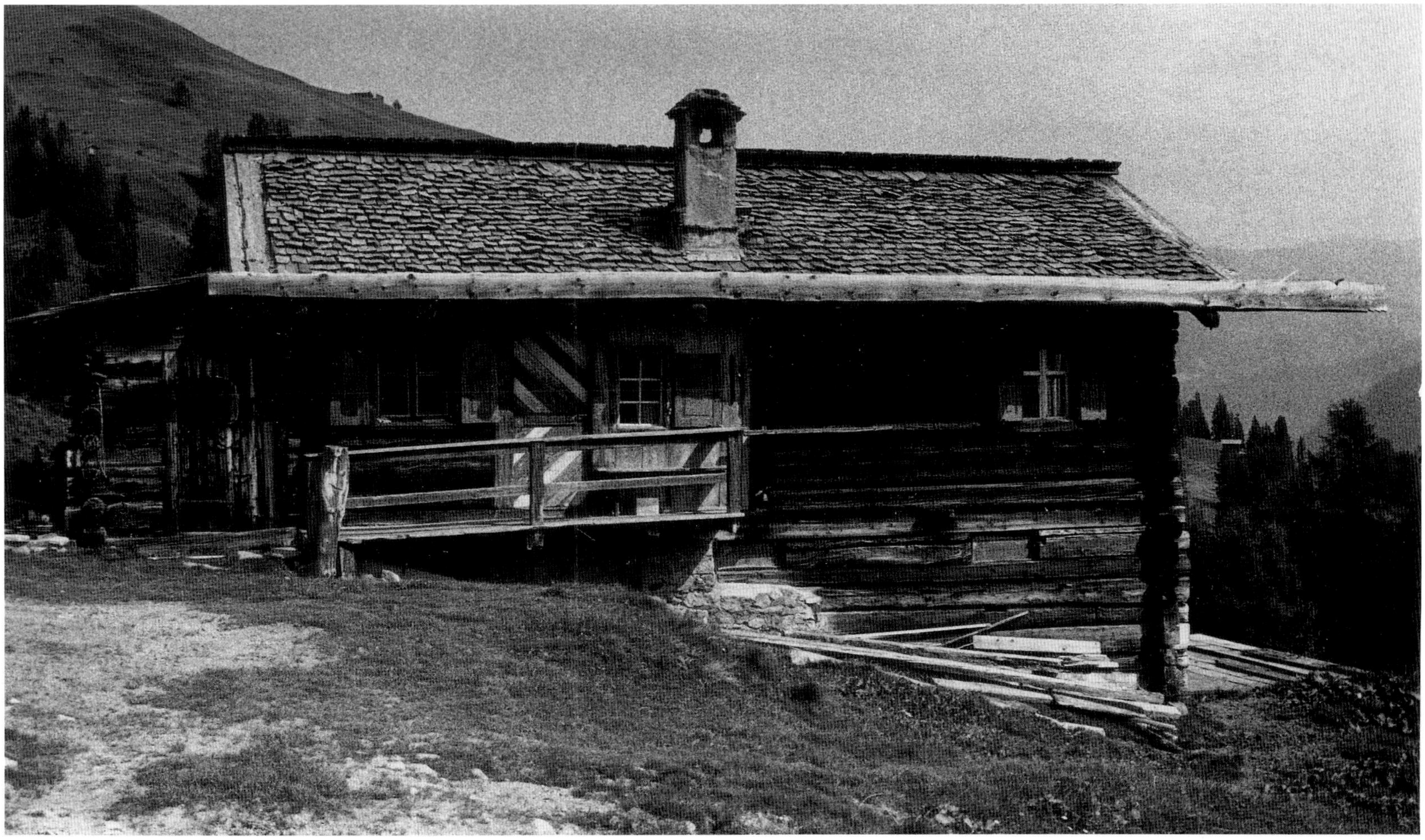

FIG 1 Exterior of the Stafelalp cabin, 1989

FIG 2 Ground plan of the Stafelalp cabin, adapted from Kornfeld (1979), p.84

FIG 3 Kitchen of the Stafelalp cabin showing the wooden table which appears in [50], as it existed in September 1989

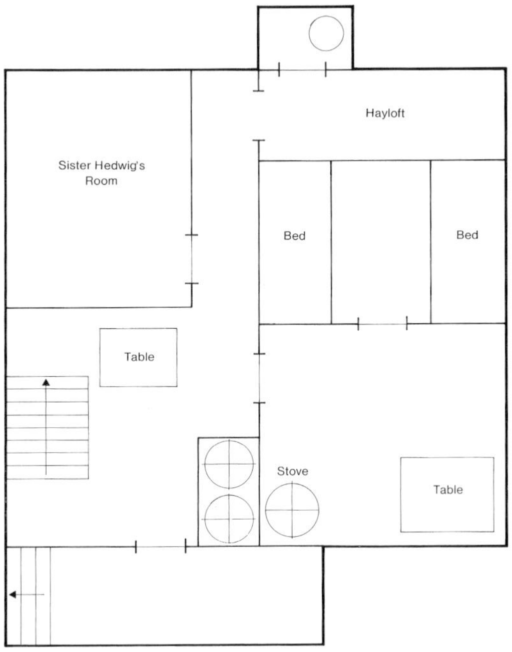

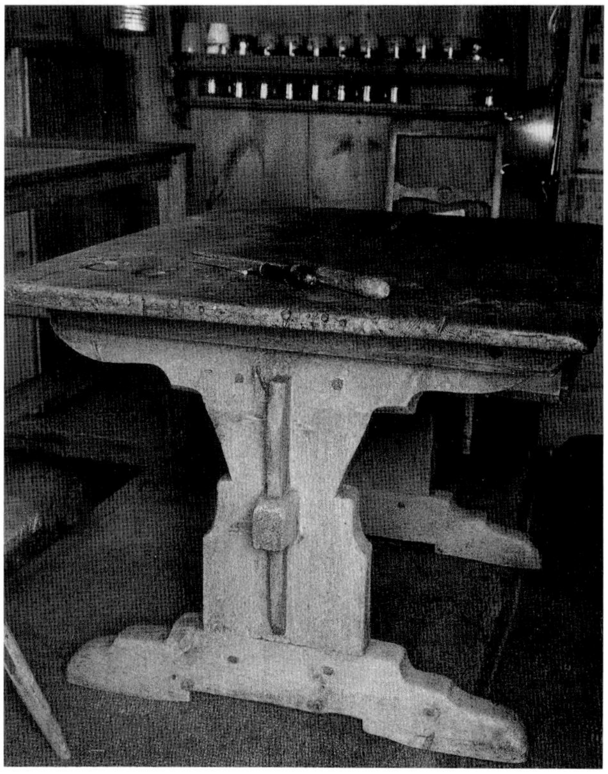

Ernst Ludwig Kirchner 1880–1938

51 The Junkerboden under Snow[1]

Oil on canvas, 100 × 120 cm
Signed upper right: 'E.L.Kirchner'[2]; affixed to back of stretcher, a tracing of the original estate stamp, inscribed: 'Da/Aa 79'[3]
The canvas has been lined with a modern lining canvas and fixed to a new stretcher, causing an apparent flattening of the paint surface. There are some minor repairs to earlier paint losses. The area of whitish paint which occupies much of the lower part of the canvas is somewhat discoloured with age[4]
Accession no.1983.7

Provenance
Estate of the artist
Galerie Alex Vömel, Düsseldorf
Fine Arts Associates, New York
Marlborough Fine Art, London/New York
Dr Max M.Stern, New York
Liselotte Bendix Stern, New York
Thyssen-Bornemisza Collection, 1983[5]

Exhibitions
New York, Fine Arts Associates, 1957, *Ernst Ludwig Kirchner*, no.13 [as '1917']
New York, Marlborough–Gerson Gallery, 1963, *Artist and Maecenas. A Tribute to Curt Valentin*, no.255 [as '1917']
London, Marlborough Fine Art, 1967, *Recent Acquisitions*, no.11 [as '1917']
New York, Marlborough–Gerson Gallery, 1968, *International Expressionism, Part I*, no.24 [as '1917']
Seattle, WN, Art Museum/Pasadena, CA, Art Museum/Boston, MA, Museum of Fine Arts, 1968–9, *Ernst Ludwig Kirchner*, no.70 [as 'ca.1936–38']
New York, Grace Borgenicht Gallery, 1983, *Ernst Ludwig Kirchner. Paintings and Works on Paper*, no.10 [as '1936–1938']

Literature
Gordon (1968), no.1018

A jarring and visually discordant impression is produced by the inconsistent handling of paint. There is a marked contrast between the upper part of the composition, where the passages depicting forests and distant peaks are finely worked, and the snowy fields which occupy most of the lower area of the picture. Here the paint, which seems of poor quality, is very loosely brushed on, almost like a kind of rough over-painting. The initial impression is that the artist changed his mind in the course of work, and covered up his first attempts at this lower part before abandoning it altogether. However, examination by means of infra-red reflectography, as well as under ultra-violet light reveals no trace of any pentimenti or earlier under-painting; on the contrary, one can only assume that this roughly brushed lower area represents a crude preparation for a more detailed and finely-painted snowscape which was intended but, for some reason, never executed.

Notes
1 The work has been known by the German title *Junkerboden im Schnee*, and is thus entitled in Gordon's oeuvre-catalogue of Kirchner's paintings: see Gordon (1968), p.414
2 See n.6 below
3 The tracing was presumably made when the canvas was transferred to a new stretcher and the original stretcher bearing the estate stamp (see n.2, p.180) discarded. The tracing paper is damaged and the inscription, especially the last figure, now only partially legible; it appears, however, to correspond to that recorded in Gordon (1968), p.414
4 I am grateful to Jim Moyes, of Momart, London, with whom I first examined and discussed [51], and to Emil Bosshard, Head of Conservation of the Thyssen-Bornemisza Collection, for supplementary information concerning the condition of the painting
5 Acquired directly from the previous owner; for a note on the Stern collection, see entry for [88]

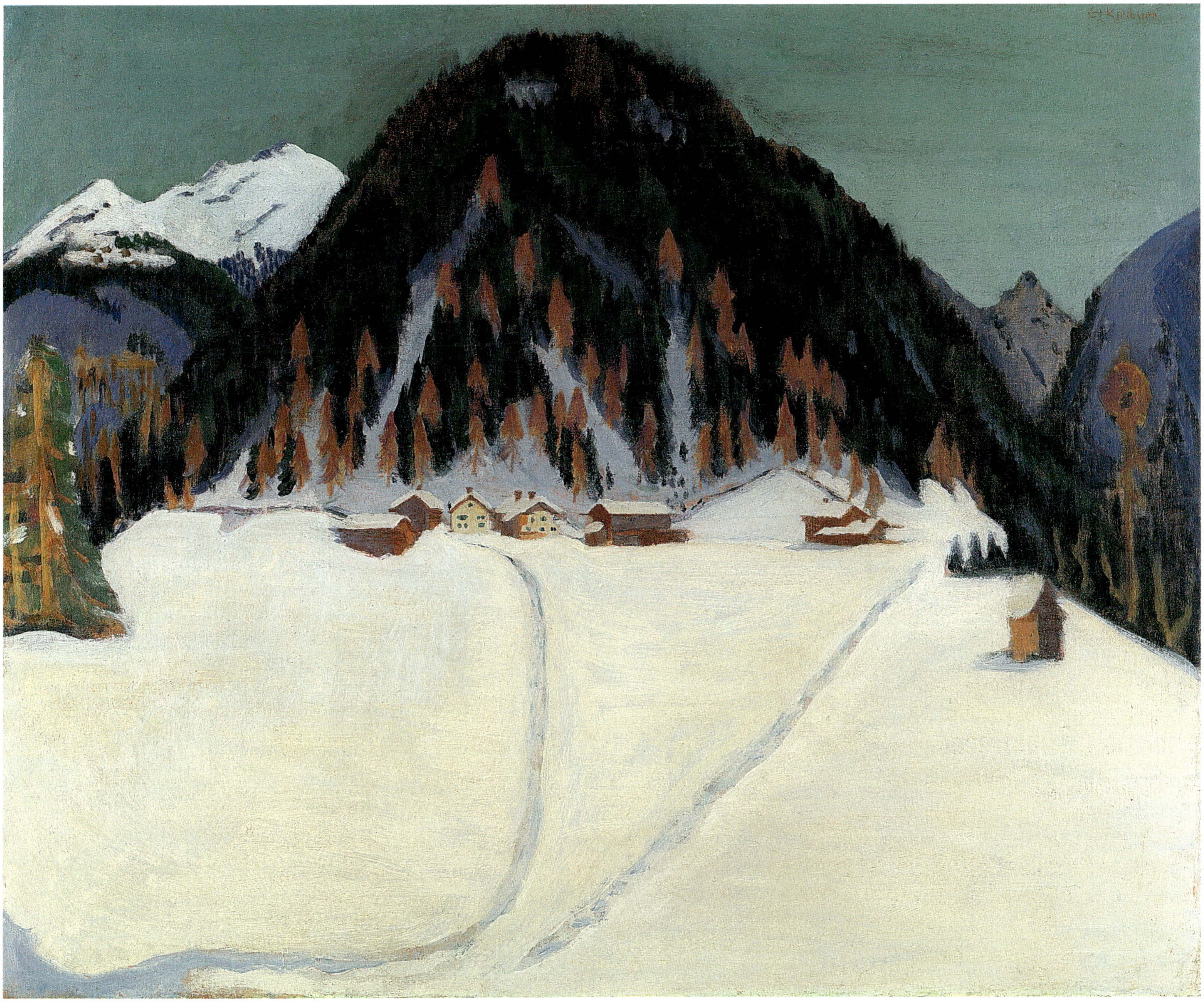

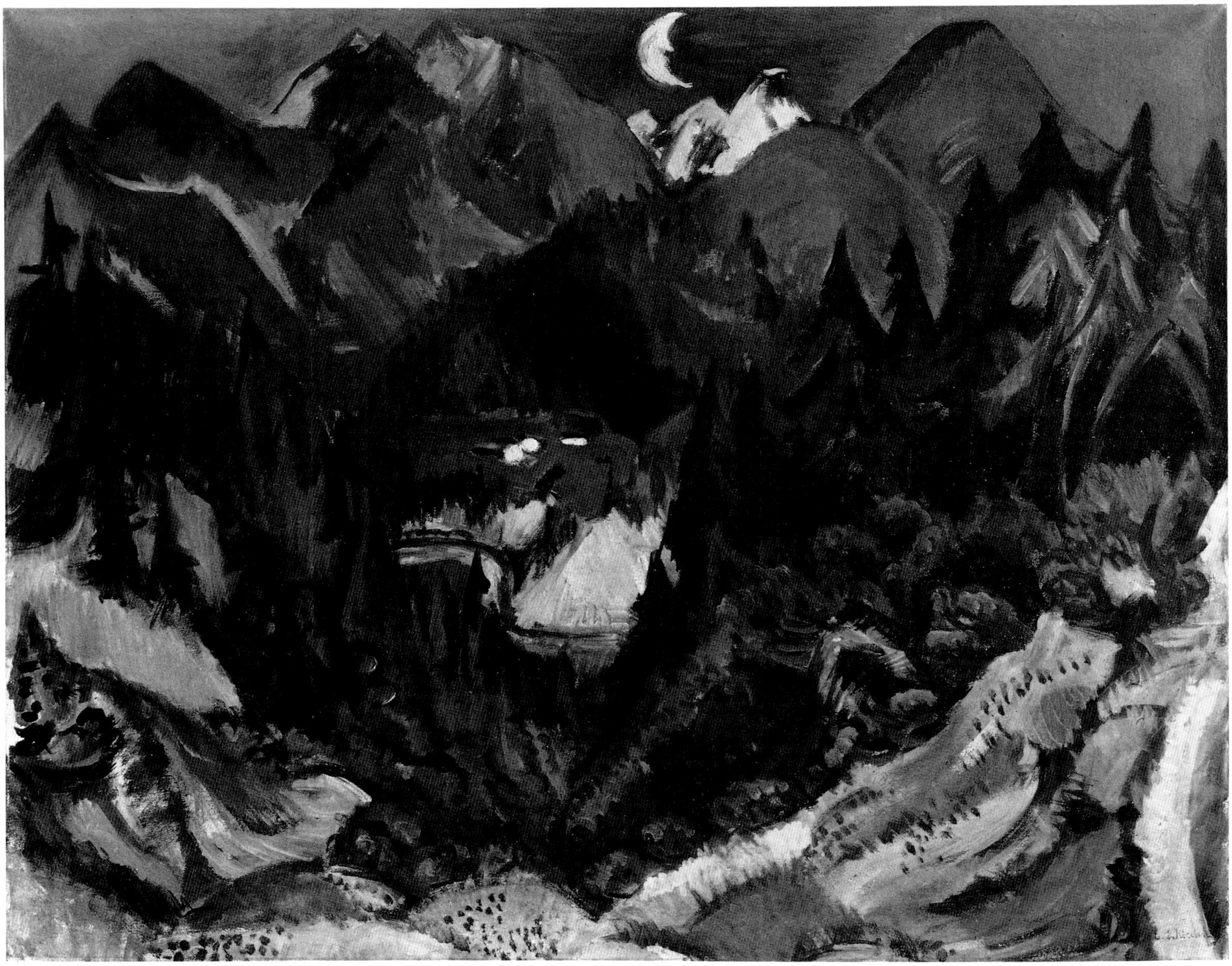

FIG 1 Ernst Ludwig Kirchner, *Junkerboden*, 1919, oil on canvas, 95 × 120 cm (Berne/Davos, Dr Eberhard W. Kornfeld)

Perhaps because of its partially unfinished appearance, as well as the seemingly 'posthumous' signature,[6] *The Junkerboden under Snow* has been ascribed to the last years of Kirchner's life, immediately prior to his suicide in June 1938. However, the date 1936–8 suggested by Gordon is not supported by any documentary evidence,[7] and on stylistic grounds it is not difficult to persuade oneself that the painting might well have been started more than a decade earlier. The subject, too, might argue for an earlier date: it was around 1919–20 that Kirchner embarked on an intensive study of the immediate environs of the Landwassertal, the flat river valley to the south of Davos, including the area around the Junkerboden with its scattered farmhouses, just as they appear in the present picture.

Kirchner represented the Junkerboden, a plateau of flat grazing land immediately above the River Sertig, on a number of occasions in paintings datable to the 1920s (see fig.1). The scene

Notes

6 The signature, seemingly not by Kirchner himself, has been scratched into the paint surface after the pigment was dry. Gordon observes that 'signatures or initials scratched into the paint surface were apparently added by Erna Kirchner [sic] following the artist's death in 1938'; see Gordon (1968), p.264

7 In exhibition catalogues from the 1950s and 1960s, the date repeatedly given for the painting is 1917. This is impossible: Kirchner was in Davos for only a

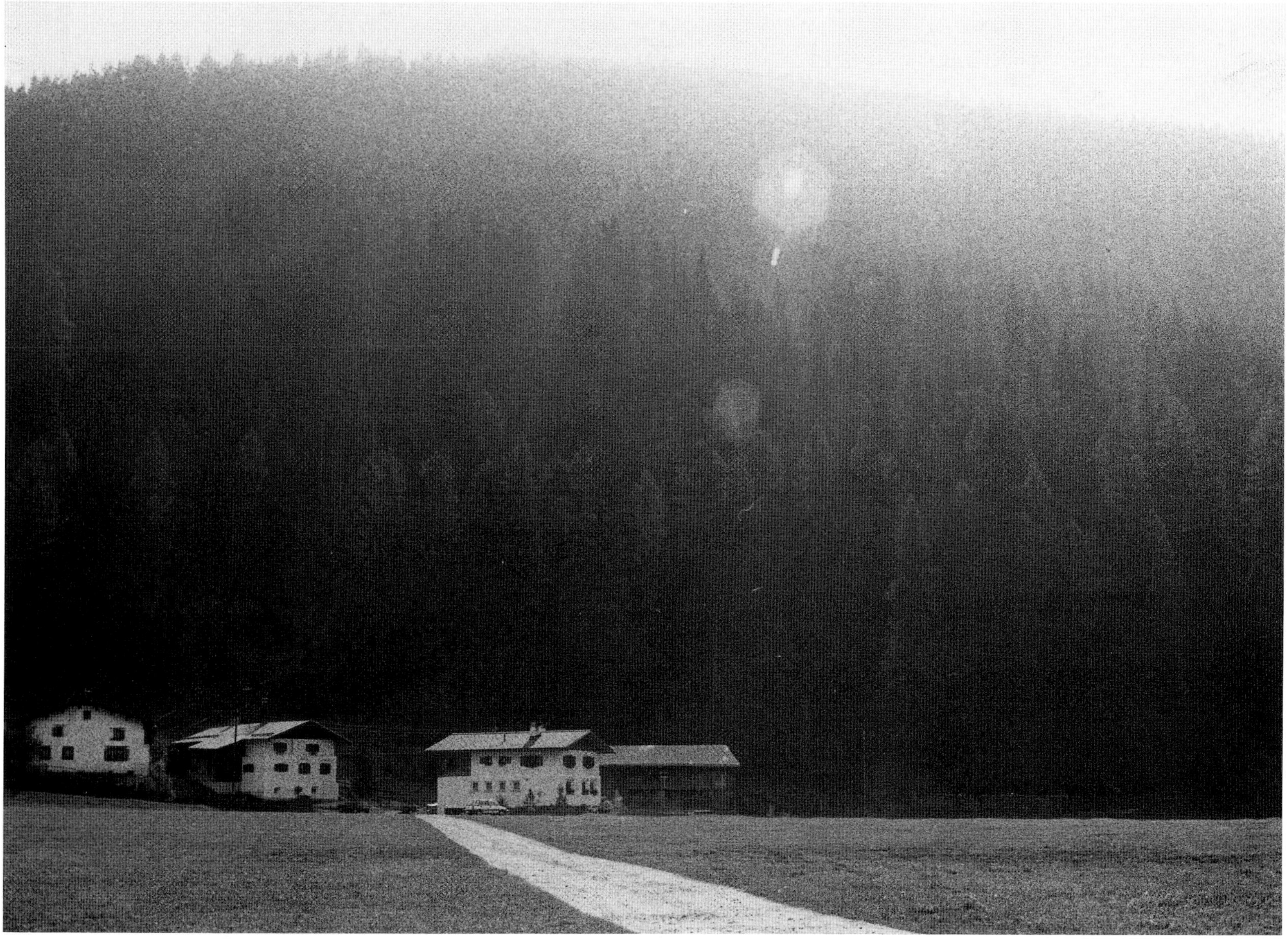

FIG 2 Frauenkirch bei Davos, the Junkerboden, looking east, 1989

few months of that year, most of his time being spent in the alpine hut on the Stafelalp (see [50]). *The Junkerboden under Snow* is, moreover, stylistically unrelated to any of Kirchner's known paintings of 1917

8 See e.g. Kirchner's letter to Gustav Schiefler dated 6 December 1923, in Grisebach (1968), pp.206ff, also cited by Claus Zoege von Manteuffel in Ketterer (1982), p.156

9 Eberhard Kornfeld, in conversation with the author, Davos, September 1989. I am grateful to Dr Kornfeld for his opinion regarding the dating of this picture

depicted in [51] is, on the other hand, to some extent an imaginary one: the artist has brought the surrounding mountains closer than they are in reality, and even included the distant Tinzenhorn, a recurrent motif in Kirchner's landscapes of the Swiss years. The mountain, which he referred to in letters and diaries simply as the 'Tinzen',[8] seems to have exerted a particular fascination on him: it appears in the background of many of his landscape paintings of his Davos period, among them *Alpine Kitchen* [50]. In real life, however, it would almost certainly have been invisible from the standpoint of the present picture.

It is also worth recording that, to judge by the recollections of those who knew him in later years, Kirchner never set up his easel outdoors to paint *en plein air*, no matter how clement the weather.[9] His Swiss landscapes, including *The Junkerboden under Snow*, are all studio pieces, and would have been worked up from sketches done, in some cases, a considerable time before.

Paul Klee 1879–1940

52 View on to a Square
Blick auf einen Platz

1912
Mixed media (watercolour, gouache, black chalk and wax crayon, with white priming over black underdrawing) on Japan paper, pasted on to a larger sheet, 16.5 × 27 cm (visible surface)
Signed lower right, in paint surface: 'Klee'; dated lower right, in border: '1912.10'; inscribed lower left, in border: 'Blick auf einen Platz'
On verso, original label: 'Der Blaue Reiter, Ausstellung, Paul Klee, Blick auf den [sic] Platz, Kat. Nr.121'
There are some losses to the lower foreground, and slight discolouration of the paper. The apparent rubbed quality of the surface may be due to the original layers having been subsequently washed away by working over the surface with a sponge or damp cloth
Accession no.1975.30

Provenance
Curt Valentin Gallery, New York
Clifford Odets, New York
The New Gallery, New York
Mr and Mrs Sidney E.Cohn, New York
Leonard Hutton Galleries, New York
Thyssen-Bornemisza Collection, 1975

Exhibitions
Munich, Kunsthandlung Hans Goltz, 1912, *Zweite Ausstellung der Redaktion Der Blaue Reiter*, no.121
Munich, Neue Kunst Hans Goltz, 1912, *Erste Gesamt-Ausstellung*, no.84[1]
Munich, Neue Kunst Hans Goltz, 1913, *V.Kollektiv-Ausstellung. Moderner Bund Schweiz*, [Klee] no.6[2]
Berlin, Der Sturm, 1913, *XV. Ausstellung/Der Moderne Bund, Schweiz*, [Klee] no.6
New York, Curt Valentin Gallery, 1954–5, *Der Blaue Reiter*, no.23 [as 'View of the Square']
Cambridge, MA, Busch-Reisinger Museum, 1955, *Artists of the Blaue Reiter*, no.27 [as 'View of the Square']
New York, Leonard Hutton Galleries, 1963, *Der Blaue Reiter*, no.64
Washington, DC, National Gallery of Art, 1969, *German Expressionist Watercolors in American Collections*, no.14
Japanese tour 1976
Brussels/Paris 1977–8, no.44
Munich, Städtische Galerie im Lenbachhaus, 1979–80, *Paul Klee, Das Frühwerk 1883–1922*, no.164

Literature
Gordon (1974), II, p.549
Charles Werner Haxthausen, 'Klees künstlerisches Verhältnis zu Kandinsky während der Münchner Jahre', in Zweite (1979), pp.98–130; also ibid. p.371

Klee first met the Blue Rider artists in Munich during the winter of 1911–12.[3] The *Blue Rider Almanac* and the two exhibitions staged by Kandinsky and Franz Marc under the Blue Rider name were important milestones in his early development, not least because they opened his eyes to a wide and hitherto unsuspected range of contemporary art.[4] Particularly interesting to Klee were the latest works of the French Cubists which he had further opportunity of seeing during his spring 1912 stay in Paris,[5] and which significantly affected the subsequent evolution of his own formal vocabulary.

Notes
1 The dealer Hans Goltz, who had mounted the second *Blaue Reiter* exhibition in his showrooms on Munich's Briennerstrasse in February 1912, opened his gallery Neue Kunst on the Odeonsplatz in Munich in October that year. Klee recorded the event in his diary ('Goltz wird Kunsthändler und eröffnet am Odeonplatz [sic] einen kleinen, sehr appetitlichen Salon'); see Klee (1957), p.284. According to his oeuvre-catalogue, [52] was one of a group of five watercolours (nos.84–8) by Klee shown at this first exhibition in Goltz's new gallery; see Geelhaar (1976), p.166 and note 62, also Gordon (1974), II, p.615
2 This exhibition, which included work by Swiss artists of the Moderner Bund, was subsequently shown from 26 April–31 May 1913 at Walden's Sturm galleries in Berlin; see Gordon (1974), I, p.94
3 Klee's first contact with Kandinsky, who lived next door but one on Munich's Ainmillerstrasse, came about through the intermediary of the artist Louis Moilliet; see Klee (1957), p.275, also Haxthausen (1981), pp.345f
4 As Haxthausen observes, until the Matisse exhibition in Munich in 1910 Klee's knowledge of the development of modern French painting had been 'at least a generation behind'; see 'Klees künstlerisches Verhältnis zu Kandinsky während der Münchner Jahre', in Zweite (1979), p.99
5 Klee was in Paris from 2–18 April 1912; during his stay he visited both Delaunay and Le Fauconnier in their studios. However, though he recorded these visits in his diary, he makes no comment regarding the works of either artist: see Klee (1957), pp.278f, also Haxthausen (1981), pp.348f

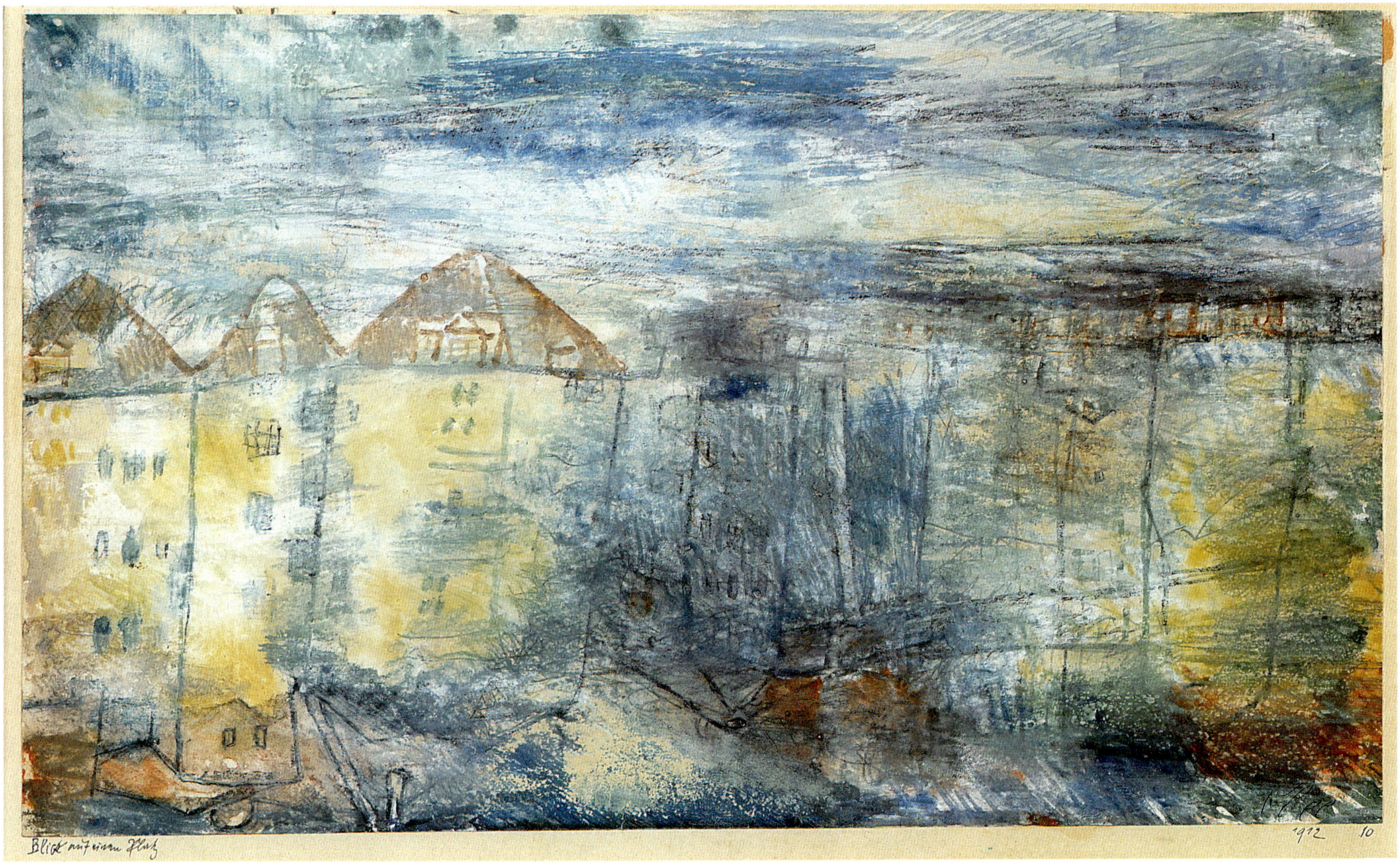

The influence of French avant-garde art is not immediately obvious in *View on to a Square*, which must have been executed early in 1912, since it was included in the second *Blaue Reiter* exhibition which opened in February that year, as evidenced by an old label on the back of the picture.[6] At this date, the only examples of Cubism Klee had seen in the original would have been four paintings and one drawing by Delaunay shown in the first *Blaue Reiter* exhibition the preceding December, together with Cubist-influenced work by Vladimir Burliuk.[7] In its high degree of abstraction and insistence on the repetition of geometric forms it none the less exhibits closer affinities with the rigorous structural logic of Cubism than with the heightened emotion and ecstatic pictorial formulations characteristic of many of the Expressionists.[8] Several of his watercolours and drawings of 1912 manifest a variety of what one writer has termed 'proto-Cubism',[9] seen particularly in their emphasis on linear-abstract rhythm and geometric pattern-making – concerns which predisposed him towards a more intensive study of Cubism proper in the course of the following winter, 1912–13.

Like a number of other works by Klee, *View on to a Square* presents us with a composition which can be 'read' in more than one way, since the right-hand part of the sheet shows a more or less literal inversion of the houses on the left which, on closer examination, turn out to have gables and attics at the bottom as well as at the top. The houses on the right, however, though still clearly visible are partially obscured by a thin layer of over-painting, so that the forms represented are discerned, quite literally, at several different 'levels', like the various layers of a palimpsest.

There is also a close relationship with another, almost contemporary watercolour entitled *Sun in Courtyard* (fig. 1), likewise based on a series of architectural forms which are simplified to the verge of abstraction and which seem just as convincing when inverted as they do the right way up. For an example of a further work by Klee which may be inverted or indeed rotated, see the following entry.

According to the artist's oeuvre-catalogue, the present watercolour was originally owned by a Dr Egger in Berne. Dr Egger was a dentist; it seems that Klee may have given it to him in lieu of payment for dental treatment.[10] Subsequently, it is thought to have been in a private collection in Japan; it has, however, not been possible to confirm its provenance prior to ownership by the Curt Valentin Gallery in New York during the 1950s.

Notes

6 *View on to a Square* was evidently a work of some importance in Klee's eyes, or at least one with which he felt reasonably satisfied, since he chose to exhibit it on no fewer than four occasions during 1912–13 (see Exhibitions); for an account of his strategy in selecting works to include in the second *Blaue Reiter* exhibition, see Wolfgang Kersten, 'Paul Klee et le "Blaue Reiter"', in *Le Cavalier Bleu*, exh. cat., Berne, Kunstmuseum, 1987, pp.261ff, 266–9

7 See Jordan (1984), pp.30ff

8 The fact that Cubism is the only art 'movement' Klee singles out for specific mention in his (admittedly somewhat superficial) review of the second *Blaue Reiter* exhibition (*Die Alpen*, VI, no.7, March 1912) suggests that he was at this stage already alive to its implications, while still experiencing some difficulty in mentally encompassing other aspects of the development of the European avant-garde. His review is reprinted in Geelhaar (1976), pp.99–100; see also Haxthausen, 'Klees künstlerisches Verhältnis zu Kandinsky . . .' in Zweite (1979), pp.104–5

9 Jordan (1984), pp.68f. Jordan notes that, in works shown at the second *Blaue Reiter* exhibition in the spring of 1912, both Klee and his *Moderner Bund* colleague Oskar Lüthy 'cubicized' their forms; he concludes, however, that 'the exact degree of Cubism, at this first stage of contact, is impossible to determine' (ibid., p.40)

10 Letter from Felix Klee to Simon de Pury, 18 May 1984 (Lugano-Castagnola, Thyssen-Bornemisza Collection, archive)

FIG 1 Paul Klee, *Courtyard* (*Sun in Courtyard*), 1913, watercolour, 19.2 × 12 cm (Private collection)

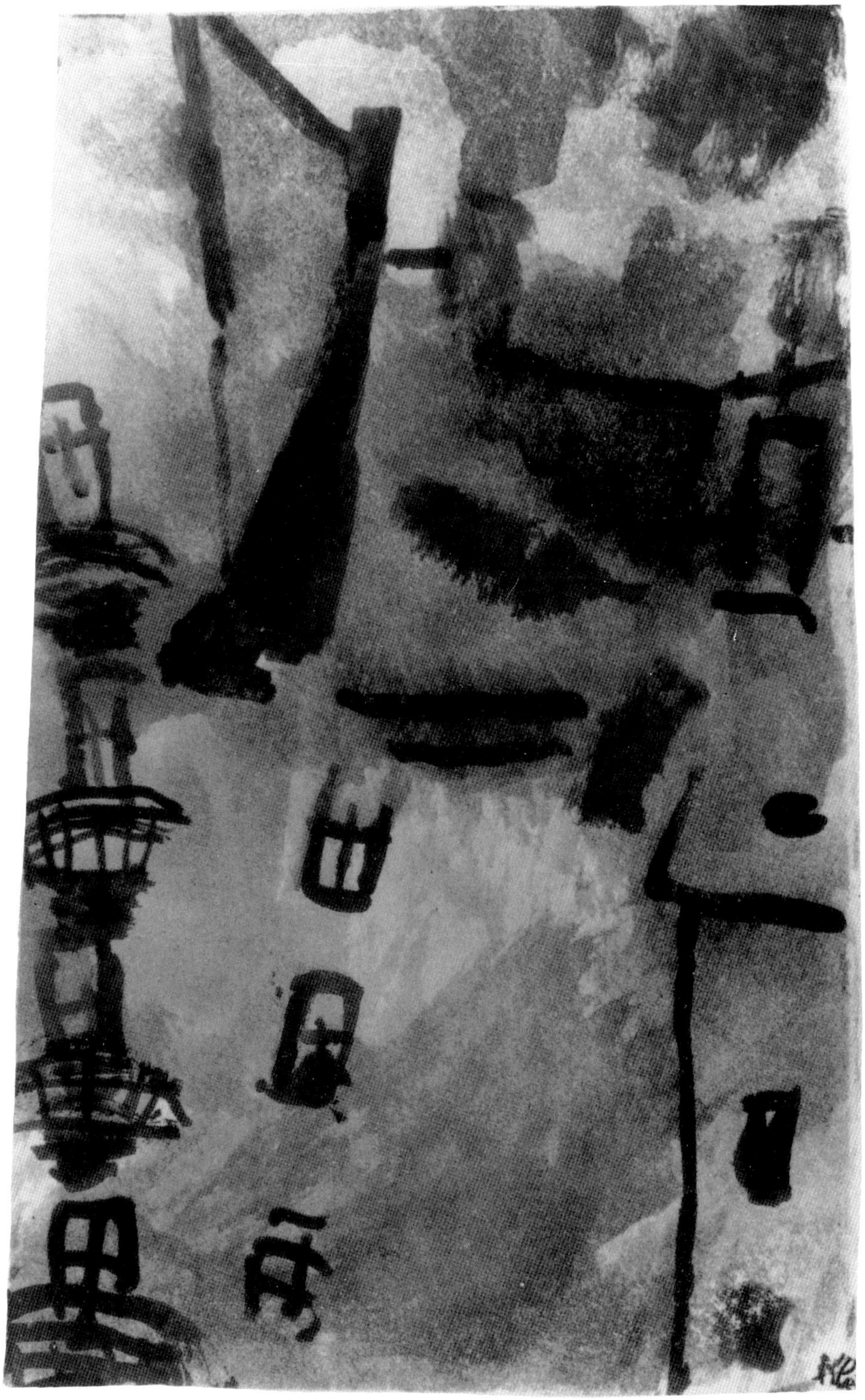

Paul Klee 1879–1940

53 Revolving House
Drehbares Haus

1921
Oil and gouache on primed cheesecloth stuck down on a larger sheet of watercolour paper, 37.7 × 52.2 cm (irregular)
Signed/dated lower right, in paint surface: 'Klee 1921'; inscribed lower left, in border: '1921/183'; lower right, in border: 'Drehbares Haus'
The work is in fragile condition. The painting is unvarnished, and paint layer is dry and brittle. There is a history of flaking and scattered losses. The support is buckled, resulting in an uneven surface
Accession no.1982.22

Provenance
Private collection, Düsseldorf
Curt Valentin Gallery, New York
Heinz Berggruen, Paris
Thyssen-Bornemisza Collection, 1982[1]

Exhibitions
Hanover, Kestner-Gesellschaft, 1952, *Paul Klee*, no.43
Budapest/Szombathely 1985–6, no.34
Cologne 1986, p.156, ill. p.157
Moscow/Leningrad, 1988, no.13
Lugano 1989, no.33
Expressionism and Modern German Painting, 1989–90, no.20
Rome 1990–91, no.30

The motif of a figure or form which can be turned or viewed from a number of different angles is one which recurs frequently in Klee's oeuvre. As already noted, in his 1912 watercolour *View on to a Square* [52] turning the sheet so as to stand the houses on their head reveals that they can be viewed equally well that way round. *Revolving House* carries the same idea still further: the house, represented merely as a diagrammatic schema of lines, is capable of being rotated on its axis, like a wheel or top.

There exists an intimate relationship between the subject depicted and the – in this case highly unusual – medium out of which the work has been created – something that is again typical of Klee. In many of his works of the 1920s, he employs unconventional materials not just for the sake of formal experimentation, but as a means of exploring the true nature of visual appearance, creating a novel form of analogy between the work of art and the work of man or nature. In this case, the piece of cheesecloth, whose loose-weave texture is apparent in many places where the paint layer is thin or non-existent, has absorbed the gouache to such an extent that the surface appears dry and crumbly, like sand or cement – the materials out of which the house depicted might have been constructed. The cheesecloth itself has been also stuck down on to the paper in such a way that its tactile, almost three-dimensional quality is immediately apparent.

Note
1 Acquired directly from the previous owner. I am grateful to M. Heinz Berggruen, Paris, for helping me to confirm the previous history of this work

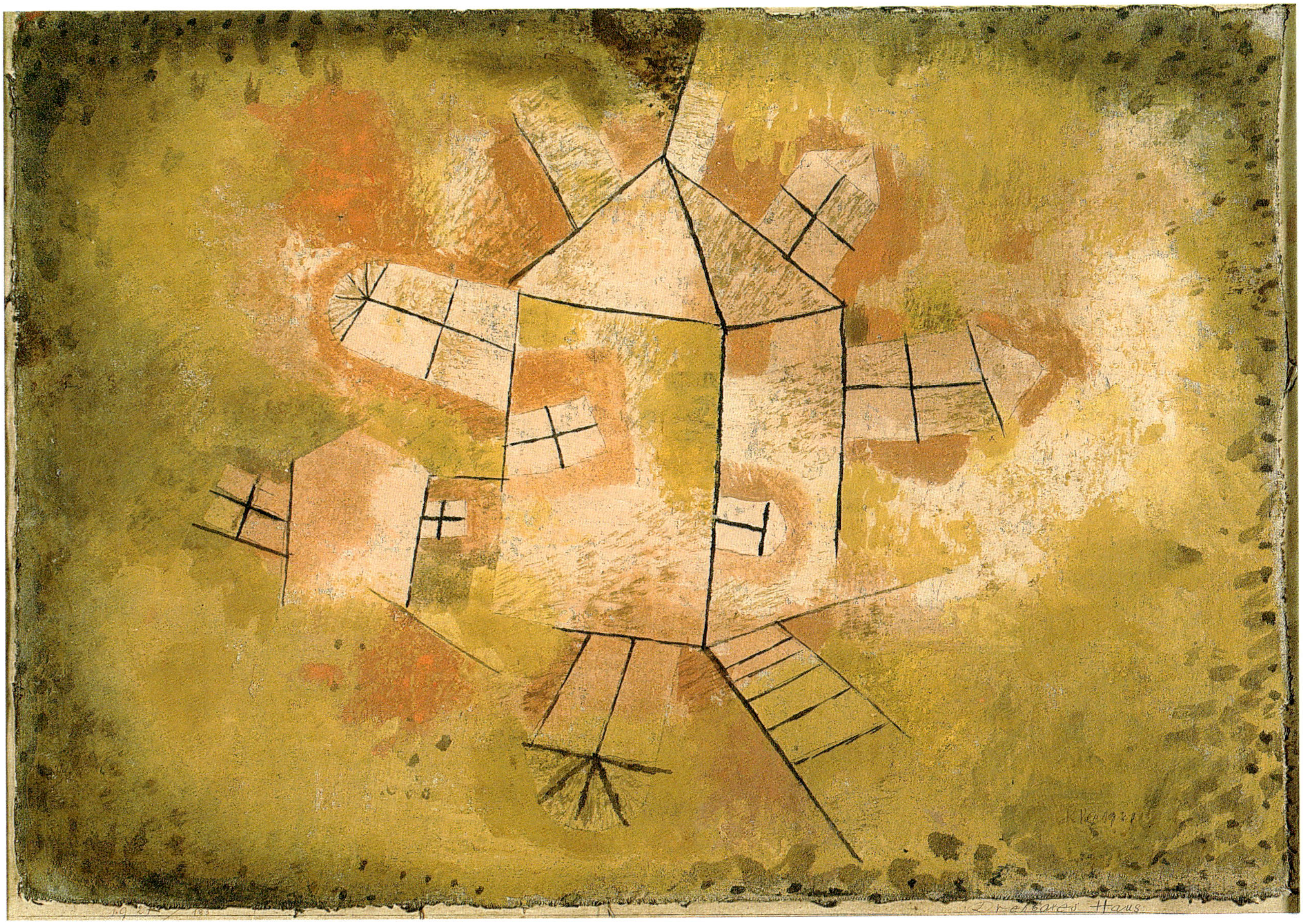

Paul Klee 1879–1940

54 Still-life with Dice
Stilleben mit dem Würfel

1923
Watercolour on wrapping paper[1] with grey wash and traces of chalk, 27 × 38 cm
Signed upper centre: 'Klee'; inscribed in lower border, in pen: '1923.22 Stilleben <mit dem Würfel>'
There is a history of flaking, and some losses, particularly associated with the tear at right of sheet. Paper is slightly convex-warped
Accession no.1963.5

Provenance
Estate of the artist
Lily Klee, Berne
Douglas Cooper, London
Galerie Berggruen, Paris
Robert Hendrickx, Brussels
Marlborough Fine Art, London
Galerie des Arts Anciens et Modernes, Schaan, Liechtenstein
Thyssen-Bornemisza Collection, 1963

Exhibitions
London, Tate Gallery, 1945, *Paul Klee*, no.62
London, Marlborough Fine Art, 1962, *Painters of the Bauhaus*, no.108
Bremen 1975, no.39
Japanese tour 1976
Saint Paul de Nice, Fondation Maeght, 1977, *Paul Klee*, no.60
Brussels/Paris 1977–8, no.46
Lugano 1978, no.52

Literature
Kiel (1974), p.62, ill. p.63
Jürgen Glaesemer, *Paul Klee. Die farbigen Werke im Kunstmuseum Bern*, Berne 1976, p.210, no.91

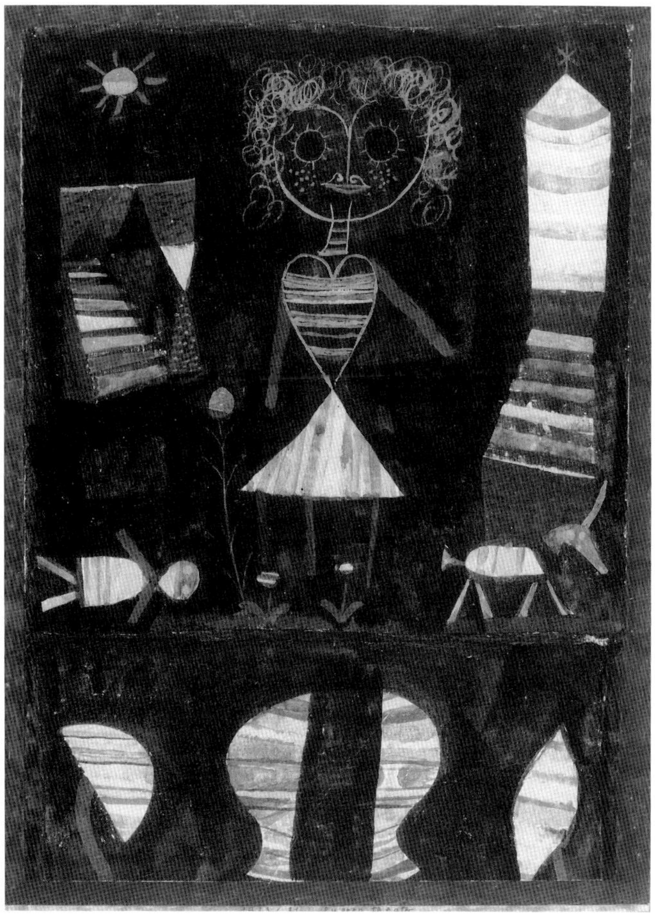

FIG 1 Paul Klee, *Puppet Theatre*, 1923, watercolour, 52 × 37.6 cm (Berne, Kunstmuseum, Paul Klee-Stiftung, inv. no.F33)

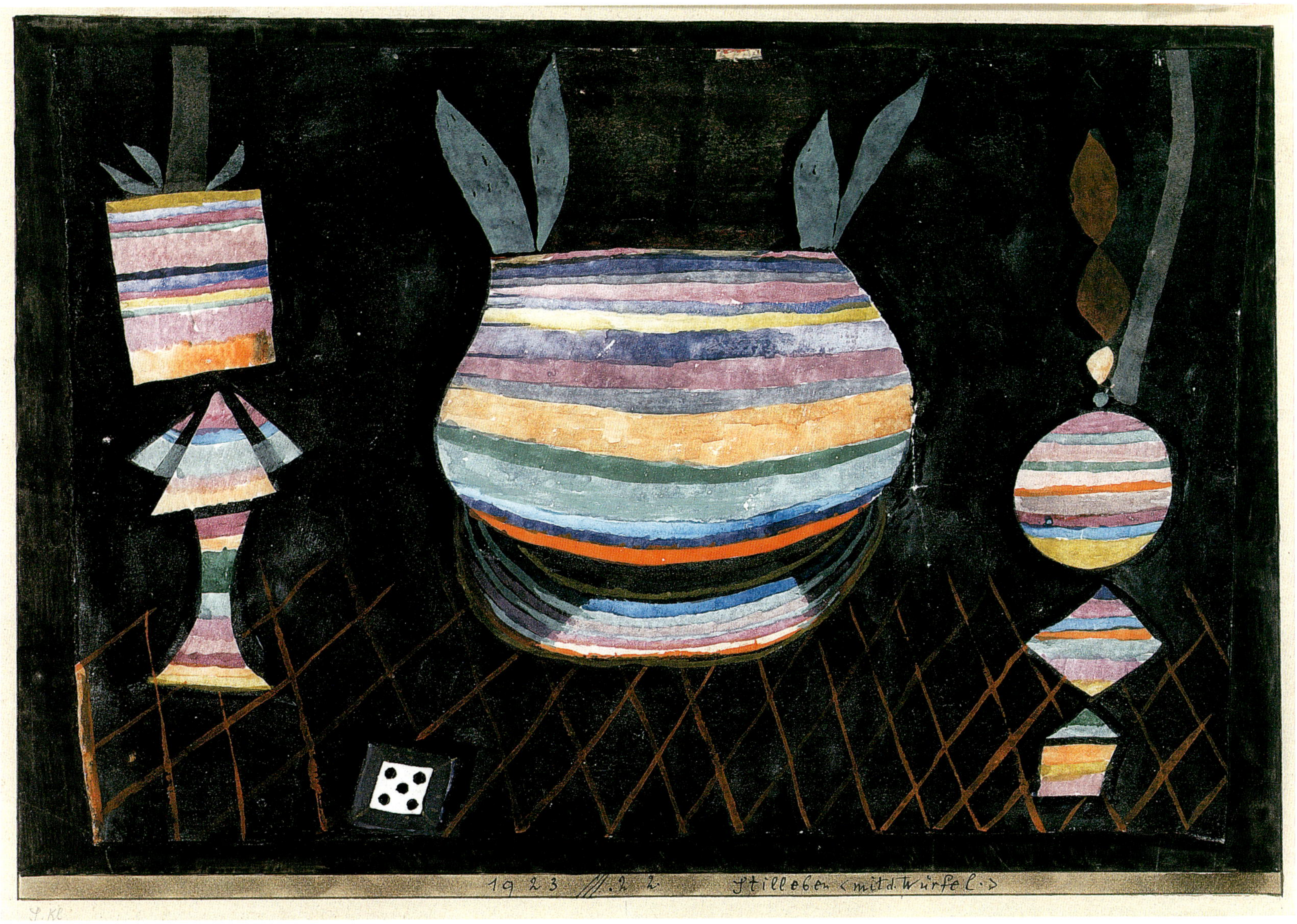

Still-life with Dice originally formed part of a larger watercolour composition in an unusually tall vertical format, the remaining portion of which, entitled *Puppet Theatre*, is now in the Kunstmuseum in Berne (fig.1).

Klee cut up his own drawings and watercolours surprisingly often – more than seventy times during the years 1914–23. In the majority of instances he divided his works into two or (occasionally) more parts which he then re-combined, often altering the relationship between top and bottom, left and right, or rotating the fragments of paper through 90 or 180 degrees.[2] In a smaller number of cases, he used scissors and paste to create a new pair of related but independent works, compositionally autonomous, to each of which he gave its own title and inventory number, as happened with [54].

The repertoire of still-life subjects to be found in *Still-life with Dice* reappears in a number of other works by Klee – the dice itself, for example, which also features in the 1927 still-life painting with pots, fruit and an Easter egg now in the Berggruen Collection of the Metropolitan Museum of Art, New York (see [55] fig.2, p.229).

The present watercolour has been pasted on to a larger sheet of heavier paper on which has been drawn a 'frame' consisting of a black background with, at the bottom, a drawn border filled in with wash. To the right of the flower bowl is a small tear in the watercolour paper, perhaps a consequence of the dividing up of the original sheet.

Notes

1 According to the entry in Klee's oeuvre-catalogue: see letter from Felix Klee to Simon de Pury, 18 May 1984 (Lugano-Castagnola, Thyssen-Bornemisza Collection, archive). I am grateful to the director and staff of the Paul Klee Foundation, Berne, for additional information drawn from Klee's oeuvre-catalogue; also to Dr Christian Geelhaar, Basle, for his advice on the present work

2 For an examination of Klee's 'deconstructive-constructive' method of cutting up and re-combining the fragments of his watercolours and drawings see the detailed study by Wolfgang Kersten, *Paul Klee, 'Zerstörung, der Konstruktion zuliebe'?*, v of *Studien zur Kunst- und Kulturgeschichte*, Marburg (Jonas) 1987

Paul Klee 1879–1940

55 Omega 5 (295) 'Dummy'

Omega 5 (295) 'Attrappe'[1]

1927
Oil and watercolour on canvas stuck down on board, 57.3 × 43 cm
Signed/dated lower left: 'Klee 1927'; inscribed: 'Omega 5 Attrappen'
The canvas has ben affixed to a piece of board some 10 mm larger, which thus forms a kind of border to the actual painting, though the paint surface continues up to the edges of the board. The inscription is scratched into the paint surface at the extreme lower left edge of the board
There are scattered drying cracks in the paint layer. The supporting board exhibits a pronounced convex warp, and is buckled at the edges. Otherwise condition is good
Accession no.1976.8

Provenance
Curt Valentin Gallery, New York
Marjorie Eaton, Ojai, CA
Galerie Berggruen, Paris
Hanover Gallery, London
Mr and Mrs Arnold Maremont, Winnetka, IL
Galerie Beyeler, Basle
Galleria Internazionale, Milan
Thyssen-Bornemisza Collection, 1976

Exhibitions
Humlebaek, Louisiana Museum of Modern Art, 1971–2, *Klee – Kandinsky*, no.94
Saint Paul de Nice, Fondation Maeght, 1977, *Paul Klee*, no.79
Brussels/Paris 1977–8, no.45
Lugano 1978, no.53
Cologne, Kunsthalle, 1979, *Paul Klee. Das Werk der Jahre 1919–1933*, no.225, ill. p.266
Australian tour 1979–80, no.52
Budapest/Szombathely 1985–6, no.35
Luxemburg/Munich/Vienna 1988, no.38
Lugano 1989, no.34
Expressionism and Modern German Painting, 1989–90, no.21
Rome 1990–91, no.31

Literature
Geelhaar (1973), p.107, ill. p.108

Many of his paintings of the years – a decade in all – Klee spent at the Bauhaus are directly or indirectly related to his teaching: studies of the spatial relations of objects, modelling in light and shade, gradations of colour. Others are more a poetic expression of his intense interest in the laws of nature, especially those governing the origin and development of organic life – an interest which assumed a new, more scientific aspect during his time at the Bauhaus.[2] It is to this second category that the present painting – one of a series of works he entitled *Omega* – belongs.

As so often with Klee, the title (or subsidiary title) here bears a significant yet tangential relationship to the painting, causing us to ponder the work rather than explaining it. 'Attrappen' are literally dummies, evidently an allusion to the bell-like shapes suspended tantalisingly before our eyes. These might almost deceive us into thinking that they were some kind of artificial construction, made perhaps from paper or cardboard, something like a

Notes
1 Though the work is inscribed 'Attrappen' the title is recorded as 'Attrappe' in Klee's oeuvre-catalogue, the manuscript of which is in the Kunstmuseum, Berne (see n.1, p.225)
2 For a detailed examination of Klee's interest in scientific theory, see the seminal study by Sara Lynn Henry, *Paul Klee, Nature and Modern Science, the 1920s*, Ann Arbor, MI (UMI) 1976

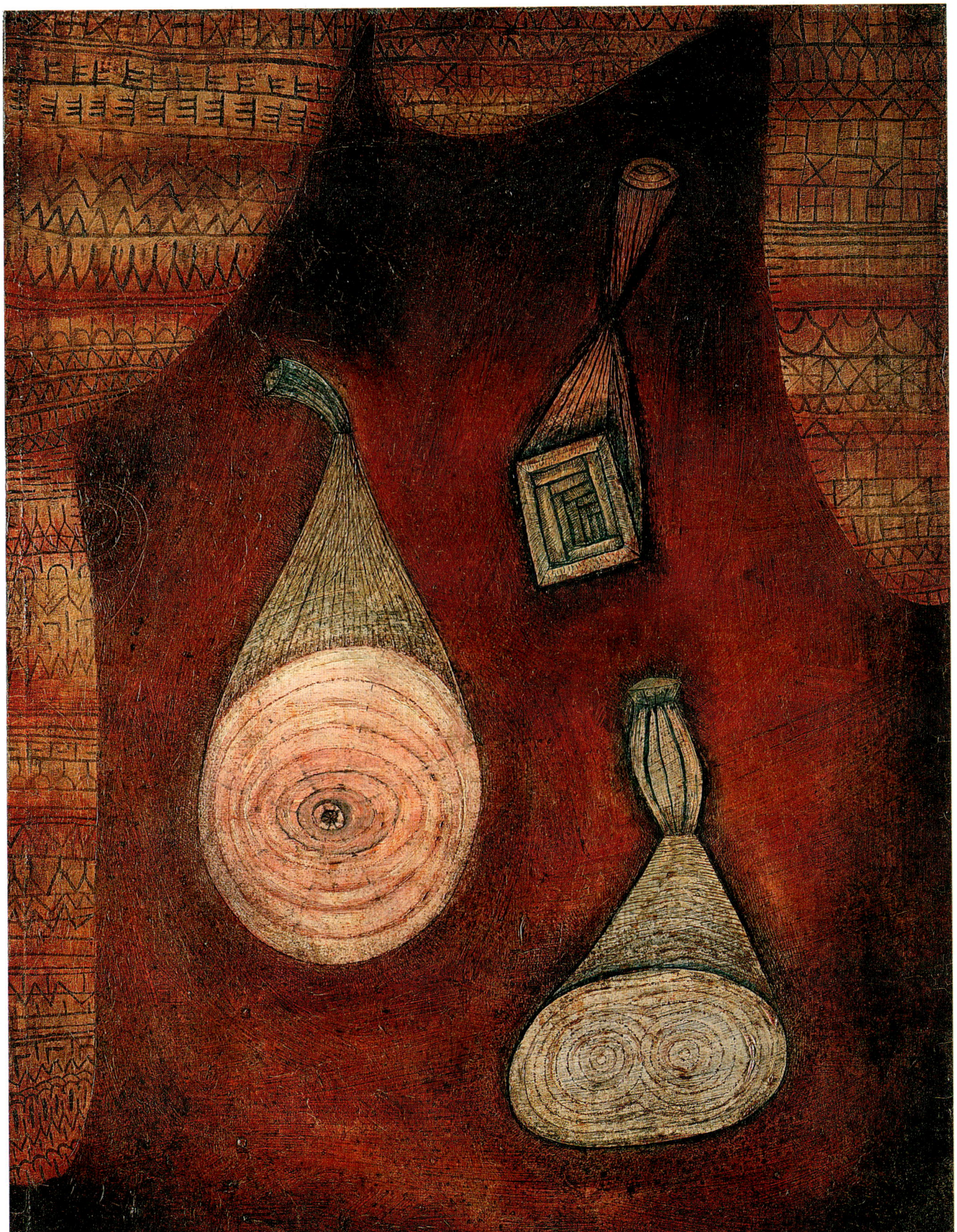

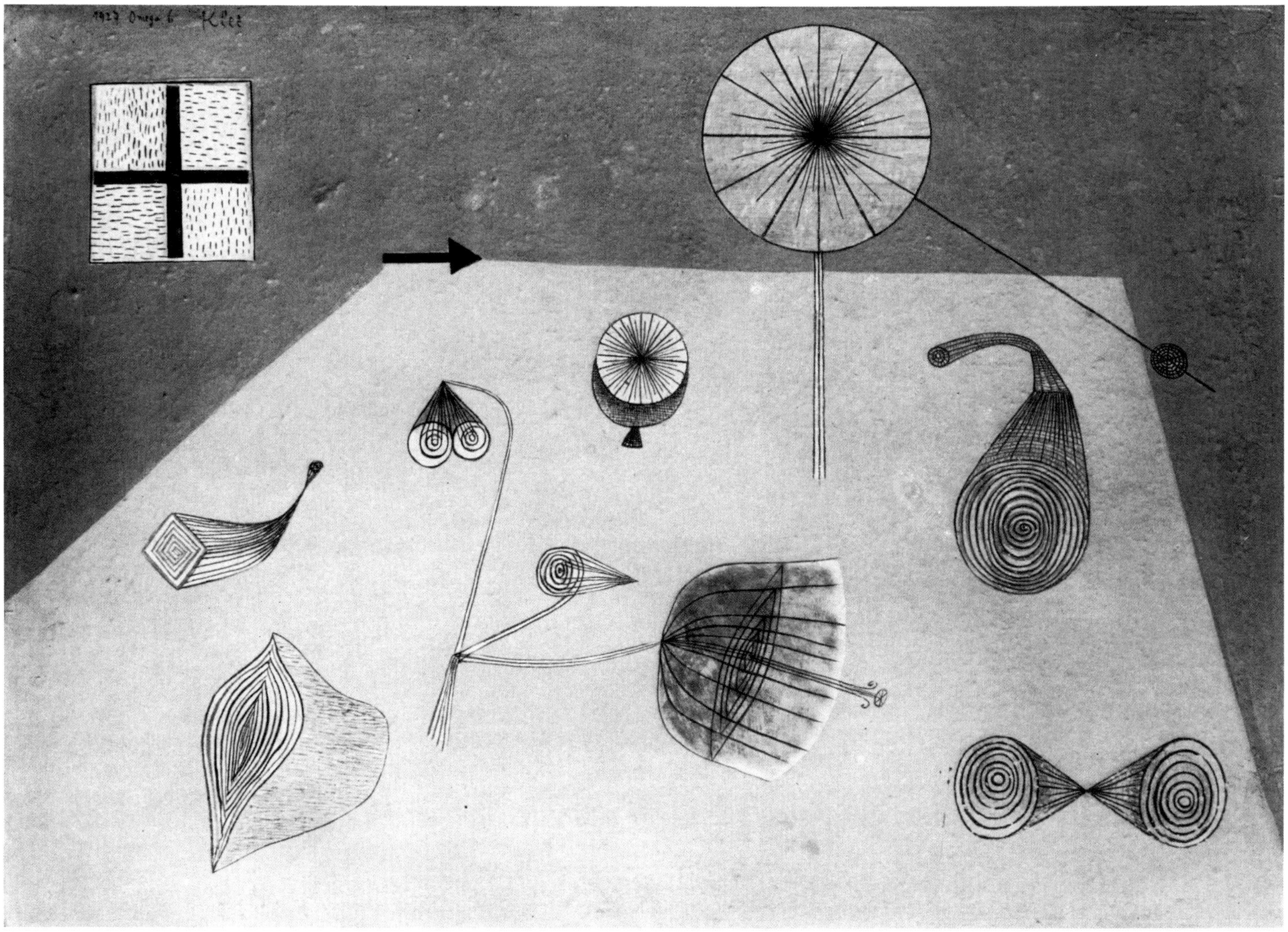

matchbox or a Chinese lantern, were they not sliced open to display the growth rings that mark them out as organic forms. The contrast between these curiously dessicated-looking objects and the sensuous appeal of the rich purple-red background is clearly deliberate and at the same time faintly ironic.

In a letter dated 10 March 1991, Sabine Rewald of the Metropolitan Museum of Art, New York, pointed out the resemblance between these curious suspended forms which are the dominant feature of *Omega 5* and the type of cut-off hams or sausages that sometimes appear as illustrations in children's picture-books.[3] To the present author, it appears more probable that the reference intended here is to some kind of organic or vegetal being – a variety of fruit, perhaps – especially given the striking similarity between *Omega 5* and the immediately following work in the series, *Omega 6* (fig. 1), in which fruit, flower, seed and tuberous root are laid out as in a still-life arrangement on a table. One of these, a bell-shaped form with a curved stalk like a pear, is identical to that which appears at extreme left in the Thyssen Collection's painting, even to the extent of being sliced open to reveal the growth rings already referred to.

As noted by Sara Lynn Henry, from 1923 onwards Klee repeatedly wrote about penetrating

FIG 1 Paul Klee, *Omega 6 (297) 'Time of the Plants'*, 1927, oil and watercolour on wood, 39 × 52.5 cm (Rome, Private collection)

Notes

3 A suggestion also advanced by Emil Bosshard, Head of Conservation of the Thyssen-Bornemisza Collection (in conversation, Lugano, May 1991). Though my interpretation of its iconography diverges somewhat from theirs, I am grateful to both Sabine Rewald and Emil Bosshard for sharing with me their opinion on the painting

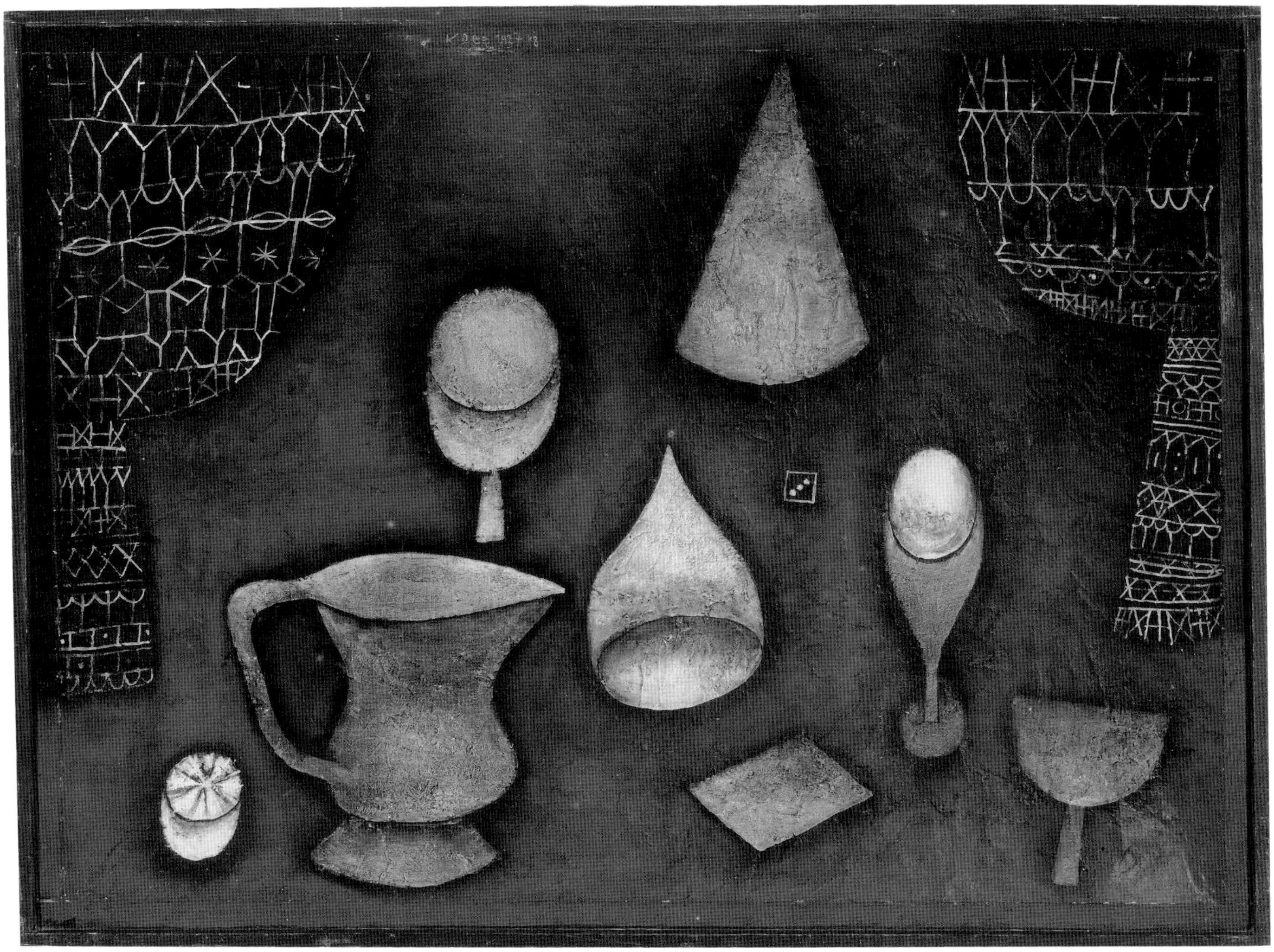

FIG 2 Paul Klee, *Still-life*, 1927, oil on gypsum construction, 47.9 × 64.1 cm (New York, Metropolitan Museum of Art, The Beggruen Klee Collection, inv. no.1984.315.49)

the external shell of natural objects in order not merely to lay bare their inner being, but also to expose the dynamic forces determining growth, development and change.[4] In his essay 'Wege des Naturstudiums' (Ways of Studying Nature), published in the celebrated Bauhaus album of 1923, he describes the way in which mankind 'dissects things, revealing their inner essence by means of cross-sections whose number and type condition our perception of the character of the object. This process of making the interior visible is achieved in part by the scalpel, in part by more refined instruments capable of bringing the structure and dynamics of the material object clearly before our eyes.'[5] In his drawings, subsequently elaborated in the form of diagrams used as an adjunct to his teaching, he devised a formal method for studying the dynamic forces which affect the growth of natural, especially vegetal forms, numerous examples of which are to be found in his pedagogical sketchbooks.

Among Klee's other works of this period, *Omega 5* is closely related to a further still-life painting of 1927, now in the Berggruen Klee collection of the Metropolitan Museum of Art, New York (fig.2), in which pots, fruit and an Easter egg are likewise framed by curtains and placed against an intensely painted, opaque background.

4 Henry, op. cit., p.53ff
5 Paul Klee, 'Wege des Naturstudiums', in *Staatliches Bauhaus Weimar 1919–1923*, Weimar/Munich (Bauhausverlag) 1923, pp.24–5, repr. in Geelhaar (1976), pp.124–6

Oskar Kokoschka 1886–1980

56 Portrait of Max Schmidt

1914
Oil on canvas, 90 × 57.5 cm
Initialled/dated lower left: 'OK 20.iii.14'
The painting is unvarnished; there is a history of cracking and flaking to the paint layer and some evidence of losses previously restored. The canvas has been relined
Accession no.1982.29

Provenance
Atelier Friedrich Otto Schmidt, Vienna/Budapest
F. Kleinberger & Co., New York
Marlborough Fine Art, London
Professor Edgar Horstmann, Hamburg
Galerie Beyeler, Basle
Thyssen-Bornemisza Collection, 1982

Exhibitions
London, Marlborough Fine Art, 1959, *Art in Revolt. Germany 1905–25*, no.36
London, Tate Gallery, 1962, *Oskar Kokoschka*, no.43
Florence 1964, no.313
Zurich, Kunsthaus, 1966, *Oskar Kokoschka*, no.31
Karlsruhe, Badischer Kunstverein, 1966, *Oskar Kokoschka, Das Portrait*, no.26
Munich, Haus der Kunst, 1971, *Oskar Kokoschka, Bildnisse von 1907–1970*, no.19
Basle, Galerie Beyeler, 1982, *Portraits et Figures*, no.58
Modern Masters from the Thyssen-Bornemisza Collection, 1984–6, no.62
Lugano 1989, no.40
Essen, Museum Folkwang, 1990, *Vincent van Gogh und die Moderne 1890–1914*, no.195
Amsterdam, Rijksmuseum Vincent van Gogh, 1990–91, *Vincent van Gogh en de moderne Kunst 1890–1914*, no.104

Literature
Wingler (1958), no.94, p.304[1]

The well-known firm of Friedrich Otto Schmidt, furnishers and interior decorators, was established in 1853 in Vienna, where it still exists today; there was later a subsidiary branch in Budapest. By the turn of the century it numbered among its clients leading members of the Austrian Imperial family and aristocracy, as well as the Viennese *haute bourgeoisie*. It was also frequently represented at exhibitions of furniture and applied art held in Vienna by the Österreichisches Museum für Angewandte Kunst.

During the early 1900s there were three brothers principally involved in the running of the firm: Max Schmidt, the owner; Carl Leo Schmidt (known as Leo), responsible for the Viennese side of the business, who became owner after Max's death in 1935; and Hugo Schmidt, who rose to the rank of captain in the Austrian navy.[2] It was these three brothers who were depicted

Notes

1 The painting recorded and reproduced on p.304 of Wingler's 1958 oeuvre-catalogue of Kokoschka's work is in fact the triple portrait of the three Schmidt brothers, of which [56] is the central portion. Described as a sketch, this triple portrait was evidently unknown to Wingler in the original, since he lists neither its whereabouts nor its dimensions

2 I am indebted to present members of the Schmidt family in Vienna, in particular Frau Irene Schmidt and her daughter, Frau Irene Lorenz, who provided information regarding the family, and allowed me to publish the photographs reproduced here as figs.1, 2; also to Dr Vera J.Behal, of the Österreichisches Museum für Angewandte Kunst, Vienna, for information about the history of the firm. In addition, my thanks to Johann Winkler, director of the Oskar Kokoschka Documentation Centre at Pöchlarn, Austria, for sharing with me the results of his researches in connection with his own revised edition of Wingler's oeuvre-catalogue of the artist's work

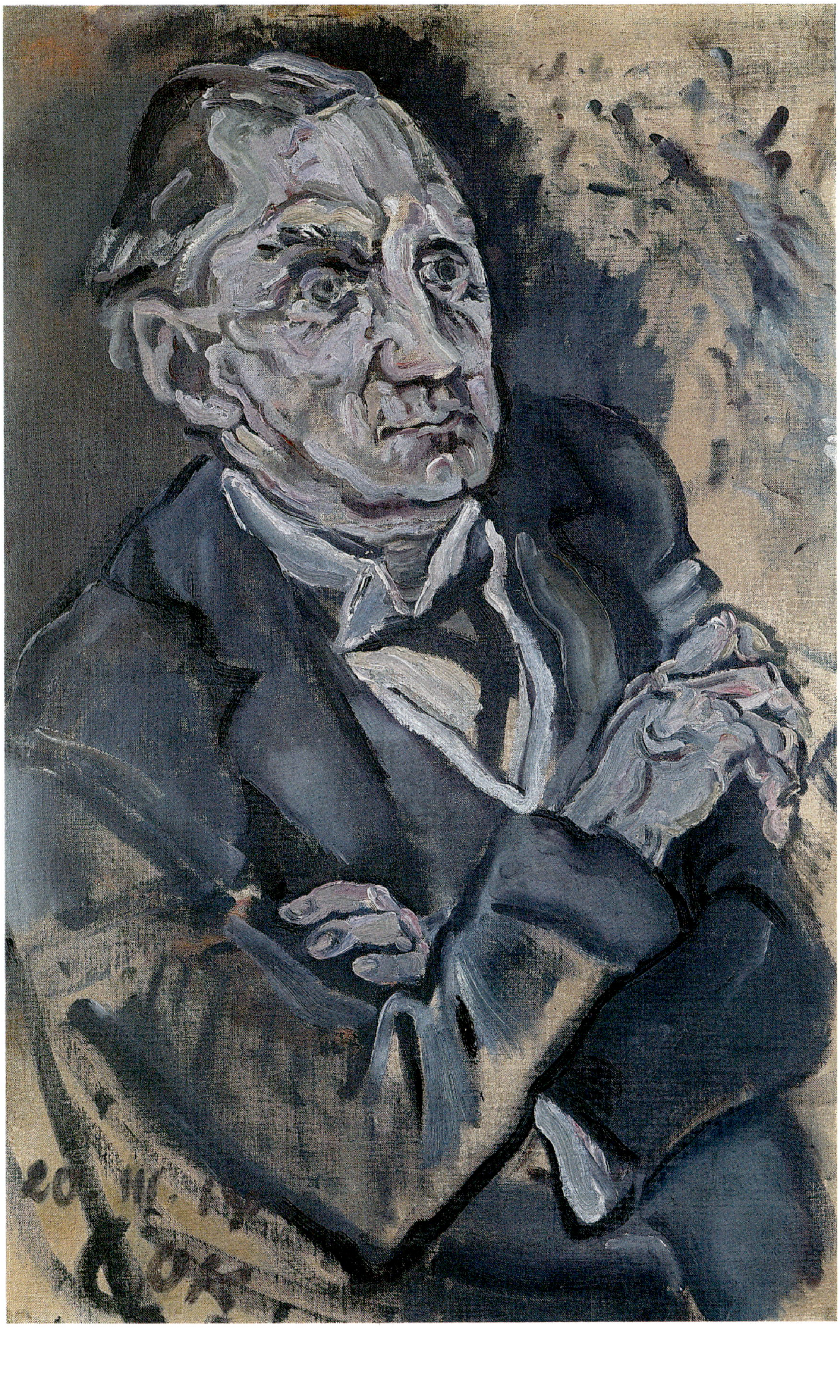

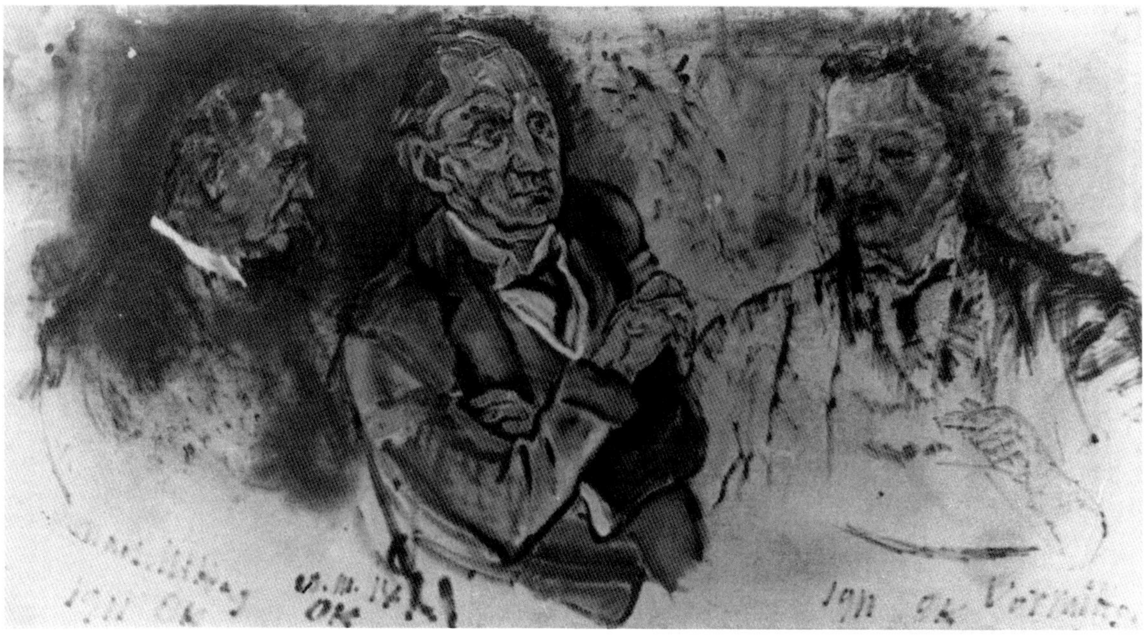

FIG 1 Oskar Kokoschka, *The Schmidt Brothers*, 1911/14, oil on canvas, dimensions unknown (original state)

by Kokoschka in what was originally a triple portrait, of which the present painting is a fragment, in the order (left to right) Hugo, Max, Leo (see fig.1).

One peculiarity of the triple portrait is that each of the three likenesses was individually dated by the artist: the flanking figures to 1911 and inscribed (on the left) *Nachmittag* (afternoon) and (on the right) *Vormittag* (morning); the central figure to 1914 and given a precise date (20th March). Seemingly, therefore, the original painting was the product of at least two distinct phases of work; it may also have subsequently been abandoned as unfinished. The central likeness is important in the context of Kokoschka's oeuvre since, by dating it to a precise day, the artist has provided a rare fixed point by reference to which other stylistically congruent works of this period can convincingly be related.

There appears to be no documentation regarding the commissioning or original creation of the triple portrait; it had, however, been dismembered by 1959, when three individual portraits of the Schmidt brothers were offered for sale at Sotheby's in London.[3] The same three portraits were also included in the exhibition *Art in Revolt* held in London in the autumn of that year,[4] the text of the catalogue reproducing word for word the entries in the Sotheby's sale catalogue. In both, however, as well as mis-identifying the left-hand figure from the original triple portrait as 'Ernst', the present portrait was, in all probability for the first time, christened 'Gino Schmidt', the name by which it has subsequently been known.[5]

The portrait of Hugo Schmidt is, apparently, destroyed. The portrait of Leo is now in a private collection in London. By 1962 at the time of the Kokoschka retrospective exhibition at the Tate Gallery, the portrait of Max was in the collection of Professor Edgar Horstmann in Hamburg;[6] it was still in his possession in 1966 at the time of the Zurich and Karlsruhe exhibitions. It was offered for sale by Hauswedell & Nolte in Hamburg in 1979;[7] hence via the Galerie Beyeler, Basle (1982), to the present owner.

It has been claimed on several occasions that the triple portrait of the Schmidt brothers was cut up with Kokoschka's consent.[8] There does not, however, appear to exist any firm evidence for this assertion. Olda Kokoschka recalled that her husband appeared less than pleased, perhaps even shocked by the news that the canvas had been divided into three.[9] It also seems unlikely that the initials and date now visible in the lower left corner of the *Portrait of Max Schmidt* are by the artist's own hand. Seen under ultra-violet light, they seem hesitant in execution, and consist of a pigment texturally different from any other employed in the portrait.

Notes

3 *Highly Important Impressionist and Modern Paintings and Drawings*, 6 May 1959, lots 130–2

4 Cat. nos.34–6. The exhibition took place during October–November 1959

5 It is not clear why the name 'Gino' should have been attached to the portrait; as far as it is possible to ascertain, it was not a name which ever existed in the Schmidt family, not even as a nickname

6 The painting was not reproduced in the catalogue of the Tate exhibition; the entry refers to the triple portrait, but this is evidently a mistake as revealed by the dimensions, which are those of the present picture

7 *Auktion 231 (Moderne Kunst)*, 8–9 June 1979, lot 664

8 For example, in the catalogue of the 1979 Hamburg auction: see n.7

9 Letter to the author dated 18 February 1991; according to her recollection, Kokoschka was also deeply saddened by the news that the portrait of Hugo Schmidt had been destroyed. I am grateful to Mrs Kokoschka for helping to confirm a number of details concerning the Thyssen Collection's painting

10 According to Kokoschka's own account: see Kokoschka (1974), p.51

11 Albert Ehrenstein, *Menschen und Affen*, Berlin 1925, quoted after Werkner (1986), p.102. For a more sophisticated account of Kokoschka's portraiture, see Edward Timms, 'Kokoschka's Pictographs – a contextual reading', *Word and Image. A Journal of Verbal/Visual Enquiry*, VI, no.1 (January–March 1990): 4–17

12 Kokoschka (1974), p.34

13 Wingler (1958), no.36; see also Hodin (1966), pp.96–7

14 Wingler (1958), no.15

FIG 2 Portrait photograph of Max Schmidt (Irene Schmidt, Vienna)

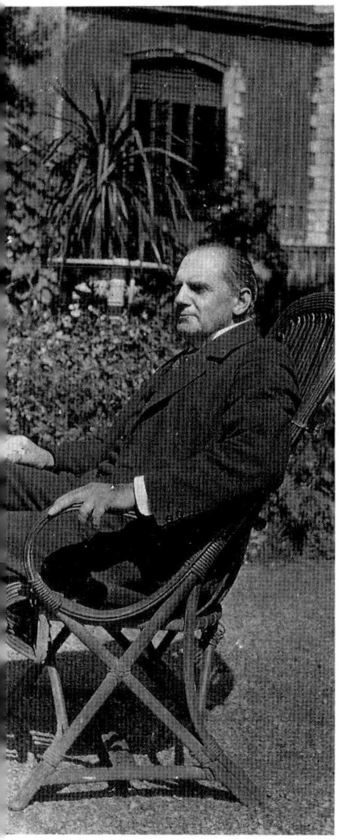

There are also traces of in-filling at the extreme lower left, and what may be the barest vestiges of an earlier signature, which had evidently been defaced by cutting the canvas. The photograph of the triple portrait in its original state shows initials and date in a slightly different position to that in which they now appear. The canvas has, however, been cut in such a way that it is impossible to draw any firm conclusions from the surviving visual evidence.

It has often been maintained that Kokoschka's aim in portraiture was to render a 'psychological likeness', disdaining mere physical veracity. He was even charged with having 'X-ray vision' – for example, by the architect Adolf Loos, a close friend of his at this time.[10] The poet and essayist Albert Ehrenstein, whom Kokoschka also painted in 1914, observed: 'In an eerie way, in painting hands and heads he lays bare the spiritual skeleton of those whom he portrays. This kind of gruesome psychotomy might be compared to vivisection.'[11] To some extent, such assertions derive from the artist's own statements about his work. For example, in his autobiography published in 1971, he observed that he did not consider it his task as a portraitist to 'enumerate physical details like five fingers, two ears, one nose', considering such attributes trivial by comparison with that 'flash of the eye that betrays an inner movement'.[12] On the other hand, he describes in no less vivid prose his struggle to capture the 'myriad wrinkles' on the face of Auguste Forel in his 1910 portrait of the Swiss biologist,[13] which made the old man's skin seem to Kokoschka like an ancient parchment. And indeed, many of his portraits of these pre-war years are remarkable for their stubborn determination to capture a physical likeness. What he, in most cases, omits in these paintings is any reference to the wealth, the social standing, the intellectual or professional pursuits of his sitters. We find no pictorial allusion to Forel's eminence as a scientist nor, for example, to Loos's profession as an architect in Kokoschka's famous portrait of 1909.[14]

In the Thyssen Collection's portrait of Max Schmidt, we might equally search in vain for any indication of the sitter's place in society, or of his activities as a businessman and entrepreneur. On the other hand, the portrait evokes a visage remarkably similar to that captured in a old family photograph (fig.2). Evidently, in the case of the present work, Kokoschka's preoccupation with psychological truth, with what he termed the 'inner life' of the subject, did not exclude the possibility of exactly recording the features, as well as (strikingly) the expression of his sitter.

Oskar Kokoschka 1886–1980

57 Pontresina

1952
Oil on canvas, 91 × 130 cm
Initialled lower right: 'OK'
The picture is painted on commercial pre-primed canvas. It is unvarnished and, apart from two small tears towards the lower left corner of the canvas, is in pristine condition
Accession no.1970.38

Provenance
Willy Hahn, Stuttgart
Senta Hildebrand, Munich
Galerie R.N.Ketterer, Campione d'Italia
Thyssen-Bornemisza Collection, 1970

Exhibitions[1]
Darmstadt, Mathildenhöhe, 1954, *Das Bild der Landschaft 1945–1954*, no.101
Pittsburgh, PA, Carnegie Institute, 1955, *The 1955 Pittsburgh International Exhibition of Contemporary Painting*, no.158
Munich, Haus der Kunst, 1956, *Grosse Kunstausstellung*, no.377
Munich, Haus der Kunst, 1958, *Oskar Kokoschka*, no.139
Vienna, Künstlerhaus, 1958, *Oskar Kokoschka*, no.144
Brunswick, Haus Salve Hospes/Bremen, Kunsthalle/Hameln, Kunstkreis/Pforzheim, Kunst- und Gewerbeverein, 1960, *Der späte Kokoschka*, no.26
Munich, Haus der Kunst, 1966, *Grosse Kunstausstellung*, no.730
Bremen 1975, no.40
Lugano 1975, no.150
Villingen-Schwenningen, Beethovenhaus, 1976, *Oskar Kokoschka zum 90. Geburtstag*, no.8
Brussels/Paris 1977–8, no.47
Lugano 1978, no.56
St Moritz, Parkhausrondelle, 1985, *Das Oberengadin in der Malerei. 18. Jahrhundert biz zur Gegenwart*, ill. p.157

Literature
Wingler (1958), no.377
R.N.Ketterer, *Moderne Kunst IV*, Campione d'Italia (Galerie R.N.Ketterer) 1967, p.112, no.89, ill. p.113
R.N.Ketterer, *Moderne Kunst V*, Campione d'Italia (Galerie R.N.Ketterer) 1968, p.114, no.92, ill. p.115
R.N.Ketterer, *Moderne Kunst VI*, Campione d'Italia (Galerie R.N.Ketterer) 1969, p.104, no.58, ill. p.105
Kiel (1974), p.82, ill. p.83
See also the chronology compiled by Katharina Schulz, in *Oskar Kokoschka 1886–1980*, exh. cat., London, Tate Gallery, 1986, pp.337ff, 359

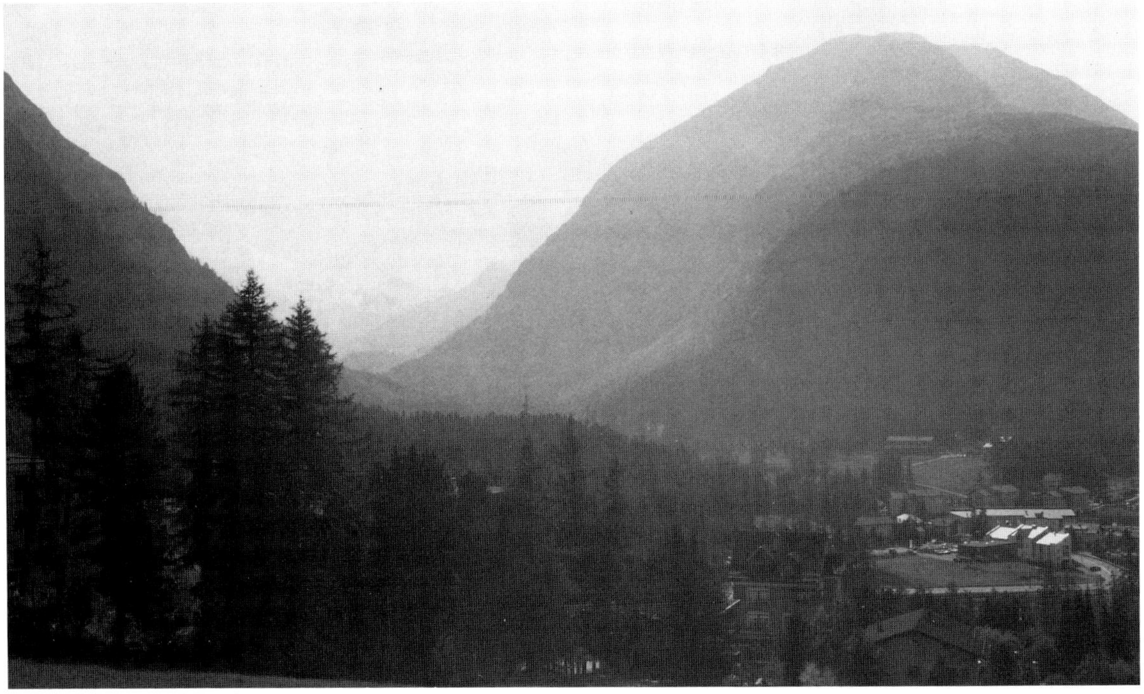

FIG 1 The town of Pontresina, looking south

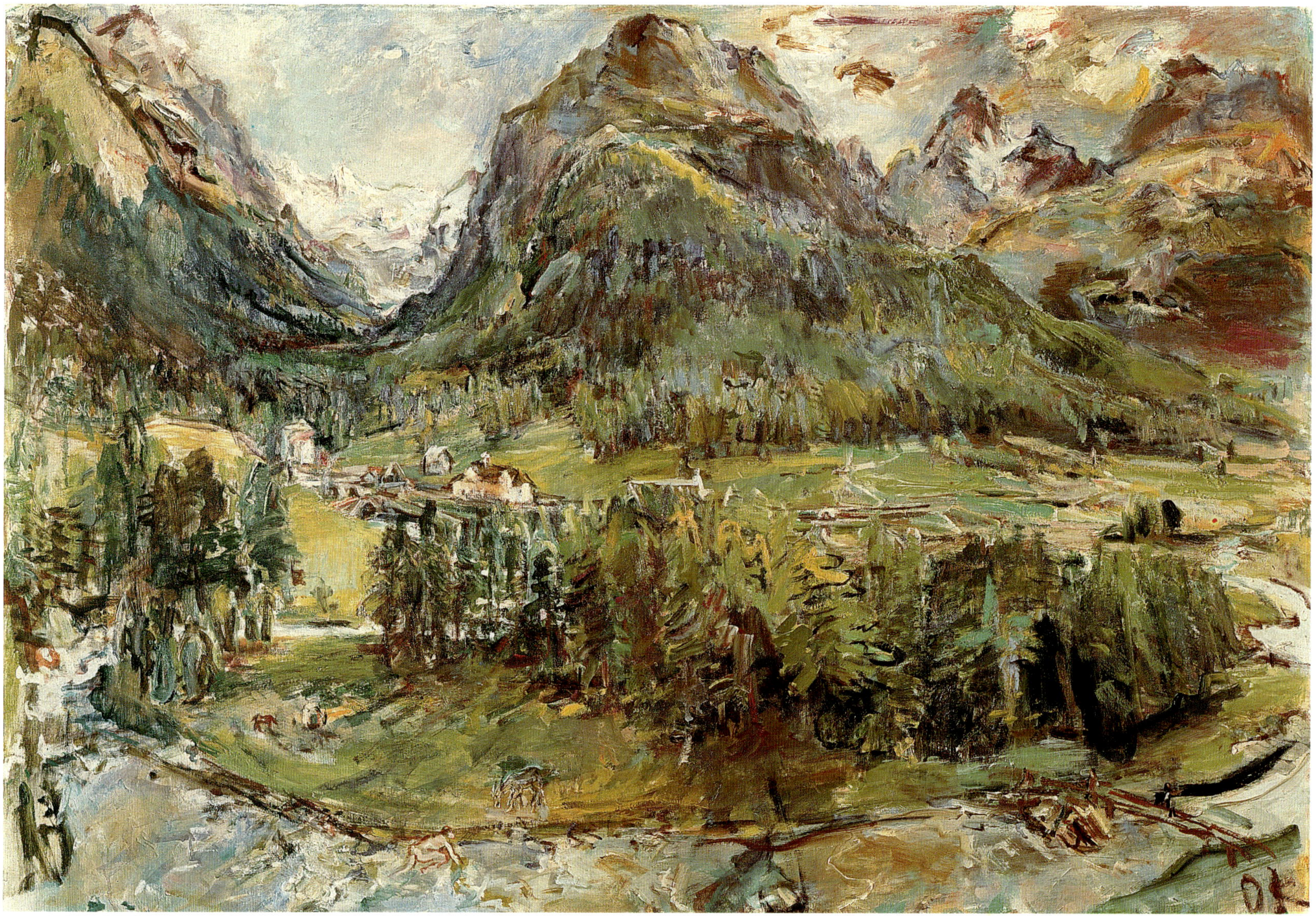

Notes
1 I am grateful to Johann Winkler, Director of the Oskar Kokoschka Documentation Centre at Pöchlarn, for information concerning early exhibitions at which the painting was shown
2 For an account of Hahn's friendship with Kokoschka see Ketterer (1988/II), pp.213f
3 Information kindly supplied by Marianne Feilchenfeldt, Zurich, letter to the author, 3 September 1990

Kokoschka was a frequent visitor to Switzerland from 1947 onwards, though it was not until 1953 that he finally settled at Villeneuve, on the eastern shore of Lake Geneva. The lakes and mountains of his new homeland were to provide him with the subject matter for a succession of landscape paintings of sweeping grandeur and intensity, of which *Pontresina* is an outstanding example.

The previous summer, 1952, the artist had visited the area of the Engandine on his way from Salzburg to Zurich. To judge by his itinerary, the present picture must have been painted during August of that year. It depicts the small town of Pontresina, a few kilometres to the east of St Moritz. The vantage point is some way above the town, looking south towards the high peaks of the Piz Bernina and beyond. However, as so often in his later landscapes and cityscapes, the picture embraces far more than could in reality have been seen from a single viewpoint. The accompanying photograph (fig.1), taken in September 1989, conveys some idea of the actual location.

The painting was acquired directly from the artist by Kokoschka's close friend, the collector and musician Willy Hahn.[2] In 1958 it was sold on Hahn's behalf to a private collector in Munich, whence via the Galerie R.N.Ketterer to the present owner.[3]

Oskar Kokoschka 1886–1980

58 Flowers in a Vase

1961
Watercolour on paper, 65 × 47 cm
Signed/dated lower right: 'O.Kokoschka 61'
In good condition
Accession no.1972.11

Provenance
Galerie R.N.Ketterer, Campione d'Italia
Thyssen-Bornemisza Collection, 1972

Literature
On Kokoschka's flower studies, see Doris Wild, *Oskar Kokoschka, Blumenaquarelle. Sechs mehrfarbige Wiedergaben*, Zurich (Rascher) 1948, and *Oskar Kokoschka, Blumenaquarelle. Zweite Blumenmappe mit sechs mehrfarbigen Wiedergaben und einer Einführung von Doris Wild*, Zurich/Stuttgart (Rascher) 1962

As Heinz Spielmann points out, Kokoschka used water-based paints (watercolour, gouache) only at certain periods of his life, and only in rather precise ways.[1] Leaving aside the very early figure drawings, which are occasionally embellished with watercolour, the most important works in this medium date from the years in Dresden during and immediately after the First World War, from the artist's stay in England and Scotland between 1938 and 1946, and from his last years in Switzerland.

Though Kokoschka continued to travel extensively during the 1960s, including to North Africa, Turkey and the USA, the home to which he returned from all his journeys was at Villeneuve on Lake Geneva, where he and his wife Olda had bought a plot of land in 1951. He was passionately attached to the house and gardens at Villeneuve, the house being completed by 1953. During the late fifties and throughout the sixties, he made numerous watercolour studies of flowers, and of bushes and shrubs in the garden. Among these are the present work, which is dated 1961, and the following three watercolours [59], [60] and [61] from 1967–8.

Note
1 See Heinz Spielmann, *Kokoschka-Fälschungen (Sonderdruck aus den Weltkunst-Ausgaben 1983)*, 'Kokoschka-Fälschungen IV: Zu Fälschungen der Aquarelle und Gouachen (Verzeichnis der gefälschten, gefälscht signierten oder falsch zugeschriebenen Aquarelle und Gouachen aus dem Archiv des Künstlers)'

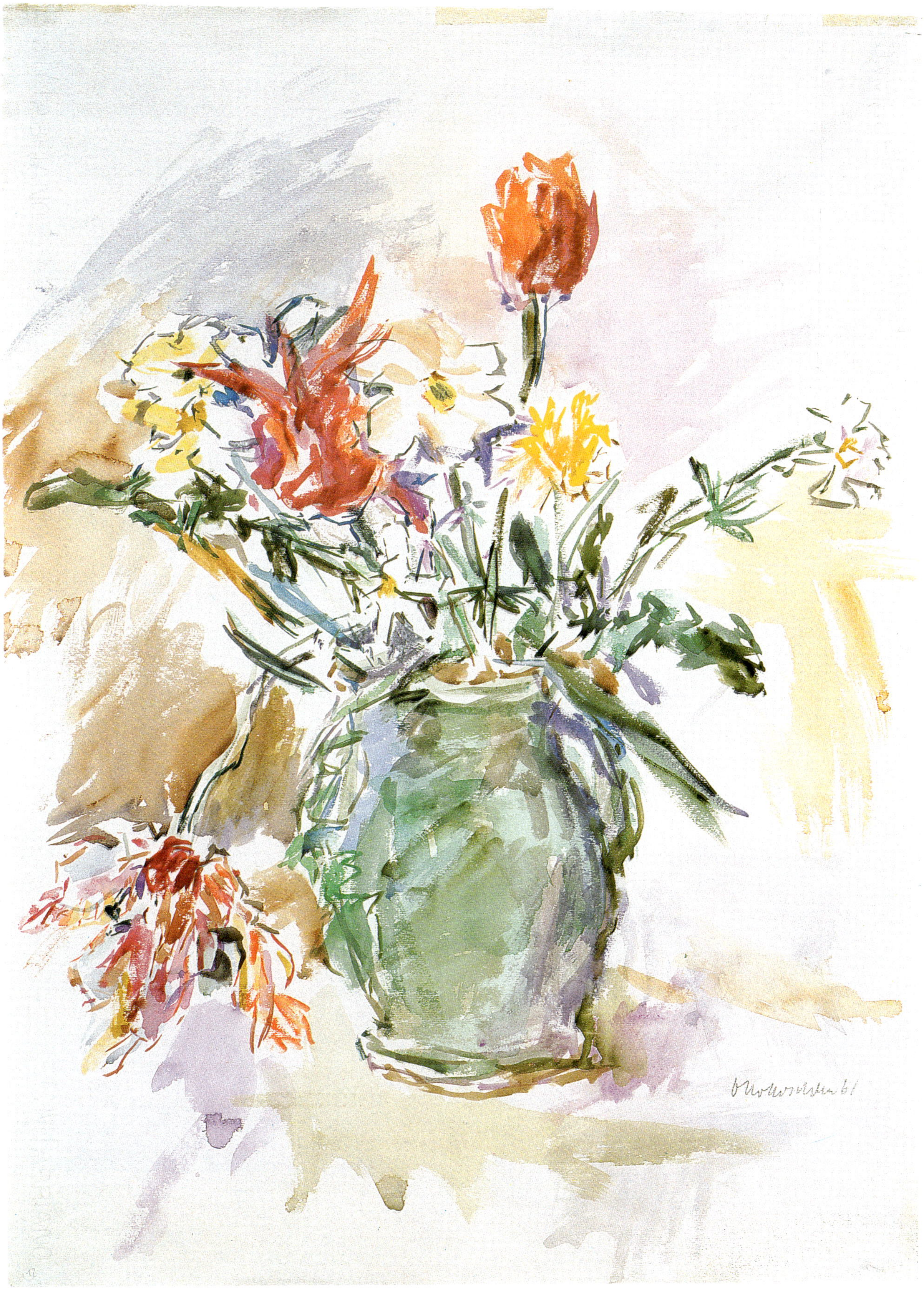

Oskar Kokoschka 1886–1980

59 Tulips and Peonies

1967
Watercolour on paper, 65.5 × 50 cm
Signed/dated lower left: 'O.Kokoschka 1967'
In good condition
Accession no.1970.27

Provenance
Galerie R.N.Ketterer, Campione d'Italia
Thyssen-Bornemisza Collection, 1970

Literature
R.N.Ketterer, *Moderne Kunst VI*, Campione d'Italia (Galerie R.N.Ketterer) 1969, no.64, p.111, ill.

The poet and critic Edouard Roditi recalled visiting Kokoschka at Villeneuve during the late 1950s, where he conducted a lengthy interview subsequently published in his book *Dialogues on Art*. At the end of the interview, Kokoschka made a particular point of showing Roditi some of his flower pieces:

> I was about to leave, when Kokoschka produced a folder of water-colours which he began to show me. They were exquisite studies of details of his garden, of the effects of light and shadow on flowers and shrubs. One could feel that they had all been painted in a completely relaxed mood, with the mastery achieved at the climax of a life devoted to drawing and painting, but also with the wonder and delight of a child or a mystic ... the water-colours that he was showing me had the same quality of wisdom and of wonder as those of a whole school of mystical painters of the Far East, the Taoist and Zen artists of China and Japan who were able to discover, as he, order and beauty in the confusion of natural appearances.[1]

See also entry for [58].

Note
1 Roditi (1980), p.88

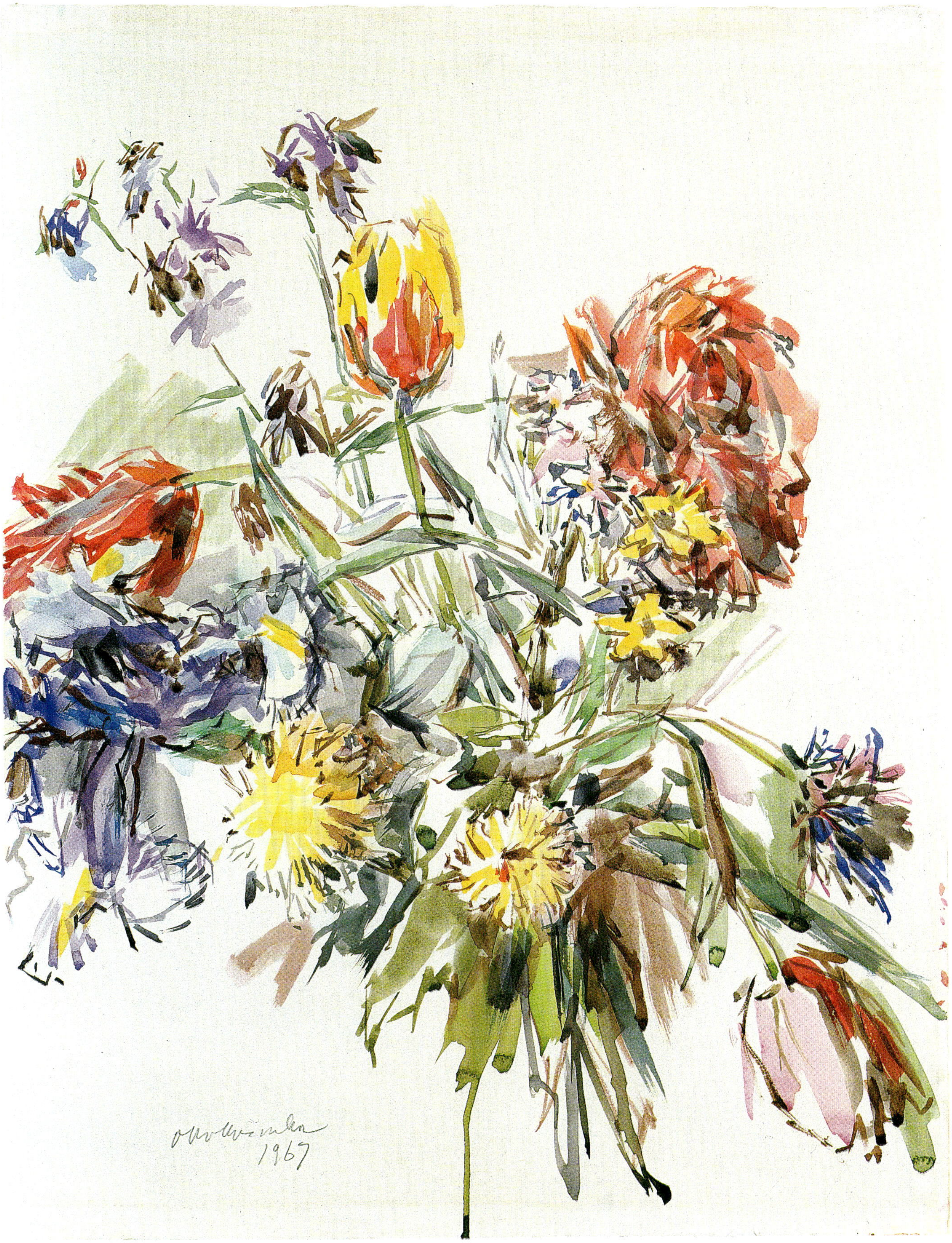

Oskar Kokoschka 1886–1980

60 Bouquet of Flowers (Tulips and Lilac)

1968
Watercolour on paper, 65.5 × 47.5 cm
Signed/dated lower right: 'O.Kokoschka 1968'
In good condition
Accession no.1970.25

Provenance
Galerie R.N.Ketterer, Campione d'Italia
Thyssen-Bornemisza Collection, 1970

Literature
R.N.Ketterer, *Moderne Kunst VI*, Campione d'Italia (Galerie R.N.Ketterer) 1969, no.60, p.107, ill.

See entry for [58].

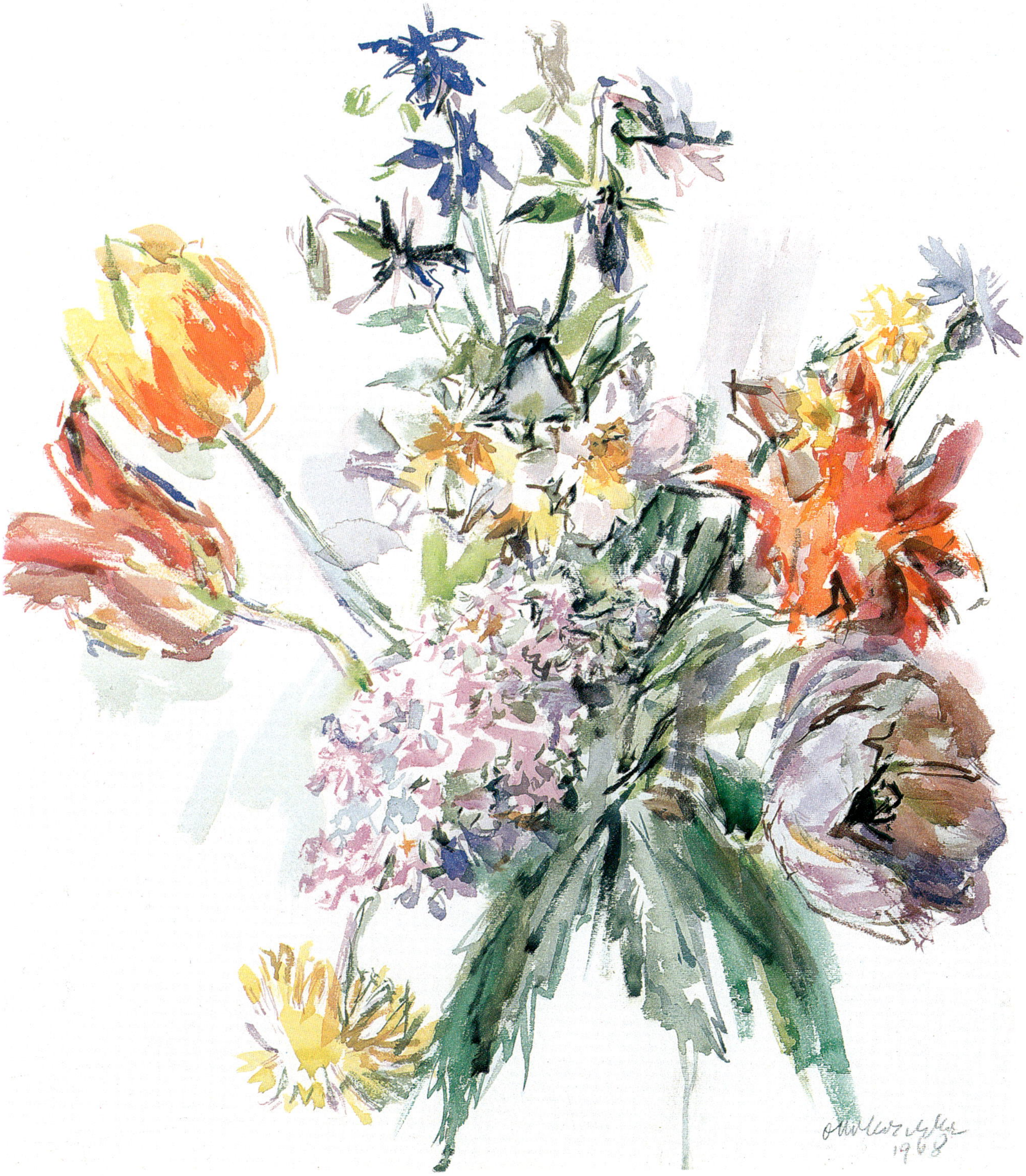

Oskar Kokoschka 1886–1980

61 Tulips and Narcissi (Spring Flowers)

1968
Watercolour on paper, 64 × 49 cm
Signed/dated lower right: 'O.Kokoschka 68'
In good condition
Accession no.1970.26

Provenance
Galerie R.N.Ketterer, Campione d'Italia
Thyssen-Bornemisza Collection, 1970

Literature
R.N.Ketterer, *Moderne Kunst VI*, Campione d'Italia (Galerie R.N.Ketterer) 1969, p.110, no.63, ill.
See also Heinz Spielmann, *Kokoschka-Fälschungen* (*Sonderdruck aus den Weltkunst-Ausgaben 1983*), 'Kokoschka-Fälschungen IV: Zu Fälschungen der Aquarelle und Gouachen (Verzeichnis der gefälschten, gefälscht signierten oder falsch zugeschriebenen Aquarelle und Gouachen aus dem Archiv des Künstlers)', no.347

In November 1981, a copy after this watercolour was offered for sale in Munich.[1] At first accepted as authentic by the artist's widow, Olda Kokoschka, it was subsequently identified as a forgery. As Spielmann remarks, the increasing prices attained at auction by Kokoschka's authentic watercolours and flower studies made them an attractive target for imitators. In the present case, the fact that the original had been reproduced in colour, together with a note of medium and dimensions, in the catalogue *Moderne Kunst VI* would have made the forger's task all the easier.

See also entries for [58] and [59].

Note
1 See the catalogue of the 158th auction, Karl & Faber, Munich (26–7 November 1981, lot 1314). I am indebted to Hofrat Mag. Dr Alice Strobl, Vienna, who is compiling a complete catalogue of Kokoschka's drawings and watercolours, for bringing this reference to my attention, also to Direktor Dr Heinz Spielmann, Schleswig, for further information concerning forgeries after Kokoschka's works

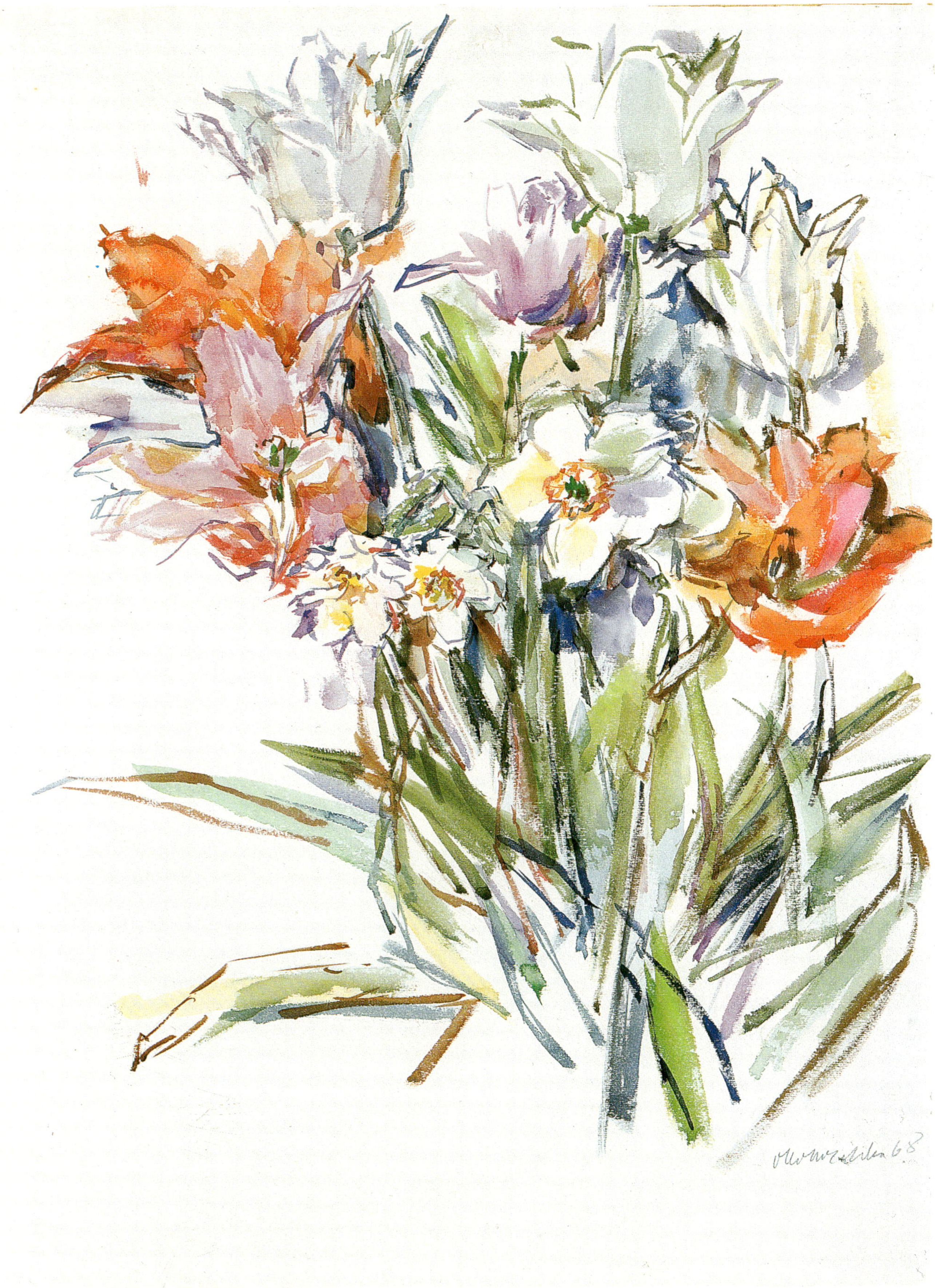

August Macke 1887–1914

62 Hussars (Hussars on a Sortie)
Husaren (Ausreitende Husaren)

1913
Oil on canvas, 37.5 × 56.1 cm
Inscribed on stretcher: 'August Macke Ausreitende Husaren 1913'; on back of canvas: 'August Macke Husaren 1913'; also estate stamp: 'Nachlass August Macke'
In good condition. The painting is unvarnished
Accession no.1980.50

Provenance
Estate of the artist
Galerie Karin Hielscher, Munich
Georg Schäfer, Schweinfurt
Leonard Hutton Galleries, New York
Thyssen-Bornemisza Collection, 1980

Exhibitions
Hanover, Kestner-Gesellschaft, 1935, *August Macke*, no.46
Luxemburg/Munich/Vienna 1988, no.49

Literature
Vriesen (1957), no.337

According to Vriesen's oeuvre-catalogue of Macke's paintings, *Hussars* (or *Hussars on a Sortie*) was painted in 1913 in the artist's studio in Bonn. It is therefore datable to the earlier part of the year, much of which had been taken up with plans for exhibitions: the showing of Rhenish Expressionists at the Kunsthandlung Friedrich Cohen in Bonn in July 1913, in which Macke played a leading role, and the famous *Erster Deutscher Herbstsalon* (First German *Salon d'automne*), which took place in Berlin in the autumn of that year, and for which he had obtained funding from his wife's uncle, the industrialist and collector Bernhard Koehler.[1] In September, Macke travelled to Berlin to assist in hanging the exhibition; at the end of the month, after the *Herbstsalon* had opened, he moved with his family to Hilterfingen on Lake Thun in Switzerland, where he remained – with interruptions – until June the following year.[2]

In October 1908 Macke had enlisted as a volunteer in the 160th Rhenish Infantry Regiment, initially for one year, returning for shorter periods of military service at intervals thereafter. It seems as if his experience of the army left little trace in his pictorial oeuvre, which certainly does not abound in military subjects: *Hussars* is exceptional in that respect. Indeed, it is remarkable that the Thyssen Collection should possess not one, but two such untypical works by Macke (compare [63]). Though there are numerous depictions of the human figure and of animals to be found in his paintings of 1913 and 1914, these depictions are for the most part gentle, lyrical and seemingly timeless in character, having little in common with the agitated and dramatic mood of the present work.

The picture is painted in what is for Macke an unusually abbreviated manner, the body of the nearest horse, for example, being indicated only in summary fashion, with details of flanks, haunches and accoutrements left largely to the imagination. Rather, the artist is here principally concerned with the representation of rapid movement, the multiple legs of the further horses leading one to suppose that he had, by this date, largely absorbed the lessons of

Notes
1 On Koehler's role as collector and patron of the arts, see Silvia Schmidt, 'Bernhard Koehler – ein Mäzen und Sammler August Mackes und der Künstler des "Blauen Reiter"', *Zeitschrift des Deutschen Vereins für Kunstwissenschaft*, XLII, no.3 (1988): 76–91
2 See the biography printed in Güse (1986), pp.167–70

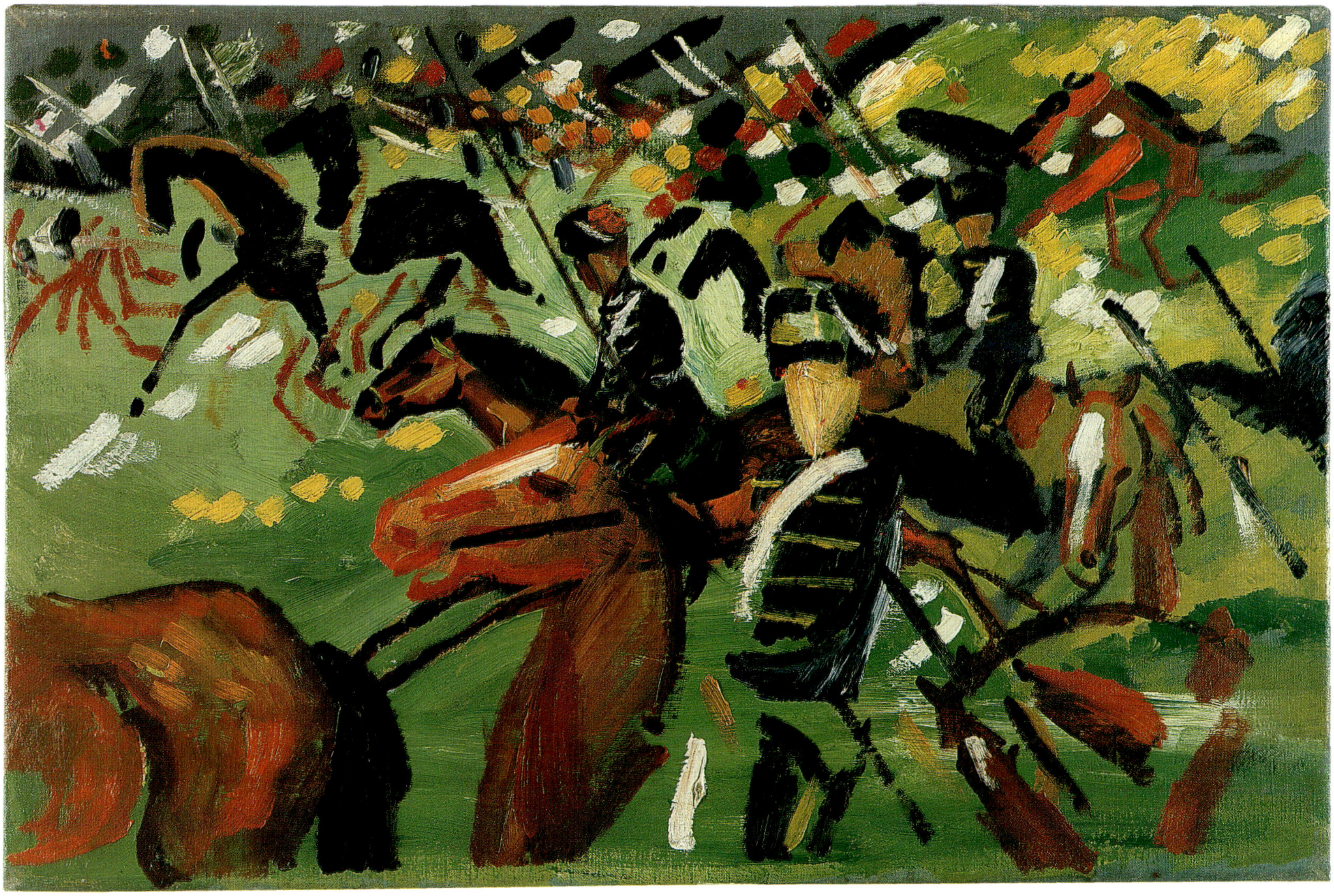

3 At the Futurist exhibition shown at the Kunstsalon Feldmann in October 1912: see ibid., p.167

4 *Fifteen German Expressionist Paintings from the Georg Schäfer Collection, Schweinfurt*, 27 June 1978, lot 9

Italian Futurist painting, examples of which he would have had the opportunity of seeing in Cologne the preceding year.[3]

With his contributions to the Cologne *Sonderbund* and the *Blue Rider* exhibition behind him, his experiences as an organizer of exhibitions and champion of the new, it is not difficult to imagine that Macke saw himself in a Quixotic role, tilting at the windmills of philistinism and reaction, and that the hussars in the present painting had, for him at least, an allegorical significance, riding out to do battle with the foe, spearheading the movement to bring about a new art. On the other hand, it is equally possible that the work is without specific reference to contemporary political or artistic events; in any case, it is almost certainly an imaginary rather than an actual scene the artist has chosen to depict.

Hussars was for some years part of the famous collection owned by Georg Schäfer in Schweinfurt. In 1978, together with other items from the Schäfer collection, it was offered for sale at Christie's, London,[4] and subsequently acquired by Leonard Hutton Galleries, New York, from whom it was purchased by the present owner.

August Macke 1887–1914

63 Circus
Zirkus

1913
Oil on board, 47 × 63.5 cm
Unsigned/undated. On back of board, vestiges of old label of the Sturm Gallery, Berlin, with the date 1913 written in pen; though remains of further inscriptions (presumably name of artist and title of work) are still visible, they are now indecipherable
The cardboard support is slightly convex-warped. Some scratches in the pigment layer have been repaired. Otherwise condition is good
Accession no.1988.21

Provenance
Private collection
Thyssen-Bornemisza Collection, 1988

Exhibitions
Lugano 1989, no.28
Expressionism and Modern German Painting, 1989–90, no.22
Rome 1990–91, no.32

Literature
Vriesen (1957), no.413[1]
Ursula Heiderich, 'Zirkusszene von August Macke. Ein neuentdecktes Gemälde aus dem Jahr 1913', *Kunst und Antiquitäten. Zeitschrift für Kunstfreunde, Sammler und Museen*, no.1 (1988): 80–84[2]
See also Janice McCullagh, 'The Tightrope Walker: An Expressionist Image', *Art Bulletin*, LXVI, no.4 (December 1984): 633–44

The subject of the present painting is unusual in Macke's oeuvre, which rarely shows any dramatic incident such as depicted here: a bareback rider has fallen from her horse, and an anxious group of acrobats bends over her and prepares to carry her off. Their concerned expressions, however, are partially concealed by a thin layer of over-painting. The drama of the subject is conveyed by gesture, not by facial expression.

Macke painted relatively few oil paintings of acrobats and circus artists. Closest of all to *Circus* in both style and subject is his 1914 version of another circus scene, the *Tightrope Walker*, now in the Städtisches Kunstmuseum, Bonn (fig.1). Such themes are, on the other hand,

Notes
1 See n.6
2 I am grateful to Dr Ursula Heiderich, Syke-Okel, for her assistance, and her advice in connection with the picture

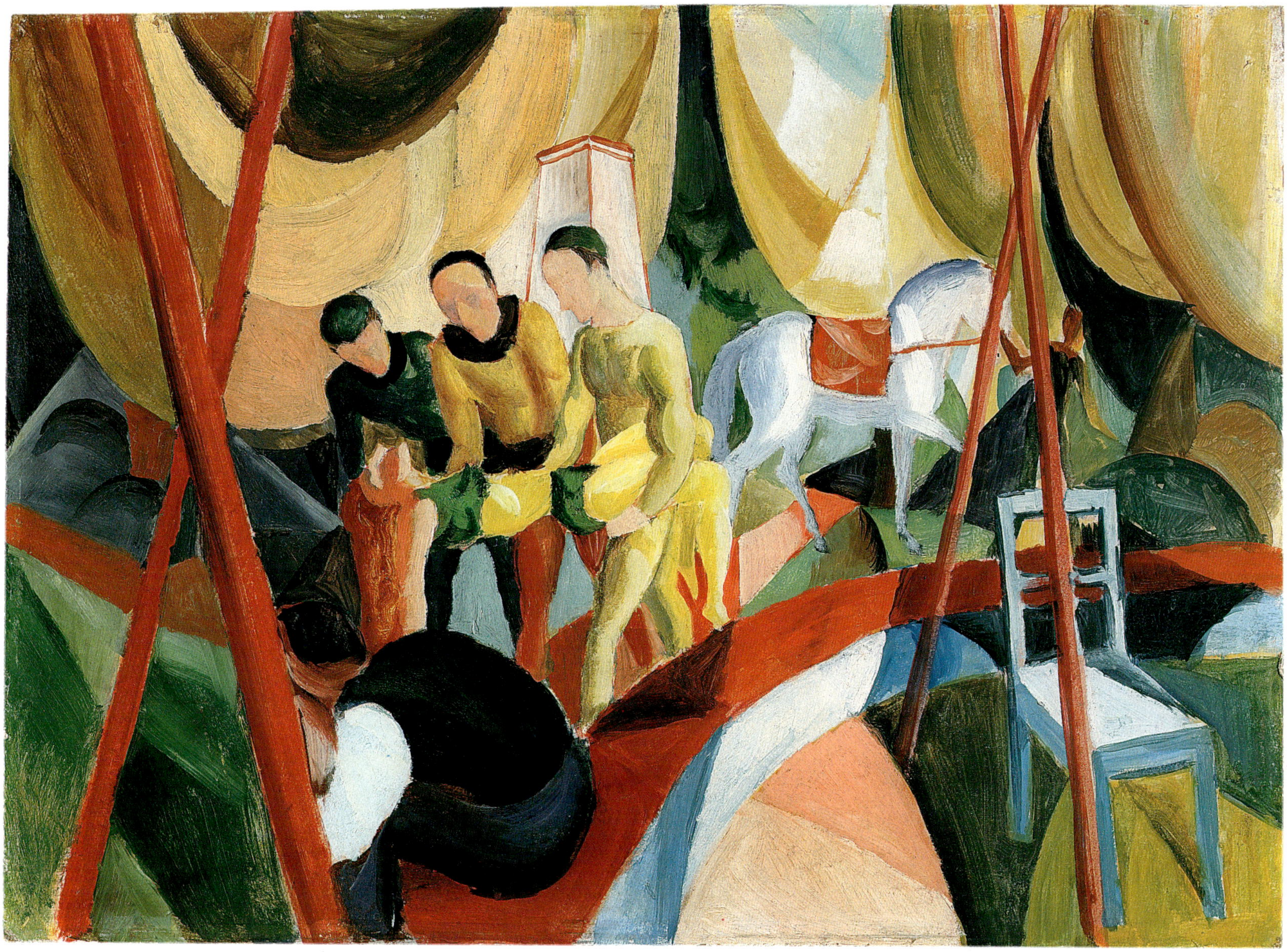

represented more frequently in his watercolours and drawings. Two works on paper, in particular, exhibit an especially close relationship to the Thyssen Collection's *Circus* painting: the drawing entitled *Fallen* (*Gestürzt*) of 1911 (fig.3) and the charcoal drawing *Circus Scene* of 1913–14 (fig.4).

Two factors may have been influential in causing Macke to occupy himself with the depiction of acrobats and circus scenes during the autumn and winter of 1913–14: his move to Hilterfingen in Switzerland, where he and his family rented a house on the shore of Lake Thun, and his friendship with the Swiss artist Louis Moilliet, with whom he travelled to North Africa in April 1914 (see *Woman on a Divan* [66]). According to Elisabeth Macke's recollections, a Swiss family of circus artists by the name of Knie would sometimes perform on warm evenings in the open air on the market square in Hilterfingen. She particularly remembered the death-defying stunts of the tightrope walkers, with the high wire stretched way above the darkened square: 'an unusual spectacle in richly contrasting colours such as one rarely sees. It all made a deep artistic impression on August, who translated these experiences in masterly fashion into numerous drawings and paintings.'[3] But it is also significant that Moilliet was himself working

Notes

3 Erdmann-Macke (1962), p.231

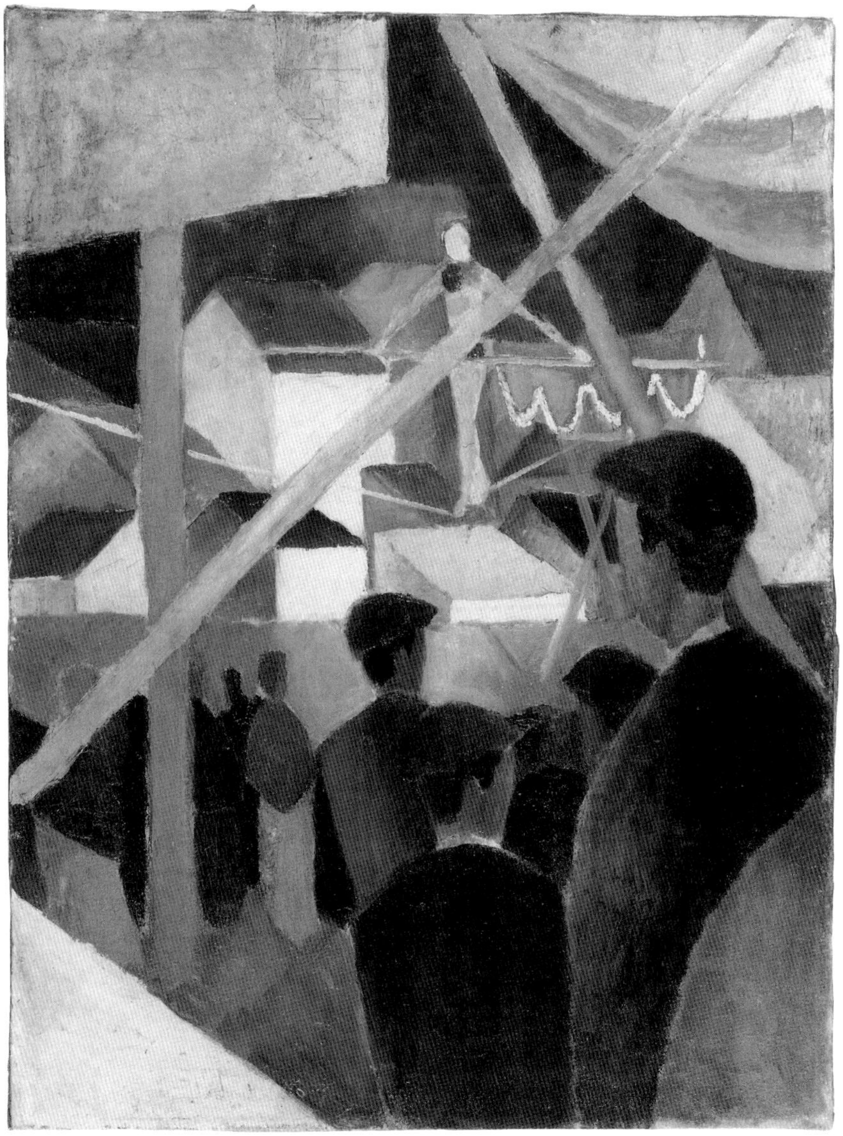

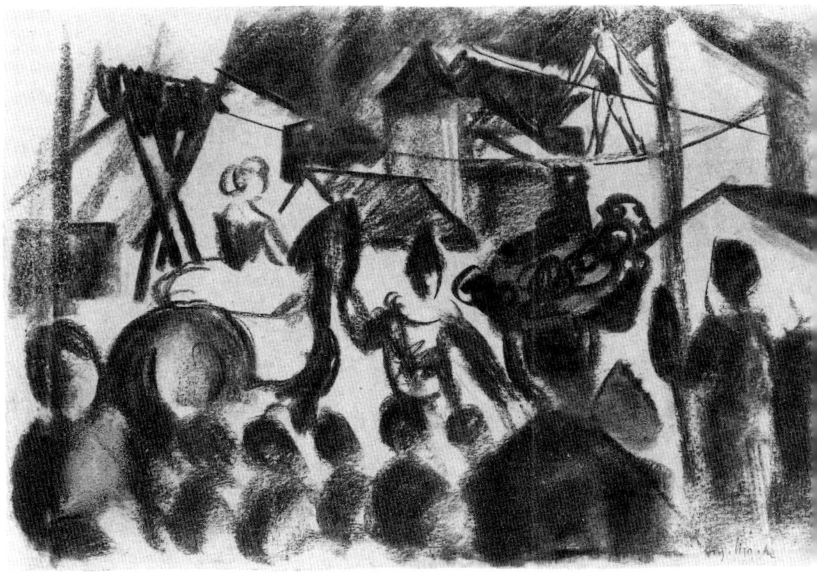

FIG 1 August Macke, *Tightrope Walker*, 1914, oil on canvas, 82 × 60 cm (Bonn, Städtisches Kunstmuseum, inv. no.G 3266)

FIG 2 August Macke, *Circus Scene: Tightrope Walker, Bareback Rider and Clown*, charcoal, 24.2 × 34.7 cm (Bonn, Städtisches Kunstmuseum, inv. no.Z 533 [81])

on a large circus painting at this time (*In the Circus*, 1914–15, Basle, Kunstmuseum).[4] He and Macke were constantly together during this period, and it appears that Macke advised him on the completion of his picture, even assisting him in its execution. Moilliet subsequently acknowledged the debt he owed to Macke, especially for having explained to him Delaunay's ideas on colour.[5]

Macke's *Circus* remained unknown for a long time, and has only recently been rediscovered. When first examined, an old label was found on the back of the painting, indicating that it had been shown at Walden's Sturm gallery in Berlin. Though the name of the artist was illegible, vestiges of a typewritten title 'Zirkus', together with a handwritten 'II' and the date 1913 could still be deciphered. Ursula Heiderich, in her article announcing the discovery, on the evidence of a notebook preserved in the Macke-Archiv in Münster identified the painting with no.36 in a handwritten list of works exhibited at Der Sturm in January 1914, the 'II' having been added by Elisabeth Macke in order to distinguish it from another circus painting shown as no.25 in the same exhibition.[6] The subsequent history of the work remains unclear until it was acquired by a private collector after the end of the Second World War.

4 See Werner Schmalenbach, 'Louis Moilliet', in Güse (1982), pp.152ff; also Brigitte Kaul, 'Louis Moilliet und die Reise nach Tunesien 1914', in ibid., pp.158ff
5 Kaul, op. cit., p.161
6 Vriesen, who evidently could not have known the present work in the original, identified the painting 'Zirkuszene II' from Macke's handwritten list with no.246 in his catalogue raisonné of the artist's work. Heiderich suggests that it is, on the contrary, identical with Vriesen no.413; see Heiderich, op. cit., p.83

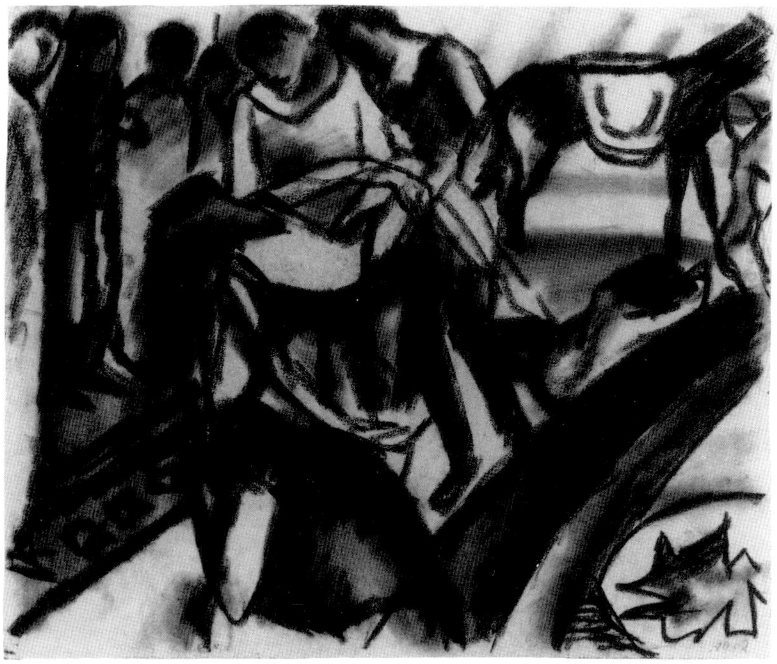

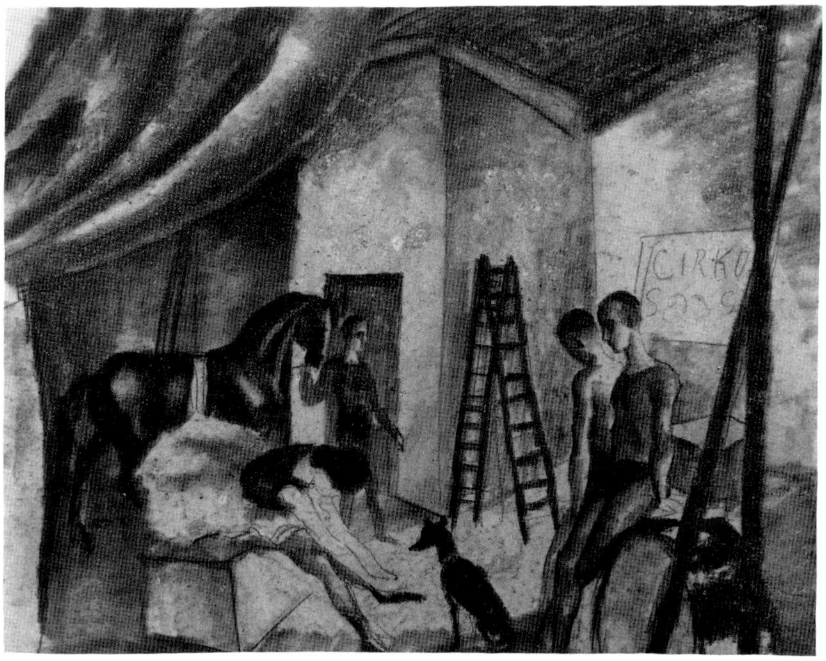

FIG 3 August Macke, *Fallen*, 1911, black chalk, 27 × 32 cm (Private collection)

FIG 4 August Macke, *Circus Scene*, 1913–14, charcoal, 30 × 40 cm (Private collection)

August Macke 1887–1914

64 Promenade à Trois
Spaziergang zu Dreien

1914
Oil on canvas, 56.3 × 33.7 cm
Signed/dated on back of canvas: 'August Macke 1914'; inscribed on stretcher: 'August Macke Spaziergang zu Dreien'
Extensive cupping, with many traces of previous lifting of the paint layer, since secured. The painting is unvarnished. The canvas has been nailed to the front of the stretcher
Accession no.1962.8

Provenance
Estate of the artist
Private collection, Bonn
Galerie Aenne Abels, Cologne
Thyssen-Bornemisza Collection, 1962

Exhibitions
Munich 1949, no.186
Basel, Kunsthalle, 1950, *Der Blaue Reiter 1908–14. Wegbereiter und Zeitgenossen*, no.152
New York, Fine Arts Associates, 1952, *August Macke*, p.13, no.18 [as 'Trio']
The Hague, Gemeentemuseum, 1953–4, *August Macke*, no.66
Amsterdam, Stedelijk Museum, 1954, *August Macke*, no.26
Zurich, Kunsthaus, 1954, *August Macke 1887–1914*, no.57
Brunswick, Kunstverein, 1954, *August Macke 1887–1914. Oelbilder, Aquarelle und Handzeichnungen 1907–1914*, no.82
Münster, Kunstverein/Westfälisches Landesmuseum, 1957, *August Macke. Gedenkausstellung zum 70. Geburtstag*, no.99
Munich, Städtische Galerie im Lenbachhaus, 1962, *August Macke*, no.154
Bremen 1975, no.42
Lugano 1975, no.36
Brussels/Paris 1977–8, no.53
Lugano 1978, no.64
Modern Masters from the Thyssen-Bornemisza Collection, 1984–6, no.70
Münster, Westfälisches Landesmuseum/Bonn, Kunstmuseum/Munich, Städtische Galerie im Lenbachhaus, 1986–7, *August Macke. Gemälde, Aquarelle, Zeichnungen*, no.122
Lugano 1989, no.29

Literature
Vriesen (1957), no.477
Kiel (1974), p.90, ill. p.91
Güse (1986), p.470

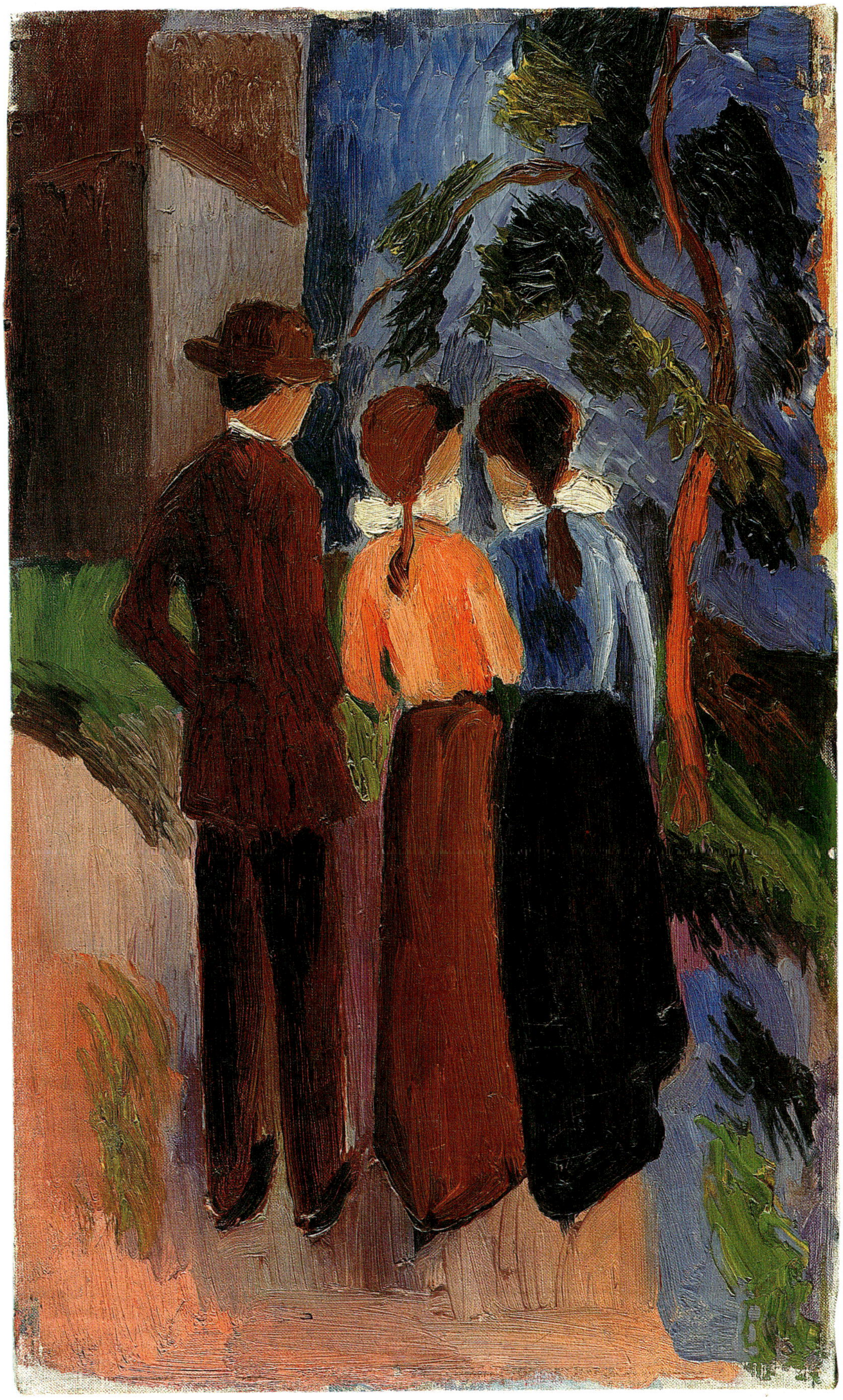

According to Macke's biographer, Gustav Vriesen, *Promenade à Trois* was painted in the artist's studio in Bonn in July 1914. This assertion is supported by the existence of a sketchbook in use in Bonn during June–July 1914, which contains several figure studies of promenanding groups, including on p.33 a drawing identified as *Drei Mädchen im Freien* (Three Girls in the Open Air: fig.1).[1] In style and subject, however, the painting is clearly linked with the other *Promenade* pictures of winter 1913–14, executed at Hilterfingen, on Lake Thun in Switzerland, where Macke and his family rented a villa, the Haus Rosengarten, from September 1913 onwards.

At Hilterfingen, Macke embarked on a series of, for the most part, multi-figure compositions, the dominant theme of which is that of the stroll or promenade, often along the lakeside or through shaded gardens, the figures almost invariably seen in half profile or from behind. These are among the most important of his mature works. The influence of Delaunay, so apparent in his paintings of 1912–13 with their abstract forms and broken planes of colour, is here less obvious, and Macke has achieved a new-found subtlety and confidence in his handling of colour.

Macke left Hilterfingen for Bonn early in June 1914, breaking his journey for a couple of weeks in Kandern; his presence in Bonn is documented only after 19th June. No oil paintings can be dated to early June 1914, since his materials had been sent directly from Hilterfingen to Bonn; in Kandern, Macke concentrated particularly on watercolours, including designs for objects of decorative art.[2] *Promenade à Trois* can thus be ascribed with some precision to the weeks between 19th June and 8th August 1914, the date on which Macke, now a lieutenant in the 160th Rhenish infantry regiment, left for the Western Front.[3] He was killed in action in France on 26 September 1914.

Notes

1 See Heiderich (1987), II, p.1113, ill. p.1112

2 Ibid., I, p.152

3 See chronology printed in Güse (1986), p.178–9

FIG 1 August Macke, *Three Girls in the Open Air*, ink, 16.2 × 10.2 cm, from sketchbook LXX, June–July 1914, p.33 (Münster, Westfälisches Landesmuseum für Kunst und Kulturgeschichte, Macke Archive)

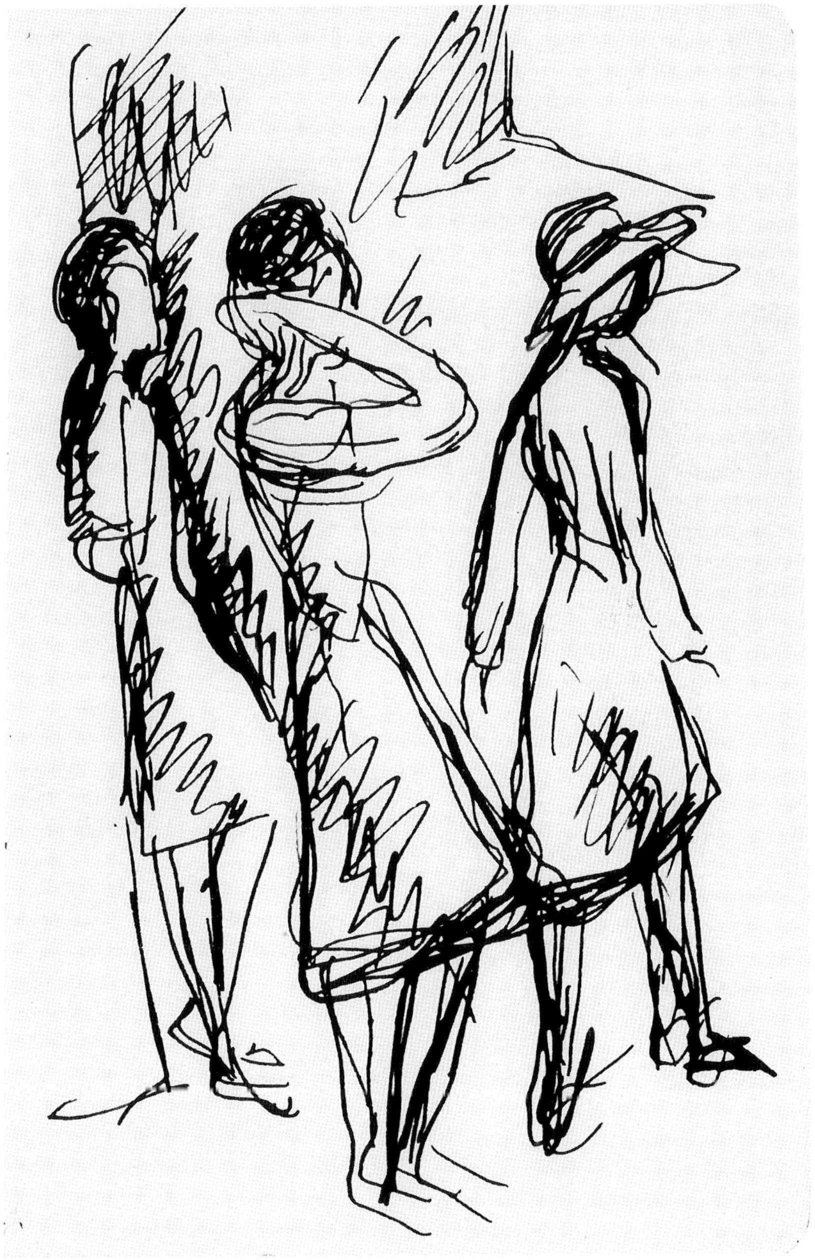

August Macke 1887–1914

65 Flowers

*c*1913
Watercolour, Indian and coloured inks on paper, 28.5 × 23.5 cm
Unsigned/undated
On the verso, estate stamp, inscribed: 'V[riesen] 262'; with further inscription relating to an earlier inventory of the artist's coloured drawings: 'F[arbige] T[usche] Nr.30'
Paper is somewhat yellow; otherwise condition is good
Accession no.1969.9

Provenance
Lothar Erdmann, Bonn
Elisabeth Erdmann-Macke, Bonn
Galerie Aenne Abels, Cologne
Thyssen-Bornemisza Collection, 1969

Exhibitions
Hanover, Kestner-Gesellschaft, 1935, *August Macke*, no.84
Bielefeld, Städtisches Kunsthaus, 1957, *Macke 1887–1914. Aquarell-Ausstellung*, no.262
Bremen 1975, no.43
Münster, Westfälisches Landesmuseum/Bonn, Kunstmuseum/Munich, Städtische Galerie im Lenbachhaus, 1986–7, *August Macke. Gemälde, Aquarelle, Zeichnungen*, no.154

Literature
Vriesen (1957), no.A-262
Kiel (1974), p.87 with ill.
Güse (1986), p.478

This watercolour is closely related to several of Macke's 1912 designs for embroideries based on ornamental plant forms. It may have been intended as a study for a fabric design or for some object of applied art.[1]

Note
1 On Macke's ornamental designs see Dominik Bartmann, 'Elemente der Tradition und Avantgarde in Mackes kunsthandwerklichen Arbeiten', in Güse (1986), pp.141–8

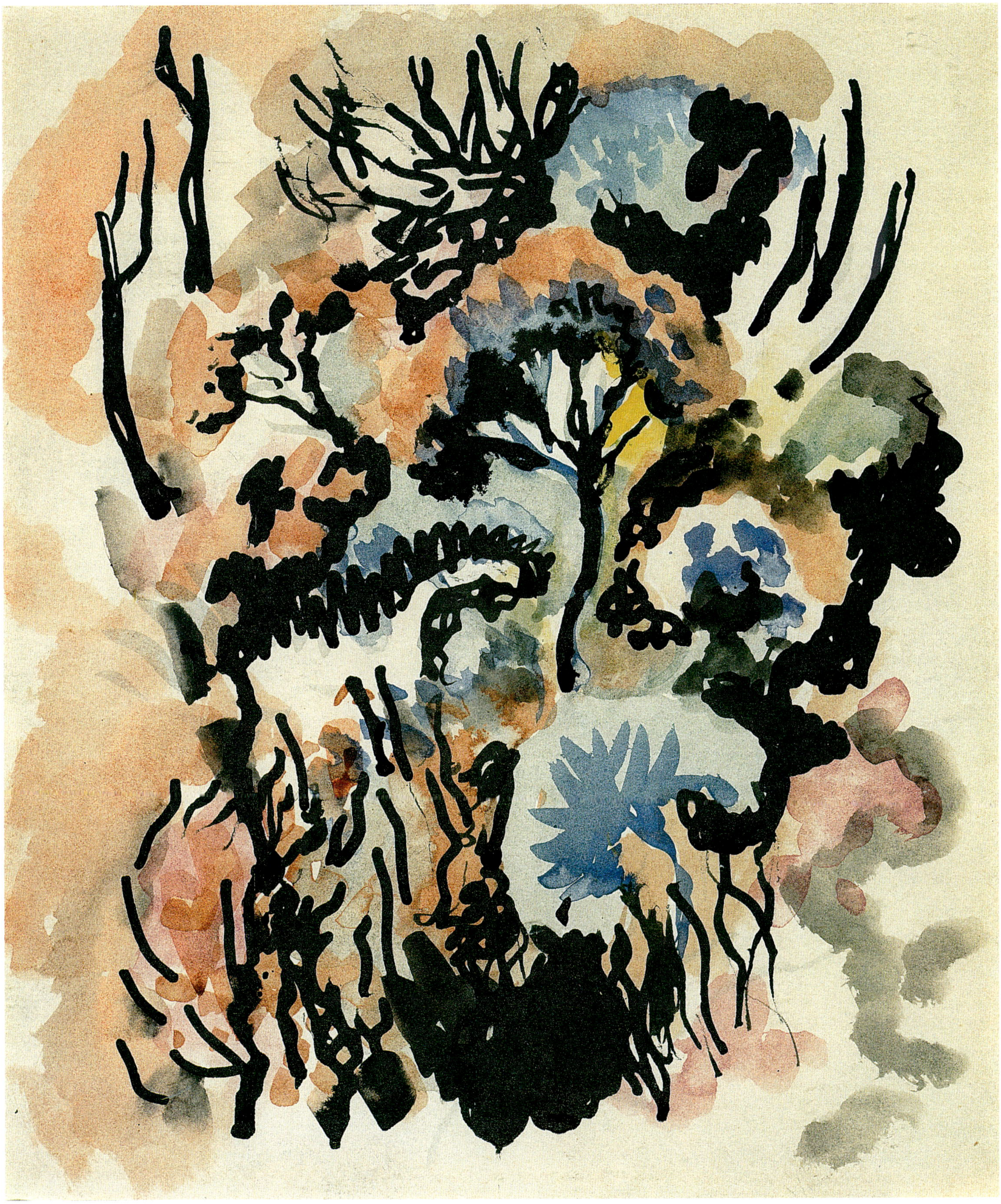

August Macke 1887–1914

66 Woman on a Divan

1914
Watercolour on paper, 27 × 20 cm
Unsigned/undated; on back of sheet, estate stamp, inscribed 'Aquarell aus Tunis 1914. Frau auf Ruhebett' and 'August Macke. Frau auf Ruhebett (Tunis) 1914.'[1] The handwritten number '8', also inscribed on the back of the sheet, relates to an earlier inventory of the artist's Tunisian watercolours
In good condition
Accession no.1969.10

Provenance
Estate of the artist
Dr Wolfgang Macke, Bonn
Private collection, Willich bei Krefeld
Galerie R.N.Ketterer, Campione d'Italia
Thyssen-Bornemisza Collection, 1969

Exhibitions
Cologne, Museen der Stadt Köln in der alten Universität, 1947, *August Macke Gedächtnisausstellung*, no.171
Trier, Werkschule, 1947, *August Macke Gedächtnisausstellung*, no.66
Berne, Kunsthalle, 1948, *Lehmbruck – Macke – Marc*, no.113
Oldenburg, Kunstverein, 1948–9, *August Macke, Gemälde, Aquarelle und Zeichnungen*, no.61
Bochum, Richard-Baltz-Haus, 1949, *August Macke Gedächtnisausstellung*, no.61
Duisburg, Städtisches Kunstmuseum, 1949, *August Macke*, no.91
Dortmund, Museum am Ostwall, 1949, *August Macke Gedächtnisausstellung*, no.95
Munich 1949, no.210
New York, Fine Arts Associates, 1952, *August Macke*, p.14, no.3
The Hague, Gemeentemuseum, 1953–4, *August Macke*, no.102
Amsterdam, Stedelijk Museum, 1954, *August Macke*, no.57
Zurich, Kunsthaus, 1954, *August Macke 1887–1914*, no.95
Brunswick, Kunstverein, 1954, *August Macke 1887–1914. Oelbilder, Aquarelle und Handzeichnungen 1907–1914*, no.167
Bonn, Städtische Kunstsammlungen, 1955, *Tunisaquarelle von August Macke 1914*, no.8
Kassel, Museum Fridericianum, 1955, *documenta* [1], no.343
Münster, Kunstverein/Westfälisches Landesmuseum, 1957, *August Macke Gedenkausstellung zum 70. Geburtstag*, no.117
Bielefeld, Städtisches Kunsthaus, 1957, *Macke 1887–1914. Aquarell-Ausstellung*, no.461
Reutlingen, Spendhaus, 1958, *August Macke*, no.103
London, Marlborough Fine Art, 1959, *Art in Revolt. Germany 1905–25*, no.82
Bremen 1975, no.44
Münster, Westfälisches Landesmuseum/Bonn, Kunstmuseum/Munich, Städtische Galerie im Lenbachhaus, 1986–7, *August Macke. Gemälde, Aquarelle, Zeichnungen*, no.189

Literature
Vriesen (1957), no.A-461
R.N.Ketterer, *Moderne Kunst VI*, Campione d'Italia (Galerie R.N.Ketterer) 1969, p.122, no.73, ill. p.123
Kiel (1974), p.88, ill. p.89
Ernst Gerhard Güse, 'Raum und Fläche – Europa und der Orient. Zu August Mackes Tunis-Aquarellen', in Güse (1982), pp.134f
Güse (1986), pp.111, 483–4
Moeller (1989), p.14 and fig.58
See also Klee (1957), p.311; G. Büsch, W. Holzhausen *et al.*, *Die Tunisreise. Aquarelle und Zeichnungen von August Macke*, Cologne (DuMont) 1958; Uta Laxner, *Stilanalytische Untersuchungen zu den Aquarellen der Tunisreise 1914: Macke, Klee, Moilliet*, Bonn 1967

Note
1 As Güse observes, none of the titles given to the Tunisian watercolours can be ascribed with certainty to the artist himself. It seems likely that the inscriptions on the back of *Woman on a Divan* would have been added by Macke's widow Elisabeth after his death, and that the title was her own invention, possibly in collaboration with the artist Louis Moilliet: see Güse (1982), p.130

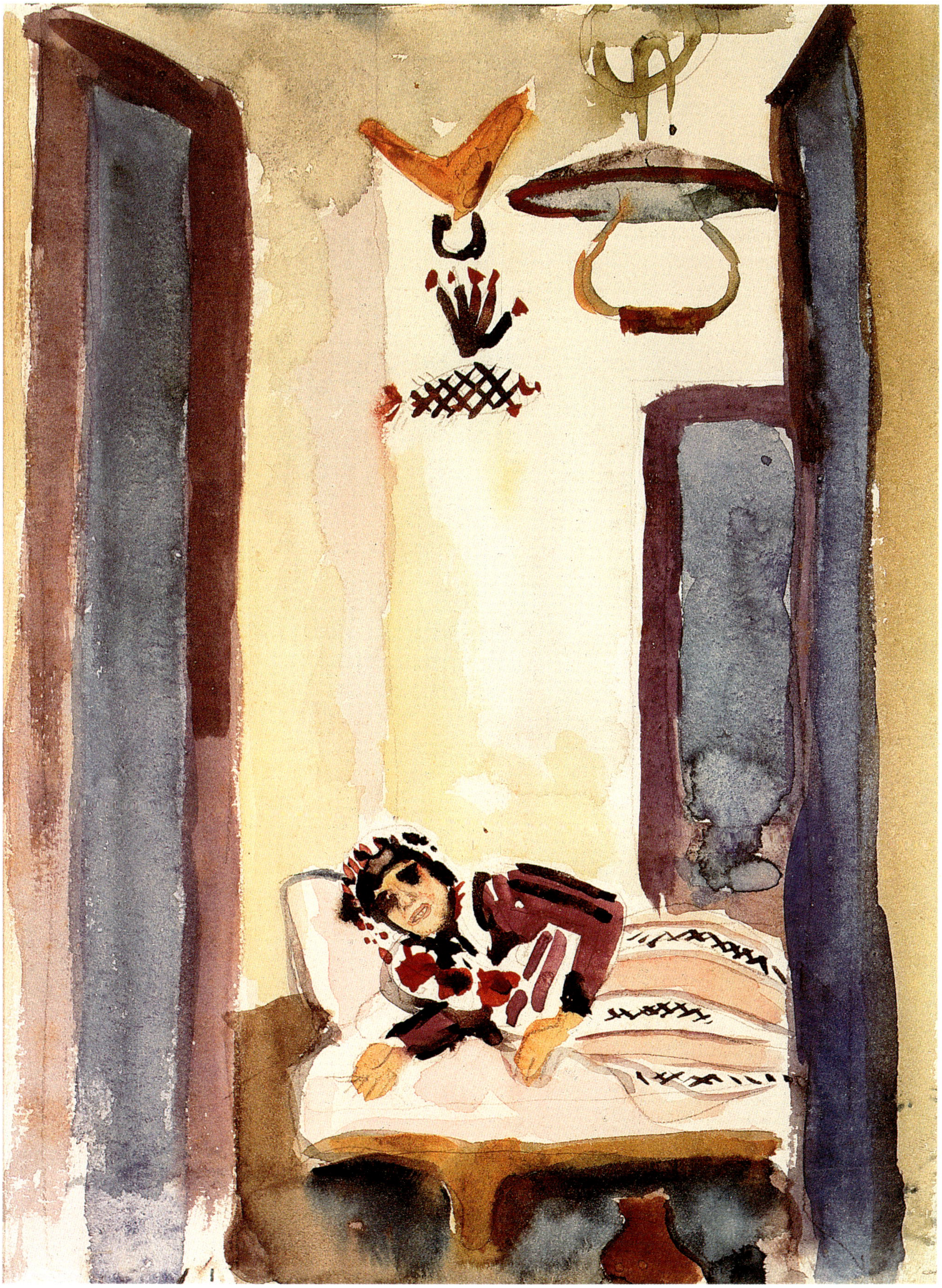

Woman on a Divan is one of a celebrated group of works, some thirty-eight in number, known as the Tunisian watercolours, which Macke painted during a visit to North Africa he made in April 1914, accompanied by his friends Paul Klee and Louis Moilliet. Of the three, only Moilliet had been there before, and presumably had some knowledge of the realities of life in Tunisia. Perhaps for this reason, it was he who produced the smallest number of works directly inspired by the experience of this 1914 visit.[2] For Klee and Macke, on the other hand, Tunisia came as a revelation, not only because it provided a wealth of 'exotic' motifs, but also because of the intensity of its light and brilliance of its colours. By Klee's own account, this experience marked the beginning of his liberation as a colourist.[3]

Macke's mastery of brilliant, luminous colour had come somewhat earlier, accelerated by his acquaintance with both the theories and paintings of Delaunay. Like Klee, he produced a succession of watercolours based on architectural and topographical themes drawn from Tunis itself and from locations such as Kairouan and Hammamet; he, however, was the only one of the three artists to treat directly themes inspired by the souk, the harem and the brothel.

Relatively few works of art can be dated with confidence not merely to a particular year or a particular month, but to a particular day. In this instance, however, letters from Macke to his wife Elisabeth and her uncle Bernhard Koehler, Klee's diaries and Moilliet's recollections[4] allow us to reconstruct the chronology of the trip and the circumstances under which [66] was created with a fair degree of precision. The three friends docked at the port of Tunis on Tuesday 7 April 1914. Their second full day in the city, Thursday 9 April, was according to Klee's account bright but windy, and the artists paid a visit to the harbour area, painting and sketching.[5] On the same day, they also penetrated the brothel quarter;[6] inspired by this visit, Macke painted and drew a number of depictions of street girls and harem scenes, of which *Woman on a Divan* is one.

Broadly speaking, Macke's Tunisian drawings and watercolours may be divided into two groups: a larger group of works, executed directly in front of the motif, which reflect his experiences and impressions of this unfamiliar and colourful environment, and a somewhat smaller number of more calculated and intricate compositions almost certainly worked up after the event – the product of memory and reflection. Quite apart from any stylistic considerations, the circumstances of its creation alone suggest that *Woman on a Divan* should be ascribed to this latter group of works done from memory. In his diaries, Klee recorded that it would have been tempting to try to photograph some of the more picturesque scenes and inhabitants, but that the ladies of pleasure would permit everything except photography: 'as soon as they see a camera, they vanish';[7] while according to Moilliet's recollection, their visit to the brothel quarter was thought to be sufficently risky to necessitate taking a police escort.[8] These accounts lend support to the hypothesis that Macke would scarcely have attempted drawing or sketching on the spot, and that works such as *Woman on a Divan* or *Three Girls in front of a House* (fig.1) would have been worked up later, though almost certainly on the same day, perhaps even within hours of the actual visit.

Notes

2 Only three watercolours and a small number of sketches and drawings, according to Brigitte Kaul, 'Louis Moilliet und die Reise nach Tunesien 1914', in Güse (1982), pp.158f. Moilliet had first visited Tunis in 1908, returning the following year for a longer stay which encompassed the winter and spring of 1909–10

3 'Die Farbe hat mich. Ich brauche nicht mehr nach ihr zu haschen. Sie hat mich für immer, ich weiss das . . . ich und die Farbe sind eins. Ich bin Maler.' (Klee, op. cit., pp.307–8)

4 In conversation with Walter Holzhausen: see W. Holzhausen, 'Die Tunisreise, Erinnerung und Geschichte', in Macke (1958), pp.18–24

5 Klee (1957), p.298

6 Macke wrote to Elisabeth the following day, 10 April 1914, describing the 'splendid sight' of the women standing in doorways sunning themselves, 'as colourful and clear as stained-glass windows'; the letter is reprinted in Erdmann-Macke (1962), pp.241–2

7 Klee (1957), p.311

8 Macke (1958), p.18; Güse (1982), p.134

FIG 1 August Macke, *Three Girls in Front of a House*, 1914, watercolour, 26.5 × 21 cm (Private collection)

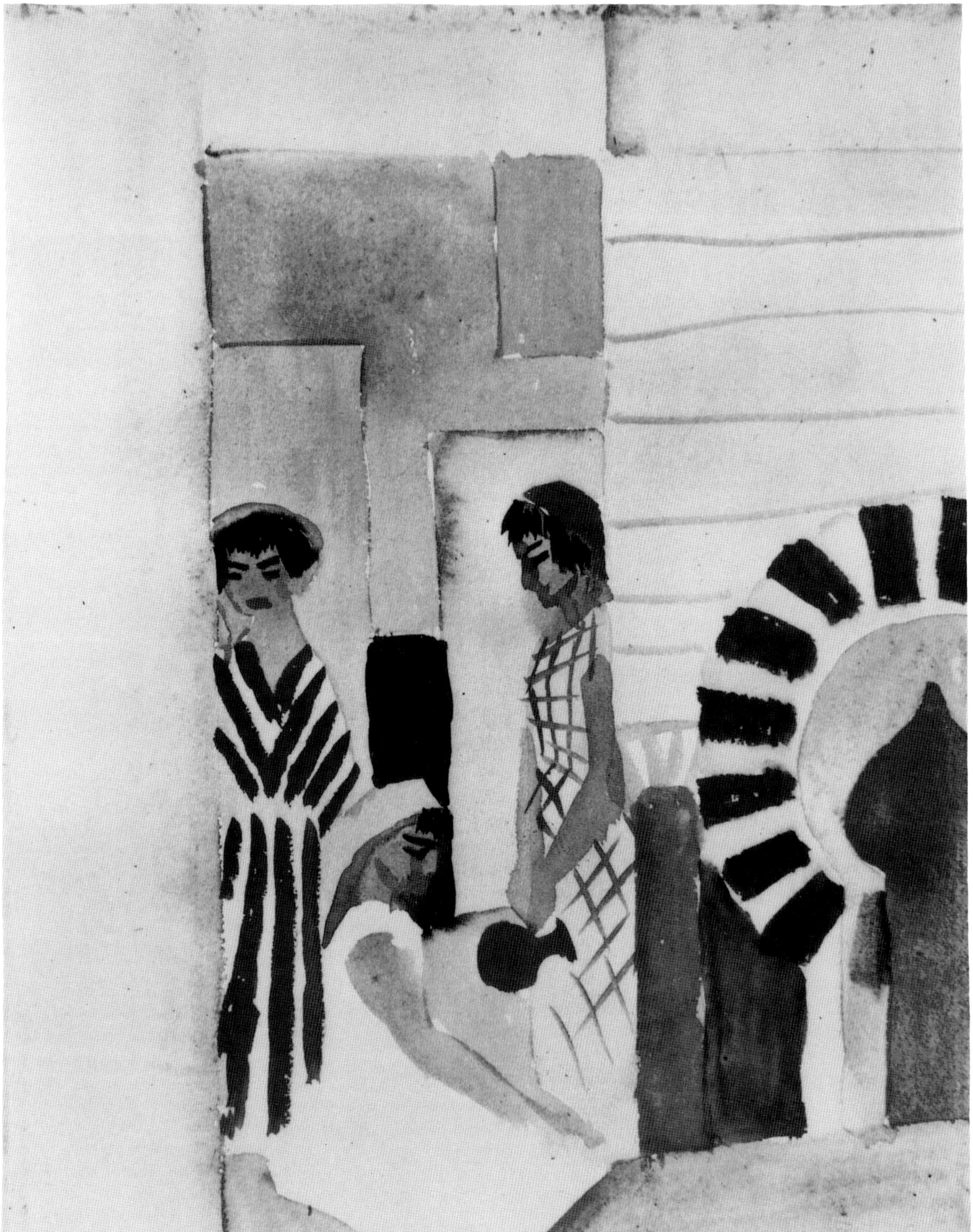

Jeanne Mammen 1890–1976

67 Street Girl
Strassenmädchen

*c*1913–14 (?)
Pastel and white chalk on paper mounted on board, 46.5 × 40.7 cm
Unsigned/undated; inscribed on back of board: 'Strassenmädchen'; with estate stamp: 'Nachlass Jeanne Mammen'
The work was previously in poor condition, in all probability the result of damage suffered many years or even decades ago in the artist's studio. At the time of its purchase in 1980, the drawing showed signs of oxidation staining and exhibited numerous water stains and abrasions. The paper had lifted and cockled in several places, resulting in colour loss and an uneven surface appearance. There were also a number of scratches, and two small tears at the extreme edges of the paper.
The sheet was restored in May 1990. The conspicuous water stains were mechanically broken down with a scalpel, and the areas of colour loss touched and stumped in with fine brush and pastel. The tears at the edges were repaired and the work was attached to new acid-free board, and reset in the original mount and frame[1]
Accession no.1980.61

Provenance
Estate of the artist
Fischer Fine Art, London
Thyssen-Bornemisza Collection, 1980

Exhibitions
London, Fischer Fine Art, 1980, *Jeanne Mammen 1890–1976. Works from 1914–1930*, no.55

Literature
See *Jeanne Mammen 1890–1976*, herausgegeben von der Jeanne Mammen-Gesellschaft in Verbindung mit der Berlinischen Galerie, v of *Bildende Kunst in Berlin*, Berlin/Stuttgart (Edition Cantz) 1978; Dorothea von Stetten, 'Jeanne Mammen Ante Portas', in *Jeanne Mammen 1890–1976. Gemälde, Aquarelle, Zeichnungen, Lithographien*, exh. cat., Reutlingen, Hans Thoma-Gesellschaft, 1981

Jeanne Mammen was the daughter of a German businessman who settled in Paris during the years before the First World War. She studied art first at the Académie Julian but then, attracted perhaps by the presence of artists such as Delville and Khnopff, enrolled at the Académie Royale des Beaux-Arts in Brussels, where she studied painting and drawing between 1908 and 1910. French and Belgian Symbolism was the most important formative influence on her early work, as evidenced by her illustrations for Flaubert's *Tentation de Saint Antoine*, a book which fascinated artists of quite different persuasions over a period of many decades, among them Rops, Redon and Beckmann.[2] Her literary interests embraced the writings of authors such as Huysmans, Wilde and E.T.A.Hoffmann; in 1931–2 she produced a cycle of seven lithographic illustrations for Pierre Louÿs's *Chansons de Bilitis* (which also inspired, among others, the composer Claude Debussy). In 1967 her translation of Rimbaud's *Les Illuminations* was published by Insel-Verlag, Frankfurt.

Forced to flee France by the outbreak of the Great War, Jeanne Mammen moved to Berlin in 1916, where her new 'realistic' style soon brought her to the attention of society and fashion magazines, as well as satirical journals such as *Jugend* and *Simplicissimus*. Active as an illustrator during the 1920s and early 1930s, during which period the human figure is the most important theme in her art, the advent of the Nazis in 1933 marked the onset of a period of isolation during which it was virtually impossible either to sell or to exhibit her work. In contrast to the officially sanctioned tendency, Mammen's paintings of the Nazi period became defiantly cubo-expressionistic in style; after 1945 she began constructing relief figures out of wire – figures subsequently incorporated into her paintings. During the post-war decades, the dominant tendency in her work was a kind of lyrical abstractionism, but she also experimented with a variety of media, including collages constructed out of tin-foil.

Notes
1 I am indebted to Roy Graf, of Plan Conservation Ltd, Reading, who was responsible for restoring the sheet, for allowing me to examine the work with him prior to treatment and for providing information both before and after restoration was completed. It is on this information that the accompanying remarks on condition are largely based
2 Compare entry for [4]
3 I am grateful to Professor Eberhard Roters, one of the founder members of the Jeanne Mammen-Gesellschaft, Berlin, for his opinion on the dating of this work

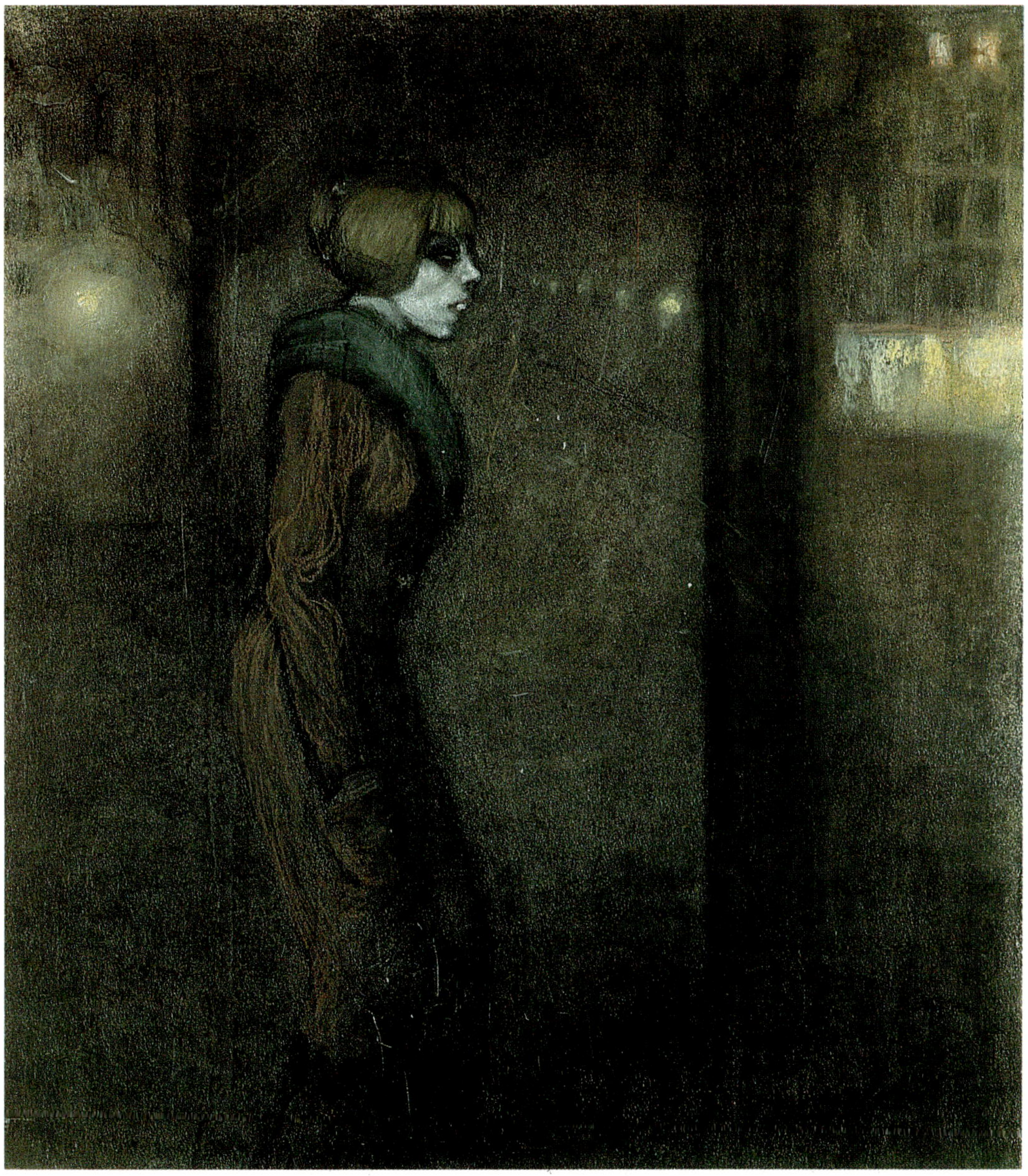

In the course of a creative life which extended over some seven decades, Mammen rarely signed and, as a matter of principle, never dated her pictures, believing that knowledge of the date at which it was created added nothing to one's understanding or appreciation of a work of art. For this reason, leaving aside a small number of documented works (for example, the published illustrations), any attempt at dating can only be undertaken on the basis of stylistic criteria, and is fraught with difficulty. To judge by its style, the present pastel would appear to mark the transition between her symbolist and realistic periods, and should hence be ascribed, albeit tentatively, to the years around 1913–14.[3]

Technically, the artist's handling of the medium in *Street Girl* and the effect produced are extremely subtle. The large areas of dark-toned pastel, heavily worked, succeed in conveying the murky darkness of the street, while subsequent touches of softer pastel evoke flickering street lights and (at extreme right) the brighter lights of a shop window, seen through the fog. The figure of the street girl herself, positioned between two trees only the dim outlines of which are seen, has a ghostly pallor, the high tones of the face and especially the cheeks created by the application of white chalk contrasting starkly with the heavily kohl-rimmed eyes.

Franz Marc 1880–1916

68 The Dream
Der Traum

1912
Oil on canvas, 100.5 × 135.5 cm
Signed lower right: 'Marc'; signed on back of canvas: 'Fz Marc Sindelsdorf'; inscribed on stretcher: 'Franz Marc – "Der Traum". Besitzer Kandinsky'
The painting is unvarnished. The canvas is tight with some bulges along the top edge. There are small areas of cracking immediately above the back of the foreground horse and a few surface scratches. Otherwise condition is good
Accession no.1978.15

Provenance
Estate of Wassily Kandinsky
Nina Kandinsky, Paris
Leonard Hutton Galleries, New York
Thyssen-Bornemisza Collection, 1978

Exhibitions
Frankfurt am Main, Kunstsalon Ludwig Schames, 1912, *Franz Marc*, no.2
Berlin, Der Sturm, 1913, *14. Ausstellung. Franz Marc*
Munich, Neue Secession, 1916, *Franz Marc Gedächtnisausstellung*, no.108
Berlin, Der Sturm, 1916, *46. Ausstellung. Franz Marc Gedächtnisausstellung. Gemälde und Aquarelle/Holzschnitte*, no.14
Wiesbaden, Nassauischer Kunstverein, 1917, *Franz Marc Gedächtnisausstellung*, no.38
Berlin, Nationalgalerie (Kronprinzenpalais), 1922, *Gedächtnis-Ausstellung Franz Marc*
New York, Brooklyn Museum, 1926–7, *International Exhibition of Modern Art*, no.91[1]
New York, Leonard Hutton Galleries, 1963, *Der Blaue Reiter*, no.14
Munich, Städtische Galerie im Lenbachhaus, 1963, *Franz Marc*, no.125
Hamburg, Kunstverein, 1963–4, *Franz Marc. Gemälde, Gouachen, Zeichnungen, Skulpturen*, no.40
Florence 1964, no.384
Marseilles, Musée Cantini, 1965, *Expressionisme Allemand 1900–1920*, no.108
Turin, Galleria Civica d'Arte Moderna, 1971, *Il Cavaliere Azzurro*, ill. p.149
New York, Leonard Hutton Galleries, 1977, *Der Blaue Reiter und sein Kreis*, no.50 [as '1911']
Lugano 1978, no.67
Australian tour 1979–80, no.31
USA tour 1982–4, no.10
Modern Masters from the Thyssen-Bornemisza Collection, 1984–6, no.73
Budapest/Szombathely 1985–6, no.36
Lugano 1989, no.27
Expressionism and Modern German Painting, 1989–90, no.23
Rome 1990–91, no.33

Literature
Schardt (1936), I/1912/27
Lankheit (1970), no.172
Lankheit (1976), p.84

In retrospect, his friend Kandinsky strenuously denied the charge that Franz Marc was merely an animal painter.[2] In fact, animals are by far the most frequently occurring subject in his art, much of which has to do with seeing the world or nature though animals' eyes[3] – what Marc himself called the 'animalization of art'.[4] Only rarely do human figures play any significant role in his paintings after 1910 – the years of his artistic maturity. There is, however, a number of works which treat the theme of the pastoral, depicting figures in a landscape setting, and

Notes
1 Also shown in revised form New York, Anderson Galleries/Buffalo, NY, Albright Art Gallery/Toronto, Art Gallery. *The Dream* was no.51 at the Anderson Galleries and no.55 at both Buffalo and Toronto: see Bohan (1982), especially pp.48f, 148–9
2 'Franz Marc' (1936), in Lindsay (1982), pp.793f, 795; see also 'Unsere Freundschaft', in Lankheit (1960), p.47
3 See, e.g., Lankheit (1978), pp.99–100 ('Aufzeichnungen auf Blättern in Quart', originally published in Franz Marc, *Briefe, Aufzeichnungen und Aphorismen*, Berlin 1920, pp.121f; trans. as 'How Does a Horse See the World?', in Herschel B.Chipp, *Theories of Modern Art*, University of California Press 1968, pp.178f)
4 'Über das Tier in der Kunst' (edited version of a letter dated April 1910 to Reinhard Piper), in Reinhard Piper, *Das Tier in der Kunst*, Munich (R.Piper & Co.) 1910, p.190, repr. in Lankheit (1978), p.98

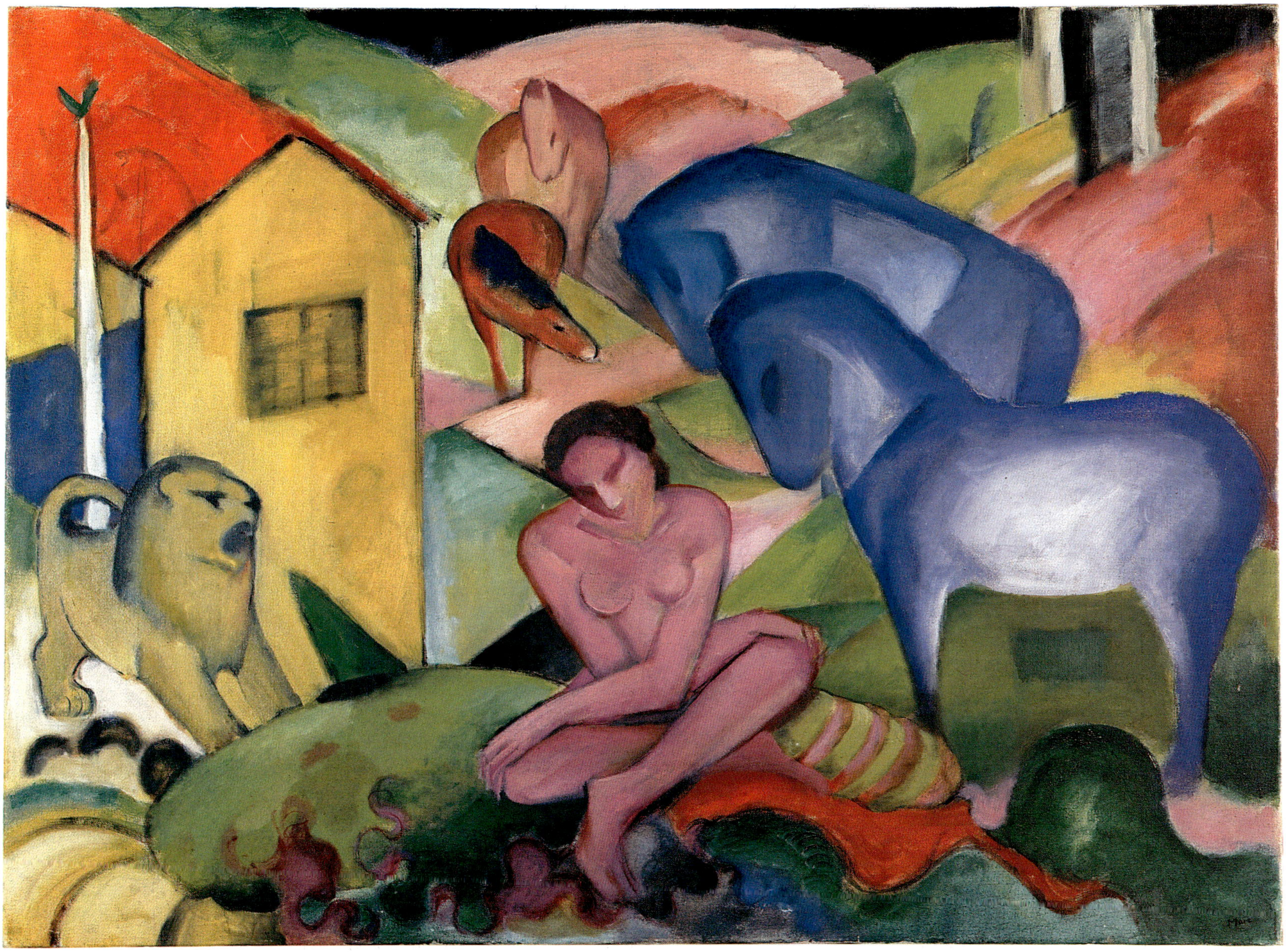

displaying in more than one instance an evident debt to the work of Gauguin.[5] There is also a small group of paintings from the period 1912–13, for the most part on a grand scale and clearly allegorical in intent, which show humans in harmony with nature and animals, placed in an imaginary or mythical setting: a kind of idyllic or arcadian landscape related perhaps to the traditional subject of the Garden of Delights, a theme which Kandinsky also treated. It is to this latter group of paintings that *The Dream* belongs.

Closest of all in both style and subject to the present work is another painting of 1912 entitled *The Shepherds* (fig.1),[6] which depicts a motionless horse keeping watch over two naked figures, one apparently sunk in reverie in a cross-legged posture very similar to that employed in *The Dream*, the other asleep or perhaps even dead, since the body appears to have been laid out on a rock which might be thought to bear a somewhat sinister resemblance to a mortuary slab. Intended, perhaps, is an ironic reversal of roles: the human shepherds, who should be keeping watch over their animals, watched over by the beasts of the field. There is also an evident similarity with a further 1912 painting, *The Waterfall* (fig.2), which includes three crouching nude female figures, very similar to the central figure in *The Dream*, and also an animal – in this case apparently a tiger – approaching out of a landscape background at the extreme left.

More distantly related to [68] is a painting datable to the beginning of 1913, likewise entitled *Dream* (fig.3), which again shows animals watching over a sleeping figure. This slightly later version of the subject bears a dedication to the 'Prince of Thebes' – an allusion to the German poetess Else Lasker-Schüler, whom Marc greatly admired, and to whom he also addressed a series of coloured postcards under her adopted pseudonym 'Prince Yussuf of Thebes'.[7]

If, however, the Thyssen Collection's version of the subject is indeed an allegorical painting,

Notes

5 See for example Lankheit (1970), no.125, in which the allusion to Gauguin is unmistakable. Lankheit suggests that the group of paintings to which *The Dream* belongs may also have been inspired by Marc's renewed interest in the work of Gauguin (whose paintings had been exhibited in Munich in August 1910) and also of Hans von Marées: see Lankheit (1976), loc. cit.

6 Lankheit (1970), no.173

7 See *Franz Marc, Botschaften an den Prinzen Jussuf. Mit einem Geleitwort von Maria Marc und einer Einführung von Georg Schmidt*, Munich (R.Piper & Co.) 1954; Peter-Klaus Schuster (ed.), *Franz Marc. Postcards to Prince Jussuf*, Munich (Prestel) 1988

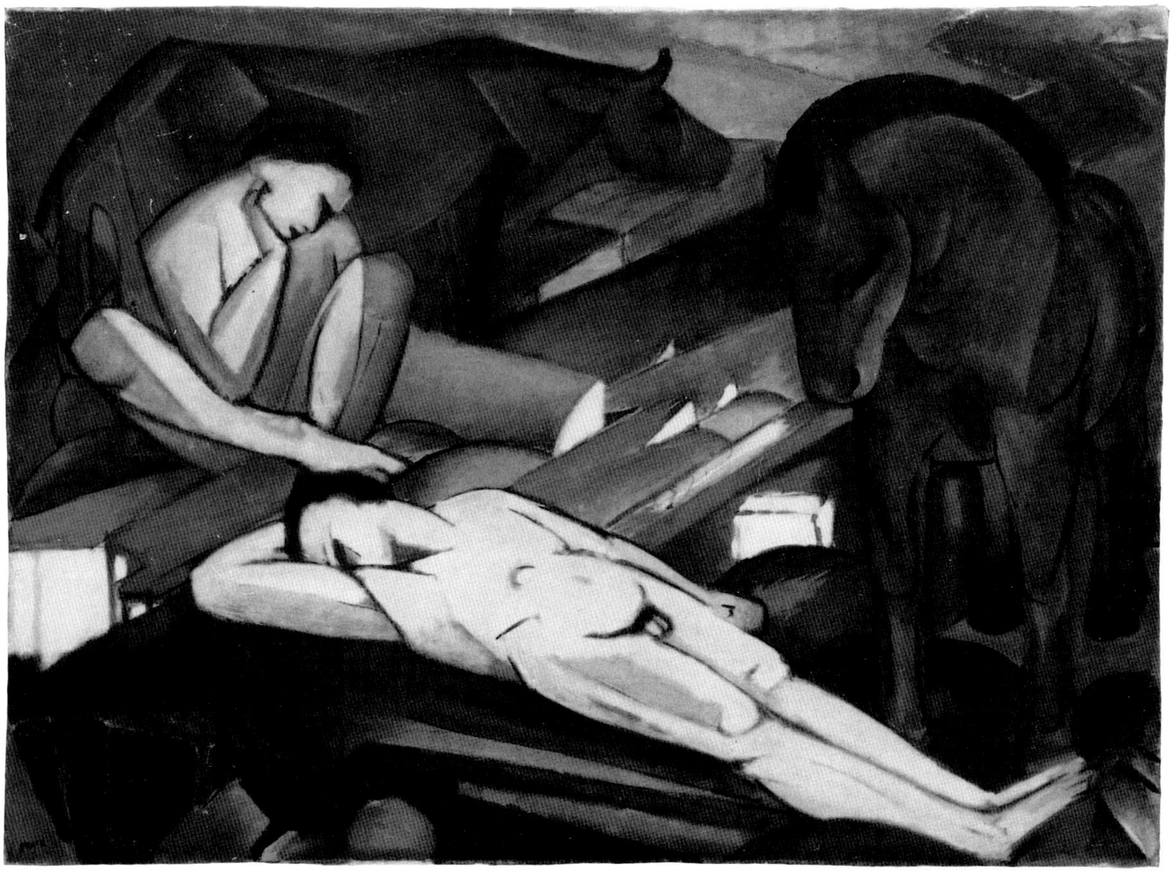

FIG 1 Franz Marc, *The Shepherds*, 1912, oil on canvas, 100 × 135 cm (Private collection)

FIG 2 Franz Marc, *The Waterfall*, 1912, oil on canvas, 164 × 158 cm (Los Angeles, CA, Robert Gore Rifkind Collection)

FIG 3 Franz Marc, *Dream*, 1913, oil on paper on card, 76 × 101 cm (Berne, Kunstmuseum, inv. no.1642)

8 See Lankheit (1976), loc. cit. ('... vielleicht hat darin das Erlebnis des "Blauen Reiters" in allegorischer Umschreibung einen orphischen Niederschlag gefunden'); Lankheit suggests that it was thus no coincidence that Marc gave *The Dream* to Kandinsky
9 Roethel (1982), no.354
10 See Klaus Lankheit (ed.), *Wassily Kandinsky – Franz Marc. Briefwechsel. Mit Briefen von und an Gabriele Münter und Maria Marc*, Munich (R.Piper & Co.) 1983, pp.280, 287, 293
11 See n.1
12 Bohan, op. cit., ch.2. *The Dream* was also reproduced as the only illustration accompanying the foreword Dreier wrote for *Modern Art at the Sesqui-Centennial Exhibition*, exh. cat., New York, Societé Anonyme, Inc., 1926, n.p., in which she makes specific allusion to Marc's influence on modern painting
13 Ibid., p.55

the allegory is far from straightforward. There is no motivic key which would enable us to decipher the meaning of the picture, nor does it retail any specific narrative or sequence of events. Rather, *The Dream* is, as Marc's biographer Klaus Lankheit observes, permeated by a poetic meaning which eludes rational explication – a kind of Orphic rhapsody in which the ideas that lay behind the genesis of the *Blue Rider Almanac* perhaps found symbolic expression.[8]

Shortly after its execution, Marc exchanged *The Dream* with Kandinsky in return for the latter's *Improvisation 12 (Rider)* of 1910, now in the Bayerische Staatsgemäldesammlungen, Munich.[9] Temporarily in Gabriele Münter's possession after Kandinsky's return to Russia at the outbreak of war, the picture was exhibited on numerous occasions during the decade after Marc's death. It was lent at the request of his widow Maria to the 1916–17 Franz Marc memorial exhibition at the Munich Neue Secession, and at the Nassauischer Kunstverein, Wiesbaden; in this connection it is referred to on several occasions in correspondence between Maria Marc and Gabriele Münter.[10] It was also lent by Kandinsky himself to the *International Exhibition of Modern Art* assembled by Katherine Dreier's Societé Anonyme, and shown in New York, Buffalo and Toronto during the winter of 1926–7.[11]

Dreier had visited Kandinsky at the Bauhaus in 1922, and again in early summer 1926 in connection with preparations for the *International Exhibition*. She was a staunch admirer of his art and shared his theosophical and mystical interests.[12] She was also especially fond of Marc's painting: he was one of only two artists represented posthumously at the Societé Anonyme exhibition, which was otherwise devoted exclusively to contemporary art.[13] There can be little doubt that this exhibition did a great deal to enhance Marc's reputation in the United States, as well as that of modern German painting generally.

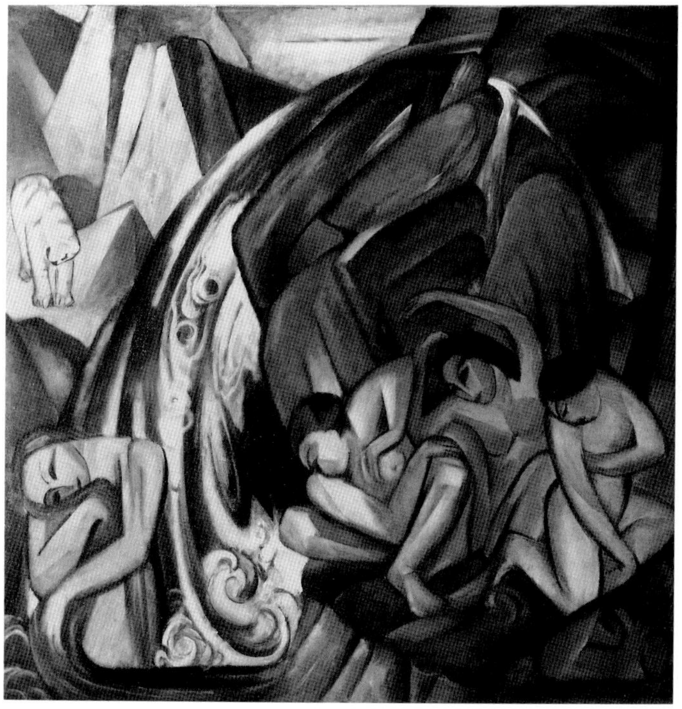

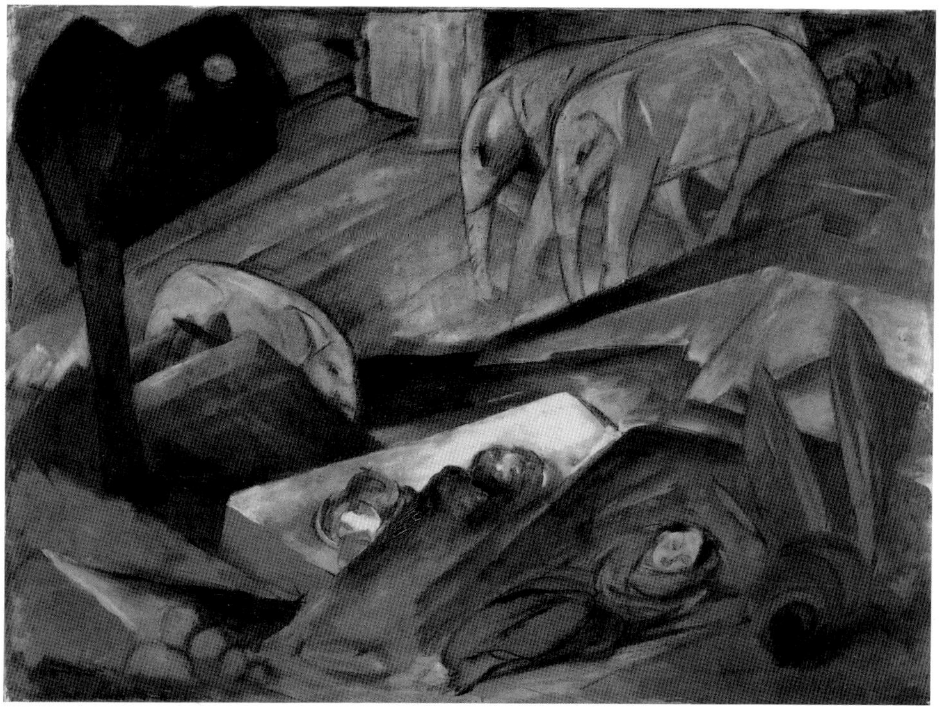

Franz Marc 1880–1916

69 Goblet with Fox and Deer

1915
Mixed media, 16 × 11.7 cm
Inscribed by the artist: 'Alfred Mayer kredenzt im Kriegsjahr 1915 von f.m.'
The paper has become somewhat yellow and the metal partly oxidized. There are a number of paint losses to the upper part of the composition
Accession no.1975.32

Provenance
Alfred Mayer, Munich
Galerie Günther Franke, Munich
Heinrich Thannhauser, Munich
Dr G.Schöne, Stettin/Berlin[1]
Stuttgarter Kunstkabinett, Stuttgart
Private collection
Herbert Klewer, Berlin
Leonard Hutton Galleries, New York
Thyssen-Bornemisza Collection, 1975

Exhibitions
Munich, Neue Secession, 1916, *Franz Marc Gedächtnisausstellung*, no.163
Berlin, Galerie Nierendorf, 1936, *Franz Marc Gedächtnisausstellung*, no.38
Berlin, Brücke-Museum/Essen, Museum Folkwang/Tübingen, Kunsthalle, 1989–90, *Franz Marc. Zeichnungen und Aquarelle*, no.186
Rome 1990–91, no.34

Literature
Schardt (1936), II/1915/1
Lankheit (1970), no.501
Lankheit (1976), p.150

In addition to paintings, sculptures and graphic works, Marc executed a series of coloured postcards, and also made a small number of designs for objects of applied art, including tapestries, painted screens, door furniture and decorated beakers and dishes. In some ways, *Goblet with Fox and Deer* recalls the latter.

According to the artist's widow, Maria Marc,[2] this was the only watercolour done by her husband during his time as a soldier in the First World War. It bears an inscription in Marc's own hand: 'dedicated to Alfred Mayer in the year of war 1915 by f.m.' It originally formed part of a visitors' book belonging to Mayer, a writer and patron of Franz Marc and a close friend of both Marc and Kandinsky during their Munich years.[3] It was executed as consequence of a visit Marc paid to Mayer while on home leave from the Front; since he had leave only twice in the course of 1915, in early July and early November, it can be dated with some precision to the latter half of that year.[4]

The work represents a goblet or tankard with a reclining blue (mythical?) creature, tentatively identified as a fox, in the foreground, behind it a roebuck with blue antlers. It is executed in an unusual combination of media: gouache, watercolour, lacquer, plus silver-painted paper pasted-on; the area representing the inside of the rim of the goblet is in fact a hole cut out of the sheet of paper, which has been filled by pasting in the additional piece of silver-painted paper. The fact that *Goblet with Fox and Deer* was considered significant enough to be included both in the memorial exhibition held at the Neue Secession in Munich in the year of the artist's death, and in the 1936 commemorative exhibition organized by the Galerie Nierendorf in Berlin, is worthy of note.

Notes

1 Professor Dr med. G.Schöne was senior doctor in charge of the hospital in Stettin; he acquired *Goblet with Fox and Deer* in *c*1930. He subsequently moved to the Landhausklinik of the Red Cross in Berlin-Wilmersdorf, according to information supplied by Professor Klaus Lankheit (letter to the author, 6 December 1990). I am grateful to Professor Lankheit for supplying many of the factual details on which the accompanying entry is based

2 In interview with Professor Klaus Lankheit, *c*1948; see n.1

3 Mayer is referred to on a number of occasions in correspondence between Gabriele Münter and Maria Marc, with whom he remained on friendly terms both during and after the war; see Klaus Lankheit (ed.), *Wassily Kandinsky – Franz Marc. Briefwechsel. Mit Briefen von und an Gabriele Münter und Maria Marc*, Munich (R.Piper & Co.) 1983, pp.268, 280, 284, 289

4 It has not been possible to determine to which period of leave, July or November 1915, the execution of [69] should be ascribed

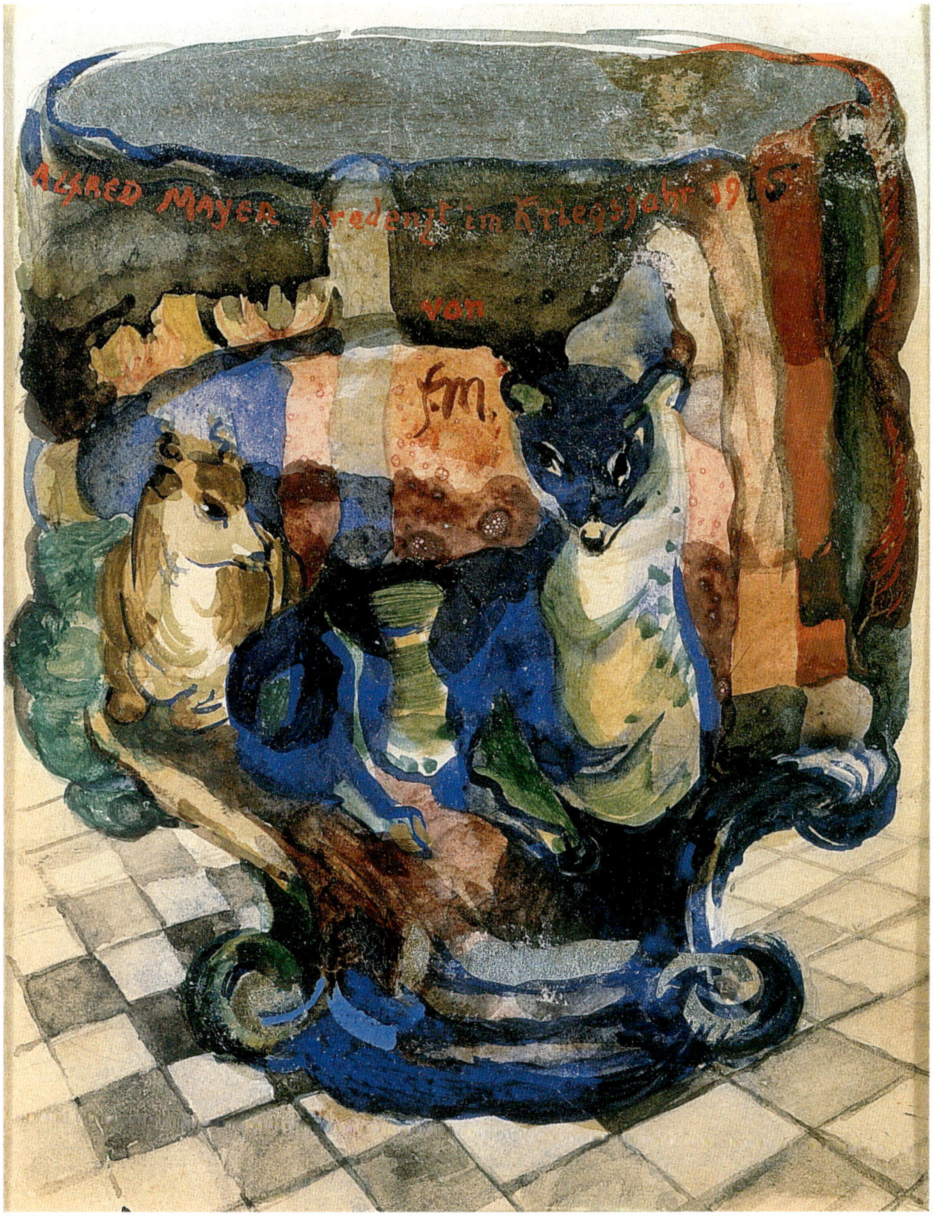
ALFRED MAYER kredenzt im Kriegsjahr 1915
von
F.M.

Ludwig Meidner 1884–1966

70 The Corner House (Villa Kochmann, Dresden)[1]

1913
Oil on canvas on board, 97.2 × 78 cm
Signed/dated (twice); lower right: 'LM 1913'; lower left: 'LM 19.. [indecipherable]'
There is a history of flaking and scattered paint losses previously restored, perhaps by the artist. The original canvas has been stuck down on a piece of cardboard, probably in the course of restoration. The painting is unvarnished, and there is marked surface grime. Otherwise condition is good
Accession no.1980.28

Provenance
Collection of the artist
Walter Kirste, Recklinghausen
Private collection, Hamburg
Private collection, Switzerland
Fischer Fine Art, London
Thyssen-Bornemisza Collection, 1980

Exhibitions
Recklinghausen, Städtische Kunsthalle/Berlin, Haus am Waldsee/Darmstadt, Kunsthalle, 1963–4, *Ludwig Meidner*, no.14
Hamburg, Kunsthalle, 1977, *Kunst, was ist das?*, ill. p.201
Moscow, Pushkin Museum/Leningrad, Hermitage/ Frankfurt am Main, Städelsches Kunstinstitut, 1978, *Deutsche Malerei 1890–1918*, no.73
Modern Masters from the Thyssen-Bornemisza Collection, 1984–6, no.74
Lugano 1989, no.38
Expressionism and Modern German Painting, 1989–90, no.24
Essen, Museum Folkwang, 1990, *Vincent van Gogh und die Moderne 1890–1914*, no.187
Amsterdam, Rijksmuseum Vincent van Gogh, 1990–91, *Vincent van Gogh en de moderne Kunst 1890–1914*, no.143

Literature
Grochowiak (1966) pp.77f, 99 and col. pl.XII
Kunz (1973), p.49
Victor H.Miesel, 'Ludwig Meidner', in Meidner (1978), p.8
Peter-Klaus Schuster (ed.), *Delaunay und Deutschland*, exh. cat., Munich, Haus der Kunst, 1985, pp.276, 459–60 and cat. no.225,[2] ill. p.277
C.M.Joachimedes, N.Rosenthal, W.Schmied (eds.), *German Art in the 20th Century*, exh. cat., London, Royal Academy of Arts, 1985, p.26, ill fig.8
Eliel (1989), p.19 and fig.15

The most important influences on Meidner's pre-1914 work are, in essence, the same as those which may be detected in the early work of Grosz (compare *Metropolis* [17]): that of French Cubism, in particular the 'Orphic Cubism' of Delaunay, and of Italian Futurism. Meidner would, like Grosz, have been aware of the most recent development of both movements through the activities of Herwarth Walden's Sturm gallery in Berlin. He could have seen Italian Futurist paintings in the original not later than the autumn of 1913, at Walden's famous *Erster Deutscher Herbstsalon* (First German *Salon d'automne*) which opened at Der Sturm in September

Notes
1 In Grochowiak's 1966 monograph, which was written in consultation with the artist, the painting is entitled *Das Eckhaus* ('The Corner House' or 'House on the Corner'). However, in a list of works in his possession compiled by Meidner in July 1916, what is evidently the present painting is entered under the title 'Landschaft: Landhaus in Dresden, 1913' (Landscape: Country House in Dresden, 1913); see Kunz, loc. cit. The title 'Landhaus' is also inscribed on one of two drawings closely related to the painting (see fig.3)
2 Though the painting is included under this number in the catalogue of the exhibition *Delaunay und Deutschland* held at the Haus der Kunst, Munich during 1985–6, it was not in fact shown, since it was then on tour as part of the exhibition *Modern Masters from the Thyssen-Bornemisza Collection*: for full reference see p.27

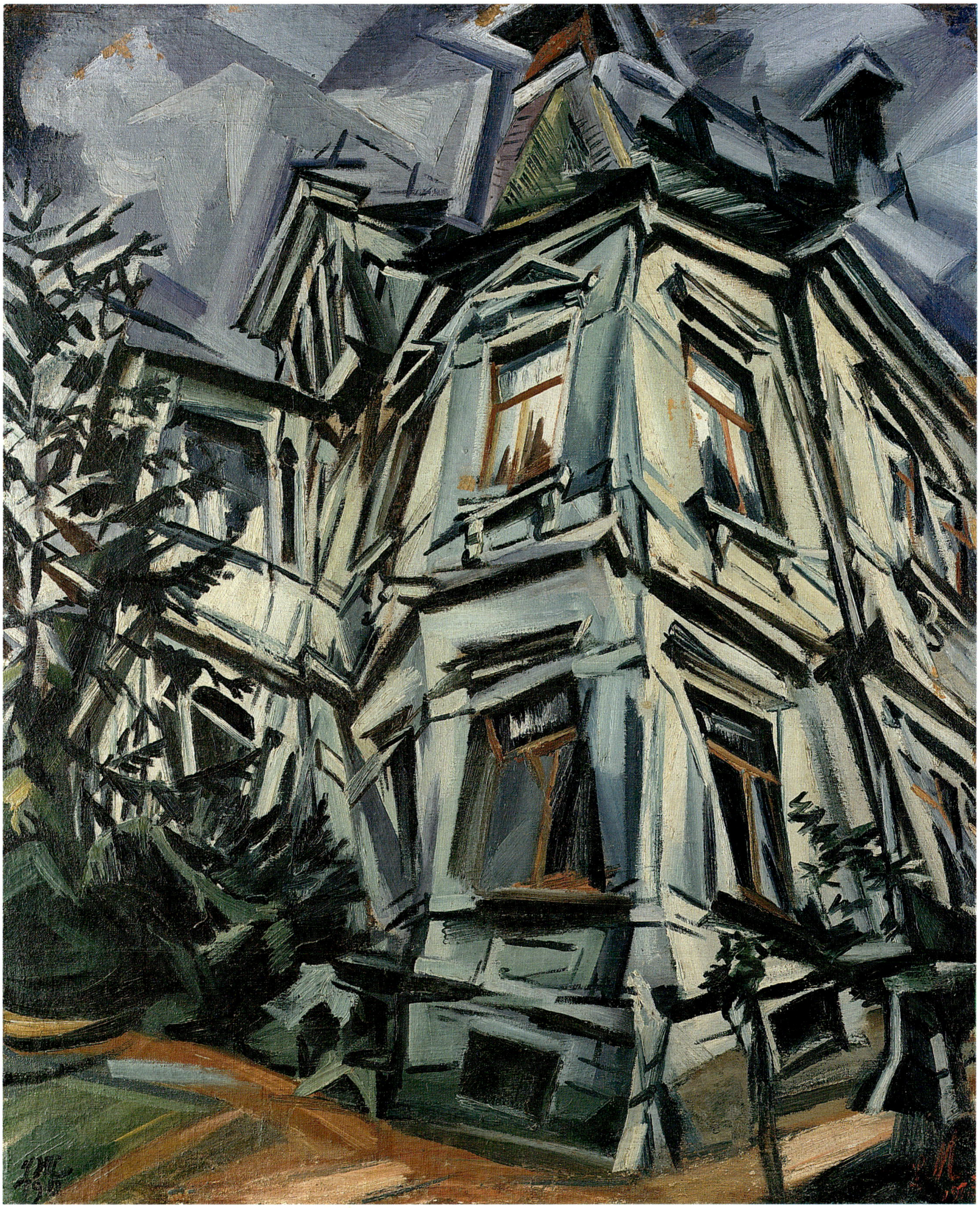

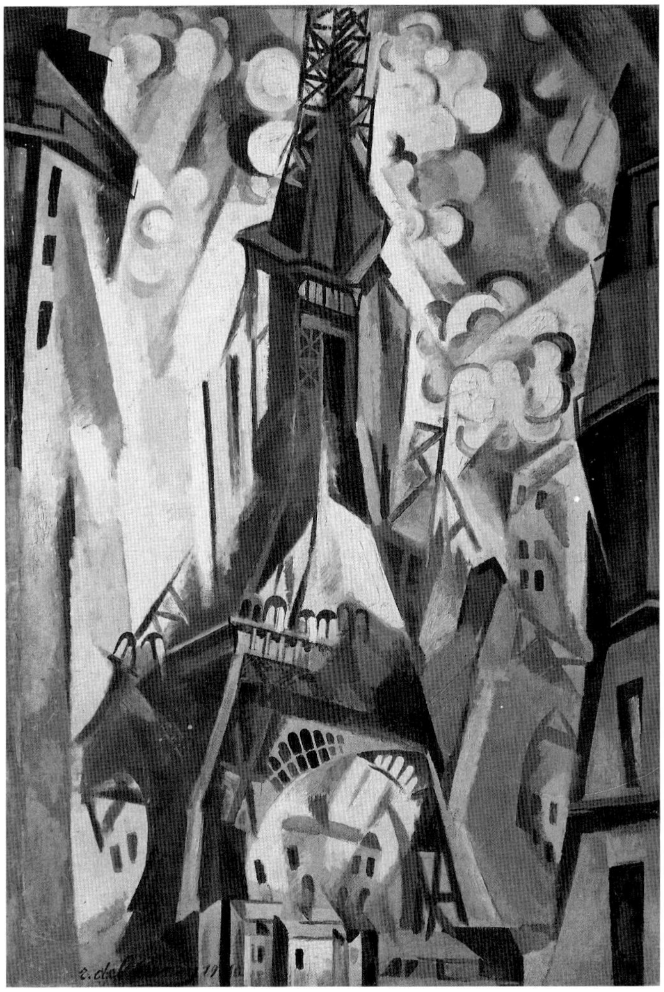

FIG 1 Robert Delaunay, *The Eiffel Tower*, 1910–11, oil on canvas, 195.5 × 129 cm (Basle, Kunstmuseum, Emanuel Hoffmann-Stiftung, inv. no.H. 1943.4)

FIG 2 Ludwig Meidner, drawing related to *The Corner House*, 1913, pencil, dimensions unknown (Private collection)

of that year. His first acquaintance with Delaunay's work would probably have occurred even earlier; it is recorded that he met the French artist in person at the Café Josti in Berlin,[3] an encounter which must have taken place during the course of Delaunay's visit in connection with the opening of his one-man exhibition at Der Sturm in January 1913. They also exchanged postcards and photographs of their works,[4] and Meidner subsequently acknowledged that certain of his paintings, including *The Corner House*, were attempts to achieve comparable effects to those Delaunay had attained in his Paris cityscapes, in particular his depictions of the Eiffel Tower (fig.1).[5]

However, in *The Corner House*, Meidner employs Delaunay's deconstructive-analytic style to his own highly individual purpose. As J.P.Hodin has observed, the French artist's Eiffel Tower paintings culminate in a series of formal abstractions, whereas *The Corner House* is remarkable for its air of imminent dissolution, of impending collapse, as if the angular forms found in Delaunay's work have been turned into the symbolic expression of an emotional or spiritual state. 'The acute angles', writes Hodin, 'which in Delaunay's early works (the Eiffel Tower pictures of *c*1910) take on a quasi-expressionistic character, yield to the formalist-constructive element [of the later paintings] ... in the case of Meidner, of Kokoschka and other German Expressionists, on the contrary, they become transformed into the symbolic manifestation of a spiritual condition.'[6]

Notes

3 Grochowiak, p.224

4 See *Delaunay und Deutschland*, pp.459–60

5 Kunz (1973), p.39 (entry in Meidner's journal dated 4 September 1915; in this entry, the artist refers to the present painting by the alternative title 'Landhaus', see also n.1 above)

6 '... wo die aus dem Kubismus und Futurismus stammenden spitzen Winkel, die im frühen Werk von Delaunay (Die Eiffelturmbilder um 1910) ... einen quasi-expressionistischen Charakter angenommen hatten, der bei diesen Künstlern ins Konstruktiv-Formale ausmündete, von Meidner jedoch, von Kokoschka und von anderen deutschen Expressionisten in den symbolischen Ausdruck einer seelischen Situation umgeprägt wurden.' See Hodin (1973), p.42

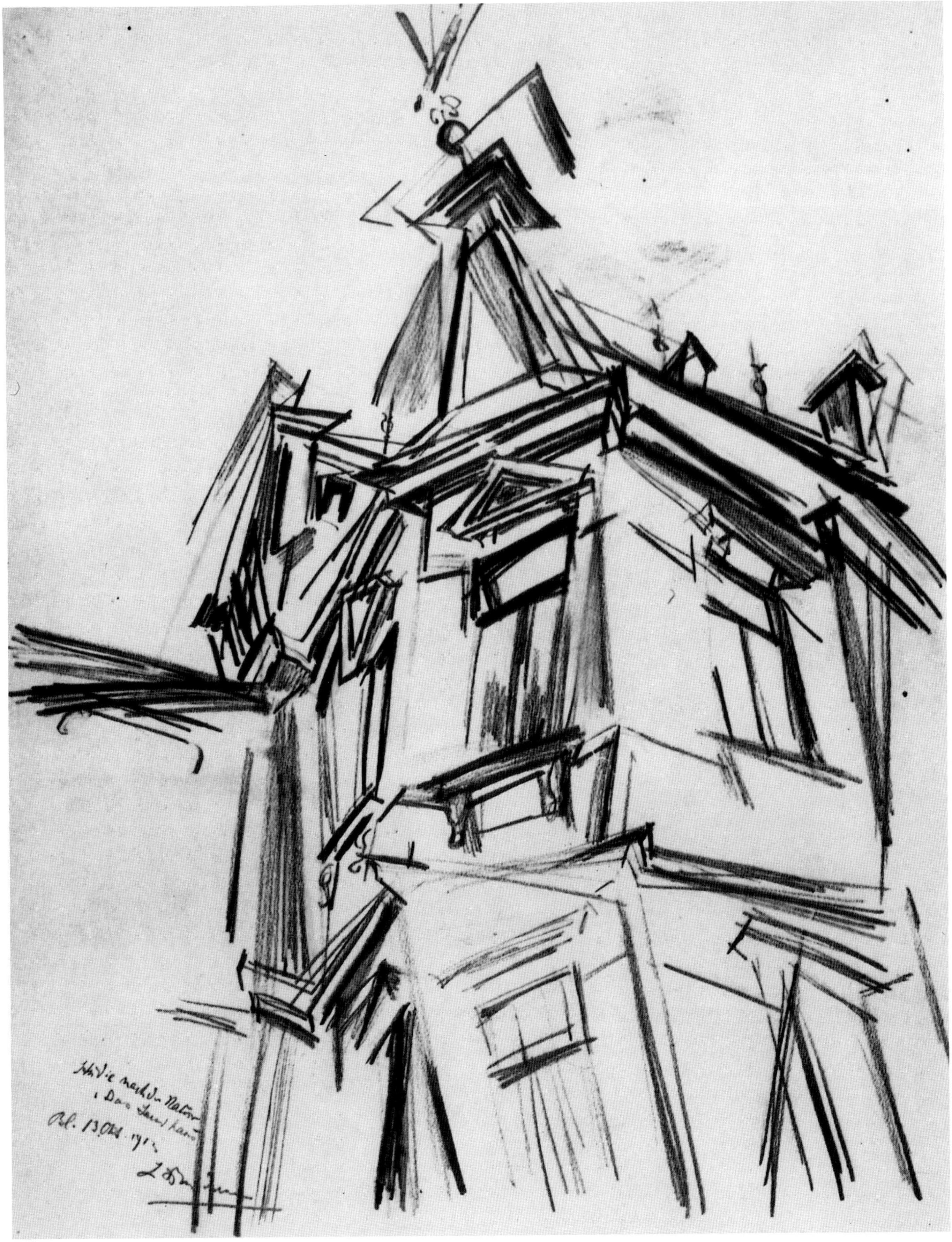

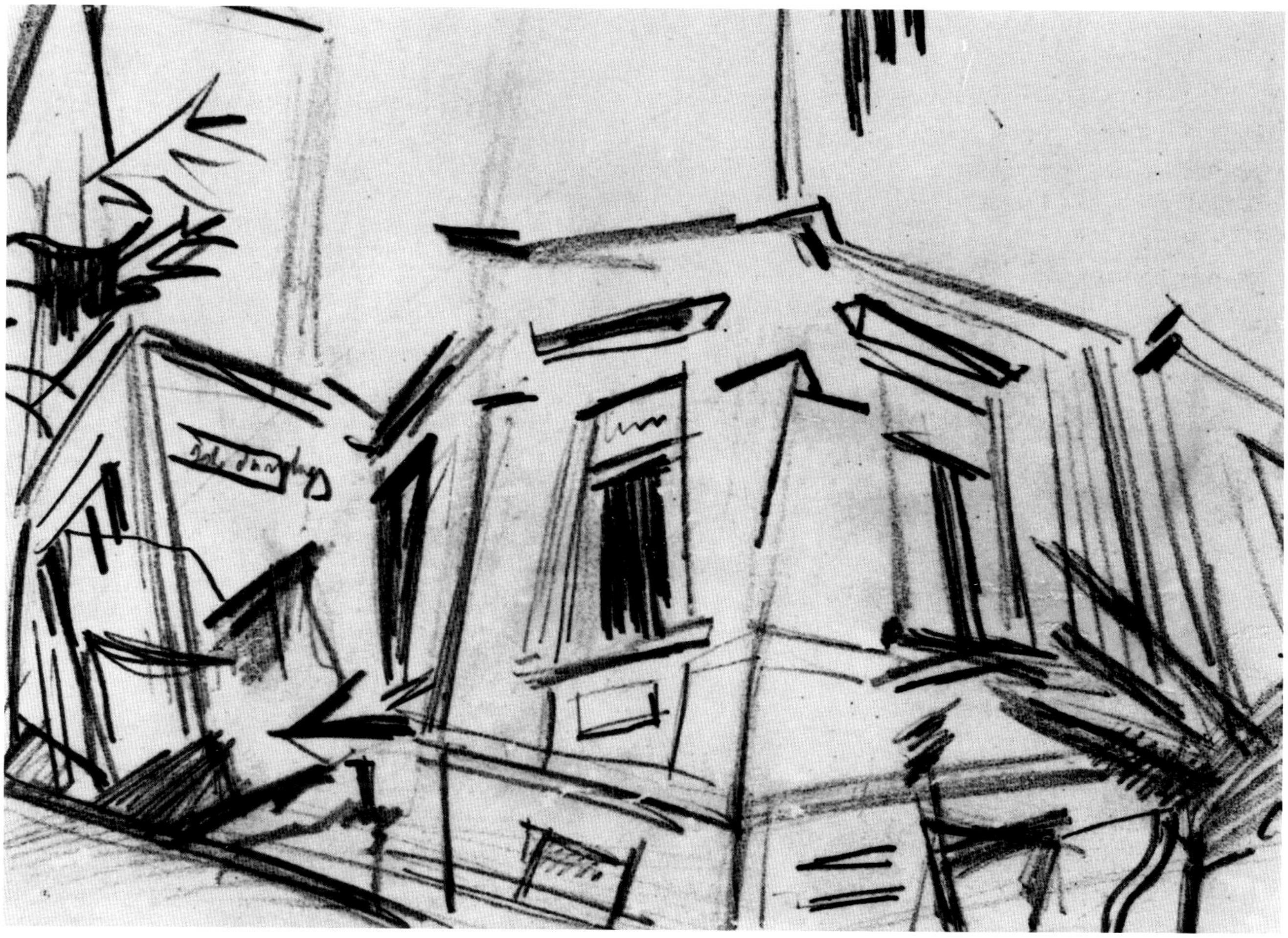

FIG 3 Ludwig Meidner, *The Country House*, 1913, pencil, 51.5 × 39 cm
(formerly Stuttgart, Galerie Valentien,
present location unknown)

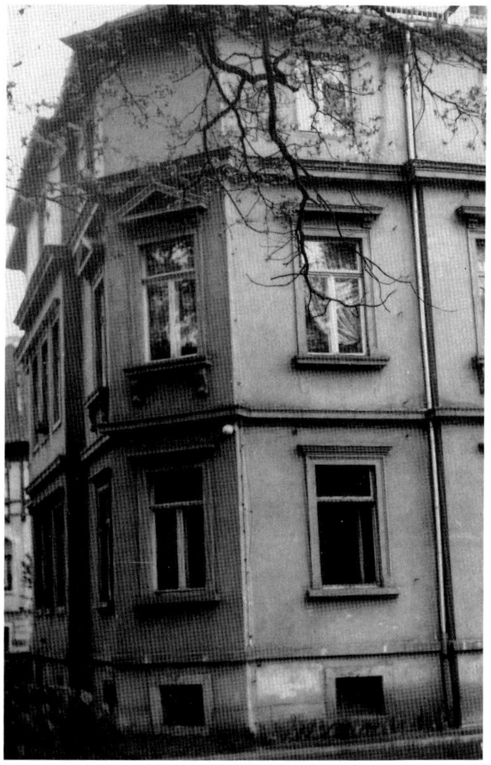

FIG 4 Dresden,
Loschwitzerstrasse 10, present state

In tracing the origins of the painting, several authors have referred to the existence of preparatory studies. Thomas Grochowiak in his 1966 monograph, still the principal source of reliable information on Meidner, writes of 'sketches' in which the artist 'observed the Corner House from various sides and angles, as if circling round an object with a camera'.[7] Victor H. Miesel, in the catalogue of the Meidner exhibition held at the University of Michigan in 1978, refers to a 'carefully drawn series of views made from different vantage points',[8] though apparently no such drawings were included in the exhibition.[9] Despite the existence of a number of studies datable to 1913 which are vaguely akin in subject and mood to *The Corner House*,[10] the present author has been able to find evidence of only two drawings directly related to the painting, neither of which can plausibly be described as 'carefully drawn': a pencil sketch, undated, formerly in the estate of the artist in Darmstadt and now in a private collection (fig.2), which shows the upper part of the façade of the building, and a far more detailed drawing which in composition closely resembles the finished painting (fig.3), and which is signed and dated by the artist, with an inscription: 'Studie nach der Natur "Das Landhaus", Bl[eistift]. 13. Okt. 1913' (Study from nature 'The Country House', pencil, 13 October 1913).[11] This inscription allows us to date the execution of the painting with relative precision.

Other than this, relatively little is known about the circumstances of its creation beyond what is printed in Grochowiak's monograph, based largely on the artist's own recollections. According to this account, *The Corner House* dates from a brief visit Meidner made to Dresden in the autumn of 1913. The owner of the house, Franz Kochmann, who had made his fortune as proprietor of a liquor shop in Kattowitz, had recently bought a lithographic firm in Dresden; it was at his instigation that Meidner returned there the following spring, accompanied by his friend, the poet Ernst Wilhelm Lotz, armed with plans to start publishing an illustrated journal and albums of prints.[12] This intended collaboration appears, however, to have been forestalled by the outbreak of war in August that year, in which Lotz was killed.

The Villa Kochmann – the 'corner house' depicted in Meidner's painting – still exists today, albeit in a somewhat altered state. A comparison with the accompanying photograph (fig.4), taken in 1991, shows that the veranda at extreme left – a dominant feature in the painting – has been demolished, and the characteristic roof line obliterated by the addition of a new top storey. Many of the details of the façade, on the other hand, have survived, in particular the distinctive form of the window openings, some with detached triangular pediments above, and even the guttering and the drainpipe, which look much the same as they did in 1913. The photograph also shows that Meidner's rendering is considerably more faithful to reality than has often been thought. The corner of the building, in particular, does indeed form an oblique angle of roughly 45 degrees, instead of following the right-angle of the adjoining streets, while the painting also reproduces more or less accurately the three cornices which run around the house at different heights.

The businessman Franz Kochmann appears to have bought the house and plot of land occupying the corner of Residenzstrasse and Alemannenallee in the then still independent Dresden suburb of Blasewitz in 1913. In 1921, Blasewitz was incorporated into greater Dresden, at which point the street changed its name to Loschwitzerstrasse. Kochmann himself is listed in the city's business register as owner of a factory manufacturing photographic equipment. The business, to judge from the same source, must have been relatively successful, since it still existed well into the 1930s.[13]

Notes

7 Ibid., p.77

8 Miesel, loc. cit.

9 *Delaunay und Deutschland* also refers to 'numerous drawings and prints' related to *The Corner House*, but cites as an example only the drawing reproduced here as fig.3; see Schuster, op. cit., p.460

10 See for example the 1913 ink drawing *Strasse* (Street), now in the Fishman collection in Milwaukee, reproduced in Eliel (1989), fig.16; though Eliel points specifically to what she sees as the similarity with *The Corner House*, the drawing in fact shows only a rather generalized street scene, including a building on the corner which bears no more than a passing resemblance to the house depicted in the Thyssen Collection's painting

11 A print of this latter drawing is preserved in the Meidner archive in Darmstadt. The drawing itself was illustrated in *Ludwig Meidner*, exh. cat., Recklinghausen/Berlin/Darmstadt, 1963, no.72, where its dimensions are given as 51.5 × 39 cm and the owner identified as the Galerie Valentien, Stuttgart; its present whereabouts are unknown. I am grateful to Annelise Loth, Darmstadt, for kindly providing information and for making available to me photographs of the drawings illustrated here

12 'Wir hatten die Absicht, mit Hilfe unseres ... Mäzens Franz Kochmann, der neben anderen Firmen auch eine lithographische Anstalt hatte, eine Zeitschrift zu gründen, die wir beide gemeinsamen zu redigieren beabsichtigten.' See Ludwig Meidner, 'Dichter, Maler und Cafés', in Kunz (1973), p.17

13 Information supplied by Bernd Hünlich, Radebeul

Otto Mueller 1874–1930

71 Two Female Nudes in a Landscape

c1922 (?)
Oil on burlap, 100 × 138 cm
Initialled upper right: 'OM'; signed on back of canvas: 'Otto Mueller', also inscribed on verso at lower right: 'KM 1928.126'[1]
The paint layer is very dry and brittle. There are numerous pronounced cracks, also a history of flaking and losses, some consolidated. The painting is unvarnished
Accession no.1968.4

Provenance
Private collection
Stuttgarter Kunstkabinett, Stuttgart
Hugo Gouthier, Paris
Thyssen-Bornemisza Collection, 1968

Exhibitions
New York, Marlborough–Gerson Gallery, 1968, *International Expressionism, Part I*, no.39[2]
Turin, Galleria Civica d'Arte Moderna, 1971, *Il Cavaliere Azzurro*, ill. p.125
Bremen 1975, no.54
Lugano 1975, no.25
Brussels/Paris 1977–8, no.63
Lugano 1978, no.78
Modern Masters from the Thyssen-Bornemisza Collection, 1984–6, no.81
Lugano 1989, no.22
Expressionism and Modern German Painting, 1989–90, no.26
Rome 1990–91, no.35

Literature
Kiel (1974), p.96, ill. p.97
See also Buchheim (1963), nos.109, 148; Karsch (1974), nos.109, 148

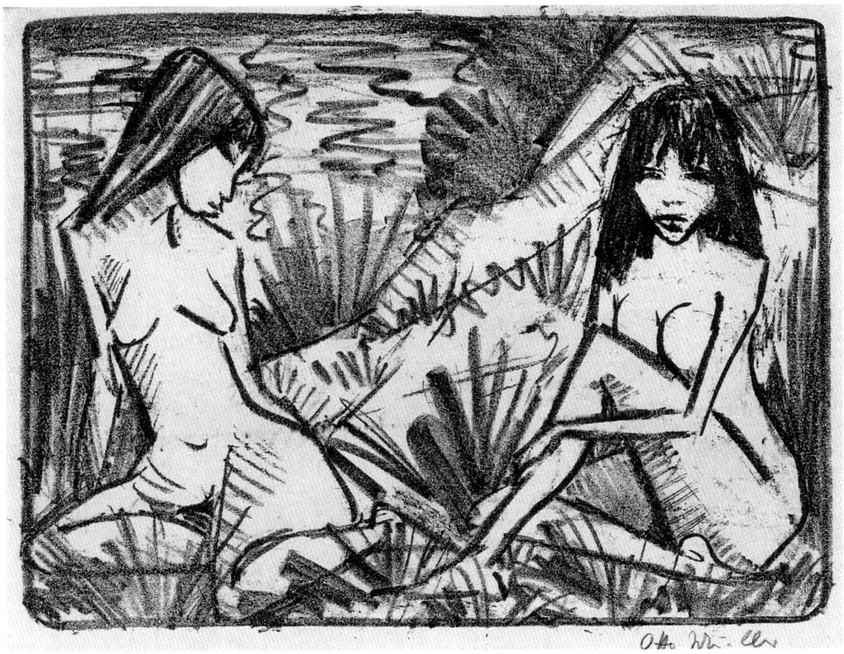

FIG 1 Otto Mueller, *Two Girls seated among Dunes (II)*, 1921–2, lithograph, 29 × 39 cm (Berlin, Galerie Nierendorf)

In 1919, Mueller wrote on the occasion of an exhibition at Cassirer's in Berlin: 'My main aim is to express my response to landscape and people with the utmost simplicity. My model was and still is the art of the ancient Egyptians, including its purely technical aspect . . .'[3]

Like the rest of the Brücke group, which he joined in 1910, Mueller was preoccupied with the portrayal of nude figures in a landscape. His range of subject matter is, however, far more restricted than that of the other members of the group, consisting almost exclusively of female bathers, gypsy youths and amorous couples.

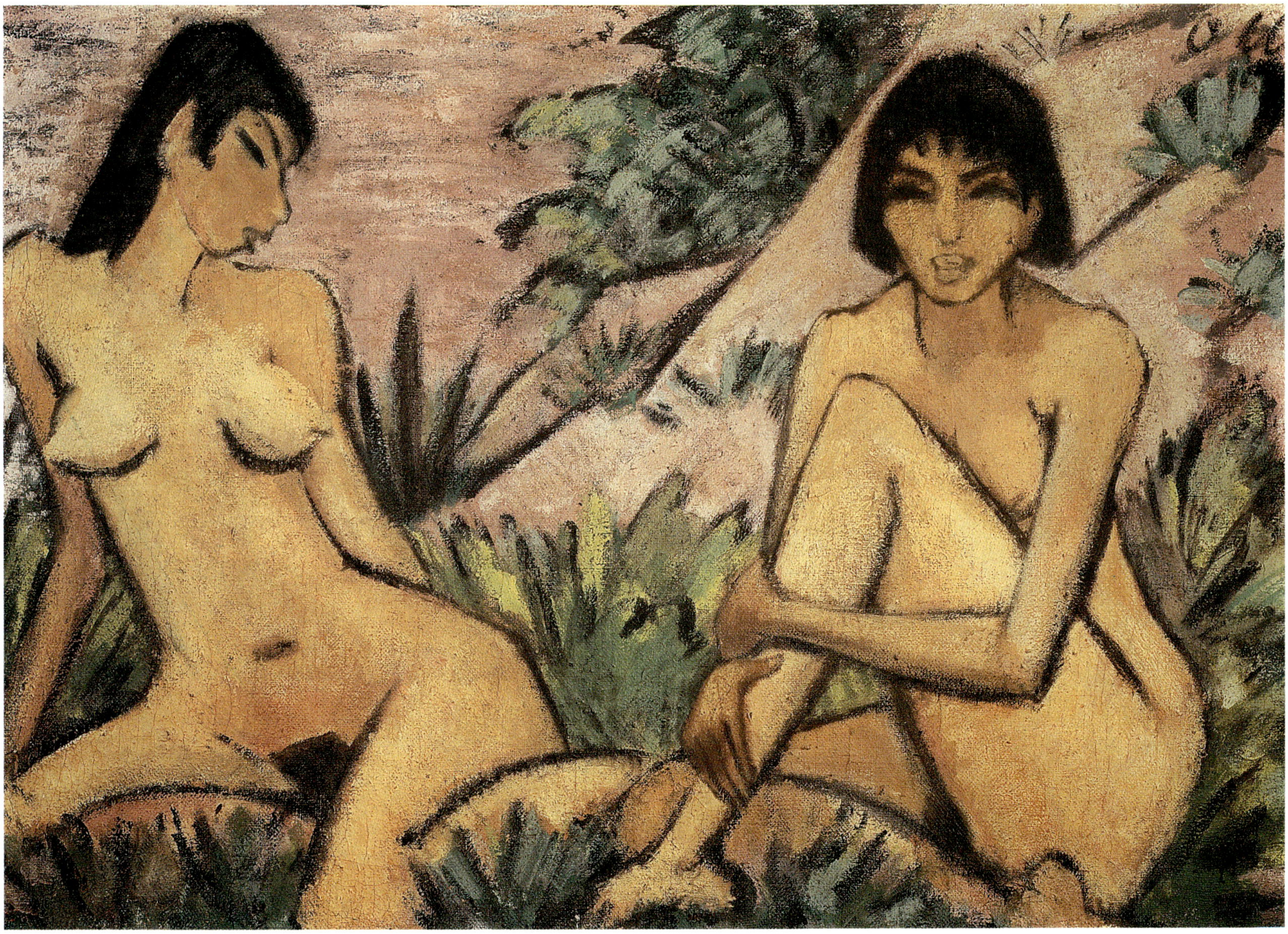

Notes
1 The inscription refers presumably to an exhibition in 1928 in which the painting was shown, perhaps the one-man show of Mueller's work organized by the Galerie Ferdinand Möller in Berlin in February and March of that year; see Roters (1984), p.301
2 The painting was both recorded and reproduced in this 1968 catalogue, but not included in the exhibition
3 Quoted after *Entartete Kunst. Bildersturm vor 25 Jahren*, exh. cat., Munich, Haus der Kunst, 1962, n.p.
4 Karsch (1974), no.109

Mueller very rarely dated any of his works and made no record of their chronology. This, together with his limited range of subjects and relative lack of stylistic development, makes the dating of his paintings problematic in the extreme. There are, however, two lithographs which are closely related to *Two Female Nudes in a Landscape*, both datable to the period 1920–22, which provide at least a point of comparison. One of these, usually dated *c*1920,[4] shows the same two figures in reverse, though the landscape background remains the same as in the painting. The other (fig.1) reproduces almost exactly the composition of [71]; this lithograph was published as part of a portfolio of prints by the Graphisches Kabinett J.B.Neumann, Berlin, in 1922 in an edition of thirty numbered copies.

On the basis of its close resemblance with these two lithographs, a date of *c*1922 for the present painting is suggested here. At all events, it seems likely that its execution may with reasonable confidence be ascribed to the early 1920s, shortly after the artist's appointment as Professor at the Academy of Fine Arts in Breslau, a post which Mueller held from 1919 until his death in 1930.

Otto Mueller 1874–1930

72 Nude by a Woodland Pool

*c*1920–22 (?)
Watercolour and crayon on paper, 50 × 40 cm
Signed lower right: 'Otto Mueller'
The paper is wavy. Otherwise condition is good
Accession no.1974.56

Provenance
Sommer Collection, Ronco
Galerie R.N.Ketterer, Campione d'Italia
Thyssen-Bornemisza Collection, 1974

Exhibitions
Bremen 1975, no.55
Lugano 1978, no.77

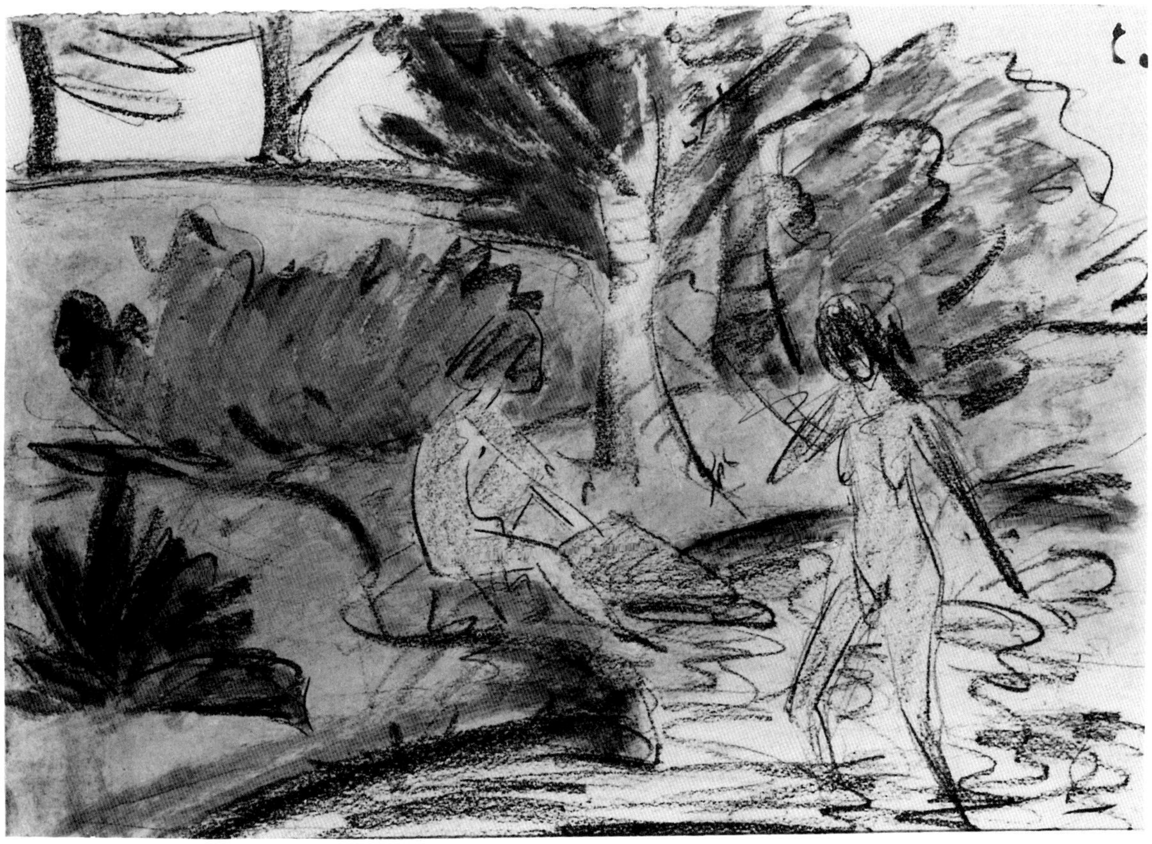

The present sheet belongs to a group of works executed in watercolour and coloured crayons depicting bathing scenes, to which the undated *Two Girls Bathing in a Woodland Pool* (fig.1) also belongs. The dating of Mueller's works on paper is no less problematic than that of his oil paintings (see [71]). None the less, on the basis of both subject and style, a date of *c*1920–22 is tentatively advanced here.

FIG 1 Otto Mueller, *Two Girls Bathing in a Woodland Pool*, undated, watercolour and crayon, 52.5 × 69 cm (Feldafing, Lothar-Günther Buchheim)

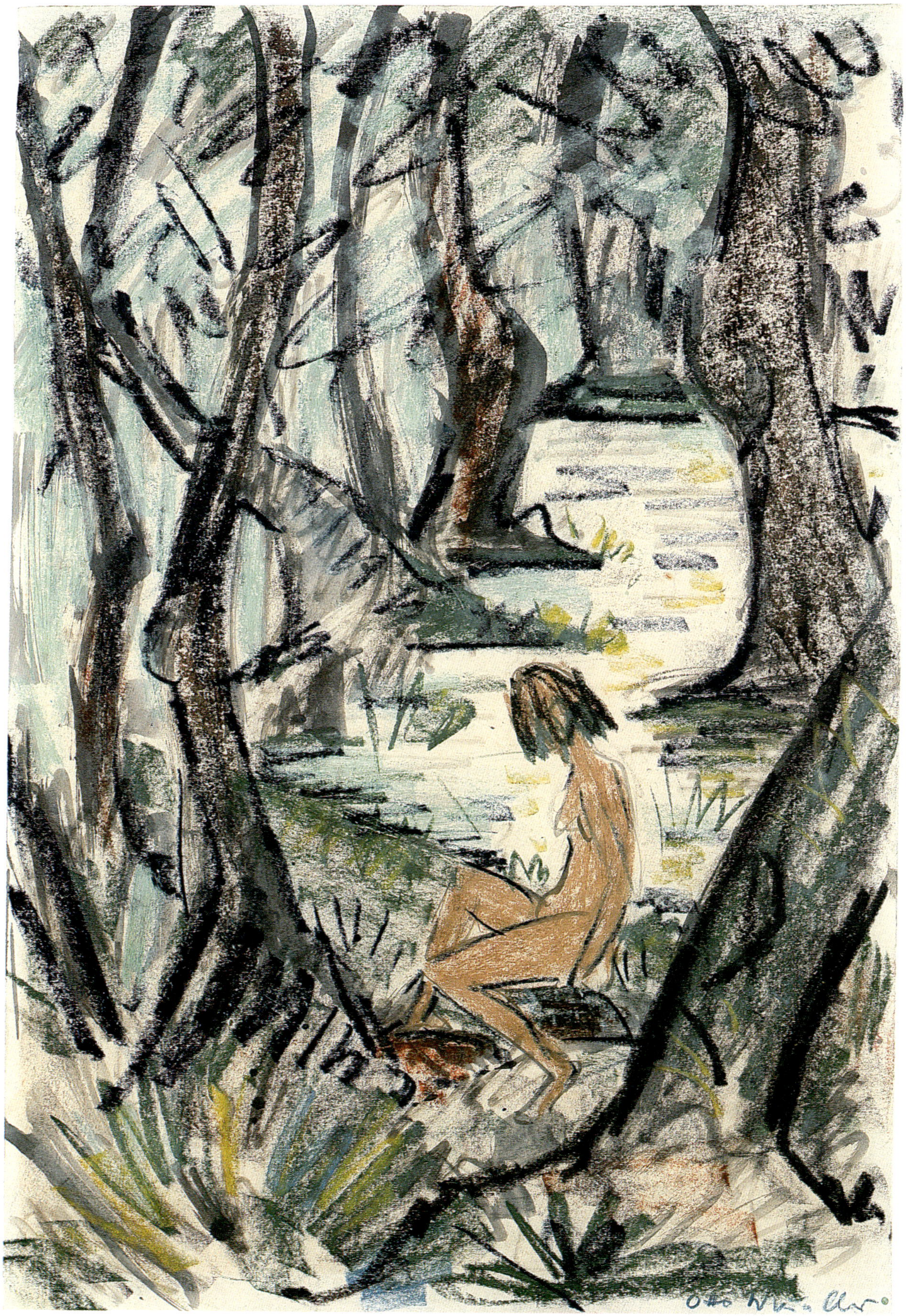

Gabriele Münter 1877–1962

73 Self-portrait

*c*1908
Oil on board, 49 × 33.6 cm
Unsigned/undated. Inscribed in pencil on back of board: 'G. Münter Selbststudie zwischen 1909 u. 14', also inventory number 'P59' and estate stamp: 'Gabriele Münter Nachlass'
On back of board, the sketchy outline of a face, perhaps the beginnings of the under-drawing for another portrait, evidently abandoned
In good condition. The painting is unvarnished
Accession no.1985.17

Provenance
Estate of the artist
Gabriele Münter and Johannes Eichner Foundation
Robert Gore Rifkind Collection, Los Angeles, CA
Sotheby's, New York
Thyssen-Bornemisza Collection, 1985[1]

Exhibitions
New York, Leonard Hutton Galleries, 1966, *Gabriele Münter, 1877 to 1962. Fifty Years of her Art: Paintings 1906–1956*, no.28 [as '1910']
Lugano 1989, no.32
Expressionism and Modern German Painting, 1989–90, no.25
Rome 1990–91, no.36

Literature
Alessandra Comini, 'Gender or Genius? The Women Artists of German Expressionism', in Norma Broude and Mary D. Garrard (eds.), *Feminism and Art History: Questioning the Litany*, New York (Harper & Row) 1982, pp.281f[2]
See also 'Gabriele Münter über sich selbst', *Das Kunstwerk*, II, no.7 (1948): 25; Roditi (1980), pp.133–54; Anne Mochon, *Gabriele Münter: Between Munich and Murnau*, exh. cat., Cambridge, MA, Harvard University, Busch-Reisinger Museum, 1980; Kenneth Lindsay, 'Gabriele Münter and Wassily Kandinsky: What They Meant To Each Other', *Arts Magazine*, LVI, no.4 (December 1981): 56–62

Portraiture and especially self-portraiture were important to Münter – unlike Kandinsky, her companion of these pre-war years in Munich, who paid scant attention when depicting others, and never portrayed himself.[3] In an interview given many years later to the writer and critic Edouard Roditi, she recalled that she had always concentrated in her work on 'depicting nature as I saw it or felt it . . . on obtaining a kind of psychological likeness which would convey the personality of my model or the mood of the moment.'[4] The same acuity of psychological penetration characterizes the present self-portrait, which shows a woman already past thirty who had achieved a measure of independence as an artist, certain of the career she wished to follow, and increasingly confident about her own aims as a painter.

At the time this picture was painted, Münter was closely associated with other Munich artists including Kandinsky, Jawlensky, Marianne von Werefkin and Vladimir Bekhteev, all of them Russians, who in 1909 formally constituted themselves as an exhibiting society to which they gave the name Neue Künstler-Vereinigung München (New Artists' Association of Munich). The NKVM as it soon became known did not represent any particular national or stylistic tendency. Rather, in Münter's words it was merely 'a group of friends who shared a common passion for painting as a form of self-expression. Each of us was interested in the work of the other members . . . much as each of us was also interested in the health and happiness of the

Notes
1 Acquired at auction, 14 May 1985 (*Impressionist and Modern Paintings and Sculpture, Part I*, lot 54)
2 See also the same author's 'State of the Field 1980: The Women Artists of German Expressionism', *Arts Magazine*, LV, no.3 (November 1980): 147–53
3 See Lindsay, op. cit., p.59
4 Roditi (1980), p.140

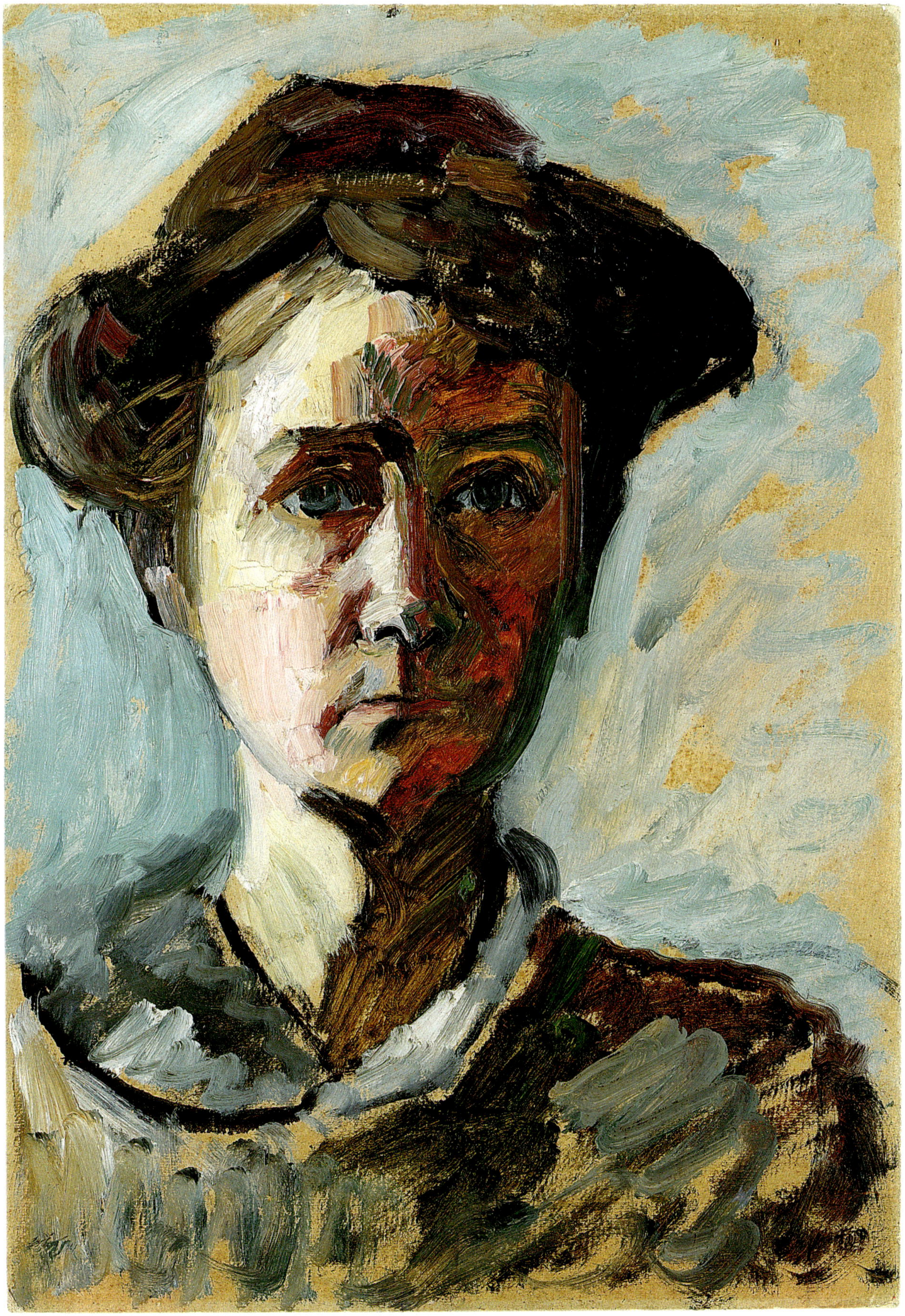

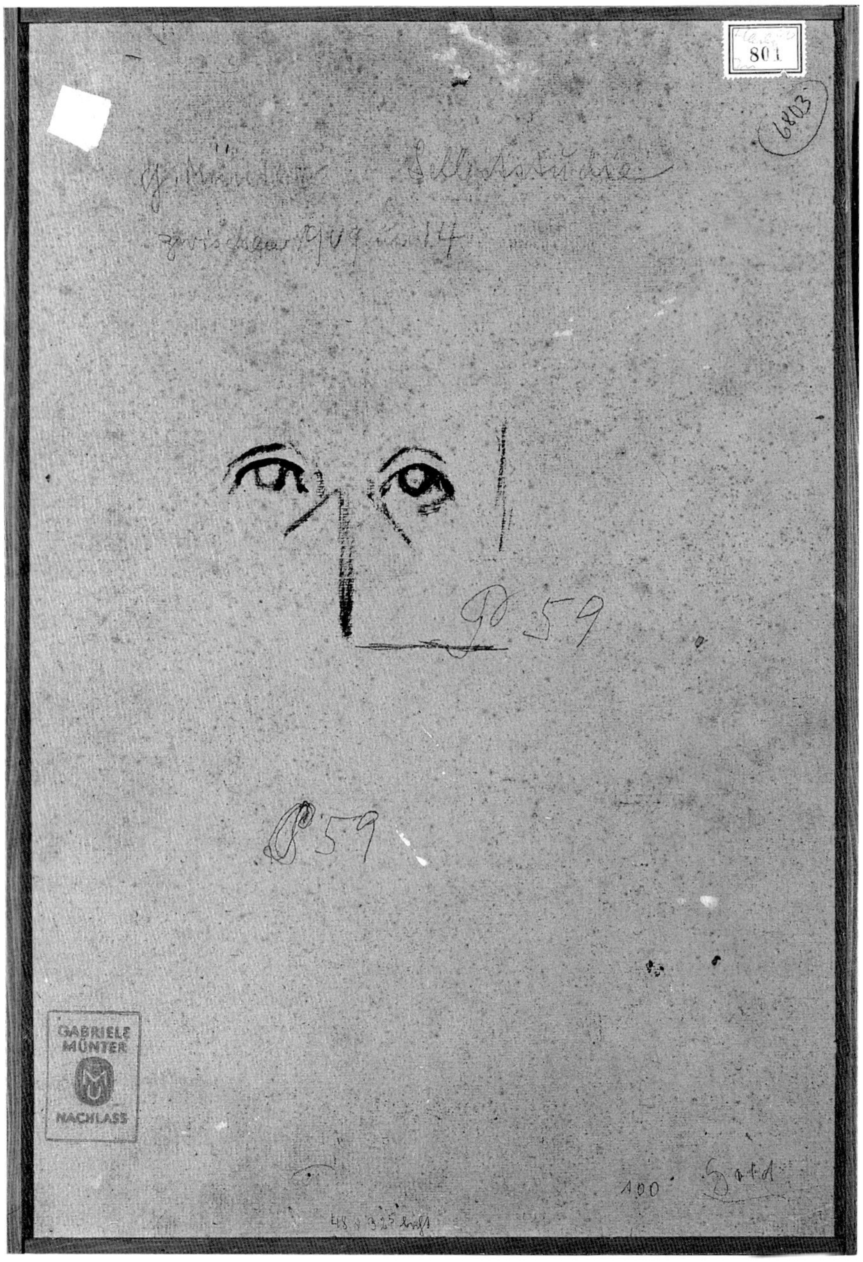

[73] *verso*

others. But we were still far from considering ourselves as a group or a school of art . . .'[5] And indeed, stylistically there is little in Münter's work at this time to link her own stubborn naturalism with the Fauve-inspired lyricism of Jawlensky, or the increasingly radical abstractions of Kandinsky who, in the foreword to the catalogue of a 1916 exhibition of her work, wrote about what he called Münter's 'calm, immediate, one might almost say innocent attitude to the world'.[6]

As depicted by herself, the artist's features here betray rather more of the quiet determination which enabled her to pursue her own goals, relatively unaffected by the dominant personalities of figures like Kandinsky and Jawlensky whose influence she none the less acknowledged. Of her relationship with both and the development of her own art, she recalled in an undated jotting: 'If, stylistically speaking, I was influenced by anybody – which during the years 1903–13 was to some extent the case – it was probably van Gogh, via the intermediary of Jawlensky and his theories (talk of synthesis). However, that is not to compare him with what Kandinsky meant to me. He loved my talent, understood it, defended and furthered it.'[7]

Notes

5 Ibid., pp.145–6

6 From the German manuscript of Kandinsky's essay 'On the Artist', in the archive of the Gabriele Münter- und Johannes Eichner-Stiftung, Munich, quoted after *Sammlungskatalog 1: Der Blaue Reiter*, 2nd edn., Munich (Städtische Galerie im Lenbachhaus), 1966, p.125. Such specific references to Münter's personality and art were in fact omitted from the published version of the essay, which appeared in Swedish under the title 'Om Konstnären' in the catalogue of the exhibition held at the Carl Gummeson Gallery in Stockholm in spring 1916: see Lindsay (1982), pp.407ff

7 Quoted after *Sammlungskatalog 1: Der Blaue Reiter*, p.122. Münter's manuscript is now in the archive of the Gabriele Münter- und Johannes Eichner-Stiftung, Munich

The *Self-portrait* remained in the artist's possession until her death in 1962. In 1966, a trust was established under the title 'Gabriele Münter- und Johannes Eichner-Stiftung' to administer her estate which at that time, in addition to her two houses and her own personal fortune, included numerous paintings, drawings, watercolours and graphic works as well as manuscripts, letters and books. Until the early 1980s, a number of works from the estate were sold either privately or through dealers, among them the present *Self-portrait* which was acquired by the Kunsthandlung Resch in Gauting in March 1970. In November 1972 it was offered for sale by the Galerie Wolfgang Ketterer in Munich,[8] where it was acquired by the American collector Robert Gore Rifkind; thence via Sotheby's, New York, to the present owner.[9]

Despite the inscription on the reverse which, though seemingly by the artist herself, was almost certainly added years after the event – perhaps during the 1930s – on stylistic grounds the painting should probably be dated no later than the beginning of 1909. The pronounced chiaroscuro which distinguishes the treatment of the facial features would argue strongly for such a date: by 1909–10, such a manner of depiction had given way to a flatter handling of paint, with areas of pigment often delimited by heavy countours, quite unlike the still impressionistic handling characteristic of [73].[10]

8 Auction no.8 (28 November 1972, lot 846)
9 I am grateful to Robert Gore Rifkind, Los Angeles, CA, also to his Registrar, Christine Vigiletti, for supplying details of the painting's acquisition and subsequent disposal by the Robert Gore Rifkind Collection
10 I am grateful both to Dr Armin Zweite and to Professor Reinhold Heller of the University of Chicago for their opinion on the dating of this portrait

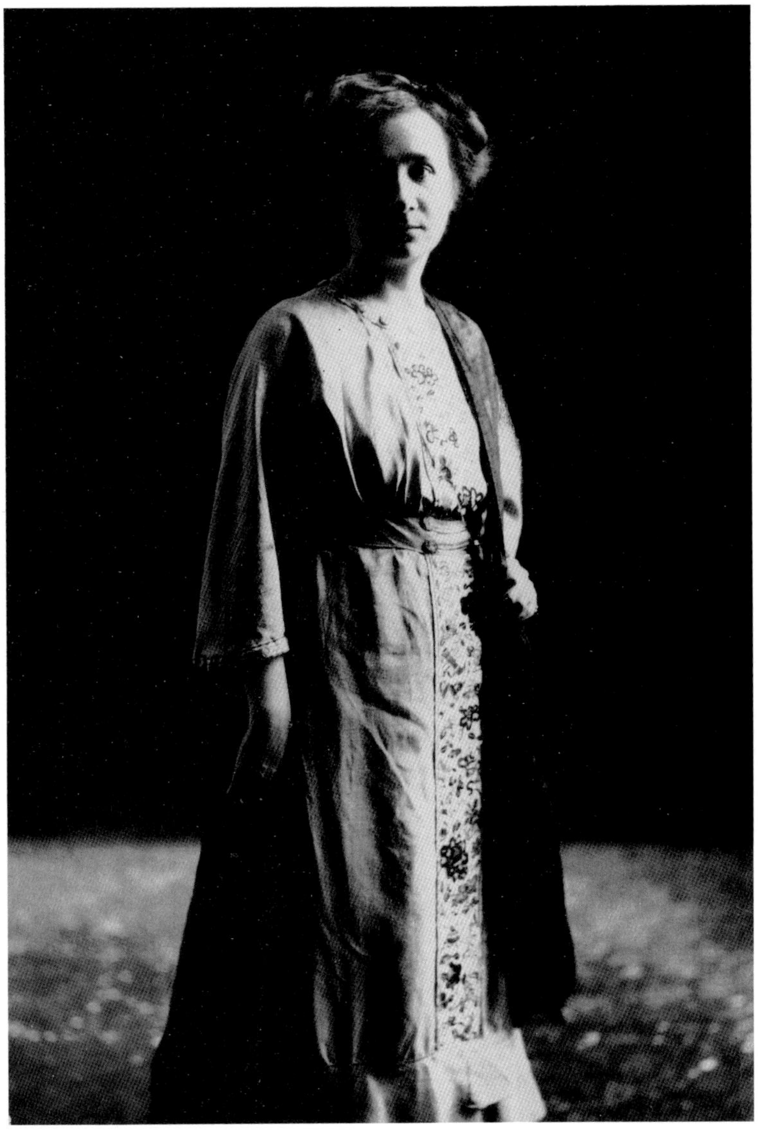

FIG 1 Portrait photograph of Gabriele Münter, June 1910 (Gabriele Münter- und Johannes Eichner-Stiftung, Munich)

Gabriele Münter 1877–1962

74 Murnau

1924
Oil on canvas, 51 × 38 cm
Signed/dated lower right: 'Münter Murnau 1924'; inventory number 'L97' inscribed on back of canvas, also estate stamp: 'Gabriele Münter Nachlass'
The picture is painted on pre-primed commercial canvas, which has been fixed to a new stretcher. The canvas itself appears to have been cut from a larger piece and re-used; a vertical crease some 25 mm from the present left-hand edge shows where it must previously have been folded around the original stretcher. Otherwise condition is good[1]
Accession no.1970.22

Provenance
Estate of the artist
Gabriele Münter and Johannes Eichner Foundation[2]
Galerie Aenne Abels, Cologne
Thyssen-Bornemisza Collection, 1970

Exhibitions
Rome 1990–91, no.37

Literature
See Eichner (1957), pp.178ff, 210–11

As already noted in connection with *Murnau: Houses on the Obermarkt* [34], in summer 1908 Kandinsky and Münter returned to Bavaria where, the following year, Münter bought a house in the market village of Murnau. To this day, the house is known to some of the older villagers as the 'house of the Russians', doubtless because so many of the artists who congregated there during the years before the First World War were Kandinsky's compatriots, among them Jawlensky, the painter Marianne von Werefkin, the sculptor Moissej Kogan and the dancer Aleksandr Sakharov.

Notes
1 I am grateful to Emil Bosshard, Head of Conservation of the Thyssen-Bornemisza Collection, for providing additional information regarding this painting
2 Like [73], the present landscape was de-accessioned by the Gabriele Münter- und Johannes Eichner-Stiftung (see p.281) in 1970 and sold to the Kunsthandling Resch in Gauting. I am indebted to the president of the board of trustees of the Münter–Eichner Stiftung, Dr Armin Zweite, for information concerning the sale of this painting

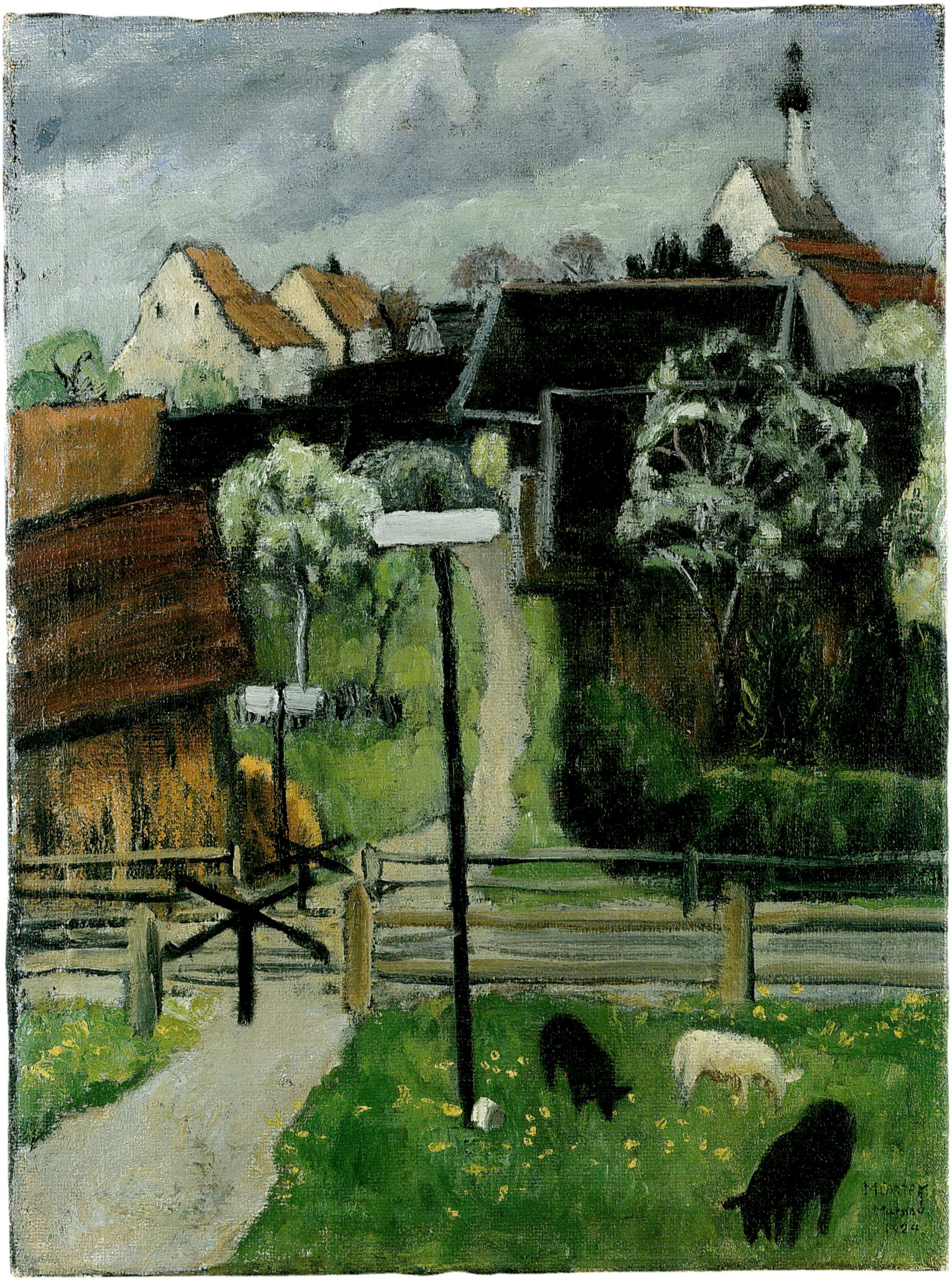
Münter
Murnau
1924

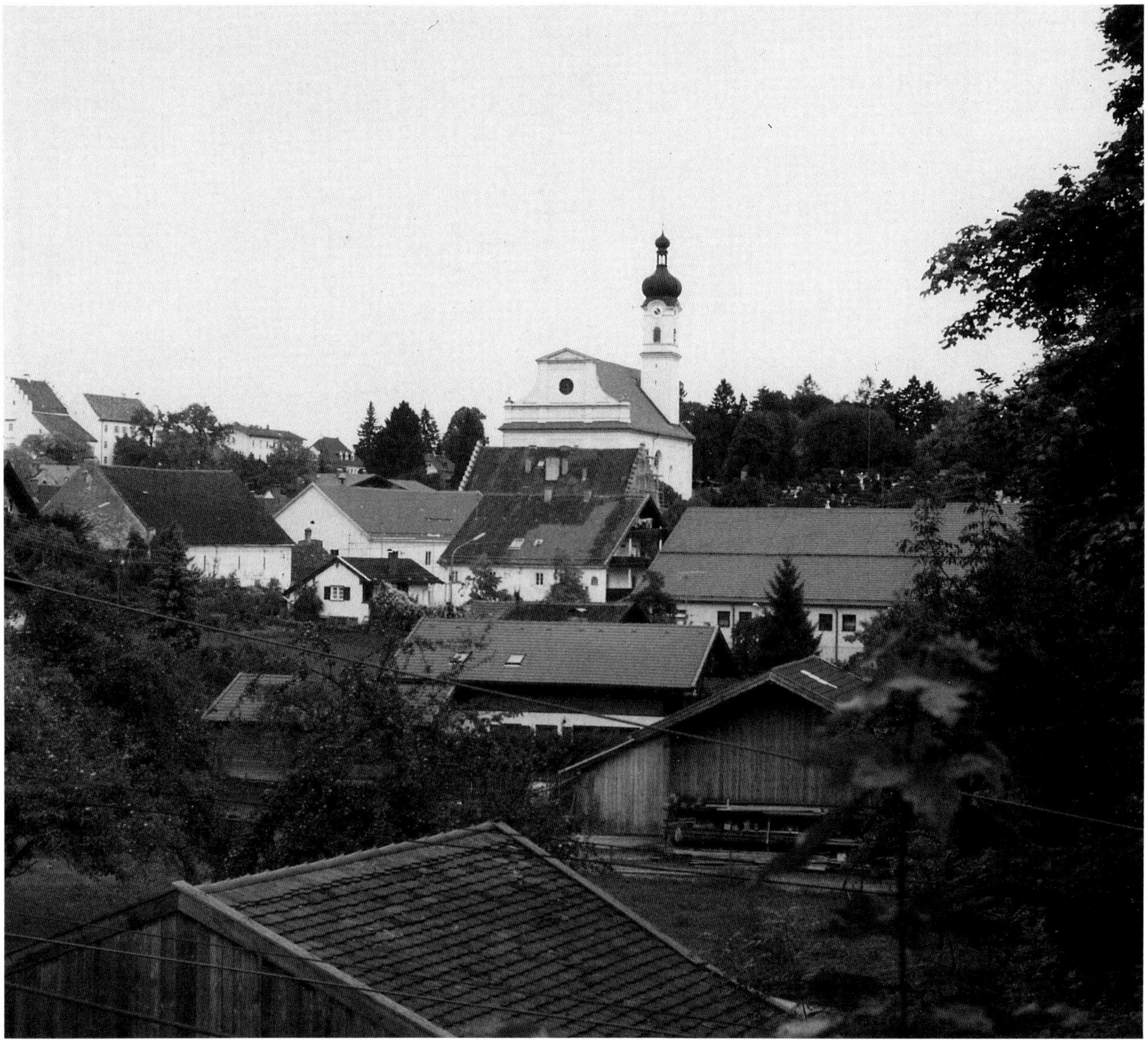

FIG 1 Murnau seen from the west, 1988

Notes

3 On the details of Kandinsky and Münter's wartime relationship, see Barnett (1989), pp.10ff, 69ff; also Gisela Kleine, *Gabriele Münter und Wassily Kandinsky*, Frankfurt (Insel) 1990, especially pp.453ff

4 According to the artist's 'Notizkalendar' for 1924, she was in Murnau during the last ten days of March, nearly the whole of May and late June to early July. The present work is probably identical with the picture she entitled *Studie 3: Bahnübergang*, which according to her notes was painted on 12 May. I am indebted to Professor Reinhold Heller of the University of Chicago, who is preparing a complete catalogue of Münter's paintings, for communicating to me this information derived from the archives of the Gabriele Münter- und Johannes Eichner-Stiftung, Munich

5 See Uta Schedler *et al.*, *Murnau am Staffelsee: St. Nikolaus und seine Nebenkirchen*, 4th edn., Munich (Schnell & Steiner) 1984, pp.2ff.

Having returned to Russia after the outbreak of hostilities, Kandinsky met Münter for the last time on neutral soil, in Stockholm, in the winter of 1915–16.[3] After the ending of their relationship and his marriage to Nina Andreevskaia in 1917, Münter prolonged her stay in Scandinavia until the war was over, returning to Germany only in 1920. However, she kept on the house in Murnau; the village and its surroundings provided the subject matter of many of her landscape paintings of the early twenties, among them *Murnau*.[4]

The 'house of the Russians' is situated on the outskirts of Murnau, the garden side of the house looking towards the centre of the village. The present picture is painted from a standpoint close to the bottom of the garden, with the parish church of St Nikolaus and its cluster of adjacent buildings prominent in the background.[5]

After the lapse of more than half a century, the surroundings have changed in several respects. In particular, the footpath across the railway line, which still separates the house from the village itself, has disappeared and been replaced by a road bridge. None the less, several of the buildings which feature prominently in Münter's painting have survived. A recent photograph (fig.1), taken from a standpoint close to that from which the picture must have been painted, gives an idea of the location.

It is interesting to compare Kandinsky's 1908–9 painting of Murnau, seen from a very similar standpoint just below the 'house of the Russians' (fig.2), with Münter's treatment of the same subject. Both artists have in a number of important respects 'adjusted' reality, in Kandinsky's case abbreviating many of the architectural details, massing the buildings more closely together and making the slope up to the centre of the village appear much steeper than it really is. Münter's painting, on the other hand, rather surprisingly omits altogether one of the most striking features of the church, its unashamedly Baroque façade with gable and oculus which, as far as it is possible to ascertain, must have looked very much the same in 1924 as it does today.

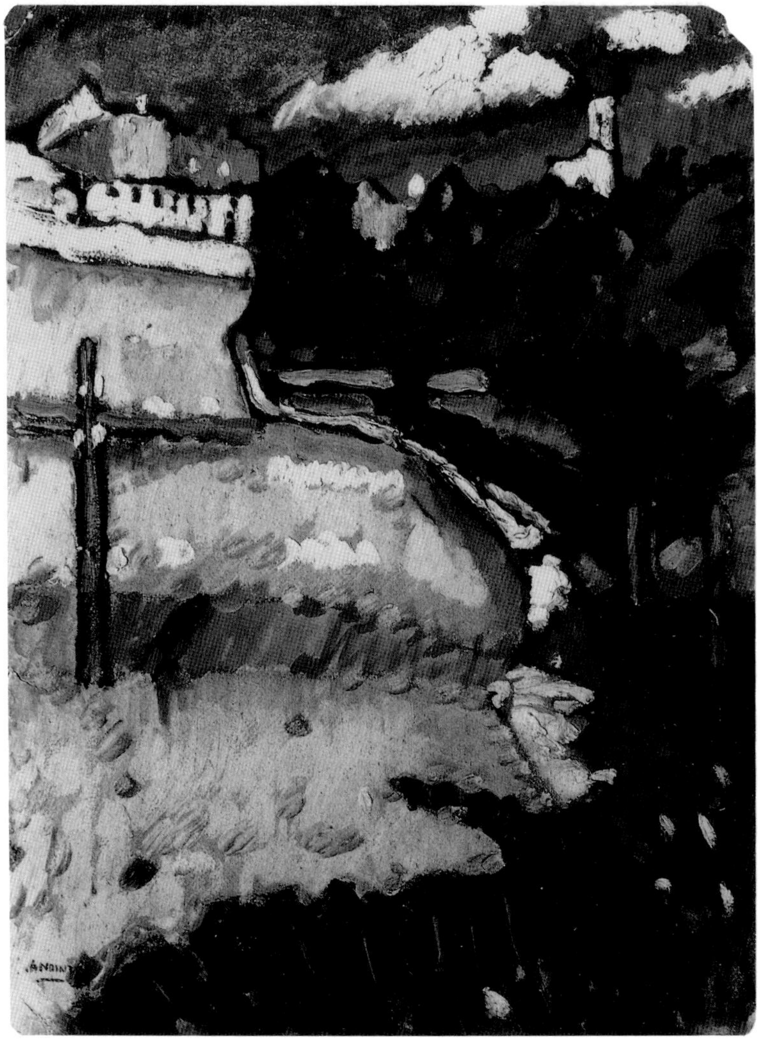

FIG 2 Wassily Kandinsky, *Study for Church in Murnau*, 1908–9, oil and tempera on board, 44.5 × 32.8 cm (Omsk, Regional Museum of Fine Arts, inv. no.Zh-444)

Edvard Munch 1863–1944

75 Evening
Aften

1888
Oil on canvas, 75 × 100.5 cm
Signed/dated lower right: 'Edvard Munch 1888'
Small tears in the canvas have been repaired and the picture relined with a glue lining. There are minute scattered losses, with some evidence of retouching. Otherwise condition is good
Accession no.1967.7

Provenance
J.Sejersted Bødtker, Oslo
Thorvald Johnsen, Oslo
Private collection, USA
Galerie des Arts Anciens et Modernes, Schaan, Liechtenstein
Thyssen-Bornemisza Collection, 1967

Exhibitions
Kristiania [Oslo], 1888, *Kunstudstillingen*, no.108
Berlin, Nationalgalerie, 1927, *Edvard Munch*, no.16
Oslo, Nasjonalgalleriet, 1927, *Edvard Munch*, no.32 [as 'Den gule hatt']
Oslo, Kunstnernes Hus, 1932, *Høstutstillingen gjennem de første 25 år 1882–1907*, no.199 [as 'Portrett (søsteren med gul hatt)']
Boston, MA, Institute of Contemporary Arts, 1950, *Edvard Munch*, no.5[1] [as 'The Evening Hour']
The Hague, Gemeentemuseum, 1951–2, *Edvard Munch*, no.5 [as 'Avonduur']
Warsaw, Muzeum Narodowe, 1959, *Edvard Munch, malarstwo i grafika*, no.3
Frankfurt am Main, Steinernes Haus (Kunstverein), 1962–3, *Edvard Munch*, no.4
New York, Solomon R.Guggenheim Museum, 1965, *Edvard Munch*, no.5
Australian tour, 1979–80, no.7
Hamburg, Kunsthalle, 1986, *Eva und die Zukunft*, no.77
Lugano 1989, no.3

Literature
Jens Thiis, *Edvard Munch og hans samtid*, Oslo (Gylendal Norsk Forlag) 1933, pp.145–8
Arve Moen, *Edvard Munch. Nature and Animals*, Oslo (Norsk Kunstreproduksjon) 1958, pp.16–18
Otto Benesch, *Edvard Munch*, London (Phaidon) 1960, pp.7, 131
Gösta Svenaeus, *Edvard Munch. Das Universum der Melancholie*, Lund (Vetenskaps Societeten) 1968, pp.148–50
Trygve Nergaard, 'Despair', in Munch (1978), pp.122–3
Stang (1979), pp.63–4 and fig.78
Eggum (1984), pp.51–2 and fig.88
Heller (1984), p.41
Werner Hofmann (ed.), *Eva und die Zukunft. Das Bild der Frau seit der Französischen Revolution*, exh. cat., Hamburg, Kunsthalle, 1986, pp.153–4

The painting has also been known as *Evening Hour* (or *Evening Hour with the Artist's Sister Laura*) and *The Yellow Hat*, though the evidence for these titles remains uncertain. The title used here, *Evening* (Norwegian: *Aften*) is that under which the work was first shown at the annual Autumn Exhibition (*Høstutstilling*) in Kristiania in 1888.[2]

It has several times been stated that the picture was painted at Åsgårdstrand, a resort a few miles to the south of Oslo, where Munch rented a holiday house in the summer of 1889.[3] This, however, seems highly improbable. It was not until the autumn of 1888 that he visited Åsgårdstrand for the first time, whereas *Evening* has unmistakably the air of a summer painting, and is indeed referred to as such in, for example, Ragna Stang's book on the artist.[4]

Notes
1 Exhibition also shown in Washington, New York, Detroit, Minneapolis, Colorado Springs, Los Angeles, San Francisco, Pittsburgh, Chicago and Saint Louis during 1950–51
2 On the early history of the Autumn Exhibition see Schneede (1984), pp.7f. Schneede notes that, although initially independent of the state, as early as the 'third year of its existence' (i.e. 1884) the exhibition had started to enjoy official patronage
3 For example by Moen, op. cit., p.16, who also states, incorrectly, that Munch purchased the house at Åsgårdstrand in 1888. Munch in fact continued to rent for some years, buying a house there only in 1897: see *Edvard Munch. Sommernacht am Oslofjord, um 1900*, exh. cat., Mannheim, Städtische Kunsthalle, 1988 (Kunst + Dokumentation, no.12); also Eggum (1984), p.285
4 Stang (1979), p.63. Since, moreover, the picture was ready for the opening of the Autumn Exhibition at the beginning of October 1888, for this reason also it seems likely that it must have been begun at least several months previously, during the summer of that same year, and must therefore have been painted somewhere other than at Åsgårdstrand

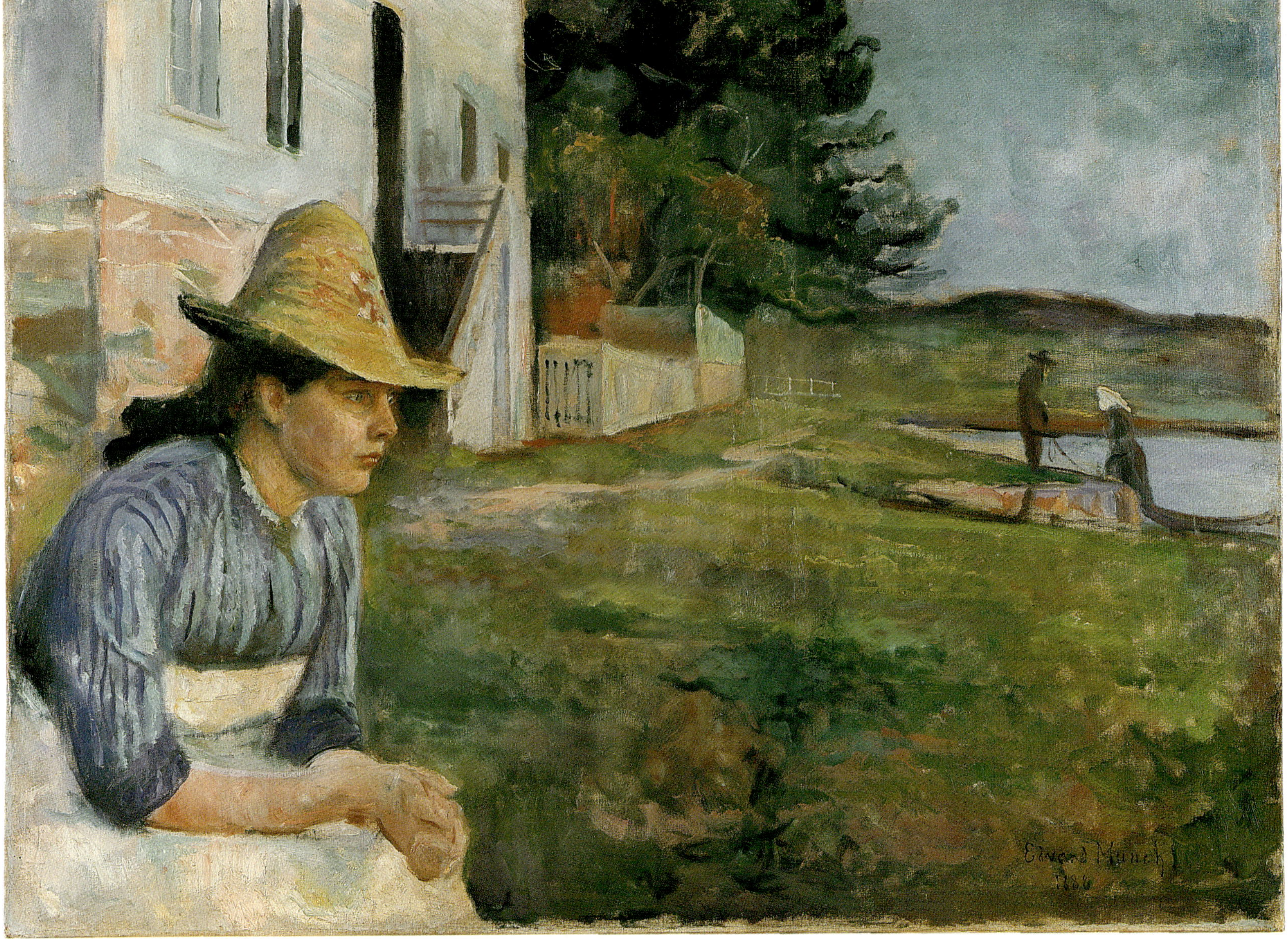
Edvard Munch
1886

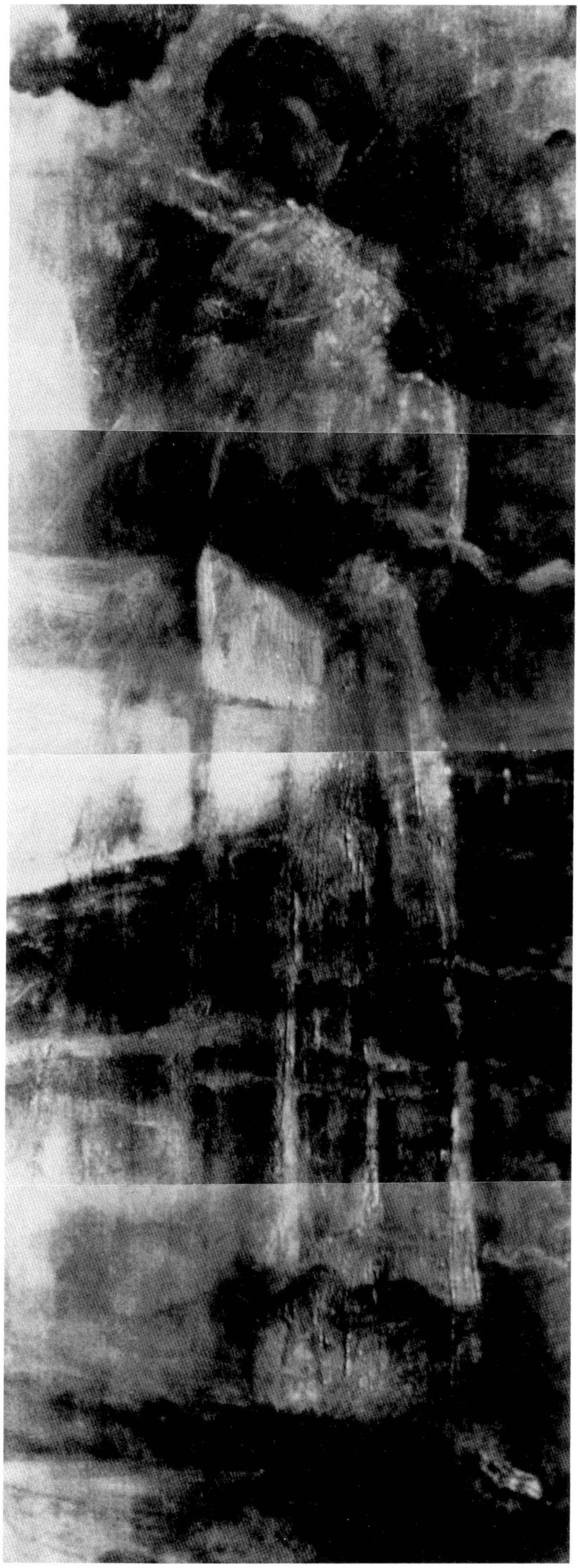

FIG 1 central detail of *Evening* under infra-red reflectography

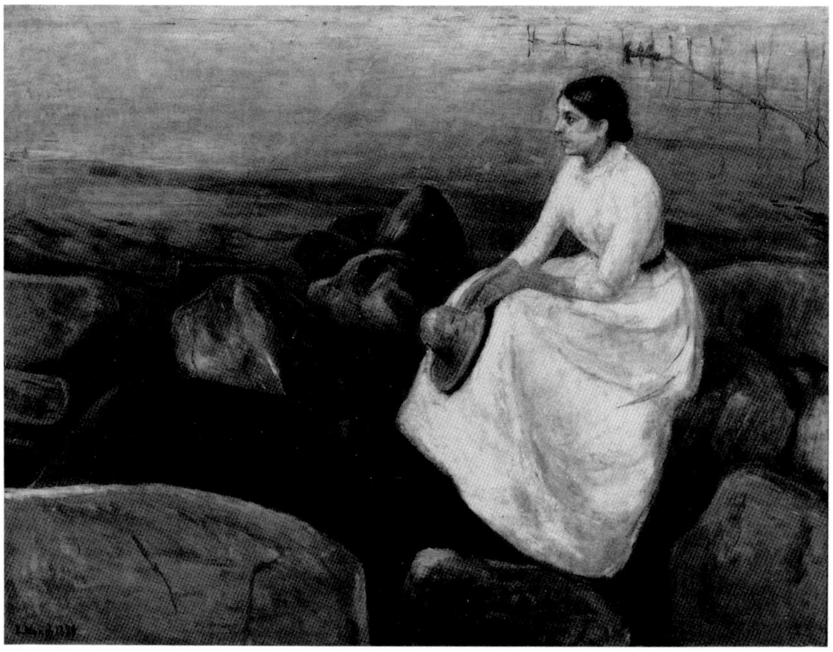

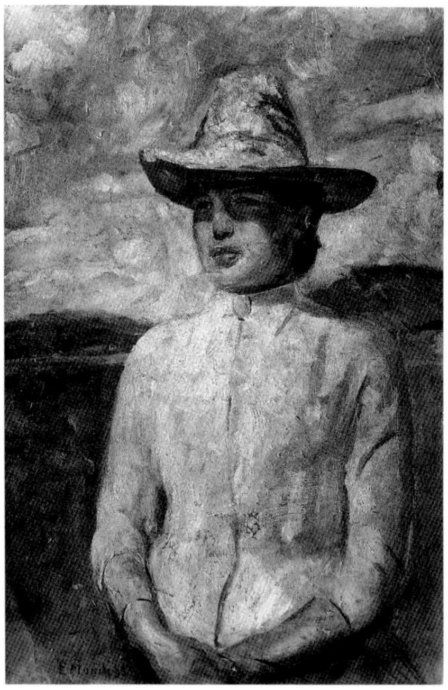

FIG 2 Edvard Munch, *Inger on the Beach*, 1889, oil on canvas, 126.5 × 162 cm (Bergen, Rasmus Meyers Samlinger)

FIG 3 Edvard Munch, *Inger in the Sunshine*, 1888, oil on board, 73 × 46 cm (Bergen, Rasmus Meyers Samlinger)

Moreover Jens Thiis, whose 1933 monograph was written in collaboration with Munch and who was a close personal friend, refers to the painting by the title *Evening at Vrengen*.[5] Munch visited Vrengen, a tiny hamlet somewhat further from Oslo than Åsgårdstrand, roughly equidistant from Sandefjord and Tonsberg on the western shore of Oslofjord, in the summer of 1888, staying with his friend, the painter Karl Doernberger.[6] In all probability, *Evening* was painted there in the course of this summer 1888 visit.

The young woman with the yellow hat, seated in the left foreground staring out of the picture, is Munch's younger sister Laura Cathrine (1867–1926). Laura seems to have been particularly associated in his mind with the theme of melancholy, perhaps because of her precarious mental state. There are several references to her bouts of depressive illness, and she spent periods in the asylum at Gaustad from 1894 to 1896,[7] where Munch made a number of studies related to the later painting *Melancholy (Laura)* of 1899 (Munch Museum, Oslo).

The picture as we see it today is no longer as it first appeared, but has at some point been overpainted: there was originally another female figure placed almost centrally within the composition, standing slightly behind the seated girl with yellow hat (compare fig.1).[8] The artist's intention in painting out this figure was presumably both to stress the asymmetry of the composition, and to emphasize the disjunction between sitter and landscape, characteristics which are found repeatedly in his work of the 1890s.

Svenaeus has pointed to the possible influence of artists such as Daumier and Degas, as well as that of Japanese woodblock prints, in the placing of the truncated foreground figure close to the surface plane of the picture. However, apart from any such formal similarities, the deliberate 'unbalancing' of the composition in so many of his paintings of the late eighties and early nineties was a device which Munch elaborated over a number of years, and which quite clearly had a specific emotional resonance for him. In other works of this period, the asymmetrical placing of a figure, staring into space against a landscape background, is linked both with the themes of isolation, melancholy and depression, and with the subject of evening, as in the colour woodcut *Evening/Melancholy* of 1896[9]; compare also the oil painting *Melancholy: the Yellow Boat* (1892–3; Nasjonalgalleriet, Oslo).

Evening has also been compared on several occasions with Munch's painting of his other sister Inger, done the following year (fig.2). In its handling of paint, however, it is far closer to the half-length *Inger in the Sunshine* of 1888 (fig.3). Both *Evening* and *Inger in the Sunshine* may

Notes

5 The only other writer to refer to the painting consistently by the title *Evening at Vrengen* is Ragna Stang, Thiis's daughter: see Stang (1979), pp.63–4 and list of plates, p.306

6 See Langaard (1961), p.17

7 Stang (1979), p.169; Eggum (1984), pp.51, 137, 155. Laura died of cancer in 1926

8 Examination of the picture by means of infra-red reflectography reveals that the shadowy form beneath the surface paint layer is a standing figure of a woman with centre parting clad in a long dress, represented frontally and occupying almost exactly the centre of the composition (see fig.1). The faint image of another female figure observed by Nergaard standing at the top of the steps leading into the house is not, however, a first thought subsequently obscured by over-painting, but is made up of a few summary and indistinct brushstrokes laid on top of the main surface layer of paint: see Nergaard, loc. cit.

9 Schiefler (1907), no.82

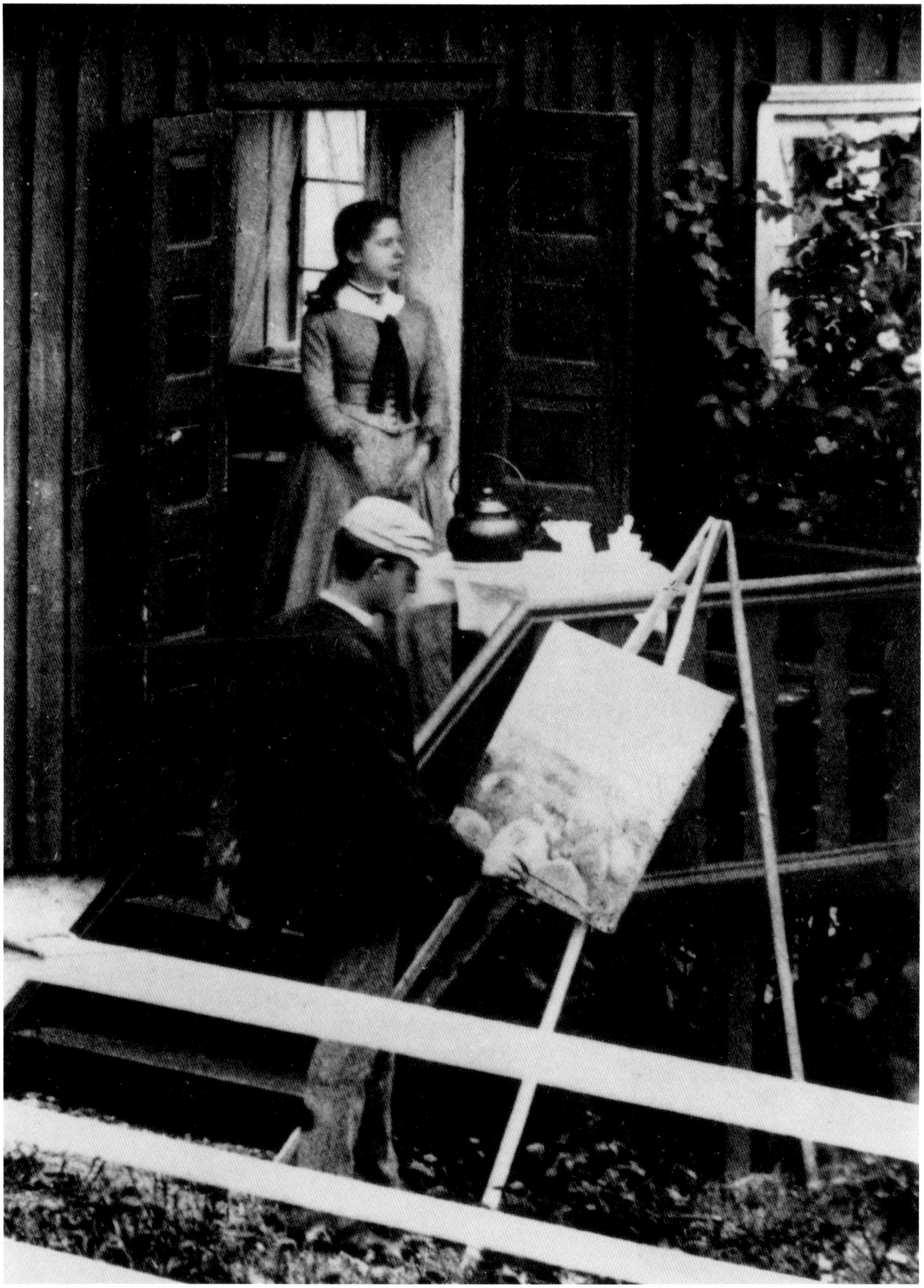

FIG 4 Munch painting in front of his rented house in Åsgårdstrand, with his sister Laura standing in the doorway, summer 1889 (Munch Museum, Oslo)

seem in retrospect a surprising return to naturalism after the astonishing first version of *The Sick Child* (see p.292). The critics, however, failed to notice Munch's partial accomodation to the prevailing taste of his time, and his works shown at the Autumn Exhibition of 1888 were in general greeted scathingly. The newspaper *Aftenposten* wrote:

> E. Munch's *Evening* (no.108), depicting a girl with a large violet face under a yellow straw hat sitting in a blue field outside a white house, occupies an even lower place. The whole thing is so indescribably poor in every respect that it appears almost comic ... Accepting pictures of this kind for exhibition reveals either a complete misunderstanding of one's task and one's duty or a complete lack of artistic understanding, helping simply to debase art in the eyes of the general public, while at the same time young artists themselves are thereby confused and led astray.[10]

A closely related painting by Munch, depicting Laura seated in the foreground wearing the same yellow straw hat, was offered for sale by Sotheby's, New York, in October 1990 under the title *Sisters in the Garden* (fig.5).[11] Much looser and more Impressionistic in its handling of paint, it may well have been a preliminary study for *Evening*. Like the original version of [75] prior to over-painting, it includes in the middle distance a standing female figure, perhaps Inger. In *Sisters in the Garden*, however, the psychological tensions which must have been evident in *Evening* when first exhibited in 1888 are underlined by the way in which both figures are shown gazing into space, staring fixedly in opposite directions, out of the picture.

Notes

10 *Aftenposten*, no.604 (Friday, 5 October 1888), p.1, also quoted by Thiis, op. cit., p.148. I am indebted to Helen Skåtun for locating and translating the original newspaper review and to Dr Marit Werenskiold, of the University of Oslo, for providing information regarding early exhibitions of Munch's work, and for her helpful comments on the foregoing catalogue entry

11 Sotheby's, New York, sale 6083 (*19th and 20th Century Scandinavian Painting and Sculpture*, 26 October 1990, lot 191)

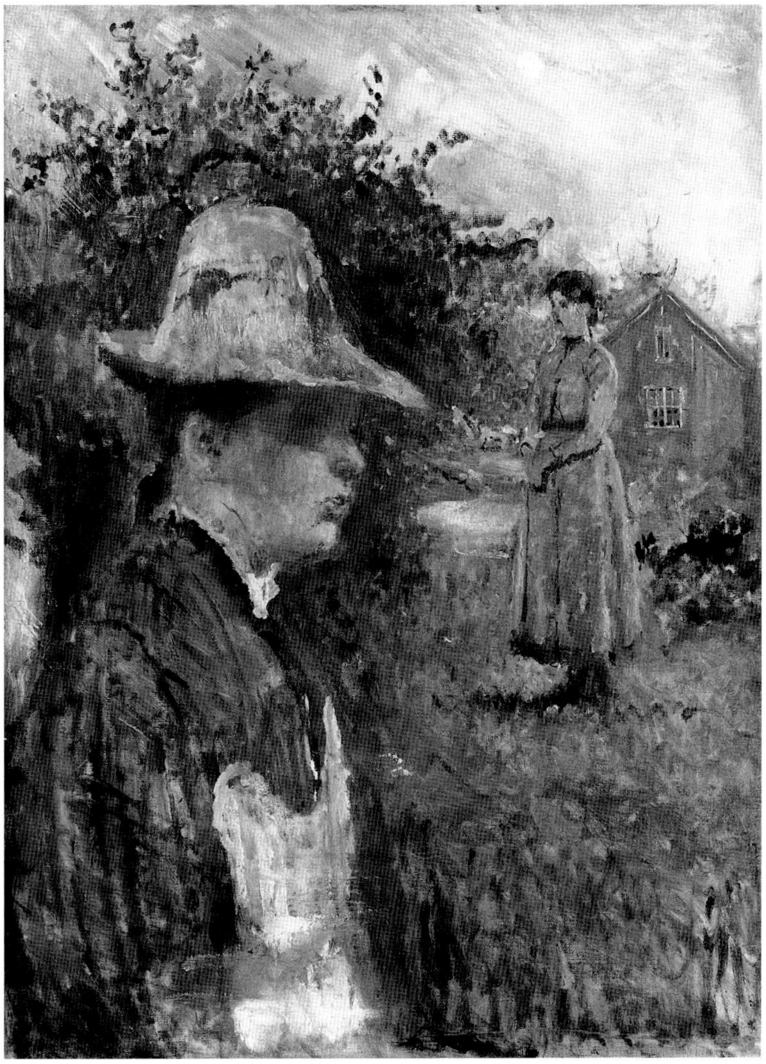

FIG 5 Edvard Munch, *Sisters in the Garden*, 1888, oil on canvas, 85.1 × 62.2 cm (Sotheby's, Inc., New York)

Edvard Munch 1863–1944

76 The Sick Child[1]

1896
Lithograph printed in two colours on heavy wove paper, 42.1 × 56.5 cm (image)
Signed lower right in pencil, in the border: 'E. Munch'
First state, prior to signature in the lithographic stone
Apart from a couple of tears at the upper edge of the sheet, since repaired, condition is good
Accession no.1973.45

Provenance
Clarence and Jane Franklin, New York
Kornfeld & Klipstein, Berne
Thyssen-Bornemisza Collection, 1973[2]

Literature
Schiefler (1907), no.59
Arne Eggum, 'The Theme of Death', in Munch (1978), pp.143ff
Prelinger (1983), pp.76f and col. pl.50
See also Alley (1981), pp.548f; Schneede (1984); *Edvard Munch. Sein Werk in Schweizer Sammlungen*, exh. cat., Basle, Kunstmuseum, 1985, p.12

This representation of the averted face of the sick child, apparently staring though an unseen window, is a virtual replica of the principal figure which appears in Munch's oil paintings of the same title. This subject seems to have been of great significance for him: he painted no fewer than six oil versions of *The Sick Child* between 1885–6 and *c*1927. This lithographic version is closest in composition to the painting of 1896, now in the Gothenburg Art Museum (fig.1),[3] and even more intimately related to a pastel of the head of the girl done in the same year.[4] Munch had previously reworked the composition of the whole painting, rather than just the head, in the form of a drypoint with roulette which shows the figure reversed, and which is distinguished by the addition of a seemingly unrelated landscape adjoining the lower border.[5] A further drypoint, of smaller dimensions, likewise shows the head of the figure reversed (i.e. to the left); this print, in one or more colours, is comparatively rare.[6]

Notes
1 The title used by Schiefler in his catalogue of Munch's graphic works, which was compiled with the artist's collaboration, is *Das kranke Mädchen* – literally, 'the sick girl'. However, those publications on Munch which have appeared in English have almost invariably opted for the title used here
2 Acquired at auction, 22 June 1973 (*Auktion 150: Graphik von Edvard Munch – Henri de Toulouse-Lautrec*, lot 14). I am grateful to Dr Eberhard W. Kornfeld, Berne, for providing information regarding this sale
3 This 'replica' was painted for the industrialist Olaf Schou: see Eggum, op. cit., pp.150, 152 and n.41
4 Ibid., p.150, fig.8
5 Schiefler (1907), no.7
6 12.7 × 16.8 cm; Schiefler (1907), no.60

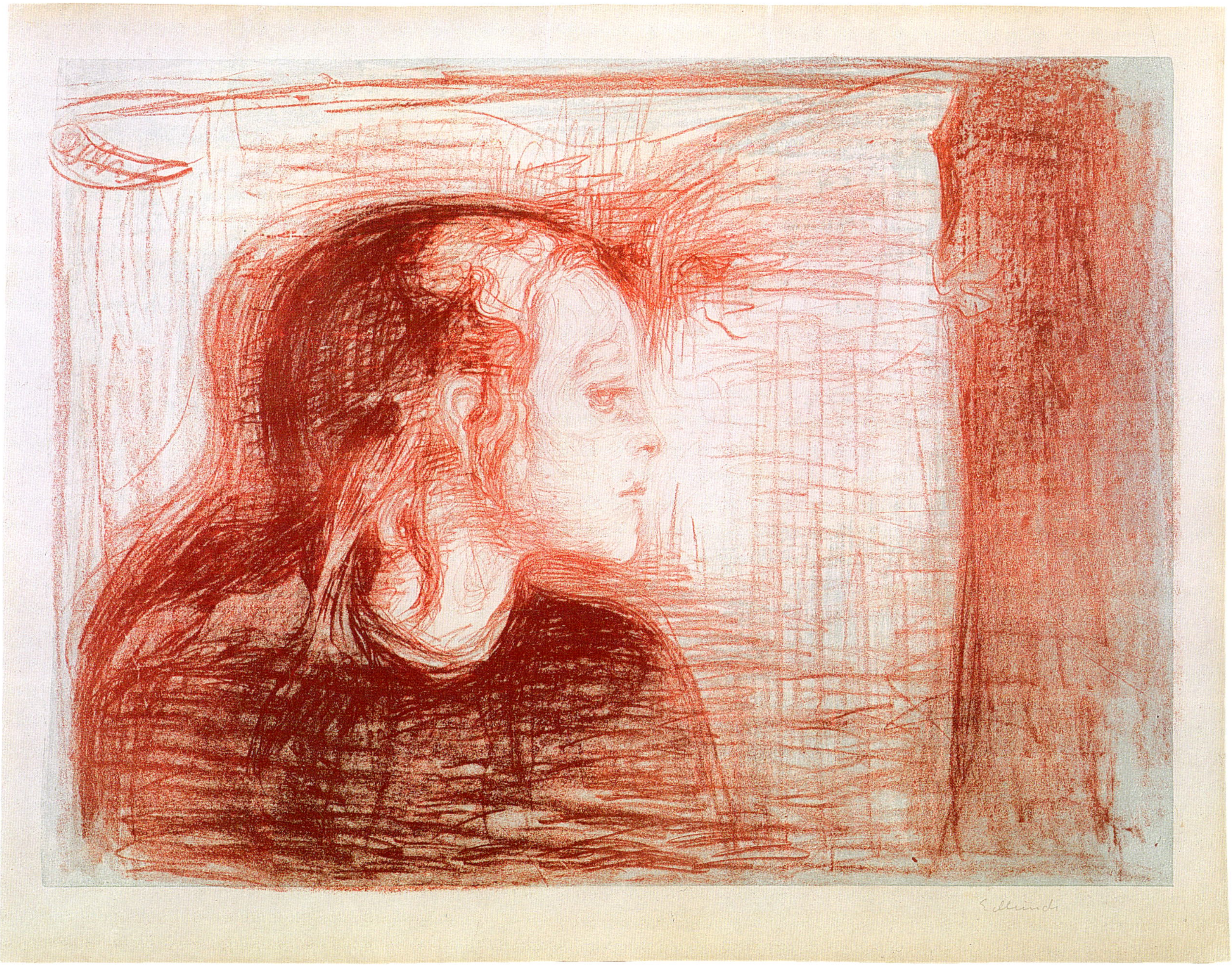

The subject of the dying child has often been related by Munch's biographers to the death of his favourite sister Sophie from tuberculosis in 1877 at the age of fifteen. According to the artist's own recollection, this incident left an indelible scar on his memory and seems in later life to have given rise to an extended series of works which revolve around the themes of sickness, death and bereavement. Sophie's death was evidently still vivid in his mind nearly twenty years afterwards: he described the event in a passage in a letter probably written in the mid-1890s, in other words at almost exactly the same time as the creation of [76]: 'her eyes became red – I could not believe that death was so inevitable, so near at hand ... how strange she felt – the room was different – it was as though she was seeing it though a veil – her body seemed to be weighed down with lead – she was so tired.'[7]

Several commentators have, on the other hand, pointed out that Munch's statements regarding the autobiographical content of his art ('I painted not what I saw, but what I had seen')[8] should not be taken too literally.[9] The subject of the sick child was a frequent one in Scandinavian painting at this time: it had also been treated, for example, by his teacher Christian Krohg, who had intervened on the younger artist's behalf in the controversy provoked by the showing of the first oil version of Munch's *The Sick Child* at the Autumn Exhibition in Kristiania in 1886.[10] Nor is it a matter of any straightforward identification of the subject as representing the death of Munch's sister: on the contrary, there is evidence to show that the girl portrayed was not Sophie at all, but the 11-year-old Betzy Nielsen, whom he had encountered while accompanying his physician father, Dr Christian Munch, on one of his visits, to a house in the east end of Oslo, during the winter of 1885.[11] According to Betzy's own recollections, set down many decades after the event, Dr Munch had been called to attend to the broken leg of her 5-year-old brother; Betzy observed the proceedings with mixed emotions compounded of sympathy and anxiety, while Munch observed Betzy, whose demeanour perhaps called to mind memories of his dead sister. It appears that he then asked Betzy's parents to allow her to pose for *The Sick Child*; her features are also recognizable in other works of 1886, for example the oil painting *Redheaded Girl with a White Rat* (Basle, Oeffentliche Kunstsammlung).

Munch himself regarded the lithographic version of *The Sick Child* as his most important print;[12] it was also his first colour lithograph. It exists in at least three states, and in various colours.[13] The sheet in the Thyssen-Bornemisza Collection represents the earliest known state, prior to signature in the lithographic stone. It was done under the supervision of the printer Auguste Clot during the artist's 1896 stay in Paris. In collaboration with Clot, and by means of two or more stones, Munch was able to experiment with a wide range of colour combinations, varying the colours and sequence of printing stones in a purely intuitive and to all appearances random fashion,[14] so that the known versions of the print range from the colouristically subtle to the strikingly garish. This example is printed in two colours: a burgundy red over a bluish ground, a combination only rarely encountered and which is in this instance peculiarly effective.

Notes

7 *Edvard Munchs brev: Familien*, Oslo (Munch Museum) 1949, cited after Stang (1979), p.34

8 Edvard Munch, *Livsfrisens tilblivelse*, cited after Schneede (1984), p.43

9 See, for example, Carla Lathe, *Edvard Munch and his Literary Associates*, exh. cat., Norwich, University of East Anglia, 1979, p.1: 'It is a mistake to believe that he produced simply autobiographical paintings ... He was interested and curious about other people ... above all he was able to express other people's emotions ... if any of his paintings were based on personal experience, there was a considerable interval of time and effort between the original sensation and the process of recreating it.'

10 Schneede, pp.14, 19ff; for a reproduction of Krohg's *The Sick Child* of 1880–81 see ibid., p.21, fig.14

11 Alley, loc. cit; see also *Edvard Munch, Sein Werk in Schweizer Sammlungen*, p.12

12 Ingrid Langaard, *Edvard Munch. Modningsår*, Oslo 1960, p.453, cited after Prelinger, loc. cit.

13 See Eggum, loc. cit. and n.39

14 Munch's friend Paul Herrmann, who was with him in Paris and visited Clot's studio, described in vivid terms witnessing the creation of *The Sick Child*, and the seemingly random succession of colours employed: see Eggum, op. cit., p.152; also Prelinger, loc. cit.

FIG 1 Edvard Munch, *The Sick Child*, 1896, oil on canvas, 121.5 × 118.5 cm (Gothenburg, Göteborgs Konstmuseum)

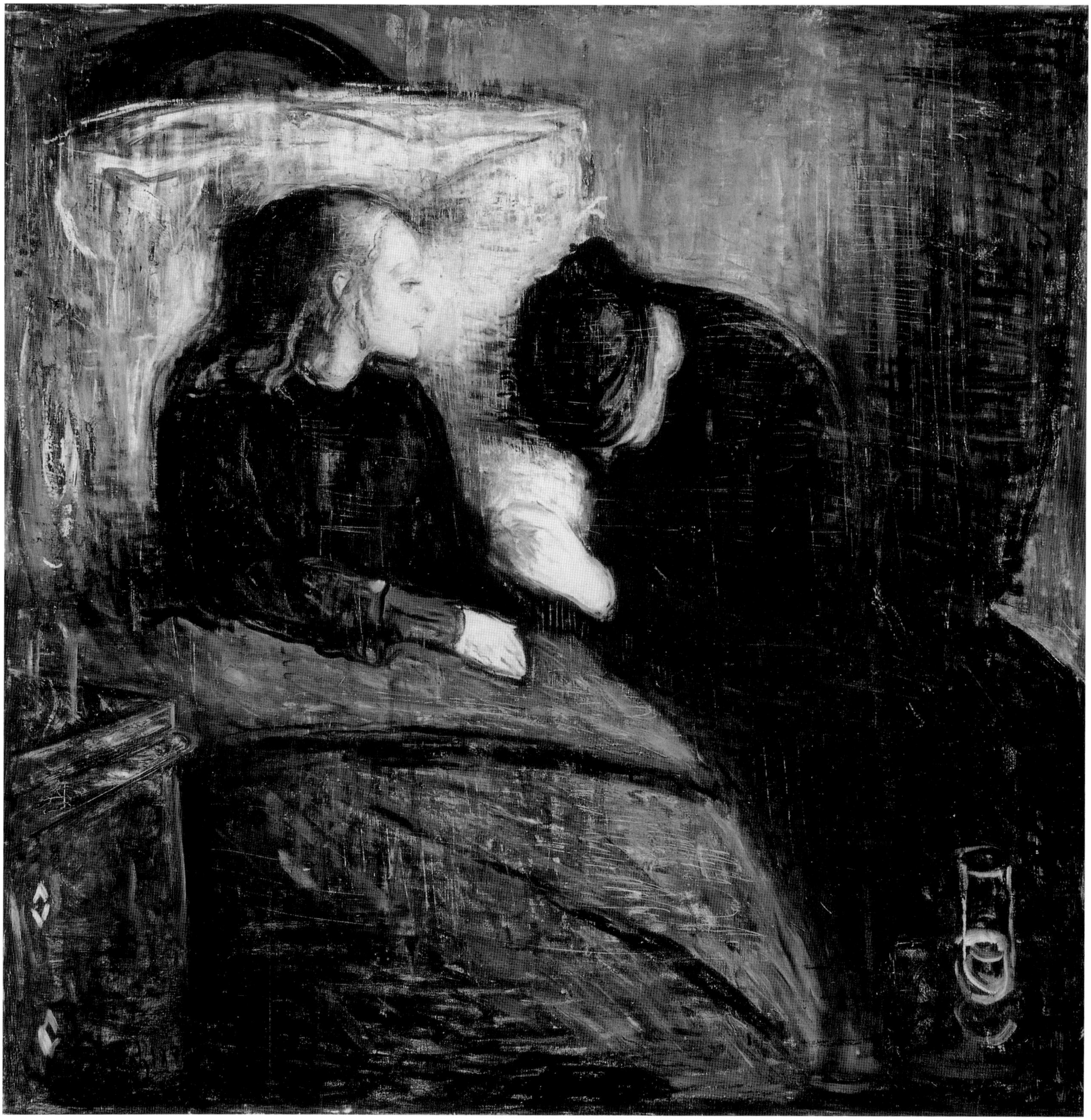

Edvard Munch 1863–1944

77 Encounter in Space
Begegnung im Weltall[1]

1899
Three-colour woodcut on very thin greyish paper, 18.5 × 25.2 cm (image)
Signed lower right in pencil in the border: 'Edv. Munch'
In good condition
Accession no.1973.44

Provenance
Clarence and Jane Franklin, New York
Kornfeld & Klipstein, Berne
Thyssen-Bornemisza Collection, 1973[2]

Literature
Schiefler (1907), no.135
Prelinger (1983), pp.82, 95 and col. pl.63

That the encounter depicted here is of a sexual nature is evidenced by the spermatazoa which also feature in other graphic works by Munch, for example in the border of the lithograph version of *Madonna* of 1895.[3] That it is of a cosmic character is revealed not merely by the title, but also by the dense black of the void against which the floating male and female figures are set. Similar floating forms are found elsewhere in Munch's oeuvre, and are usually associated with some kind of encounter or confrontation between the sexes, as in the lithograph *Lovers in Waves* of 1896;[4] compare the drawing *Moonlight Glides over your Face* of 1894–5, now in the Munch Museum, Oslo.[5] There also exists a version of *Encounter in Space* in the medium of drypoint.[6]

As Prelinger observes, this woodcut has been printed from a single block, cut into three pieces and inked separately: the woman (in this example, bluish-green), the man (brick red) and the background (black). White contour lines around the cut-out shapes echo the strings of white sperm floating in the void and at the same time emphasize the separation of the figures one from another. Their positioning is, from a psychological standpoint, crucial: as so often in Munch's work, it is the female who is made to appear the dominant force, striving purposefully ahead and upwards; the male, by comparison, seems abject, despondent, incapable of action.

As in the case of other woodcuts in which Munch employed the same technique of sawing into a single block and inking the parts separately (for example, *Man's Head in Woman's Hair* or *Women on the Shore*),[7] the block has been subject to considerable wear. In particular, small pieces have evidently broken off at points close to the position of the feet of both the male and the female figures; in a number of impressions, including [77], the corresponding areas of colour loss have been filled in by hand.

Encounter in Space is known in only a relatively small number of impressions. According to Schiefler, the few examples on thin white, as opposed to brownish paper, were hand-printed by the artist. In the case of [77], the support has the appearance of a very thin laid paper; it is, however, greyish rather than white in colour, and may signify an artist's proof or trial state of this print.

Notes
1 The title is that used by Schiefler in his catalogue of Munch's graphic works, which was compiled with the artist's collaboration; it may thus be regarded as authentic
2 Acquired at auction, 22 June 1973 (*Auktion 150: Graphik von Edvard Munch – Henri de Toulouse-Lautrec*, lot 29). I am grateful to Dr Eberhard W. Kornfeld, Berne, for providing information regarding this sale
3 Schiefler (1907), no.33
4 Schiefler (1907), no.71
5 See Munch (1978), p.260, cat. no.243, ill. p.243
6 Entitled by Schiefler *Begegnung im Weltenraum*: see Schiefler (1907), no.151
7 See Prelinger (1983), col. pls.62 and 64
8 Schiefler (1907), p.106

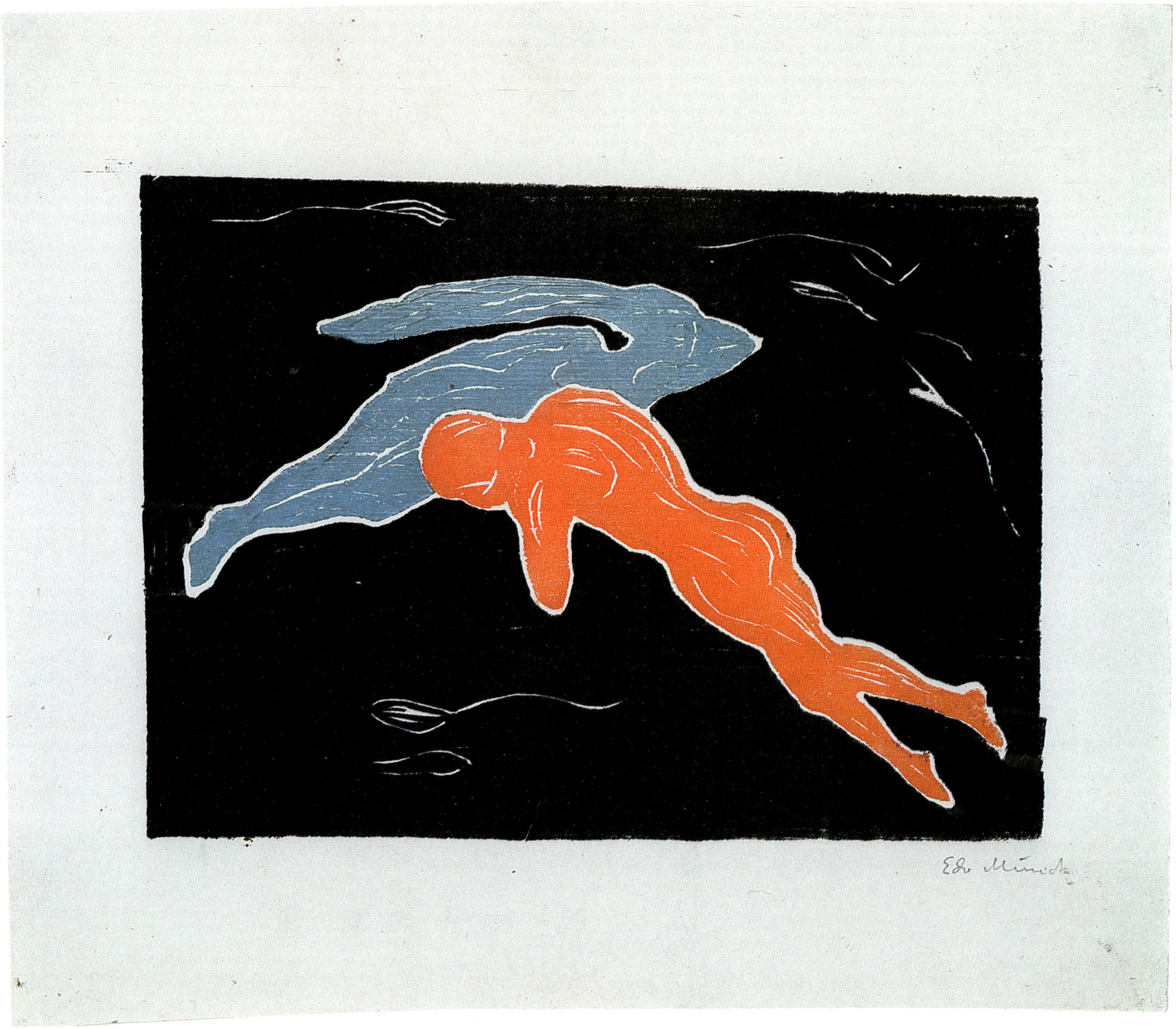

Emil Nolde 1867–1956

78 Red Flowers
Rote Blumen[1]

1906
Oil on canvas, 52.4 × 55.8 cm
Signed/dated lower centre: 'Nolde 06'
Condition fair. There is a history of scattered losses and old repairs. The canvas has been relined with wax–resin adhesive and put on a new stretcher. The painting is unvarnished
Accession no.1980.12

Provenance
Ernst Rump, Hamburg[2]
Aenne Morseth-Rump, Hamburg
Christiane Aubergé-Rump, London
Thyssen-Bornemisza Collection, 1980[3]

Exhibitions
Hagen, Museum Folkwang, 1907, *Emil Nolde*[4]
Hamburg, Galerie Commeter, 1910, *Emil Nolde*[5]
Nagoya, City Art Museum, 1988, *Perspective of Twentieth Century Paintings*, no.6
Lugano 1989, no.18
Rome 1990–91, no.38

Literature
Ernst Rump, *Lexikon der bildenden Künstler Hamburgs . . .*, Hamburg (Otto Bröcker & Co.) 1912, p.96 [as 'Gartenweg']
Urban (1987), no.172

Red Flowers was painted on the island of Alsen in the Baltic in the summer of 1906. The sense of joyful celebration of nature with which the picture is imbued belies the circumstances under which it was created. This was for Nolde a time of great poverty and distress. He was virtually penniless, and more or less dependent on the charity of friends like Hans Fehr. His wife Ada was ill and travelling from sanatorium to sanatorium in search of a cure. He himself was deeply dissatisfied with the progress of his art, and by his own account experienced the utmost difficulty in completing or even starting a picture.[6]

However, that summer he embarked on a series of small-scale flower and garden paintings, many of them done in the gardens of neighbours like Burchard or Anna Wied, who were sometimes his only human contact during the months on Alsen, where he and Ada rented a fisherman's cottage from 1903 onwards. In his paintings of these 'luxuriant, neatly tended gardens bordered by boxwood hedges',[7] with their riotous display of flowers, the element of colour is all-important, 'spread out carpet-wise in a vibrant surface to which order is brought by the rhythm of their application and a kind of musical harmony in the juxtaposition of shades.'[8]

Red Flowers is almost exactly contemporary with Schmidt-Rottluff's *The Little House* [102], also painted at Alsen that same summer; indeed, the two pictures may well have been executed within a few weeks of each other. A comparison between them makes clear that both artists were, at this time, responding to very similar influences, principally French Impressionism and the art of van Gogh. These influences are reflected in the vivid colours, open brushwork and heavy impasto which are the distinguishing characteristics of [78].

Nolde had come into contact with Impressionism as early as 1899–1900, during the course of an extended visit to Paris. Though it is unlikely that he saw van Gogh's paintings at this time, he was certainly aware of them by 1906 at the latest, partly as a result of the various retrospective exhibitions held in Germany the previous year, partly through his contacts with Karl Ernst Osthaus at Hagen, one of the first German museum directors to purchase examples of the Dutch artist's work.[9]

Notes
1 The title *Rote Blumen* occurs in a handlist of Nolde's paintings compiled by the artist in 1930: see Urban (1987), p.171
2 Acquired directly from the artist, 1910
3 Acquired directly from the previous owner
4 Nolde in most cases kept detailed records of when his works were sold or exhibited; these records are now in the archives of the Stiftung Seebüll Ada und Emil Nolde. In this and the following entries, indications regarding early exhibitions are taken from the two-volume oeuvre-catalogue of the paintings by the director of the Nolde-Stiftung, Martin Urban, which is based on the information contained in the archives: see Urban (1987) and (1990)
5 Exhibition subsequently shown at the Kunstverein, Essen, and at the Kunstverein in Jena: see Urban (1987), p.580
6 See Nolde (1971), pp.76f
7 Ibid., p.108
8 Urban (1970), p.16
9 See Feilchenfeldt (1988), pp.18ff

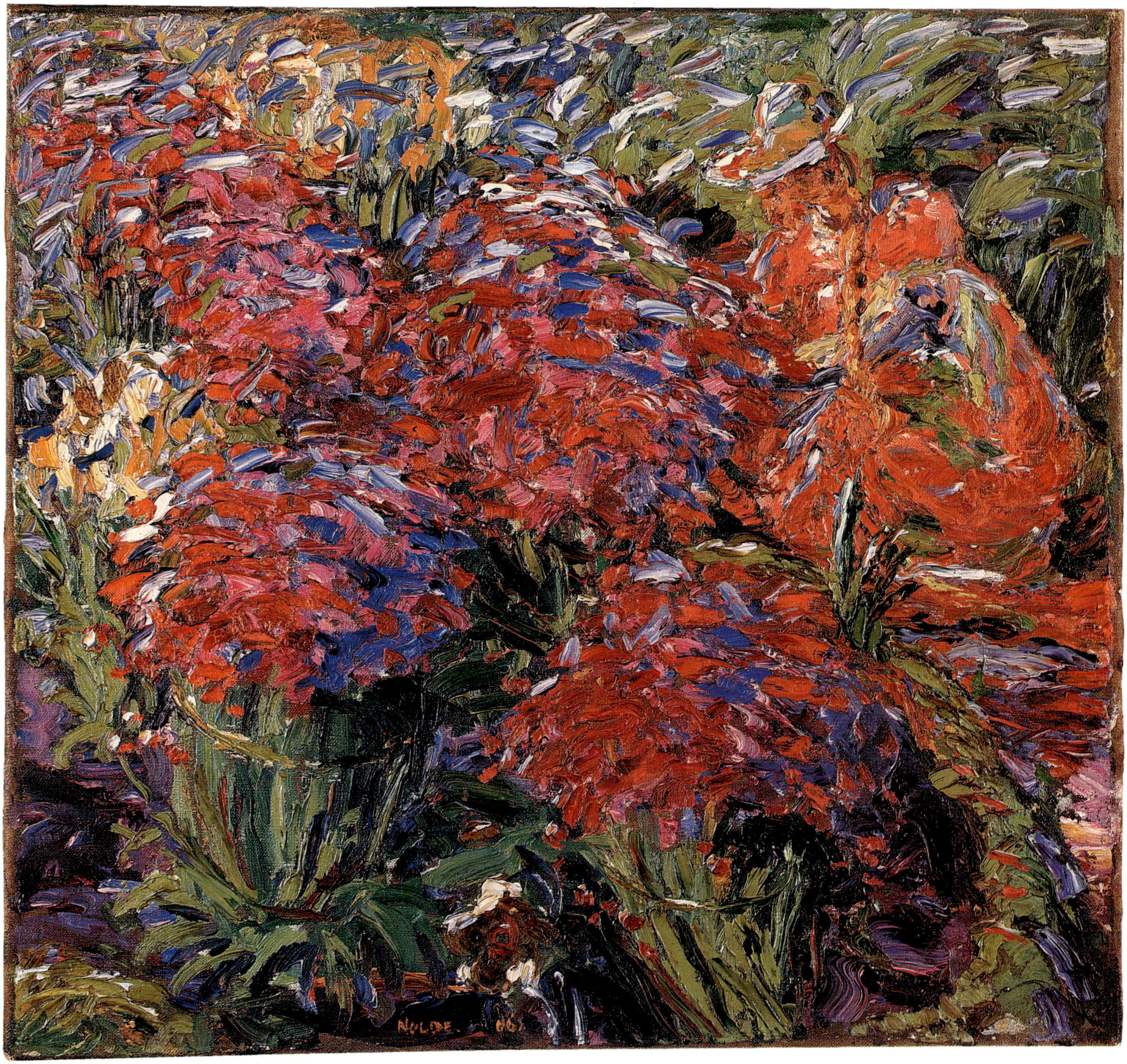
NOLDE

Emil Nolde 1867–1956

79 Summer Clouds
Sommerwolken

1913
Oil on canvas, 73.3 × 88.5 cm
Signed lower right: 'Emil Nolde'; inscribed on stretcher: 'Emil Nolde: "Sommerwolken"'[1]
The painting is unvarnished and has become rather dirty. The canvas is cockled along the top and bottom edges. The paint layer is brittle, and there are areas of pronounced crackle, especially in the passages of heavy impasto
Accession no.1972.12

Provenance
Collection of the artist
Kunsthalle, Kiel, Schleswig-Holsteinischer Kunstverein
Arvid Brodersen, Denmark
Gemälde-Galerie H. & G. Abels, Cologne
Private collection, London
Hauswedell & Nolte, Hamburg
Thyssen-Bornemisza Collection, 1972[2]

Exhibitions
Elberfeld, Städtisches Museum, 1914, *Nolde, Pechstein, Beckmann*
Kiel, Schleswig-Holsteinischer Kunstverein, 1920, *Rohlfs, Nolde, Barlach (Jahresausstellung 1920)*, no.80[3]
London, Marlborough Fine Art, 1964, *Emil Nolde*, no.8
London, Tate Gallery, 1964, *Painters of the Brücke*, no.149
New York, Spencer A. Samuels, 1968, *Expressionismus*, no.9
Cologne, Kunsthalle, 1973, *Emil Nolde. Gemälde, Aquarelle, Zeichnungen und Druckgraphik*, no.51
Bremen 1975, no.59
Lugano 1975, no.19
Brussels/Paris 1977–8, no.64
Lugano 1978, no.80
Australian tour 1979–80, no.32
Modern Masters from the Thyssen-Bornemisza Collection, 1984–6, no.83
Nagoya, City Art Museum, 1988, *Perspective of Twentieth Century Paintings*, no.7
Lugano 1989, no.19
Expressionism and Modern German Painting, 1989–90, no.27
Rome 1990–91, no.39

Literature
Alfred Heuer, 'Emil Nolde', *Jahrbuch für den Kreis Pinneberg*, VI (1922): 28–30
Arthur Haseloff, 'Die Kieler Kunsthalle', *Museum der Gegenwart*, I, no.2 (1930–1): 62ff, ill. p.67
R.N. Ketterer, *Moderne Kunst V*, Campione d'Ialia (Galerie R.N. Ketterer) 1968, p.159, no.126, ill.
Kiel (1974), p.102, ill. p.103
Urban (1987), no.554

For much of his life, Nolde lived on the edge of, or close to the sea, whose ever-changing aspect had a symbolic, almost mystical significance for him. The elemental forces of nature were a constant source of pictorial inspiration. In his autobiography, recalling a stormy boat trip across the Kattegat, still vivid in his imagination though it had occurred many years earlier, he reflected: 'Supposing a heavy sea had swept me overboard and I had had to struggle for my life against the elements? I wonder if I should now be able to paint the sea even more powerfully?'[4]

Notes
1 The painting is also entered under the title *Sommerwolken* in a handlist of Nolde's paintings compiled by the artist in 1930: see Urban (1987), p.483
2 Acquired at auction, 10 June 1972 (*187. Auktion*, lot 1738)
3 According to Urban (1987), p.483
4 Nolde (1971), p.108

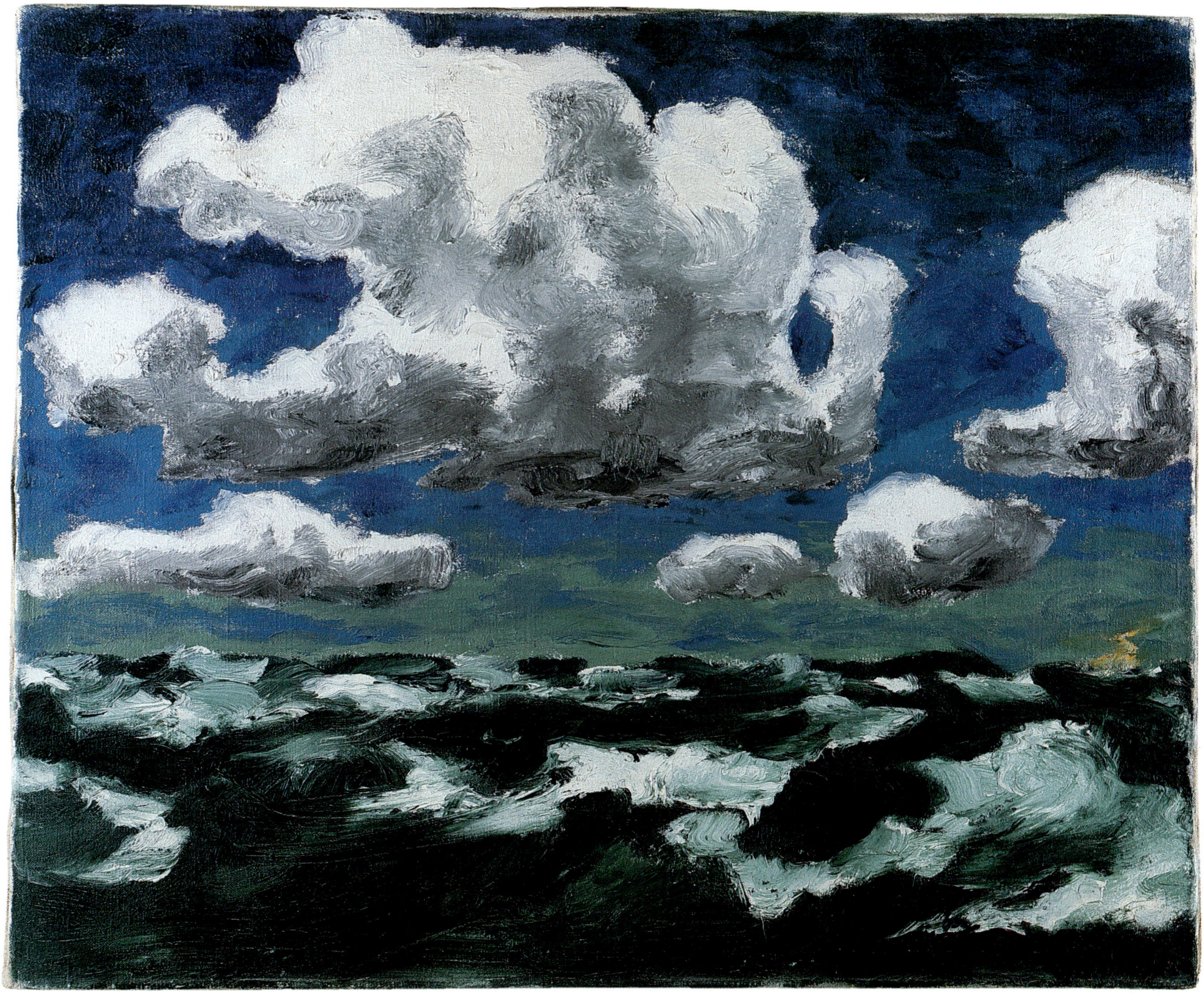

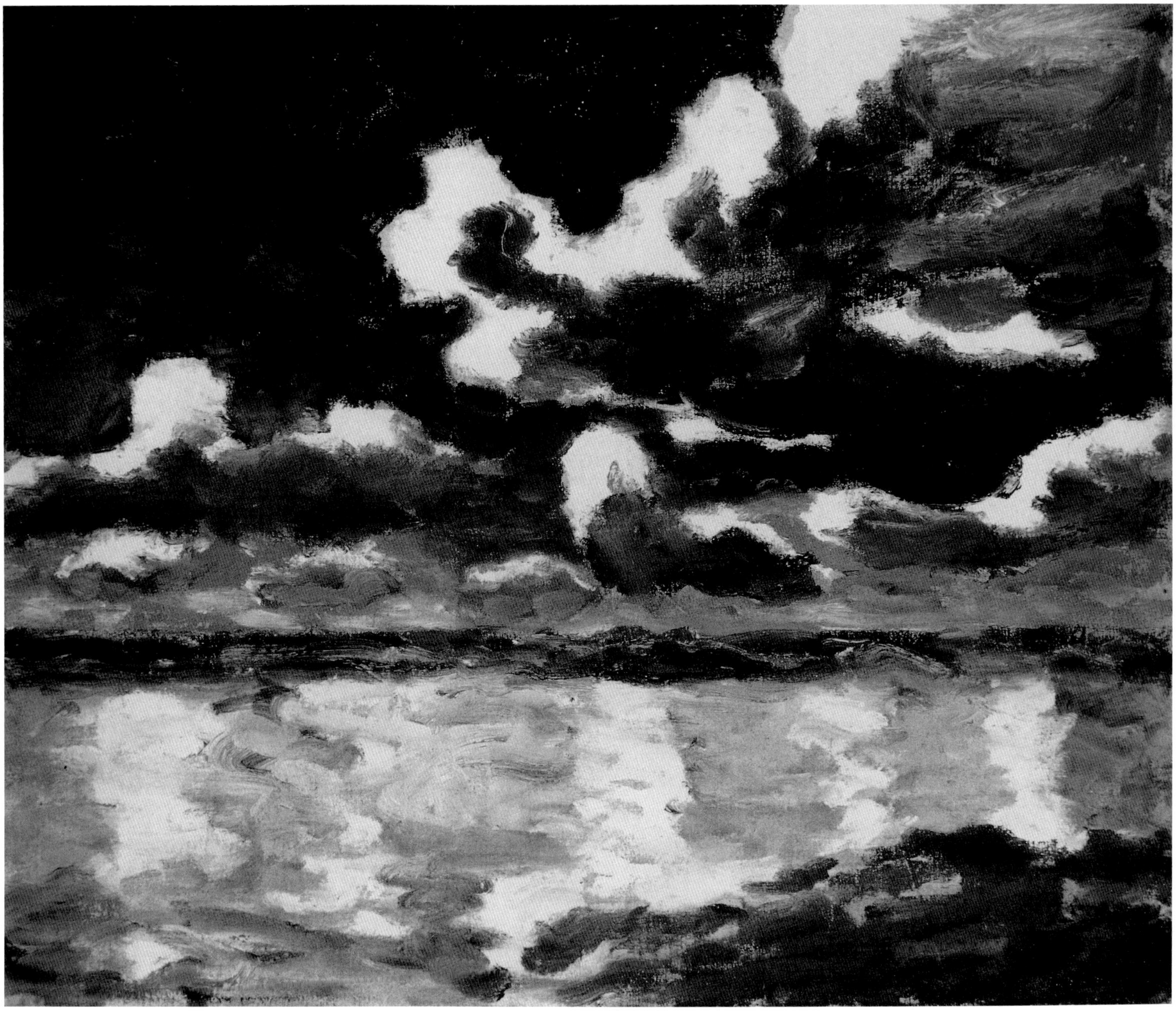

He depicted waves and sea – rarely calm, even in this supposedly summer picture – on numerous occasions throughout his career, from 1901 (an early group of paintings executed in Copenhagen)[5] until 1951, the year in which he painted his last seascape, *Autumn Sea in the Evening*.[6] In 1910–11 he produced a series of nineteen pictures entitled *Autumn Seas*. In 1913, however, he painted only one other comparable canvas of sea and heavy clouds, very similar in style, in subject and in scale to *Summer Clouds*: the painting *Wolkenspiegelung* (Reflection of Clouds) in the collection of Berthold von Bohlen und Halbach, Essen (fig. 1).

FIG 1 Emil Nolde, *Reflection of Clouds*, 1913, oil on canvas, 86 × 100 cm (Essen, Berthold von Bohlen und Halbach)

Notes

5 Urban (1970), p.32

6 Urban (1990), no.1355

Summer Clouds was acquired by the Kunsthalle in Kiel in 1921,[7] where it remained on display until its confiscation by the Nazis in 1937.[8] It was thus well known at a relatively early date, being discussed, for example, in an article by the teacher Alfred Heuer which appeared in a regional journal the year after the picture's acquisition. In addition to linking the painting with the German Romantic tradition, Heuer makes a number of perceptive remarks about the artist's handling of his subject and, more generally, about his relationship with nature:

> A triad of colours of the utmost subtlety of effect: green and blue are laid on top of one another in a lucid structure, the green of the water with its white crest suggesting at the same time the white spume of clouds in the sky. Transition from green to the blue of the sky, and the brilliant snow white of the clouds, powerful and luminous in their intensity ... towards the upper edge of the painting becoming bluer and bluer, streaming forth in all directions, unchecked, into infinity, embracing the whole world, producing an effect far exceeding the bounds of the picture: only sea and clouds and sky – the entire loneliness of Nordic seas ... How prosaic Liebermann with his impressionistic seascapes seems by comparison. How differently Böcklin attempts to enliven his sea by means of lengendary creatures, of which Nolde has no need. Only Hodler, conjuring up as if with divine hand the mountain summits of his native Switzerland, partakes of the same spirit as Nolde.[9]

7 Haseloff, loc. cit.
8 *Summer Clouds* was listed among the confiscated pictures stored at the Depository for Degenerate Art at Schloss Niederschönhausen under inventory no.14222: see Urban (1990), p.15; also Andreas Hüneke, 'On the Trail of Missing Masterpieces. Modern Art from German Galleries', in Barron (1991), pp.121ff
9 Heuer, loc. cit. I am grateful to Professor Martin Urban for drawing this article to my attention

Emil Nolde 1867–1956

80 Flower Garden
Blumengarten

1917
Oil on plywood panel, 82.5 × 64.5 cm
Signed lower right: 'Nolde'; inscribed on back of panel: 'Emil Nolde. Blumengarten. Rosen, Feuerlilien, Rittersporn' (Emil Nolde. Flower Garden. Roses, Tiger-lilies, Larkspur)[1]
The plywood panel is convex-warped and is split vertically in two places. Apart from minor cracking, however, the condition of the paint layer is good. The painting is unvarnished
Accession no.1964.8

Provenance
Estate of the artist
Ada und Emil Nolde Foundation, Seebüll
Marlborough Fine Art, London
Thyssen-Bornemisza Collection, 1964

Exhibitions
Frankfurt am Main, Kunstsalon Ludwig Schames, 1925, *Emil Nolde*, no.29
Oldenburg, Augusteum (Vereinigung für Junge Kunst), 1925, *Emil Nolde*, no.27
Altona, Altonaer Museum, 1926, *Emil Nolde*
London, Marlborough Fine Art, 1964, *Emil Nolde*, no.17
Bremen 1975, no.56
Lugano 1975, no.20
Lugano 1978, no.81
USA tour 1982–4, no.11
Modern Masters from the Thyssen-Bornemisza Collection, 1984–6, no.82

Literature
Kiel (1974), p.104, ill. p.105
Urban (1990), no.763

Flower Garden was probaby painted between May and October 1917 at Utenwarf, the remote farmhouse close to the German–Danish border which Nolde and his wife purchased in 1913. Work to make the house habitable had been delayed by their voyage to the South Seas in 1913–14. Only in July 1916 were he and Ada able to move into their new home, still unfinished because of the war.

As at Nolde's last house at Seebüll, at Utenwarf the artist took a great interest in the immediate surroundings, especially the garden. The gardens at Utenwarf and at Seebüll provided the subject of numerous paintings dating from the 1920s and 1930s.

Note
1 The title *Blumengarten* (*Rosen, Feuerlilien, Rittersporn*) is also entered in a handlist of Nolde's paintings compiled by the artist in 1930: see Urban (1990), p.141

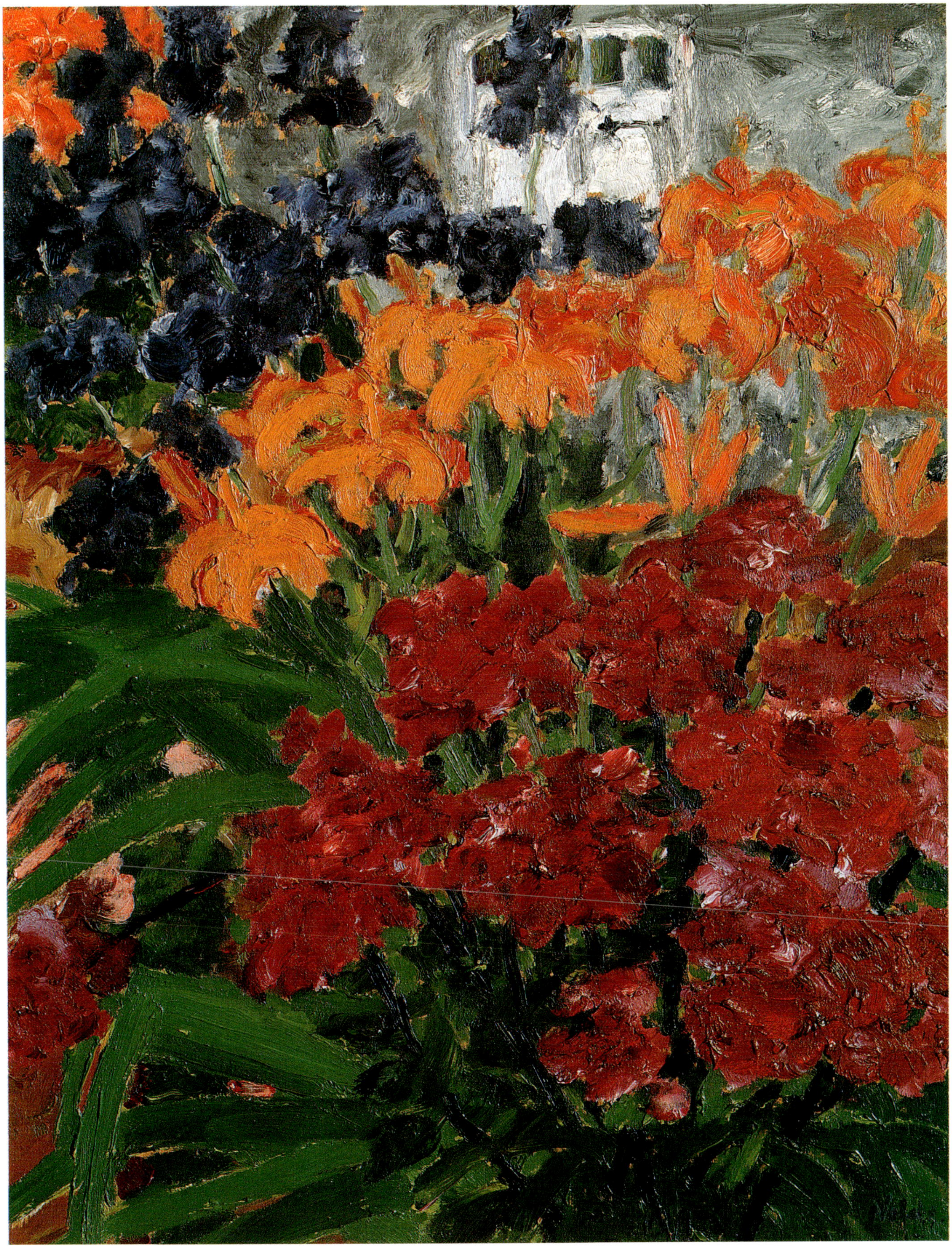

Emil Nolde 1867–1956

81 Autumn Evening
Herbstabend

1924
Oil on canvas, 73 × 100.5 cm
Signed lower left: 'Emil Nolde'
The canvas has been relined, and the original stretcher with the inscription 'Herbstabend' replaced. The canvas is uneven, with numerous distortions and bulges; there are also vertical tension cracks across the whole of the paint surface. The painting is unvarnished
Accession no.1964.9

Provenance
Estate of the artist
Ada und Emil Nolde Foundation, Seebüll
Marlborough Fine Art, London
Thyssen-Bornemisza Collection, 1964

Exhibitions
Dresden, Städtisches Kunstausstellungsgebäude, 1927, *Emil Nolde. Jubiläumsausstellung zum 60. Geburtstag*, no.140[1]
Frankfurt am Main, Kunstverein, 1928, *Emil Nolde*, no.91
Wuppertal, Kunst- und Museumsverein, 1951, *Emil Nolde*[2]
Mannheim, Städtische Kunsthalle, 1952, *Emil Nolde*, no.36
Kiel, Schleswig-Holsteinischer Kunstverein, 1952, *Emil Nolde*, no.21
Odense, Fyns Stiftsmuseum, 1956, *Emil Nolde*, no.21
Kiel, Kunsthalle, 1956–7, *Emil Nolde Gedächtnisausstellung*, no.20
Hamburg, Kunstverein/Essen, Museum Folkwang/Munich, Haus der Kunst, 1957, *Emil Nolde. Gedächtnisausstellung*, no.139
Amsterdam, Stedelijk Museum, 1958, *Emil Nolde*, no.46
Frankfurt am Main, Kunstverein, 1958, *Emil Nolde*, no.30
Zurich, Kunsthaus, 1958, *Emil Nolde*, no.51
Brussels, Palais des Beaux-Arts, 1961, *Emil Nolde*, no.40
Hanover, Kunstverein, 1961, *Emil Nolde. Oelgemalde, Aquarelle, Zeichnungen*, no.40
London, Marlborough Fine Art, 1964, *Emil Nolde*, no.24
Cologne, Kunsthalle, 1973, *Emil Nolde. Gemälde, Aquarelle, Zeichnungen und Druckgraphik*, no.92
Villingen-Schwenningen, Beethovenhaus, 1974, *Emil Nolde. Gemälde, Aquarelle, Graphik*, no.4
Bremen 1975, no.58
Madrid, Centro de Arte Reina Sofia, 1989, *Berlin, Punto de Encuentro*, no.2/27
Lugano 1989, no.20
Expressionism and Modern German Painting, 1989–90, no.28

Literature
Kiel (1974), p.106, ill. p.107
Urban (1990), no.987

From his earliest years, Nolde employed vivid colour to expressive ends. In his paintings of the 1920s and 1930s, however, he began to use more opaque, saturated colours, often having profound symbolic or emotive connotations. In his autobiography he wrote of how for him colours have a 'life of their own, weeping or laughing, dream and joy . . . vibrating like the peal of silver bells, like the sound of bronze, heralding joy, passion and love, blood and death.'[3]

Autumn Evening was almost certainly painted at Utenwarf between May and October 1924. His depictions of the surrounding countryside, 'that flat landscape where the heavy storm clouds terrify weaklings,'[4] are almost invariably devoid of figures and, as in the present case, often seem imbued with an air of menace.

According to Urban, *Autumn Evening* was one of ninety-two paintings and watercolours shown in Mannheim at the Kunsthaus Rudolf Probst in 1937, an exhibition which was banned by the authorities after three days.[5] In his autobiography, Nolde refers to the president of the Reichskunstkammer accompanied by three officials having travelled to Mannheim specifically in order to close the exhibition and forbid the gallery owner from selling his work.[6] This incident, though relatively minor in itself, is indicative of the fate his art was to suffer at the hands of the Nazi régime.

Notes
1 According to Urban (1987), p.582, there were two versions of the catalogue of this jubilee exhibition to mark the artist's 60th birthday: in the variant or 'B' version, the present painting is listed as no.159. After Dresden, the exhibition travelled to Hamburg, Kiel, Essen and Wiesbaden
2 Exhibition recorded by Urban (1990), p.315
3 Nolde (1971), p.200
4 Quoted after Urban (1970), p.26
5 See Urban (1987), p.582. No catalogue of the exhibition appears to have survived
6 Nolde (1978), p.121

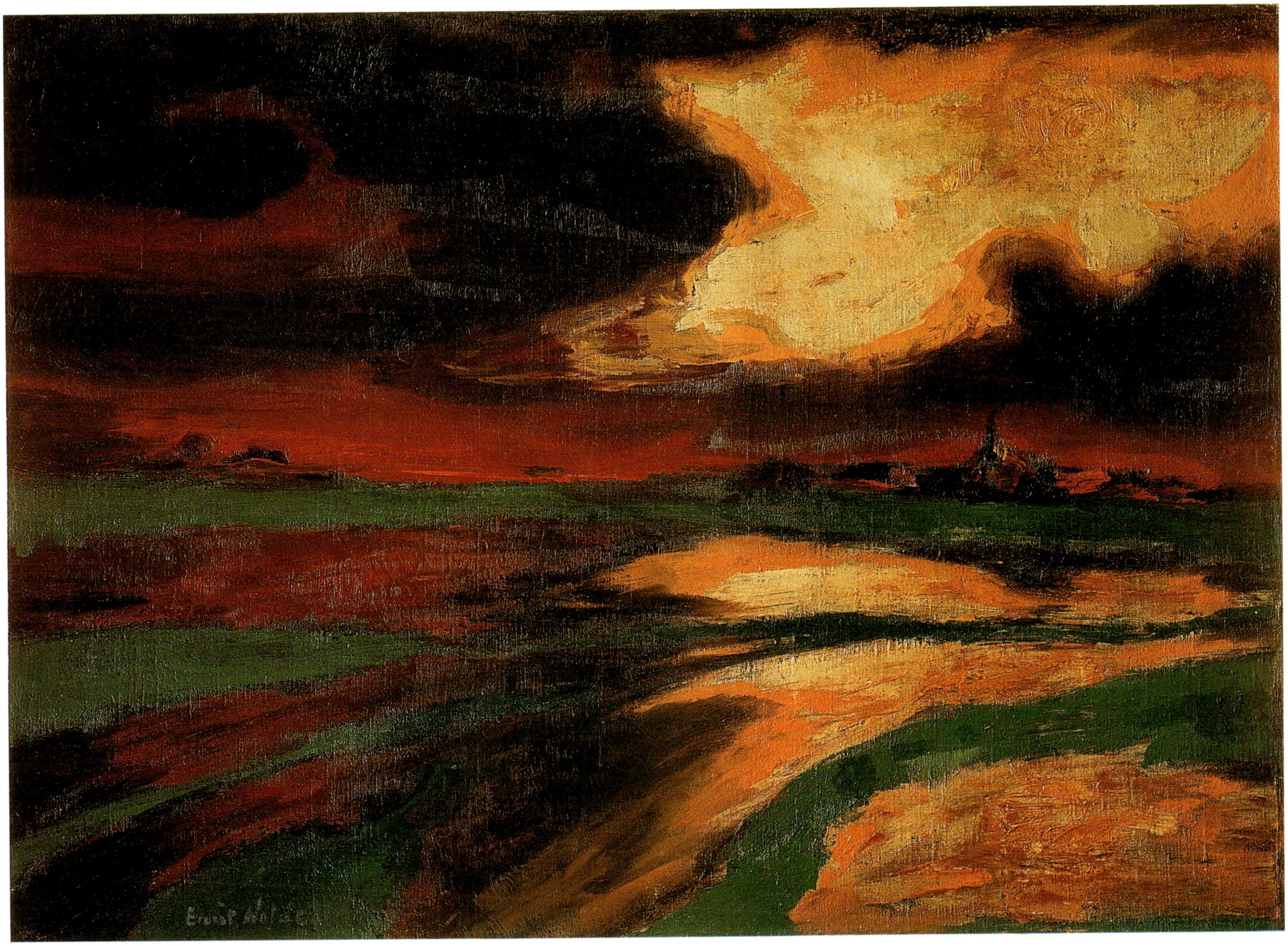

Emil Nolde 1867–1956

82 Glowing Sunflowers
Leuchtende Sonnenblumen

1936
Oil on canvas, 88.5 × 67.3 cm
Signed lower right: 'Nolde'; inscribed on stretcher: 'Emil Nolde Leuchtende Sonnenblumen'[1]
The painting has four small pin-holes or nail-holes in the four corners of the canvas. There is occasional cupping and cracking in the paint surface, which is very uneven; the canvas itself also shows some distortions. Otherwise condition is good. The painting is unvarnished
Accession no.1973.67

Provenance
Friedrich Doehlemann, Munich
Frieda Doehlemann, Munich
Galerie R. N. Ketterer, Campione d'Italia
Thyssen-Bornemisza Collection, 1973

Exhibitions
Bremen 1975, no.57
Lugano 1989, no.21
Expressionism and Modern German Painting, 1989–90, no.29
Rome 1990–91, no.40

Literature
R.N.Ketterer, *Moderne Kunst VIII*, Campione d'Italia (Galerie R.N.Ketterer) 1973, p.148, no.75, ill. p.149
Kiel (1974), p.108, ill. p.109
Urban (1990), no.1169

In 1926, the last year he was to spend at Utenwarf before moving to Seebüll, Nolde embarked on his great series of *Sunflower* paintings which was to occupy him for more than a decade. A lifelong admirer of van Gogh (he even attended the notorious van Gogh forgeries trial in Berlin in April 1932, staying from beginning to end and writing enthusiastically to his friend Hans Fehr about the 'clear-sighted, absorbing and well-reasoned verdict'),[2] he could scarcely have been unaware of the significance of his choice of this particular subject. In these paintings, which include some of his most important works of the 1930s, Nolde's religious feeling for nature is coupled with a deeply-held personal symbolism in which the tragedy of human existence is mirrored in the constantly repeated natural cycle of birth, evolution and decay.

Glowing Sunflowers was painted in 1936, by which time the National Socialists were firmly in power in Germany and Nolde's professional existence was beginning to seem increasingly precarious. The following year, many of his religious and figure paintings were removed from German museums, a number being included in the Munich *Degenerate Art* exhibition, among them his major cycle *The Life of Christ*. Curiously, in one or two cases the flower paintings and landscapes were allowed to remain, despite the fact that these categories represent an equally important and characteristic aspect of his work.[3]

Glowing Sunflowers was apparently acquired almost immediately upon its completion by the banker Friedrich Doehlemann,[4] who owned a number of important canvases by Nolde.[5] Ironically, Doehlemann was not only director of the Bayerische Gemeindebank but also president of the fund-raising committee that helped finance the building of the Haus der Deutschen Kunst in Munich, home of the 1937 *Grosse Deutsche Kunstausstellung* and Hitler's showcase for the display of work by officially approved artists.[6] When Nolde and his wife visited Munich in the summer of 1937, they stayed with Doehlemann, who accompanied them on a visit to the *Degenerate Art* exhibition.[7] His association with Nolde brought him a good deal of unwelcome attention;[8] none the less, he continued despite some personal risk to intercede on the artist's behalf, even writing to the architect Wilhelm Kreis, president of the Reichskammer für bildende Künste, in support of Nolde's work, long after Nolde himself had been expelled from the association and forbidden to paint.[9]

Notes
1 The title *Leuchtende Sonnenblumen* is also entered in a handlist of Nolde's paintings compiled by the artist in 1930: see Urban (1990), p.456
2 Ibid., p.21
3 See Martin Urban, 'The "Exhibition of Degenerate Art" in 1937 and the Disposal of Nolde's Confiscated Paintings', in Urban (1990), pp.9ff
4 Letters from Doehlemann to Nolde dated 21 January and 21 February 1937 are in the archives of the Stiftung Seebüll Ada und Emil Nolde: see Urban (1990), p.456. The picture remained in the possession of the family until being offered for sale at auction in Hamburg in the spring of 1973 (Hauswedell & Nolte, 193. *Auktion, Moderne Kunst*, lot 1460); it was acquired by the present owner in December of the same year
5 'Wir reisten nach München und waren Gäste der Kunstfreunde Döhlemann und seiner jungen Frau. Um uns herum an den Wänden hingen meine Bilder . . .'; see Nolde (1978), p.113
6 Hans-Joachim Hecker, 'Missbrauchtes Mäzenatentum? Die Gründung der Anstalt des öffentlichen Rechts "Haus der Deutschen Kunst (Neuer Glaspalast)" im Jahre 1933', in Schuster (1987), pp.56ff
7 Ibid., p.59
8 In his autobiography, Nolde notes merely that it was taken 'seriously amiss' that Doehlemann should have 'accepted a "degenerate" artist into his home. Again and again admirers of my art were obliged to a greater or lesser extent to share its fate . . .'; see Nolde (1978), p.113
9 Hecker, loc. cit.; the letter dated 23 August 1941 expelling Nolde from the Reichskammer der bildenden Künste is reproduced in Nolde (1978), p.124

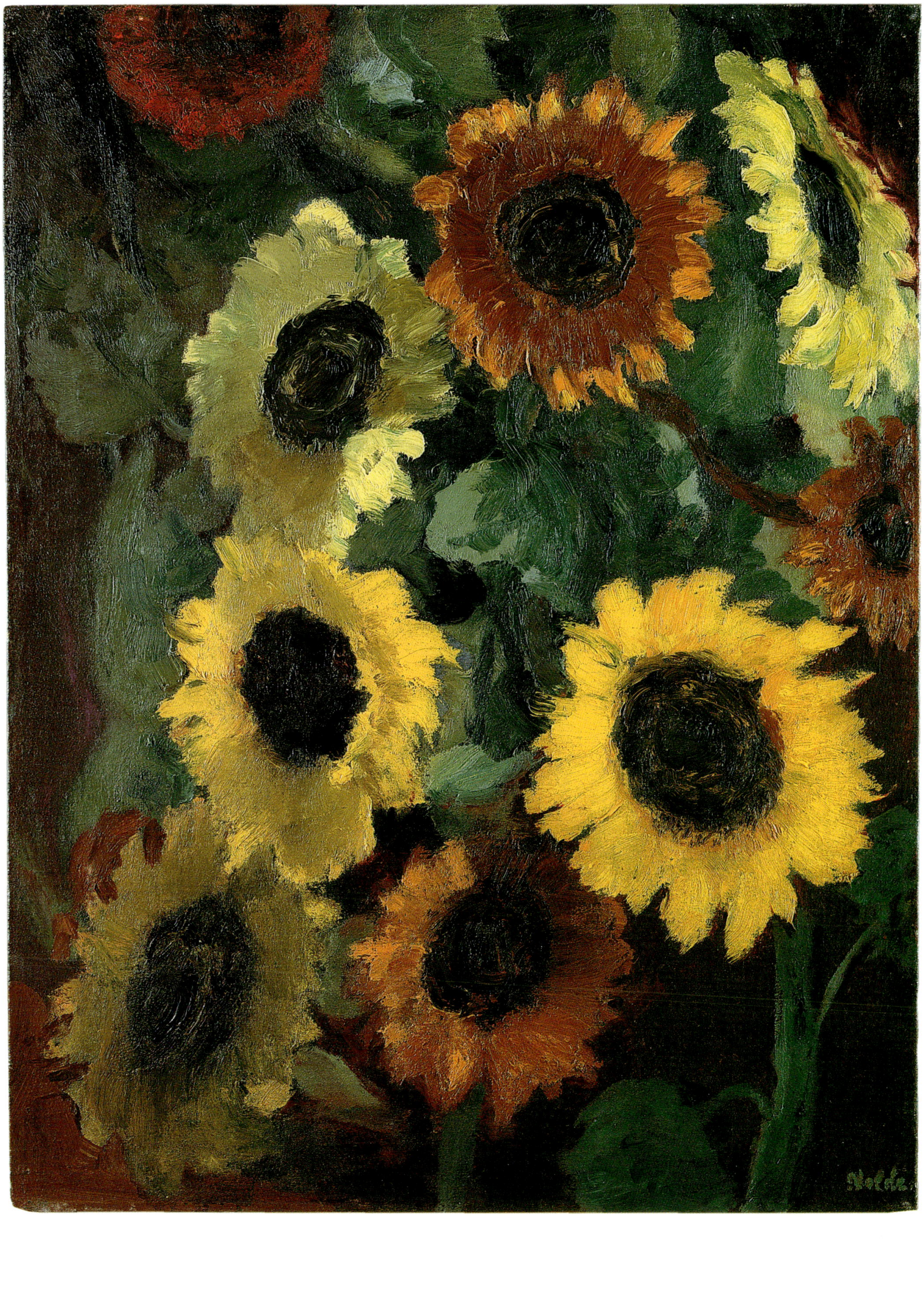

Emil Nolde 1867–1956

83 Head of a Woman

*c*1925–30
Watercolour on paper, 47.5 × 34.5 cm
Signed lower right: 'Nolde'
Paper is slightly creased; otherwise condition is good
Accession no.1970.34

Provenance
Estate of the artist
Ada und Emil Nolde Foundation, Seebüll
Galerie Nierendorf, Berlin
Parke Bernet Galleries, Inc., New York
Thyssen-Bornemisza Collection, 1970[1]

Exhibitions
Bremen 1975, no.61

Literature
Kiel (1974), p.114, ill. p.115

Despite the overwhelming number of his landscapes and flower paintings, it is the human figure which remains the central theme of Nolde's art. Throughout his career as a painter, he made watercolours, drawings and fleeting sketches of particular types: fishermen and peasants, actors and cabaret artists, the Pacific Islanders whom he encountered on his expedition to the South Seas in 1913–14.

During the years after the First World War, the farm labourers and fishing folk who inhabited the area of North Frisia around Utenwarf and Seebüll offered a repertoire of subjects to which Nolde returned again and again in his drawings and watercolours. Among these, his studies of heads such as [83] are, in reality, rapidly executed sketches rather than carefully worked-up portraits, and are for the most part representations of a particular facial type rather than of any identifiable sitter.

Note
1 Acquired at auction, 11 November 1970 (*German Expressionist and Other 20th Century Drawings, Sculpture and Paintings*, lot 8)

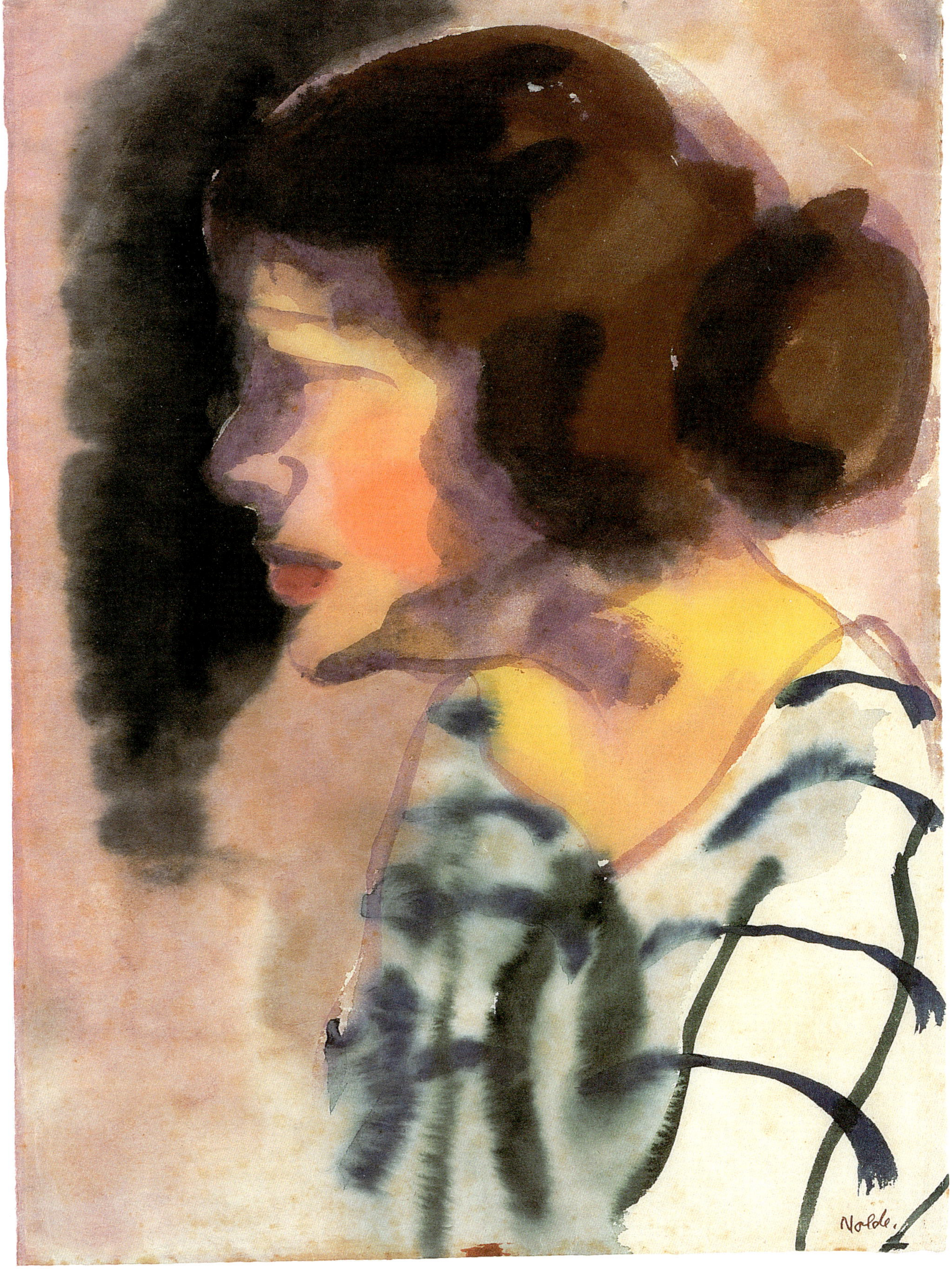
Nolde.

Emil Nolde 1867–1956

84 Summer Flowers (Red and White Poppies against Blue Sky)

*c*1930
Watercolour on paper, 45 × 33 cm
Signed lower right: 'Nolde'
History of foxing, recently treated. Now in good condition
Accession no.1965.5

Provenance
Marlborough Fine Art, London
Galerie R. N. Ketterer, Campione d'Italia
Thyssen-Bornemisza Collection, 1965

Exhibitions
Bremen 1975, no.60

Literature
R.N.Ketterer, *Moderne Kunst II*, Campione d'Italia (Galerie R.N.Ketterer) 1965, p.144, no.97, ill. p.145
Kiel (1974), p.114

Flower paintings and watercolours constitute a major part of Nolde's oeuvre of the 1920s and 1930s. He always loved flowers: in his autobiography he described the life-cycle of the flower, 'sprouting, blossoming, gleaming, glowing, bringing joy, drooping, wilting, ending up on the rubbish tip',[1] comparing its fate to that of the work of art, likewise the product of natural forces, deriving its character from the medium out of which it is created, just as a plant springs up from the soil.

Forced to abandon watercolour painting on any scale for lack of suitable materials during the period in which he was banned from any form of professional activity, it was to flower paintings he returned in the years immediately after the war, as well as to paintings based on his tiny wartime studies, the so-called 'unpainted pictures'. Watercolours of flowers are also among the last works executed during the 1950s, shortly before his death.

While the dating of Nolde's watercolours can sometimes be inferred from their subject (for example, the depictions of animals which resulted from his visits to the Berlin zoo and aquarium in 1923–4), the majority of the flower pieces, as Urban observes, can be neither arranged in a convincing chronological sequence nor dated other than by analogy with works whose date of execution is more securely documented.[2] The dates advanced here for this and the following watercolour (see [85]) are suggestions made, albeit tentatively, on the basis of style.

As regards technique, the flower studies are, in the majority of cases, 'pure' watercolours, that is to say without the use of white heightening or other opaque materials. In the present work, as in [85] the artist employs a method whereby the paper is saturated with colour, not delineating forms but seemingly conjuring them up out of the superimposed layers of pigment. His second wife Jolanthe, recalling Nolde's working methods, described how the colours would be applied 'five, six or more times, producing the most remarkable effect of depth ... patiently the brush caresses the surface, the wet paper cockles, the colour gradually accumulating in the little hollows ... Because he painted with such diluted colours, the contours would stray across the surface of the paper for up to an hour before they were finally dry ... He would paint, the paper would soak up the colour, the contours would spread as if the material had become liberated – yet the pictures were a success ... The pictures just happened, unfolding like living beings – under guidance, but with a life of their own.'[3]

Notes
1 Nolde (1971), p.100
2 Urban (1972), pp.38, 41–2
3 Jolanthe Nolde, 'Beim Malen zugeschaut', in *Emil Nolde. Gemälde, Aquarelle, Graphik*, exh. cat., Villingen-Schwenningen, Beethovenhaus, 1974, pp.45–6

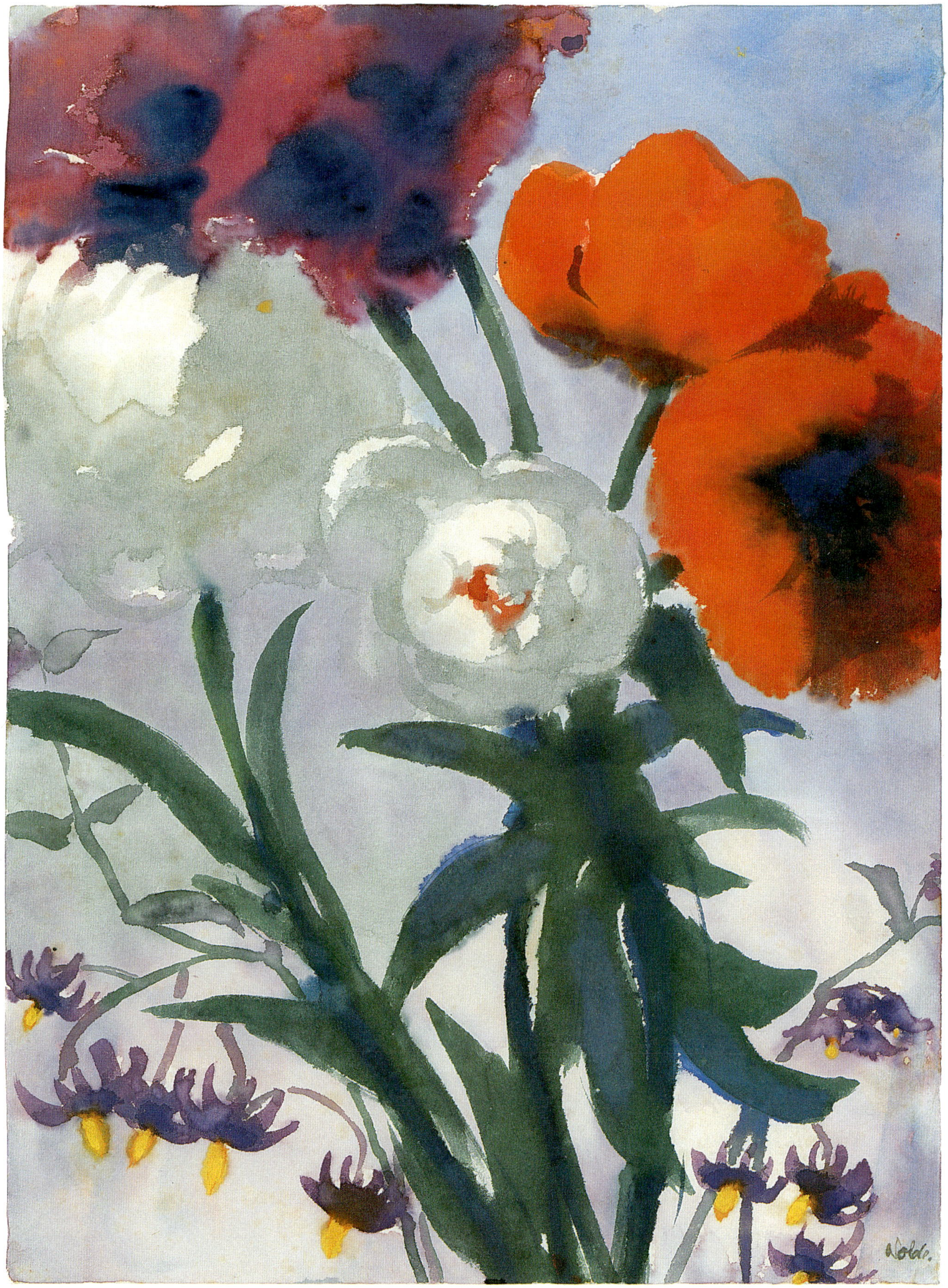
Nolde.

Emil Nolde 1867–1956

85 Iris, Tiger-lilies, Poppies

*c*1930–5,
Watercolour on paper, 47 × 34 cm
Signed lower right: 'Nolde'
The paper is slightly bulging; otherwise condition is good
Accession no.1970.31

Provenance
Private collection, West Germany
Galerie R.N.Ketterer, Campione d'Italia
Thyssen-Bornemisza Collection, 1970

Exhibitions
Bremen 1975, no.63

Literature
Kiel (1974), p.114

See preceding entry.

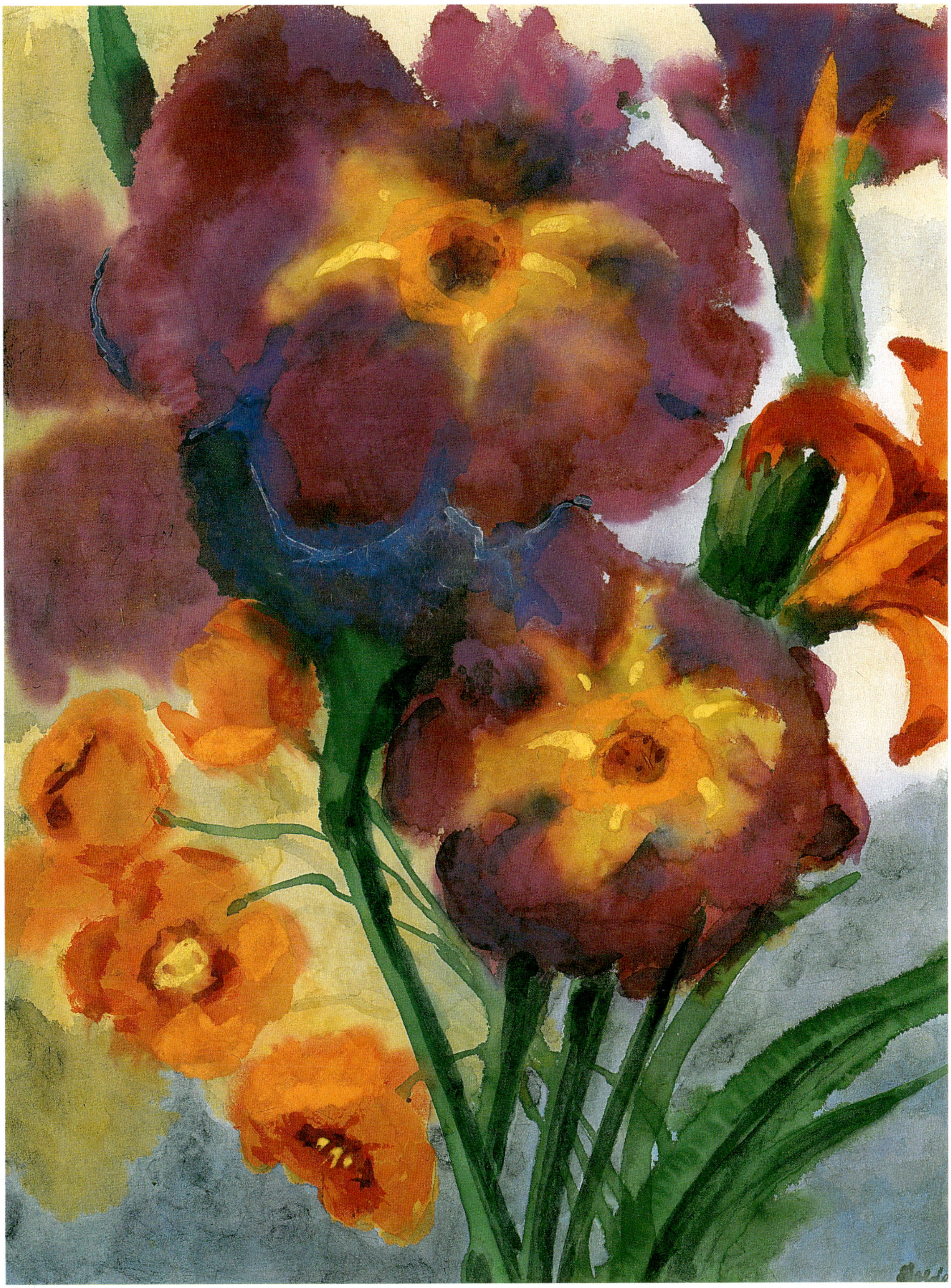

Emil Nolde 1867–1956

86 Young Couple

*c*1931–5
Watercolour on paper laid on card, 53.5 × 36.9 cm
Signed lower right: 'Nolde'[1]
The work is executed on Japan paper with extremely long fibres, known as 'Mulberry paper'. The paper itself is bulging, and the surface very uneven. There are some loose fibres around the heads and faces of the figures. Otherwise condition is good
Accession no.1961.3

Provenance
Collection of the artist
Sprengel Collection, Hanover[2]
Stuttgarter Kunstkabinett, Stuttgart
Thyssen-Bornemisza Collection, 1961[3]

Exhibitions
Munich, Galerie Günther Franke, 1947, *Emil Nolde*, no.61
Hanover, Kestner-Gesellschaft, 1948, *Emil Nolde*, no.70
Bielefeld, Städtisches Kunsthaus, 1951, *Emil Nolde. Gemälde, Aquarelle, Graphik*, no.40
Mannheim, Städtische Kunsthalle, 1952, *Emil Nolde*, no.49
Kiel, Schleswig-Holsteinischer Kunstverein, 1952, *Emil Nolde*, no.71
Düsseldorf, Kunstverein, 1953, *Emil Nolde*
London, Tate Gallery, 1956, *Emil Nolde*, no.205
Helsinki, Ateneum, 1958, *Emil Nolde*, no.38
Lübeck, Overbeck-Gesellschaft, 1960, *Emil Nolde*, no.60
Bremen 1975, no.62
Brussels/Paris 1977–8, no.65
Lugano 1978, no.82

Literature
Martin Gosebruch, *Nolde, Aquarelle und Zeichnungen*, Munich (F.Bruckmann) 1957, p.30, ill. p.65
Kiel (1974), p.110, ill. p.111

This watercolour, once owned by the Sprengel Collection in Hanover, was the first purchase of a work by an Expressionist artist made by the present Baron Thyssen-Bornemisza; it was thus the foundation stone of his now remarkable collection of twentieth-century German art. Auctioned in Stuttgart in 1961, it achieved a record price, the highest ever paid until then for a Nolde watercolour. The occasion, the tense atmosphere and fierce bidding, is described in his recollections by the dealer and auctioneer on that occasion, Roman Norbert Ketterer,[4] who subsequently became one of the most important sources of Expressionist works acquired by the Thyssen Collection.

According to Martin Urban, *Young Couple* is one of the cycle of large-scale watercolours known under the title 'fantasies' executed between 1931 and 1935.[5] Apart from its immediate colouristic appeal, it is distinguished by its air of theatricality and magical atmosphere. Our feeling that what is represented here is indeed fantasy – not the real world, but part of some fairy-tale existence – is intensified by the jewel-like, non-naturalistic colours.

Martin Gosebruch, commenting on this piece, has also pointed to its theatrical atmosphere, as well as emphasizing its colouristic subtlety and the implicit tensions between the two figures:

> The woman's coat and cap glow cinnabar red against an ultramarine background. Seen in profile, she presses to the left, while the man in green remains withdrawn and, though he reaches out to touch her, looks away from her into the far distance with limpid jewel-like eyes. Eve was the seductress, Adam, half in another world, was drawn to her, that is the age-old drama, here acted out on a brightly coloured magic stage.[6]

Notes

1 Virtually all previous catalogues state that the backing sheet is inscribed in the artist's hand 'Junges Paar' (Young Couple) – the title by which the work has always been known. However, when taken out of its frame and examined in October 1990, no inscriptions were found. I am grateful to Emil Bosshard, Head of Conservation of the Thyssen-Bornemisza Collection, for examining the work on my behalf, and for supplementary technical information concerning medium and support

2 Acquired in 1946 by Dr Bernhard Sprengel directly from the artist (letter from Frau Margrit Sprengel to the author, 24 January 1991); I am grateful to Mrs Sprengel and to the the Sprengel Museum, Hanover, for their assistance

3 At the 36th auction of the Stuttgarter Kunstkabinett, Pt.I, 3–4 May 1961, lot 374; on the Stuttgarter Kunstkabinett, the Ketterer collection, and the Galerie R.N.Ketterer, see pp.16–17

4 Ketterer (1988/I), pp.168f; see also Hans Heinrich Thyssen-Bornemisza, 'German Expressionism, a Personal Choice', in Vergo (1989), pp.9f, reprinted from *Apollo*, CXVIII, no.257 (July 1983): 76f

5 In conversation with author, Seebüll, May 1990; see also letter from Professor Urban to A.S.Berkes, 7 July 1971 (Lugano-Castagnola, Thyssen-Bornemisza Collection, archive)

6 Gosebruch, loc. cit.

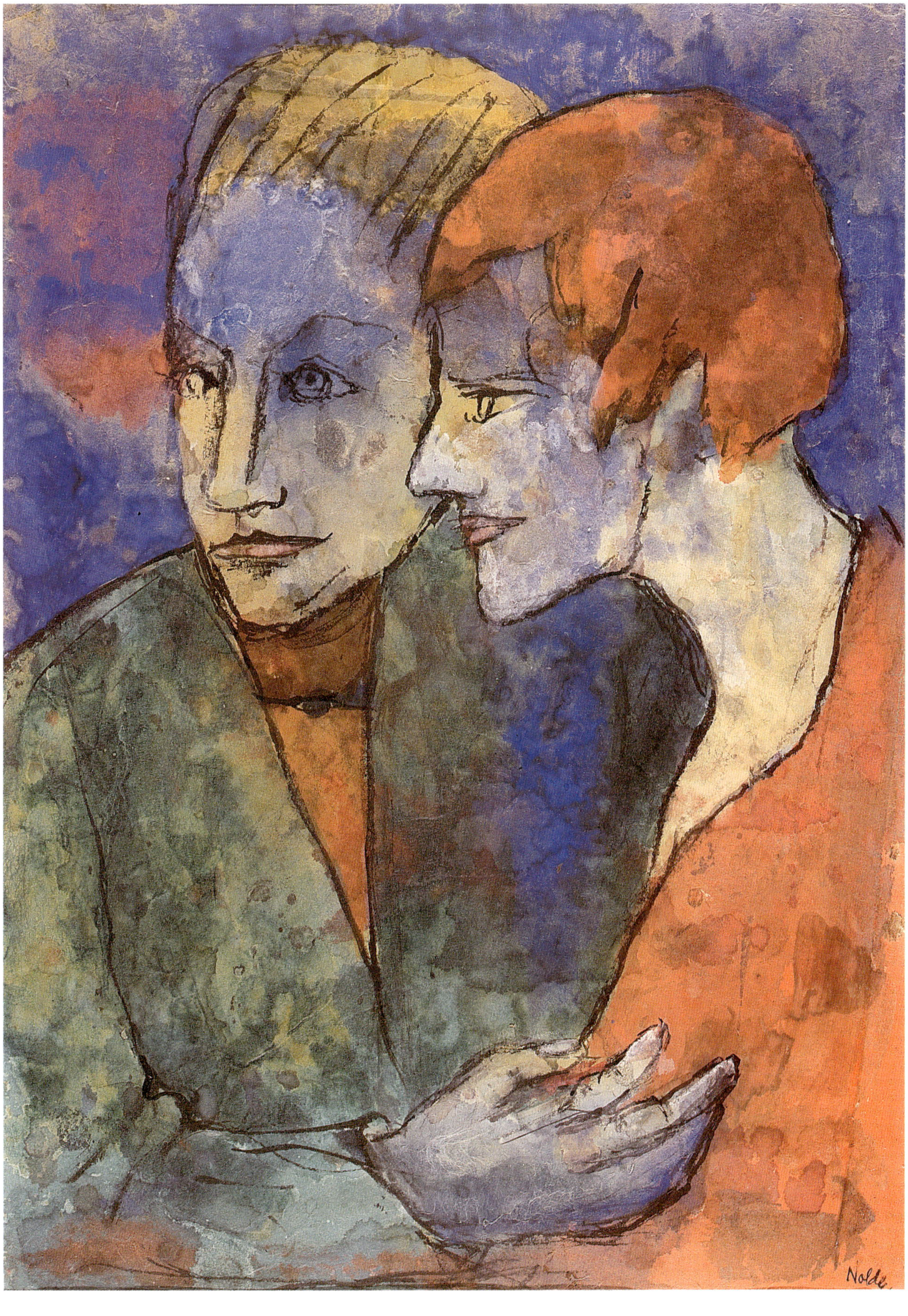
Nolde.

Emil Nolde 1867–1956

87 Landscape with Farmhouses

1946 or 1947
Watercolour on paper, 22.8 × 27.5 cm (irregular)
Signed lower right: 'Nolde'
Edges of the paper are frayed, and the surface is very uneven
Accession no.1974.24

Provenance
Estate of the artist
Ada und Emil Nolde Foundation, Seebüll
Norton Simon Collection
Sotheby's, London
Thyssen-Bornemisza Collection, 1974[1]

Exhibitions
Princeton, NJ, University Art Museum, 1972, *Selections from the Norton Simon, Inc., Museum of Art*, no.67
Bremen 1975, no.64
Lugano 1978, no.83

Literature
Kiel (1974), p.112, ill. p.113

During the summer of 1946, the year in which his wife Ada died, Nolde visited the little resort of St Peter on the North Frisian coast. Here he embarked on a series of depictions of the coastline and North Sea, sometimes showing the beach and fishing boats, more occasionally the surrounding landscape with its isolated farmhouses, such as appear in *Landscape with Farmhouses*. Returning there the following summer, he continued this series of works similar in both subject and format – the first important group of related watercolours since the 'unpainted pictures' of the war years.[2]

Notes
1 Acquired at auction, 2 April 1974 (*Impressionist and Modern Painting and Sculpture, Watercolours and Drawings*, lot 55)
2 I am indebted to Professor Martin Urban, director of the Stiftung Seebüll Ada und Emil Nolde, for his assistance in dating and identifying the subject of this watercolour

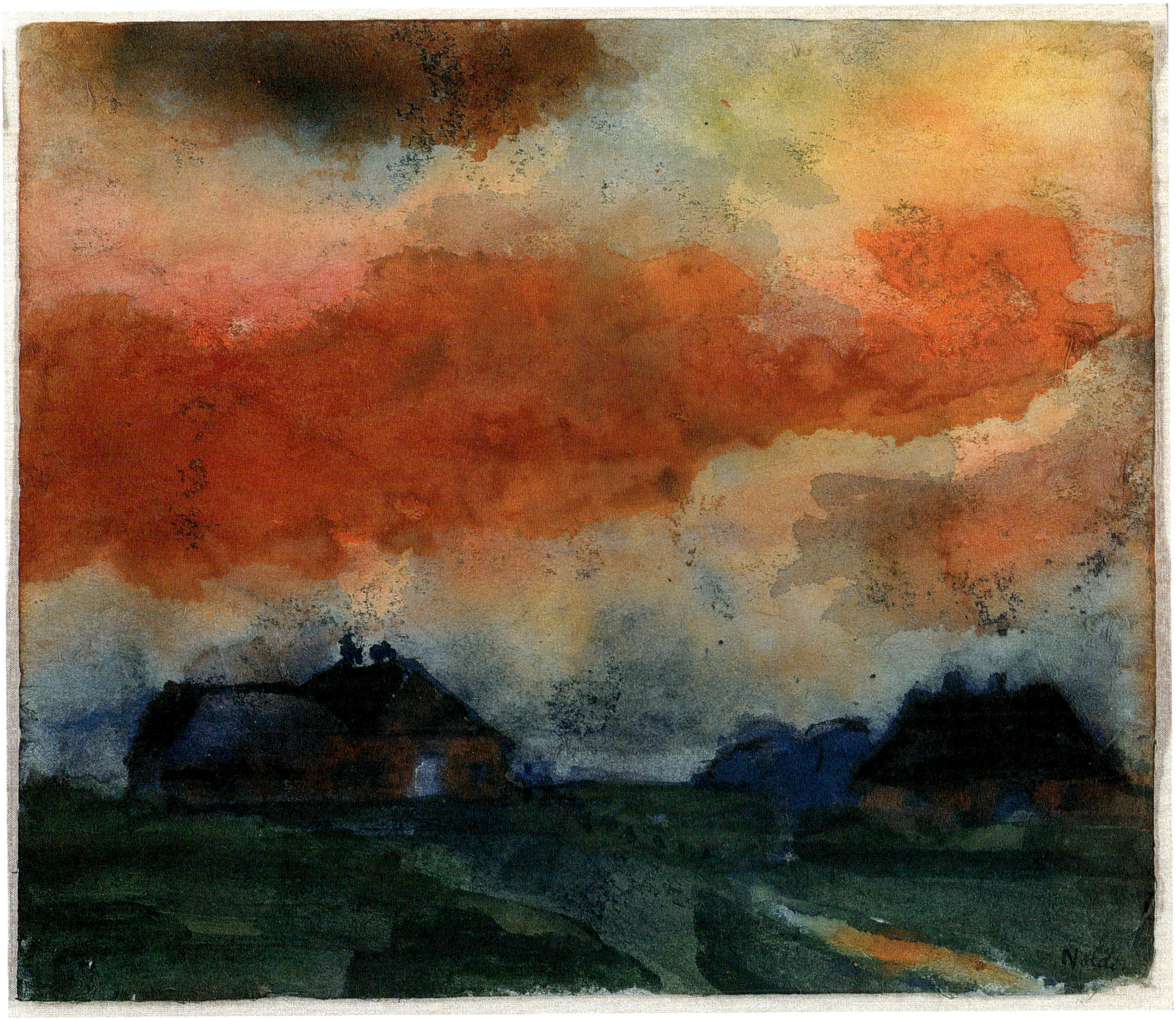

Emil Nolde 1867–1956

88 Red Cloud

Watercolour on hand-made paper, 33 × 45 cm (irregular)
Signed lower right: 'Nolde'
The paper is cockled and shows some creases. Otherwise condition is good
Accession no. 1983.9

Provenance
Dr Max M. Stern, New York
Liselotte Bendix Stern, New York
Thyssen-Bornemisza Collection, 1983[1]

This watercolour, though unquestionably genuine, is undocumented (as are most of the later works on paper) and cannot be dated accurately either on the basis of style, or by reference to the known chronology of the artist's life. Its subject, on the other hand, is almost certainly the landscape around Nolde's last home at Seebüll in North Frisia to which he had moved from Utenwarf in 1927, and where he had built for himself a house executed to his own designs. This house is now the home of the Ada and Emil Nolde Foundation.

Red Cloud was acquired from the estate of the New York psychiatrist Dr Max M. Stern. From the 1950s onwards Max Stern, who had trained as a doctor in Frankfurt before the advent of the Nazis and then emigrated to the United States by way of first Paris and then Palestine, amassed a remarkable collection of art of all periods from antiquity to the twentieth century, including Pre-Columbian, Oceanic and African art. His greatest love was, however, German Expressionism, and his collection included works of major importance not only by Nolde but also by Jawlensky, Beckmann and, most especially, Kirchner, for whom Stern felt a particular affinity. The Thyssen Collection's Kirchner painting *Junkerboden under Snow* [51] was also acquired from the same source.[2]

Notes

1 Acquired directly from the previous owner

2 I am grateful to Dr Stern's widow, Liselotte Bendix Stern, for supplying me with much interesting information regarding her late husband's collection in general, and the works by Nolde and Kirchner in particular, also biographical details on which the brief account given here is based

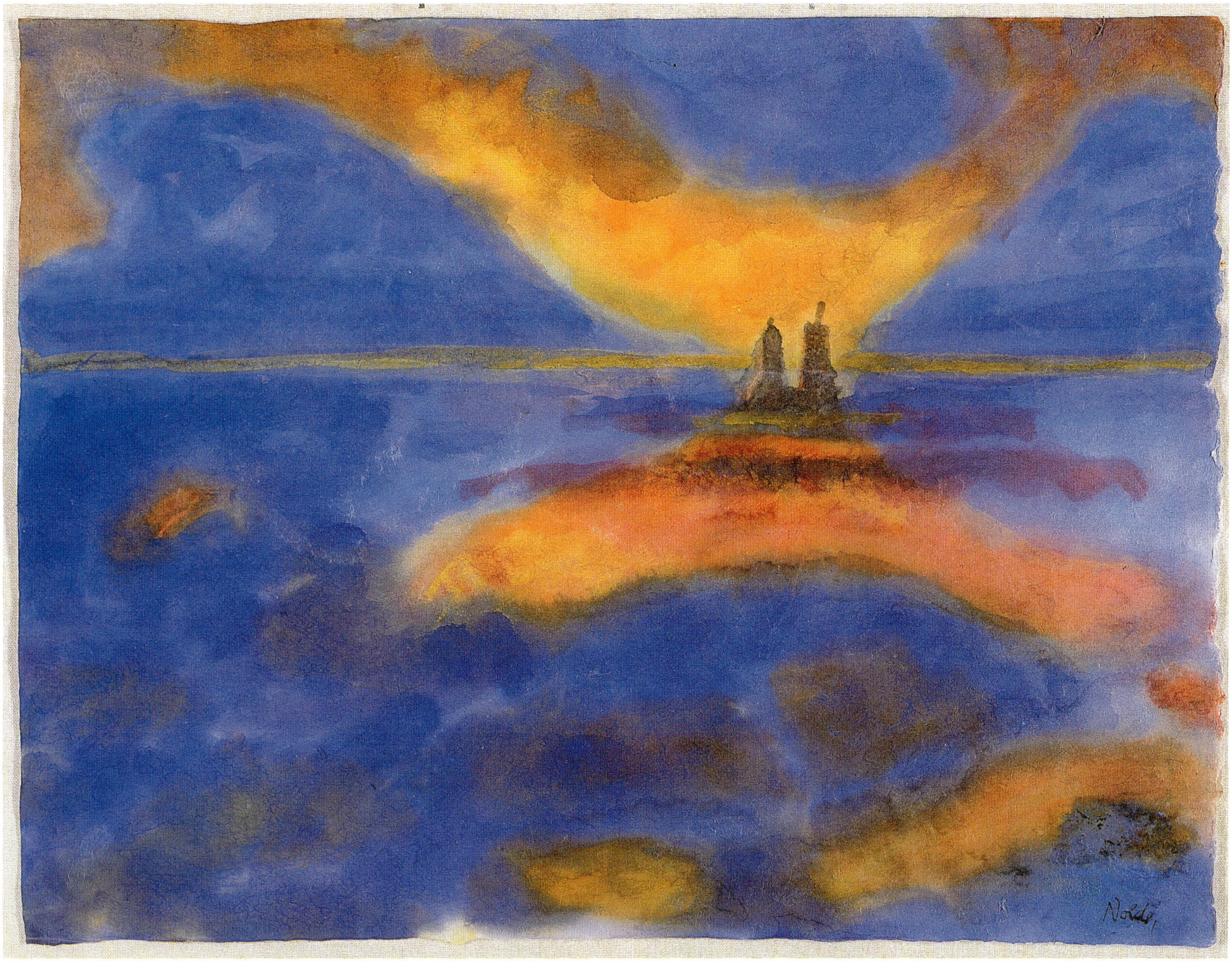
Nolde

Max Pechstein 1881–1955

89 Horse Fair
Pferdemarkt

1910
Oil on canvas, 70 × 81 cm
Initialled/dated lower right: 'HMP 1910'; inscribed on back of canvas: 'Pferdemarkt 1910 M.Pechstein'
Adhesion of the paint layer is poor, with numerous small losses, previously restored. There is a history of flaking and some cracking
Accession no.1961.16

Provenance
Collection of the artist
Nationalgalerie, Berlin
Professor Edgar Horstmann, Hamburg
Collection Roman Norbert Ketterer
Thyssen-Bornemisza Collection, 1961[1]

Exhibitions
Amsterdam, Stedelijk Museum, 1949, *Expressionisme. Van Gogh tot Picasso*, no.132
Essen 1958, no.120
Berlin, Nationalgalerie, 1959, *Max Pechstein*, no.71
Schaffhausen, Museum zu Allerheiligen/Berlin, Schloss Charlottenburg, 1959, *Triumph der Farbe. Die europäischen Fauves*, no.96
Meisterwerke des deutschen Expressionismus, 1960–61, no.145
Munich, Haus der Kunst, 1962, *Entartete Kunst. Bildersturm vor 25 Jahren*, no.132
Lausanne, Palais de Beaulieu, 1964, *Chefs-d'oeuvre des collections suisses de Manet à Picasso*, no.205
London, Tate Gallery, 1964, *Painters of the Brücke*, no.204
Paris/Munich 1966, no.255
Munich, Haus der Kunst, 1970, *Europäischer Expressionismus*, no.128
Paris, Musée National d'Art Moderne, 1970, *L'Expressionisme Européen*, no.119
Turin, Galleria Civica d'Arte Moderna, 1971, *Il Cavaliere Azzurro*, ill. p.123
Schaffhausen, Museum zu Allerheiligen, 1972, *Die Künstler der 'Brücke'*, no.152
Bremen 1975, no.66
Lugano 1975, no.30
Brussels/Paris 1977–8, no.66
Lugano 1978, no.85
Wrocław, Muzeum Narodowe, 1978–9, *Die Künstlergruppe 'Brücke', 1905–1913/Grupa 'Die Brücke'*, no.32
Poznan, Muzeum Narodowe, 1979, *Die Brücke 1905–1913*, no.32
Expressionism, a German Intuition, 1980–81, no.209
Brunswick, Kunstverein/Kaiserslautern, Pfalzgalerie, 1982, *Max Pechstein*, no.47
Modern Masters from the Thyssen-Bornemisza Collection, 1984–6, no.85
Lugano 1989, no.16
Expressionism and Modern German Painting, 1989–90, no.30

Literature
Ludwig Justi, *Von Corinth bis Klee*, Berlin (Julius Bard) 1931, p.135
Roh (1962), p.140
Pechstein (1963), pp.45f
Myers (1963), p.142.
Kiel (1974), p.116, ill. p.117
Herbert (1983), pl.x
Hünlich (1990): 177
See also Reidemeister (1970), pp.4f

Note
1 Acquired directly from the previous owner; on the Stuttgarter Kunstkabinett, the Ketterer collection, and the Galerie R.N.Ketterer, see pp.16–17

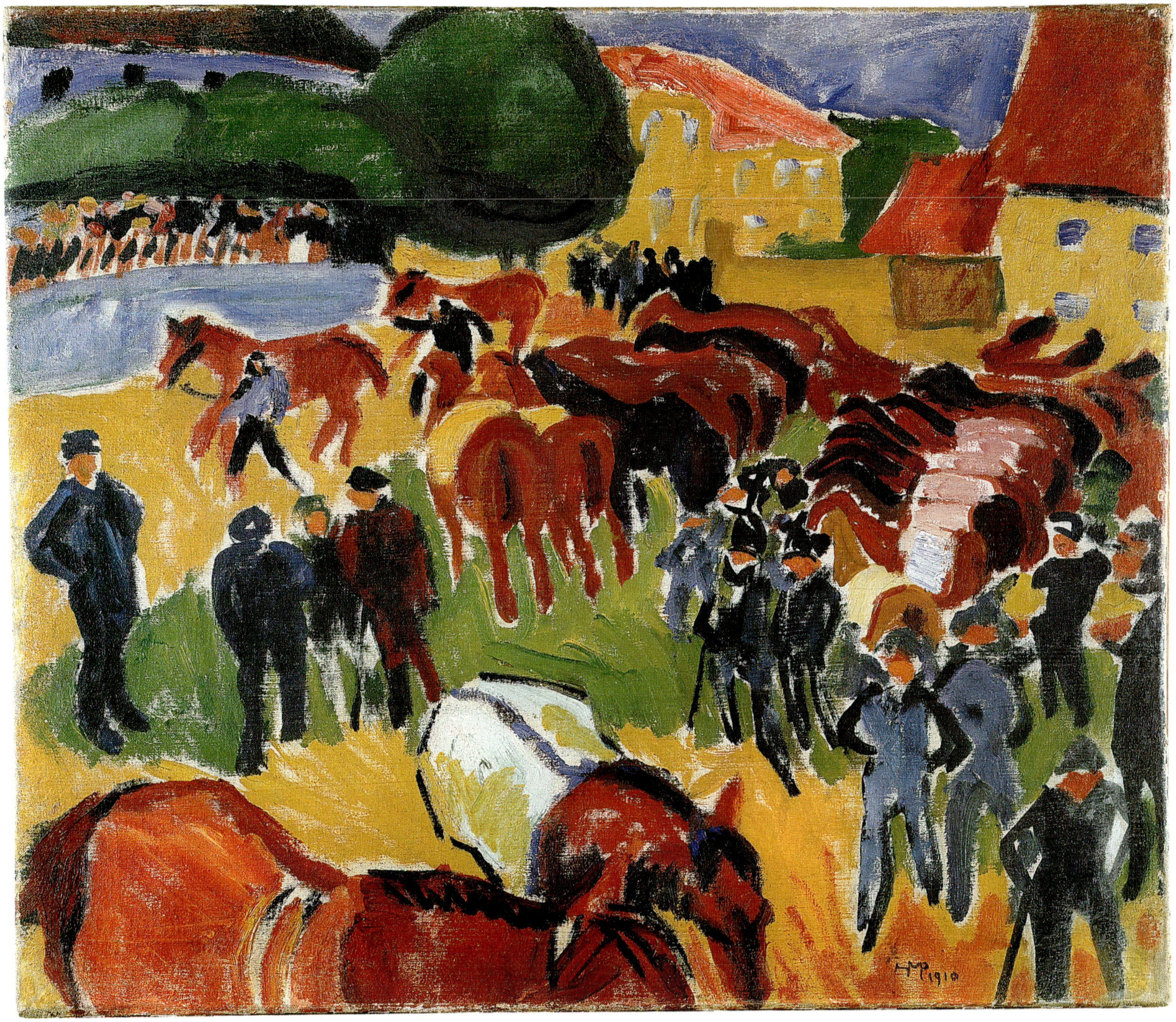
HMP 1910

Pechstein's works of the years around 1910 are, in style, quite distinct from those of the other members of the Brücke group, and display by comparison with theirs a remarkable sureness in the handling of form, and economy and concentration of pictorial means. These qualities are particularly manifest in *Horse Fair*, a painting which has in recent years become one of the best-known images of Expressionist art.

The picture was painted at Eisenberg-Moritzburg, near Dresden, during the summer of 1910, when Pechstein joined Kirchner and Heckel on an excursion to the so-called Moritzburg lakes: shallow stretches of water flanked by reeds and bushes, grouped around the sixteenth-century hunting lodge of the Elector Moritz of Saxony. The purpose of their expedition was twofold: to escape the stuffy confines of the city, and to find an environment in which, as Kirchner put it, they might grapple with the 'problem of turning new resources to the depiction of nude figures in the open air.'[2] The lakes offered an ideal setting in which he and his companions might disport themselves naked amidst shrubs and shallows, making numerous studies on the Cézannesque theme of bathers in a landscape setting.

Kirchner and Heckèl had already visited Moritzburg the previous year, in the early summer of 1909, accompanied by their girl-friends and studio models.[3] In his account of his 1910 visit, Pechstein evokes vividly the sense of sexual freedom which pervaded the Brücke artists' second summer at the lakes, the air of licence and camaraderie; he even relates how the painters were caught 'with their trousers down' by an uncomprehending and deeply suspicious local policeman.[4] He also specifically mentions the horse fair that took place from time to time at Moritzburg itself, a consequence of the proximity of a renowned local stud-farm whose fame extended far beyond the confines of Saxony.[5] In his reminiscences, he recalled how he sought to capture the 'gleaming bodies of the animals' crowded on to the square and the throng of people around them. Comparing his treatment of the theme with a contemporary postcard (fig.1), which shows the horses tethered side by side on the market-place in just the way Pechstein depicts them, one can scarcely fail to be struck by the artist's fidelity to the scene before his eyes: not merely the horses themselves, the onlookers and prospective buyers, but even the adjacent buildings and immediate environs of the square. Much that has been written about the Expressionists' subjective deformation of nature and distortive world view seems unconvincing when confronted with a painting as faithful to perceived reality as [89].

During the period immediately before and after the First World War, Pechstein was by far the best known of the Brücke artists – no doubt the cause of some jealousies, and almost certainly of various acid comments by Kirchner in later years after the dissolution of the group in 1913.[6] A significant number of his paintings entered German public collections, including *Horse Fair* which together with two seascapes, *Stormy Sea* and *Two Ships at Königsberg*, was purchased directly from the artist in May 1928 by the Nationalgalerie in Berlin for a total of 2000 marks.[7] It continued to be exhibited in the former Kronprinzen-Palais – the 'modern wing' of the Nationalgalerie – until October 1936, and is listed under no.1645 in the 1933 catalogue of the collection.[8] It was confiscated by the Nazis on 7 July 1937, when a five-man commission charged by Goebbels's propaganda ministry with organizing the infamous *Degenerate Art* exhibition, led by the painter Adolf Ziegler, first descended on the gallery.[9] Most of the works seized on this first visit, though not [89], were sent to Munich for the exhibition which opened on the 19th of that month. To judge by its number – 14138 – in the inventory of confiscations, *Horse Fair* was instead taken directly to the rented warehouse on Berlin's Köpenicker Strasse where vast quantities of paintings by 'degenerate' artists were temporarily housed. It must subsequently have been thought sufficiently valuable to be moved to the relative safety of the 'depository for degenerate art' at Schloss Niederschönhausen, thus escaping the fate of some five thousand paintings, drawings and graphic works which remained in the Köpenicker Strasse store, and which were ceremonially burned in the courtyard of Berlin's main fire station in March 1939.[10]

Less than a year after the first round of confiscations, an edict of 31 May 1938 declared the

Notes

2 Grisebach (1968), p.85

3 There may have been earlier visits. Fritz Bleyl, another founder member of the Brücke, recalled that he and Kirchner had several times been sketching in the vicinity of Moritzburg prior to the inauguration of the group in summer 1905; see Wentzel (1968): 94. However, there are no known Moritzburg paintings by either Kirchner or Heckel securely datable before 1909; see Reidemeister (1970), pp.4ff, also Hünlich (1990): 170ff

4 Pechstein, loc. cit. This anecdote would appear to be confirmed by Kirchner, who later recalled that Pechstein 'lud uns einen Process [sic] auf den Hals': see Grisebach (1968), p.75

5 Hünlich, loc. cit.

6 See for example Grisebach (1968), p.77, where Kirchner refers to Pechstein's 'lack of understanding' and recourse to merely 'decorative' colour; also ibid., p.75, where he claims that Pechstein learned 'everything he knows, or rather doesn't know' from himself and Heckel

7 According to information compiled at the time of the painting's acquisition by the present owner, *Horse Fair* was supposedly in the possession of the dealer Fritz Gurlitt in Berlin before being purchased by the Nationalgalerie. This assertion is repeated in Kiel (1974); it is not, however, substantiated by any documentary evidence, and is contradicted by information supplied by the Berlin Nationalgalerie. I am indebted to Dr Annegret Janda and Dr Jörn Grabowski of the Staatliche Museen zu Berlin, Nationalgalerie und Zentralarchiv, for providing me with the details given here regarding the acquisition and subsequent history of the painting

8 *Nationalgalerie. Verzeichnis der Gemälde und Bildwerke der Neuen Abteilung im Ehemaligen Kronprinzenpalais*, Berlin (Ernst Rathenau) 1933, p.26

9 See Annegret Janda, 'The Fight for Modern Art. The Berlin Nationalgalerie after 1933', in Barron (1991), p.113; also Roters (1984), p.166

10 For an account of this barbaric act, see Roters (1984), pp.170f

works impounded at that time to be the property of the Reich, rather than of individual museums.[11] By this date, the German government had entered into negotiations with several dealers who were entrusted with 'realizing the value' (which meant selling for hard currency) of those items considered potentially attractive to foreign buyers. Among these was *Horse Fair* which, in an inventory compiled by one of the main dealers involved, Karl Buchholz, is valued at $20.[12] Like many of the confiscated works, however, the painting was not sold abroad, in direct contravention of several successive and explicit directives by the ministry. Rather, it appears to have been acquired on commission by Buchholz himself and stored for safe-keeping until after the war. In the same manner, several of the dealers responsible for the disposal of examples of 'degenerate' art, who also included Ferdinand Möller and Bernhard A. Boehmer, succeeded in rescuing for posterity masterpieces which would otherwise almost certainly have been destroyed.

11 See p.93 and note 20

12 Now in the Bundesarchiv (former Zentrales Staatsarchiv), Potsdam (Prop.-Min. 1017, p.13 and 1018, p.59). As Roters observes, the price-tags attached to most of the works intended for disposal reflect the schizophrenia which characterizes the Nazis' thinking on the subject of 'degenerate' art. While anxious to obtain the maximum in foreign currency for the pictures removed from the museums, the very fact that this same art had been declared to be worthless meant that, for propaganda reasons, prices were set ridiculously low: see Roters (1984), pp.172f

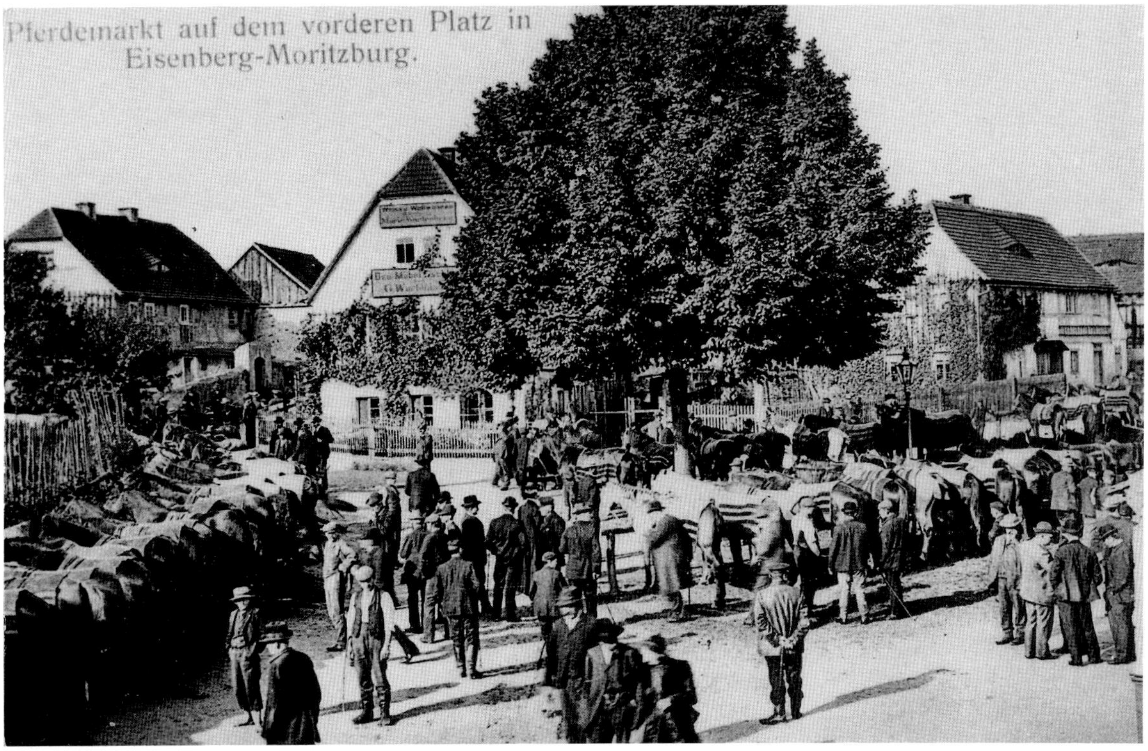

FIG 1 *The Horse Fair at Eisenberg-Moritzburg*, postcard by Hermann Seibt, Meissen, *c*1913

Max Pechstein 1881–1955

90 Summer in Nidden

1919 or 1920
Oil on canvas, 81.3 × 101 cm
Signed lower right: 'HMPechstein'
The canvas has been fitted to a new stretcher. Condition is good. The painting is unvarnished
Accession no.1961.4

Provenance
Dr Karl Lilienfeld, Berlin
Lilienfeld–Van Diemen Galleries, New York
Stuttgarter Kunstkabinett, Stuttgart
Thyssen-Bornemisza Collection, 1961[1]

Exhibitions
Cambridge, MA, Busch-Reisinger Museum, 1932, *Paintings by Max Pechstein*
San Francisco, CA, Museum of Art, 1937, *Max Pechstein*
Lausanne, Palais de Beaulieu, 1964, *Chefs-d'oeuvre des collections suisses de Manet à Picasso*, no.207
Bremen 1975, no.67
Lugano 1989, no.17
Expressionism and Modern German Painting, 1989–90, no.31
Rome 1990–91, no.41

Literature
Pechstein (1963), pp.38ff, 115f
Kiel (1974), p.118, ill. p.119
See also Günter Krüger, 'Nidden auf der Kurischen Nehrung', in Wietek (1976), pp.142–53; Werner Timm, 'Max Pechstein und die Ostsee', *Max Pechstein. Ostsee-Bilder*, exh. cat., Regensburg, Ostdeutsche Galerie, 1981, pp.5–10

The fishing village of Nidden is situated at the extreme eastern end of the Baltic in what was, until after the Second World War, known as East Prussia. It stands on the Kurische Nehrung, a long narrow spit of land dividing the sea from a shallow lagoon, the Haff. With its simple fisher-folk, its rolling sand-dunes and forests of pine and fir inhabited by elk and deer, from the late nineteenth century onwards it became a place of pilgrimage for artists, initially the painters of the Königsberg Academy, subsequently visitors from further afield, who found in this remote environment an unspoiled landscape and picturesque subjects to depict. They also saw in the continual struggle for survival waged by the primitive fishing community an image of the unity of man and nature, untouched by 'progress', the dubious benefits of civilization.

Until the First World War, communications between Nidden and the rest of the world were erratic in the extreme. Pechstein, influenced perhaps by the paintings of Eduard Bischoff-Culm shown at the Berlin Secession,[2] first visited the area in the summer of 1909. In his autobiography, he describes the difficulty of his journey from Berlin via Königsberg (now Kaliningrad), eventually reaching his destination by fishing smack. In his mind, Nidden, because of its remoteness and primitive way of life, played a role perhaps similar to that which Brittany fulfilled for Gauguin – just as one might compare Pechstein's trip to the South Seas in 1913–14 with the French artist's visits to Martinque and to Tahiti during the last years of the nineteenth century.

The following summer, 1910, he decided to join Kirchner and Heckel on their expedition to the Moritzburg lakes, near Dresden (see [89]), but in 1911 and 1912 he revisited Nidden, accompanied by his wife. Her presence as model, and the deserted landscape of dunes bordered by the lagoon on one side, the sea on the other, allowed him to resume his study of the nude figure in nature on which he had embarked at Moritzburg.

In the years immediately following the Great War, Pechstein paid two further visits to Nidden, in 1919 (his longest stay) and again in 1920. According to his autobiography, he was surprised and delighted to find the region relatively unchanged, remarking that it was he himself who had been more deeply affected by the horrors of war, so that 'the first of my new works turned out looking somewhat clumsy, hesitant and angular in form, until I became once more possessed by the untrammelled freedom which still existed there after all.'[3] Whether the

Notes
1 Acquired at the 36th auction of the Stuttgarter Kunstkabinett, 3–4 May 1961, lot 386
2 Bischoff-Culm had been painting in the vicinity of Nidden from the late 1880s onwards; see Krüger, op. cit., pp.143f
3 Pechstein (1963), pp.115–16
4 See Günter Krüger, 'Zu Arbeiten von Max Pechstein im Besitz des Altonaer Museums', *Altonaer Museum in Hamburg. Jahrbuch*, IX (1971): 9–37
5 *Art News* (17 December 1932), p.6. Though not specifically mentioned, it is highly likely that *Summer in Nidden* was included in the exhibition, which followed hard on the heels of the autumn 1932 showing of Pechstein's work at the Busch-Reisinger Museum at Harvard (see Exhibitions). It has not, however, been possible to locate a catalogue for the New York show. I am grateful to Peter Nisbet, Daimler-Benz Curator, Busch-Reisinger Museum, for drawing my attention to this exhibition and the accompanying reviews
6 Krüger, in Wietek (1976), p.147

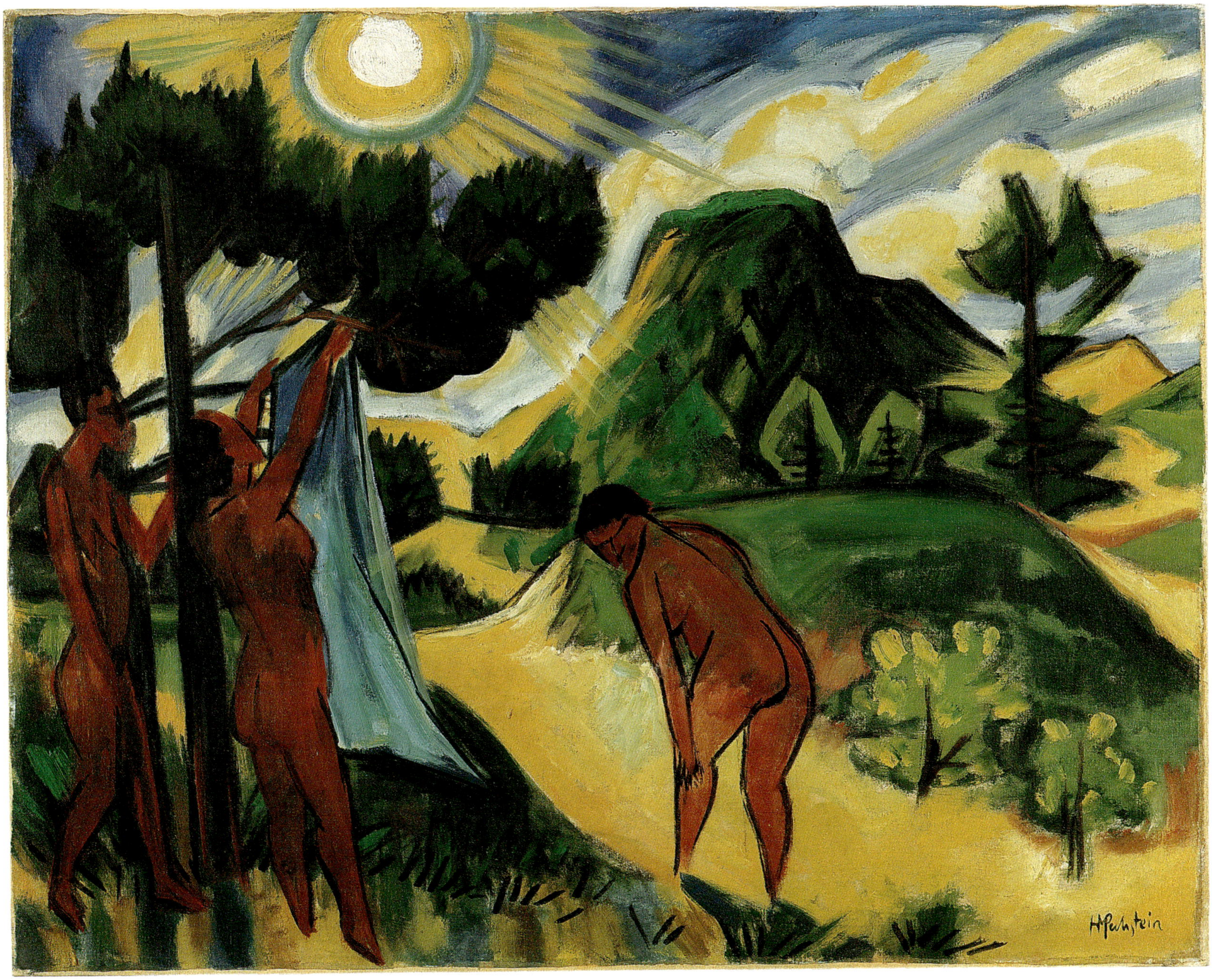

present picture dates from the first or second of these visits is, on the basis of documentary evidence, impossible to say. Stylistically, it would appear to have closer affinities with the works of 1920, especially some of the drawings and sketches contained in letters and postcards written to friends and patrons.[4]

Though, in the long term, it is Pechstein's works of the 'Brücke'-years that have attained lasting popularity, during the 1920s and 1930s his immediately post-war work was held in considerable esteem. The anonymous reviewer of the New York *Art News*, discussing an exhibition held at the Lilienfeld–Van Diemen Galleries in 1932, singled out what he termed the artist's 'middle period' for particular praise;[5] while as late as 1976, the art historian Günter Krüger, who made a special study of Pechstein and of the works of other painters active in and around Nidden, described the years 1919–20 as 'perhaps the most productive of [his] entire creative life'.[6]

Christian Rohlfs 1849–1938

91 Street in Soest

1907
Oil on canvas, 59 × 78 cm
Initialled/dated lower right: 'CR 07'
The painting is unvarnished and has become rather dirty. Otherwise condition is good
Accession no.1964.14

Provenance
Mrs Gustav Jung, Hagen-Schalksmühle
Kunsthaus Lempertz, Cologne
Thyssen-Bornemisza Collection, 1964[1]

Exhibitions
Hagen, Karl Ernst Osthaus-Museum, 1949–50, *Christian Rohlfs Gedächtnis-Ausstellung*, no.22
Bremen 1975, no.70

Literature
Vogt (1978) no.426 and p.255
See also Utermann (1984)

Rohlfs was a student at the Grand-Ducal Academy in Weimar from 1870 to 1884, where he remained, with interruptions, until 1900.[2] His work of this period shows little trace of foreign influences save for a certain loosening of his brushwork during the 1890s, brought about by his contact with French Impressionism. The years after the turn of the century, on the other hand, are marked by an increasing eclecticism, the artist responding to a variety of powerful stimuli, among which the Neo-Impressionism of Seurat and (especially) Signac and the art of van Gogh were the most significant. The impact of the latter, in particular, is seen clearly in his use of a heavily-impastoed, expressive brushstroke in his works after 1905, the year in which major van Gogh retrospective exhibitions were held in Amsterdam and in a number of German cities.[3]

Notes
1 Acquired at auction, 4 December 1964 (*Auktion 480*, lot 546)
2 See Vogt (1978), pp.7ff for an account of Rohlfs's training and early work
3 This touring exhibition was the brainchild of the Berlin dealer Paul Cassirer, in collaboration with Johanna van Gogh-Bonger. It was shown in Hamburg, Dresden, Berlin and at the Galerie Miethke in Vienna during the autumn and winter of 1905–6; see Feilchenfeldt (1988), pp.18ff

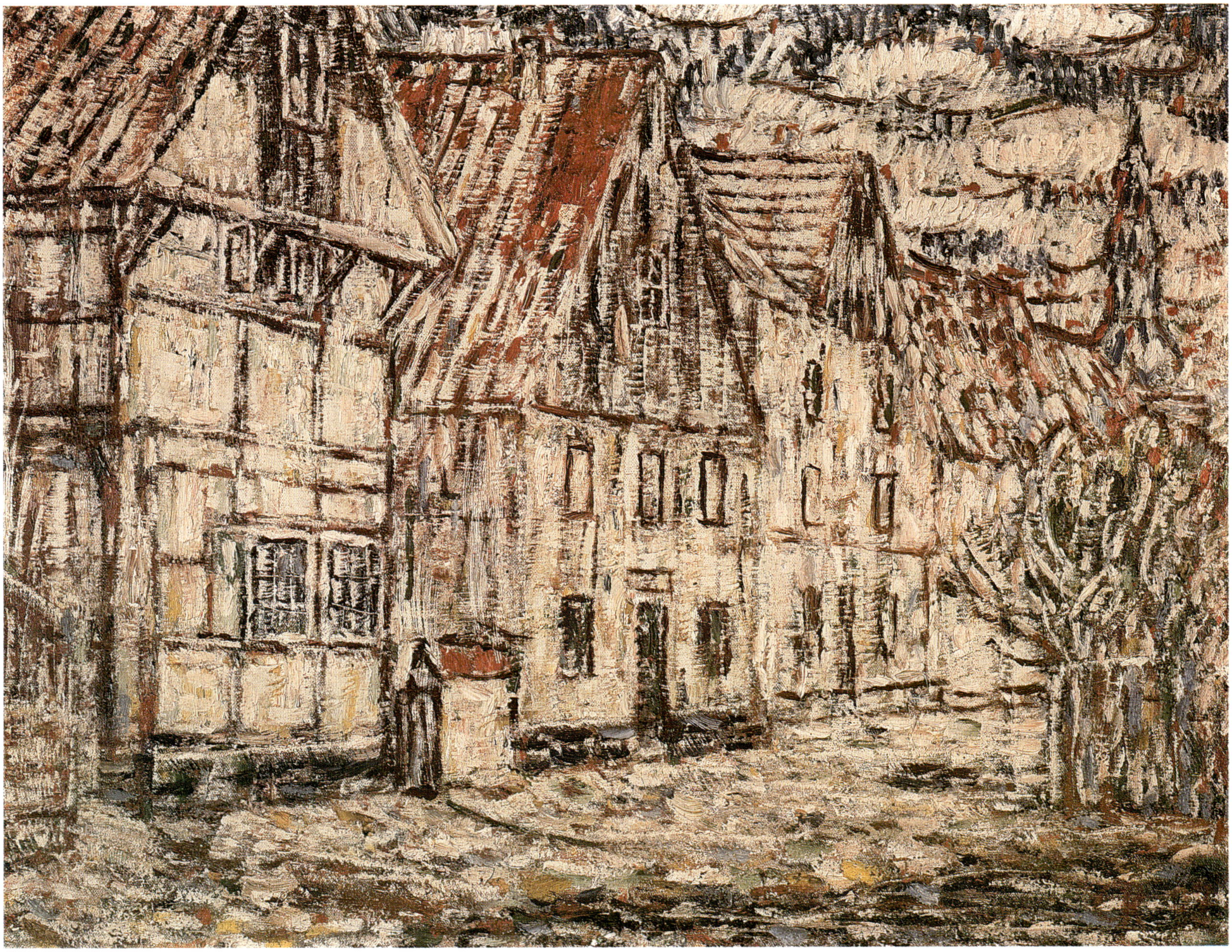

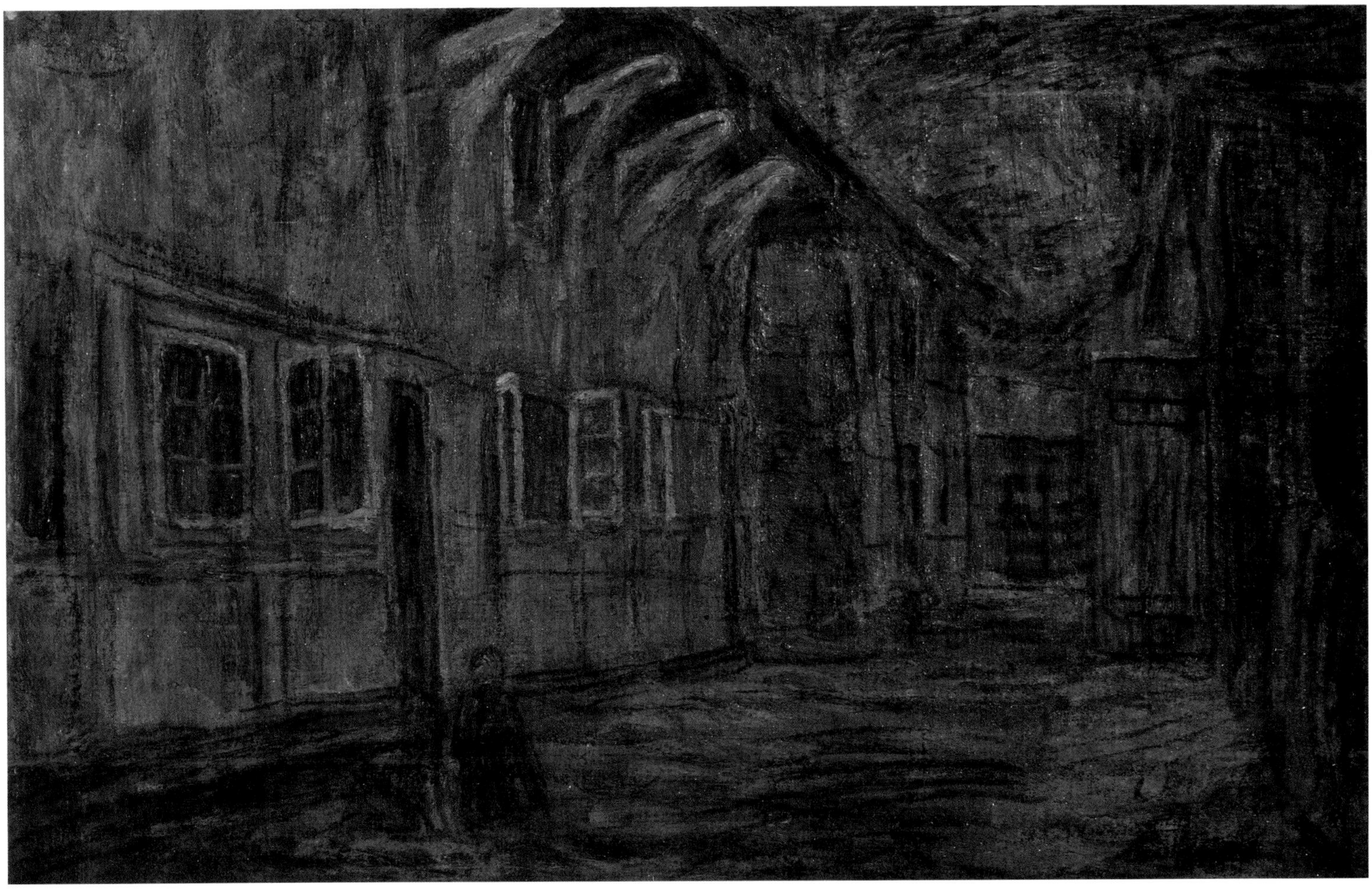

Chronologically speaking, this phase of his work begins in 1901 when Karl Ernst Osthaus, founder of the Folkwang Museum, persuaded him to establish himself in Hagen in Westphalia – part of Osthaus's campaign to make his collection there a focus for everything that was new in contemporary art.[4] From this point on, Rohlfs had available to him, and was increasingly aware of, an ever-wider range of recent and avant-garde painting. He never felt wholly comfortable, however, in Hagen, and throughout this period maintained a studio in Weimar, where the architecture provided the staple motifs for the majority of his townscapes executed up to and including the early years of this century.

In 1904, on an excursion from Hagen, he first visited the picturesque old town of Soest, which like Weimar was to play a crucial part in his life and art. By contrast with Hagen, he was so impressed by Soest, with its many churches and ancient streets with timber-framed buildings, that he returned to spend the summer of 1905 there, when he made the

Notes

4 Osthaus was the first museum director in Germany to buy paintings and drawings by van Gogh; he also exhibited works by the Dutch artist in Hagen during September–October 1905. See Paul Vogt, *Das Museum Folkwang Essen*, Cologne 1965, p.16; also Feilchenfeldt (1988), pp.20–21, and Moeller (1990), p.335

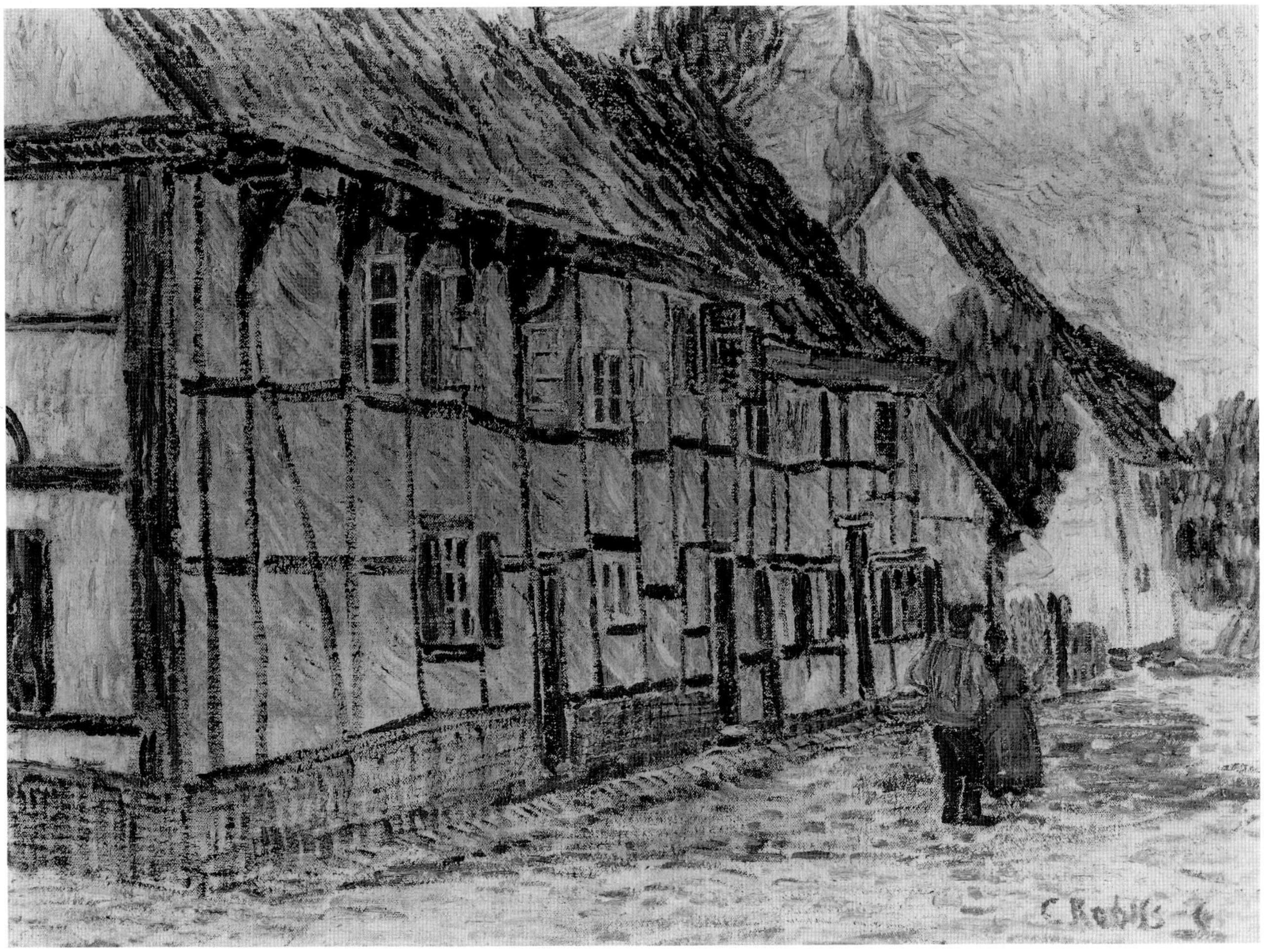

FIG 1 Christian Rohlfs, *Street in Soest*, 1906, oil on canvas, 45 × 69 cm (Witten, Märkisches Museum)

FIG 2 Christian Rohlfs, *Houses in Soest with the Tower of St Peter's Church*, 1906, oil on canvas, 59.5 × 77 cm (Rostock, Kulturhistorisches Museum, inv. no.12778)

acquaintance of Nolde. He visited Soest again in the summer of 1906, and in later years painted numerous pictures of the town and its principal buildings which are not so much literal depictions of its architecture and topography as a summing up of his experiences and impressions.

Stylistically, *Street in Soest* marks a transition from his heavily Neo-Impressionist-influenced manner of the early 1900s, still detectable in some of his other earlier views of the town,[5] to his harder, more structural style of *c*1910. Since Rohlfs was not in Soest in 1907, it must be among the pictures referred to above which were done from memory, probably in the artist's Hagen studio. His recollections of the town would, however, still have been vivid. Indeed, the present painting is closely related to another actually executed in Soest the preceding summer (fig.2) which appears to show the same street of houses, with the tower of St Peter's Church visible in the background – a work with which [91] has on occasion been confused.[6]

5 Compare, for example, the painting *Paulikirche in Soest*, 1906 (Vogt (1978), no.385: destroyed)
6 I am grateful to Professor Dr Paul Vogt, Essen, for supplementary information concerning the Thyssen Collection's painting

Christian Schad 1894–1982

92 Composition en N

1919
Wood relief with collage, 18 × 25 × 2.2 cm (irregular), mounted on hessian and set in original box frame, 32 × 43 cm (recess), 44 × 55 cm (frame)
Signed/dated on lower left edge: 'SCHAD 19'; inscribed on reverse: 'Composition en N, Christ. Schad 19'
The fragments of paper and other material of which the collage is composed are fragile and in some cases have become loose; both paper and metal have oxidized
Accession no.1980.56

Provenance
Collection of the artist
Kunstkabinett G.A.Richter, Stuttgart
Thyssen-Bornemisza Collection, 1980

Exhibitions
Geneva, Salon Néri, 1920, *Dadaïstes: Exposition Gustave Buchet/Christian Schad*
Trier, Städtisches Museum, 1971, *Christian Schad*, no.8
Milan, Palazzo Reale, 1972, *Christian Schad*, ill. [n.p.]
Wuppertal, Von der Heydt-Museum, 1975, *Schadographien*
Berlin, 15. Europäische Kunstausstellung, 1977, *Tendenzen der Zwanziger Jahre*, no.3/465
Frankfurt am Main, Städtische Galerie im Städelschen Kunstinstitut, 1977–8, *Dada in Europa*, no.3/465
Berlin, Staatliche Kunsthalle, 1980, *Christian Schad*, no.56
Cologne 1986, p.34, ill. p.35
Luxemburg/Munich/Vienna 1988, no.67

Literature
Heesemann-Wilson (1978), cat. no.283 and pp.69–72
Christian Schad, exh. cat., Berlin, Staatliche Kunsthalle, 1980, pp.70–4

The work is composed of a piece of wood, of irregular dimensions, which has been sawn and planed and painted black, on which are mounted various *objets trouvés*: a coin, bearing the Austrian Imperial arms and the inscription 'k.k. Oesterreichische Scheidemünze', set into a metal surround; a triangular piece of pigskin, with a smaller piece of greenish coloured paper pasted on top; a small piece of paper, inscribed in ink 'Come [mi s]ento bene'; a strip of lace; a metal button; a pinkish stone or pebble (or possibly a piece of shell, stuck down and painted pink); fragments of a cigarette packet, with imprint: 'High Class Carlton Cigarettes/Carlton Cigarettes Cork Tipped'; a fragment of gauze; a piece of silver paper. The whole is attached by a triangular metal hook and staple to a hessian-covered backboard recessed into the original wooden box frame.

Composition en N was executed in Geneva in 1919, where Schad had spent the greater part of the First World War. According to his recollection, it was the first in order of execution of a group of seven related wood reliefs dating from 1919–20. These were shown at an exhibition of 'Dadaïstes' organized by Schad's friend Walter Serner and held at the Salon Néri in Geneva in February 1920. It appears that the reliefs were left in the cellar after the close of the exhibition and rediscovered some forty-five years later when the gallery owner, somewhat belatedly, returned them to the artist, who by this stage had forgotten all about them.[1] The titles of one or two could be discovered from old photographs or illustrations in newspapers. For the others, Schad, who could not remember what he had originally called them, invented new titles, though not for [92], which was inscribed on the back 'Composition en N'. He himself surmised that 'N' must have stood for 'noir' (black)

> since with the exception of a little touch of colour in the appliquéd elements, the relief is as black-and-white as the Schadographs, which it closely resembles in the shape of its outlines. The same 'objets trouvés', especially flat objects such as newspaper fragments, bits of material and pieces of metal, iron rings and coins that in the Schadographs are dematerialised are here actually stuck and nailed on to the black-painted wooden surface, so as to demonstrate my hostility to tradition by means of these banal realities.[2]

Notes
1 According to *Christian Schad*, exh. cat., Berlin, Staatliche Kunsthalle, 1980, p.72. This exhibition was arranged and the catalogue entries compiled in collaboration with the artist
2 Schad's recollections are cited in a letter from G.A.Richter to Baron H.H.Thyssen-Bornemisza, 4 October 1980 (Lugano-Castagnola, Thyssen-Bornemisza Collection, archive)

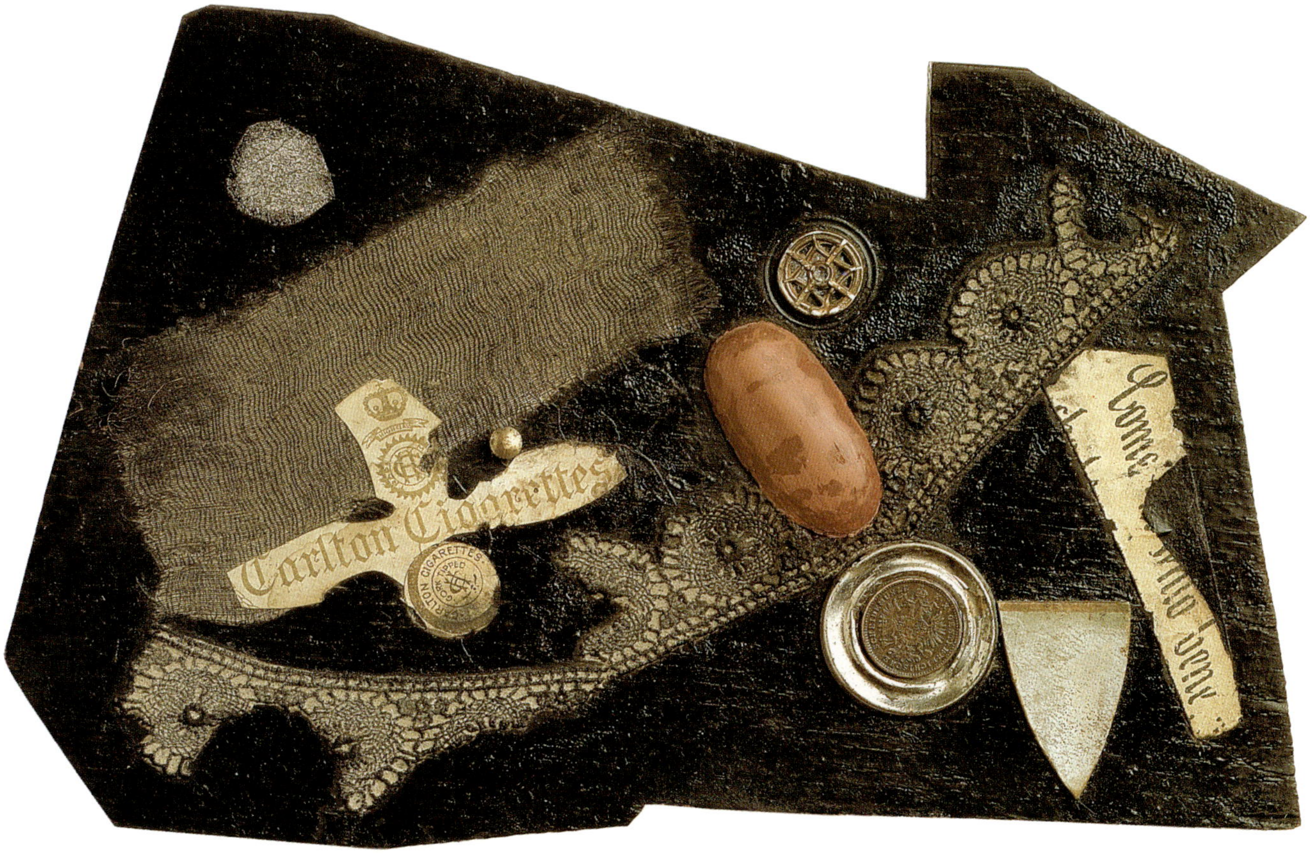

The reliefs were made out of pieces of solid wood sawn up by a friendly carpenter 'with much shaking of the head' according to the artist's designs. In these works, Schad's intention was not merely to demonstrate his 'hostility to tradition' but also to exclude, by utilizing found objects having no material or aesthetic value, what he termed the 'psychological impulse' in art – the source of his profound disagreement with Archipenko, who was also living in Geneva at this time. In Schad's own words, the 'psychological element was a relic of Expressionism and its exclusion, above all in the wood reliefs, one of the major impulses behind Dada. Any attempt to pin down one's psychological motivation would in this case have been a handicap. The greatness of Dada was that it was unencumbered by anything. It was this longing that drove us to Dada.'[3]

As Schad mentions, the Dada reliefs of 1919–20 are closely related in both form and intent to the immediately preceding 'Schadographs': photographic images, in many ways similar to Man Ray's later photograms (or 'Rayograms'), in which worthless objects, mainly the flotsam and jetsam of daily life, are taken from their original context and 'dematerialized' by being exposed to light-sensitive paper. There is also an evident point of contact with the work of Arp, who in his reliefs like *Oiseau Hippique* and *Plant Hammer*[4] juxtaposed pieces of sawn and painted wood comprising, in his case, mainly biomorphic-abstract forms. Schad, while acknowledging the similarity between his own reliefs and those of Arp, contrasted the latter's 'poetic-organic shapes' with his own 'harder, more aggressive forms ... added to which the incorporation of "non-art" objects consciously reinforced the anti-traditional message.'[5]

Possible precedents in the work of both Picasso and Tatlin (the former's 'relief constructions' of 1913–14, the latter's 'painting-reliefs' and 'counter-reliefs' of 1914–15) may likewise be noted. Schad himself, on the other hand, emphasized the 'primitivist' origins of his own wood reliefs, tracing their pedigree back to Gauguin, who

> long before Dada, even before he embarked on his Tahitian escapade, was the first to realize that art had come to a dead end, and who demanded a return to the natural, the untainted. Borrowings from primitive art and the craze for negro sculpture were the consequence, likewise new stylistic experiments which, despite their formal emancipation, remained rooted in a fine-art aesthetic. Dada's aggression, however, was directed against everything aesthetic ...[6]

3 Cited after *Christian Schad*, loc. cit.
4 *Oiseau Hippique*, painted wood, 18 × 16 cm (Fondation Arp e.V.); *Plant Hammer*, painted wood, 62 × 50 cm (Private collection). Arp's wood reliefs were first exhibited at the Kunstsalon Wolfsberg in September 1918; it is now considered that they should be ascribed to the period 1918–20, rather than 1916–17 as had previously been thought. The earliest of them thus antedates Schad's wood reliefs by no more than a few months, if at all; see Alastair Grieve, 'Arp in Zürich', in Stephen Foster and Rudolf Kuenzli (eds.), *Dada Spectrum: the Dialectics of Revolt*, Madison, WI (Coda Press)/Iowa (University of Iowa City) 1979, pp.175ff, 199
5 Christian Schad, 'Relative Realitäten', quoted after Heesemann-Wilson (1978), p.71
6 Ibid., p.69

Christian Schad 1894–1982

93 Maria and Annunziata 'from the Harbour'

Maria und Annunziata 'vom Hafen'[1]

1923
Oil on canvas, 67.5 × 55.5 cm
Signed lower left: 'Schad'
Paint film appears brittle and generally insecure. History of flaking and scattered old repairs
Accession no.1979.8

Provenance
Collection of the artist
Galerie Brockstedt, Hamburg
Galleria del Levante, Milan/Munich
Private collection, Milan
Fischer Fine Art, London
Thyssen-Bornemisza Collection, 1979

Exhibitions
Vienna, Kunsthandlung Würthle, 1927, *Christian Schad*, no.2
Berlin, Galerie Neumann–Nierendorf, 1927, *Christian Schad*
Berlin, Akademie der Künste, 1934, *Grosse Berliner Kunstausstellung*, no.259
Aschaffenburg, Museum der Stadt, 1955, *Christian Schad*
Frankfurt am Main, Kunstverein, 1956, *Christian Schad*
Frankfurt am Main, Kunstverein/Aschaffenburg, Museum der Stadt/Brunswick, Städtisches Museum, 1959–60, *Christian Schad. Bilder und Blätter*, no.9
Hildesheim, Roemer-Pelizaeus-Museum, 1960, *Christian Schad*
Remscheid, Städtisches Kulturamt, 1961, *Christian Schad*
Würzburg, Städtische Galerie, 1962, *Christian Schad*
Hamburg, Galerie Brockstedt, 1964, *Christian Schad. Gesichter der 20er Jahre*
Düsseldorf, Galerie Nebelung, 1965, *Bilder der 20er Jahre*
Rome, Galleria Il Fante di Spade, 1970, *Christian Schad. Dipinti dal 1920 al 1930*, no.4
Milan, Galleria del Levante/Munich, Galleria del Levante, 1970, *Christian Schad*, no.22
Milan, Palazzo Reale, 1972, *Christian Schad*, ill. [n.p.]
Bologna, Galleria d'Arte Stivani, 1973, *Christian Schad*, no.6
Saint Étienne, Musée d'Art et d'Industrie/Chambéry, Musée d'Art et d'Histoire, 1974, *Réalismes en Allemagne, 1919–1933*, no.102
Nuremberg, Kunsthalle, 1975, *Drei Generationen*, no.3
Vienna, Museum des 20. Jahrhunderts, 1977, *Neue Sachlichkeit und Realismus*, no.143
London, Arts Council of Great Britain, 1978–9, *Neue Sachlichkeit and German Realism of the Twenties*, no.223
Berlin, Staatliche Kunsthalle, 1980, *Christian Schad*, no.71
USA tour 1982–4, no.47
Modern Masters from the Thyssen-Bornemisza Collection, 1984–6, no.97
Lugano 1989, no.45
Bielefeld, Kunsthalle, 1990–91, *Neue Sachlichkeit – Magischer Realismus*, no.24

Literature
Schmied (1969), p.50 and fig.256
Schad (1970), no.22
Heesemann-Wilson (1978), no.72 and pp.104f
Christian Schad, exh. cat., Berlin, Staatliche Kunsthalle, 1980, pp.90–92

Note
1 The title is taken from the inventory of the artist's paintings compiled by Bettina Schad: see Schad (1970), no.22. The picture was also shown under this title in the 1980 Berlin retrospective exhibition of Schad's work, organized in collaboration with the artist

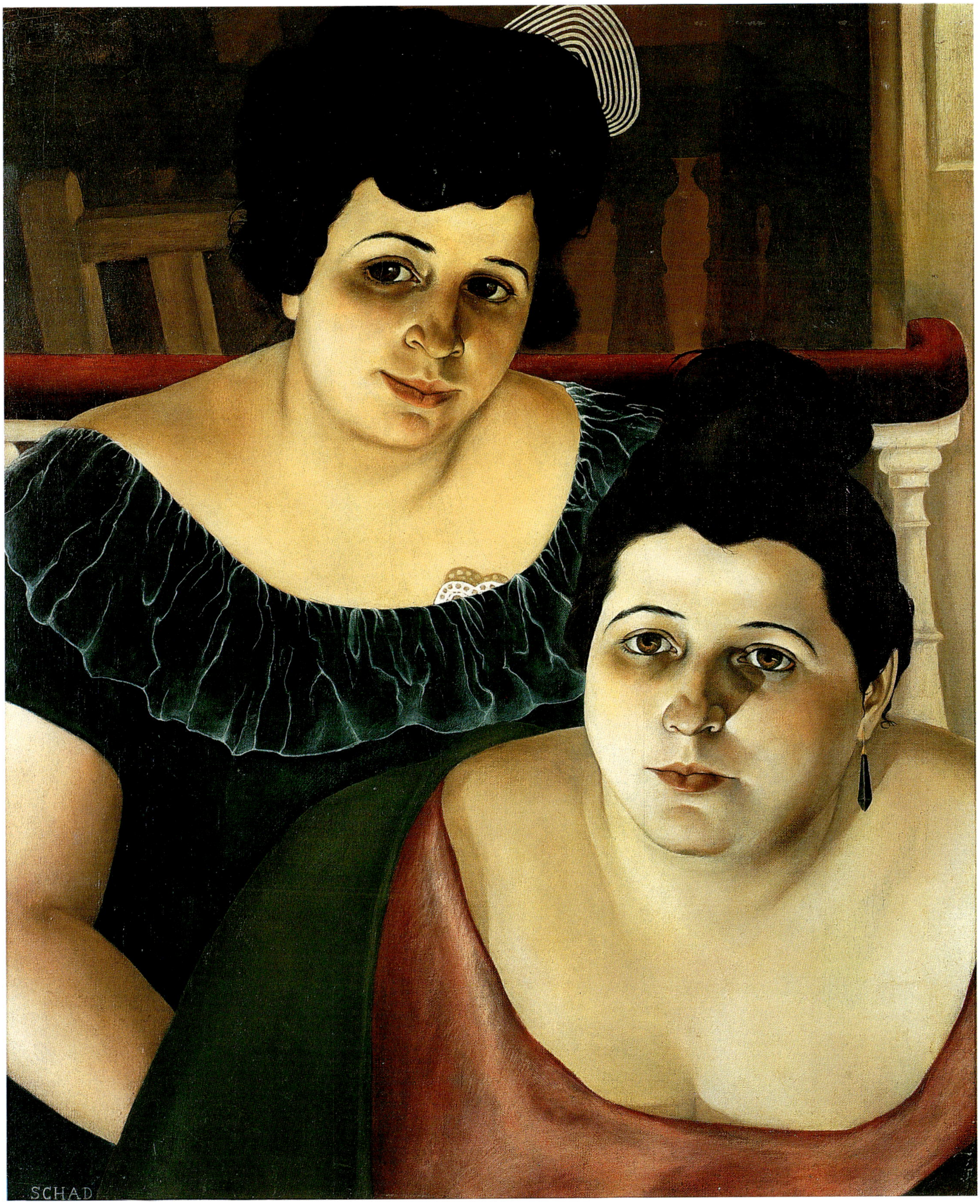
SCHAD

During the early 1920s, Schad spent the greater part of his time, albeit with interrruptions, in Italy, mainly in Naples and in Rome. This period coincides with a dramatic change not only in style, but in his whole attitude to art, characterized by a rapid shift away from his Dada-influenced manner of the preceding years in Switzerland. By his own account, this change was influenced in part by a decisive encounter which occurred during his first visit to Rome in 1920: with Raphael's painting known as *La Fornarina*,[2] then as now in the Palazzo Barberini (fig.1). According to Schad, the works of Raphael, Leonardo, Botticelli and other masters of the Italian Renaissance convinced him of the possibility of an expressive, realistic style of modern painting.[3] His works executed thereafter, including *Maria and Annunziata 'from the Harbour'*, are characterized by a lucidity and precision in the observation of nature, a kind of myopic, larger-than-life verism which link them with much of Neue Sachlichkeit painting.

However, few if any of the other painters of the Neue Sachlichkeit movement strove for so minutely detailed a manner of depiction: a mode of scrutiny so searching that it surpasses any ordinary, casual process of observing life and the world. This is seen most clearly in Schad's uncompromizing, even unflattering depiction of human flesh. Wieland Schmied, one of the first post-war art historians to write in detail about the phenomenon of the 'new objectivity', remarked that 'no painter of his time could make skin appear so vulnerable and transparent, revealing the underlying network of tiny veins, throbbing with the utmost sensuality and yet at the same time observed with such detachment, with so clinical an eye – as if the implements of the painter had become the instruments of the surgeon.'[4] In the case of [93], Schad's insistence on tiny details of drapery or flesh induces at times a sense of *un*reality, for example the way he represents the glistening skin around eyelids and nostrils, flanked by areas of deep shadow, as if the women portrayed are illuminated from beneath by the harsh light of the stage.

During his stay in Naples, whose 'volcanic soil' caused him to think 'of the here-and-now instead of the hereafter, bestowing sharper outlines on every-day life in all its various manifestations',[5] Schad painted numerous theatre and café scenes as well as depictions of gypsy children and street girls. According to his own recollection, 'Maria' and 'Annunziata' were two actresses, members of a troupe who played at the Teatro Rossini in the vicinity of the Piazza Dante. For him, they represented the incarnation of the *donna napoletana*, flaunting their finery on the streets of Naples as well as on the stage, where their appearance was greeted with enthusiasm by a devoted claque of followers.

In this double portrait, however, they have been subjected to a poetic transposition: Schad has represented them, not on the stage of the theatre, but in one of its boxes, assuming the role played by their own public, their faces intent on some action beyond our line of vision. Their bodies cut off at each side by the edge of the picture, as if a photographer, intent on capturing a likeness, had placed his camera slightly too close to the subject, one of the figures even seems to reach out beyond the frame – a device sometimes exploited in Italian Baroque portraiture, which may indeed have been another of Schad's numerous but concealed sources of inspiration.

Notes

2 At various times, the portrait has been attributed to Raphael or to one of his pupils or followers: see Leopold Dussler, *Raphael. A Critical Catalogue of his Pictures, Wall Paintings and Tapestries*, London (Phaidon) 1971, p.43

3 *Christian Schad*, p.92. For the catalogue of this 1980 Berlin retrospective, the artist himself provided draft entries and other relevant information, much of which has been incorporated into the present essay. Copies of this material were provided at the time by the organizers of the Berlin exhibition, and are now in the archive of the Thyssen-Bornemisza Collection, Lugano-Castagnola

4 Schmied, loc. cit.

5 Christian Schad, 'Relative Realitäten', quoted after *Christian Schad*, loc. cit.

FIG 1 attrib. Raphael, *Portrait of a Woman (La Fornarina)*, c1515, oil on panel, 85 × 60 cm (Rome, Galleria Nazionale, Palazzo Barberini)

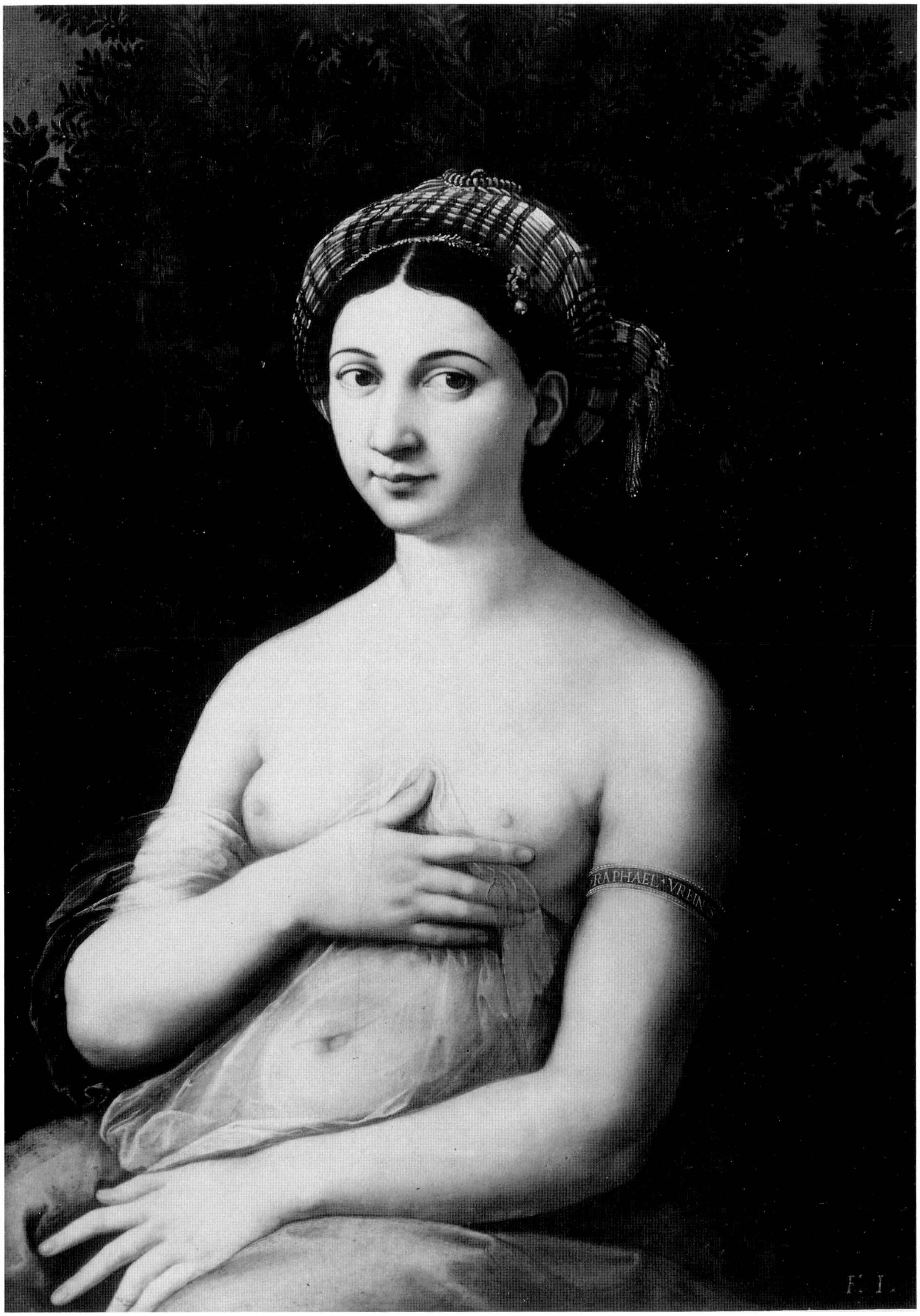

Christian Schad 1894–1982

94 Portrait of Dr Haustein

1928
Oil on canvas, 80.5 × 55 cm
Signed/dated lower right: 'Schad 28'
There is a history of scattered losses, which have been retouched. There are abrasions in the paint surface and passages of crackle, with some cupping
Accession no.1979.57

Provenance
Collection of the artist
Galerie Brockstedt, Hamburg
Galleria del Levante, Milan/Munich
Fischer Fine Art, London
Thyssen-Bornemisza Collection, 1979

Exhibitions
Berlin, Galerie Fritz Gurlitt, 1929, *Christian Schad*
Hamburg, Galerie Brockstedt, 1964, *Christian Schad. Gesichter der 20er Jahre*
Milan, Galleria del Levante, 1970, *Christian Schad, Periodo Nuova Oggettività*, no.47
Modena, Galleria Mutina, 1970, *Christian Schad*
Rome, Galleria Il Fante di Spade, 1970, *Christian Schad. Dipinti dal 1920 al 1930*, no.17
Trier, Städtisches Museum 1971, *Christian Schad*, no.23
Bologna, Galleria d'Arte Stivani, 1972, *Nuova Oggettività Tedesca, 1918–1933*, no.35
Milan, Palazzo Reale, 1972, *Christian Schad*, ill. [n.p.]
Bologna, Galleria d'Arte Stivani, 1973, *Christian Schad*, no.13
Saint Étienne, Musée d'Art et d'Industrie/Chambéry, Musée d'Art et d'Histoire, 1974, *Réalismes en Allemagne, 1919–1933*, no.107
Nuremberg, Kunsthalle, 1975, *Drei Generationen*, no.9
London, Arts Council of Great Britain, 1978–9, *Neue Sachlichkeit and German Realism of the Twenties*, no.217
Berlin, Staatliche Kunsthalle, 1980, *Christian Schad*, no.103
Paris, Centre Georges Pompidou, 1980–81, *Les Réalismes – entre Révolution et Réaction*, ill. p.521[1]
Modern Masters from the Thyssen-Bornemisza Collection, 1984–6, no.96
Berlin, Berlinische Galerie, 1987, *Ich und die Stadt*, no.178
Madrid, Centro de Arte Reina Sofia, 1989, *Berlin, Punto de Encuentro*, no.5/27
Lugano 1989, no.46
Expressionism and Modern German Painting, 1989–90, no.32
Bielefeld, Kunsthalle, 1990–91, *Neue Sachlichkeit – Magischer Realismus*, no.26

Literature
Schad (1970), no.47
Heesemann-Wilson (1978), no.97 and p.130
Stephan Leibfried and Florian Tennstedt, 'Berufsverbote und Sozialpolitik 1933. Die Auswirkungen der nationalsozialistischen Machtergreifung auf die Krankenkassenverwaltung und die Kassenärzte', *Arbeitspapiere des Forschungsschwerpunktes Reproduktionsrisiken, soziale Bewegungen und Sozialpolitik*, no.2, Bremen (Universität Bremen) 1979, d) 'Ein einzelnes Schicksal: Der Fall Dr *Hans Haustein*', p.128f
Christian Schad, exh. cat., Berlin, Staatliche Kunsthalle, 1980, p.140
Eberhard Roters and Bernhard Schulz (eds.), *Ich und die Stadt. Mensch und Grosstadt in der deutschen Kunst des 20. Jahrhunderts*, exh. cat., Berlin, Berlinische Galerie, 1987, p.246

Note
1 Exhibition also shown in revised form in Berlin: see exh. cat., *Realismus. Zwischen Revolution und Reaktion 1919–1939*, Berlin, Staatliche Kunsthalle 1981

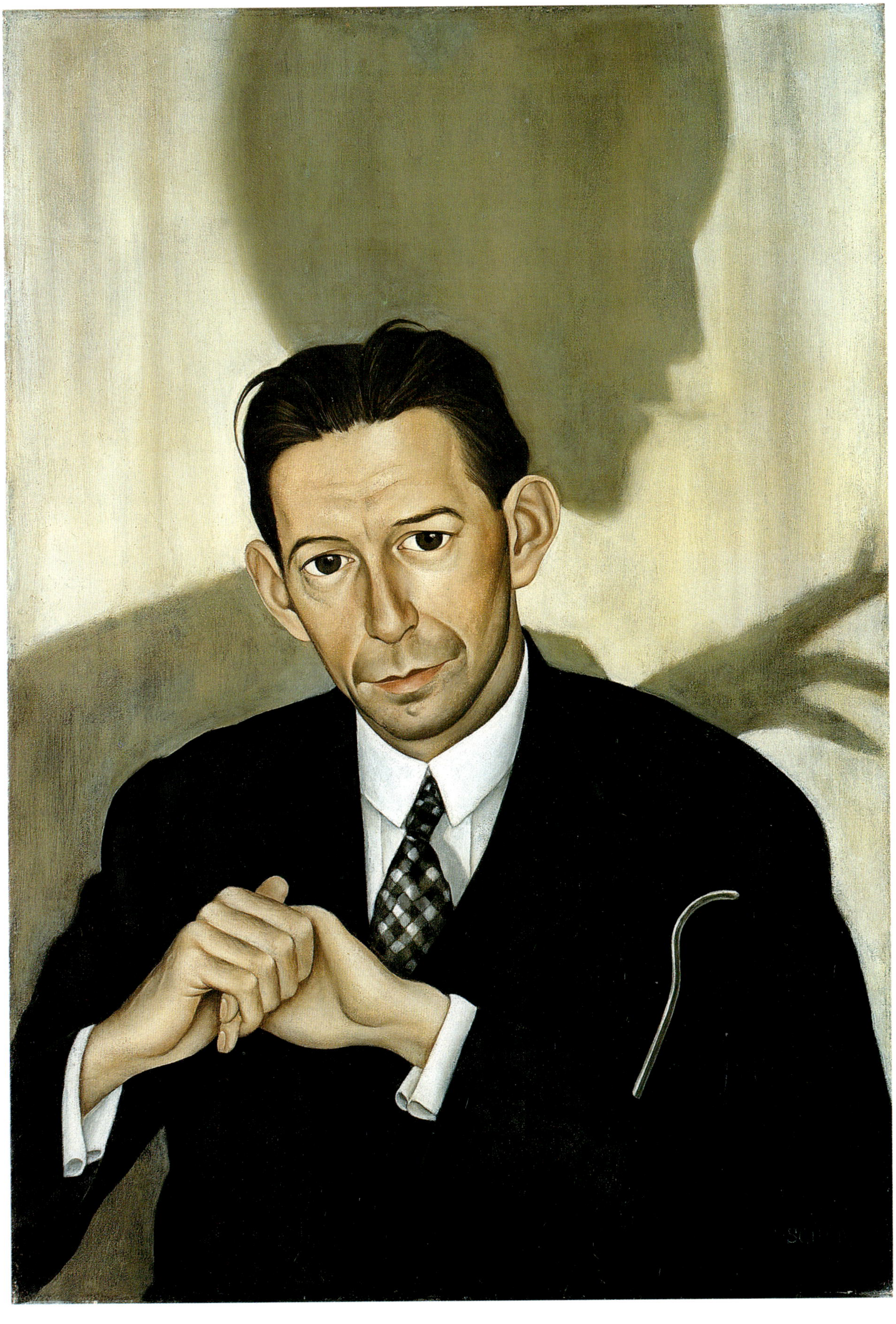

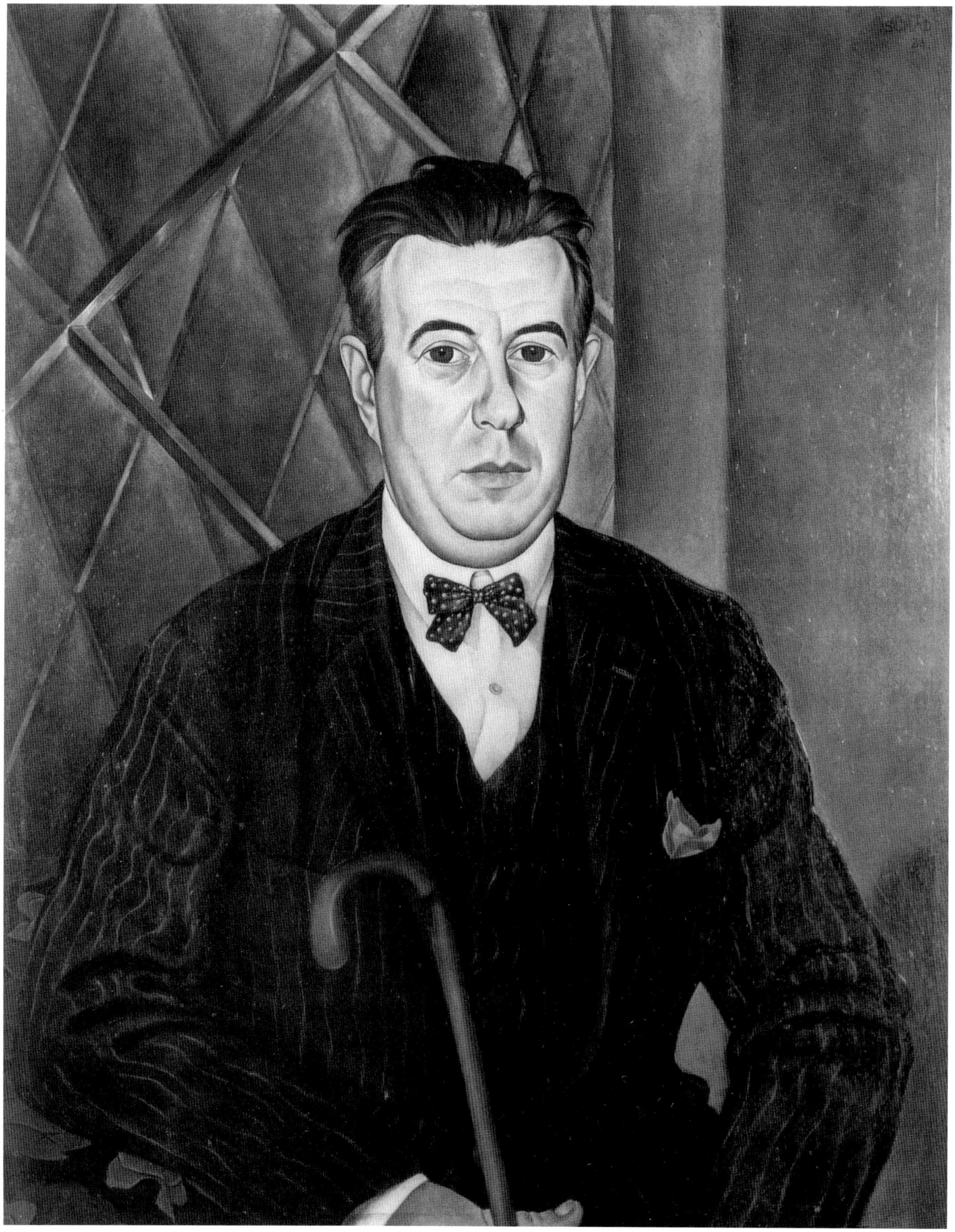

FIG 1 Christian Schad, *Portrait of Felix Bryk*, 1928, oil on canvas, 81 × 65 cm (Private collection)

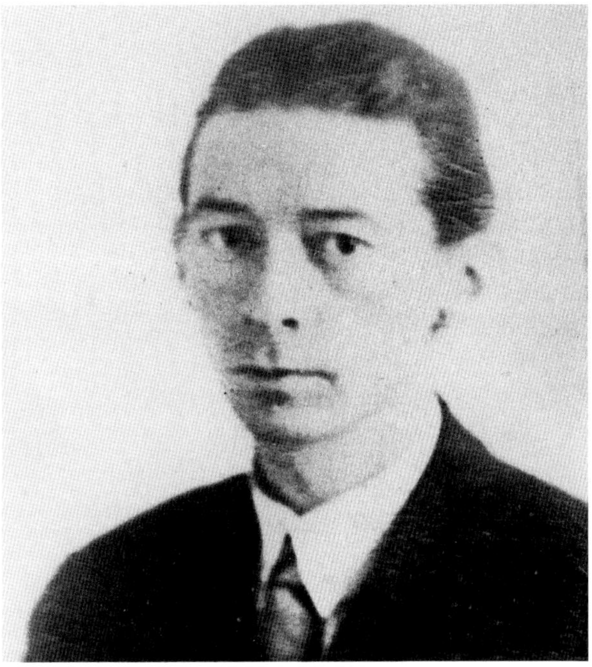

FIG 2 Photograph of Dr Hans Haustein, taken from his personal dossier, which also contains a report of his suicide (Potsdam, Bundesarchiv)

During the late 1920s, one of Schad's closest friends was the Viennese-born entymologist (and self-styled anthropologist) Felix Bryk, whose portrait he painted shortly after moving more or less permanently to Berlin in 1928 (see fig.1).[2] It was Bryk who introduced the painter to the political and literary salon presided over by Friedel Haustein, wife of the dermatologist and specialist in venereal diseases Dr Hans Haustein (1894–1933). Haustein was an expert on social hygiene who had done extensive research on tuberculosis, and on the history of medicine.[3] It is also said that he was well-known as a provider of prophylactics to the 'ladies of the profession' who frequented his practice in Berlin's Bregenzerstrasse.

Schad himself remembered Friedel Haustein for her knack of cultivating not only people who were interesting and amusing, but also those who might be useful to her husband, and that 'everyone who was anyone' in Berlin belonged to her salon, which he described as characterized by 'extreme intellectual and erotic licence, typical of 1920s Berlin . . . frequented by writers, artists and politicians, scientists, doctors and beautiful women'.[4] Among the habitués of the Haustein circle were the novelist Lion Feuchtwanger, the composer Fred Raymond and the Soviet Commissar of Enlightenment, Anatoly Lunacharsky.

In this chillingly 'clinical' portrait, the sitter is identified by one of the instruments of his profession, a catheter which protrudes oddly from the crook of his left arm. It has also been suggested that the shadow which looms threateningly behind him, with its enlarged cranium and diminutive hand, represents a human embryo and is thus likewise an allusion to Haustein's profession as doctor and specialist in sexually transmitted diseases.[5] According, however, to Schad's own recollection, the shadow is that of Haustein's mistress, a fashion model named Sonja, with whom the doctor was then infatuated.[6] The air of menace in this painting turned out to be prophetic: Haustein's liaison with Sonja led to the break-up of his marriage, whereupon his wife committed suicide. Haustein himself, who had strong socialist connections and was banned from medical practice almost as soon as the Nazis came to power, poisoned himself on 12 November 1933, having heard that he was about to be arrested by the Gestapo.

Notes

2 See *Christian Schad*, p.134; also the biography by Giovanni Testori in *Christian Schad, Periodo Nuova Oggettività*, exh. cat., Milan, Gallerie del Levante, 1970

3 Information about Haustein's career, his interests, and the manner of his death is taken either from Leibfried and Tennstedt, op. cit., or from Haustein's own curriculum vitae, preserved among his personal papers in the Bundesarchiv (former Zentrales Staatsarchiv), Potsdam. I am grateful to the director and staff of the Bundesarchiv Potsdam for placing this material at my disposal. See also Dietrich Tutzke, *Über wenig bekannte Beziehungen zwischen deutschen und sowjetischen Venerologen in der Weimarer Republik*, Leipzig (NTM-Schriftenreihe zur Geschichte der Naturwissenschaft, Technik und Medizin) 1976, p.88

4 From the notes prepared by the artist in connection with the 1980 Berlin retrospective, copies of which were provided at the time by the organizers of the exhibition, and are now in the archive of the Thyssen-Bornemisza Collection, Lugano-Castagnola. See also *Christian Schad*, p.140

5 Heesemann-Wilson (1978), p.130. This suggestion seems strangely at odds with the fact that the figure portrayed is, unmistakably, smoking a cigarette

6 See n.4

Egon Schiele 1890–1918

95 Houses on the River (The Old Town)

Häuser am Fluss (Die alte Stadt)[1]

1914
Oil on canvas, 100 × 120.5 cm
Signed/dated upper right, in cartouche: 'Egon Schiele 1914'
History of overcleaning and heavy restoration; scattered losses, especially to the edges of the canvas, and cracking have been stabilized by relining with wax–resin adhesive. The painting has been re-varnished using a thin coat of acrylic resin; residues of old varnish are visible as occasional passages of yellowish discolouration
Accession no.1978.81

Provenance
Franz Hauer, Vienna
Spira Collection, Vienna
Kunsthandlung Würthle, Vienna
Josef von Sternberg, Los Angeles, CA
Mr and Mrs Mortimer M.Denker, New York
Solomon R.Guggenheim Museum, New York
Fischer Fine Art, London
Thyssen-Bornemisza Collection, 1978

Exhibitions
Vienna, Kunsthandlung Würthle, 1925–6, *Egon Schiele*, no.29
Vienna, Hagenbund, 1928, *Gedächtnisausstellung Egon Schiele*, no.58
Los Angeles, CA, Los Angeles Museum, 1935, *From the Collection of Josef von Sternberg*, no.33
Los Angeles, CA, County Museum, 1943, *The Collection of Josef von Sternberg*, no.43
Chicago, IL, Arts Club, 1946, *Josef von Sternberg Collection*, no.21
Vienna, Österreichische Galerie (Oberes Belvedere), 1968, *Egon Schiele. Ausstellung zur 50. Wiederkehr seines Todestages*, no.47 [as 'Wachau(?)']
Birmingham, AL, Museum of Art, 1977, *Austrian Art*, no.61
Modern Masters from the Thyssen-Bornemisza Collection, 1984–6, no.98
Lugano 1989, no.39
Rome 1990–91, no.44

Literature
Nirenstein (1930), no.145 [as 'Wachau']
Kallir (1966), no.197
Leopold (1973), no.245 and p.655
Malafarina (1982), no.268
J.Kallir (1990), P.279 [as 'Houses by the River II (The Old City II)'][2]

Houses on the River was for a long time wrongly identified as a motif from the Wachau,[3] the region of Lower Austria around the towns of Krems and Stein on the Danube where Schiele in fact painted several important townscapes, among them views of the façade of the parish church at Stein and the adjacent Frauenbergkirche.[4] It has, however, been convincingly demonstrated that the subject of the present work is Krumau, a town situated on a sharp bend of the River Moldau in Southern Bohemia (now Czechoslovakia).[5] His mother's birthplace, Krumau seems to have been associated in the artist's mind with a mood of emptiness and desolation: several representations of the same subject bear the title *Dead Town*.[6] In other

Notes
1 According to Leopold, loc. cit., the artist also listed the painting under the titles *Die alte Stadt* and *Stadt-II*; on Schiele's use of alternative titles, and the problems associated with them, see Leopold (1973), p.513
2 I am grateful to Jane Kallir, of the Galerie St Étienne, New York, for making available to me material from her complete catalogue raisonné of Schiele's paintings and works on paper prior to the publication of this massive and indispensable reference work (see J.Kallir (1990)), also for her advice on this and the other Schiele entries which follow
3 Including as recently as 1984–6 in the catalogue of the exhibition *Modern Masters from the Thyssen-Bornemisza Collection* (for full reference see p.27); see, for example, the entry in the London version of the catalogue (Royal Academy of Arts, 1984, p.197), where the subject is described as the 'city of Wachau' [sic]
4 See n.9
5 Leopold (1973), p.654; also J.Kallir (1990), pp.326, 338
6 Compare, for example, three paintings of 1912, Leopold nos.205–6, 222, all of which are entitled *Tote Stadt* (Dead Town)

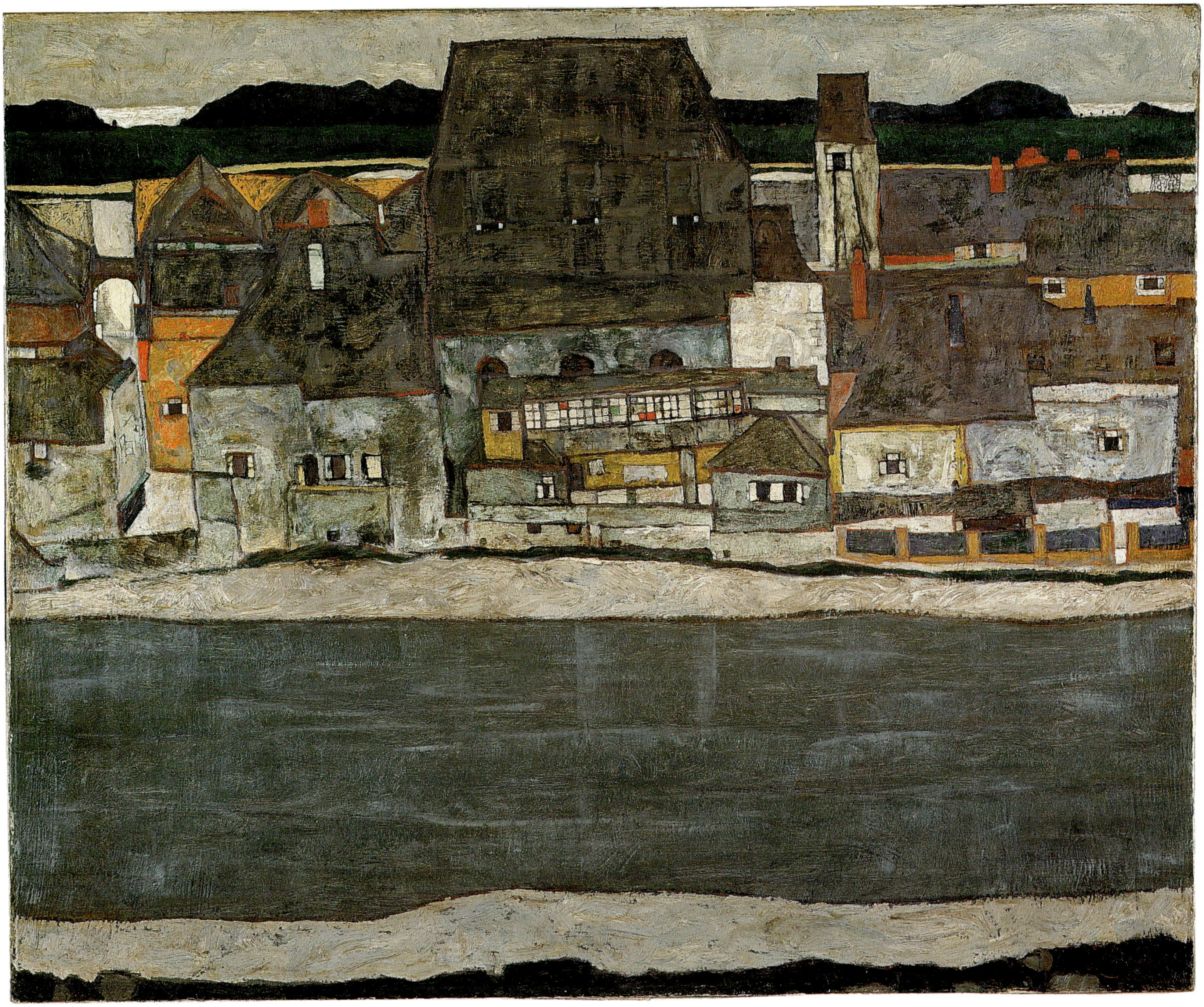

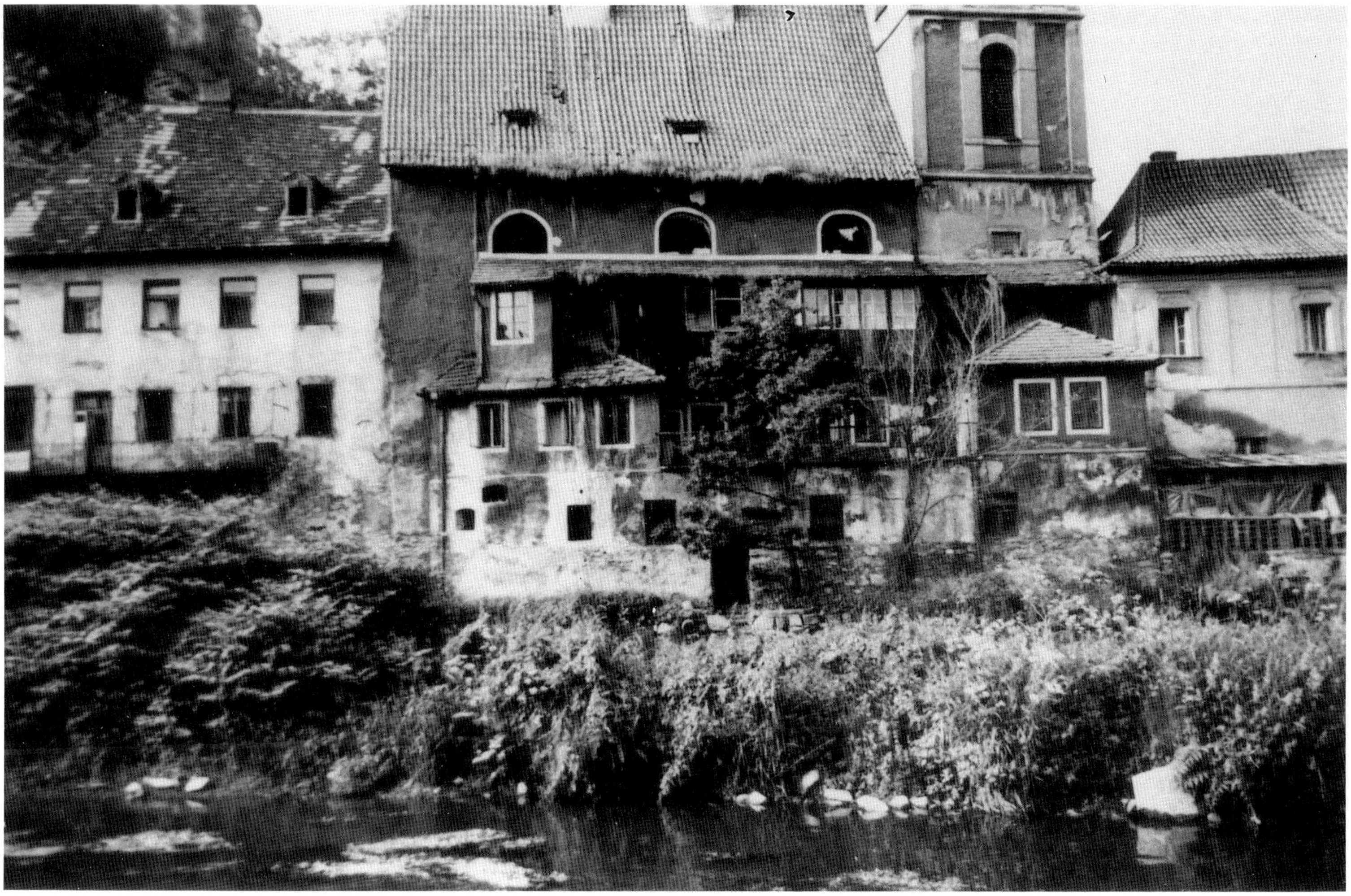

FIG 1 The Jodokus Church in Krumau, seen from the river

paintings, he invests its architecture with a curiously anthropomorphic quality, as in [95], in which the windows of the houses appear like sightless eyes gazing unseeingly down on the river.

Comparing the picture with a photograph of the actual location (see fig.1), it is striking the extent to which Schiele has departed from reality, exercising in this instance a greater-than-usual degree of artistic licence. The façade of the Jodokus church, looking on to the river, is recorded more or less faithfully, in particular the three arched windows and jumble of houses below, but the proportions of the steeply-angled roof have been totally altered, the tall church tower is reduced to a stump, and an extra (non-existent) tower has been inserted to the right of the church. In two further paintings of 1915 and 1917, Schiele treats precisely the same subject but from a much closer standpoint, adding colourful festoons of washing which hang from beneath the windows giving on to the river.[7]

It appears that *Houses on the River* was bought almost immediately upon its completion by Franz Hauer, the owner of a Viennese restaurant, the Reichenberger Griechenbeisl.[8] Having taken over the running of the restaurant from his brother-in-law, by the turn of the century Hauer had built it up into one of the capital's best known eating-places. Newly prosperous, he began to interest himself in collecting art, initially the painters of the Vienna Künstlerhaus, subsequently more avant-garde artists, especially Kokoschka and Albin Egger-Lienz. Schiele first approached him in 1912; in the short period 1912–14, Hauer was to become one of his most significant patrons, acquiring several important landscapes in addition to *Houses on the River*, among them the two versions of *The Town of Stein*.[9]

Notes

7 1915, Leopold no.263, and 1917, Leopold no.275

8 See Nebehay (1979), p.530; Leopold (1973), p.668. The restaurant still exists today at its original location on Vienna's Fleischmarkt

9 1913, Leopold nos.239–40

During the first months of 1914, the two men corresponded about the possible purchase of one or more townscapes.[10] In a letter dated 5 February, Schiele invited Hauer to visit his studio in his absence in order to inspect a picture referred to simply as 'das Stadtbild';[11] if this was [95], the painting must have been completed shortly after the beginning of the year. The artist himself, in a handwritten inventory of his paintings, listed a work entitled simply *Stadt* as the second painting of 1914 (the preceding entry on the same list, for a work entitled 'Liebespaar', has had its date changed from 1913 to 1914). Though its dimensions (100 × 110 cm) do not correspond exactly with the present work, the fact that in Schiele's list the location is given as 'Galerie Hauer, Wien' leads one to suspect that it may have been identical with *Houses on the River*.[12] (Leopold in his catalogue raisonné of the paintings, which is ordered chronologically, also places *Houses on the River* among the first paintings of 1914.) In a further letter of 8 March 1914, Schiele asks Hauer to allow him to keep 'das letzterworbene Bild' for another two or three weeks, so that he may look over it properly, implying that it had been only recently completed;[13] it is not obvious, however, to which picture he is referring.

If the dating suggested above is correct, this must be a painting done from memory or worked up from sketches, rather than in front of the motif. Schiele revisited Krumau in November 1914, in the company of Hans and Heinrich Böhler and the artist Ludwig Heinrich Jungnickel;[14] *Houses on the River* must have been completed prior to this autumn visit, since Hauer had died of peritonitis on 5 June. Schiele's previous visit to Krumau, together with his mistress Wally Neuzil, had taken place in June–July 1913.

Following Hauer's death, the painting passed through several private collections before being given by Mr and Mrs Mortimer M. Denker to the Solomon R. Guggenheim Museum, New York, in 1965. 'De-accessioned' by the museum in 1978, it was acquired through exchange by Helen Serger's gallery La Boetie, New York; thence via Fischer Fine Art, London, to the present owner.

10 'Sehr geehrter Herr Hauer! ich erwarte von Ihnen dass Sie mich am Dienstag oder Mittwoch 2–4h nachmittags besuchen werden um eines oder beide Städte zu kaufen . . .', letter dated 25 January 1914: see Nebehay (1979), p.301 ('Dokumente und Korrespondenz 1914', no.633)
11 Ibid., doc. no.637
12 See Kallir (1966), n.p. [p.81], where several pages from this list are reproduced
13 Nebehay (1979), no.643
14 Ibid., p.286

Egon Schiele 1890–1918

96 Self-portrait

1910
Charcoal and watercolour on paper, 45.7 × 31 cm
Signed/dated lower right: 'Egon Schiele 1910'
The overall condition is poor. The paper is of inferior quality, possibly a form of wrapping-paper, and may have been re-used; it is now rubbed, stained and wrinkled. There are also two very obtrusive creases, showing that the sheet has previously been folded: one vertical, running parallel with the left edge of the paper, the other horizontal, across the lower part of the sheet, passing directly through the signature. The passages of watercolour have significantly faded, and the sheet shows evidence of former attempts at restoration: what now appear in places like passages of (bistre?) wash may be due to the intervention of a previous restorer[1]
Accession no.1972.19

Provenance
La Boetie, New York[2]
Fischer Fine Art, London
Thyssen-Bornemisza Collection, 1972

Exhibitions
London, Fischer Fine Art, 1972, *Egon Schiele*, no.15
Bremen 1975, no.73
Lugano 1975, no.38
Rome 1990–91, no.43

Literature
Kiel (1974), p.122, ill. p.123
J.Kallir (1990), D.701

As with so many artists, Schiele was his own most frequent subject in portraiture. His reasons for representing himself so often were complex. He evidently regarded his own body with a mixture of fascination and distaste, sometimes depicting himself nude, exploiting the genre of self-portraiture as a way of exploring his own sexuality. Some of these nude self-portraits have a curiously voyeuristic quality, though the way in which he portrays himself is far from erotic in any normal sense. Posed photographs, on the other hand, show that he was equally intrigued by the gestural language of the mime artist, which evidently afforded new possibilities for the treatment of the human body as a vehicle for expressing emotional states, a kind of psychological or 'inner' world – one of the most important purposes of Expressionist art generally.

As Jane Kallir observes, the pose of the figure is related to that used for the foremost of the two figures in the first oil version of Schiele's composition *The Self-Seers*, likewise of 1910.[3]

Notes
1 I am grateful to Emil Bosshard, Head of Conservation of the Thyssen-Bornemisza Collection, for providing me with supplementary information regarding the condition of this work
2 According to Jane Kallir, the work had previously been offered for sale by Hauswedell & Nolte in Hamburg (sale no.180, 5 June 1971, lot 1754); see J.Kallir (1990), p.427
3 *Die Selbstseher I*, 1910: Leopold (1973), no.161; J.Kallir (1990), P.174

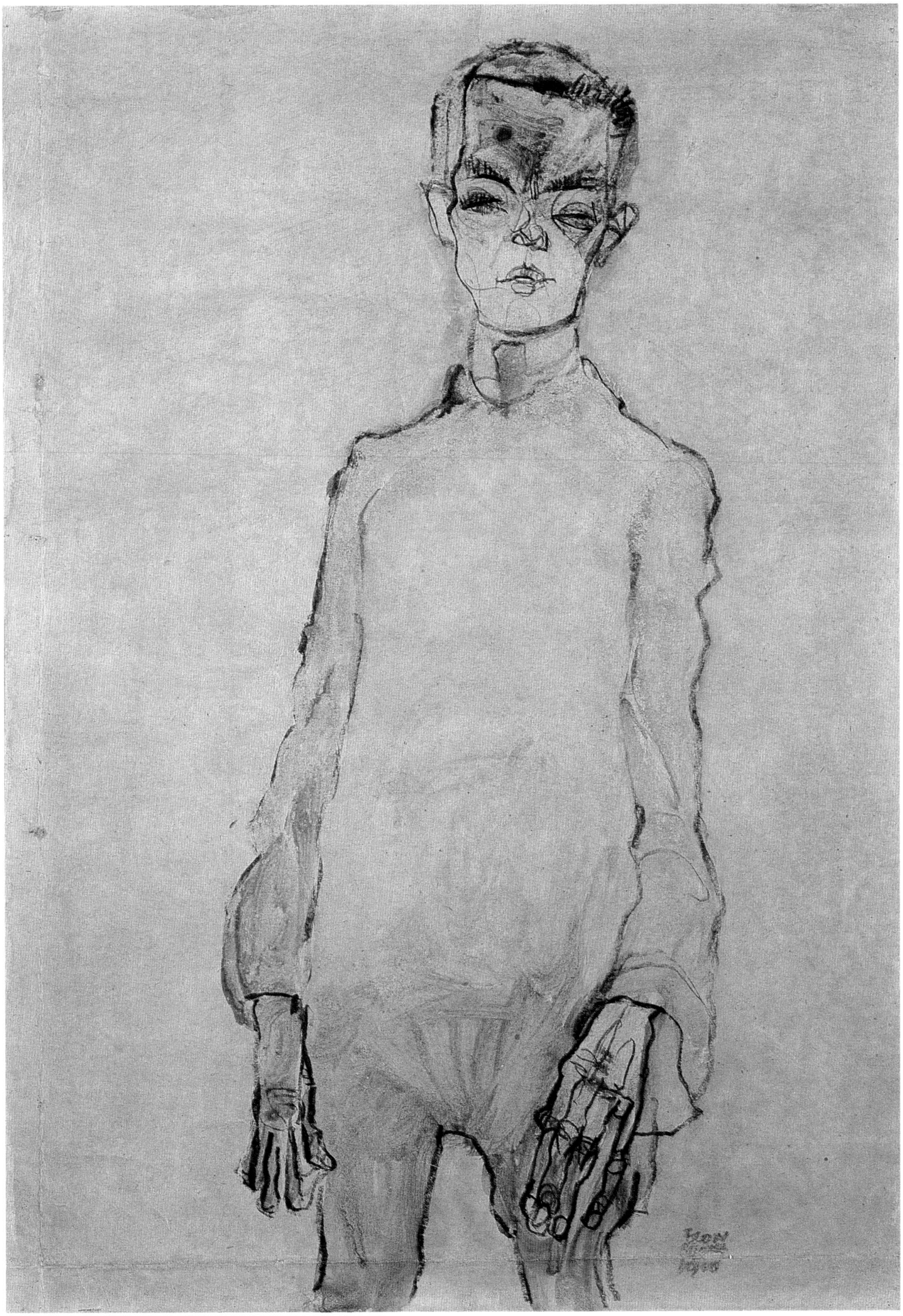

Egon Schiele 1890–1918

97 Seated Girl (Poldi Lodzinski [?])

*c*1910
Watercolour and gouache, with traces of black crayon and pencil on brown wrapping paper, 45 × 28.5 cm
Signed lower right: 'Schiele'
The paper is somewhat creased and yellowed with age. Otherwise condition is good
Accession no.1972.18

Provenance
Piccadilly Gallery, London[1]
La Boetie, New York
Fischer Fine Art, London
Thyssen-Bornemisza Collection, 1972

Exhibitions
New York, La Boetie, 1971, *Egon Schiele and his Circle*, no.32
Des Moines, IO, Art Center, 1971, *Egon Schiele and the Human Form*, no.7[2]
New York, La Boetie, 1971, *A Selection of 20th-Century Drawings*, no.144
London, Fischer Fine Art, 1972, *Egon Schiele*, no.9
Bremen 1975, no.72
Lugano 1978, no.97
Rome 1990–91, no.42

Literature
Leopold (1973), p.548
Kiel (1974), p.124, ill. p.125
Vergo (1975), p.215
Frank Whitford, *Egon Schiele*, London 1981, p.76
J.Kallir (1990), D.404

This watercolour has generally been considered a study for Schiele's oil painting *Poldi Lodzinsky* (fig.1).[3] Though the painting is signed and dated 1908, Leopold has argued convincingly that, for stylistic reasons, it should be ascribed to 1910. A date of 1910 for the present watercolour, both on stylistic grounds and on the basis of its affinity with the oil painting, likewise appears plausible.

Apart from her name, and the fact that she was allegedly the daughter of a cab driver in Krumau (Schiele's mother's birthplace: see [95]), it has not proved possible to ascertain anything regarding the identity of the young girl portrayed. The identification of the sitter has, moreover, recently been called into question by Jane Kallir, on the basis of comparison with other drawings known to be of 'Poldi'.[4]

Notes
1 The work had previously been offered for sale at auction at the Dorotheum in Vienna (sale no.580, 21 June 1968, lot 299)
2 Exhibition also shown at Columbus, OH, Gallery of Fine Arts and at the Art Institute of Chicago during 1971–2. [97] was, however, shown only in Des Moines
3 Leopold (1973), no.143; J.Kallir (1990), P.162
4 Letter to the author, 22 August 1990; see also J.Kallir (1990), p.394

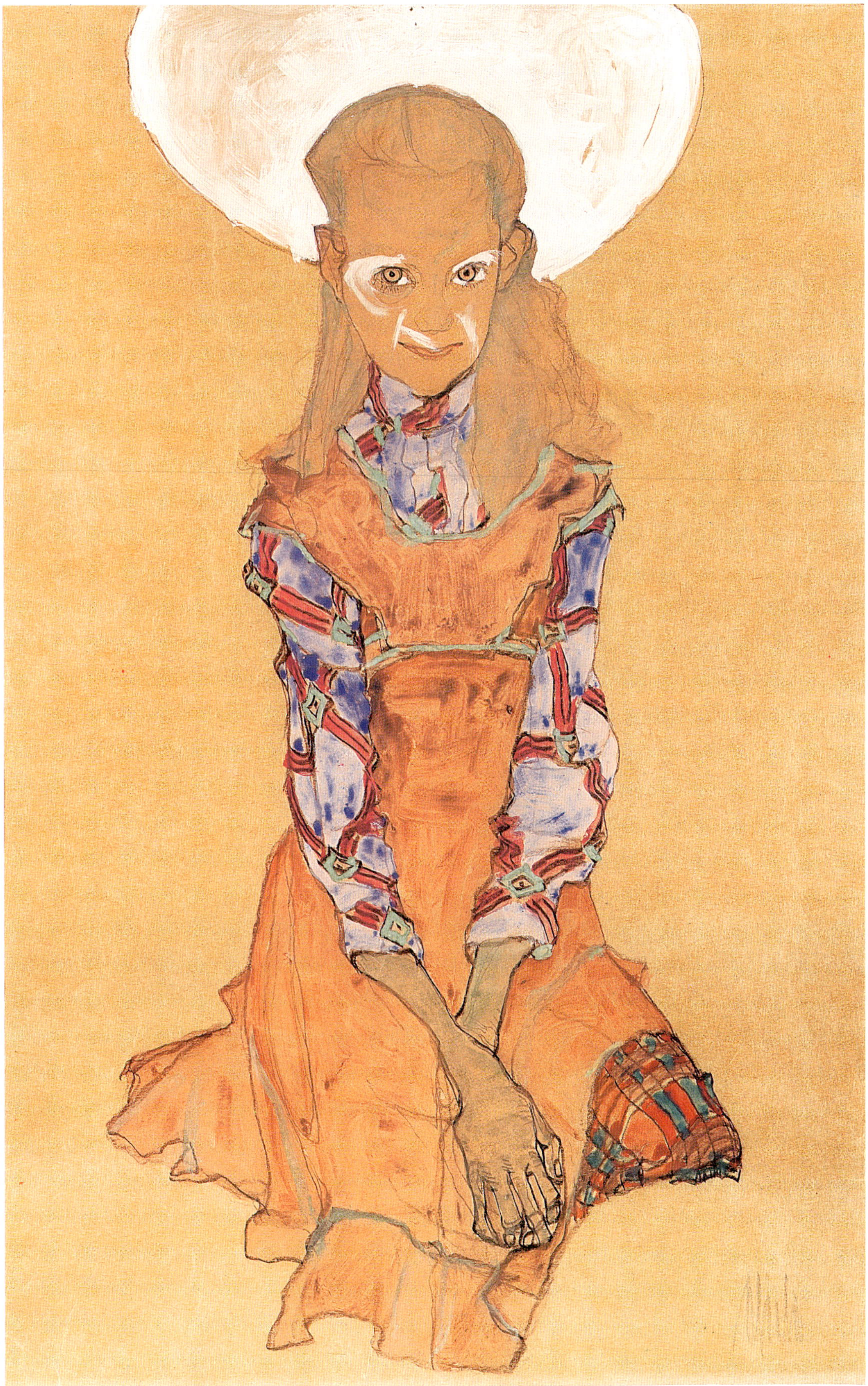

It has often been claimed that the oil painting of Poldi Lodzinsky was a study or maquette for a stained-glass window, intended for the staircase of the Palais Stoclet in Brussels, built by the Secessionist architect Josef Hoffmann between 1905 and 1911 and decorated by artists of the Viennese craft group, the Wiener Werkstätte.[5] Schiele was involved with the Wiener Werkstätte in various ways, including designing postcards for them; that he was also commissioned to work on the Palais Stoclet project is documented in letters to Ludwig Karl Strauch and Josef Hoffmann dating from the summer and autumn of 1910.[6] It seems, however, that his designs were rejected by the client, Adolphe Stoclet; not is it certain, on the basis of documentary evidence, that the Poldi Lodzinsky painting was in fact one of these rejected designs.[7] Though the geometric character of the present study, and the gouache 'halo' behind the head of the figure, make the idea of a commission for a stained-glass window seem not implausible, both these features occur in other works by Schiele from around 1910 having no relationship with any applied-art project. On the other hand, the tall vertical format of the oil painting, unusual in Schiele's oeuvre, might also suggest that he could possibly have had a staircase window in mind.

For his drawings of this period, Schiele often used a cheap, poor-quality paper – or, in this case, wrapping-paper. This may have been partly by choice: it is possible that he regarded it as suitable for rapid sketches or studies. Kallir notes that the brownish *Packpapier* employed in a number of drawings of around 1910, including the present work, has something in common with the heavily-sized 'simile Japan' that Schiele favoured, and could afford, from 1911 on:[8] relatively non-absorbent, it allowed the colour to be manipulated quickly and easily on the surface of the sheet. However, these were also years of great financial hardship, as emerges from the correspondence cited above; thus, his choice of such inexpensive materials may also have been dictated by economic circumstances.

It has on several occasions been alleged that at least part of the colouring of the present watercolour may be by another hand.[9] This allegation is, however, impossible either to confirm or to deny on the basis of purely visual inspection.

Notes

5 On the building history of the Palais Stoclet, see Vergo (1975) pp.143f; also Schweiger (1982), pp.51f

6 Nebehay (1979), p.132, doc. 104 and pp.135–6, doc. 123

7 See J.Kallir (1990), p.292

8 Letter to the author, 22 August 1990

9 See J.Kallir (1990), p.394

FIG 1 Egon Schiele, *Poldi Lodzinsky*, oil on canvas, 109.5 × 36.5 cm (Private collection)

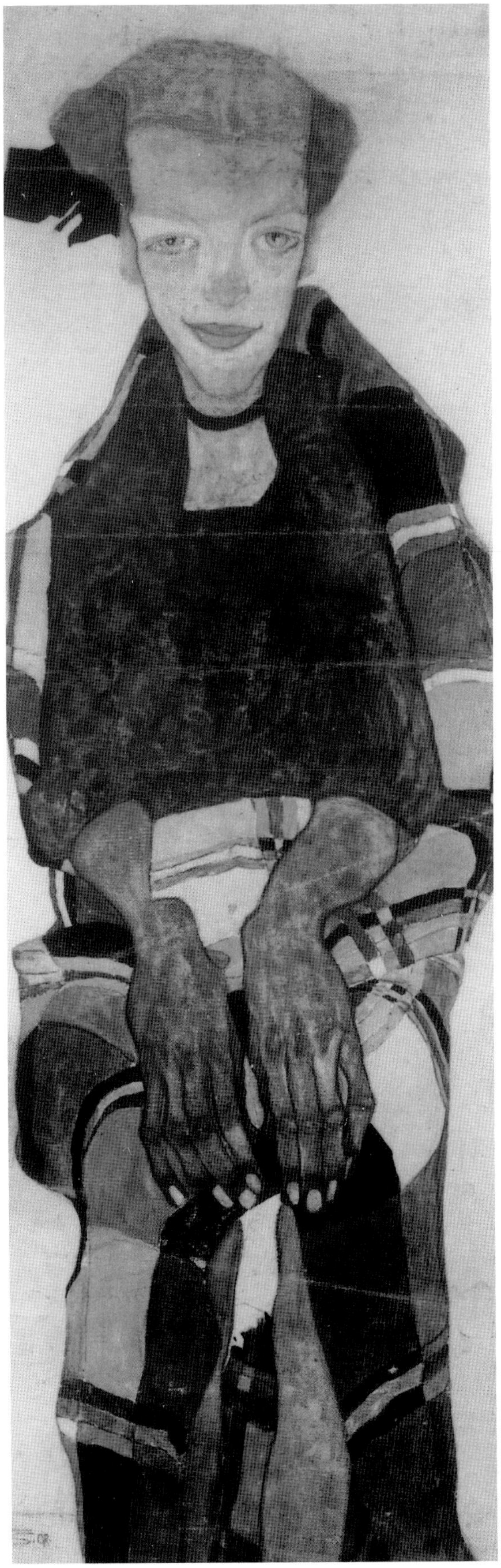

Egon Schiele 1890–1918

98 Nude Girl with Arms Outstretched[1]

1911
Watercolour, gouache and pencil on paper, 48 × 32 cm
Signed/dated centre right: 'Egon Schiele 1911'
The paper has become wrinkled, creased and yellow with age. There is a water stain close to the lower left corner of the sheet
Accession no.1977.11

Provenance
La Boetie, New York
Thyssen-Bornemisza Collection, 1977

Exhibitions
New York, La Boetie, 1969, *Selection of Major 20th Century Paintings, Sculpture and Drawings*, no.81
New York, La Boetie, 1971, *Egon Schiele and his Circle*, no.24

Literature
Malafarina (1982), no.54
J.Kallir (1990), D.778 [as 'Standing Female Nude']

Throughout his career, but especially during the period *c*1909–11, Schiele made frequent use of juvenile models, often depicted in overtly erotic or seductive poses. Frequent warnings by his friends that he should be circumspect, most especially with regard to his conduct with children, turned out to be prophetic. In 1912 he was convicted by a district court at St Pölten, Lower Austria, of offending against public morals, on the grounds that he had left indecent drawings displayed in his studio for children to see. One such drawing was ritually burnt by the judge in the course of the hearing. Far more serious charges, of abduction and forced intercourse with a child, were however dropped in the course of the eleven days Schiele spent in prison at Neulengbach awaiting trial.[2]

To modern eyes, Schiele's erotic subjects – even his depictions of children – seem neither surprising nor even very shocking. Despite his minute and obsessive recording of the details of genitalia and pubic hair, and his occasional treatment of 'taboo' subjects such as lesbianism and female masturbation, in the case of works such as *Nude Girl with Arms Outstretched* the present-day viewer is struck not so much by the erotic or voyeuristic qualities of the subject, but by the seeming note of compassion in the way the artist renders the skinny bodies and haggard faces of these for the most part street urchins and (sometimes) under-age prostitutes.

In her 1990 catalogue raisonné of Schiele's paintings and works on paper, Jane Kallir calls this work 'Standing Female Nude'. To the present author, however, it seems beyond question that the young girl portrayed is lying rather than standing. The whole weight of the figure suggests a recumbent, not an erect posture. The torso is at full stretch, the rib cage distended, the arms (though summarily indicated) flung wide – a pose almost impossible to sustain had the girl been made to stand. Nor is it clear how the blanket or shawl around the lower part of the figure could have been supported, other than in a recumbent position. Kallir herself observes that it was Schiele's frequent practice to have his models pose on a low couch or mattress while he observed them from above, perched on a stool or even ladder in search of an unconventional, plunging perspective which characterizes many of his figure drawings.[3] The pose of the figure suggests that he may well have followed this rather odd procedure in the case of the present work.

Notes
1 The accompanying essay summarizes the reasons for re-titling this work, previously known as 'Standing Female Nude'
2 For a full account of Schiele's arrest, imprisonment and trial, see Arthur Roessler (ed.), *Egon Schiele im Gefängnis. Aufzeichnungen und Zeichnungen*, Vienna/Leipzig (Carl Konegen) 1922; Alessandra Comini, *Schiele in Prison*, London (Thames & Hudson) 1973; also Nebehay (1979), pp.191ff; J.Kallir (1990), pp.127ff
3 J.Kallir (1990), p.264

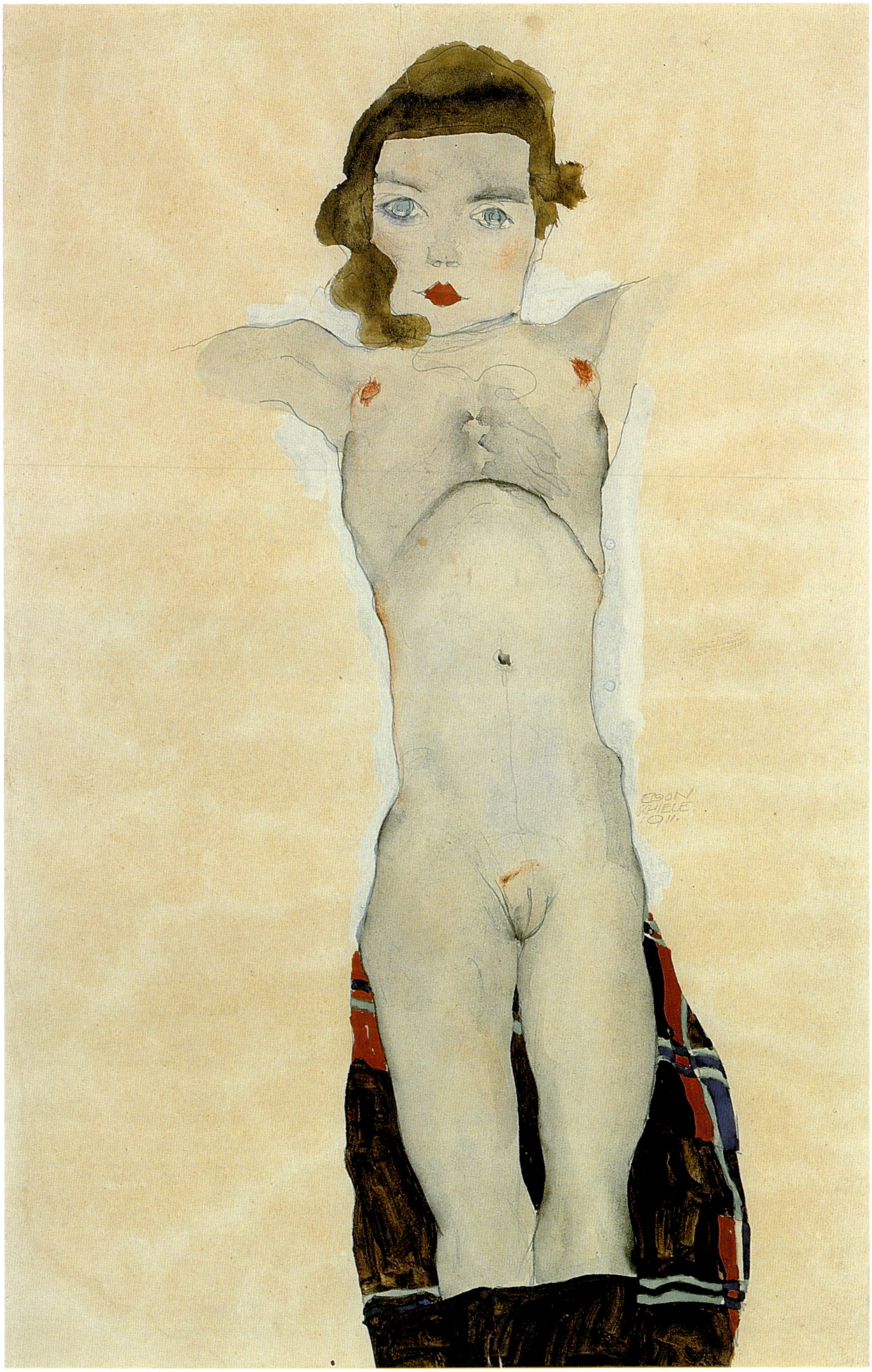
EGON
SCHIELE
1911.

Egon Schiele 1890–1918

99 Boy in a Sailor Suit (Paul Erdmann)

1915
Graphite, wax crayon and oil paint (?) on cheap drawing paper,[1] 47.5 × 31.5 cm
Signed/dated lower right, in cartouche: 'Egon Schiele 1915'
The paper is cockled and has become somewhat dirty. Otherwise condition is good
Accession no.1974.18

Provenance
Collection Erich Lederer
Sommer Collection, Ronco
Galerie R.N.Ketterer, Campione d'Italia
Thyssen-Bornemisza Collection, 1974

Exhibitions
Vienna, Antiquariat Kunsthandlung Willy Verkauf, c1970, *Kunst und Literatur des XX. Jahrhunderts*, no.433[2]
Bremen 1975, no.71
Lugano 1975, no.37
Lugano 1978, no.98

Literature
Leopold (1973), p.394 and pl.181
Kiel (1974), p.126, ill. p.127
J.Kallir (1990), D.1697

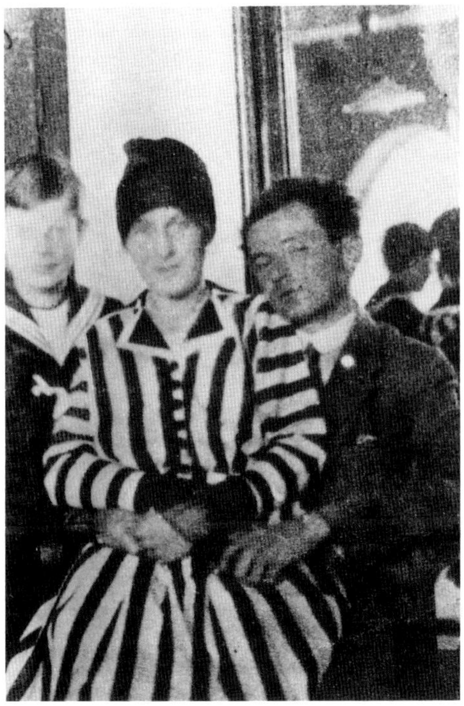

FIG 1 Paul Erdmann with Edith and Egon Schiele, 1915 (archive Alessandra Comini)

Paul was the son of Fritz Erdmann, half-brother of Schiele's wife Edith Harms. Fritz and Edith were on friendly terms especially during the war years, while Schiele himself was for part of the time away on military service.[3] Schiele drew Paul by himself and together with Edith in a succession of drawings and gouaches mostly dating from the autumn of 1915.[4] As Kallir points out, the double portraits of Paul with Edith, which at times greatly resemble Schiele's depictions of himself together with his wife, are characterized by a degree of erotic ambiguity that is somewhat startling in view of the fact that Paul was Edith's nephew.[5]

In her 1990 oeuvre-catalogue of Schiele's paintings and works on paper, Jane Kallir describes the medium employed in the present work as 'gouache, watercolour and pencil'. In a letter to the author dated 22 August 1990, she observes that to mistake Schiele's heavy gouache technique of this period for oil paint is a common error when depending on visual appearance rather than chemical testing. In a further letter dated 3 October, she adds that the use of oil would create a greasy residue or halo on the sheet. On inspection, however, there were found to be precisely such greasy marks around some of the more heavily worked passages. Whether this is in fact the result of using oil paint is difficult to determine: a similar effect might be produced by reworking passages executed in wax crayon using a solvent such as paraffin or turpentine, causing the colour to become fluid.[6] Though the present author still believes on the basis of purely visual inspection that crayon, rather than oil paint, is most likely to have been the principal medium employed, Schiele's often highly unusual techniques of this period do not yield easily to visual analysis. In the absence of chemical testing the suggestions advanced here must remain, in part, conjectural.[7]

Notes
1 See the accompanying essay for an account of the difficulties of analysing the medium in which the present work is executed
2 According to J.Kallir (1990), p.546
3 See e.g. Nebehay (1979), p.397, doc. 1131 (letter from Edith to Egon dated 14 November 1916, in which she suggests that Fritz might accompany her to the opening of an exhibition at the dealer Arnot's in Vienna, which Schiele himself was evidently unable to attend)
4 Compare J.Kallir (1990), D.1794, D.1798; see also Erwin Mitsch (ed.), *Egon Schiele in der Albertina. Die Zeichnungen und Aquarelle aus eigenem Besitz*, exh. cat., Vienna, Graphische Sammlung Albertina, 1990, nos.135, 136
5 J.Kallir (1990), p.546
6 A suggestion advanced by Emil Bosshard, Head of Conservation of the Thyssen-Bornemisza Collection. I am grateful both to Emil Bosshard and to Jane Kallir for generously sharing their opinions with me
7 See also my note on pigment and paper analysis under 'Medium and Support' on pp.23–4

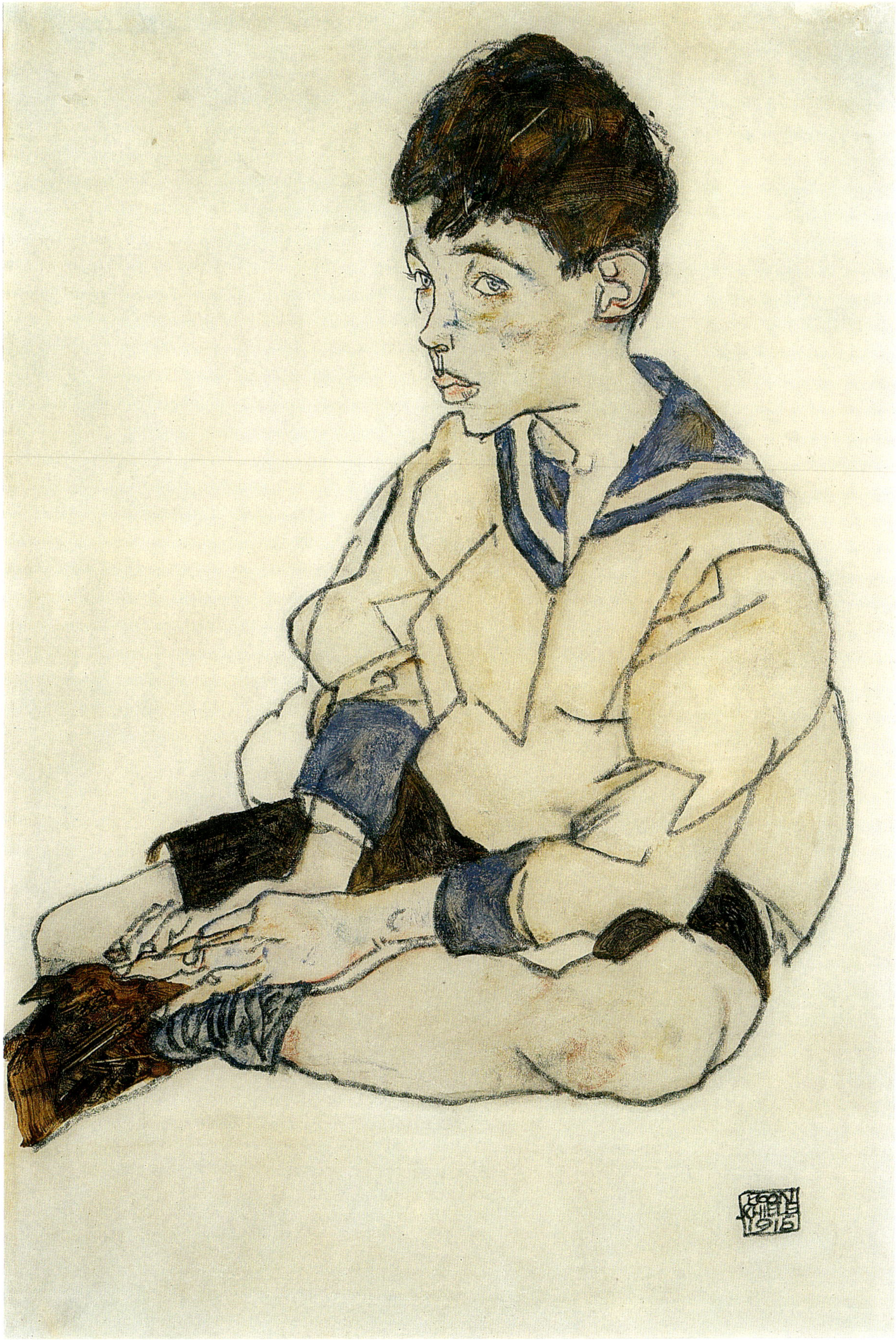
EGON
SCHIELE
1915

Oskar Schlemmer 1888–1943

100 Formation (Tri-partition)
Reihung (Dreiteilung)

1926
Pencil and watercolour on paper, 55.9 × 35.2 cm (sheet), 47.5 × 28 cm (image)
Unsigned/undated
The paper has become slightly yellow with age. Otherwise condition is good
Accession no.1976.16

Provenance
Ida Bienert, Dresden/Munich
Marlborough–Gerson Gallery, New York
Mr and Mrs Lester Francis Avnet, New York
Museum of Modern Art, New York [as loan]
Sotheby Parke Bernet, Inc., New York
Thyssen-Bornemisza Collection, 1976[1]

Exhibitions
Dresden, Sächsischer Kunstverein, Brühlsche Terrasse, 1926, *Grosse Aquarellausstellung*, no.724
Stuttgart, Kunsthaus Schaller, 1929, list no.23[2]
Munich, Haus der Kunst/Düsseldorf, Städtische Kunstsammlungen/Berlin, Schloss Charlottenburg, 1950, *Die Maler am Bauhaus*, no.253
London, Marlborough Fine Art, 1966, *Kandinsky and his Friends*, no.113
London, Marlborough Fine Art, 1967, *Recent Acquisitions*, no.50
New York, Spencer A.Samuels, 1969, *Oskar Schlemmer*, no.63
New York, Museum of Modern Art, 1971–2, *From Cézanne through Picasso. 100 Drawings from the Collection of the Museum of Modern Art*, New York, no.97[3]
Brussels/Paris 1977–8, no.73
Lugano 1978, no.99
Ascona, Museo Communale d'Arte Moderna, 1987, *Oskar Schlemmer. Opere del/Werke von 1908–1942*, no.32

Literature
Will Grohmann, *Die Sammlung Ida Bienert, Dresden*, Potsdam (Müller and I.Kiepenheuer) 1933, pp.17, 24
Hildebrandt (1952), no.631
Von Maur (1979), II, no.A-377, ill. p.297; see also I, pp.187–8 and supplement (von Maur (1982)), n.p.
Karin von Maur, 'The Art of Oskar Schlemmer', in Lehman (1986), p.60[4]

Formation (*Tri-partition*) is, as von Maur observes, the largest and most painterly of a series of eight watercolours, in various formats, executed between 1925 and 1931 which relate to Schlemmer's painting *Dreiteilung* of 1925–8 (fig.1).[5] There also exist two detailed pencil studies for the central portion of the composition. Of the eight watercolours, only one is dated,[6] and it is impossible, on the basis of documentary evidence, to be certain of the exact chronological sequence in which the remainder were executed. At least two, however, would appear to be variants upon the completed picture, rather than preparatory studies. One of these variants evidently relates to Schlemmer's intention to resume work on a new version of *Dreiteilung*, as emerges from an entry in the artist's diary dated 21 February 1931.[7]

Notes
1 The watercolour was offered for sale by Sotheby Parke Bernet, New York, in spring 1976 (sale no.3848, *Important 19th and 20th Century Drawings and Watercolors collected by the late Lester Avnet*, 18 March 1976, lot 112); it was acquired by the present owner in autumn the same year
2 Exhibition recorded by von Maur (1979), II, p.297
3 The same exhibition was shown in a revised form in various cities during 1972–4, including Auckland, Melbourne, Sydney, Honolulu, San Francisco, Otterlo, Sheffield, Milan and Lisbon
4 Catalogue of the Schlemmer retrospective exhibition shown in Baltimore, New York, San Francisco and Minneapolis during 1986–7
5 Von Maur (1979), II, G142; for the remaining watercolours see ibid., A191–2, A195–7, A299 and A440
6 See von Maur (1979), II, p.255, A197
7 Ibid., pp.310–11, A440

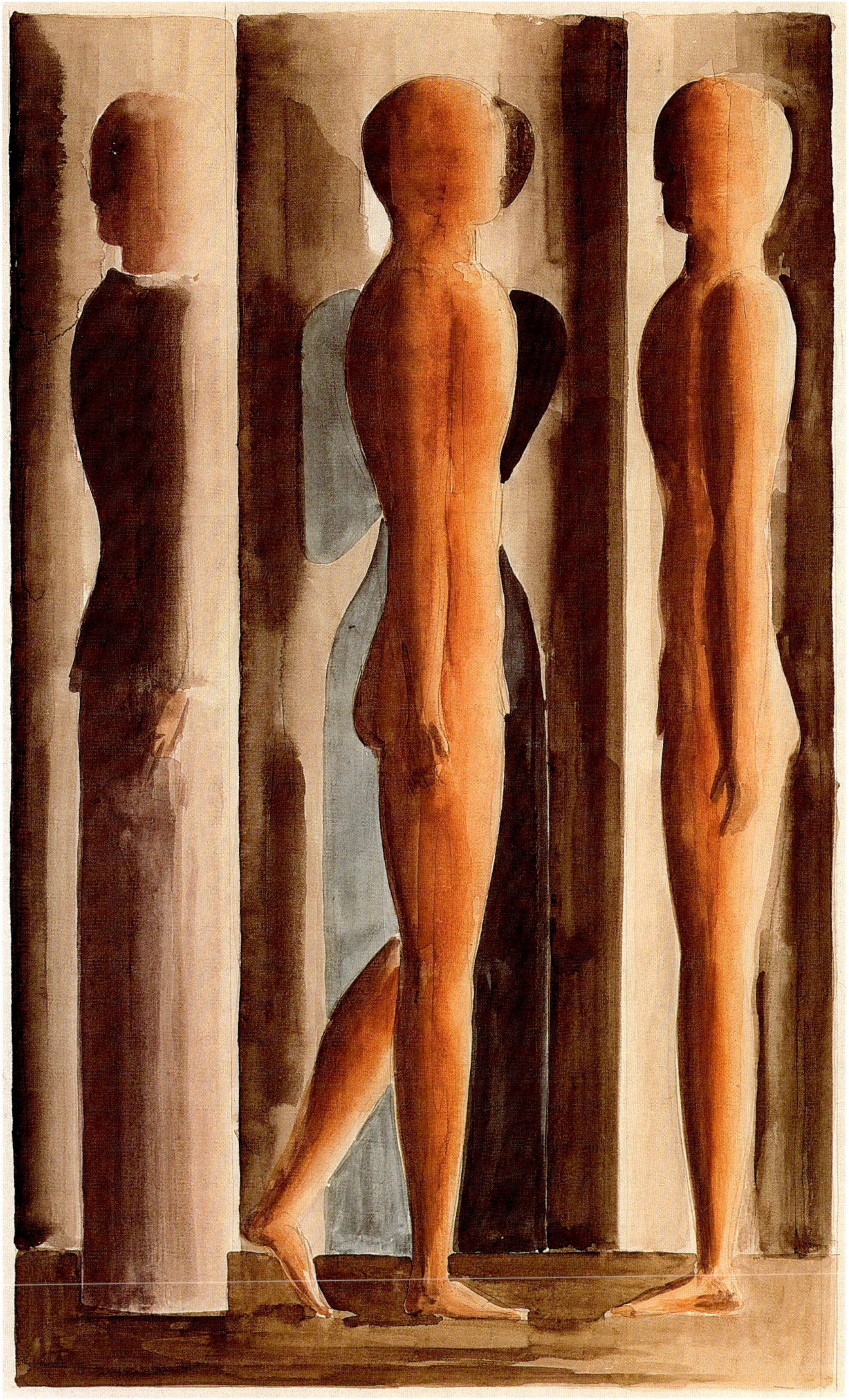

Both Grohmann (1933) and von Maur in the first edition of her oeuvre-catalogue of Schlemmer's work originally dated the present watercolour to 1929, thus placing it together with the 'retrospective' studies already referred to. However, in her 1982 supplement, von Maur revised Grohmann's dating to 1926 on the basis of a previously unnoticed exhibition which took place in Dresden in May–September that year, thus providing a *terminus ante quem* for the execution of this and two other (unrelated) watercolours by Schlemmer.[8]

Among the early studies for *Dreiteilung*, the Thyssen Collection's watercolour is remarkable for its high degree of elaboration and close affinity with the final painting, especially in the way that the principal (male) figure partially masks a shadowy female form, situated in what on closer examination turns out to be a deeply receding space in the centre of the composition. The principal difference between watercolour and painting resides in the predominantly static character of the former, the central male figure seemingly posed or frozen, whereas both in the painting and in the 1931 watercolour referred to above, the figures which occupy the middle of the three zones are clearly in motion – in the painting moving in opposite directions, in the watercolour striding together, towards the right-hand edge of the composition.

In Grohmann's 1933 monograph on the Bienert collection, the present watercolour is entitled 'Reihung'. 'Reihung' has usually been translated as 'formation', and this translation is followed here. However, the close affinity between [100] and the oil painting *Dreiteilung* has always been recognized, and both titles used. In the catalogue of the 1969 New York exhibition of Schlemmer's work, 'Dreiteilung' is rendered as 'three sections'; in the catalogue of the Schlemmer exhibition held in Baltimore in 1986,[9] in which two of the other related watercolours were shown, the somewhat misleading title 'triptych' (for which the German would be '*Triptychon*') is used. Although a neologism, 'Tri-partition', used here, seems a more accurate rendering of the original German.

Von Maur, in her 1979 monograph which accompanies her catalogue raisonné of the artist's work, sees the completed oil painting as marking the caesura between Schlemmer's hieratic figure compositions of the Bauhaus years and the more animated studies of human form characteristic of his subsequent Breslau period.[10] The title of the present work, 'formation', may reflect his particular interest in ballet and the dance generally, which found fullest expression in his designs for *Triadic Ballet*, performed as part of the experimental theatre programme at the Bauhaus. For a period of nearly three years from 1925 to 1928, Schlemmer abandoned easel painting in favour of his work for the stage; only with the preparatory studies for *Dreiteilung* did he begin once again to devote himself to two-dimensional art.

Notes

8 I am grateful to Dr Karin Frank von Maur, of the Staatsgalerie Stuttgart, for drawing my attention to this exhibition, as well as for her comments on the relationship between the Thyssen watercolour and the completed oil painting, and for providing much useful information

9 Baltimore, MD, Museum of Art, 1986–7, cat. nos.150, 151 (see n.4 above)

10 Von Maur (1979), I, pp.187–8; see also idem., 'The Art of Oskar Schlemmer', loc. cit.

FIG 1 Oskar Schlemmer, *Tri-partition*, 1925–8, oil and pencil on canvas, 134.5 × 99.5 cm (Private collection)

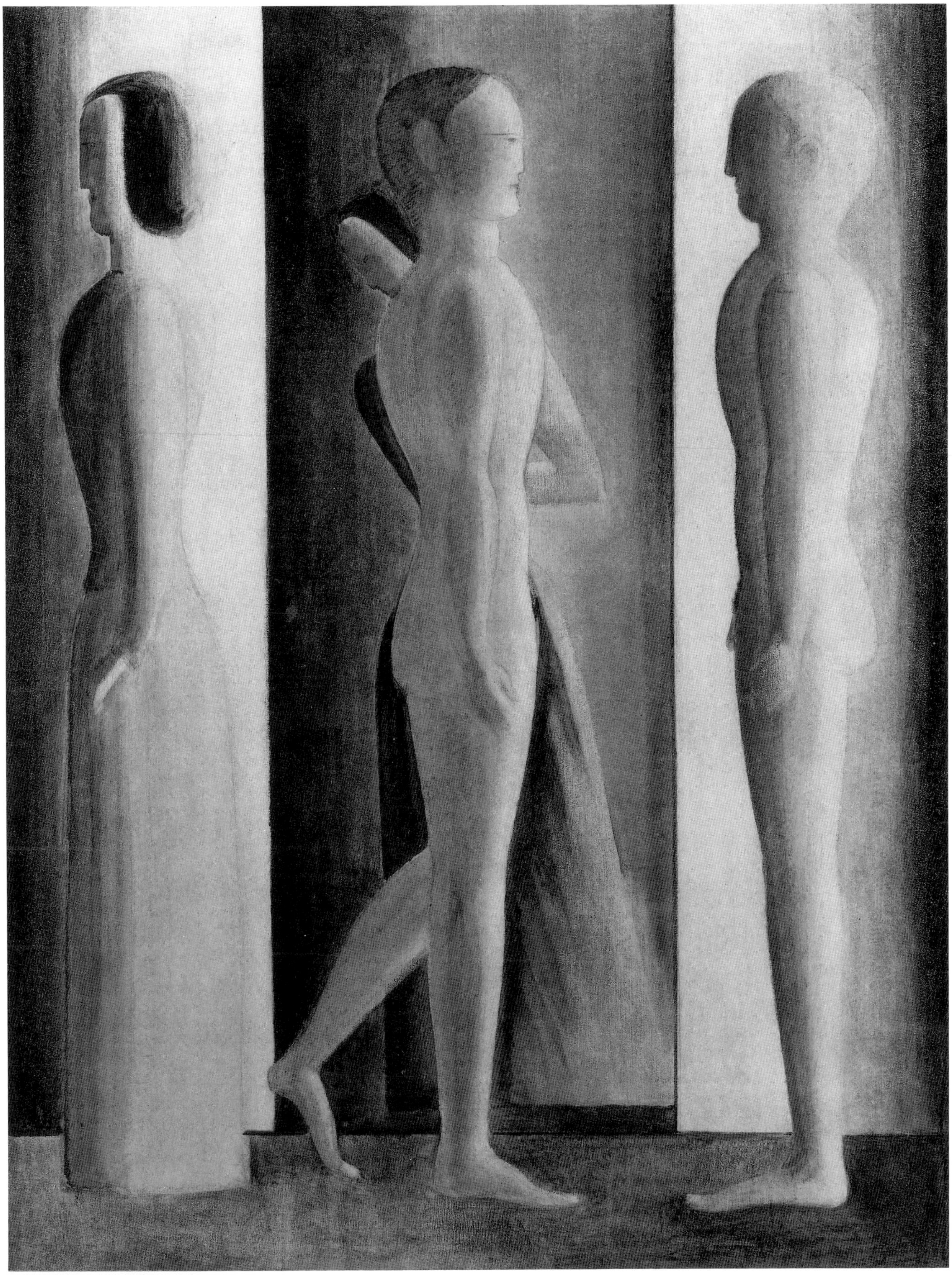

Rudolf Schlichter 1890–1955

101 Portrait of an Oriental Journalist

*c*1923–4
Oil on canvas, 73.5 × 50.5 cm
Signed lower right: 'R.Schlichter'
Condition is fair. There are stretcher creases and a number of cracks and abrasions to the paint layer. The painting is unvarnished
Accession no.1978.89

Provenance
Collection of the artist
Galleria del Levante, Milan/Munich
Fischer Fine Art, London
Thyssen-Bornemisza Collection, 1978

Exhibitions
Munich, Galleria del Levante, 1968, *Aspekte der Neuen Sachlichkeit*, no.140
Milan, Galleria del Levante, 1968, *Aspetti della Nuova Oggettività*, no.140
London, Arts Council of Great Britain, 1978–9, *Neue Sachlichkeit and German Realism of the Twenties*, no.225
Modern Masters from the Thyssen-Bornemisza Collection, 1984–6, no.99
Lugano 1989, no.48
Rome 1990–91, no.45

Literature
See Gabriele Horn (ed.), *Rudolf Schlichter 1890–1955*, exh. cat., Berlin (Staatliche Kunsthalle) 1984

Rudolf Schlichter studied at the School of Applied Arts in Stuttgart, and at the Karlsruhe Academy.[1] Called up in 1916, he was subsequently discharged from active service after embarking on a hunger strike. In 1919 he moved to Berlin, 'the centre of art against the bourgeoisie', where he became acquainted with George Grosz and John Heartfield. Together with Grosz and Heartfield, he joined the Communist Party and exhibited at the famous First International Dada Fair at the Kunsthandlung Dr Otto Burchard in Berlin in 1920.[2] Like Grosz, Hubbuch and several other painters associated with the Neue Sachlichkeit movement, Schlichter was an artist of strong political convictions. In 1924 he was a founder member of the so-called 'Rote Gruppe' (Red Group), an association of Communist artists; he was also linked with the extreme social-critical tendency within the left-wing Novembergruppe.

As in the case of Schad, Schlichter's work of the 1920s shows a transition from Dada to a strongly realist style of painting. It is, however, difficult to pigeon-hole his work of this half-decade. An article published as early as 1920 in the periodical *Das Kunstblatt* pointed to the diversity of Schlichter's art, 'the extent of his range, from abstraction to representation, from the calligraphic to the narrative. It would be tactless to try to tie [him] down to a formula, to which he himself makes no claim ...'[3] He was represented at G.F.Hartlaub's famous 1925 exhibition of the 'New Objectivity' held at the Mannheim Kunsthalle, which brought the movement to the attention of the public. Thereafter he withdrew increasingly from public and political life, and under the Nazi régime lived in almost total seclusion, though this did not prevent him from being expelled from the Reichskunstkammer in 1935. In 1938 he was arrested and imprisoned on account of his 'non-National-Socialist life-style'.[4]

Many of Schlichter's most important works of the mid-twenties are portraits. Some are images of eminent personalities from artistic and intellectual life, among them a striking portrait of the playwright Bertolt Brecht.[5] Others are of 'anonymous' middle-class or proletarian types. Here, the contempt for the bourgeoisie and for the vices of mankind generally which characterizes Grosz's work, for example, is lacking. Rather, Schlichter's aim appears to be to probe the personality of the sitter, to capture a psychological rather than a merely physical likeness, traits which link his work with much of Expressionist portraiture.

In the case of the *Portrait of an Oriental Journalist*, the identity of the subject has remained a mystery: indeed, it could even be an imaginary portrait. There seems to be no way of establishing whether there ever was such a person, or who he might have been. The date of the painting is also an approximation, but it is thought to have been painted around 1923–4.

Notes
1 The accompanying biographical details are taken from the essay by Gabriele Horn, 'Rudolf Schlichter – eine Biographie', in Horn, op. cit., p.3aff
2 See [19]
3 Carl Einstein, 'Rudolph Schlichter', *Das Kunstblatt*, 4 (1920), pp.105ff, cited after Horn, loc. cit.
4 Horn, op. cit., p.14a
5 See *Paris – Berlin 1900–1933*, exh. cat., Paris, Centre Georges Pompidou, 1978, repr. p.305

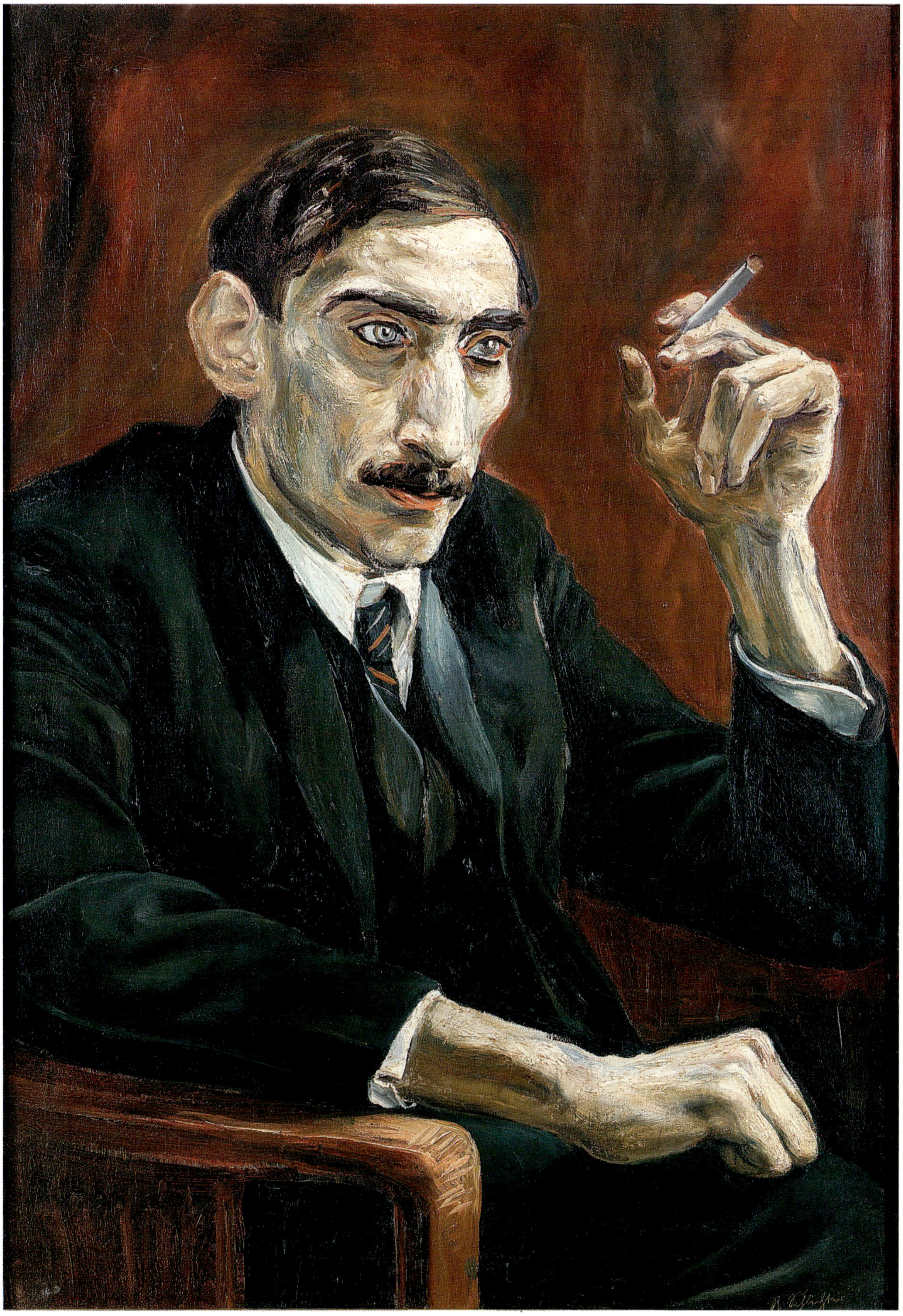

Karl Schmidt-Rottluff 1884–1976

102 The Little House

1906
Oil on board, 49.5 × 66.5 cm
Signed/dated lower left: 'K. Schmidt-Rottluff 1906'
The edges of the board are rather brittle, and are slightly convex-warped. The painting is unvarnished and the surface somewhat grimy. Otherwise condition is good
Accession no.1962.5

Provenance
Jerome Friedmann, Hamburg [before 1937][1]
Bernauer Collection, Gelsenkirchen
Stuttgarter Kunstkabinett, Stuttgart
Thyssen-Bornemisza Collection, 1962[2]

Exhibitions
Hanover, Kunstverein, 1963–4, *Karl Schmidt-Rottluff. Gemälde, Aquarelle, Graphik*, no.2[3]
Lausanne, Palais de Beaulieu, 1964, *Chefs-d'oeuvre des collections suisses de Manet à Picasso*, no.208
Berlin, Brücke-Museum, 1973, *Künstler der Brücke. Gemälde der Dresdener Jahre 1905–1910*, no.11
Bremen 1975, no.75
Schleswig, Schleswig-Holsteinisches Landesmuseum, 1984, *Karl Schmidt-Rottluff zum 100. Geburtstag*, no.2
Lugano 1989, no.10
Rome 1990–91, no.46

Literature
Grohmann (1956), p.281
Kiel (1974), p.132, ill. p.131
Wietek (1984), p.158
Thiem (1989), p.32

The Little House was painted in 1906 in the course of a visit to Nolde on the island of Alsen in the Baltic. Despite numerous references to Schmidt-Rottluff's essentially reserved nature (he did not join Kirchner and Heckel on their summer painting excursions to the Moritzburg lakes, and Pechstein later recalled that he took no part in the animated discussions which went on in the Brücke artists' studios in Dresden, preferring to sit in a corner puffing at a pipe),[4] he and Nolde seem to have undertood one another very well. The latter in his autobiography referred to Schmidt-Rottluff's 'perceptiveness and knowledge'[5] – qualities he sought to capture in his 1906 portrait *The Painter Schmidt-Rottluff* (Stiftung Seebüll Ada und Emil Nolde).[6] Thirty years later,

Notes
1 See Wietek (1984), pp.95f. for entries on collectors of Schmidt-Rottluff's work prior to 1937
2 Acquired at the 37th auction of the Stuttgarter Kunstkabinett, pt.1, 3–4 May 1962, lot 441
3 Exhibition also shown in Essen, Frankfurt and Berlin during 1963–4; though included in the catalogue, *The Little House* was, however, shown only in Hanover and Essen
4 Pechstein (1963), p.29
5 Nolde (1971), p.99
6 Urban (1987), no.180

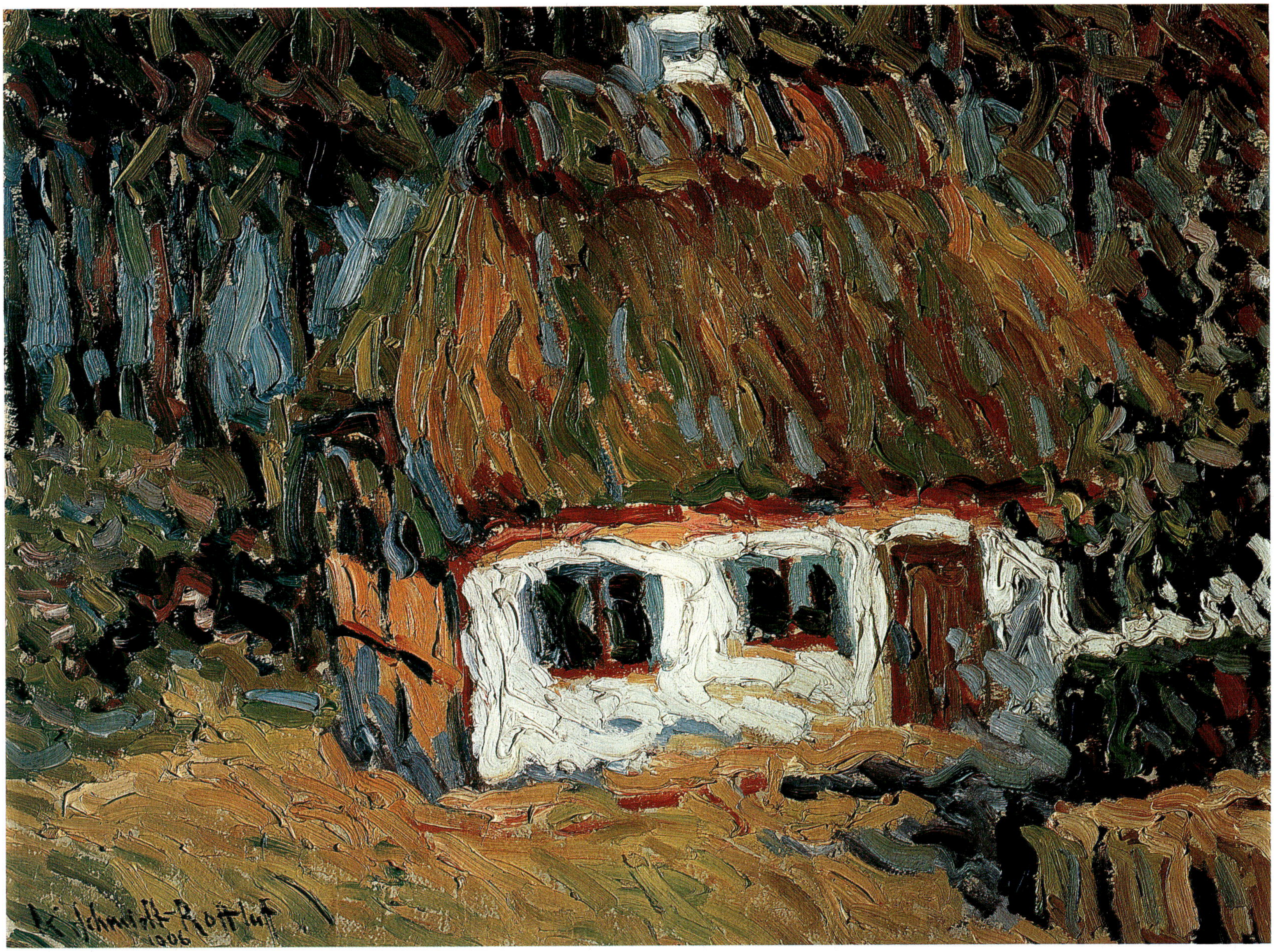

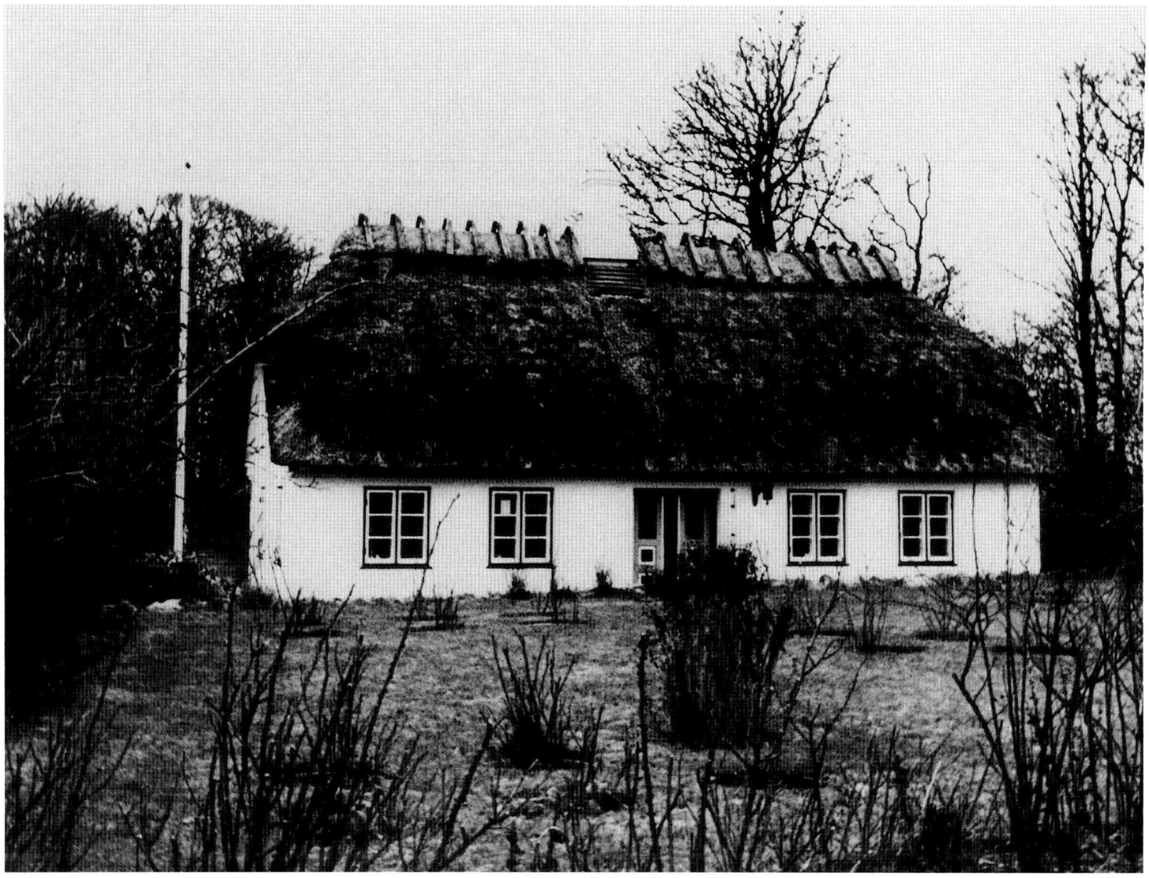

Schmidt-Rottluff paid pictorial tribute to the older artist in his painting *Homage to Nolde* (Museum Ludwig, Cologne) testimony to the enduring regard each painter felt for the other.

Schmidt-Rottluff had first written to Nolde in February 1906, urging him to join the newly-formed Brücke group. Nolde not only did so, but also invited Schmidt-Rottluff to spend the coming summer months with him on Alsen,[7] where he and his wife occupied a fisherman's cottage close to the village of Guderup. To judge by photographs it is this cottage which forms the subject of [102] – or, if not Nolde's, then another of the numerous such cottages scattered throughout the dense woodland between the village and the shoreline, of which several survive, more or less unaltered, today (see figs. 1, 2). Though the house is shown from a very close vantage point, the painting succeeds in conveying vividly the surrounding tangle of undergrowth and foliage, and the dappled effect of sunlight and shadow in this still relatively untouched forest area.

Brilliant in its colours, extraordinary for its freedom in the handling of pigment, *The Little House* is painted in the artist's loosest Impressionist-influenced manner characteristic of his early work. Only gradually did he find his way towards a more constructive style of painting of which [104], *Sun over Pine Forest* (1913), is an outstanding example.

FIG 1 Nolde's house at Guderup

FIG 2 Fisherman's cottage on Alsen, 1990

Note

7 From May to September, according to Urban (1987), p.17

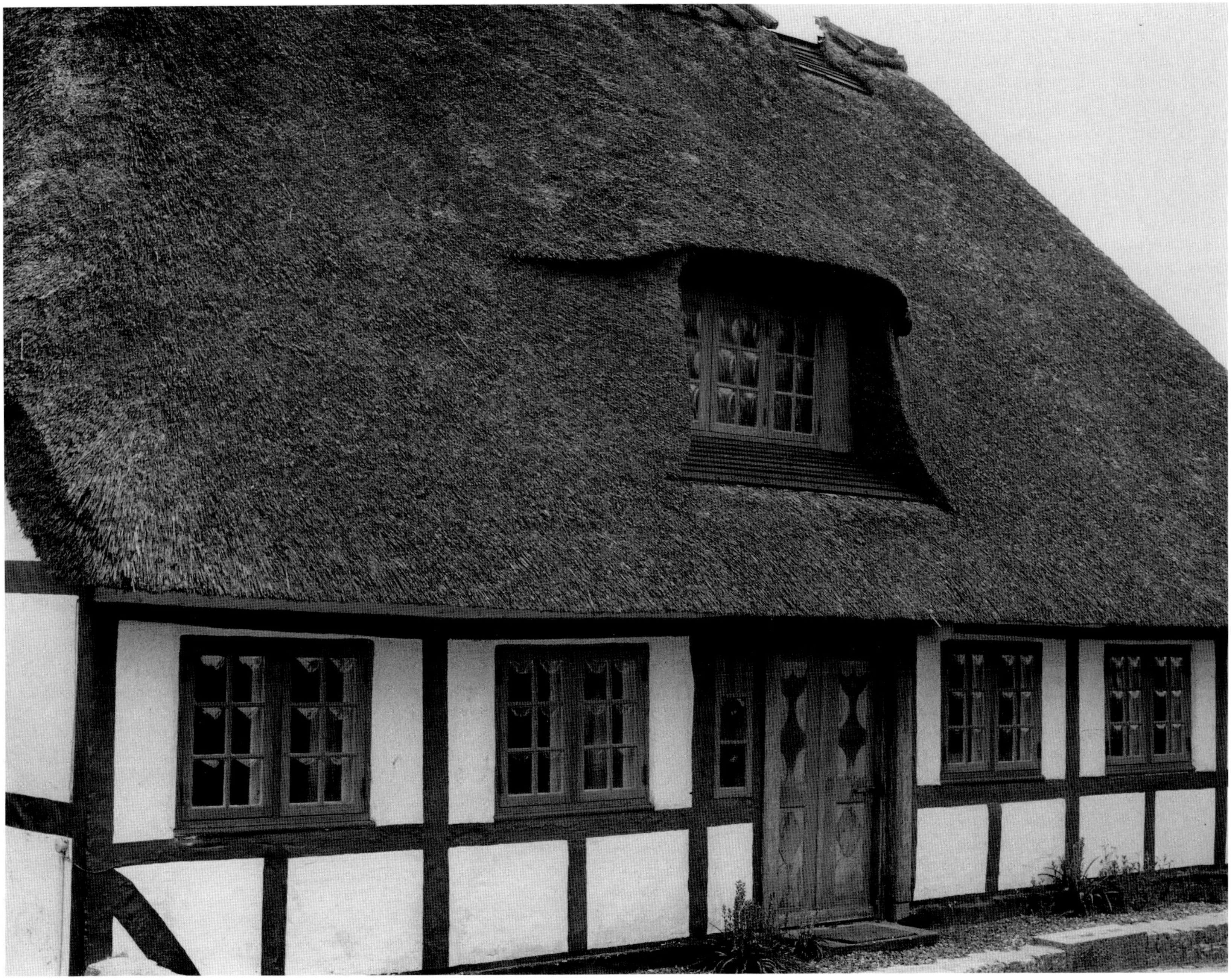

Karl Schmidt-Rottluff 1884–1976

103 Autumn Landscape in Oldenburg
Oldenburgische Herbstlandschaft

1907
Oil on canvas, 76 × 97.5 cm
Signed/dated lower right: 'S. Rottluff 1907'; inscribed on stretcher: 'Schmidt-Rottluff "Oldenburgische Herbstlandschaft"'
Surface uneven. History of flaking and previous restoration. Otherwise condition is good
Accession no.1967.5

Provenance
Collection Professor Buschkiel, Chemnitz
Herbert Kurtz, Wolframs-Eschenbach
Collection Roman Norbert Ketterer
Hugo Gouthier, Paris
Thyssen-Bornemisza Collection, 1967[1]

Exhibitions
Hamburg, Galerie Commeter, 1911, *Schmidt-Rottluff*
Berlin, Galerie Ferdinand Möller, 1919–20, *Karl Schmidt-Rottluff*[2]
Chemnitz, Kunsthütte, 1929, *15. Ausstellung des Deutschen Künstlerbundes*
Essen 1958, no.137
Ulm, Ulmer Museum, 1959, *Bilder der 'Brücke'*[3]
Meisterwerke des deutschen Expressionismus, 1960–61, no.135
New York, Marlborough–Gerson Gallery, 1968, *International Expressionism, Part I*, no.56 [as 'Farm Landscape'][4]
Munich, Haus der Kunst, 1970, *Europäischer Expressionismus*, no.18
Paris, Musée National d'Art Moderne, 1970, *L'Expressionisme Européen*, no.125
Turin, Galleria Civica d'Arte Moderne, 1971, *Il Cavaliere Azzurro*, ill. p.126
Bremen 1975, no.74
Lugano 1975, no.34
Expressionism, a German Intuition, 1980–81, no.177
USA tour 1982–4, no.5
Modern Masters from the Thyssen-Bornemisza Collection, 1984–6, no.100
Lugano 1989, no.11
Expressionism and Modern German Painting, 1989–90, no.33
Essen, Museum Folkwang, 1990, *Vincent van Gogh und die Moderne 1890–1914*, no.155
Amsterdam, Rijksmuseum Vincent van Gogh, 1990–91, *Vincent van Gogh en de moderne Kunst 1890–1914*, no.123

Literature
Grohmann (1956), pp.56, 281
Kiel (1974), p.134, ill. p.133
See also Wietek (1957), p.76[5]

The year after Schmidt-Rottluff's visit to Nolde at Alsen (see [102]), he and Heckel discovered Dangast, a tiny village on the North Sea, not far from Varel in the province (then Grand-Duchy) of Oldenburg. Schmidt-Rottluff was to return to Dangast every summer until 1912, creating in this remote environment many of his most important landscape paintings of the Brücke period: more than two-thirds of his known works of these years were produced there. As in the case of Heckel, who up to 1910 painted approximately ninety paintings in or around Dangast, the impact made by the village and its surroundings, and the landscape around Oldenburg bordering on the North Sea coast evidently made a profound impact on him. In a letter of 1921, he recalled: 'In a remarkable way, I feel strongly tied to the landscape of Oldenburg, as if it were home – more strongly, in fact, than to my real home. What attracts me is the broad sweep of the landscape and its resemblance to that of Lithuania or Russia, even if this affinity is not immediately obvious.'[6]

Schmidt-Rottluff was the youngest of all the Brücke painters, and in many ways, his early development appears somewhat halting by comparison with theirs. As late as autumn 1910 Pechstein, on the visit he paid to Dangast in the company of Heckel, was able to observe: 'Our experience in the handling of form that we had acquired [during the summer] at Moritzburg carried us much further than Schmidt-Rottluff, who had then gone scarcely beyond the bounds of the Impressionists' technique.'[7] The debt both Schmidt-Rottluff and Heckel owed to

Notes
1 Acquired directly from the previous owner
2 Exhibition recorded by Roters (1984), pp.42f, 300
3 See n.1 to p.27
4 The painting was both recorded and reproduced in this 1968 catalogue, but not included in the exhibition
5 Catalogue of the exhibition held at the Kunstverein, Oldenburg, in 1957. *Autumn Landscape in Oldenburg* is recorded as cat. no.4 on p.76; it was not, however, included in the exhibition
6 Cited after Gerhard Wietek, 'Dangast am Jadebusen', in Wietek (1976), p.173
7 Pechstein (1963), p.49

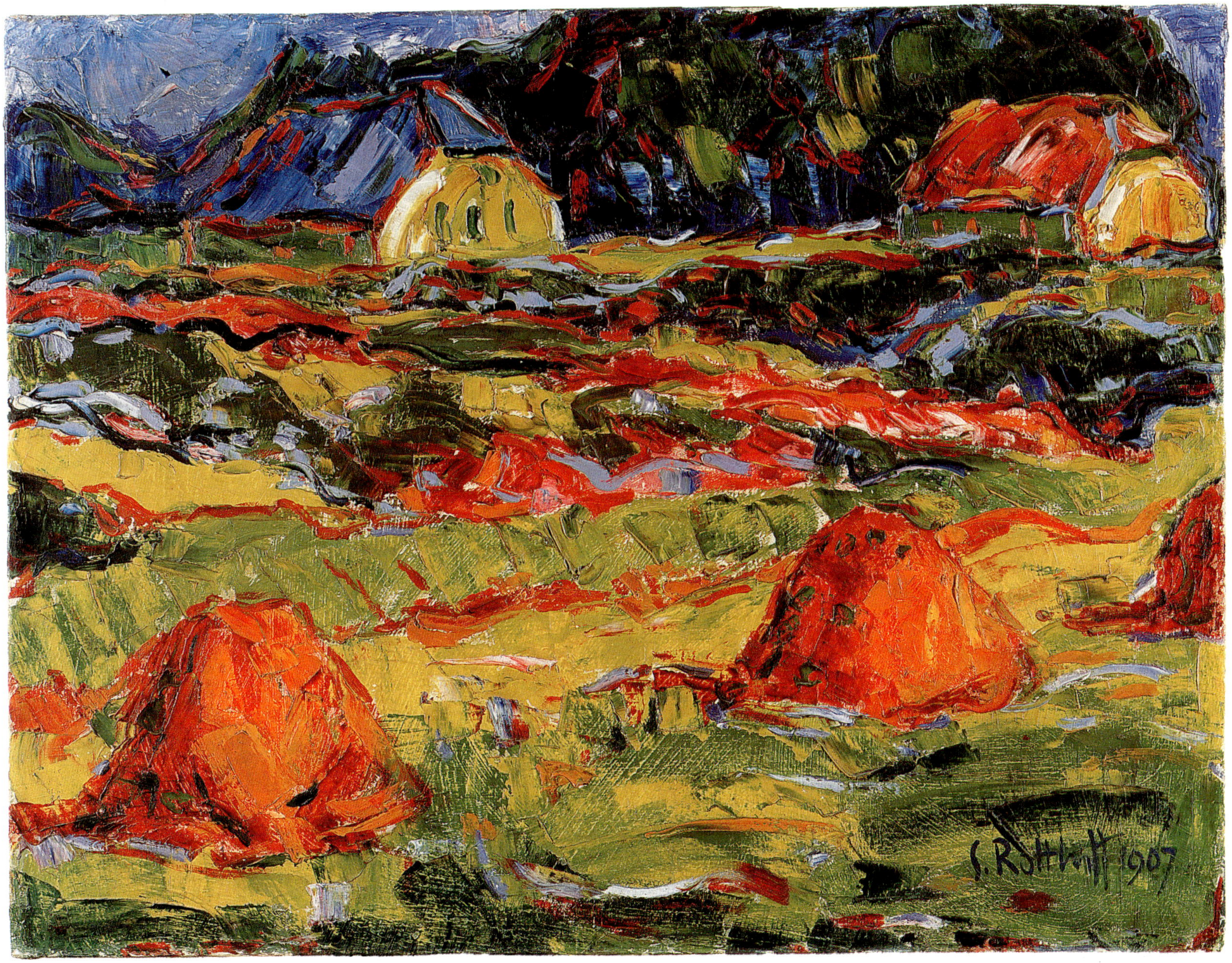

8 On the spread of van Gogh's reputation in Germany see Feilchenfeldt (1988), also Moeller (1990), pp.312ff

Impressionism is revealed by their interest in capturing the effects of light, changing weather conditions, or the precise time of day. Titles such as *Late Afternoon, Midday on the Moor,* and *After the Rain* are typical of their landscapes of this early period.

Autumn Landscape is also remarkable for its heavy brushwork and dependence on colour rather than tonal contrasts to produce its effect: in particular, the deliberate clash of red and green, also found in Heckel's exactly contemporary Dangast painting *Brickworks* [22]. At this point, both artists were responding in an immediate and spontaneous way to the example of van Gogh, though more to his use of colour and handling of paint than to his symbolism or subject matter.[8] In the present painting, however, the rather turgid brushwork and reliance on heavy impasto to create form contrast with Heckel's increasingly rapid and nervous handling of paint characteristic of his work of this period.

Karl Schmidt-Rottluff 1884–1976

104 Sun over Pine Forest[1]

1913
Oil on canvas, 77 × 90.5 cm
Signed/dated lower right: 'S. Rottluff 1913'
Extensive history of previous restoration, with in-filling of scattered losses
Accession no.1961.14

Provenance
Dr Wilhelm Niemeyer, Hamburg
Collection Roman Norbert Ketterer
Thyssen-Bornemisza Collection, 1961[2]

Exhibitions
Berlin, Schloss Charlottenburg, 1954, *Karl Schmidt-Rottluff zum 70. Geburtstag*, no.23 [as 'Sonne im Fichtenwald']
Mannheim, Städtische Kunsthalle, 1955, *Maler in Nidden*, no.50 [as 'Sonne über dem Föhrenwald']
Essen 1958, no.160
Ulm, Ulmer Museum, 1959, *Bilder der 'Brücke'*[3]
Meisterwerke des deutschen Expressionismus, 1960–61, no.139
Hanover, Kunstverein, 1963–4, *Karl Schmidt-Rottluff. Gemälde, Aquarelle, Graphik*, no.44[4]
Florence 1964, no.524
London, Tate Gallery, 1964, *Painters of the Brücke*, no.263
Paris/Munich 1966, no.275
Berlin, Deutsche Gesellschaft für bildende Künste/Lausanne, Musée Cantonal des Beaux-arts, 1968–9, *Berlin XX. Jahrhundert/Berlin XXe Siècle: de l'expressionisme à l'art contemporain*, no.50
Munich, Haus der Kunst, 1970, *Europäischer Expressionismus*, no.317
Paris, Musée National d'Art Moderne, 1970, *L'Expressionisme Européen*, no.128
Hamburg, Altonaer Museum, 1974, *Schmidt-Rottluff: Gemälde. Landschaften aus sieben Jahrzehnten*, no.13
Bremen 1975, no.76
Australian tour 1979–80, no.34
Schleswig, Schleswig-Holsteinisches Landesmuseum, 1984, *Karl Schmidt-Rottluff zum 100. Geburtstag*, no.22
Lugano 1989, no.12
Expressionism and Modern German Painting, 1989–90, no.34
Rome 1990–91, no.47

Literature
Ernst Gosebruch, 'Schmidt-Rottluff', *Genius. Zeitschrift für alte und werdende Kunst*, II, no.1 (1920): 10, ill. p.7
Eckart von Sydow, *Die deutsche expressionistische Kultur und Malerei*, Berlin (Furche) 1920, p.114
Grohmann (1956), pp.67, 286
Wietek (1963), p.11
Brix (1972), p.30
Kiel (1974), p.136, ill. p.135
Herbert (1983), pl.XVIII
Wietek (1984), p.101, ill. p.184
See also Günter Krüger, 'Nidden auf der Kurischen Nehrung', in Wietek (1976), pp.142–53; Werner Timm, 'Max Pechstein und die Ostsee', *Max Pechstein. Ostsee-Bilder*, exh. cat., Regensburg, Ostdeutsche Galerie, 1981, pp.5–10; Wietek (1990)

Sun over Pine Forest is one of a group of works painted between May and August 1913, while Schmidt-Rottluff was staying at Nidden on the east Baltic coast. This sojourn produced a rich crop of paintings and watercolours: Wietek suggests that at least thirty oil paintings were done that summer at Nidden,[5] of which he reproduces no fewer than fifteen. As regards subject, these works can be grouped into three categories: depictions of the coastline and of fishing boats; studies of figures in landscape; and views of the forests of pine and fir surrounding the scattered fishermen's cottages of Nidden itself. It is to the last category that [104] belongs.

Notes
1 The painting has most commonly been known by the German title *Sonne im Kiefernwald*; for other titles, all of which mean more or less the same, see Exhibitions
2 Acquired directly from the previous owner; on the Stuttgarter Kunstkabinett, the Ketterer collection, and the Galerie R.N.Ketterer, see pp.16–17
3 See n.1 to p.27
4 Exhibition also shown in Essen, Frankfurt and Berlin during 1963–4; though included in the catalogue, *Sun over Pine Forest* was, however, shown only in Hanover and Essen
5 Wietek (1963), p.3

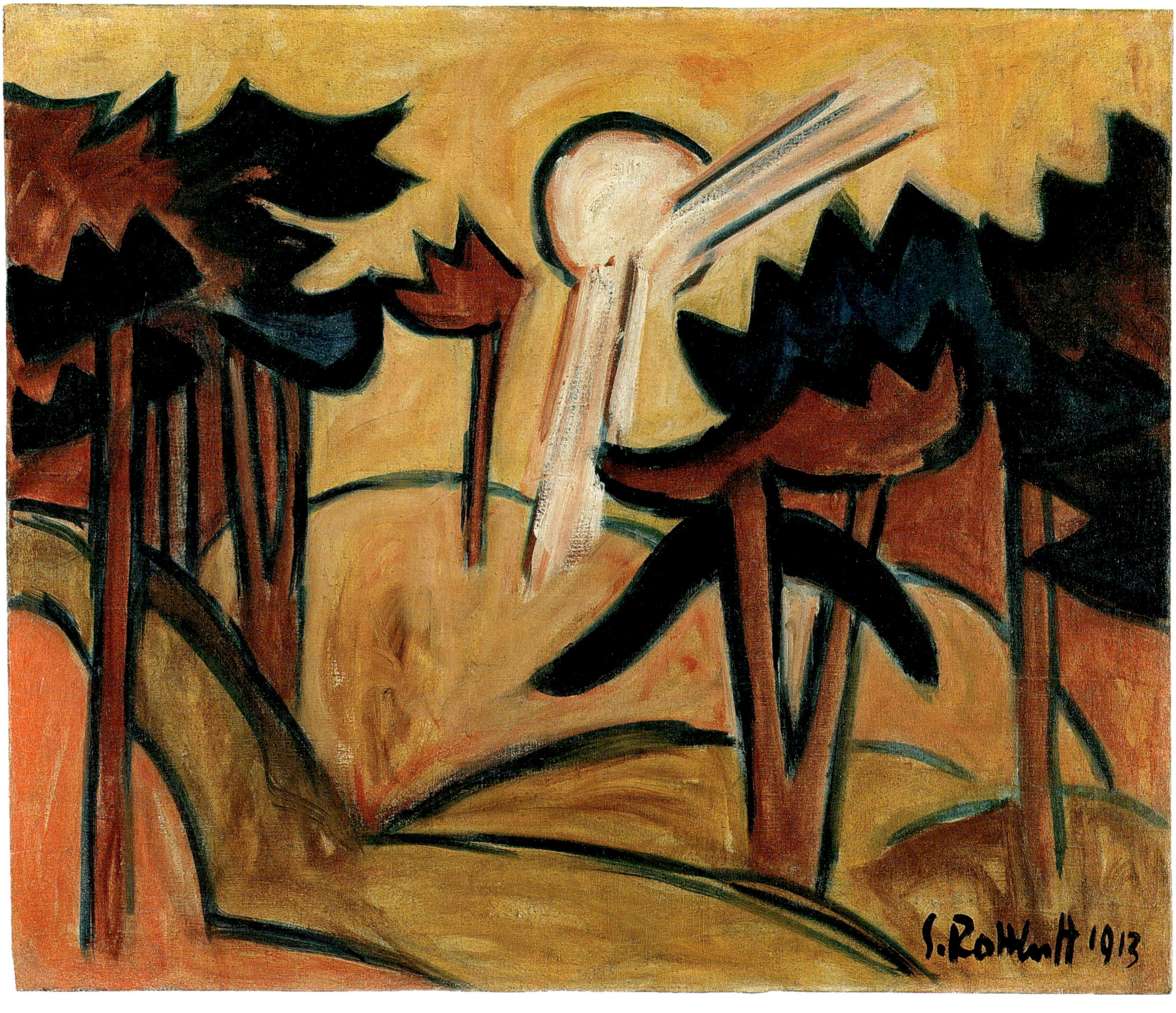
S. Rottluff 1913

It was Pechstein who had recommended Nidden as an 'artists' paradise' (which it was later to become).[6] He had first visited the 'Kurische Nehrung', the spit of land on which Nidden stands, in 1909, returning there two summers later. On both occasions he lodged with the fisherman Martin Sakuth, and it was Sakuth who likewise befriended Schmidt-Rottluff during the latter's 1913 visit.

Schmidt-Rottluff's earlier work had been deeply influenced by Impressionism (compare [102]). After 1910, however, he began gradually to eliminate the merely incidental element of perceived reality, concentrating more on the placing of form against form in what the art historian Will Grohmann described as a 'symbolic-heraldic manner ... putting plane against plane, renouncing all detail, and reducing form to bare essentials.'[7] This tendency reaches its high-point in his paintings of 1912–13, which display an even greater monumentality, partly as a result of his increasing concern with the constructive forms of French Cubism which he and the other Brücke artists had the opportunity of seeing at the Cologne Sonderbund exhibition of summer 1912. Schmidt-Rottluff's art of this period is, however, informed by a part-decorative, part-expressive tendency which is lacking in Cubism. Particularly striking in *Sun over Pine Forest* are the gaunt and hieratic shapes of the trees, which have been likened to 'monuments of a cult religion';[8] but they also reveal an anthropomorphic aspect, like arms and fingers reaching into the sky.[9]

The painting originally formed part of the important collection belonging to the art historian Wilhelm Niemeyer in Hamburg, who during the 1910s and 1920s was, together with Rosa Schapire, among the foremost adherents and collectors of Schmidt-Rottluff's art.[10]

Compare also Max Pechstein, *Summer in Nidden* [90].

Notes

6 By 1929 no less a personage than Thomas Mann had leased an area of ground there and had a holiday home erected, despite the fact that in 1923 the area had come under Lithuanian administration: see Krüger, op. cit., p.147

7 Grohmann (1956), pp.67f

8 Wietek (1963), p.12

9 Jill Lloyd has also pointed to the possible influence exerted by the more 'spiritual' version of Cubism practised by the Czech artist Bohumil Kubista, who joined the Brücke group in 1911: see Lloyd (1987), p.103

10 See also the article by Gerhard Wietek, 'Wilhelm Niemeyer und Karl Schmidt-Rottluff', *Nordelbingen. Beiträge zur Kunst- und Kulturgeschichte*, XLIX (1979): 112–22

FIG 1 [90] Max Pechstein, *Summer in Nidden*

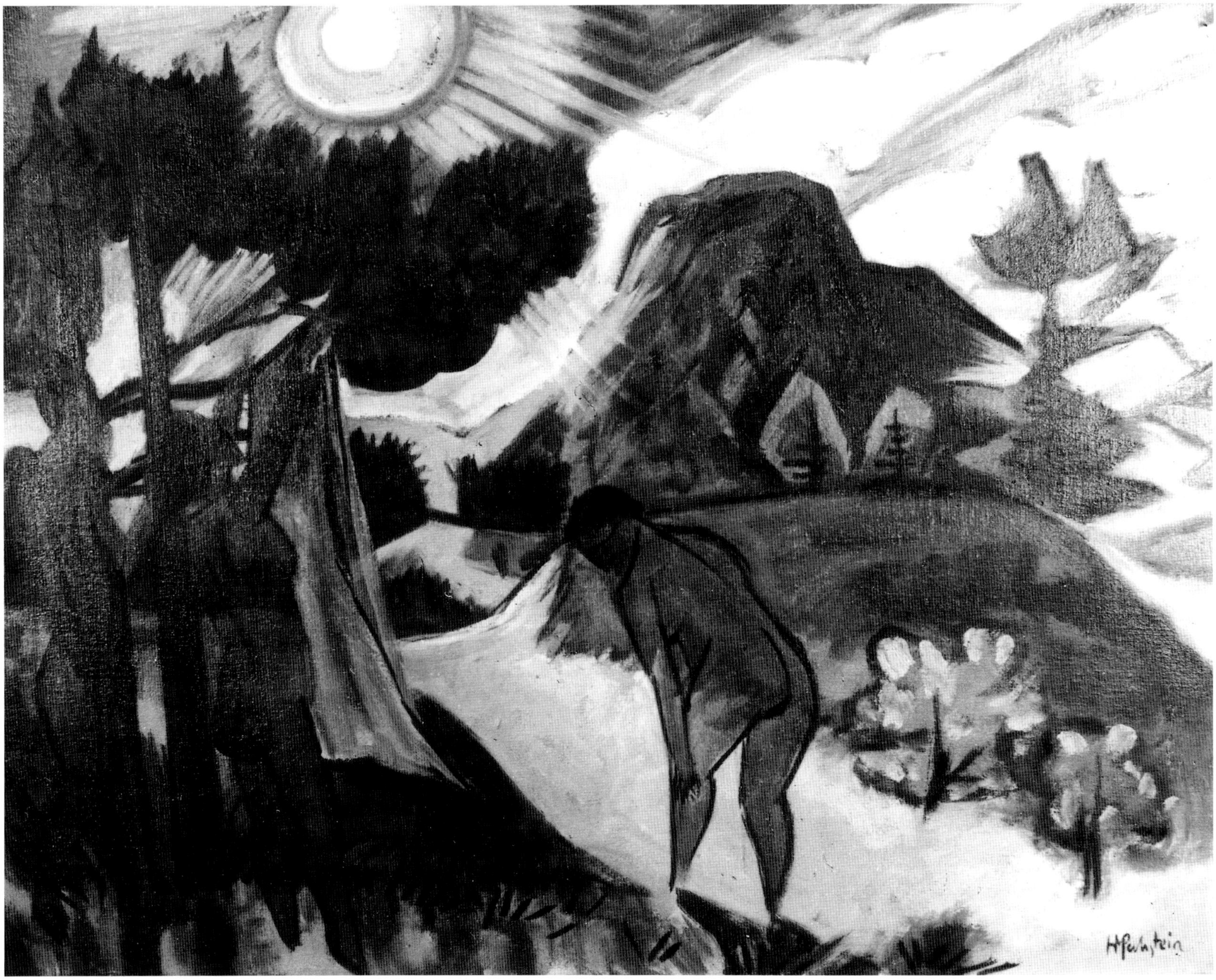

Karl Schmidt-Rottluff 1884–1976

105 The Village of Dangast

1909
Watercolour on paper, 52.5 × 65.5 cm
Signed/dated lower right: 'S.Rottluff 1909'
Paper is slightly yellow and shows some foxing
Accession no.1970.28

Provenance
Dr Viktor Peters, Leipzig
Galerie Motte, Geneva
Thyssen-Bornemisza Collection, 1970[1]

Exhibitions
Dresden, Kunstsalon Emil Richter, 1909[2]
Leipzig, Kunstverein, 1915, *Schmidt-Rottluff. Werke von 1905–1915*
Berlin, Galerie Ferdinand Möller, 1922, *Karl Schmidt-Rottluff – Aquarelle*
Dresden, Galerie Kühl und Kühn, 1925, *Sonder-Ausstellung Schmidt-Rottluff. Gemälde, Aquarelle, Graphik und Plastik*
Bremen 1975, no.77
Lugano 1978, no.100
Bremen, Kunsthalle/Munich, Städtische Galerie im Lenbachhaus, 1989, *Karl Schmidt-Rottluff Retrospektive*, no.354

Literature
Kiel (1974), p.138, ill. p.137 [as 'Farmhouses in Dangast']
Thiem (1989), pp.33–4, 291

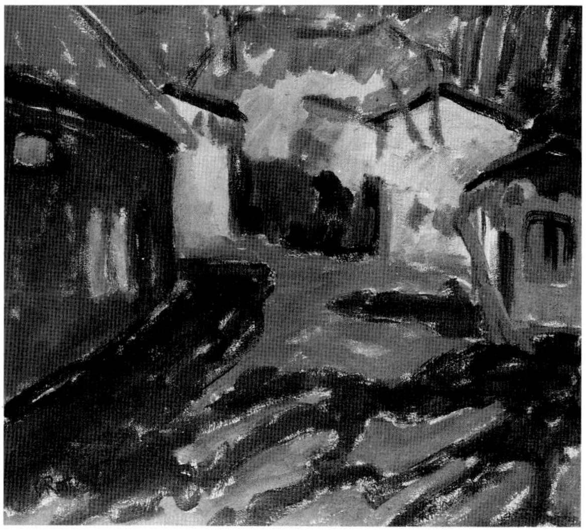

FIG 1 Karl Schmidt-Rottluff, *Farmyard in Dangast*, 1910, oil on canvas, 86.5 × 94.5 cm (Berlin, Staatliche Museen Preussischer Kulturbesitz, Nationalgalerie)

Though Heckel had originally suggested Dangast as a suitable location for painting, it was Schmidt-Rottluff who remained more consistently faithful to the village and its surroundings, returning there every summer from 1907 until 1912. He would sometimes spend more than half the year there, arriving as early as April and leaving as late as November. In correspondence dating from the years around 1908–1910, he gave 'Dangastermoor, near Varel' as his permanent abode, returning to the city only for short periods during the winter months.[3] This way of life perhaps suited his more solitary nature, as well as enabling him to maintain close links with the Oldenburg Artists' Association, by which he set great store, and in whose exhibitions he participated.[4] Being in North Germany also brought him into personal contact with figures such as Wilhelm Niemeyer, Rosa Schapire and Gustav Schiefler, all collectors or protagonists of his art, all of whom lived in or close to Hamburg, where Schmidt-Rottluff rented a small studio from 1910.[5]

The present watercolour was painted in Dangast in 1909, almost certainly during the early summer of that year, since it was included in an exhibition of work by Brücke artists held in Dresden by the Kunstsalon Richter which opened in June.[6] It was for many years owned by the Leipzig collector Dr Viktor Peters, one of the principal adherents of Expressionism in painting, and of Nolde and Schmidt-Rottluff in particular.[7]

Notes
1 Acquired at auction, 12 June 1970, lot 89
2 June 1909, mixed exhibition of works by Brücke artists, including Amiet, Heckel, Kirchner, Pechstein and Schmidt-Rottluff: see chronology in Thiem (1989), pp.80–81
3 See Ewald Gässler, 'Schmidt-Rottluff, der Kunstsammler Francksen und der Oldenburger Künstlerbund' in Thiem (1989), pp.17–22
4 Ibid., pp.18f
5 Ibid., pp.80f; also Wietek (1984), pp.10ff
6 See n.2 above. Schmidt-Rottluff had arrived back in Dangast in April 1909
7 See Gunther Thiem, 'Meine Geschichte mit Schmidt-Rottluff, 1933–1976', in Thiem (1989), pp.59f

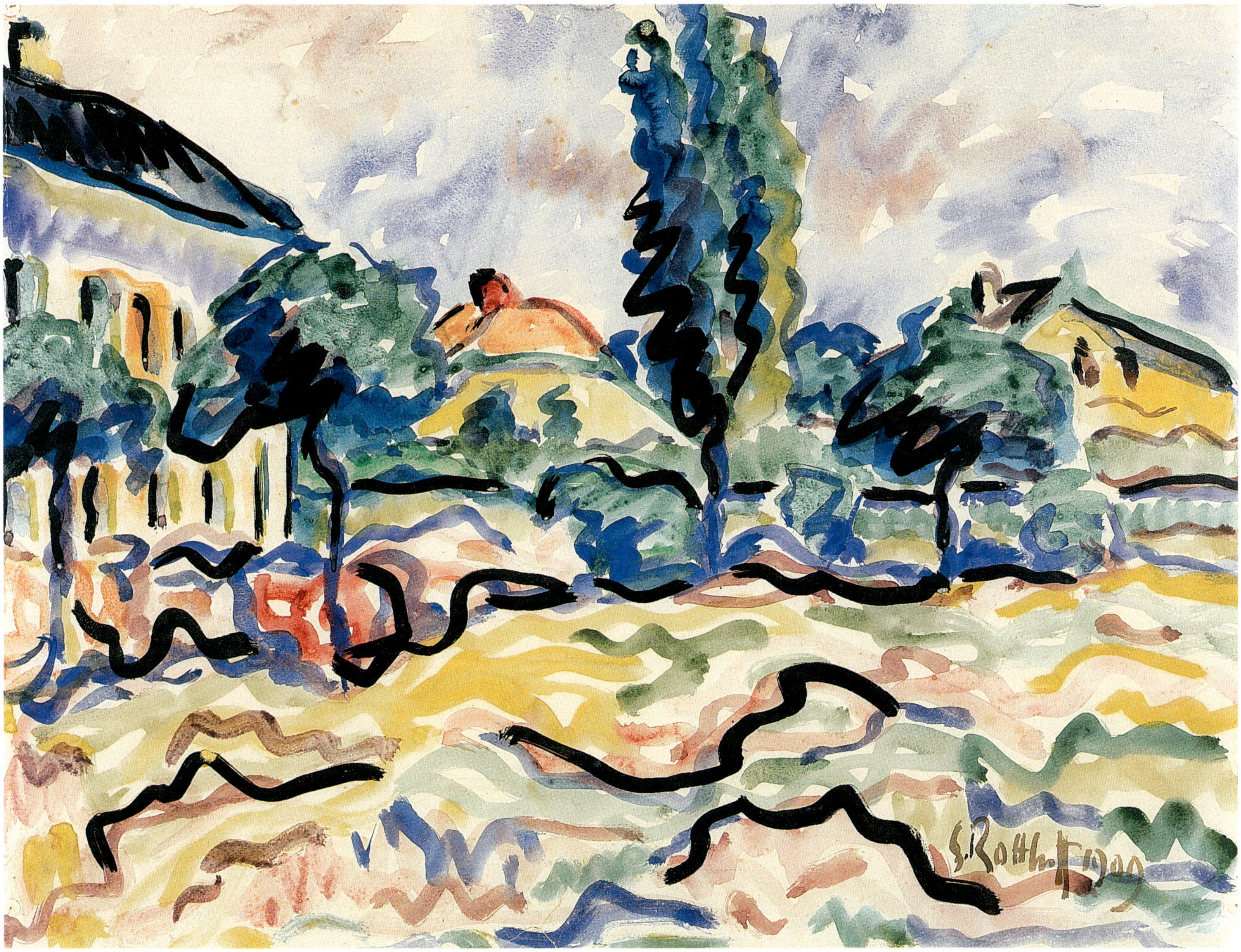

1909 was a year in which Schmidt-Rottluff painted comparatively few oils, but which saw a remarkable flowering of his watercolour technique. Attractive in themselves, vivid in their colours and distinguished by a new fluency and spontaneity in the application of paint, the Dangast watercolours of 1909 mark an important transition from the relative opacity and heavy impasto of his 1907–8 oils (compare [103]) to the far greater clarity and formal control which are the distinguishing characteristics of his work from 1910 onwards.[8]

The Village of Dangast is referred to as 'Farmhouses in Dangast' in Hanna Kiel's 1974 catalogue of modern paintings in the Thyssen-Bornemisza Collection, but it is not clear whence this title derives. Kiel also observes that the watercolour is a 'first version of the oil-painting of 1910'. In fact, there is no oil painting by Schmidt-Rottluff depicting precisely the same subject; the picture Kiel had in mind may have been *Farmyard in Dangast* (fig.1), which shows a similar though not identical view of farms and houses.

8 The stylistic development reflected in Schmidt-Rottluff's Dangast watercolours of 1908–9 is discussed in greater detail in Armin Zweite, 'Das Erleben transzendentaler Dinge im Irdischen', in Thiem (1989), pp.33–4

Karl Schmidt-Rottluff 1884–1976

106 Reflecting Clouds
Spiegelnde Wolken[1]

1936
Watercolour on paper, 51 × 68 cm
Signed lower left: 'S. Rottluff'
The watercolour has become a little faded and the paper slightly cockled. Otherwise condition is good
Accession no.1974.54

Provenance
Collection of the artist
Professor Leopold Reidemeister, Berlin
Roswitha Haftmann, Zurich[2]
Thyssen-Bornemisza Collection, 1974

Literature
See Thiem (1989), p.95

Reflecting Clouds is one of a group of oils and watercolours painted on Lake Leba, in the vicinity of Rumbke in Eastern Pomerania, which take as their subject reflections in water. The best known of these is the oil painting *Reflecting Lake*, also of 1936, now in the Folkwang Museum in Essen.[3]

Schmidt-Rottluff spent his summers in this remote locality from 1932 until 1943.[4] Though his environment was one of farmers and fisher-folk, human figures play little part in these depictions of his surroundings, which are devoted mainly to the representation of landscape forms.

Notes
1 Title and date are inscribed in Schmidt-Rottluff's hand on an old photograph of the work, now in the collection of Professor Gerhard Wietek, Hamburg. I am indebted to Professor Wietek, in latter years a friend of the artist, for his advice on Schmidt-Rottluff generally, and this watercolour in particular
2 I am grateful to Frau R.Haftmann, Zurich, for helping to establish a complete provenance for this work
3 Grohmann (1956), p.302, ill. p.225; see also Thiem (1989), no.296
4 See chronology printed in Thiem (1989), pp.77ff, 95

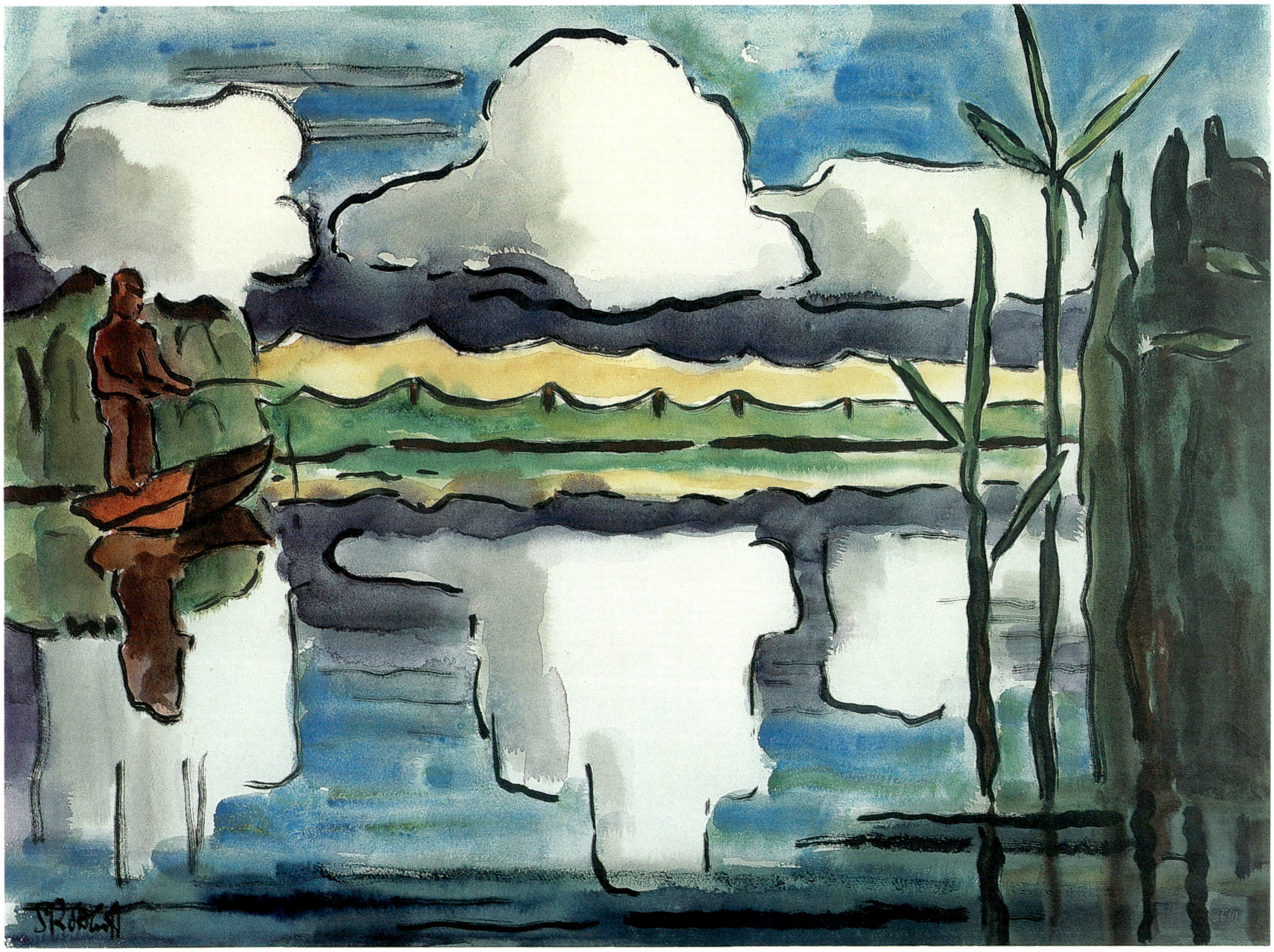

Bibliography

Alley (1981)
Ronald Alley, *Catalogue of the Tate Gallery's Collection of Modern Art other than Works by British Artists*, London (Tate Gallery/Sotheby Parke Bernet) 1981

Barnett (1980)
Vivian Endicott Barnett, 'Kandinsky Watercolours', in *Kandinsky Watercolours. A Selection from the Solomon R. Guggenheim Museum and the Hilla von Rebay Foundation*, New York (Solomon R. Guggenheim Foundation) 1980

Barnett (1989)
Vivian Endicott Barnett, *Kandinsky and Sweden*, Malmö (Konsthall)/ Stockholm (Moderna Museet) 1989

Barnett (1990)
Vivian Endicott Barnett, 'Fairy Tales and Abstraction: Stylistic Conflicts in Kandinsky's Art 1915–1921', in Anders Rosdahl (ed.), *New Perspectives on Kandinsky*, Malmö (Malmö Konsthall/ Sydsvenska Dagbladet) 1990, pp.99–109

Barnett (1992)
Vivian Endicott Barnett, *Kandinsky Watercolours. Catalogue Raisonné, Volume I, 1900–1921*, London (Sotheby's) 1992

Barron (1988)
Stephanie Barron (ed.), *German Expressionism 1915–1925. The Second Generation*, Munich (Prestel) 1988

Barron (1991)
Stephanie Barron (ed.), *'Degenerate Art'. The Fate of the Avant-Garde in Nazi Germany*, Los Angeles, CA (County Museum of Art) 1991

Berend-Corinth (1958)
Charlotte Berend-Corinth, *Die Gemälde von Lovis Corinth. Werkkatalog. Verfasst von Charlotte Berend-Corinth. Mit einer Einführung von Hans Konrad Röthel*, Munich (F. Bruckmann) 1958

Bohan (1982)
Ruth L. Bohan, *The Societé Anonyme's Brooklyn Exhibition – Katherine Dreier and Modernism in America*, Ann Arbor, MI (UMI Research Press) 1982

Brix (1972)
Karl Brix, *Karl Schmidt-Rottluff*, Vienna/Munich (Anton Schroll & Co.) 1972

Buchheim (1963)
Lothar-Günther Buchheim, *Otto Mueller, Leben und Werk. Mit einem Werkverzeichnis der Graphik Otto Muellers von Florian Karsch*, Feldafing (Buchheim) 1963

Chiappini (1989)
Rudy Chiappini (ed.), *Alexej Jawlensky*, Milan (Electa) 1989

Corinth (1979)
Lovis Corinth. Eine Dokumentation. Zusammengestellt und erläutert von Thomas Corinth, Tübingen (Ernst Wasmuth) 1979

Däubler (1916)
Theodor Däubler, 'George Grosz', *Die weissen Blätter*, III (1916): 167–70

Däubler (1919)
Theodor Däubler, *Im Kampfe um die moderne Kunst*, III of *Tribüne der Kunst und Zeit* (ed. Kasimir Edschmid), Berlin (Erich Reiss) 1919

Dube (1964)
Annemarie and Wolf-Dieter Dube, *Erich Heckel. Das Graphische Werk. I Holzschnitte*, New York (Ernest Rathenau) 1964

Dube (1965)
Annemarie and Wolf-Dieter Dube, *Erich Heckel. Das Graphische Werk. II Radierungen, Lithographien*, New York (Ernest Rathenau) 1965

Dube (1967)
Annemarie and Wolf-Dieter Dube, *E. L. Kirchner. Das Graphische Werk*, 2 vols, Munich (Prestel) 1967

Dube (1972)
Wolf-Dieter Dube, *The Expressionists*, London (Thames & Hudson) 1972

Dube-Heynig (1984)
Annemarie Dube-Heynig, *Ernst Ludwig Kirchner. Postkarten und Briefe an Erich Heckel im Altonaer Museum in Hamburg. Herausgegeben von Roman Norbert Ketterer unter Mitwirkung von Wolfgang Henze*, Cologne (DuMont) 1984

Eichner (1957)
Johannes Eichner, *Kandinsky und Gabriele Münter. Von Ursprüngen moderner Kunst*, Munich (F. Bruckmann) n.d. [1957]

Eliel (1989)
Carol S. Eliel, *The Apocalyptic Landscapes of Ludwig Meidner*, Munich (Prestel) 1989

Eggum (1984)
Arne Eggum, *Edvard Munch. Paintings, Sketches and Studies*, London (Thames & Hudson) 1984

Erdmann-Macke (1962)
Elisabeth Erdmann-Macke, *Erinnerung an August Macke*, Stuttgart (W. Kohlhammer) 1962

Erpel (1985)
Fritz Erpel, *Max Beckmann: Leben im Werk. Die Selbstbildnisse*, Munich (C.H. Beck) 1985

Feilchenfeldt (1988)
Walter Feilchenfeldt, *Vincent van Gogh and Paul Cassirer, Berlin. The Reception of van Gogh in Germany from 1901 to 1914* (Cahier Vincent no.2), Amsterdam (Van Gogh Museum)/Zwolle (Waanders) 1988

Feininger (1944)
Lyonel Feininger – Marsden Hartley, exh. cat., New York (Museum of Modern Art) 1944, repr. New York (Arno Press) 1966

Felix (1983)
Zdenek Felix (ed.), *Erich Heckel 1883–1970. Gemälde, Aquarelle, Zeichnungen und Graphik*, Munich (Prestel) 1983

Fischer (1972)
Friedhelm W. Fischer, *Max Beckmann, Symbol und Weltbild. Grundriss zu einer Deutung des Gesamtwerkes*, Munich (Wilhelm Fink) 1972

Flavell (1988)
M. Kay Flavell, *George Grosz. A Biography*, New Haven, CT/London (Yale University Press) 1988

Gabler (1980)
Karlheinz Gabler (ed.), *E. L. Kirchner. Dokumente. Fotos, Schriften, Briefe*, Aschaffenburg (Museum der Stadt Aschaffenburg) 1980

Gabler (1983)
Karlheinz Gabler (ed.), *Erich Heckel und sein Kreis. Dokumente, Fotos, Briefe, Schriften, herausgegeben von der Städtischen Galerie der Stadt Karlsruhe*, Zurich-Stuttgart (Belser) 1983

Geelhaar (1973)
Christian Geelhaar, *Paul Klee and the Bauhaus*, Bath (Adams & Dart) 1973

Geelhaar (1976)
Christian Geelhaar (ed.), *Paul Klee Schriften. Rezensionen und Aufsätze*, Cologne (DuMont) 1976

Glaser (1924)
Curt Glaser, Julius Meier-Graefe, Wilhelm Fraenger and Wilhelm Hausenstein, *Max Beckmann*, Munich (R. Piper & Co.) 1924

Göpel (1976)
Erhard and Barbara Göpel (eds.), *Max Beckmann. Katalog der Gemälde*, 2 vols, Berne (Kornfeld) 1976

Gordon (1966)
Donald E. Gordon, 'Kirchner in Dresden', *Art Bulletin*, XLVIII, nos. 3–4 (September–December 1966): 335–66

Gordon (1968)
Donald E. Gordon, *Ernst Ludwig Kirchner*, Cambridge, MA (Harvard University Press) 1968

Gordon (1974)
Donald E. Gordon, *Modern Art Exhibitions 1900–1916*, 2 vols, Munich (Prestel) 1974

Gordon (1987)
Donald E. Gordon, *Expressionism: Art and Idea*, New Haven, CT/London (Yale University Press) 1987

Grisebach (1968)
Lothar Grisebach, *E. L. Kirchners Davoser Tagebuch. Eine Darstellung des Malers und eine Sammlung seiner Schriften*, Cologne (DuMont) 1968

Grochowiak (1966)
Thomas Grochowiak, *Ludwig Meidner*, Recklinghausen (Aurel Bongers) 1966

Grohmann (1956)
Will Grohmann, *Karl Schmidt-Rottluff*, Stuttgart (W. Kohlhammer) 1956

Grohmann (1961/1)
Will Grohmann, *Wassily Kandinsky. Leben und Werk*, 2nd edn., Cologne (DuMont) 1961

Grohmann (1961/2)
Will Grohmann, *E. L. Kirchner*, New York (Arts, Inc.) 1961

Grosz (1946)
A Little Yes and a Big No. The Autobiography of George Grosz, New York (Dial Press) 1946

Grosz (1979)
H. Knust (ed.), *George Grosz. Briefe 1913–1959*, Hamburg (Rowohlt) 1979

Güse (1977)
Ernst-Gerhard Güse, *Das Frühwerk Max Beckmanns. Zur Thematik seiner Bilder aus den Jahren 1904–1914*, VI of *Kunstwissenschaftliche Studien* (ed. Alexander Perrig), Frankfurt am Main/Berne 1977

Güse (1982)
Ernst-Gerhard Güse (ed.), *Die Tunisreise. Klee, Macke, Moilliet*, Stuttgart (Hatje) 1982

Güse (1986)
Ernst-Gerhard Güse (ed.), *August Macke. Gemälde, Aquarelle, Zeichnungen*, Munich (F. Bruckmann) 1986

Haesaerts (1957)
Paul Haesaerts, *James Ensor*, London (Thames & Hudson) 1957

Haxthausen (1981)
Charles Werner Haxthausen, *Paul Klee. The Formative Years*, New York/London (Garland) 1981

Heesemann-Wilson (1978)
Andrea Heesemann-Wilson, *Christian Schad, Expressionist, Dadaist und Maler der Neuen Sachlichkeit. Leben und Werk bis 1945*, Ph.D. diss., Göttingen (Georg-August-Universität) 1978

Heiderich (1987)
Ursula Heiderich, *August Macke, Die Skizzenbücher*, 2 vols, Stuttgart (Hatje) 1987,

Heller (1984)
Reinhold Heller, *Munch. His Life and Work*, London (John Murray) 1984

Heller (1988)
Reinhold Heller, *Brücke. German Expressionist Prints from the Granvil and Marcia Specks Collection*, exh. cat., Evanston, IL, Northwestern University, Mary and Leigh Block Gallery, 1988

Henze (1980)
Anton Henze, *Ernst Ludwig Kirchner, Leben und Werk*, Stuttgart/Zurich (Belser) 1980

Henze (1983)
Anton Henze, *Erich Heckel, Leben und Werk*, Stuttgart/Zurich (Belser) 1983

Herbert (1983)
Barry Herbert, *German Expressionism. Die Brücke and Der Blaue Reiter*, London (Jupiter Books) 1983

Hess (1961)
Hans Hess, *Lyonel Feininger*, London (Thames & Hudson)/New York (Abrams) 1961

Hess (1974)
Hans Hess, *George Grosz*, London (Studio Vista) 1974

Hildebrandt (1952)
Hans Hildebrandt, *Oskar Schlemmer, Leben und Werk*, Munich (Prestel) 1952

Hodin (1966)
J. P. Hodin, *Oskar Kokoschka. The Artist and his Time*, London (Cory, Adams and Mackay) 1966

Hodin (1973)
J. P. Hodin, *Ludwig Meidner, seine Kunst, seine Persönlichkeit, seine Zeit*, Darmstadt (Justus von Liebig) 1973

Hubbuch (1981)
Helmut Goettl, Wolfgang Hartmann, Michael Schwarz (eds.), *Karl Hubbuch 1891–1979*, Munich (Prestel) 1981

Hünlich (1988)
Bernd Hünlich, 'E. L. Kirchners Dresdener Freundin "Dodo" Doris Grosse', *Dresdener Kunstblätter. Zweimonatsschrift der Staatl. Kunstsammlungen Dresden*, XXXII/5 (1988): 137–47

Hünlich (1990)
Bernd Hünlich, 'Moritzburger Ortsmotive der "Künstlergruppe Brücke". Werke von Fritz Bleyl, Erich Heckel, Ernst Ludwig Kirchner und Hermann Max Pechstein', *Dresdener Kunstblätter. Zweimonatsschrift der Staatl. Kunstsammlungen Dresden*, XXXIV/6 (1990): 170–82

Jähner (1986)
Horst Jähner, *Künstlergruppe Brücke. Geschichte – Leben und Werk ihrer Maler*, 2nd edn., Stuttgart (W.Kohlhammer) 1986

Jordan (1984)
Jim M.Jordan, *Paul Klee and Cubism*, Princeton, NJ (Princeton University Press) 1984

O.Kallir (1966)
Otto Kallir [pseud. Otto Nirenstein], *Egon Schiele. Oeuvre-Katalog der Gemälde*, Vienna (Paul Zsolnay) 1966

J.Kallir (1990)
Jane Kallir, *Egon Schiele. The Complete Works*, New York (Abrams) 1990

Karsch (1974)
Otto Mueller zum 100. Geburtstag. Das Graphische Gesamtwerk. Mit einer Einleitung von Florian Karsch, Berlin (Galerie Nierendorf) 1974

Kessler (1971)
Charles Kessler (ed.), *The Diaries of a Cosmopolitan. Count Harry Kessler, 1918–1937*, London (Weidenfeld & Nicolson) 1971

Ketterer (1982)
Roman Norbert Ketterer (ed.), *Ernst Ludwig Kirchner. Drawings and Pastels.* With the co-operation of Wolfgang Henze. Introduction and commentaries on the plates by Claus Zoege von Manteuffel. Biography and bibliography by Hans Bolliger, New York (Alpine Fine Arts Collection) 1982

Ketterer (1988/I)
Roman Norbert Ketterer, *Dialoge.* [I] *Stuttgarter Kunstkabinett, Moderne Kunst*, Stuttgart/Zurich (Belser) 1988

Ketterer (1988/II)
Roman Norbert Ketterer, *Dialogue.* [II] *Bildende Kunst, Kunsthandel*, Stuttgart/Zurich (Belser) 1988

Kiel (1974)
Hanna Kiel, *The Thyssen-Bornemisza Collection of Modern Paintings*, Castagnola 1974

Klee (1957)
Felix Klee (ed.), *Tagebücher von Paul Klee 1898–1918*, Cologne (DuMont) 1957

Kokoschka (1974)
Oskar Kokoschka, *My Life*, trans. by David Britt, London (Thames & Hudson) 1974

Kornfeld (1979)
Eberhard W.Kornfeld, *Ernst Ludwig Kirchner. Nachzeichnung seines Lebens. Katalog der Sammlung von Werken von Ernst Ludwig Kirchner im Kirchner-Haus Davos*, Berne (Kornfeld) 1979

Kunz (1973)
Ludwig Kunz (ed.), *Ludwig Meidner. Dichter, Maler und Cafés*, Zurich (Die Arche) 1973

Lackner (1967)
Stephan Lackner, *Ich erinnere mich gut an Max Beckmann*, Mainz (Florian Kupferberg) 1967

Lackner (1977)
Stephan Lackner, *Max Beckmann*, New York (Abrams) 1977

Langaard (1961)
Johan H.Langaard and Reidar Revold, *Edvard Munch fra År til År/A Year by Year Record of Edvard Munch's Life*, Oslo (H.Aschehoug) 1961

Lankheit (1960)
Klaus Lankheit (ed.), *Franz Marc im Urteil seiner Zeit*, Cologne (DuMont) 1960

Lankheit (1970)
Klaus Lankheit, *Franz Marc. Katalog der Werke*, Cologne (DuMont) 1970

Lankheit (1976)
Klaus Lankheit, *Franz Marc. Sein Leben und seine Kunst*, Cologne (DuMont) 1976

Lankheit (1978)
Klaus Lankheit (ed.), *Franz Marc. Schriften*, Cologne (DuMont) 1978

Legrand (1971)
Francine-Claire Legrand, *Ensor, cet inconnu*, Brussels (La Renaissance du Livre) 1971

Lehman (1986)
Arnold L.Lehman and Brenda Richardson (eds.), *Oskar Schlemmer*, exh. cat., Baltimore, MD, Baltimore Museum of Art, 1986

Leopold (1973)
Rudolf Leopold, *Egon Schiele. Paintings, Watercolours, Drawings*, London (Phaidon) 1973

Lewis (1971)
Beth Irwin Lewis, *George Grosz. Art and Politics in the Weimar Republic*, Madison, WI/London (Wisconsin University Press) 1971

Lindsay (1982)
Kenneth C.Lindsay and Peter Vergo (eds.), *Kandinsky. Complete Writings on Art*, 2 vols, Boston, MA (G.K.Hall)/London (Faber & Faber) 1982

Lloyd (1987)
Jill Patricia Lloyd, *Primitivism and Modernity in the Art of Die Brücke and Emil Nolde before 1914*, unpublished Ph.D. diss., University of London, 1987

Lloyd (1991)
Jill Lloyd, *German Expressionism. Primitivism and Modernity*, New Haven, CT/London (Yale University Press) 1991

Löffler (1981)
Fritz Löffler, *Otto Dix 1891–1969. Oeuvre der Gemälde*, Recklinghausen (Aurel Bongers) 1981

Lorenzer (1989)
Anna Barbara Lorenzer, 'Studien zur Maltechnik von Otto Dix in der Schaffenszeit von 1910–1933', *Zeitschrift für Kunsttechnologie und Konservierung*, III, no.1 (1989): 113–48

Luckhardt (1987)
Ulrich Luckhardt, *Lyonel Feininger: Die Karikaturen und das zeichnerische Frühwerk*, X of *Beiträge zur Kunstwissenschaft*, Munich (Scaneg) 1987

Luckhardt (1989)
Ulrich Luckhardt, *Lyonel Feininger*, Munich (Prestel) 1989

Macke (1958)
G.Busch, W.Holzhausen *et al.*, *Die Tunisreise. Aquarelle und Zeichnungen von August Macke*, Cologne (DuMont) 1958

Malafarina (1982)
Gianfranco Malafarina, *L'Opera di Schiele*, Milan (Rizzoli) 1982

von Maur (1979)
Karin von Maur, *Oskar Schlemmer. Oeuvrekatalog der Gemälde, Aquarelle, Pastelle und Plastiken*, 2 vols, Munich (Prestel) 1979

von Maur (1982)
Karin von Maur, *Oskar Schlemmer. Monographie und Oeuvrekatalog: Nachträge, Ergänzungen und Berichtigungen*, Munich (Prestel) 1982

Meidner (1978)
Ludwig Meidner. An Expressionist Master. Drawings and Prints from the D.Thomas Bergen Collection. Paintings from the Marvin and Janet

Fishman Collection, exh. cat., Ann Arbor, MI, University of Michigan Museum of Art, 1978

Moeller (1989)
Magdalena M. Moeller, *August Macke. Die Tunisreise*, Munich (Prestel) 1989

Moeller (1990)
Magdalena M. Moeller, 'Van Gogh und die Rezeption in Deutschland bis 1914', in Georg-W. Költzsch (ed.), *Vincent van Gogh und die Moderne 1890–1914*, exh. cat., Essen, Museum Folkwang, 1990

Moeller (1991)
Magdalena M. Moeller (ed.), *Expressionistische Grüsse. Künstlerpostkarten der 'Brücke' und des 'Blauen Reiter'*, Stuttgart (Hatje) 1991

Munch (1978)
Edvard Munch. Symbols and Images, Washington, DC (National Gallery of Art) 1978

Munch (1988)
Edvard Munch. Sommernacht am Oslofjord, um 1900, Mannheim (Städtische Kunsthalle) 1988 (Kunst + Dokumentation, no.12)

Myers (1963)
Bernard S. Myers, *Expressionism. A Generation in Revolt*, London (Thames & Hudson) 1963

Nebehay (1979)
Christian M. Nebehay, *Egon Schiele 1890–1918. Leben, Briefe, Gedichte*, Salzburg (Residenz) 1979

Nolde (1965)
Emil Nolde, *Welt und Heimat. Die Südseereise 1913–1918*, 2nd edn., Cologne (DuMont) 1965

Nolde (1967)
Emil Nolde, *Das Eigene Leben. Die Zeit der Jugend 1867–1902*, 3rd edn., Cologne (DuMont) 1967

Nolde (1971)
Emil Nolde, *Jahre der Kämpfe 1902–1914*, 3rd edn., Cologne (DuMont) 1971

Nolde (1978)
Emil Nolde, *Reisen, Ächtung, Befreiung 1919–1946*, Cologne (DuMont) 3rd edn., 1978

Nirenstein (1930)
Otto Nirenstein, *Egon Schiele. Persönlichkeit und Werk*, Vienna (Paul Zsolnay) 1930

Pechstein (1963)
Leopold Reidemeister (ed.), *Max Pechstein. Erinnerungen*, Munich (List) 1963

Pese (1989)
Claus Pese, *Franz Marc. Leben und Werk*, Stuttgart/Zurich (Belser) 1989

Prelinger (1983)
Elizabeth Prelinger, *Edvard Munch, Master Printmaker. An examination of the artist's works and techniques based on the Philip and Lynn Straus Collection*, New York/London (Norton) 1983

Rakitin (1979)
Vasily Rakitin, 'Zwischen Himmel und Erde oder wie befreit man das Rationale vom trockenen Rationalismus', in *Wassily Kandinsky. Die erste sowjetische Retrospektive*, exh. cat., Frankfurt am Main, Schirn Kunsthalle, 1989, pp.79–88

Reidemeister (1970)
Leopold Reidemeister, *Künstler der Brücke an den Moritzburger Seen 1909–1911. Erich Heckel, Ernst Ludwig Kirchner, Max Pechstein. Ein Beitrag zur Geschichte der Künstlergruppe Brücke*, Berlin (Brücke-Museum) 1970

Reifenberg (1949)
Benno Reifenberg and Wilhelm Hausenstein, *Max Beckmann*, Munich (R. Piper & Co.) 1949

Reinhardt (1977)
Georg Reinhardt, 'Die frühe Brücke. Beiträge zur Geschichte und zum Werk der Dresdner Künstlergruppe "Brücke" der Jahre 1905 bis 1908', *Brücke-Archiv*, 9/10 (1977/8)

Rigby (1976)
Ida Katherine Rigby, *Karl Hofer*, New York (Garland) 1976

Roditi (1980)
Edouard Roditi, *Dialogues on Art*, rev. edn., Santa Barbara, CA (Ross-Erikson) 1980

Roethel (1970)
Hans Konrad Roethel, *Kandinsky. Das Graphische Werk*, Cologne (DuMont) 1970

Roethel (1982)
Hans K. Roethel and Jean K. Benjamin, *Kandinsky. Catalogue Raisonné of the Oil Paintings*, I, London (Sotheby's) 1984

Roethel (1984)
Hans K. Roethel and Jean K. Benjamin, *Kandinsky. Catalogue Raisonné of the Oil Paintings*, II, London (Sotheby's) 1982

Roh (1962)
Franz Roh, *'Entartete' Kunst. Kunstbarbarei im Dritten Reich*, Hanover (Fackelträger-Verlag Schmidt-Küster) 1962

Rosenthal (1989)
Mark Rosenthal, *Franz Marc*, Munich (Prestel) 1989

Roters (1984)
Eberhard Roters, *Galerie Ferdinand Möller. Die Geschichte einer Galerie für Moderne Kunst in Deutschland 1917–1956*, Berlin (Gebr. Mann) 1984

Rotzler (1978)
Willy Rotzler, *Johannes Itten. Werke und Schriften. Herausgegeben von Willy Rotzler. Werkverzeichnis von Anneliese Itten*, 2nd edn., Zurich (Orell Füssli) 1978

Rudenstine (1976)
Angelica Zander Rudenstine, *The Guggenheim Museum Collection: Paintings 1880–1945*, 2 vols, New York (Solomon R. Guggenheim Foundation) 1976

Schad (1970)
Bettina Schad, 'Christian Schad, Werkverzeichnis. Bilder von 1920–1930', in *Christian Schad. Generalkatalog des Werkes und bibliographische Notizen von Bettina Schad*, exh. cat., Milan/Munich, Galleria del Levante, 1970

Schardt (1936)
Alois J. Schardt, *Franz Marc*, Berlin (Rembrandt) 1936

Scheidig (1965)
Walther Scheidig, *Christian Rohlfs*, Dresden (VEB Verlag der Kunst) 1965

Schiefler (1907)
Gustav Schiefler, *Verzeichnis der graphischen Werke Edvard Munchs bis 1906*, Berlin (Bruno Cassirer) 1907

Schiefler (1926)
Gustav Schiefler, *Die Graphik E. L. Kirchners*, I, Berlin-Charlottenburg (Euphorion) 1926

Schmied (1969)
Wieland Schmied, *Neue Sachlichkeit und Magischer Realismus in*

Deutschland 1918–1933, Hanover (Fackelträger-Verlag Schmidt-Küster) 1969

Schneede (1979)
Uwe M. Schneede, *George Grosz. His Life and Work*, London (Gordon Fraser) 1979

Schneede (1984)
Uwe M. Schneede, *Edvard Munch, Das Kranke Kind. Arbeit an der Erinnerung*, Frankfurt am Main (Fischer Taschenbuch Verlag) 1984

Schulz-Hoffmann (1984)
Carla Schulz-Hoffmann and Judith C. Weiss (eds.), *Max Beckmann Retrospective*, Munich (Prestel) 1984

Schuster (1987)
Peter-Klaus Schuster (ed.), *Die 'Kunststadt' München 1937. Nationalsozialismus und 'Entartete Kunst'*, Munich (Prestel) 1987

Schweiger (1982)
Werner J. Schweiger, *Wiener Werkstätte. Kunst und Handwerk 1903–1932*, Vienna (Christian Brandstätter) 1982

Schweiger (1983)
Werner J. Schweiger, *Der junge Kokoschka*, Vienna/Munich (Christian Brandstätter) 1983

Spalek (1977)
John M. Spalek et al., *German Expressionism in the Fine Arts: A Bibliography*, Los Angeles, CA (Hennessey & Ingalls) 1977

Stang (1979)
Ragna Stang, *Edvard Munch. The Man and the Artist*, London (Gordon Fraser) 1979

Thiem (1989)
Gunther Thiem and Armin Zweite (eds.), *Karl Schmidt-Rottluff Retrospektive*, Munich (Prestel) 1989

Tricot (1985)
Xavier Tricot, *Ensoriana*, Ostend (L'Hareng Saur) 1985

Uhr (1990)
Horst Uhr, *Lovis Corinth*, Berkeley, CA/Los Angeles, CA (California University Press) 1990

Urban (1970)
Martin Urban, *Emil Nolde – Landscapes. Watercolours and Drawings*, London (Pall Mall) 1970

Urban (1972)
Martin Urban, *Emil Nolde – Blumen und Tiere. Aquarelle und Zeichnungen*, 2nd edn., Cologne (DuMont) 1972

Urban (1987)
Martin Urban, *Emil Nolde. Catalogue Raisonné of the Oil-Paintings*, I, London (Sotheby's) 1987

Urban (1990)
Martin Urban, *Emil Nolde. Catalogue Raisonné of the Oil-Paintings*, II, London (Sotheby's) 1990

Utermann (1984)
Wilfried Utermann (ed.), *Christian Rohlfs und die Stadt Soest in seinem Werk*, exh. cat., Soest, Galerie Utermann, 1984

Vergo (1975)
Peter Vergo, *Art in Vienna, 1898–1918. Klimt, Kokoschka, Schiele and their Contemporaries*, London (Phaidon) 1975

Vergo (1989)
Peter Vergo, *Expressionism. Masterpieces from the Thyssen-Bornemisza Collection*, Milan (Electa) 1989

Vogt (1965)
Paul Vogt, *Erich Heckel*, Recklinghausen (Aurel Bongers) 1965

Vogt (1972)
Paul Vogt, *Geschichte der deutschen Malerei im 20. Jahrhundert*, Cologne (DuMont) 1972

Vogt (1978)
Paul Vogt, *Christian Rohlfs. Oeuvre-Katalog der Gemälde*, Recklinghausen (Aurel Bongers) 1978

Vriesen (1957)
Gustav Vriesen, *August Macke*, 2nd edn., Stuttgart (W. Kohlhammer) 1957

Weiler (1959)
Clemens Weiler, *Alexej Jawlensky*, Cologne (DuMont) 1959

Weiler (1970)
Clemens Weiler, *Alexej Jawlensky. Köpfe, Gesichte, Meditationen*, Hanau (Hans Peters) 1970

Wentzel (1968)
Hans Wentzel, 'Fritz Bleyl, Gründungsmitglied der "Brücke"', *Kunst in Hessen und am Mittelrhein*, VIII (1968): 89–105

Werenskiold (1974)
Marit Werenskiold, 'Die Brücke und Edvard Munch', *Zeitschrift des deutschen Vereins für Kunstwissenschaft*, XXVIII, nos. 1–4 (1974): 140–52

Werenskiold (1984)
Marit Werenskiold, *The Concept of Expressionism*, Oslo (Universitetsforlaget) 1984

Werkner (1986)
Patrick Werkner, *Physis und Psyche. Der oesterreichische Frühexpressionismus*, Vienna/Munich (Herold) 1986

Whitford (1986)
Frank Whitford, *Oskar Kokoschka. A Life*, London (Thames & Hudson) 1986

Wietek (1957)
Gerd Wietek, *Maler der 'Brücke' in Dangast von 1907 bis 1912*, exh. cat., Oldenburg, Kunstverein, 1957

Wietek (1963)
Gerhard Wietek, *Karl Schmidt-Rottluff. Bilder aus Nidden 1913*, Stuttgart (Reclam) 1963

Wietek (1974)
Gerhard Wietek, 'Erich Heckels erster Aufenthalt an der Flensburger Förde im Jahre 1913', *Nordelbingen. Beiträge zur Kunst- und Kulturgeschichte*, XLIII (1974): 144–53

Wietek (1976)
Gerhard Wietek (ed.), *Deutsche Künstlerkolonien und Künstlerorte*, Munich (Karl Thiemig) 1976

Wietek (1984)
Gerhard Wietek, *Karl Schmidt-Rottluff in Hamburg und Schleswig-Holstein*, Neumünster (Karl Wacholtz) 1984

Wietek (1990)
Gerhard Wietek, *Franz Radziwill – Wilhelm Niemeyer. Dokumente einer Freundschaft*, Oldenburg (Isensee) 1990

Wingler (1958)
Hans Maria Wingler, *Oskar Kokoschka. The Work of the Painter*, Salzburg (Galerie Welz) 1958

Zweite (1979)
Armin Zweite (ed.), *Paul Klee. Das Frühwerk 1883–1922*, Munich (Prestel) 1979

Zweite (1983)
Armin Zweite (ed.), *Alexej Jawlensky 1864–1941*, Munich (Prestel) 1983

Photographic acknowledgements

Grateful acknowledgement is made to Giuseppe Pennisi for taking the colour photographs of paintings in the Thyssen-Bornemisza Collection reproduced in this catalogue. The following are thanked for kindly supplying copyright monochrome photographic material and for granting their permission to reproduce it.

Figure numbers follow square-bracketed catalogue numbers.

BASLE
Galerie Beyeler [52] 1
Kunstmuseum [70] 1

BERGEN
Rasmus Meyers Samlinger [75] 2, 3

BERLIN
Galerie Nierendorf [19] 1, [71] 1
Staatliche Museen Preussischer Kulturbesitz/Jörg P. Anders [6] 4, [18] 1, [105] 1
Brücke-Museum [24] 1
Staatliche Museen zu Berlin [91] 2
Ullstein Bilderdienst [19] 2
Dr Wolfram Gabler [48] 4, [49] 3

BERNE
Dr Eberhard W. Kornfeld [45] 1, [51] 1
Kunstmuseum [54] 1, [68] 3

BONN
Städtisches Kuntsmuseum [63] 1, 2

CAMBRIDGE, MA
Harvard University Art Museums [10] 3, [13] 2

CAMPIONE D'ITALIA
Dr Wolfgang Henze (Foto-Archiv Hans Bolliger – Roman Norbert Ketterer) [44] 1, 4, [46] 1

CHICAGO, IL
Art Institute of Chicago [46] 4

CLEVELAND, OH
Cleveland Museum of Art [48] 3

COLOGNE
Agfa Foto-Historama im Wallraf-Richartz-Museum/Museum Ludwig [6] 2

DARMSTADT
Hessisches Landesmuseum [48] 1
Ludwig Meidner-Nachlass [70] 2, 3

DORTMUND
Galerie Utermann [46] 5

DÜSSELDORF
Kunstsammlung Nordrhein-Westfalen [47] 1

ESSEN
Museum Folkwang [22] 2

FELDAFING
Lothar-Günther Buchheim [72] 1

FRANKFURT AM MAIN
Städelsches Kunstinstitut [46] 3, 6

GOTHENBURG
Göteborgs Konstmuseum [76] 1

HALLE
Staatliche Galerie Moritzburg [1] 1

HAMBURG
Altonaer Museum, Norddeutsches Landesmuseum [44] 3, [49] 1
Ulrich Luckhardt [10] 1, 2, [13] 1
Professor Gerhard Wietek [102] 1

HANOVER
Niedersächisches Landesmuseum, Landesgalerie [5] 1

HEMMENHOFEN
Estate of Erich Heckel [24] 1, 2, [25] 1

KARLSRUHE
Staatliche Kunsthalle [29] 2

LONDON
BFI Stills, Posters and Designs [12] 1

LOS ANGELES, CA
Robert Gore Rifkind Collection [68] 2

LUGANO
Emil Bosshard [49] 4, [75] 1
Thyssen-Bornemisza Collection/Foto Brunel [16] 1, [20] *verso*, [33] 1, [73] *verso*

MALIBU, CA
The J. Paul Getty Museum [9] 2

MÜNSTER
Westfälisches Landesmuseum [64] 1

MUNICH
Bayerische Staatsgemäldesammlungen [6] 1, [26] 1, [29] 1, [68] 1, [100] 1
Gabriele Münter und Johannes Eichner-Stiftung [32] 1, [73] 1
Museum in der Stuck Villa [4] 3
Städtische Galerie im Lenbachhaus [36] 2, 3, [37] 1, [40] 1

MURNAU
Maja Beckmann [2] 1

NEW YORK
Vivian E. Barnett [39] 1, [40] 2, [74] 2
Galerie St Etienne/Jane Kallir [95] 1, [97] 1, [98] 1
Metropolitan Museum of Art [55] 2
Museum of Modern Art [4] 1
Sotheby's, Inc. [75] 4 (© Sotheby's 1990)

NORTHAMPTON, MA
Smith College Museum of Art [44] 2

OSLO
Munch Museum [75] 5

OSTEND
Xavier Tricot [9] 1

PITTSBURGH, PA
University of Pittsburgh, archive of the late Donald E. Gordon [46] 2

POTSDAM
Bundesarchiv [94] 1

PRINCETON, NJ
Peter M. Grosz [17] 3

RADEBEUL
Bernd Hünlich [70] 4, [89] 1

ROME
Istituto Centrale per il Catalogo e la Documentazione [93] 1

SEEBÜLL
Nolde-Stiftung [79] 1

ST LOUIS, MO
The Saint Louis Art Museum [4] 2

STUTTGART
Staatsgalerie [17] 1, [49] 2

SYKE-OKEL
Dr Ursula Heiderich [63] 2, 3

VIENNA
Irene Schmidt [56] 1, 2
Österreichisches Museum für Angewandte Kunst [1] 2, [30] 2

WITTEN
Märkisches Museum der Stadt Witten [91] 1

WATERVILLE, ME
Colby College Art Museum [48] 2

WUPPERTAL
Von der Heydt-Museum [6] 3

ZURICH
Kunsthaus [30] 1

Remaining photographs supplied by the author

Index of artists

Page numbers in bold refer to the main entry for each artist represented in the Collection; page numbers in italics refer to comparative illustrations

Amiet, Cuno 11n, 56n, 372n
Archipenko, Alexander 333
Arp, Hans 333
Ažbè, Anton 144

Balla, Giacomo 80
Bauer, Rudolf 162, 178
Beckmann, Max **30–45**, 8, 15, 18, 52n, 96, 132, 260, 320
Bekhteev, Vladimir 278
Berend-Corinth, Charlotte 46n, 48
Bilibin, Ivan 174
Bischoff-Culm, Eduard 326
Bleyl, Fritz 180, 182, 186n, 324n
Böcklin, Arnold 303
Botticelli 336
Breuer, Marcel 134
Burliuk, Vladimir 220

Carrà, Carlo 14
Cézanne, Paul 180
Corinth, Lovis **46–49**, 8, 41, 96
Cross, Henri-Edmond 188

Daumier, Honoré 289
Degas, Edgar 289
Delaunay, Robert 12, 72, 86, 90n, 218n, 220, 249, 252, 258, 268f, *270*
Delville, Jean 260
Derain, André 14n, 115
Dexel, Walter 14
Dix, Otto **50–55**, 6, 15, 20, 90
Doernberger, Karl 289
Dongen, Kees van **56–63**, 7, 115

Ederer, Carl 130
Egger-Lienz, Albin 344
Ensor, James **64–67**, 7
Erbslöh, Adolf 114n

Feininger, Lyonel **68–87**, 8, 13–14, 16n, 20, 41, 169n
Friesz, Othon 115

Gärtner, Friedrich von 161
Gauguin, Paul 11, 146, 195ff, 264, 326, 333, *195*
Gogh, Vincent van 7, 11–12, 56, 111, 146, 180, 280, 298, 308, 328, 330n, 367
Gothein, Werner 208
Grabar, Igor 144
Gropius, Walter 8, 52, 74, 86n
Grosz, George **88–107**, 15, 18, 20, 268, 360
Gütersloh, Albert Paris von 33

Heartfield, John 101, 102, 360
Heckel, Erich **108–129**, 6, 7, 8n, 9ff, 13, 17, 19, 184, 186n, 192ff, 208, 209, 324, 326, 362, 366f, 372

Henrich, Albert **130–131**
Herzfelde, Wieland 101, 102
Hettner, Otto 114n
Hodler, Ferdinand 146, 303
Hoerle, Heinrich 16
Hofer, Karl **132–133**, 7, 18
Hoffmann, Josef 350
Hogarth, William 94
Hubbuch, Karl **134–137**, 360

Itten, Johannes **138–143**, 8, 18–19

Jawlensky, Alexei **144–151**, 8, 12–13, 154, 169n, 278f, 282, 320
Jawlensky, Andreas 146
Jungnickel, Ludwig Heinrich 345

Kandinsky, Wassily **152–179**, 6, 8, 11ff, 18, 20, 26, 32, 41, 144f, 186f, 218, 220n, 262ff, 266, 278f, 282ff, *285*
Kanoldt, Alexander 15, 90
Kardowsky, Dmitri 144
Kassak, Lajos 14
Kaulbach, Friedrich August 34
Keller, Ludwig 130
Khnopff, Fernand 260
Kirchner, Ernst Ludwig **180–217**, 6, 8n, 9ff, 13–14, 16–17, 19, 22, 26, 41, 96, 118, 124, 320, 324, 326, 362, 372n
Klee, Paul **218–229**, 7–8, 12ff, 23, 41, 141, 169n, 258
Kogan, Moissej 282
Kokoschka, Oskar **230–243**, 6, 9, 41, 48, 270, 344
Kollwitz, Käthe 52
Kreis, Wilhelm 308
Krohg, Christian 294
Kubin, Alfred 72
Kubista, Bohumil 370n

Le Fauconnier, Henri 218n
Léger, Fernand 56
Leonardo 336
Liebermann, Max 41, 48, 303
Lissitzky, El 14
Loos, Adolf 233
Luce, Maximilien 188
Lüthy, Oskar 220n

Macke, August **244–259**, 12ff, 146n
Malevich, Kazimir 166f
Mammen, Jeanne **260–261**, 18
Männchen, Adolf 130
Marc, Franz **262–267**, 11ff, 20, 218
Marées, Hans von 132, 264n
Marquet, Albert 115
Matisse, Henri 56, 115, 146, 161, 218n
Meidner, Ludwig **268–273**, 6, 19, 90
Mense, Carlo 15, 90

Mertens, Hans 16
Miró, Joan 170
Moholy-Nagy, László 14
Moilliet, Louis 218n, 248f, 256n, 258
Mueller, Otto **274–277**, 96, 118, 122, 184n
Münter, Gabriele **278–285**, 6, 12, 20, 146, 152f, 156, 172, 175, 265, 266n
Munch, Edvard **286–297**, 7–8, 9, 20, 22, 181, 196n

Nolde, Emil **298–321**, 6, 7, 11, 16, 18, 20, 41, 48, 118, 126, 188, 331, 362f, 366, 372

Oehme, F.E. 120
Orlik, Emil 134

Pechstein, Max **322–327**, 10–11, 18, 48, 56, 115, 192, 324n, 362, 366, 368f, 372n, *371*
Peterhans, Walter 134
Picasso, Pablo 14, 333
Pissarro, Camille 180

Radziwill, Franz 114, 115n
Raphael 336, *337*
Ray, Man 56, 333
Redon, Odilon 260
Reimann, Walter 77
Repin, Il'ya 144
Rodchenko, Alexander 14, 168
Rohlfs, Christian **328–331**, 18
Röhrig, Walter 77
Rops, Félicien 260
Rousseau, Henri 11
Rubens, Sir Peter Paul 66n
Rysselberghe, Théo van 186f

Schad, Christian **332–341**, 11, 18n, 360
Schiele, Egon **342–355**, 9, 20, 33
Schlemmer, Oskar **356–359**, 14, 16
Schlichter, Rudolf **360–361**, 130
Schmidt-Rottluff, Karl **362–375**, 6, 8n, 9ff, 17, 20, 41, 56n, 110–111, 114, 118, 298
Scholz, Georg 15, 90
Schrimpf, Georg 90
Seiwert, Franz-Wilhelm 16
Seurat, Georges 188, 328
Signac, Paul 180, 186f, 328
Slevogt, Max 48, 52
Spatz, Willy 130
Stepanova, Varvara 168
Strauch, Ludwig Karl 350
Stuck, Franz von 45, *45*

Tatlin, Vladimir 101, 166, 333
Thoms, Ernst 16
Tränkler, Alfons Maria 130

Vallotton, Félix 186
Velde, Henry van de 212
Verkade, Jan 151
Vlaminck, Maurice 115

Warm, Hermann 77
Watteau, Jean-Antoine 66
Werefkin, Marianne 146, 154, 278, 282

Ziegler, Adolf 324